Building Web Services with Java

MAKING SENSE OF XML, SOAP, WSDL, AND UDDI

Second Edition

Steve Graham
Doug Davis
Simeon Simeonov
Glen Daniels
Peter Brittenham
Yuichi Nakamura
Paul Fremantle
Dieter König
Claudia Zentner

DEVELOPER'S
LIBRARY

Sams Publishing, 800 East 96th Street, Indianapolis, Indiana 46240

Building Web Services with Java, Second Edition

International Standard Book Number: 0-672-32641-8

Library of Congress Catalog Card Number: 2004091343

Printed in the United States of America

First Printing: July 2004

07 06 05 04   4 3 2 1

Trademarks

Warning and Disclaimer

Bulk Sales

Sams Publishing offers excellent discounts on this book when ordered in quantity for bulk purchases or special sales. For more information, please contact

U.S. Corporate and Government Sales

1-800-382-3419

corpsales@pearsontechgroup.com

For sales outside of the U.S., please contact

International Sales

1-317-428-3341

international@pearsontechgroup.com

Associate Publisher
Michael Stephens

Acquisitions Editor
Todd Green

Development Editor
Tiffany Taylor

Managing Editor
Charlotte Clapp

Senior Project Editor
Matthew Purcell

Indexer
Larry Sweazy

Proofreader
Eileen Dennie

Technical Editors
Alan Moffet
Alan Wexelblat
Marc Goldford
Kunal Mittal

Publishing Coordinator
Cindy Teeters

Designer
Gary Adair

Contents at a Glance

Table of Contents

About the Authors

Steve Graham is a Senior Technical Staff Member in IBM's Systems Group and a member of the IBM Academy of Technology. Steve is an architect in the On Demand Architecture group. He has spent the last several years working on service-oriented architectures as part of IBM's Web Services Initiative and IBM's On Demand Initiative. Most recently, Steve has applied service-oriented concepts to problems in Grid computing as part of the Open Grid Services Architecture work in the Global Grid Forum. Prior to this, Steve worked as a technologist and consultant with various emerging technologies such as Java and XML, and before that he was an architect and consultant with the IBM Smalltalk consulting organization. Before joining IBM, Steve was a developer with Sybase, a consultant, and a faculty member in the Department of Computer Science at the University of Waterloo. Steve holds a BMath and MMath in computer science from the University of Waterloo and an MBA from the Kenan Flagler Business School at University of North Carolina, Chapel Hill.

Doug Davis works as an architect in the Emerging Technology organization of IBM. Previous activities include being the technical lead of IBM's Emerging Technologies/Web Services Toolkit, being one of IBM's representatives in the W3C XML Protocol working group, and working on WebSphere's Machine Translation project, TeamConnection, and IBM's FORTRAN 90 compiler. Doug has a bachelor of science degree from the University of California at Davis and a master's degree in computer science from Michigan State University.

Simeon Simeonov is a Principal at Polaris Venture Partners in Boston, where he helps early-stage IT companies accelerate their growth. Prior to joining Polaris, Sim was Vice President of Emerging Technologies and Chief Architect at Macromedia. Earlier, Sim was a founding member and Chief Architect at Allaire. Sim has played a key role in eight v1.0 product initiatives. His innovation and leadership have brought about category-defining products with significant market impact: the first Web application server (Allaire ColdFusion), the best open-source Web services engine (Apache Axis) and the first rich Internet application platform (Macromedia Flash/Flex). Sim has been working with XML and precursors to Web services since 1997 and has developed standards in this space at W3C, JCP, and OASIS. Sim has a master's degree in computer science from Boston University and bachelor's degrees in computer science, economics, and mathematics from Macalester College.

Glen Daniels is the Standards Strategist for Sonic Software, creator of the first Enterprise Service Bus. Glen bridges the gap between Sonic's development organization and the evolving world of standards. He is one of the primary designers and developers for the Apache Axis project, is a member of the Apache Software Foundation, and participates actively in organizations like the W3C, OASIS, and the JCP. Prior to Sonic, he was a principal software engineer at Macromedia and Allaire, where he architected new initiatives and helped to bring the company into the Web services era. When not at standards meetings or writing code, he enjoys playing music, cooking, and spending time with his friends, his family, and his two amazing cats.

Peter Brittenham is a Senior Technical Staff Member working in the IBM Emerging Technology group. Peter is currently an architect applying service-oriented architecture concepts to IBM's Autonomic Computing initiative. Prior to this, he was the lead architect for the IBM Web Services Toolkit, which provided a preview of emerging Web service technologies. Peter also was one of the IBM representatives to the Web Services Interoperability (WS-I) organization. In this role, he was responsible for the architecture and overall development of the first release of the Java version of the WS-I Test Tools. Peter has a BS in business administration from Boston University and an MS in computer science from Marist College.

Yuichi Nakamura leads the XML & Security group at the IBM Tokyo Research Laboratory. He joined IBM in 1990 and has worked in several areas such as object-oriented systems, multi-agent systems, B2B e-commerce, and knowledge engineering. Since 1999 he has been working on Web services, addressing security, caching, and performance. Yuichi contributed to the Apache Axis project during its start-up phase, and he has been contributing to the development of security and cache components for IBM's WebSphere Application Server. He received an MSc and a PhD in applied physics from Osaka University.

Paul Fremantle is a Senior Technical Staff Member in IBM's Software division, based in the Hursley Park laboratory near Winchester in England. Paul works on IBM's Enterprise Service Bus initiative and other Web services activities in the WebSphere product. Paul has been working on Web services and XML at IBM since 1999, when he wrote early XML utilities for IBM's alphaWorks website. Since then he has co-authored *The XML Files*, an IBM redbook, as well as a number of articles on J2EE and Web services both in print and on the Web. Paul's involvement on the WebSphere Application Server includes architectural responsibility for the first SOAP support, the Web Services Invocation Framework, and the Web Services Gateway. Paul is the co-lead of the JWSDL standard in the Java Community Process and has initiated two open-source projects. Paul has an MSc in computation and an MA in mathematics and philosophy, both from Balliol College, Oxford.

Dieter König is a software architect for workflow systems at the IBM Germany Development Laboratory. He joined the laboratory in 1988 and has worked on Resource Measurement Facility for z/OS, MQSeries Workflow, and WebSphere Process Choreographer. Dieter is a member of the OASIS WS-BPEL Technical Committee, which is working toward an industry standard based on the Business Process Execution Language for Web Services (BPEL4WS) specification. He holds a master's degree (Dipl.inform.) in computer science from the University of Bonn, Germany.

Claudia Zentner is an architect working for IBM's Software Group at the IBM Development Laboratory in Böblingen, Germany. Since joining IBM in 1989, she has worked on various middleware projects. For many years Claudia has been focusing on workflow, starting with FlowMark and MQSeries Workflow; currently she is an architect for the process choreography component of the WebSphere Business Integration offering. Claudia graduated in computer science from the University of Cooperative Education in Stuttgart, Germany.

Acknowledgments

Steve Graham

Once again, to Karen, Erin, and Jessie, my family, my inspiration. For all the moments sacrificed to create this book, my most heartfelt thanks for your understanding. My thanks to my co-workers at IBM for providing an excellent environment for creative work.

My thanks also to the staff at Sams, particularly Tiffany Taylor and Michael Stephens, for the hard work that went into making this project a reality.

Romans 12:2.

Doug Davis

Thanks to my parents, family, and friends, without whose support and guidance none of the joys in my life would be possible. Lin—thanks to your never-ending patience and understanding, we managed to make it through another one! Sorry for forcing you to learn far more about Web services than you ever feared. :-)

Sim Simeonov

As always, my deepest thanks to Pyrra: my true love and a constant source of inspiration. Second editions are not easy when the topic of writing is changing as fast as Web services are evolving. Thanks go to all that helped me keep my finger on the pulse of the industry, notably, the good people working with Web services at Service Integrity, WebLayers, Orbitz, Amazon.com, eBay, CA, BMC, IBM, BEA, Microsoft, ZapThink, Burton Group, AT&T, GE, Ford, Bank of America, Wachovia, Fidelity, Morgan Stanley, Merck, and *Web Services Journal*.

Many thanks to Tiffany, Todd, and Mike at Sams for supporting us all the way!

Glen Daniels

I would like to thank my friends and family (not to mention the rest of the authoring team) for putting up with my overloaded schedule, and everyone at Sams for their great work pulling the book together. Also thanks to all the readers of the first edition who've made great comments and suggestions—we hope you like the new one!

Peter Brittenham

To my wife Abby, and my children Josh, Greg, and Jessica, thank you for your continued patience and support.

Yuichi Nakamura

To my wife Michiyo, my daughter Arisa, and my son Ryotaro. Thank you for your support and patience. My thanks to my colleagues at IBM for providing this great environment to work on Web services.

My thanks also to the staff at Sams, Tiffany, Todd, and Mike. Particularly, I thank Tiffany for her English editing on my chapter.

Paul Fremantle

To Jane, for being my supporter, friend, and advocate and making me laugh. To my children Anna and Dan for keeping me sane and driving me crazy. Thanks to my colleagues, especially Sanjiva Weerawarana, Tony Storey, Beth Hutchison, and Chris Sharp, for making my working environment challenging and fun, and to John Carter for being a great manager while I wrote this book. Finally, thanks to Tiffany, Todd, and Mike at Sams for all their hard work, and to Steve for all his encouragement to us all.

Dieter König

To my wife Rita and my sons Daniel, Sebastian, Maximilian, and Jonas. Thank you for your patience and support during this adventure.

Claudia Zentner

To Anneliese, Christian, Marion, and all my friends, thanks for your support and patience.

We Want to Hear from You!

As the reader of this book, *you* are our most important critic and commentator. We value your opinion and want to know what we're doing right, what we could do better, what areas you'd like to see us publish in, and any other words of wisdom you're willing to pass our way.

As an associate publisher for Sams Publishing, I welcome your comments. You can email or write me directly to let me know what you did or didn't like about this book—as well as what we can do to make our books better.

Please note that I cannot help you with technical problems related to the topic of this book. We do have a User Services group, however, where I will forward specific technical questions related to the book.

When you write, please be sure to include this book's title and author as well as your name, email address, and phone number. I will carefully review your comments and share them with the author and editors who worked on the book.

Email: feedback@samspublishing.com
Mail: Michael Stephens
             Associate Publisher
             Sams Publishing
             800 East 96th Street
             Indianapolis, IN 46240 USA

For more information about this book or another Sams Publishing title, visit our Web site at www.samspublishing.com. Type the ISBN (excluding hyphens) or the title of a book in the Search field to find the page you're looking for.

Introduction

WELCOME TO THE WORLD OF WEB SERVICES! Web services is an evolving collection of standards, specifications, and implementation technologies that are showing great value in the world of application integration and distributed computing. Web services continue to evolve to address more sophisticated computing scenarios, and the authors of this book are excited to bring you into what is widely believed to be the next generation of distributed computing.

Before we get going, we need to clarify some things about the purpose and structure of the book. Let's talk about them now.

Goals of This Book

The overall goal of this book is to familiarize you with the concept of Web services and what it will take to incorporate Web services as part of your business. We'll introduce the concept of Web services and give you a framework that describes how you can understand the various standards associated with Web services, such as Simple Object Access Protocol (SOAP), Web Services Description Language (WSDL), and Universal Description Discovery and Integration (UDDI). We'll help position Web services from a business and technical perspective, explaining and demonstrating how Web services can be used to address various business problems.

Another goal of this book is to help developers understand the issues and details related to building Web services using the techniques covered by this book. What pieces are required when you're planning a Web services strategy? What things do you need to take care of when you're developing Web services? We provide lots of examples to demonstrate these approaches. We also review in detail the Apache Axis Web services infrastructure with our examples.

Assumed Background

This book is meant for computing technical professionals with some experience building Web applications and distributed computing systems. You don't need to be a seasoned veteran of the distributed object wars to appreciate this book, but some familiarity with Web-based architectures and techniques such as HTTP and HTML is assumed. If you don't have any experience with these techniques, some of the material could be a little confusing—particularly some of the code examples—but you should still be able to get a lot out of the book.

We assume you're familiar with Java, in particular the Java servlet technology. We also briefly discuss the relationship between Enterprise JavaBeans (EJBs) and Web services, so some familiarity with EJBs is helpful as well. If you need to supplement your understanding of these techniques, many good books on programming with Java, JSP, servlets, and EJBs are available on the market.

You'll also discover that the Extensible Markup Language (XML) is at the core of all things dealing with Web service. Although we devote an entire chapter to explaining the core pieces of XML needed to build Web services, the more understanding of XML you have, the more successful you'll be in building Web services.

Philosophy

The concepts and standards involved in Web services are very much interdependent. It's difficult to cover each topic in isolation, because it's the combination of these concepts and standards that makes Web services important to distributed computing.

The philosophy of this book can be summarized by four points: pragmatics, progressive disclosure, a continuous example, and a service-oriented architecture framework.

Pragmatics

In this book, we try to get to programming examples and running code as quickly as possible. In particular, we focus on building and consuming SOAP-based Web services using the Java-based Apache Axis Web services infrastructure. Whereas we emphasize that Web services are fundamentally programming language neutral, ultimately, any given Web service is implemented in some programming language technology. In the case of this book, we've chosen Java—probably not a surprise to you, given our title. Where issues of interoperability with Web services written in other programming languages appear, we note them. Detailed coverage of other Web services implementation approaches, such as Microsoft's .NET, is beyond the scope of this book.

Progressive Disclosure

After an overview of Web services, we start with the fundamentals of XML and then layer on new concepts, motivated by a business computing problem. These layers produce a series of Web services technology stacks. For each of the technologies and standards in the Web services arena, we focus on explaining the technology from the perspective of the problems it solves, balancing the explanation of the technology itself.

Business Example

The technologies and standards that make up the Web services concept are each examined in the context of an example (which we discuss later in this introduction). The use of the example adds insight to the explanation of Web services in the text of the book and supports the progressive disclosure approach as we follow the example, adding the layers of Web services technology to the solution. This technique helps position various best-practices approaches to Web service development and deployment. You can download the source code for these running examples from `www.samspublishing.com`. When you reach that page, enter this book's ISBN number (0672326418) in the search box to access information about the book and a Downloads link.

Service-Oriented Architecture

The examples and Web services concepts are discussed in the context of Service-Oriented Architecture (SOA), which we introduce in Chapter 1, "Web Services Overview and Service-Oriented Architectures." We use the SOA framework to help position the various Web services concepts in the context of a bigger picture.

Overview of the Book's Composition

This book is divided into three major parts: "Web Services Basics," "Enterprise Web Services," and "Web Services in the Real World." Chapters 1 through 6 describe the core concepts of Web services; you need to have a thorough understanding of this subject matter to be successful with any Web services development project. Chapters 7 through 12 are organized around Web services topics that have an enterprise computing focus. The topics discussed in this section address technical subjects that usually crop up when you're building "real" information technology solutions. The last part of the book, Chapters 13 through 15, deals with development pragmatics that we've gleaned from real-world experience with Web services. Let's take a closer look at the topics in each of the chapters.

Chapter 1 begins the book with an explanation of what the Web services approach is all about. We describe what a Web service is, what standards and technologies are associated with Web services, and what problems can be solved using Web services. We use this chapter to introduce the Service-Oriented Architecture (SOA) conceptual framework and begin to explain how the various Web services standards such as SOAP, WSDL, and UDDI fit together. This chapter will give you a solid conceptual basis for the rest of the book.

Before we can get into the core Web services standards, we take a brief side trip to explain XML in Chapter 2, "XML Primer." Because XML is at the heart of all the Web services standards and techniques, it's important for you understand it well. XML is a huge topic, but we focus our examination of XML on what you'll need to know in order to understand the rest of the Web services topics.

After the review of XML, Chapter 3, "The SOAP Protocol," dives in to the core mechanism of invoking a Web service. We review the topic of XML messaging in a distributed computing environment, focusing on the SOAP messaging standard from the W3C. SOAP forms the core basis of communication between a service requestor and a service provider in a Web services environment, and it's the foundation on which you can build the kinds of business-level extensions we'll discuss later in the book.

Chapter 4, "Describing Web Services," introduces the important notion of service description, which is key to making Web services a great application integration technology for building loosely coupled systems. This chapter discusses how Web services use service description to address the problem of communicating the details the service requestor needs to know about the Web service in order to properly understand how (and why) to invoke it.

Chapter 5, "Implementing Web Services with Apache Axis," refines your understanding of SOAP in the context of a particular SOAP infrastructure: the Apache Axis project. This chapter dives into the details of how Axis works and how you can use it to both consume Web services and deploy your own.

Now, you need to understand how the service requestor got the service description in the first place. Chapter 6, "Discovering Web Services," picks up where Chapter 4 left off, discussing the various techniques for Web service discovery, such as UDDI. This chapter examines the standards related to finding what Web services are provided by businesses with which a company might want to collaborate.

Chapter 7, "Web Services and J2EE," adds detail to the core concepts introduced in Chapters 1 through 6. This chapter explains how the Web services concepts map to Java 2 Enterprise Edition (J2EE). Chapter 7 explains how to build Web services using Axis and using the JSR109 Java standard.

In Chapter 8, "Web Services and Stateful Resources," we review how the notion of stateful resources can be combined with Web services, by introducing the concepts of WS-Addressing, a referencing or pointer mechanism in Web services; WS-Resource Framework, a specification for associating Web services with stateful resources; and WS-Notification, a mechanism for doing publish-subscribe style of asynchronous messaging. This work is an emerging standard for use in Grid computing and systems management as well as e-business computing. (For more information on Grid computing, we recommend that you browse www.globalgridforum.org.)

The very important issue of Web services security is discussed in Chapter 9, "Securing Web Services." This chapter reviews existing security technologies and takes a closer look at the mapping from Web services security to those technologies. This chapter also reviews how Web services security technologies are integrated into enterprise applications using the J2EE model.

In many applications, it's critical to verify whether a message is sent or received by another party. Chapter 10, "Web Services Reliable Messaging," explores a Web services specification that was written to try to overcome certain problems with Web services by adding a reliability aspect to SOAP.

Chapter 11, "Web Services Transactions," examines how Web services deal with transactions. In an enterprise setting, it's likely that Web services will need to be invoked and coordinated under the scope of a single unit of work. In this chapter, we examine a group of specifications that describe how to do this with Web services.

Web services allow designers to build applications that more closely resemble the business processes they automate. Chapter 12, "Orchestrating Web Services," describes how to build Web services by coordinating or orchestrating simpler Web services into a business process (which is also a Web service). This chapter introduces the Business Process Execution Language for Web Services (BPEL4WS) specification.

Chapter 13, "Web Services Interoperability," explores the Do's and Don'ts of building Web services that interoperate with other Web services. The Web Service Interoperability (WS-I) Organization has developed a series of guidelines that help developers use the Web services specifications in a consistent way across vendors. This chapter examines the work of this organization.

Chapter 14, "Web Services Pragmatics," deals with a list of issues that you may encounter when you're building and deploying Web services in the real world.

Chapter 15 provides a forward-looking epilogue, "Web Services Futures," which speculates on some possible future uses of Web services technologies.

> **Note**
>
> This book introduces quite a few terms with which you might not be familiar. We've included a glossary at the back of the book that acts as a great reference guide to the terminology we use. We'll annotate the first use of each term appearing in the glossary using the 📖 symbol.

Introducing SkatesTown

Before we get started, let's introduce the fictional company we'll use for our examples throughout this book: SkatesTown. We'll follow SkatesTown as the company exploits Web services to improve its business.

SkatesTown is a small but growing business in New York that was founded by three mechanically inclined friends with a passion for skateboards. They started by designing and selling custom prebuilt boards out of Dean Carroll's garage, and word soon spread about the quality of their work. They came up with some innovative new construction techniques, and within months they had orders piling up. Now SkatesTown has a small manufacturing operation in Brooklyn, and the company is selling boards, clothing, and equipment to stores around the city. Dean, Frank Stemkowski, and Chad Washington couldn't be happier about how their business has grown.

Of the three, Chad is the real gearhead, and he has been responsible for most of the daring construction and design choices that have helped SkatesTown get where it is today. He's the president and head of the team. Frank, gregarious and a smooth talker ever since childhood, now handles marketing and sales. Dean has tightly tracked the computer revolution over the years, and he's chief technical officer for the company.

A few years back, Dean realized that networking technology was going to be big, and he wanted to make sure that SkatesTown could catch the wave and utilize distributed computing to leverage its business. This focus turned out to be a great move.

Dean set up a Web presence so SkatesTown could help its customers stay up to date without requiring a large staff to answer phones and questions. He also built an online order-processing system to help streamline the flow of the business with network-enabled clients. In recent months, more and more stores who carry SkatesTown products have been using the system to great effect.

Our Story Begins

At present, Dean is pretty happy with the way things are working with SkatesTown's electronic commerce systems. But there have been a few problems, and Dean is sure that the systems could be even better. He realizes that as the business grows, the manual tasks associated with order gathering and inventory resupply will limit the company's success. Always one to watch the horizon, Dean has heard the buzz about Web services, and he wants to know more. At the urging of a friend, he got in touch with Al Rosen, a contractor for Silver Bullet Consulting (SBC). Silver Bullet specializes in Web services solutions, and after a couple of meetings with Al, Dean was convinced—he hired SBC to come in, evaluate SkatesTown's systems, and help the company grow into a Web service–enabled business.

As we move through the rest of the book, we'll keep an eye on how SkatesTown uses technologies like XML and, later, SOAP, WSDL, UDDI, and the rest of the Web services stack to increase efficiency and productivity, and establish new and valuable relationships with its customers and business partners. Silver Bullet, as you'll see, usually lives up to its name.

I

Web Services Basics

1

Web Services Overview and Service-Oriented Architectures

OKAY, ENOUGH WITH THE HYPE. Some have said that Web services promised to be everything to everyone, but clearly that isn't going to happen. Where is the business benefit behind the Web services technologies? That's what this book will attempt to explain, in the context of exploring the technologies themselves. Several things do seem to be true:

- According to many industry analyst reports, Web services are being used by the vast majority of Fortune 500 businesses.
- Web services technology promises to help small and medium businesses participate more effectively in supply chains of large organizations.
- Information technology (IT) vendors have adopted Web services (more or less) as a major part of their software strategy.
- The Web services industry is dominated by standards activities, minimizing the likelihood of the technology being dominated by a single vendor.

That being said, several concerns remain:

- Widespread adoption, particularly after several pilot projects are completed, has been slow to happen. Some people speculate that the business climate after 2000 was too conservative, and the dot-com bubble made businesses shy of shiny new technology.
- Standards are being developed, but this is happening at a majestic (slow) pace. Tooling and runtime support will follow, but when? Security standards have just recently been finalized, and infrastructure products supporting those standards have yet to be ubiquitously deployed. Additional concerns are lack of finalized reliable messaging and transaction standards. Some analysts claim that the Web services hype wasn't about the technology's promise (it's well positioned to deliver value),

but rather about the rate and pace of its maturity: It's a lot harder to get industry standards adopted than it's to drive proprietary technologies.

- Best practices are slow in coming. Without a good base of solid implementation experience, there will continue to be a lot of thrashing around as businesses figure out what to use this technology for.

- Business process design is just beginning to take a service-oriented approach. Until this happens, many powerful benefits of Web services won't be realized.

So how can we move forward? We talk about adoption pragmatics toward the end of the book, in Chapter 14, "Web Services Pragmatics"; until then, it's important for developers to understand the individual technologies and standards that make up the Web services landscape. Discussing these technologies in the context of a scenario, like the SkatesTown scenario we return to throughout the book, is one excellent way to get a basic understanding of Web services. After you learn the basic concepts, technology, and terminology, the next step is for you to implement, practice, summarize, and discuss.

In this chapter, we'll provide the basic terminology and set of concepts that put the remainder of the book into context. We'll define what we mean by a *Web service* 📖 and describe situations in which Web services play an important role. We'll describe a simple framework, called *service-oriented architecture* 📖, which helps structure the application of Web services technologies. We'll also provide a framework, in the form of an "interoperability" stack that positions how the various Web services technologies including *SOAP* 📖, *Web Services Description Language (WSDL)* 📖, and *Universal Description Discovery and Integration (UDDI)* 📖 relate. The rest of the book, then, is an elaboration of the basic concepts presented here.

What Is a Web Service?

This is a book about building Web services. We can't describe how to build a Web service without first clarifying what we mean by *Web service*.

Web services have gained a lot of momentum since the term was introduced in the year 2000. Many software vendors (large and small) have Web services initiatives and products. In fact, some vendors are in the second or third version of their Web services product offerings! Many organizations are involved in the refinement of Web services standards. Early in the evolution of Web services there seemed to be a slow convergence toward a common understanding of what the term means—there was no single, universally adopted definition of what is meant by the term *Web service*. This situation was reminiscent of the early days of object-oriented programming: Not until the concepts of inheritance, encapsulation, and polymorphism were well defined did object-oriented programming become accepted into the mainstream of development methodologies.

Several major Web services infrastructure providers published their definitions for a Web service. And through the process of open standards development, a commonly accepted term emerged. The Web services Architecture working group of the *World Wide*

Web Consortium 🕮 (W3C, which manages the evolution of the SOAP and WSDL specifications) developed the following definition for a Web service:

> A Web service is a software system designed to support interoperable machine-to-machine interaction over a network. It has an interface described in a machine-processable format (specifically WSDL). Other systems interact with the Web service in a manner prescribed by its description using SOAP messages, typically conveyed using HTTP with an XML serialization in conjunction with other Web-related standards.

One important point is that a Web service need not necessarily exist on the World Wide Web. This is an unfortunate historical naming issue. A Web service can live anywhere on the network, Inter- or intranet. In fact, Web services have little to do with the browser-centric, HTML-focused World Wide Web. (Sometimes the names we choose in the IT industry don't make a lot of sense; they simply take on a life of their own.)

Another important point is that a Web service's implementation and deployment platform details aren't relevant to a program that's invoking the service. A Web service is available through its declared API and invocation mechanism (network protocol, data encoding schemes, and so on). This is analogous to the relationship between a Web browser and a Web application server: Very little shared understanding exists between the two components. The Web browser doesn't care if the Web application server is Apache Tomcat, Microsoft Internet Information Services Server, or IBM WebSphere. The shared understanding is that they both speak HTTP and converse in HTML or a limited set of MIME types. Similarly, the Web application server doesn't care what kind of client is using it—various brands of Web browsers or even non-browser clients. This minimal shared understanding between components allows Web services to form a system of loosely coupled components.

Business Perspective

Web services have become an important concept for business people; they're quickly becoming a significant part of a business IT strategy. The vast majority of the Fortune 500 has already adopted Web services in some fashion. Although Web services–based systems are mainly deployed for internal application purposes, a growing minority (around 40–50% according to recent surveys) of companies are beginning to use Web services with their customers, suppliers, and business partners.

To a business person, the Web services approach is all about integration: integrating application functionality within an organization or integrating applications between business partners (in a supply chain, for example). The scenario in this book illustrates this approach. Application integration allows time and cost efficiencies for receiving purchase orders, answering status inquiries, processing shipment requests, and so on. The important point is that application integration is enabled without tight lock-in to any particular business partner. If another supplier has better prices, shipping terms, or quality assurance, then a company's reorder systems can be easily repositioned to use that supplier;

doing so is as easy as pointing a Web browser at a different Web site. With a broader adoption of Web services and XML document format standards, this style of dynamic business partner integration will become more broadly used. The Web services technology has become so important in business that it's even appearing in business school curriculums. One of the authors of this book recently completed an MBA degree; Web services were featured in several of the courses!

The systems integration thought isn't new. The IT industry has offered numerous integration technologies; many were proprietary, some were based on open standards. Web services reflect the application of a trend broadly accepted in the IT community: adoption of open standards. With Web services acting as a ubiquitous integration infrastructure supported by most organizations, the task of building cross-organizational information systems (such as a supply chain) becomes much easier and less expensive.

When systems are easy and inexpensive to integrate, an organization's reach to suppliers, customers, and other business partners is extended, yielding cost savings, flexible business models, better customer service, higher customer retention, and so on. This fact is driving change in the way organizations think about building IT systems, particularly those involving integration of existing software programs and those of suppliers, customers, and business partners. Just as IT is fundamental to the efficient operations of an organization, Web services–based systems integration will be fundamental to flexible, lightweight systems integration—for internal application integration within an organization over an intranet and external partner integration over the Internet or extended virtual private network.

So, from a business perspective, a Web service is a business process or step within a business process that is made available over a network to internal and/or external business partners to achieve a business goal. The key is ease of integration, particularly between organizations, allowing business systems to be built quickly by combining Web services built internally with those of business partners.

Technical Perspective

From a technical perspective, a Web service is nothing more than a collection of one or more related operations that are accessible over a network and are described by a service description. At this level, the Web services concept isn't new. With Web services, the IT industry is trying to address the fundamental challenge of distributed computing that has been around for decades: locating and accessing remote components. The big difference is that now the industry is approaching this problem using open technology (XML and Internet protocols) and open standards managed by broad consortia such as *OASIS* 📖 and the W3C.

The role of loose coupling can't be overemphasized. Instead of building an application as a collection of tightly coupled components or subroutines, all of which are well known to the developer at coding time, the Web services approach is much more dynamic. The focus with Web services is on the interface: the contract between a Web service and the component invoking it. Of course, this approach isn't new; what *is* new is the way that Web services combine the loosely coupled component-based approach to software development with the lessons learned from the World Wide Web—particularly the important role of simple, open standards to achieve ubiquitously deployed infrastructure capabilities.

Service-Oriented Architectures

Early in the Web services technology evolution, we noticed a pattern that we called *service-oriented architecture (SOA)*. SOA is a simple concept, which makes it applicable to a wide variety of Web services situations.

In an SOA, all software components (or functional units that are visible for other entities to invoke or consume over the network) are modeled as services. That is, the architectural premise is that all business tasks or business processes that are built in software are designed as services to be consumed over a network.

In an SOA, the focus of design is the service's interface. This is similar to component-based software engineering approaches we've seen. However, a major difference is that the focus of application design is shifted to composing services invoked over a network. In the SOA approach, the designer isn't building a program, a functional unit for one purpose/use only; rather, they're building a service that has a well-defined interface and that can potentially be used in multiple business contexts.

Because SOA is focused on building applications using components with well-defined interfaces, it allows applications to be loosely coupled. Applications are integrated at the interface (contract) level, not at the implementation level. This allows greater flexibility, because applications are built to work with any implementation of a contract, not to take advantage of a feature or idiosyncrasy of a particular implementation. For example, different service providers (of the same interface) can be dynamically chosen based on policies (such as price, other QoS guarantees, current transaction volume, and so on).

Figure 1.1 depicts the main roles and operations in an SOA. Any service-oriented architecture contains three roles: a *service requestor* 📖, a *service provider* 📖, and a *service registry* 📖:

- A *service provider* is responsible for creating a *service description* 📖, deploying that service in a runtime environment that makes it accessible by other entities over the network, publishing that service description to one or more service registries, and receiving Web service invocation messages from one or more service requestors. A service provider, then, can be any company that hosts a Web service made available on a network. You can think of a service provider as the "server side" of a client-server relationship between the service requestor and the service provider.

- A *service requestor* is responsible for finding a service description published to one or more service registries and is responsible for using service descriptions to bind to or invoke Web services hosted by service providers. Any consumer of a Web service can be considered a service requestor. You can think of a service requestor as the "client side" of a client-server relationship between the service requestor and the service provider.

- The *service registry* is responsible for advertising Web service descriptions published to it by service providers and for allowing service requestors to search the collection of service descriptions contained within the service registry. The service registry role is simple: to be a matchmaker between service requestor and service provider. Once the service registry makes the match, it's no longer needed in the picture; the rest of the interaction takes place directly between the service requestor and the service provider for the Web service invocation.

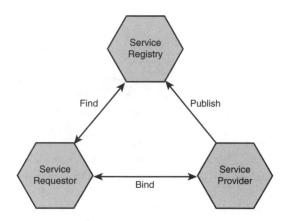

Figure 1.1 Service-oriented architecture

Each of these roles can be played by any program or network node. In some circumstances, a single program might fulfill multiple roles; for example, a program can be a service provider, providing a Web service to downstream consumers, as well as a service requestor, itself consuming Web services provided by others.

An SOA also includes three operations: *publish* 📖, *find* 📖, and *bind* 📖. These operations define the contracts between the SOA roles:

- The *publish* operation is an act of service registration or service advertisement. It acts as the contract between the service registry and the service provider. When a service provider publishes its Web service description to a service registry, it's advertising the details of that Web service to a community of service requestors. The details of the publish API depend on how the service registry is implemented. In certain simple or *direct publish* scenarios, the service registry role is played by the network itself, with publish being an act of moving the service description into a Web application server's directory structure. Other services registry implementations, such as UDDI, define a sophisticated implementation of the publish operation.

- The *find* operation is the logical dual of the publish operation. It's the contract between a service requestor and a service registry. With the find operation, the service requestor states a search criteria, such as type of service, various other aspects of the service such as quality of service guarantees, and so on. The service registry matches the find criteria against its collection of published Web service descriptions. The result of the find operation is a list of service descriptions that match the find criteria. Of course, the sophistication of the find operation varies with the implementation of the service registry role. Simple service registries can provide a find operation with nothing more sophisticated than an unparameterized HTTP GET. This means the find operation always returns all Web services published to the service registry, and it's the service requestor's job to figure out which Web service description matches its needs. UDDI, of course, provides extremely powerful find capabilities.

- The *bind* operation embodies the client-server relationship between the service requestor and the service provider. It can be quite sophisticated and dynamic, such as on-the-fly generation of a client-side proxy based on the service description used to invoke the Web service; or it can be a static model, where a developer hand-codes the way a client application invokes a Web service.

The key to SOA is the service description. It's the service description that is published by the service provider to the service registry. It's the service description that is retrieved by the service requestor as a result of the find operation. It's a service description that tells the service requestor everything it needs to know in order to bind to or invoke the Web service provided by the service provider. The service description also indicates what information (if any) is returned to the service requestor as a result of the Web service invocation.

Each time an SOA is deployed, different technologies may fulfill each role. Chapter 6, "Discovering Web Services," discusses various options for implementing a service registry and goes into great detail on the UDDI service registry technology. Chapter 4, "Describing Web Services," discusses service description in detail. Chapters 3 and 5, "The SOAP Protocol" and "Implementing Web Services with Apache Axis," focus on the use of SOAP to fulfill the bind operation. Chapter 9, "Securing Web Services," discusses how to make Web services more secure. Chapters 10 and 11, "Web Services Reliable Messaging" and "Web Services Transactions," describe how to make invoking Web services reliable and transactable. In Chapter 12, "Orchestrating Web Services," you'll learn how to build applications by stitching services together using a workflow technique.

The choices of which techniques to use are driven by business needs. How secure does a Web service invocation need to be? There is a price to pay for security (in complexity and performance); sometimes it's worth paying, and other times the risk doesn't warrant the cost. Is reliable message delivery important? For some Web services invocations, it clearly is; for others, it isn't obvious that the complexity and the performance price are warranted. The same is true for transactions and the other Web services capabilities discussed in this book.

Why Is SOA So Important?

SOA is an important trend within the IT community. There is a lot of discussion among analysts and developers about the term. Why all the fuss?

With the SOA approach to application architecture, your view of the entire software portfolio is different. SOA augments and grows your application portfolio. Existing applications can be easily converted to services, to be consumed by existing or new applications. Your portfolio of applications gradually shifts to become a portfolio of components exposed as services and applications composed of services (service orchestrations).

Eventually, monolithic, tightly coupled, inflexible applications will be replaced by SOA-architected applications. This won't happen overnight, but rather will take place in an evolutionary fashion, driven by business needs.

With an SOA, organizations will be better able to construct software to integrate business processes and respond rapidly to changes in the business environment: the arrival of a new supplier or competitor, a shift of business model, a postmerger combination of IT assets, the opportunity to outsource a business process, and so on. When parts of the solution to the new business system were built by autonomous organizations, an SOA approach is the best approach to stitch the solution together. More than any technical consideration, this concept of implicit, seamless software integration as a major business benefit is one of the main drivers for service orientation.

The SOA approach isn't lost on vendors of prepackaged software applications. Many major application vendors are at the forefront of Web services standards and SOA practices. The forward-thinking among the software vendors recognize this new SOA emphasis and are incrementally moving their product offerings away from tightly coupled, shrink-wrapped software suites toward more flexible, mix-and-match, loosely coupled SOA architectures of services. This approach will ease their customers' task of integrating packaged software components with existing business systems and processes.

Another important benefit of SOA comes from the notion of bringing IT concepts and business concepts closer together. Previously, technical architectures reflected too much technical detail and hid the underlying business process. With SOA, it's easier to focus on modeling business processes and tasks as services and building business systems as workflow combinations of these underlying services. With a closer modeling of the business system in technology, it becomes easier to isolate the parts of the system that need changing to reflect those tasks in the business process that need changing. With an SOA approach, technical details of the service are hidden behind the interface, and the designer's attention is focused on jointly (or unilaterally) designing useful service interfaces.

Thus the combination of a closer IT model of the business, together with loose coupling, provides the overall business benefit of SOA. The benefit boils down to good choice of service. What service interface design yields most benefit to the organization, and which is most useful to important service requestors? Which existing applications can be refactored or wrapped as services and let you quickly get to the point of building SOAs from existing IT investments? Which business processes will provide the biggest benefit if they're built or refactored as services? These are important questions to address when you're considering adopting SOA.

SOA and Web Services: Related but Distinct

Although Web services and SOA are often thought about in combination, these two terms are distinct. SOA is an architectural concept, an approach to building systems that focuses on a loosely coupled set of components (services) that can be dynamically composed. Web services, on the other hand, is one approach to building an SOA. Web services provides a standard for a particular set of XML-based technologies that can be used to build SOA systems.

Trends in E-Business

Interoperability, particularly between heterogeneous distributed systems components, has been one of the major themes in software engineering in general, and application integration in particular, for the last decade. It's unfortunate that the seamless interoperability vision is still a dream. Brittleness in all current architectures is preventing software from achieving this vision. *Brittleness* comes from tightly coupled systems that generate dependencies at every level in the system. One of the most important lessons we learned as developers and architects is that systems need to be able to find resources (software or otherwise) automatically, when and as needed, without human intervention. This ability frees business people to concentrate on their business and customers rather than worry about IT complexities. At the same time, it frees system developers to concentrate on enabling their business and their customers rather than deal with interoperability headaches by writing glue code and patching systems together.

Trends in application design are moving from rigid structures to flexible architectures. Trends in business partner interactions are moving from static agreements to more dynamic agreements. In a so-called *value-network* approach, competition isn't between individual companies but rather between value-networks of business partners that can best cooperate and adapt to changing market needs.

We're seeing these trends in many places, from operating system–level systems management efforts such as Grid computing all the way to packaged business application suites. A flexible, dynamically reconfigurable stack of software components is being built, heralding the era when software systems are less brittle and less expensive to configure, maintain, and change.

Trends in B2B integration are moving from a proprietary technology-based integration to business process–based integration using open standards. There is a corresponding shift in programming and architecture models to enable these trends: from tightly coupled applications to loosely coupled services.

On the technical side, major shifts have occurred toward flexibility and interoperability, through open and widely accepted standards. The first major shift happened almost three decades ago with the advent of TCP/IP as an open platform for networking. This step enabled such important and pervasive architectures as client-server computing. It took the advent of the World Wide Web for the next major shift, with HTML and HTTP providing the first truly universal open and portable user interface. Next, Java gave us truly open portable programming, and finally XML brought with it open portable data exchange. The next step in this evolution of open standards is the integration step. How do all these ingredients come together to facilitate the next evolution of e-business? Web services.

One aspect of more loosely coupled systems is reflected in the move from Remote Procedure Call (RPC) interfaces toward a messaging or *document-centric* 📖 model of distributed computing interface. With a document-centric approach, the interface to the Web service becomes much simpler and more flexible. An RPC interface presenting a fixed set of parameters in a fixed order is quite brittle. Small changes to information (for example, a new requirement for an expiration date on a credit card) require a new interface to be created, published, and understood by the service requestor. With a document-centric approach, the new information can be added to the document schema defined in the Web service interface. Programs that use the older schema don't necessarily break when the new XML element is added (this is a property of XML namespaces that you will see in Chapter 2, "XML Primer"). This approach yields Web services interfaces that are much more flexible, resulting in systems that are adaptive.

Why Do We Need Web Services?

The beginning of this chapter explained the motivation for application-to-application integration over the Internet to address the current challenges of distributed computing and B2B integration in particular. Since late 1999, the software industry has been rapidly evolving XML-based Web services technologies as the approach to solving these problems. Why build a completely new distributed computing stack based on Web services?

"Because Web services use XML" isn't the right answer. It's a correct observation, but it doesn't answer the crucial question as to why using XML makes such a big difference. At a basic level, there are three key reasons why existing distributed computing approaches are inferior to Web services for solving the problems of e-business:

- The scope of problems they try to address
- The choice of available technology
- Industry dynamics around standards control and innovation

This section will discuss those three key reasons and summarize with a discussion of characteristics of a good Web service.

Scoping the Problem

Traditional distributed computing mechanisms have typically evolved around technical architectures rather than broader problems of application integration. For example, CORBA evolved as a solution to the problem of implementing rich distributed object architectures. At the time, it was implicitly assumed that this was the right approach to getting applications to communicate with one another. As we discussed earlier, experience has shown that RPCs aren't always the best architecture for this requirement. The need for loosely coupled applications and business process automation has shown the benefits of exchanging messages containing data (typically a business document) between the participants of e-business interactions, a so-called document-centric approach. Distributed computing specifications address messaging as a computing architecture; however, there has been no unifying approach that brings RPCs and document-centric messaging to the same level of importance—until Web services, that is.

Web services have evolved not around predefined architectures but around the problem of application integration. This is an important distinction. The choice of problem scope defines the focus of a technology initiative. Web services technologies have been designed from the ground up to focus on the problems of application integration. As a result, we can do things outside the scope of traditional distributed computing approaches:

- Support both document-centric messaging and RPCs
- Transport encoded data from both applications and business documents
- Work over open Internet protocols such as HTTP and SMTP

In other words, Web services are better suited for the task than what we've used so far, because we've built them with this in mind. COM/CORBA/RMI are great technologies for tying together distributed objects on the corporate network. However, the e-business application integration problem is best tackled by Web services.

Core Technologies

Because Web services address a much more broadly scoped problem, they use much more flexible technologies than traditional distributed computing approaches. Further, with Web services, we can leverage all that we've learned about connecting and integrating applications since we began doing distributed computing. These two factors put Web services on a better technology foundation for solving the problems of e-business than traditional distributed computing approaches.

Later, in the "Web Services Interoperability Stack" section, we introduce a hierarchical organization of the technologies and standards associated with Web services. It's possible to compare the Web services approach to traditional distributed computing approaches level-by-level to see why the technical foundation of Web services is more appropriate for the problems it needs to solve. Rather than going through this lengthy process, let's focus on two key capabilities: the ability to represent data structures and the ability to describe these data structures.

Data encoding is a key weakness for traditional distributed computing approaches, particularly those that are programming language independent. Sure, they typically have a mechanism to represent simple data (numbers, strings, booleans, date-time values, and so on), basic arrays, and structures with properties. However, mapping existing complex datatypes in applications to the underlying data encoding mechanisms was difficult. Adding new native datatypes was practically impossible. The fact that data was encoded in binary formats further complicated matters.

Web services address these issues by using XML to represent information. XML's text-based form eliminates byte-ordering concerns. The wide availability of XML processing tools makes participation in the world of Web services relatively easy. XML's hierarchical structure (achieved by the nesting of XML elements) allows changes at some level of nesting in an XML document to be made without worrying about the effect on other parts of the document. Also, the expressive nature of attributes and nested elements makes it easier to represent complex data structures in XML than in the pure binary formats traditionally used by COM and CORBA, for example. In short, XML makes working with arbitrary data easier.

The choice of XML brought another advantage to Web services: the ability to describe datatypes and validate whether data coming on the wire complies with its specification. This happens through the use of XML meta-languages such as XML Schema.

Industry Dynamics

Momentum is a very important aspect of the dynamics of software innovation. Great problems lead to great opportunities. The desire to capitalize on the opportunities generates momentum around a set of initiatives targeted at solving the problem. This momentum is the binding force of our industry. This is how major innovation takes place on a broad scale. The challenge of e-business application integration is great; this is why all the key players in the industry are focused on it. Customer need, market pressure, and the desire to be part of the frontier-defining elite have pushed many companies to become deeply engaged with Web services.

Good things are bound to happen. Consider this: The last time every one of the key infrastructure vendors was focused on the same set of issues was during the early days of e-business when the industry was trying to address the challenges of building Web applications. The net result was a new model for application development that leveraged the Web browser as a universal client and the Web application server as a universal backend. In short, trust that some of the very best minds in the industry working together under the aegis of organizations such as the W3C and OASIS will be able to come up with a good solution to the problems of e-business integration.

Parallelism is key to building real momentum and increasing the bandwidth of innovation. Traditional distributed computing efforts could not achieve this kind of parallelism because they were driven either by a single vendor (Microsoft promoting COM, for example) or by a large, slow organization such as the Object Management Group (OMG), which owns the CORBA standards. In both cases, the key barrier to fast progress was the centralized management of standards. Any change had to be approved by the body owning the standard. And Microsoft and OMG owned all of COM and CORBA, respectively. Open-source efforts such as the Linux operating system and projects of the Apache Software Foundation fundamentally generate momentum because people working on them can have a direct influence on the end product. The momentum of Web services is real because standardization work is going on in parallel at the W3C, OASIS, and many other horizontal and vertical industry standards organizations.

Further, the major players so far have shown a commitment to do a lot of innovation out in the open.

The interesting thing from a technical perspective is that XML has something to do with the ability of Web service standardization to be parallelized. XML has facilities (namespaces and schema) that enable the decentralized evolution of XML-based standards without preventing the later composition of these standards in the context of a single solution. For example, if group A owns some standard and group B is trying to build an extension to the standard, then with some careful use of XML, group B can design the extensions such that:

- Its extension can be published independently of the standard.
- Its extension can be present in cases where the standard is used.
- Applications that don't understand the extension won't break if the extension is present.
- Applications that need the extension will work only if the extension is present.

The industry's focus on Web services combines the right scope (e-business application integration) with the right technologies (XML-based standards) and the potential for significant parallelism and high-bandwidth innovation. This is why Web services will be successful.

What Makes a Good Web Service?

An IT project should exhibit many (but not all) of the following characteristics before you should consider modeling the solution using SOA and Web services:

- The problem has a distributed computing nature: parts of the solution exist in multiple network endpoints.
- The solution needs to consist of components built and run by different organizations. If there is a single point of control or administration that can resolve any issue that may arise, you have a broad range of solution choices that can be imposed by this single administrative control. A multiplicity of partners favors the dynamic binding nature and XML protocols associated with Web services.
- The components that need to be integrated have heterogeneous platforms (operating system, application server, programming language).
- The business process should be automated; various characteristics of the solution can't require a human interaction for each step. If a human can be involved, standard World Wide Web technologies such as browsers, JSPs, and servlets will do.
- The business process, and/or the set of components that make up the business process, change with some frequency. For a dynamic business environment, a flexible solution is required.
- The business process needs to be policy driven; decisions made within the logic of the business process need to be based on externalizable policies (which may themselves change with some rapidity).

- The business process isn't core and has the potential for outsourcing. With a Web services approach, outsourcing the business process minimizes the perturbation to those systems that interface with the outsourced process.

- Data needs to be available to more than just the core applications that generate/maintain the data. Rapid situation detection and response decision-making may require accessing data in non-traditional ways. Web services is a simple approach to making information accessible to all sorts of different requestors.

The Web Service Opportunity

The Web services approach is an application integration concept; it's a set of technologies that provides access to business functionality, such as purchase order processing. Often, the business functionality already exists in the form of legacy transaction processing systems, existing Web applications, Enterprise JavaBeans, and so on. Web services technology is about access and application integration; it isn't an implementation technology.

Organizations use Web services technology in two broad categories: application integration and business-to-business (B2B) partner integration over the Internet. In either of these categories, Web services can range in sophistication from simple request/response functions such as a credit card check to complicated multi-party, multi-stage, long-running business transactions such as a supply configuration and order system. Web services can be invoked by PC-based programs, mainframe systems, Web browsers, or even small mobile devices such as cell phones or personal digital assistants (PDAs).

In addition to application integration and B2B, we'll discuss another growing use of Web services: B2C, or building systems with a human interface component using Web services.

Application Integration

Gartner defines *application integration* as "making independently designed application systems work together." The need for better-integrated applications is huge. Here are just a few examples from the public Internet and corporate networks:

- Forrester estimates that more than 50% of Fortune 1000 enterprises have over 50 legacy or packaged applications that need to be integrated—in spite of the functional and business needs. The opportunity cost of not integrating these applications is huge.

- *CIO Magazine*'s Tech Poll recently showed that more than 85% of surveyed companies have an IT application backlog, weighed heavily toward integrating existing systems as opposed to buying new systems.

- Have you ever forgotten some of your passwords? If single sign-on (SSO) is broadly deployed, you won't have to remember so many passwords.

- Have you ever chosen not to buy from a Web site offering you the best terms because you didn't have an account set up and you didn't want to spend the time registering? If eWallets work broadly on the Web, this won't be a problem.

- Email is the life blood of companies. Much relevant business information is sent and received through email, often outside the context of enterprise systems. A whole industry of companies has sprung up to address this lack of integration across multiple domains: sales automation, collaboration, resource planning, and so on.

- One large financial institution takes more than a week to process a change of address. The institution thinks that it can generate up to 10% more profit per customer if only it can process the change in less than 24 hours. It's been trying for years to integrate several applications to do this without success.

End users, IT, and business executives want more integration and information leverage between the applications they use every day. IDC estimates that the size of the application integration software market in the United States is approaching $5 billion. The United States systems integration (consulting) market, at the same time, was about $38 billion. Most of that is pure labor (as opposed to hardware and software) cost, and much of it is spent on integrating systems as opposed to building new systems. Two things become clear from this analysis: First, the total market size for integration is tens of billions for the United States alone. Second, services and not products account for the majority of that amount.

To harness the value potential of applications, we need much more integration. The only way to achieve this is to significantly lower the cost of integration across the board. There is a problem, however: The low product-to-service ratio in the integration space puts a constraint on both the rate of growth of the market and the cost of integration projects. Screen scraping, data mapping, and building bridges between incompatible APIs aren't scalable activities—they require trained personnel and a lot of time. When technology picks up its pace, IT services can't keep up. Unless enterprises fundamentally change their dependence on integration services, they won't be able to leverage the powerful trends in computing, storage, connectivity, and standardization. Nor will they be able to leverage the full value potential of integrated distributed applications. Companies will be stuck with integration backlogs that forever exceed their resources, both monetary and human.

The Web services approach offers an attractive set of technologies by which existing legacy systems can be wrappered as Web services and made available for integration with other systems within the organization. Applications exposed as Web services are accessible by other applications running on different hardware platforms and written in different programming languages. Using this approach, the complexity of these systems can be encapsulated behind industry-standard XML protocols. Pair-wise system integration projects can be replaced with one-to-many systems interactions based on Web services. The promise of higher-level interoperability initiatives is that over time we'll be able to develop the set of standards, technologies, and tools that will enable small and large businesses to easily integrate systems internally; then they can mix and match the implementation of various activities within a business process, maintaining the option to outsource any or all of these activities if doing so makes business sense.

B2B

Another key driver behind the rise of Web services is the continuing evolution of B2B computing. B2B computing is about integrating the business systems of two or more companies to support cross-enterprise business processes such as supply chain management. B2B applications can be as simple as automated credit card validation or as complex as the full automation of the multi-billion-dollar supply chain of a Fortune 100 company. The challenges of building B2B applications combined with their huge market potential drove rapid innovation that has taken the industry from simple *business-to-consumer (B2C)* 📖 applications to SOAP-enabled Web services in a matter of five years.

Integration of Human Interaction with Systems: B2C

Online HTML-based applications are consumer oriented. The classic example of a B2C Web application is the Amazon book search. To access this functionality, a human being needs to use a Web browser to navigate the company's site through multiple page transitions, input information using Web forms, submit them, and get the results back in human-readable form. The only way to automate this process is to simulate how a human uses the system. Doing so involves reverse-engineering the Web application to see how it moves data between pages, passing the data automatically from page to page, and, finally, parsing any data contained in the response HTML of pages. This screen-scraping approach was popular in the early years of the Web (1995–97), but it's very error prone. The only true way to integrate applications on the Web is to use a B2B-focused solution.

Because B2B applications are designed to have other applications as their clients, they're fundamentally different from B2C applications. Table 1.1 summarizes some of these differences for Java applications. Both types of application are unrestricted as to the type of backend they can use—typically, Java classes or Enterprise JavaBeans (EJBs). (We discuss how Web services work with EJBs in more detail in Chapter 7, "Web Services and J2EE.") This is where the similarities end, however.

To customize backend logic, B2C applications use servlets or Java ServerPages (JSPs) hosted in a servlet engine. B2B applications customize their backends using straight Java code (often EJBs) hosted inside a Web service engine. B2C applications communicate with a browser over HTTP. B2B applications can use any of the open Internet protocols such as HTTP, SMTP, or FTP, or proprietary networks such as EDI. B2C applications handle data over the straight HTTP protocol. Input comes as GET parameters (on the URL/query string) or as POST parameters from Web forms. Only strings can be exchanged; any other datatypes, even numbers, need to be encoded as strings. For output, data is mixed together with formatting rules inside HTML pages. This is in marked contrast with B2B applications, which use XML for both data input and output. XML is perfect for B2B computing because it's programming language- and platform-neutral, it can represent arbitrary data structures, it's easy to process, and it can be validated independently of its processing. B2C applications need a UI (typically HTML, although some use Java applets) because their clients are humans. B2B applications have no UI because their clients are other applications.

Table 1.1 **Comparing B2C and B2B Java Applications**

Area B2C	Application	B2B Application
Backend logic	Java classes and EJBs	Java classes and EJBs
Controller logic	Servlets and JSPs	Web service engine
Communication protocol	HTTP	HTTP/S, SMTP, FTP, TCP/IP, EDI, JMS, RMI/IIOP…
Data input	HTTP GET/POST parameters	XML
Data output	HTML	XML
UI	HTML + script	N/A
Client	Human behind a browser	Software application

Justifying Web Services

Information technology investments must be evaluated against all other competing potential uses of a firm's capital and other resources. This evaluation usually involves doing a *net present value* analysis to determine a dollar value of the costs and the benefits over time, and distilling this analysis into a single current value that can be compared with other investments. If the estimated value of the benefits doesn't exceed the cost, the project isn't financially justifiable.

The task is to understand the categories of costs and benefits for a Web services project. We've outlined some of the benefits in this chapter; they're summarized as follows:

- Application integration can be done in a faster and cheaper manner.
- Application integration can be done in ways that were hard to cost-justify with previous technologies. For example, the platform neutrality of Web services allows designers to combine business systems with all sorts of devices (such as PDAs, cell phones, normal desktops, server-based applications) with service providers of all shapes and sizes from small ones (such as radio frequency ID tags) to more traditional Web applications and mainframe systems.
- Time to market is reduced for new IT systems that support new or modified business processes. This is largely achieved by wrappering existing functionality. If the function exists, but only in a form that's hard to integrate, a simple adapter or wrapper function will quickly and cheaply enable other applications to exploit the existing function.

- The use of standards provides two major benefits. First, the team has a growing choice of runtime and tooling products. Second, customers avoid proprietary lock-in to a single vendor's technology, reducing the vendor's pricing power.

- The relatively low cost of entry, often leveraging existing Web infrastructure, allows small and medium sized businesses to participate in Web services applications of many partners, large and small.

- Interface-based development, using self-describing service descriptions, reduces the time to integrate applications, because less information is necessary to interact (for services you provide and those of partners that you consume).

The cost categories with Web services are fairly traditional for IT systems development; they include cost of tooling and runtimes, training costs for developers, testing costs, and consulting costs. Web services reduces some of these costs. Many Web services technologies are being layered into existing operating system and Web application platforms (such as Microsoft .NET and IBM WebSphere). This means that additional costs for the core Web services runtime and tooling can often be avoided. Because the Web services approach provides a means to wrapper existing software, more software is reused. With higher reuse, you reduce new software development and therefore lower overall costs.

An Iterative Approach to Adopting Web Services

Many development organizations increase benefits and reduce development risks by using an incremental approach to Web services. This approach is often characterized by the following four steps:

1. *Learn about the technologies.* Attend conferences, read articles, read books (like this one), and talk to vendors and analysts.

2. *Experiment.* Start with a small pilot project, to get a sense for the current state of the art of the technology and pragmatically separate what is real from and what is promise. Do several pilot projects to increase understanding among your organization's developers and get a sense of how your business's problems might be solved with this technology.

3. *Synthesize the learning into policies.* Make organization-wide commitments to platforms, tools, and technologies. Be ready to iterate the policies as your team's learning increases and as the standards and products evolve.

4. *Iterate the projects into production.* Become familiar with the issues related to putting Web services into production.

By taking an iterative approach, an organization can more effectively learn how to apply Web services to its business problems. With an SOA approach, you should find that the business strategy and the IT strategy are easier to coordinate.

Web Services Interoperability Stack

The Web services concept has been under iterative development since late 1999. The industry has seen Web services start from humble beginnings in the first version of XML messaging using SOAP, WSDL 1.1, and the initial version of UDDI as a service registry standard. Since that time, dozens of other Web services–related specifications have been introduced by various organizations; this book reviews many of them in detail.

To help position these technologies, we've developed the interoperability stack shown in Figure 1.2. You can think of Web services as a layered set of technologies. Note that this depiction shows a conceptual relationship between the technologies—the actual combination of technologies in a solution will vary. Most Web services solutions will use only a subset of the technologies.

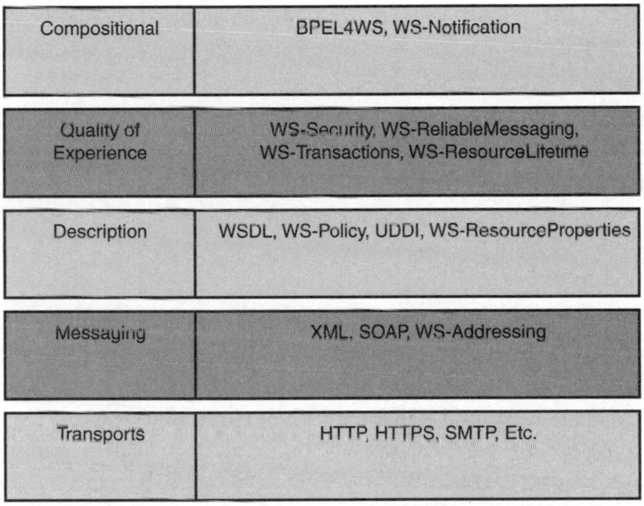

Compositional	BPEL4WS, WS-Notification
Quality of Experience	WS-Security, WS-ReliableMessaging, WS-Transactions, WS-ResourceLifetime
Description	WSDL, WS-Policy, UDDI, WS-ResourceProperties
Messaging	XML, SOAP, WS-Addressing
Transports	HTTP, HTTPS, SMTP, Etc.

Figure 1.2   Web services interoperability stack

Let's examine each of the layers in the stack and briefly overview the associated Web services technologies.

Transport Layer

At the base of the stack is the transport layer. Web services is basically a messaging mechanism, so it's reasonable to think about message transport technologies at the base of any Web services conceptualization. Web services are essentially transport neutral: A Web service message can be transported using the ubiquitous HTTP or HTTPS protocol, as well as via more specialized transport mechanisms such as JMS. Although transport mechanisms are fundamental to Web services, this book doesn't examine details of any transport. If you aren't comfortable with your understanding of network transport protocols, don't worry—Web services insulate the designer from most of the details and implications of the message transport layer.

Messaging Layer

At the messaging layer are fundamental Web services technologies such as XML, SOAP, and WS-Addressing. Web services use XML as the format of message payloads between the requestor and the provider. XML is the basic language of all the Web services description techniques we discuss in this book. If you're unfamiliar with XML, please examine Chapter 2; it will tell you everything you need to know about XML to be proficient with Web services.

One of the most popular and mature Web services standards is SOAP. The SOAP specification defines a simple enveloping mechanism that defines the basis of most Web services messages. SOAP was one of the original Web services standards, and its second version (SOAP 1.2) has been standardized within the W3C. We cover SOAP in great detail in Chapter 3.

WS-Addressing is a specification proposed by BEA, IBM, and Microsoft to standardize the concept of a *Web services pointer*. As you'll see in Chapter 8, "Web Services and Stateful Resources," WS-Addressing is used to allow Web services to refer to other Web services in a standard fashion.

Description Layer

As we mentioned previously, *service descriptions*—additional descriptive meta-data associated with Web services deployed on a network—help SOA systems achieve the looser coupling and dynamic binding features they're known for. The technologies listed at this layer include WSDL, WS-Policy, UDDI, and WS-ResourceProperties.

Web Services Description Language (WSDL) is the most mature and important form of Web services meta-data formats. With WSDL, developers describe the functional characteristics of their Web services: What operations does the service provide? What input and output messages are associated with those operations? WSDL 2.0 is nearing completion of the standardization process in the W3C. A related specification, WS-Policy, is one approach to augmenting WSDL with additional descriptive power, allowing a Web service's description to include statements about its capabilities beyond the raw functional or method signature level. We cover WSDL and WS-Policy in Chapter 4.

The notion of Web services registries and additional discovery-oriented meta-data is also important. The Universal Description Discovery and Integration (UDDI) specification is the most widely acknowledged specification for Web services registries. We cover UDDI in Chapter 6.

WS-ResourceProperties is a recently introduced specification describing the relationship between state information and Web services. WS-ResourceProperties is an important component of the WS-ResourceFramework proposed by Computer Associates, Globus, HP, and IBM to address the overall relationship between Web services and stateful resources. We cover this topic in detail in Chapter 8.

Quality of Experience Layer

The fourth layer in the stack is populated by specifications related to the quality of experience of the Web services solution. At this layer are technologies that clarify certain capabilities and requirements of Web services related to transactions, security, and reliable messaging. The technologies listed at this level are WS-Security, WS-ReliableMessaging, WS-Transactions, and WS-ResourceLifetime.

WS-Security (see Chapter 9) is a family of related specifications that clarify how a Web service interaction can be done in a secure fashion. WS-Security addresses concepts such as trust relationships in Web services environment and identity of Web services requestors.

WS-ReliableMessaging (see Chapter 10) is a proposed standard to address how Web services messaging can be done in a fashion that leaves the requestor and provider no doubt as to whether any particular message was received.

WS-Transactions (see Chapter 11) is a series of related specifications that clarify how Web services invocations are related to transactional contexts and so-called *ACID* semantics.

Compositional Layer

At the compositional layer are the BPEL4WS and WS-Notification specifications. The purpose of specifications at this level is to describe how other Web services are combined or composed.

BPEL4WS is a proposed standard to address how Web services can be combined into higher-level business processes by describing workflows or orchestrations of Web services invocations. BPEL4WS is covered in detail in Chapter 12.

WS-Notification is a recently published specification that addresses how to publish and subscribe (pub/sub) notification messages in a Web services environment. This specification is discussed in Chapter 8.

Understanding the Web Services Interoperability Stack

It's important to note that the constellation of Web services standards and specifications continues to evolve. Some of the earlier Web services specifications have entered their second or third version. Many of these specifications have undergone formal standardization within an open standards body. Other specifications are newer and have yet to be introduced to a standards body. We expect these specifications to continue to mature. We don't, however, anticipate that many more Web services specifications will be forthcoming. We dedicate the last chapter of this book to our speculation on what the future holds for Web services.

Don't let all the WS-* specifications intimidate you. Web services address a complicated problem: loosely coupled, dynamically configured heterogeneous distributed computing. However, the technology is doing this in a clever way. Instead of building Web services as a single, monolithic 1000+-page specification, the community has chosen to incrementally deliver a series of smaller, purpose-focused specifications. Each specification deals with its own domain (such as security, reliable messaging, or transactions) in isolation. The notion of *composability* allows designers to combine the specifications to build a complete Web services system. Each Web services specification is designed to compose with the others. For example, does WS-ReliableMessaging define its own security standard to address security issues related to reliable messaging? No. WS-ReliableMessaging, like the rest of the WS-★ specifications, depends on other WS-★ specifications. The job of a Web services designer is to determine which specifications their system needs and implement them accordingly. Is it important to the business function that Web services messages be delivered reliably? If so, use WS-ReliableMessaging; if not, don't use it. Is it important that Web services invocations be done in a transactional context? If so, use WS-Transactions; if not, then you don't need to use it.

To help the designer determine how to combine the various WS-★ specifications, the Web services community initiated an organization called the Web services Interoperability organization (WS-I). The purpose of WS-I is to standardize combinations of Web services specifications that can be used to increase the level of interoperability between Web services. We discuss the work done in WS-I as part of Chapter 13, "Web Services Interoperability."

Summary

In this chapter, we've provided you with a definition for Web services and helped position where these technologies will benefit businesses. We've also provided a conceptual framework—service-oriented architecture—that you can use to think about problems related to Web services. We outlined how the Web services technologies can be used for application integration within a business and between businesses. We discussed the benefits and costs to using Web services.

We also introduced the alphabet soup of Web services technologies and illustrated an organizational framework around an interoperability stack. The rest of this book builds on what we've introduced here.

2

XML Primer

Since its introduction in 1998, Extensible Markup Language (XML) has revolutionized how we think about structuring, describing, and exchanging information. The ways in which XML is used in the software industry are many and growing. Certainly for Web services the importance of XML is paramount; all key Web service technologies are based on it.

One great thing about XML is that it's constantly changing and evolving. However, this can also be its downside. New problems require new approaches and uses of XML that drive aggressive technological innovation. The net result is a maelstrom of invention—a pace of change so rapid that it leaves most people confused. To say that you're using XML is meaningless. Are you using DTDs or XML Schema and, if so, whose? How about XML Namespaces, XML Encryption, XML Signature, XPointer, XLink, XPath, XSLT, XQuery, XKMS, RDF, SOAP, WSDL, UDDI, XAML, BPEL, WSIA, WSRP, or WS-Whatever? Does your software use SAX, DOM, JAXB, JAXP, JAXM, JAXR, or JAX-RPC? It's easy to get lost, to drown in the acronym soup. You're interested in Web services (you bought this book, remember?). How much do you really need to know about XML?

The truth is pleasantly surprising. First, many XML technologies you might have heard about aren't relevant to Web services. You can safely forget half the acronyms you wish you knew more about. Second, even with relevant technologies, you need to know only a few core concepts. (The 80/20 rule doesn't disappoint.) Third, this chapter is all you need to read and understand to be able to handle the rest of the book and make the most of it.

This chapter will develop a set of examples around SkatesTown's processes for submitting POs and generating invoices. The examples cover all the technologies we've listed here.

If you're an old hand at XML who understands the XML namespace mechanism and feels at home with schema extensibility and the use of xsi:type, you should go straight to Chapter 3, "The SOAP Protocol," and dive into Web services. If you can parse and process a significant portion of the previous sentence, you should skim this chapter to get a quick refresher of some core XML technologies. And if you're someone with more limited XML experience, don't worry—by the end of this chapter, you'll be able to hold your own.

XML is here to stay. The XML industry is experiencing a boom. XML has become the de facto standard for representing structured and semistructured information in textual form. Many specifications are built on top of XML to extend its capabilities and enable its use in a broader range of scenarios. One of the most exciting areas of use for XML is Web services. The rest of this chapter will introduce the set of XML technologies and standards that are the foundation of Web services:

- *XML instances*—The rules for creating syntactically correct XML documents
- *XML Schema*—A standard that enables detailed validation of XML documents as well as the specification of XML datatypes
- *XML Namespaces*—Definitions of the mechanisms for combining XML from multiple sources in a single document
- *XML processing*—The core architecture and mechanisms for creating, parsing, and manipulating XML documents from programming languages as well as mapping Java data structures to XML

Document- Versus Data-Centric XML

Generally speaking, there are two broad application areas of XML technologies. The first relates to document-centric applications, and the second to data-centric applications. Because XML can be used in so many different ways, it's important to understand the difference between these two categories.

Document-Centric XML

Because of its SGML origins, in the early days of its existence, XML gained rapid adoption within publishing systems as a mechanism for representing semistructured documents such as technical manuals, legal documents, and product catalogs. The content in these documents is typically meant for human consumption, although it could be processed by any number of applications before it's presented to humans. The key element of these documents is semistructured marked-up text.

The following markup is a perfect example of XML used in a document-centric manner. The content is directed toward human consumption—it's part of the FastGlide skateboard user guide. The content is semistructured. The usage rules for tags such as `<B>`, `<I>`, and `<LINK>` are loosely defined; they could appear just about anywhere in the document:

```
<H1>Skateboard Usage Requirements</H1>
<P>In order to use the <B>FastGlide</B> skateboard you have to
have:</P>
<LIST>
```

```
<ITEM>A strong pair of legs.</ITEM>
<ITEM>A reasonably long stretch of smooth road surface.</ITEM>
<ITEM>The impulse to impress others.</ITEM>
</LIST>
<P>If you have all of the above, you can proceed to <LINK
HREF="Chapter2.xml">Getting on the Board</LINK>.</P>
```

Data-Centric XML

By contrast, data-centric XML is used to mark up highly structured information such as the textual representation of relational data from databases, financial transaction information, and programming language data structures. Data-centric XML is typically generated by machines and is meant for machine consumption. XML's natural ability to nest and repeat markup makes it the perfect choice for representing these types of data.

Consider the example in Listing 2.1. It's a purchase order (PO) from the Skateboard Warehouse, a retailer of skateboards to SkatesTown. The order is for 5 backpacks, 12 skateboards, and 1,000 SkatesTown promotional stickers (this is what the stock-keeping unit [SKU] 008-PR stands for).

Listing 2.1 **Purchase Order in XML**

```
<po id="43871" submitted="2004-01-05" customerId="73852">
   <billTo>
      <company>The Skateboard Warehouse</company>
      <street>One Warehouse Park</street>
      <street>Building 17</street>
      <city>Boston</city>
      <state>MA</state>
      <postalCode>01775</postalCode>
   </billTo>
   <shipTo>
      <company>The Skateboard Warehouse</company>
      <street>One Warehouse Park</street>
      <street>Building 17</street>
      <city>Boston</city>
      <state>MA</state>
      <postalCode>01775</postalCode>
   </shipTo>
   <order>
      <item sku="318-BP" quantity="5">
         <description>Skateboard backpack; five pockets</description>
      </item>
      <item sku="947-TI" quantity="12">
         <description>Street-style titanium skateboard.</description>
      </item>
      <item sku="008-PR" quantity="1000">
```

Listing 2.1 **Continued**

```
      </item>
   </order>
</po>
```

The use of XML is very different from the previous user guide example:

- The ratio of markup to content is high. The XML includes many types of tags. There is no long-running text.
- The XML includes machine-generated information; for example, the PO's submission date uses a date-time format of *year-month-day*. A human authoring an XML document is unlikely to enter a date-time value in this format.
- The tags are organized in a highly structured manner. Order and positioning matter, relative to other tags. For example, `<description>` must be under `<item>`, which must be under `<order>`, which must be under `<po>`. The `<order>` tag can be used only once in the document.
- Markup is used to describe what a piece of information *means* rather than how it should be presented to a human.

In short, if you can easily imagine the XML as a data structure in your favorite programming language, you're probably looking at a data-centric use of XML. An example Java class that could, with a bit more work, be used to represent the PO data is shown here:

```
class PO
{
    int id;
    Date submitted;
    int customerId;
    Address billTo;
    Address shipTo;
    Item order[];
}
```

Document Lifetime

Document- and data-centric uses of XML can differ in one other significant aspect: the lifetime of the XML document. Typically, XML documents for human consumption (such as technical manuals and research papers) live a long time because the information they contain can be used for a long time. On the other hand, some data-centric XML may live for only a few milliseconds. Consider the example of a database that is returning the results of a query in XML format. The whole operation takes several milliseconds. After the query is used, the data is discarded. Further, no real XML document exists—the XML is just bits on a wire or bits in an application's data structure. Still, for convenience purposes, we'll use the term *XML document* to refer to any whole piece of XML. To identify parts of a whole XML document, this book uses the highly technical term *chunk*.

Web services are about data-centric uses of XML. Through the rest of this chapter and the rest of this book, we'll purposefully ignore discussing document-centric XML.

XML Instances

The structure and formatting of XML in an XML document must follow the rules of the XML instance syntax. The term *instance* 📖 is used to explicitly distinguish the difference between the use of some particular type of XML and its specification. This usage parallels the difference in object-oriented terminology between an object instance and an object type.

Document Prolog

XML documents contain an optional *prolog* 📖 followed by a *root element* 📖 that holds the contents of the document. Typically the prolog serves up to three roles:

- Identifies the document as an XML document
- Includes any comments about the document
- Includes any meta-information about the content of the document

A document is identified as an XML document through the use of a *processing instruction* 📖. Processing instructions (PIs) are special directives to the application that will process the XML document. They have the following syntax:

```
<?PITarget ...?>
```

PIs are enclosed in `<?` ... `?>`. The PI target is a keyword meaningful to the processing application. Everything between the PI target and the `?>` marker is considered the contents of the PI.

In general, data-oriented XML applications don't use application-specific processing instructions. Instead, they tend to put all information in elements and attributes. However, you should use one standard processing instruction—the *XML declaration* 📖—in the XML document prolog to determine two important pieces of information: the version of XML in the document and the character encoding. Here's an example:

```
<?xml version="1.0" encoding="UTF-8"?>
```

The `version` parameter of the `xml` PI tells the processing application the version of the XML specification to which the document conforms. (W3C released an updated XML specification, XML 1.1, in early 2004; but all examples in this book use the 1.0 version of XML, which came in 1998.) The `encoding` parameter is optional. It identifies the character set of the document. The default value is `"UTF-8"`.

> **Note**
>
> UTF-8 (RFC 2279) stands for Unicode Transformation Format-8. It's an octet (8-bit) lossless encoding of
> characters from the Universal Character Set (UCS), aka Unicode (ISO 10646). UTF-8 is an efficient represen-
> tation of English because it preserves the full US-ASCII character range. One ASCII character is encoded in 8
> bits, whereas some Unicode characters can take up to 48 bits. UTF-8 encoding makes it easy to move XML
> on the Internet using standard communication protocols such as HTTP, SMTP, and FTP. XML is international-
> ized by design and can support other character encodings such as Unicode and ISO/IEC 10646. However, for
> simplicity and readability purposes, this book will use UTF-8 encoding for all samples.

If you omit the XML declaration, the XML version is assumed to be 1.0, and the processing application will try to guess the encoding of the document based on clues such
as the raw byte order of the data stream. This approach has problems, and whenever
interoperability is of high importance—such as for Web services—applications should
provide an explicit XML declaration and use UTF-8 encoding.

XML document prologs can also include comments that pertain to the whole document. Comments use the following syntax:

```
<!-- Sample comment and more ... -->
```

Comments can span multiple lines but can't be nested (comments can't enclose other
comments). The processing application will ignore everything inside the comment markers. Some of the XML samples in this book use comments to provide you with useful
context about the examples in question.

With what we've discussed so far, we can extend the PO example from Listing 2.1 to
include an XML declaration and a comment about the document (see Listing 2.2).

Listing 2.2 **XML Declaration and Comment for the Purchase Order**

```
<?xml version="1.0" encoding="UTF-8"?>
<!-- Created by Bob Dister, approved by Mary Jones -->
<po id="43871" submitted="2004-01-05" customerId="73852">
   <!-- The rest of the purchase order will be the same as before -->
   ...
</po>
```

In this case, po is the root element of the XML document.

Elements

The term *element* 📖 is a technical name for the pairing of a start tag and an end tag in
an XML document. In the previous example, the po element has the start tag `<po>` and
the end tag `</po>`. Every start tag must have a matching end tag and vice versa.
Everything between these two tags is the *content* 📖 of the element. This includes any
nested elements, text, comments, and so on.

Element names can include all standard programming language identifier characters
(`[0-9A-Za-z]`) as well as the underscore (_), hyphen (-), and colon (:), but they must

begin with a letter. `customer-name` is a valid XML element name. However, because XML is case-sensitive, `customer-name` isn't the same element as `Customer-Name`.

According to the XML Specification, elements can have three different *content types* 📖: *element-only* content 📖, *mixed* content 📖, or *empty* content 📖. Element-only content consists entirely of nested elements. Any whitespace separating elements isn't considered significant in this case. Mixed content refers to any combination of nested elements and text. All elements in the purchase order example, with the exception of `description`, have element content. Most elements in the skateboard user guide example earlier in the chapter had mixed content.

Note that the XML Specification doesn't define a text-only content model. Outside the letter of the specification, an element that contains only text is often referred to as having *data* content; but, technically speaking, it has mixed content. This awkwardness comes as a result of XML's roots in SGML and document-oriented applications. However, in most data-oriented applications, you'll never see elements whose contents are both nested elements and text. The content will typically be one or the other, because limiting it to be either elements or text makes processing XML much easier.

The syntax for elements with empty content is a start tag immediately followed by an end tag, as in `<emptyElement></emptyElement>`. This is too much text, so the XML Specification also allows the shorthand form `<emptyElement/>`. For example, because the last item in our PO doesn't have a nested `description` element, it has empty content. Therefore, we could have written it as follows:

```
<item sku="008-PR" quantity="1000"/>
```

XML elements must be strictly nested. They can't overlap, as shown here:

```
<!-- This is correct nesting -->
<P><B><I>Bold, italicized text in a paragraph</I></B></P>

<!--Bad syntax: overlapping I and B tags -->
<P><I><B>Bold, italicized text in a paragraph</I></B></P>

<!-- Bad syntax: overlapping P and B tags -->
<B><P><I>Bold, italicized text in a paragraph</I></B></P>
```

The notion of an XML document root implies that there is only one element at the very top level of a document. For example, the following wouldn't be a valid XML document:

```
<first>I am the first element</first>
<second>I am the second element</second>
```

It's easy to think of nested XML elements as a hierarchy. For example, Figure 2.1 shows a hierarchical tree representation of the XML elements in the purchase order example together with the data (text) associated with them.

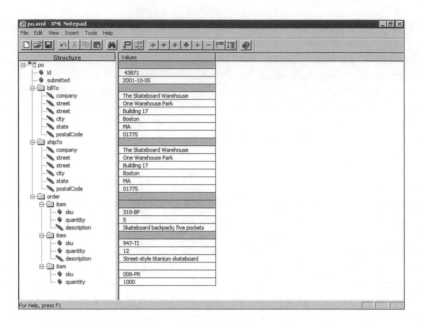

Figure 2.1   Tree representation of XML elements in a purchase order.

Unfortunately, it's often difficult to identify XML elements precisely in the hierarchy. To aid this task, the XML community has taken to using genealogy terms such as *parent*, *child*, *sibling*, *ancestor*, and *descendant*. Figure 2.2 illustrates the terminology as it applies to the order element of the PO:

- Its parent (the element immediately above it in the hierarchy) is po.

- Its ancestor is po. Ancestors are all the elements above a given element in the hierarchy.

- Its siblings (elements on the same level of the hierarchy and that have the same parent) are billTo and shipTo.

- Its children (elements that have this element as a parent) are three item elements.

- Its descendants (elements that have this element as an ancestor) are three item elements and two description elements.

Attributes

The start tags for XML elements can have zero or more *attributes* 📖. An attribute is a name-value pair. The syntax for an attribute is a name (which uses the same character set as an XML element name) followed by an equal sign (=), followed by a quoted value. The XML Specification requires the quoting of values; you can use both single and double quotes, provided they're correctly matched. For example, the po element of our PO has three attributes, id, submitted, and customerId:

```
<po id="43871" submitted="2004-01-05" customerId="73852"> ... </po>
```

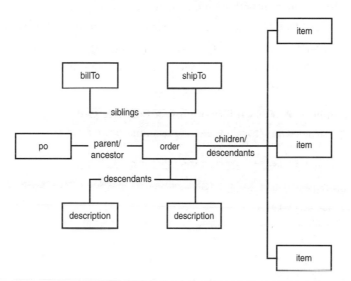

Figure 2.2   Common terminology for XML element relationships

A family of attributes whose names begin with xml: is reserved for use by the XML Specification. Probably the best example is xml:lang, which identifies the language of the text used in the content of the element that has the xml:lang attribute. For example, we could have written the description elements in our purchase order example to identify the description text as English:

```
<description xml:lang="en">Skateboard backpack; five pockets</description>
```

Note that applications processing XML aren't required to recognize, process, and act based on the values of these attributes. The key reason the XML Specification identified these attributes is that they address common use-cases; standardizing them aided interoperability between applications.

Without any meta-information about an XML document, attribute values are considered to be pieces of text. In the previous example, the ID might look like a number and the submission date might look like a date, but to an XML processor, they will both be strings. This behavior causes headaches when processing data-oriented XML, and it's one of the primary reasons most data-oriented XML documents have associated meta-information described in XML schemas (introduced later in this chapter).

XML applications are free to attach any semantics they choose to XML markup. A common use-case leverages attributes to create a basic linking mechanism within an XML document. The typical scenario involves a document that has duplicate information in multiple locations. The goal is to eliminate information duplication. The process has three steps:

1. Put the information in the document only once.

2. Mark the information with a unique identifier.

3. Refer to this identifier every time you need to refer to the information.

The purchase order example offers the opportunity to try this technique (see Listing 2.3). As shown in the example, in most cases, the bill-to and ship-to addresses will be the same.

Listing 2.3   **Duplicate Address Information in a Purchase Order**

```
<po id="43871" submitted="2004-01-05" customerId="73852">
   <billTo>
      <company>The Skateboard Warehouse</company>
      <street>One Warehouse Park</street>
      <street>Building 17</street>
      <city>Boston</city>
      <state>MA</state>
      <postalCode>01775</postalCode>
   </billTo>
   <shipTo>
      <company>The Skateboard Warehouse</company>
      <street>One Warehouse Park</street>
      <street>Building 17</street>
      <city>Boston</city>
      <state>MA</state>
      <postalCode>01775</postalCode>
   </shipTo>
   ...
</po>
```

There is no reason to duplicate this information. Instead, we can use the markup shown in Listing 2.4.

Listing 2.4   **Using ID/IDREF Attributes to Eliminate Redundancy**

```
<po id="43871" submitted="2004-01-05" customerId="73852">
   <billTo id="addr-1">
      <company>The Skateboard Warehouse</company>
      <street>One Warehouse Park</street>
      <street>Building 17</street>
      <city>Boston</city>
      <state>MA</state>
      <postalCode>01775</postalCode>
   </billTo>
```

Listing 2.4   **Continued**

```
<shipTo href="addr-1"/>
...
</po>
```

We followed the three steps described previously:

1. We put the address information in the document only once, under the `billTo` element.

2. We uniquely identified the address as `"addr-1"` and stored that information in the `id` attribute of the `billTo` element. We only need to worry about the uniqueness of the identifier within the XML document.

3. To refer to the address from the `shipTo` element, we use another attribute, `href`, whose value is the unique address identifier `"addr-1"`.

The attribute names `id` and `href` aren't required but nevertheless are commonly used by convention.

You might have noticed that now both the `po` and `billTo` elements have an attribute called `id`. This is fine, because the attribute names are unique within the context of the two elements.

> **Elements Versus Attributes**
>
> Given that information can be stored in both element content and attribute values, sooner or later the question of whether to use an element or an attribute arises. This debate has erupted a few times in the XML community and has claimed many casualties.
>
> One common rule is to represent structured information using markup. For example, you should use an `address` element with nested `company`, `street`, `city`, `state`, `postalCode`, and `country` elements instead of including a whole address as a chunk of text.
>
> Even this simple rule is subject to interpretation and the choice of application domain. For example, the choice between
>
> ```
> <work number="617.219.2000">
> ```
>
> and
>
> ```
> <work>
>    <area>617</area>
>    <number>219.2000</number>
> </work>
> ```
>
> depends on whether your application needs to have phone number information in granular form (for example, to perform searches based on the area code only).
>
> In other cases, only personal preference and stylistic choice apply. We might ask if SkatesTown should have used
>
> ```
> <po>
>    <id>43871</id>
> ```

```
        <submitted>2004-01-05</submitted>
        <customerId>73852</customerId>
        ...
    </po>
```

instead of

```
    <po id="43871" submitted="2004-01-05" customerId="73852">
        ...
    </po>
```

There's no good way to answer this question without adding stretchy assumptions about extensibility needs and so on.

In general, whenever humans design XML documents, you'll see more frequent use of attributes. This is true even in data-oriented applications. On the other hand, when XML documents are automatically "designed" and generated by applications, you may see more prevalent use of elements. The reasons are somewhat complex; Chapter 3 will address some of them.

Character Data

Attribute values as well as the text and whitespace between tags must follow precisely a small but strict set of rules. Most XML developers think of this character data as mapping to the string data type in their programming language of choice. Unfortunately, things aren't that simple.

Encoding

First, and most important, all character data in an XML document must comply with the document's encoding. Any characters outside the range of characters that can be included in the document must be escaped and identified as *character references* 📖. The escape sequence used throughout XML uses the ampersand (&) as its start and a semicolon (;) as its end. The syntax for character references is an ampersand, followed by a pound/hash sign (#), followed by either a decimal character code or lowercase *x* followed by a hexadecimal character code, followed by a semicolon. Therefore, the 8-bit character code 128 is encoded in a UTF-8 XML document as €.

Unfortunately, for obscure document-oriented reasons, there is no way to include character codes 0 through 7, 9, 11, 12, or 14 through 31 (typically known as *nonwhitespace control characters* 📖 in ASCII) in XML documents. Even a correctly escaped character reference won't do. This situation can cause unexpected problems for programmers whose string data types sometimes end up with these values.

Whitespace

The rules for whitespace handling are also a legacy from the document-centric world XML came from. It isn't important to completely define these rules here, but a couple of them are worth mentioning:

- An XML processor is required to convert any carriage return (CR) character it sees in the XML document, as well as the sequence of a carriage return and a line feed (LF) character, into a single LF character.

- Whitespace can be treated as either significant or insignificant. The set of rules for how applications are notified about either of these has caused more than one debate in the XML community.

Luckily, most data-oriented XML applications care little about whitespace.

Entities

In addition to character references, XML documents can define *entities* 📖 as well as references to them (*entity references* 📖). Entities typically aren't important for data-oriented applications, and we won't discuss them in detail. However, all XML processors must recognize several predefined entities that map to characters that can be confused with markup delimiters. These characters are less than (<); greater than (>); ampersand (&); apostrophe, aka single quote ('); and quote, aka double quote ("). Table 2.1 shows the syntax for escaping these characters.

Table 2.1   **Predefined XML Character Escape Sequences**

Character	Escape Sequence
<	&lt;
>	&gt;
&	&amp;
'	&apos;
"	&quot;

For example, to include a chunk of XML as text rather than markup inside an XML document, you should escape all special characters:

```
<example-to-show>
    &lt;?xml version=&quot;1.0&quot;?&gt;
    &lt;rootElement&gt;
        &lt;childElement id=&quot;1&quot;&gt;
            The man said: &quot;Hello, there!&quot;.
        &lt;/childElement&gt;
    &lt;/rootElement&gt;
</example-to-show>
```

The result is not only reduced readability but also a significant increase in the size of the document, because single characters are mapped to character escape sequences whose length is at least four characters.

To address this problem, the XML Specification has a special multi-character escape construct. The name of the construct, the *CDATA section* 📖, refers to the section holding character data. The syntax is `<![CDATA[`, followed by any sequences of characters

allowed by the document encoding that don't include]]>, followed by]]>. Therefore, you can write the previous example much more simply as follows:

```
<example-to-show><![CDATA[
    <?xml version="1.0"?>
    <rootElement>
        <childElement id="1">
            The man said: "Hello, there!".
        </childElement>
    </rootElement>
]]></example-to-show>
```

A Simpler Purchase Order

Based on the information in this section, we can re-write the PO document as shown in Listing 2.5.

Listing 2.5   **Improved Purchase Order Document**

```
<?xml version="1.0" encoding="UTF-8"?>
<!-- Created by Bob Dister, approved by Mary Jones -->
<po id="43871" submitted="2004-01-05" customerId="73852">
    <billTo id="addr-1">
        <company>The Skateboard Warehouse</company>
        <street>One Warehouse Park</street>
        <street>Building 17</street>
        <city>Boston</city>
        <state>MA</state>
        <postalCode>01775</postalCode>
    </billTo>
    <shipTo href="addr-1"/>
    <order>
        <item sku="318-BP" quantity="5">
            <description>Skateboard backpack; five pockets</description>
        </item>
        <item sku="947-TI" quantity="12">
            <description>Street-style titanium skateboard.</description>
        </item>
        <item sku="008-PR" quantity="1000"/>
    </order>
</po>
```

XML Namespaces

An important property of XML documents is that they can be composed to create new documents. This is the most basic mechanism for reusing XML. Unfortunately, simple composition creates the problems of recognition and collision.

To illustrate these problems, consider a scenario where SkatesTown wants to receive its POs via the XML messaging system of XCommerce Messaging, Inc. The format of the messages is simple:

```
<message from="..." to="..." sent="...">
   <text>
      This is the text of the message.
   </text>
   <!-- A message can have attachments -->
   <attachment>
      <description>Brief description of the attachment.</description>
      <item>
         <!-- XML of attachment goes here -->
      </item>
   </attachment>
</message>
```

Listing 2.6 shows a complete message with a PO attachment.

Listing 2.6   **Message with Purchase Order Attachment**

```
<message from="bj@bjskates.com" to="orders@skatestown.com"
   sent="2004-01-05">
   <text>
      Hi, here is what I need this time. Thx, BJ.
   </text>
   <attachment>
      <description>The PO</description>
      <item>
         <po id="43871" submitted="2004-01-05" customerId="73852">
            <billTo id="addr-1">
               <company>The Skateboard Warehouse</company>
               <street>One Warehouse Park</street>
               <street>Building 17</street>
               <city>Boston</city>
               <state>MA</state>
               <postalCode>01775</postalCode>
            </billTo>
            <shipTo href="addr-1"/>
            <order>
               <item sku="318-BP" quantity="5">
                  <description>
                     Skateboard backpack; five pockets
                  </description>
               </item>
               <item sku="947-TI" quantity="12">
                  <description>
```

Listing 2.6 **Continued**

```
                    Street-style titanium skateboard.
                </description>
            </item>
            <item sku="008-PR" quantity="1000"/>
          </order>
        </po>
      </item>
    </attachment>
</message>
```

It's relatively easy to identify the two problems mentioned earlier in the composed document:

- *Recognition*—How does an XML processing application distinguish between the XML elements that describe the message and the XML elements that are part of the PO?

- *Collision*—Does the element `description` refer to attachment descriptions in messages or order item descriptions? Does the `item` element refer to an item of attachment or an order item?

Very simple applications might not be bothered by these problems. After all, the knowledge of what an element means can reside in the application logic. However, as application complexity increases and the number of applications that need to work with a particular composed document type grows, the need to clearly distinguish between the XML elements becomes paramount. The XML Namespaces specification brings order to the chaos.

Namespace Mechanism

The problem of collision in composed XML documents arises because of the likelihood that elements with common names (description, item, and so on) will be reused in different document types. This problem can be addressed by *qualifying* an XML element name with an additional *identifier* that's much more likely to be unique within the composed document. In other words:

Qualified name (aka QName) = Namespace identifier + Local name

This approach is similar to the way namespaces are used in languages such as C++ and C# and to the way package names are used in the Java programming language.

The problem of recognition in composed XML documents arises because no good mechanism exists to identify all elements belonging to the same document type. Given namespace qualifiers, the problem is addressed in a simple way—all elements that have the same namespace identifier are considered together.

For identifiers, XML Namespaces uses *Uniform Resource Identifiers* (URIs), which are described in RFC 2396. URIs are nothing fancy, but they're very useful. They can be locators, names, or both. URI locators are known as *Uniform Resource Locators* 📖 (URLs), a term familiar to anyone using the Web. URLs are strings such as `http://www.skatestown.com/services/POSubmission` and `mailto:orders@skatestown.com`.

Uniform Resource Names 📖 (URNs) are URIs that are globally unique and persistent. *Universally Unique Identifiers* 📖 (UUIDs) are perfect for use as URNs. UUIDs are 128-bit identifiers that are designed to be globally unique. Typically, they combine network card (Ethernet) addresses with a high-precision timestamp and an increment counter. An example URN using a UUID is `urn:uuid:2FAC1234-31F8-11B4-A222-08002B34C003`. UUIDs are used as unique identifiers in Universal Description Discovery and Integration (UDDI) as detailed in Chapter 6, "Web Services Registries."

Namespace Syntax

Because URIs can be long and typically contain characters that aren't allowed in XML element names, the syntax of including namespaces in XML documents involves two steps:

1. A namespace identifier is associated with a *prefix*, a name that contains only legal XML element name characters with the exception of the colon (:).

2. Qualified names are obtained as a combination of the prefix, the colon character, and the local element name, as in `myPrefix:myElementName`.

Listing 2.7 shows an example of the composed XML document using namespaces.

Listing 2.7 **Message with Namespaces**

```
<msg:message from="bj@bjskates.com" to="orders@skatestown.com"
    sent="2004-01-05" xmlns:msg="http://www.xcommercemsg.com/ns/message"
xmlns:po="http://www.skatestown.com/ns/po">
  <msg:text>
    Hi, here is what I need this time. Thx, BJ.
  </msg:text>
  <msg:attachment>
    <msg:description>The PO</msg:description>
    <msg:item>
      <po:po id="43871" submitted="2004-01-05" customerId="73852">
        <po:billTo id="addr-1">
          <po:company>The Skateboard Warehouse</po:company>
          <po:street>One Warehouse Park</po:street>
          <po:street>Building 17</po:street>
          <po:city>Boston</po:city>
          <po:state>MA</po:state>
          <po:postalCode>01775</po:postalCode>
        </po:billTo>
        <po:shipTo href="addr-1"/>
```

Listing 2.7   **Continued**

```
            <po:order>
                <po:item sku="318-BP" quantity="5">
                    <po:description>
                        Skateboard backpack; five pockets
                    </po:description>
                </po:item>
                <po:item sku="947-TI" quantity="12">
                    <po:description>
                        Street-style titanium skateboard.
                    </po:description>
                </po:item>
                <po:item sku="008-PR" quantity="1000"/>
            </po:order>
        </po:po>
    </msg:item>
  </msg:attachment>
</msg:message>
```

In this example, the elements prefixed with msg are associated with a namespace whose identifier is http://www.xcommercemsg.com/ns/message, and those prefixed with po are associated with a namespace whose identifier is http://www.skatestown.com/ns/po. The prefixes are linked to the complete namespace identifiers by the attributes on the top message element beginning with xmlns: (xmlns:msg and xmlns:po). XML processing software has access to both the prefixed name and the mapping of prefixes to complete namespace identifiers.

Adding a prefix to every element in the document decreases readability and increases document size. Therefore, XML Namespaces lets you use a default namespace in a document. Elements belonging to the default namespace don't require prefixes. Listing 2.8 makes the msg namespace the default.

Listing 2.8   **Using Default Namespaces**

```
<message from="bj@bjskates.com" to="orders@skatestown.com"
    sent="2004-01-05" xmlns ="http://www.xcommercemsg.com/ns/message"
    xmlns:po="http://www.skatestown.com/ns/po">
    <text>
        Hi, here is what I need this time. Thx, BJ.
    </text>
    <attachment>
        <description>The PO</description>
        <item>
            <po:po id="43871" submitted="2004-01-05" customerId="73852">
                ...
            </po:po>
```

Listing 2.8   **Continued**

```
        </item>
    </attachment>
</message>
```

Default namespaces work because the content of any namespace-prefixed element is considered to belong to the namespace of its parent element—unless, of course, the element is explicitly defined to be in another namespace with its own xmlns-type attribute. We can use this to further clean up the composed XML document by moving the PO namespace declaration to the po element (see Listing 2.9).

Listing 2.9   **Using Nested Namespace Defaulting**

```
<message from="bj@bjskates.com" to="orders@skatestown.com"
    sent="2004-01-05" xmlns="http://www.xcommercemsg.com/ns/message">
    <text>
        Hi, here is what I need this time. Thx, BJ.
    </text>
    <attachment>
        <description>The PO</description>
        <item>
            <po:po id="43871" submitted="2004-01-05" customerId="73852"
                xmlns:po="http://www.skatestown.com/ns/po">
                <billTo id="addr-1">
                    ...
                </billTo>
                <shipTo href="addr-1"/>
                <order>
                    ...
                </order>
            </po:po>
        </item>
    </attachment>
</message>
```

This example shows an efficient, readable syntax that eliminates the recognition and collision problems. XML processors can identify the namespace of any element in the document.

Namespace-Prefixed Attributes

Attributes can also have namespaces associated with them. Initially, it might be hard to imagine why a capability like this would be useful for XML applications. The common use-case scenario is the desire to extend the information provided by an XML element without having to make changes directly to its document type.

A concrete example might involve SkatesTown wanting to have an indication of the priority of items in POs. High-priority items could be shipped immediately, without waiting for any back-ordered items to become available. SkatesTown's automatic order-processing software doesn't understand item priorities; they're just hints that tell the fulfillment system how it should react in case of back-ordered items.

A simple implementation could involve extending the `item` element with an optional `priority` attribute. However, doing so could cause a problem for the order-processing software, which doesn't expect to see such an attribute. A better solution is to attach priority information to items using a namespace-prefixed `priority` attribute. Because the attribute will be in a namespace different from that of the `item` element, the order-processing software will ignore it.

The example in Listing 2.10 uses this mechanism to make the backpacks high priority and the promotional materials low priority. By default, any items without a `priority` attribute, such as the skateboards, are presumed to be of medium priority.

Listing 2.10 **Adding Priority to Order Items**

```
<message from="bj@bjskates.com" to="orders@skatestown.com"
    sent="2004-01-05" xmlns="http://www.xcommercemsg.com/ns/message">
    <text>
        Hi, here is what I need this time. Thx, BJ.
    </text>
    <attachment>
        <description>The PO</description>
        <item>
            <po:po id="43871" submitted="2004-01-05" customerId="73852"
                xmlns:po="http://www.skatestown.com/ns/po">
                xmlns:p="http://www.skatestown.com/ns/priority">
                ...
                <po:order>
                    <po:item sku="318-BP" quantity="5" p:priority="high">
                        <po:description>
                            Skateboard backpack; five pockets
                        </po:description>
                    </po:item>
                    <po:item sku="947-TI" quantity="12">
                        <po:description>
                            Street-style titanium skateboard.
                        </po:description>
                    </po:item>
                    <po:item sku="008-PR" quantity="1000" p:priority="low"/>
                </po:order>
            </po:po>
        </item>
    </attachment>
</message>
```

> **Dereferencing URIs**
>
> All the examples in this section use namespace URIs that are URLs. A natural question arises: What is the resource at that URL? The answer is that it doesn't matter. XML Namespaces doesn't require that a resource be there. The URI is used entirely for identification purposes.
>
> This could cause problems for applications that see an unknown namespace in an XML document and have no way to obtain more information about the elements and attributes that belong to that namespace. In the next section, you'll see a mechanism that addresses this issue.

XML Schemas

XML provides a flexible set of structures that can represent many different types of document- and data-oriented information. XML offers an optional feature called Document Type Definitions (DTDs). A document associated with a DTD has a set of rules regarding the elements and attributes that can be part of the document and where they can appear. DTDs offer the basic mechanism for defining a *vocabulary* 📖 specifying the structure of XML documents in an attempt to establish a contract (how an XML document will be structured) between multiple parties working with the same type of XML.

DTDs came into existence because people and applications needed to be able to treat XML at a higher level than a collection of elements and attributes. Well-designed DTDs attach meaning to the XML syntax in documents. At the same time, DTDs fail to address the common needs of namespace integration, modular vocabulary design, flexible content models, and tight integration with data-oriented applications. This failure comes as a direct result of XML's SGML origins and the predominantly document-centric nature of SGML applications. To address these issues, the XML community, under the leadership of the W3C, took up the task of creating a meta-language for describing both the structure of XML document and the mapping of XML syntax to data types. After long deliberation, the effort produced the final version of the XML Schema specification in March 2001. All the Web services specifications use XML Schema for defining their vocabularies.

Well-Formedness and Validity

The presence of schema information allows us to distinguish the concepts of *well-formedness* 📖 and *validity* 📖. If a document subscribes to the rules of XML syntax (as described in the section "XML Instances"), it's considered well-formed. Well-formedness implies that XML processing software can read the document without any basic errors associated with parsing, such as invalid character data, mismatched start and end tags, multiple attributes with the same name, and so on. The XML Specification mandates that if any well-formedness constraint isn't met, the XML parser must immediately generate a nonrecoverable error. This rigid mandate makes it easy to separate the doings of the software focused on the *logical structure* 📖 of an XML document (what the markup means) from the mundane details of the *physical structure* 📖 of the document (the markup syntax).

However, well-formedness isn't sufficient for most applications. Consider, for example, the SkatesTown order-processing application. When an XML document is submitted to the application, it doesn't care whether the document is well-formed XML but that the document is a PO in the specific XML format it requires. The notion of *format* applies to the set of rules describing SkatesTown's POs: "The document must begin with a po element that has three attributes (`id`, `submitted`, and `customerId`), which will be followed by a `billTo` element, ..." and so on. In other words, before a submitted document is processed, it must be identified as a valid PO.

This is how the notion of validity comes in. Schemas offer an automated, declarative mechanism for validating the contents of XML documents as they're parsed. Therefore, XML applications can limit the amount of validation they need to perform. If the SkatesTown PO-processing application couldn't delegate validation to the XML processor, it would have to express all validation rules directly in code. Code is procedural in nature and much harder to maintain than schemas, which are declarative and have readable XML syntax.

To handle validity checks, schemas enable the following:

- Identification of the elements that can be in a document
- Identification of the order and relation between elements
- Identification of the attributes of every element and whether they're optional or required or have some other special properties
- Identification of the datatype of attribute content

Last but not least, schemas offer significant capabilities for modular vocabulary design that let you reuse and repurpose existing vocabularies.

XML Schema Basics

In a nutshell, XML Schema is both powerful and complex. It's powerful because it allows for much more expressive and precise specification of the content of XML documents. It's complex for the same reason. The specification is broken into three parts:

- *XML Schema Part 0: Primer* is a non-normative document that tries to make sense of XML Schema by parceling complexity into small chunks and using many examples.
- *XML Schema Part 1: Structures* focuses primarily on serving the needs of document-oriented applications by laying out the rules for defining the structure of XML documents.
- *XML Schema Part 2: Datatypes* builds on the structures specification with additional capabilities that address the needs of data-oriented applications such as defining reusable datatypes, associating XML syntax with schema datatypes, and mapping these to application-level data.

Part 0 is meant for general consumption, whereas Parts 1 and 2 are deeply technical and require a skilled and determined reader. The rest of this section will provide an introduction to XML Schema that is biased toward schema usage in data-oriented applications. You should gain sufficient understanding of structure and datatype specifications to comprehend and use common Web service schemas. Still, because XML Schema is fundamental to Web services, we recommend that you go through the primer document of the XML Schema specification.

One way to visualize the structure of a document is as a tree of possible element and attribute combinations. For example, Figure 2.3 shows the document structure for POs as expressed by a popular XML processing tool. The image uses some syntax from regular expressions to visualize the multiplicity of elements: question mark (?) stands for optional (zero or one), asterisk (*) stands for any (zero or more), and plus (+) stands for at least some (one or more).

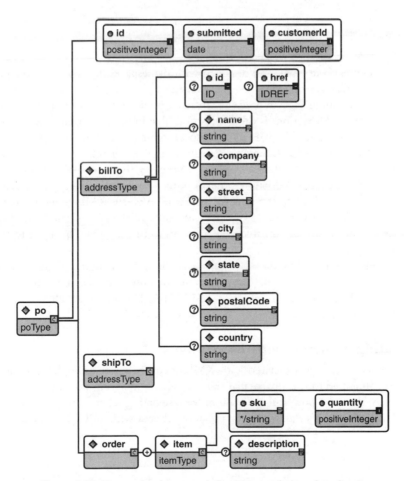

Figure 2.3 Document structure defined by purchase order schema

Listing 2.11 shows the basic structure of the SkatesTown PO schema.

Listing 2.11   **Basic XML Schema Structure**

```
<?xml version="1.0" encoding="UTF-8"?>
<xsd:schema xmlns="http://www.skatestown.com/ns/po"
            xmlns:xsd="http://www.w3.org/2001/XMLSchema"
            targetNamespace="http://www.skatestown.com/ns/po">

    <xsd:annotation>
      <xsd:documentation xml:lang="en">
         Purchase order schema for SkatesTown.
      </xsd:documentation>
    </xsd:annotation>


    ...


</xsd:schema>
```

Schema are expressed in XML and designed with namespaces in mind from the ground up. In this particular schema document, all elements belonging to the schema specification are prefixed with `xsd:`. The prefix's name isn't important, but `xsd:` (which comes from XML Schema Definition) is the convention. The prefix is associated with the `http://www.w3.org/2001/XMLSchema` namespace, which identifies the W3C Recommendation of the XML Schema specification. The default namespace of the document is set to be `http://www.skatestown.com/ns/po`, the namespace of the SkatesTown PO. The schema document needs both namespaces to distinguish between XML elements that belong to the schema specification versus XML elements that belong to POs. Finally, the `targetNamespace` attribute of the `schema` element identifies the namespace of the documents that will conform to this schema. This is set to the PO schema namespace.

The schema is enclosed by the `xsd:schema` element. The content of this element is other schema elements that are used for element, attribute, and datatype definitions. The `annotation` and `documentation` elements can be used liberally to attach auxiliary information to the schema.

Associating Schemas with Documents

Schemas don't have to be associated with XML documents. For example, applications can be preconfigured to use a particular schema when processing documents. Alternatively, there is a powerful mechanism for associating schemas with documents. Listing 2.12 shows how to associate the previous schema with a PO document.

Listing 2.12   **Associating Schemas with Documents**

```
<?xml version="1.0" encoding="UTF-8"?>
<po:po xmlns:po="http://www.skatestown.com/ns/po"
       xmlns:xsi="http://www.w3.org/2001/XMLSchema-instance"
       xsi:schemaLocation="http://www.skatestown.com/ns/po
                           http://www.skatestown.com/schema/po.xsd"
       id="43871" submitted="2004-01-05" customerId="73852">

    . . .

</po:po>
```

First, because the PO schema identifies a target namespace, PO documents are required to use namespaces to identify their elements. The PO document uses the po prefix for this task.

Next, the document uses another namespace—http://www.w3.org/2001/XMLSchema-instance—which has a special meaning. It defines a number of attributes that are part of the schema specification. These attributes can be applied to elements in instance documents to provide additional information to a schema-aware XML processor. By convention, most documents use the namespace prefix xsi: (for XML Schema: Instance).

The binding between the PO document and its schema is established via the xsi:schemaLocation attribute. This attribute contains a pair of values. The first value is the namespace identifier whose schema's location is identified by the second value. Typically, the second value is a URL, but specialized applications can use other types of values, such as an identifier in a schema repository or a well-known schema name. If the document used more than one namespace, the xsi:schemaLocation attribute would contain multiple pairs of values.

Simple Types

Prior to the arrival of schemas, one of the biggest problems with XML processing was that XML had no notion of datatypes, even for simple values such as the character data content of an element or an attribute value. Because of this limitation, XML applications included a large amount of validation code. For example, even a simple PO requires the following validation rules, which are outside the scope of the XML Specification:

- Attributes id and customerId of the po element must be positive integers.
- Attribute submitted of the po element must be a date in the format *yyyy-mm-dd*.
- Attribute quantity of the item element must be a positive integer.
- Attribute sku (stock keeping unit) of the item element must be a string with this format: three digits, followed by a dash, followed by two uppercase letters.

XML schemas address these issues in two ways. First, the specification comes with a large set of predefined basic datatypes such as string, positiveInteger, and date, which you

can use directly. For custom data types, such as the values of the sku attribute, the specification defines a powerful mechanism for defining new types. Table 2.2 shows some of
the commonly used predefined schema types with examples of their use.

Table 2.2 **Predefined XML Schema Simple Types**

Simple Type	Examples (Delimited by Commas)	Notes
string	Confirm this is electric	
base64Binary	GpM7	
hexBinary	0FB7	
integer	–126789, –1, 0, 1, 126789	
positiveInteger	1, 126789	
negativeInteger	–126789, –1	
nonNegativeInteger	0, 1, 126789	
nonPositiveInteger	–126789, –1, 0	
decimal	–1.23, 0, 123.4, 1000.00	
boolean	true, false	
	1, 0	
time	13:20:00.000	
	13:20:00.000–05:00	
dateTime	1999-05-31T13:20:00.000–05:00 (May 31, 1999 at 1.20pm Eastern Standard Time, which is 5 hours behind Coordinated Universal Time)	
duration	P1Y2M3DT10H30M12.3S (1 year, 2 months, 3 days, 10 hours, 30 minutes, and 12.3 seconds)	
date	1999-05-31	
Name	shipTo	XML Name type
QName	po:USAddress	XML Namespace QName
anyURI	http://www.example.com/, http://www.example.com/doc.html#ID5	
ID		XML ID attribute type
IDREF		XML IDREF attribute type

The information in this table comes from the XML Schema Primer.

A note on ID/IDREF attributes: An XML processor is required to generate an error if a
document contains two ID attributes with the same value or an IDREF with a value that

has no matching `ID` value. This makes `ID`/`IDREF` attributes perfect for handling attributes such as `id` and `href` in SkatesTown's PO `address` element.

Extending Simple Types

The process for creating new simple datatypes is straightforward. The new type must be derived from a *base type*: a predefined schema type or another already-defined simple type. The base type is *restricted* along a number of *facets* to obtain the new type. The facets identify various characteristics of the types, such as

- `length`, `minLength`, `maxLength`—The exact, minimum, and maximum character length of the value
- `pattern`—A regular expression pattern for the value
- `enumeration`—A list of all possible values
- `whiteSpace`—The rules for handling whitespace in the value
- `minExclusive`, `minInclusive`, `maxInclusive`, `maxExclusive`—The range of numeric values that are allowed
- `totalDigits`—The number of decimal digits in a numeric value
- `fractionDigits`—The number of decimal digits after the decimal point

Of course, not all facets apply to all types. For example, the notion of fraction digits makes no sense for a date or a name. Tables 2.3 and 2.4 cross-link the predefined types and the facets that are applicable for them.

Table 2.3 **XML Schema Facets for Simple Types**

Simple Type	Facets					
	length	minLength	maxLength	pattern	enumeration	whiteSpace
string	✔	✔	✔	✔	✔	✔
base64Binary	✔	✔	✔	✔	✔	✔
hexBinary	✔	✔	✔	✔	✔	✔
integer				✔	✔	✔
positiveInteger				✔	✔	✔
negativeInteger				✔	✔	✔
nonNegativeInteger				✔	✔	✔
nonPositiveInteger				✔	✔	✔
decimal				✔	✔	✔
boolean				✔		✔
time				✔	✔	✔
dateTime				✔	✔	✔
duration				✔	✔	✔
date				✔	✔	✔

Table 2.3 **Continued**

Simple Type	Facets					
	length	minLength	maxLength	pattern	enumeration	whiteSpace
Name	✔	✔	✔	✔	✔	✔
QName	✔	✔	✔	✔	✔	✔
anyURI	✔	✔	✔	✔	✔	✔
ID	✔	✔	✔	✔	✔	✔
IDREF	✔	✔	✔	✔	✔	✔

The information in this table comes from the XML Schema Primer.

The facets listed in Table 2.4 apply only to simple types that have an implicit order.

Table 2.4 **XML Schema Facets for Ordered Simple Types**

Simple Types	Facets					
	Max Inclusive	Max Exclusive	Min Inclusive	Min Exclusive	Total Digits	Fraction Digits
integer	✔	✔	✔	✔	✔	✔
positiveInteger	✔	✔	✔	✔	✔	✔
negativeInteger	✔	✔	✔	✔	✔	✔
nonNegativeInteger	✔	✔	✔	✔	✔	✔
nonPositiveInteger	✔	✔	✔	✔	✔	✔
decimal	✔	✔	✔	✔	✔	✔
time	✔	✔	✔	✔		
dateTime	✔	✔	✔	✔		
duration	✔	✔	✔	✔		
date	✔	✔	✔	✔		

The information in this table comes from the XML Schema Primer.

The syntax for creating new types is simple. For example, the schema snippet in Listing 2.13 defines a simple type for purchase order SKUs. The name of the type is skuType. It's based on a string, and it restricts the string to the following pattern: three digits, followed by a dash, followed by two uppercase letters.

Listing 2.13   **Using Patterns to Define a String's Format**

```
<xsd:simpleType name="skuType">
   <xsd:restriction base="xsd:string">
      <xsd:pattern value="\d{3}-[A-Z]{2}"/>
   </xsd:restriction>
</xsd:simpleType>
```

Listing 2.14 shows how to force purchase order IDs to be greater than 10,000 but less than 100,000, and also how to define an enumeration of all U.S. states.

Listing 2.14   **Using Ranges and Enumerations**

```
<xsd:simpleType name="poIdType">
   <xsd:restriction base="xsd:integer">
      <xsd:minExclusive value="10000"/>
      <xsd:maxExclusive value="100000"/>
   </xsd:restriction>
</xsd:simpleType>

<xsd:simpleType name="stateType">
   <xsd:restriction base="xsd:string">
      <xsd:enumeration value="AK"/>
      <xsd:enumeration value="AL"/>
      <xsd:enumeration value="AR"/>
      ...
   </xsd:restriction>
</xsd:simpleType>
```

Complex Types

In XML Schema, simple types define the valid choices for character-based content such as attribute values and elements with character content. *Complex types* 📖, on the other hand, define complex content models, such as those of elements that can have attributes and nested children. Complex type definitions address both the sequencing and multiplicity of child elements as well as the names of associated attributes and whether they're required or optional.

The syntax for defining complex types is straightforward:

```
<xsd:complexType name="typeName">
   <xsd:someTopLevelModelGroup>
      <!-- Sequencing and multiplicity constraints for
           child elements defined using xsd:element -->
   </xsd:someTopLevelModelGroup>
   <!-- Attribute declarations using xsd:attribute -->
</xsd:complexType>
```

The element `xsd:complexType` identifies the type definition. There are many different ways to specify the model group of the complex type. The most commonly used top-level model group elements you'll see are

- `xsd:sequence`—A sequence of elements
- `xsd:choice`—Allows one out of a number of elements
- `xsd:all`—Allows a certain set of elements to appear once or not at all but in any order
- `xsd:group`—References a model group that is defined someplace else

These could be further nested to create more complex model groups. The `xsd:group` model group element is covered later in this chapter in the section "Content Model Groups."

Inside the model group specification, child elements are defined using `xsd:element`. The model group specification is followed by any number of attribute definitions using `xsd:attribute`.

For example, one possible way to define the content model of the PO address used in the `billTo` and `shipTo` elements is shown in Listing 2.15. The name of the complex type is `addressType`. Using `xsd:sequence` and `xsd:element`, it defines a sequence of the elements name, company, street, city, state, postalCode, and country.

Listing 2.15 Schema Fragment for the Address Complex Type

```
<xsd:complexType name="addressType">
   <xsd:sequence>
      <xsd:element name="name" type="xsd:string" minOccurs="0"/>
      <xsd:element name="company" type="xsd:string" minOccurs="0"/>
      <xsd:element name="street" type="xsd:string"
                   maxOccurs="unbounded"/>
      <xsd:element name="city" type="xsd:string"/>
      <xsd:element name="state" type="xsd:string" minOccurs="0"/>
      <xsd:element name="postalCode" type="xsd:string"
                   minOccurs="0"/>
      <xsd:element name="country" type="xsd:string" minOccurs="0"/>
   </xsd:sequence>
   <xsd:attribute name="id" type="xsd:ID"/>
   <xsd:attribute name="href" type="xsd:IDREF"/>
</xsd:complexType>
```

The multiplicities of these elements' occurrences are defined using the `minOccurs` and `maxOccurs` attributes of `xsd:element`. The value of zero for `minOccurs` renders an element's presence optional (? in the document structure diagrams). The default value for `minOccurs` is 1. The special `maxOccurs` value `"unbounded"` is used for the street element to indicate that at least one must be present (+ in the document structure diagrams).

As we mentioned earlier, every element is associated with a type using the type attribute xsd:element. In this example, all elements have simple character content of type string, identified by the xsd:string type. It might seem unusual that the namespace prefix is used inside an attribute value. It's true, the XML Namespaces specification doesn't explicitly address this use of namespace prefixes. However, the idea is simple. A schema can define any number of types. Some of them are built into the specification, and others are user-defined. The only way to know for sure which type is being referred to is to associate the type name with the namespace from which it's coming. What better way to do this than to prefix all references to the type with a namespace prefix?

After the model group definition come the attribute definitions. In this example, xsd:attribute defines attributes id and href of types ID and IDREF, respectively. Both attributes are optional by default.

Now, consider a slightly more complex example of a complex type definition—the po element's type (see Listing 2.16).

Listing 2.16   **Schema Fragment for the Purchase Order Complex Type**

```
<xsd:complexType name="poType">
   <xsd:sequence>
      <xsd:element name="billTo" type="addressType"/>
      <xsd:element name="shipTo" type="addressType"/>
      <xsd:element name="order">
         <xsd:complexType>
            <xsd:sequence>
               <xsd:element name="item" type="itemType"
                            maxOccurs="unbounded"/>
            </xsd:sequence>
         </xsd:complexType>
      </xsd:element>
   </xsd:sequence>
   <xsd:attribute name="id" use="required"
                  type="xsd:positiveInteger"/>
   <xsd:attribute name="submitted" use="required"
                  type="xsd:date"/>
   <xsd:attribute name="customerId" use="required"
                  type="xsd:positiveInteger"/>
</xsd:complexType>
```

The poType introduces three interesting aspects of schemas:

- It shows how easy it is to achieve basic reusability of types. Both the billTo and shipTo elements refer to the addressType defined previously. Note that because this is a user-defined complex type, a namespace prefix isn't necessary.

- The association between elements and their types can be implicit. The order element's type is defined inline as a sequence of one or more item elements of type itemType. This is convenient because it keeps the schema more readable and prevents the need to define a global type that is used in only one place.

- The presence of attributes can be required through the use="required" attribute-value pair of the xsd:attribute element. To give default and fixed values to attributes, you can also use the aptly named default and fixed attributes of xsd:attribute.

The Purchase Order Schema

With the information gathered so far, we can completely define the SkatesTown purchase order schema (Listing 2.17).

Listing 2.17   **The Complete SkatesTown Purchase Order Schema** (po.xsd)

```
<?xml version="1.0" encoding="UTF-8"?>
<xsd:schema xmlns="http://www.skatestown.com/ns/po"
            xmlns:xsd="http://www.w3.org/2001/XMLSchema"
            targetNamespace="http://www.skatestown.com/ns/po">

   <xsd:annotation>
      <xsd:documentation xml:lang="en">
         Purchase order schema for SkatesTown.
      </xsd:documentation>
   </xsd:annotation>

   <xsd:element name="po" type="poType"/>

   <xsd:complexType name="poType">
      <xsd:sequence>
         <xsd:element name="billTo" type="addressType"/>
         <xsd:element name="shipTo" type="addressType"/>
         <xsd:element name="order">
            <xsd:complexType>
               <xsd:sequence>
                  <xsd:element name="item" type="itemType"
                               maxOccurs="unbounded"/>
               </xsd:sequence>
            </xsd:complexType>
         </xsd:element>
      </xsd:sequence>
      <xsd:attribute name="id" use="required"
                     type="xsd:positiveInteger"/>
      <xsd:attribute name="submitted" use="required"
                     type="xsd:date"/>
      <xsd:attribute name="customerId" use="required"
                     type="xsd:positiveInteger"/>
   </xsd:complexType>
```

Listing 2.17 **Continued**

```xsd
<xsd:complexType name="addressType">
    <xsd:sequence>
        <xsd:element name="name" type="xsd:string" minOccurs="0"/>
        <xsd:element name="company" type="xsd:string" minOccurs="0"/>
        <xsd:element name="street" type="xsd:string"
                    maxOccurs="unbounded"/>
        <xsd:element name="city" type="xsd:string"/>
        <xsd:element name="state" type="xsd:string" minOccurs="0"/>
        <xsd:element name="postalCode" type="xsd:string"
                    minOccurs="0"/>
        <xsd:element name="country" type="xsd:string" minOccurs="0"/>
    </xsd:sequence>
    <xsd:attribute name="id" type="xsd:ID"/>
    <xsd:attribute name="href" type="xsd:IDREF"/>
</xsd:complexType>

<xsd:complexType name="itemType">
    <xsd:sequence>
        <xsd:element name="description" type="xsd:string"
                    minOccurs="0"/>
    </xsd:sequence>
    <xsd:attribute name="sku" use="required">
        <xsd:simpleType>
            <xsd:restriction base="xsd:string">
                <xsd:pattern value="\d{3}-[A-Z]{2}"/>
            </xsd:restriction>
        </xsd:simpleType>
    </xsd:attribute>
    <xsd:attribute name="quantity" use="required"
                    type="xsd:positiveInteger"/>
</xsd:complexType>
</xsd:schema>
```

Global Versus Local Elements and Attributes

Everything should look familiar except perhaps the standalone definition of the po element after the schema annotation. This brings us to the important topic of local versus global elements and attributes. Any element or attribute defined inside a complex type definition is considered local to that definition. Conversely, any element or attribute defined at the top level (as a child of xsd:schema) is considered global.

All global elements can be document roots. That is the main reason why most schemas define a single global element. In the case of the SkatesTown PO, the po element must be the root of the PO document and is hence defined as a global element.

The notion of global attributes might not make much sense at first, but these attributes are very convenient. You can use them (in namespace-prefixed form) on any element in a document that allows them. The item priority attribute discussed in the section "XML Namespaces" is defined with the short schema in Listing 2.18.

Listing 2.18   **Defining the Priority Global Attribute Using a Schema**

```
<?xml version="1.0" encoding="UTF-8"?>
<xsd:schema xmlns="http://www.skatestown.com/ns/priority"
            targetNamespace="http://www.skatestown.com/ns/priority"
            xmlns:xsd="http://www.w3.org/2001/XMLSchema">
   <xsd:attribute name="priority" use="optional" default="medium">
      <xsd:simpleType>
         <xsd:restriction base="xsd:string">
            <xsd:enumeration value="low"/>
            <xsd:enumeration value="medium"/>
            <xsd:enumeration value="high"/>
         </xsd:restriction>
      </xsd:simpleType>
   </xsd:attribute>
</xsd:schema>
```

Basic Schema Reusability

The concept of reusability is important for XML Schema. Reusability deals with the question of how to best leverage existing assets in new projects. In schemas, the assets include element and attribute definitions, content model definitions, simple and complex datatypes, and whole schemas. We can roughly break down reusability mechanisms into two kinds: basic and advanced. The basic reusability mechanisms address the problems of using existing assets in multiple places. Advanced reusability mechanisms address the problems of modifying existing assets to serve needs that are different than those for which the assets were originally designed.

This section will address the following basic reusability mechanisms:

- Element references
- Content model groups
- Attribute groups
- Schema includes
- Schema imports

Element References

In XML Schema, you can define elements using a name and a type. Alternatively, element declarations can refer to preexisting elements using the ref attribute of xsd:element as follows, where a globally defined comment element is reused for both person and task complex types:

```
<xsd:element name="comment" type="xsd:string"/>

<xsd:complexType name="personType">
   <xsd:sequence>
      <xsd:element name="name" type="xsd:string"/>
      <xsd:element ref="comment" minOccurs="0"/>
   </xsd:sequence>
</xsd:complexType>

<xsd:complexType name="taskType">
   <xsd:sequence>
      <xsd:element name="toDo" type="xsd:string"/>
      <xsd:element ref="comment" minOccurs="0"/>
   </xsd:sequence>
</xsd:complexType>
```

Content Model Groups

Element references are perfect for reusing the definition of a single element. However, if your goal is to reuse all or part of a content model, then element groups are the way to go. Element groups are defined using xsd:group and are referred to using the same mechanism used for elements. The following schema fragment illustrates the concept. It extends the previous example so that instead of a single comment element, public and private comment elements are reused as a group:

```
<xsd:group name="comments">
   <xsd:sequence>
      <xsd:element name="publicComment" type="xsd:string"
                   minOccurs="0"/>
      <xsd:element name="privateComment" type="xsd:string"
                   minOccurs="0"/>
   </xsd:sequence>
</xsd:group>

<xsd:complexType name="personType">
   <xsd:sequence>
      <xsd:element name="name" type="xsd:string"/>
      <xsd:group ref="comments"/>
   </xsd:sequence>
</xsd:complexType>

<xsd:complexType name="taskType">
   <xsd:sequence>
```

```
        <xsd:element name="toDo" type="xsd:string"/>
        <xsd:group ref="comments"/>
    </xsd:sequence>
</xsd:complexType>
```

Attribute Groups

The same reusability mechanism can be applied to commonly used attribute groups. The following example defines the ID/IDREF combination of id and href attributes as a referenceable attribute group. It's then applied to both the person and the task type:

```
<xsd:attributeGroup name="referenceable">
    <xsd:attribute name="id" type="xsd:ID"/>
    <xsd:attribute name="href" type="xsd:IDREF"/>
</xsd:attributeGroup>

<xsd:complexType name="personType">
    <xsd:sequence>
        <xsd:element name="name" type="xsd:string"/>
    </xsd:sequence>
    <xsd:attributeGroup ref="referenceable"/>
</xsd:complexType>

<xsd:complexType name="taskType">
    <xsd:sequence>
        <xsd:element name="toDo" type="xsd:string"/>
    </xsd:sequence>
    <xsd:attributeGroup ref="referenceable"/>
</xsd:complexType>
```

Schema Includes and Imports

Element references and groups as well as attribute groups provide reusability within the same schema document. However, when you're dealing with very complex schema or trying to achieve maximum reusability, you'll often need to split a schema into several documents. The schema *include* and *import* mechanisms allow these documents to reference one another.

Consider the scenario where SkatesTown is intent on reusing the schema definition for its address type for a mailing list schema. SkatesTown must solve three small problems:

- Put the address type definition in its own schema document
- Reference this schema document from the purchase order schema document
- Reference this schema document from the mailing list schema document

Pulling the address definition into its own schema is as easy as a cut-and-paste operation (see Listing 2.19). Even though this is a different document than the main purchase order schema, they both define portions of the SkatesTown PO namespace. The binding between schema documents and the namespaces they define isn't one-to-one. It's explicitly identified by the `targetNamespace` attribute of the `xsd:schema` element.

Listing 2.19 **Standalone Address Type Schema**

```
<?xml version="1.0" encoding="UTF-8"?>
<xsd:schema xmlns="http://www.skatestown.com/ns/po"
            xmlns:xsd="http://www.w3.org/2001/XMLSchema"
            targetNamespace="http://www.skatestown.com/ns/po">

   <xsd:annotation>
      <xsd:documentation xml:lang="en">
         Address type schema for SkatesTown.
      </xsd:documentation>
   </xsd:annotation>

   <xsd:complexType name="addressType">
      <xsd:sequence>
         <xsd:element name="name" type="xsd:string" minOccurs="0"/>
         <xsd:element name="company" type="xsd:string" minOccurs-"0"/>
         <xsd:element name="street" type="xsd:string"
                     maxOccurs="unbounded"/>
         <xsd:element name="city" type="xsd:string"/>
         <xsd:element name="state" type="xsd:string" minOccurs="0"/>
         <xsd:element name="postalCode" type="xsd:string"
                     minOccurs="0"/>
         <xsd:element name="country" type="xsd:string" minOccurs="0"/>
      </xsd:sequence>
      <xsd:attribute name="id" type="xsd:ID"/>
      <xsd:attribute name="href" type="xsd:IDREF"/>
   </xsd:complexType>

</xsd:schema>
```

Referring to this schema is also easy. Instead of having the address type definition inline, the PO schema needs to include the address schema using the `xsd:include` element. During the processing of the PO schema, the address schema will be retrieved and the address type definition will become available (see Listing 2.20).

Listing 2.20 **Referring to the Address Type Schema**

```
<?xml version="1.0" encoding="UTF-8"?>
<xsd:schema xmlns="http://www.skatestown.com/ns/po"
            xmlns:xsd="http://www.w3.org/2001/XMLSchema"
            targetNamespace="http://www.skatestown.com/ns/po">
```

Listing 2.20   **Continued**

```
<xsd:include
    schemaLocation="http://www.skatestown.com/schema/address.xsd"/>

    . . .
</xsd:schema>
```

The mailing list schema is very simple. It defines a single `mailingList` element that contains any number of contact elements whose type is `address`. Being an altogether different schema than that used for POs, the mailing list schema uses a new namespace: `http://www.skatestown.com/ns/mailingList`. Listing 2.21 shows one possible way to define this schema.

Listing 2.21   **Mailing List Schema**

```
<?xml version="1.0" encoding="UTF-8"?>
<xsd:schema xmlns="http://www.skatestown.com/ns/po"
            xmlns:xsd="http://www.w3.org/2001/XMLSchema"
            targetNamespace="http://www.skatestown.com/ns/mailingList">

    <xsd:include
        schemaLocation="http://www.skatestown.com/schema/address.xsd"/>

    <xsd:annotation>
        <xsd:documentation xml:lang="en">
            Mailing list schema for SkatesTown.
        </xsd:documentation>
    </xsd:annotation>

    <xsd:element name="mailingList">
        <xsd:sequence>
            <xsd:element name="contact" type="addressType"
                         minOccurs="0" maxOccurs="unbounded"/>
        </xsd:sequence>
    </xsd:element>

</xsd:schema>
```

This example uses `xsd:include` to bring in the schema fragment defining the address type. There is no problem with that approach. However, there might be a problem with authoring mailing-list documents. The root of the problem is that the `mailingList` and `contact` elements are defined in one namespace (`http://www.skatestown.com/ns/mailingList`), whereas the elements belonging to the address type—`name`, `company`, `street`, `city`, `state`, `postalCode`, and `country`—are defined in another (`http://www.skatestown.com/ns/po`). Therefore, the mailing list document must reference both namespaces (see Listing 2.22).

Listing 2.22   **Mailing List That References Two Namespaces**

```
<?xml version="1.0" encoding="UTF-8"?>
<list:mailingList xmlns:list="http://www.skatestown.com/ns/mailingList"
   xmlns:addr="http://www.skatestown.com/ns/po"
   xmlns:xsi="http://www.w3.org/2001/XMLSchema-instance"
   xsi:schemaLocation="http://www.skatestown.com/ns/mailingList
                       http://www.skatestown.com/schema/mailingList.xsd
                       http://www.skatestown.com/ns/po
                       http://www.skatestown.com/schema/address.xsd">
   <contact>
      <addr:company>The Skateboard Warehouse</addr:company>
      <addr:street>One Warehouse Park</addr:street>
      <addr:street>Building 17</addr:street>
      <addr:city>Boston</addr:city>
      <addr:state>MA</addr:state>
      <addr:postalCode>01775</addr:postalCode>
   </contact>
</list:mailingList>
```

Ideally, when reusing the address type definition in the mailing list schema, we want to hide the fact that it originates from a different namespace and treat it as a true part of the mailing list schema. Therefore, the `xsd:include` mechanism isn't the right one to use, because it makes no namespace changes. The reuse mechanism that will allow the merging of schema fragments from multiple namespaces into a single schema is the import mechanism. Listing 2.23 shows the new mailing list schema.

Listing 2.23   **Importing Rather Than Including the Address Type Schema**

```
<?xml version="1.0" encoding="UTF-8"?>
<xsd:schema xmlns="http://www.skatestown.com/ns/po"
            xmlns:xsd="http://www.w3.org/2001/XMLSchema"
            xmlns:addr="http://www.skatestown.com/ns/po"
            xmlns:xsi="http://www.w3.org/2001/XMLSchema-instance"
            xsi:schemaLocation="http://www.skatestown.com/ns/po
               http://www.skatestown.com/schema/address.xsd"
            targetNamespace="http://www.skatestown.com/ns/mailingList">

   <xsd:import namespace="http://www.skatestown.com/ns/po"/>

   <xsd:annotation>
      <xsd:documentation xml:lang="en">
         Mailing list schema for SkatesTown.
      </xsd:documentation>
   </xsd:annotation>

   <xsd:element name="mailingList">
      <xsd:sequence>
```

Listing 2.23   **Continued**

```
        <xsd:element name="contact" type="addr:addressType"
                     minOccurs="0" maxOccurs="unbounded"/>
    </xsd:sequence>
  </xsd:element>

</xsd:schema>
```

Although the mechanism is simple to describe, it takes several steps to execute:

1. Declare the namespace of the address type definition and assign it the prefix `addr`.

2. Use the standard `xsi:schemaLocation` mechanism to hint about the location of the address schema.

3. Use `xsd:import` instead of `xsd:include` to merge the contents of the PO namespace into the mailing list namespace.

4. When referring to the address type, use its fully qualified name: `addr:addressType`.

The net result is that the mailing list instance document has been simplified (see Listing 2.24).

Listing 2.24   **Simplified Instance Document That Requires a Single Namespace**

```
<?xml version="1.0" encoding="UTF-8"?>
<list:mailingList xmlns:list="http://www.skatestown.com/ns/mailingList"
  xmlns:xsi="http://www.w3.org/2001/XMLSchema-instance"
  xsi:schemaLocation="http://www.skatestown.com/ns/mailingList
                      http://www.skatestown.com/schema/mailingList.xsd">
  <contact>
     <company>The Skateboard Warehouse</company>
     <street>One Warehouse Park</street>
     <street>Building 17</street>
     <city>Boston</city>
     <state>MA</state>
     <postalCode>01775</postalCode>
  </contact>
</list:mailingList>
```

Advanced Schema Reusability

The previous section demonstrated how you can reuse types and elements as is from the same or a different namespace. This capability can go a long way in some cases, but many real-world scenarios require more sophisticated reuse capabilities. Consider, for example, the format of the invoice that SkatesTown will send to the Skateboard Warehouse based on its PO (see Listing 2.25).

Listing 2.25   **SkatesTown Invoice Document**

```xml
<?xml version="1.0" encoding="UTF-8"?>
<invoice:invoice xmlns:invoice="http://www.skatestown.com/ns/invoice"
   xmlns:xsi="http://www.w3.org/2001/XMLSchema-instance"
   xsi:schemaLocation="http://www.skatestown.com/ns/invoice
                       http://www.skatestown.com/schema/invoice.xsd"
   id="43871" submitted="2004-01-05" customerId="73852">
   <billTo id="addr-1">
      <company>The Skateboard Warehouse</company>
      <street>One Warehouse Park</street>
      <street>Building 17</street>
      <city>Boston</city>
      <state>MA</state>
      <postalCode>01775</postalCode>
   </billTo>
   <shipTo href="addr-1"/>
   <order>
      <item sku="318-BP" quantity="5" unitPrice="49.95">
         <description>Skateboard backpack; five pockets</description>
      </item>
      <item sku="947-TI" quantity="12" unitPrice="129.00">
         <description>Street-style titanium skateboard.</description>
      </item>
      <item sku="008-PR" quantity="1000" unitPrice="0.00">
         <description>Promotional: SkatesTown stickers</description>
      </item>
   </order>
   <tax>89.89</tax>
   <shippingAndHandling>200</shippingAndHandling>
   <totalCost>2087.64</totalCost>
</invoice:invoice>
```

The invoice document has many of the features of a PO document, with a few important changes:

- Invoices use a different namespace: http://www.skatestown.com/ns/invoice.
- The root element of the document is invoice, not po.
- The invoice element has three additional children: tax, shippingAndHandling, and totalCost.
- The item element has an additional attribute: unitPrice.

How can we leverage the work done to define the PO schema in defining the invoice schema? This section will introduce the advanced schema reusability mechanisms that make this possible.

Design Principles

Imagine that purchase orders, addresses, and items were represented as classes in an object-oriented programming language such as Java. We could create an invoice object by subclassing item to invoiceItem (which adds unitPrice) and po to invoice (which adds tax, shippingAndHandling, and totalCost). The benefit of this approach is that any changes to related classes such as address will be automatically picked up by both POs and invoices. Further, any changes in base types such as item will be automatically picked up by derived types such as invoiceItem.

The following pseudocode shows how this approach might work:

```
public class Address { ... }

public class Item
{
   public String sku;
   public int quantity;
}

public class InvoiceItem extends Item
{
   public double unitPrice;
}

public class PO
{
   public int id;
   public Calendar submitted;
   public int customerId;
   public Address billTo;
   public Address shipTo;
   public Item order[];
}

public class Invoice extends PO
{
   public double tax;
   public double shippingAndHandling;
   public double totalCost;
}
```

Everything looks good except for one important detail. You might have noticed that Invoice shouldn't subclass PO, because the order array inside an invoice object must hold InvoiceItems and not just Item. The subclassing relationship will force you to work with Items instead of InvoiceItems. Doing so will weaken static type-checking and require constant downcasting, which is generally a bad thing in well-designed object-oriented systems. A better design for the Invoice class, unfortunately, requires some duplication of PO's data members:

```
public class Invoice
{
    public int id;
    public Calendar submitted;
    public int customerId;
    public Address billTo;
    public Address shipTo;
    public InvoiceItem order[];
    public double tax;
    public double shippingAndHandling;
    public double totalCost;
}
```

Note that subclassing Item to get InvoiceItem is a good decision because InvoiceItem is a pure extension of Item. It adds new data members; it doesn't require modifications to Item's data members, nor does it change the way they're used.

Extensions and Restrictions

The analysis from object-oriented systems can be directly applied to the design of SkatesTown's invoice schema. The schema defines the invoice element in terms of pre-existing types such as addressType, and the invoice's item type reuses the already-defined purchase order item type via *extension* (see Listing 2.26).

Listing 2.26   **SkatesTown Invoice Schema**

```xml
<?xml version="1.0" encoding="UTF-8"?>
<xsd:schema xmlns="http://www.skatestown.com/ns/invoice"
    targetNamespace="http://www.skatestown.com/ns/invoice"
    xmlns:xsd="http://www.w3.org/2001/XMLSchema"
    xmlns:po="http://www.skatestown.com/ns/po">

    <xsd:import namespace-"http://www.skatestown.com/ns/po"
       schemaLocation="http://www.skatestown.cm/schema/po.xsd"/>

    <xsd:annotation>
       <xsd:documentation xml:lang="en">
          Invoice schema for SkatesTown.
       </xsd:documentation>
    </xsd:annotation>

    <xsd:element name="invoice" type="invoiceType"/>

    <xsd:complexType name="invoiceType">
       <xsd:sequence>
          <xsd:element name="billTo" type="po:addressType"/>
          <xsd:element name="shipTo" type="po:addressType"/>
          <xsd:element name="order">
```

Listing 2.26   **Continued**

```
        <xsd:complexType>
          <xsd:sequence>
            <xsd:element name="item" type="itemType"
                         maxOccurs="unbounded"/>
          </xsd:sequence>
        </xsd:complexType>
      </xsd:element>
      <xsd:element name="tax" type="priceType"/>
      <xsd:element name="shippingAndHandling" type="priceType"/>
      <xsd:element name="totalCost" type="priceType"/>
    </xsd:sequence>
    <xsd:attribute name="id" use="required"
                   type="xsd:positiveInteger"/>
    <xsd:attribute name="submitted" use="required"
                   type="xsd:date"/>
    <xsd:attribute name="customerId" use="required"
                   type="xsd:positiveInteger"/>
  </xsd:complexType>

  <xsd:complexType name="itemType">
    <xsd:complexContent>
      <xsd:extension base="po:itemType">
        <xsd:attribute name="unitPrice" use="required"
                       type="priceType"/>
      </xsd:extension>
    </xsd:complexContent>
  </xsd:complexType>

  <xsd:simpleType name="priceType">
    <xsd:restriction base="xsd:decimal">
      <xsd:minInclusive value="0"/>
    </xsd:restriction>
  </xsd:simpleType>

</xsd:schema>
```

By now the schema mechanics should be familiar. The beginning of the schema declares the PO and invoice namespaces. The PO schema has to be imported because it doesn't reside in the same namespace as the invoice schema.

The invoiceType schema address type is defined in terms of po:addressType, but the order element's content is of type itemType and not po:itemType. That's because the invoice's itemType needs to extend po:itemType and add the unitPrice attribute. This happens at the next complex type definition. In general, the schema extension syntax, although somewhat verbose, is easy to use:

```
<xsd:complexType name="...">
  <xsd:complexContent>
    <xsd:extension base="...">
      <!-- Optional extension content model -->
      <!-- Optional extension attributes -->
    </xsd:extension>
  </xsd:complexContent>
</xsd:complexType>
```

The content model of extended types contains all the child elements of the base type plus any additional elements added by the extension. Any attributes in the extension are added to the attribute set of the base type.

Last but not least, the invoice schema defines a simple price type as a non-negative decimal number. The definition happens via restriction of the lower boundary of the decimal type using the same mechanism introduced in the section on simple types.

The restriction mechanism in schemas applies not only to simple types but also to complex types. The syntax is similar to that of extension:

```
<xsd:complexType name="...">
  <xsd:complexContent>
    <xsd:restriction base="...">
      <!-- Content model and attributes -->
    </xsd:restriction>
  </xsd:complexContent>
</xsd:complexType>
```

The concept of restriction has a precise meaning in XML Schema. The declarations of the type derived by restriction are very close to those of the base type but more limited. There are several possible types of restrictions:

- Multiplicity restrictions
- Deletion of optional elements
- Tighter limits on occurrence constraints
- Provision of default values
- Provision of types where there were none, or narrowing of types

For example, we can extend the address type by restriction to create a corporate address that doesn't include a name:

```
<xsd:complexType name="corporateAddressType">
  <xsd:complexContent>
    <xsd:restriction base="addressType">
      <xsd:sequence>
        <!-- Add maxOccurs="0" to delete optional name element -->
        <xsd:element name="name" type="xsd:string"
                     minOccurs="0" maxOccurs="0"/>
```

```
      <!-- The rest is the same as in addressType -->
      <xsd:element name="company" type="xsd:string"
                   minOccurs="0"/>
      <xsd:element name="street" type="xsd:string"
                   maxOccurs="unbounded"/>
      <xsd:element name="city" type="xsd:string"/>
      <xsd:element name="state" type="xsd:string"
                   minOccurs="0"/>
      <xsd:element name="postalCode" type="xsd:string"
                   minOccurs="0"/>
      <xsd:element name="country" type="xsd:string"
                   minOccurs="0"/>
    </xsd:sequence>
    <xsd:attribute name="id" type="xsd:ID"/>
    <xsd:attribute name="href" type="xsd:IDREF"/>
  </xsd:restriction>
 </xsd:complexContent>
</xsd:complexType>
```

The Importance of xsi:type

The nature of restriction is such that an application that is prepared to deal with the base type can certainly accept the derived type. In other words, you can use a corporate address type directly inside the billTo and shipTo elements of POs and invoices without a problem. Sometimes, however, it might be convenient to identify the actual schema type used in an instance document. XML Schema allows you to do this through the use of the global xsi:type attribute. This attribute can be applied to any element to signal its actual schema type, as Listing 2.27 shows.

Listing 2.27 **Using** xsi:type

```
<?xml version="1.0" encoding="UTF-8"?>
<po:po xmlns:po="http://www.skatestown.com/ns/po"
       xmlns:xsi="http://www.w3.org/2001/XMLSchema-instance"
       xsi:schemaLocation="http://www.skatestown.com/ns/po
                           http://www.skatestown.com/schema/po.xsd"
       id="43871" submitted="2004-01-05" customerId="73852">
  <billTo xsi:type="po:corporateAddressType" >
    <company>The Skateboard Warehouse</company>
    <street>One Warehouse Park</street>
    <street>Building 17</street>
    <city>Boston</city>
    <state>MA</state>
    <postalCode>01775</postalCode>
  </billTo>
  ...
</po:po>
```

Although derivation by restriction doesn't require the use of xsi:type, derivation by extension often does. The reason is that an application prepared for the base schema type is unlikely to be able to process the derived type (it adds information) without a hint. But why would such a scenario ever occur? Why would an instance document contain data from a type derived by extension in a place where the schema expects a base type?

XML Schema allows derivation by extension to be used in cases where it really shouldn't be used, as in the case of the invoice and PO datatypes. In these cases, you must use xsi:type in the instance document to ensure successful validation. Consider a scenario where the invoice type was derived by extension from the PO type:

```
<xsd:complexType name="invoiceType">
   <xsd:complexContent>
      <xsd:extension base="po:poType">
         <xsd:element name="tax" type="priceType"/>
         <xsd:element name="shippingAndHandling" type="priceType"/>
         <xsd:element name="totalCost" type="priceType"/>
      </xsd:extension>
   </xsd:complexContent>
</xsd:complexType>
```

Remember, extension doesn't change the content model of the base type; it can only add to the content model. Therefore, this definition will make the item element inside invoices of type po:itemType, not invoice:itemType. The use of xsi:type (see Listing 2.28) is the only way to add unit prices to items without violating the validity constraints of the document imposed by the schema. An imperfect analogy from programming languages is that xsi:type provides the true type to downcast to when you're holding a reference to a base type.

Listing 2.28 **Using xsi:type to Correctly Identify Invoice Item Elements**

```
<order>
   <item sku="318-BP" quantity="5" unitPrice="49.95"
         xsi:type="invoice:itemType">
      <description>Skateboard backpack; five pockets</description>
   </item>
   <item sku="947-TI" quantity="12" unitPrice="129.00"
         xsi:type="invoice:itemType">
      <description>Street-style titanium skateboard.</description>
   </item>
   <item sku="008-PR" quantity="1000" unitPrice="0.00"
         xsi:type="invoice:itemType">
      <description>Promotional: SkatesTown stickers</description>
   </item>
</order>
```

This example shows a use of xsi:type that comes as a result of poor schema design. If, instead of extending PO, the invoice type is defined on its own, the need for xsi:type disappears. However, sometimes even good schema design doesn't prevent the need to identify actual types in instance documents.

Imagine that, due to constant typos in shipping and billing address postal codes, SkatesTown decides to become more restrictive in its document validation. The company defines three types of addresses that are part of POs and schema. The types have the following constraints:

- Address—Same as always
- USAddress—Country isn't allowed, and the ZIP Code pattern "\d{5}(-\d{4})?" is enforced
- UKAddress—Country is fixed to UK, and the postal code pattern "[0-9A-Z]{3} [0-9A-Z]{3}" is enforced

To get the best possible validation, SkatesTown's applications need to know the exact type of address that is being used in a document. Without using xsi:type, the PO and invoice schema will each have to define nine (three squared) possible combinations of billTo and shipTo elements: billTo/shipTo, billTo/shipToUS, billTo/shipToUK, billToUS/shipTo, and so on. It's better to stick with billTo and shipTo and use xsi:type to get exact schema type information.

There's More

This completes the whirlwind tour of XML Schema. Much material useful for data-oriented applications falls outside the scope of what is included in this chapter; we'll introduce some information throughout the book as needed.

Processing XML

So far, this chapter has introduced the key XML standards and explained how they're expressed in XML documents. The final section of the chapter focuses on processing XML, with a quick tour of the specifications and APIs you need to know to be able to generate, parse, and process XML documents in your Java applications.

Basic Operations

The basic XML processing architecture shown in Figure 2.4 consists of three key layers. At far left are the XML documents an application needs to work with. At far right is the application. In the middle is the infrastructure layer for working with XML documents, which is the topic of this section.

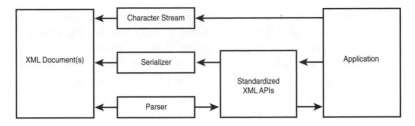

Figure 2.4 Basic XML processing architecture

For an application to be able to work with an XML document, it must first be able to parse the document. *Parsing* is a process that involves breaking the text of an XML document into small identifiable pieces (*nodes*). Parsers break documents into pieces such as start tags, end tags, attribute value pairs, chunks of text content, processing instructions, comments, and so on. These pieces are fed into the application using a well-defined API implementing a particular parsing model. Four parsing models are commonly used:

- *Pull parsing* —The application always has to ask the parser to give it the next piece of information about the document. It's as if the application has to "pull" the information out of the parser (hence the name of the model). The XML community has not yet defined standard APIs for pull parsing. However, because pull parsing is becoming popular, this could happen soon.

- *Push parsing* —The parser sends notifications to the application about the types of XML document pieces it encounters during the parsing process. The notifications are sent in reading order, as they appear in the text of the document. Notifications are typically implemented as event callbacks in the application code, and thus push parsing is also commonly known as *event-based parsing*. The XML community created a de facto standard for push parsing called *Simple API for XML (SAX)* . SAX is currently released in version 2.0.

- *One-step parsing* —The parser reads the whole XML document and generates a data structure (a *parse tree*) describing its contents (elements, attributes, PIs, comments, and so on). The data structure is typically deeply nested; its hierarchy mimics the nesting of elements in the parsed XML document. The W3C has defined a *Document Object Model (DOM)* for XML. The XML DOM specifies the types of objects that are included in the parse tree, their properties, and their operations. The DOM is so popular that one-step parsing is typically referred to as *DOM parsing*. The DOM is a language- and platform-independent API. It offers many obvious benefits but also some hidden costs. The biggest problem with the DOM APIs is that they often don't map well to the native data structures of programming languages. To address this issue for Java, the Java community has started working on a Java DOM (JDOM) specification whose goal is to simplify the manipulation of document trees in Java by using object APIs tuned to the common patterns of Java programming.

- *Hybrid parsing* 📖—This approach combines characteristics of the other three parsing models to create efficient parsers for special scenarios. For example, one common pattern combines pull parsing with one-step parsing. In this model, the application thinks it's working with a one-step parser that has processed the whole XML document from start to end. In reality, the parsing process has just begun. As the application keeps accessing more objects on the DOM (or JDOM) tree, the parsing continues incrementally so that just enough of the document is parsed at any given point to give the application the objects it wants to see.

The reasons there are so many different models for parsing XML have to do with trade-offs between memory efficiency, computational efficiency, and ease of programming. Table 2.5 identifies some of the characteristics of the parsing models. In the table, *control of parsing* refers to who manages the step-by-step parsing process. Pull parsing requires that the application do that; in all other models, the parser takes care of this process. *Control of context* refers to who manages context information such as the level of nesting of elements and their location relative to one another. Both push and pull parsing delegate this control to the application; all other models build a tree of nodes that makes maintaining context much easier. This approach makes programming with DOM or JDOM generally easier than working with SAX. The price is memory and computational efficiency, because instantiating all these objects takes up time and memory. Hybrid parsers attempt to offer the best of both worlds by presenting a tree view of the document but doing incremental parsing behind the scenes.

Table 2.5 **XML Parsing Models and Their Trade-offs**

Model	Control of parsing	Control of context	Memory efficiency	Computational efficiency	Ease of programming
Pull	Application	Application	High	Highest	Low
Push (SAX)	Parser	Application	High	High	Low
One-step (DOM)	Parser	Parser	Lowest	Lowest	High
One-step (JDOM)	Parser	Parser	Low	Low	Highest
Hybrid (DOM)	Parser	Parser	Medium	Medium	High
Hybrid (JDOM)	Parser	Parser	Medium	Medium	Highest

In the Java world, a standardized API—*Java API for XML Processing (JAXP)* 📖—exists for instantiating XML parsers and parsing documents using either SAX or DOM. Without JAXP, Java applications weren't completely portable across XML parsers because different parsers, despite following SAX and DOM, had different APIs for creation, configuration, and parsing of documents. JAXP is currently released in version 1.2. It doesn't support JDOM yet because the JDOM specification isn't complete at this point.

Although XML parsing addresses the problem of feeding data from XML documents into applications, XML output addresses the reverse problem—applications generating XML documents. At the most basic level, an application can directly output XML markup. In Figure 2.4, this is indicated by the application working with a character stream. This isn't difficult to do, but handling the basic syntax rules (attributes quoting, special character escaping, and so on) can become cumbersome. In many cases, it might be easier for the application to construct a data structure (DOM or JDOM tree) describing the XML document that should be generated. Then, the application can use a *serialization* 📖 process to traverse the document tree and emit XML markup corresponding to its elements. This capability isn't directly defined in the DOM and JDOM APIs, but most XML toolkits make it very easy to do just that.

Data-Oriented XML Processing

When you're thinking about applications working with XML, it's important to note that all the mechanisms for parsing and generating XML described so far are *syntax-oriented*. They force the application to work with concepts such as elements, attributes, and pieces of text. This is similar to applications that use text files for storage being forced to work with characters, lines, carriage returns (CR), and line feeds (LF).

Typically, applications want a higher-level view of their data. They aren't concerned with the *physical structure* of the data, be it characters and lines in the case of text files or elements and attributes in the case of XML documents. They want to abstract this away and expose the *meaning* or semantics of the data. In other words, applications don't want to work with syntax-oriented APIs; they want to work with *data-oriented* APIs. Therefore, typical data-oriented XML applications introduce a data abstraction layer between the syntax-oriented parsing and output APIs and application logic (see Figure 2.5).

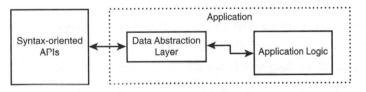

Figure 2.5   Data abstraction layer in XML applications

When working with XML in a data-oriented manner, you'll typically use one of two approaches: *operation-centric* and *data-centric*.

The Operation-Centric Approach

The operation-centric approach works in terms of custom-built APIs for certain operations on the XML document. The implementation of these APIs hides the details of XML processing. Only non-XML types are passed through the APIs.

Consider, for example, the task of SkatesTown trying to independently check the total amount on the invoices it's sending to its customers. From a Java application perspective, a good way to implement an operation like this would be through the interface shown in Listing 2.29.

Listing 2.29 `InvoiceChecker` **Interface**

```
package com.skatestown.invoice;

import java.io.InputStream;

/**
 * SkatesTown invoice checker
 */
public interface InvoiceChecker {
    /**
     * Check invoice totals.
     *
     * @param       invoiceXML Invoice XML document
     * @exception    Exception  Any exception returned during checking
     */
    void checkInvoice(InputStream invoiceXML) throws Exception;
}
```

The implementation of `checkInvoice()` must do the following:

1. Obtain an XML parser.
2. Parse the XML from the input stream.
3. Initialize a running total to zero.
4. Find all order items, and calculate item subtotals by multiplying quantities and unit prices. Add the item subtotals to the running total.
5. Add tax to the running total.
6. Add shipping and handling to the running total.
7. Compare the running total to the total on the invoice.
8. If there is a difference, throw an exception.
9. Otherwise, return.

The most important aspect of this approach is that any XML processing details are hidden from the application. It can happily deal with the `InvoiceChecker` interface, never knowing or caring about how `checkInvoice()` works.

The Data-Centric Approach

An alternative is the data-centric approach. Data-centric XML computing reduces the problem of working with XML documents to that of mapping the XML to and from application data and then working with the data independently of its XML origins. Application data covers the common datatypes developers work with every day: boolean values, numbers, strings, date-time values, arrays, associative arrays (dictionaries, maps, hash tables), database recordsets, and complex object types. Note that in this context, DOM tree objects aren't considered true application data because they're tied to XML syntax. The process of converting application data to XML is called *marshalling* 📖. The XML is a serialized representation of the application data. The process of generating application data from XML is called *unmarshalling* 📖.

For example, the XML invoice markup could be mapped to the set of Java classes introduced in the schema section (see Listing 2.30).

Listing 2.30   **Java Classes Representing Invoice Data**

```
class Address { ... }

class Item { ... }

class InvoiceItem extends Item { ... }

class Invoice
{
    int id;
    Date submitted;
    int customerId;
    Address billTo;
    Address shipTo;
    InvoiceItem order[];
    double tax;
    double shippingAndHandling;
    double totalCost;
}
```

Schema Compilers

The traditional approach for generating XML from application data has been to custom-code the way data values become elements, attributes, and element content. The traditional approach of working with XML to produce application data has been to parse it using a SAX or a DOM parser. Data structures are built from the SAX events or the DOM tree using custom code. However, there are better ways to map data to and from XML using technologies specifically built for marshalling and unmarshalling data to and from XML. Enter schema compilation tools.

Schema compilers are tools that analyze XML schema and code-generate marshalling and unmarshalling modules specific to the schema. These modules work with data structures tuned to the schema. Figure 2.6 shows the basic process for working with schema compilers. The schema compiler needs to be invoked only once; then the application can use the code-generated modules like any other API.

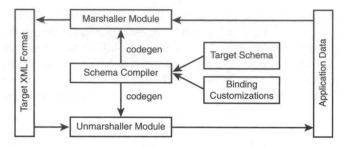

Figure 2.6   Using a schema compiler.

Binding Customization

In some cases, the object types generated by the schema compiler offer a good enough API for working with the types and elements described in the target schema. The application can use these classes directly. Other cases may require customization of the default binding of XML types to object types. That is where the binding customizations come in: They provide additional information to the schema compiler about how the binding between XML and application structures should happen.

There are two main reasons for applying customization:

- *To deal with predefined application data structures*—This reason applies in environments where the application already has defined object types to represent the concepts described in the schema. An example is a PO processing system that was designed to receive inputs from a human-facing UI and an EDI data feed. Now, the system must be extended to handle XML POs. The task is to map the XML of POs to the existing application data structures. There is zero chance that the default mapping defined by the schema compiler will do this in a satisfactory manner.

- *To simplify the API*—This reason for applying customization is driven by programming convenience. Sometimes the conventions of schema design don't map well to the conventions of object-oriented design. For example, localized text is often represented in schema as a subelement with an `xml:lang` attribute identifying the language. Most applications represent this construct as a string object property whose value is determined by the active internationalization locale. Further, there is often more than one way to express a schema type in a programming language. For example, should an `xsd:decimal` be mapped to a `BigDecimal`, `double`, or `float` in Java? The right answer depends on the application.

Common examples of customizations include the following:

- Changing the names of namespaces, object types, and object properties; for example, mapping the `customerID` attribute to the `_cid` object property.
- Defining the type mapping, especially for simple types, as the previous `xsd:decimal` mapping example suggested.

- Choosing which subelements to map to object properties and whether to map them as simple types or as properties that are objects themselves, as the localized text example suggested.

- Specifying how repeated types should be mapped to collection types in programming languages. For example, should the order items in POs be represented by a simple array type, a dynamic array type, or some other data structure such as a list?

The Java community has defined a standard set of tools and APIs for mapping schema types to Java data structures called *Java Architecture for XML Binding (JAXB)* 📖. JAXB took a long time to develop because the problems it was trying to address were very complex. Initially, the work targeted DTD-to-Java mapping. This, and the fact that JAXB was JSR-31 in the Java Community Process (JCP), gives you an idea of how long JAXB has taken to evolve. Because of its long history, JAXB isn't yet fully aligned with the latest thinking about XML type mapping for Web services. The good news is that JAXB now supports a significant part of XML Schema and is ready for production use. JAXB 2.0 will synchronize JAXB with JAX-RPC (the Java APIs for remote procedure calls using Web services), which will make JAXB even better suited for use with Web services.

Chapters 3 and 5 ("Implementing Web Services with Apache Axis") introduce advanced data-mapping concepts specific to Web services as well as more sophisticated mechanisms for working with XML. The rest of this section will offer a taste of XML processing by implementing the checkInvoice() API described earlier using both a SAX and a DOM parser as well as JAXB.

SAX-Based checkInvoice()

The basic architecture of the JAXP SAX parsing APIs is shown in Figure 2.7. It uses the common abstract factory design pattern. First, you must create an instance of SAXParserFactory that is used to create an instance of SAXParser. Internally, the parser wraps a SAXReader object that is defined by the SAX API. JAXP developers typically don't have to work directly with SAXReader. When the parser's parse() method is invoked, the reader starts firing events to the application by invoking certain registered callbacks.

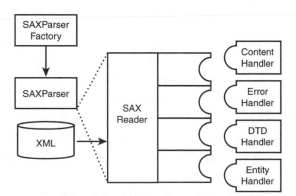

Figure 2.7   SAX parsing architecture

Working with JAXP and SAX involves four important Java packages:

- `org.xml.sax`—Defines the SAX interfaces
- `org.xml.sax.ext`—Defines advanced SAX extensions for DTD processing and detailed syntax information
- `org.xml.sax.helpers`—Defines helper classes such as `DefaultHandler`
- `javax.xml.parsers`—Defines the `SAXParserFactory` and `SAXParser` classes

Here is a summary of the key SAX-related objects:

- `SAXParserFactory`—A `SAXParserFactory` object creates an instance of the parser determined by the system property `javax.xml.parsers.SAXParserFactory`.
- `SAXParser`—The `SAXParser` interface defines several kinds of `parse()` methods. In general, you pass an XML data source and a `DefaultHandler` object to the parser, which processes the XML and invokes the appropriate methods in the handler object.
- `DefaultHandler`—Not shown in Figure 2.7, `DefaultHandler` implements all SAX callback interfaces with null methods. Custom handlers subclass `DefaultHandler` and override the methods they're interested in receiving.

The following list contains the callback interfaces and some of their important methods:

- `ContentHandler`—Contains methods for all basic XML parsing events:

  `void startDocument()`
  Receive notification of the beginning of a document.

  `void endDocument()`
  Receive notification of the end of a document.

  `void startElement(String namespaceURI, String localName,`
  `                  String qName, Attributes atts)`
  Receive notification of the beginning of an element.

  `void characters(char[] ch, int start, int length)`
  Receive notification of character data.

- `ErrorHandler`—Contains methods for receiving error notification. The default implementation in `DefaultHandler` throws errors for fatal errors but does nothing for nonfatal errors, including validation errors:

  `void error(SAXParseException exception)`
  Receive notification of a recoverable error (for example, a validation error).

  `void fatalError(SAXParseException exception)`
  Receive notification of a nonrecoverable error (for example, a well-formedness error).

- `DTDHandler`—Contains methods for dealing with XML entities.
- `EntityResolver`—Contains methods for resolving the location of external entities.

SAX defines an event-based parsing model. A SAX parser invokes the callbacks from these interfaces as it's working through the document. Consider the following sample document:

```
<?xml version="1.0" encoding="UTF-8"?>
<sampleDoc>
   <greeting>Hello, world!</greeting>
</sampleDoc>
```

An event-based parser will make the series of callbacks to the application as follows:

```
start document
start element: sampleDoc
start element: greeting
characters: Hello, world!
end element: greeting
end element: sampleDoc
end document
```

Because of the simplicity of the parsing model, the parser doesn't need to keep much state information in memory. This is why SAX-based parsers are fast and highly efficient. The flip side to this benefit is that the application has to manage any context associated with the parsing process. For example, for the application to know that the string "Hello, world!" is associated with the `greeting` element, it needs to maintain a flag that is raised in the start element event for `greeting` and lowered in the end element event. More complex applications typically maintain a stack of elements that are in the process of being parsed. Here are the SAX events with an added context stack:

```
start document               ()
start element: sampleDoc     (sampleDoc)
start element: greeting      (sampleDoc, greeting)
characters: Hello, world!    (sampleDoc, greeting)
end element: greeting        (sampleDoc, greeting)
end element: sampleDoc       (sampleDoc)
end document                 ()
```

With this information in mind, building a class to check invoice totals becomes relatively simple (see Listing 2.31).

Listing 2.31 **SAX–Based Invoice Checker** (`InvoiceCheckerSAX.java`)

```java
package com.skatestown.invoice;

import java.io.InputStream;
import org.xml.sax.Attributes;
import org.xml.sax.SAXException;
import javax.xml.parsers.SAXParser;
import javax.xml.parsers.SAXParserFactory;
import org.xml.sax.helpers.DefaultHandler;

/**
 * Check SkatesTown invoice totals using a SAX parser.
 */
public class InvoiceCheckerSAX
    extends DefaultHandler
    implements InvoiceChecker
{
    // Class-level data
    // invoice running total
    double runningTotal = 0.0;
    // invoice total
    double total = 0.0;

    // Utility data for extracting money amounts from content
    boolean isMoneyContent = false;
    double amount = 0.0;

    /**
     * Check invoice totals.
     * @param      invoiceXML     Invoice XML document
     * @exception Exception      Any exception returned during checking
     */
    public void checkInvoice(InputStream invoiceXML) throws Exception {
        // Use the default (non-validating) parser
        SAXParserFactory factory = SAXParserFactory.newInstance();
        SAXParser saxParser = factory.newSAXParser();

        // Parse the input; we are the handler of SAX events
        saxParser.parse(invoiceXML, this);
    }

    // SAX DocumentHandler methods
    public void startDocument() throws SAXException {
        runningTotal = 0.0;
        total = 0.0;
        isMoneyContent = false;
    }
```

Listing 2.31 **Continued**

```java
public void endDocument() throws SAXException {
    // Use delta equality check to prevent cumulative
    // binary arithmetic errors. In this case, the delta
    // is one half of one cent
    if (Math.abs(runningTotal - total) >= 0.005) {
        throw new SAXException(
            "Invoice error: total is " + Double.toString(total) +
            " while our calculation shows a total of " +
            Double.toString(Math.round(runningTotal * 100) / 100.0));
    }
}

public void startElement(String namespaceURI,
                         String localName,
                         String qualifiedName,
                         Attributes attrs) throws SAXException {
    if (localName.equals("item")) {
        // Find item subtotal; add it to running total
        runningTotal +=
            Integer.valueOf(attrs.getValue(namespaceURI,
                "quantity")).intValue() *
            Double.valueOf(attrs.getValue(namespaceURI,
                "unitPrice")).doubleValue();
    } else if (localName.equals("tax") ||
               localName.equals("shippingAndHandling") ||
               localName.equals("totalCost")) {
        // Prepare to extract money amount
        isMoneyContent = true;
    }
}

public void endElement(String namespaceURI,
                       String localName,
                       String qualifiedName) throws SAXException {
    if (isMoneyContent) {
        if (localName.equals("totalCost")) {
            total = amount;
        } else {
            // It must be tax or shippingAndHandling
            runningTotal += amount;
        }
        isMoneyContent = false;
    }
}

public void characters(char buf[], int offset, int len)
```

Listing 2.31 **Continued**

```
        throws SAXException {
        if (isMoneyContent) {
            String value = new String(buf, offset, len);
            amount = Double.valueOf(value).doubleValue();
        }
    }
}
```

InvoiceCheckerSAX must implement the InvoiceChecker interface in order to provide the checkInvoice() functionality. It also subclasses DefaultHandler to obtain default implementations for all SAX callbacks. This way, the implementation can focus on overriding only the relevant callbacks.

The class members runningTotal and total maintain state information about the invoice during the parsing process. The class members isMoneyContent and amount are necessary in order to maintain parsing context. Because events about character data are independent of events about elements, we need the isMoneyContent flag to indicate whether we should attempt to parse character data as a dollar amount for the tax, shippingAndHandling, and totalCost elements. After we parse the text into a dollar figure, we save it into the amount member variable and wait until the endElement() callback to determine what to do with it.

The checkInvoice() method implementation shows how easy it is to use JAXP for XML parsing. Parsing an XML document with SAX only takes three lines of code.

At the beginning of the document, we have to initialize all member variables. At the end of the document, we check whether there is a difference between the running total and the total cost listed on the invoice. If there is a problem, we throw an exception with a descriptive message. Note that we can't use an equality check because no exact mapping exists between decimal numbers and their binary representation. During the many additions to runningTotal, a tiny error will be introduced in the calculation. So, instead of checking for equality, we need to check whether the difference between the listed and the calculated totals is significant. *Significant* in this case would be any amount greater than half a cent, because a half-cent difference can affect the rounding of a final value to a cent.

The parser pushes events about new elements to the startElement() method. If the element we get a notification about is an item element, we can immediately extract the values of the quantity and unitPrice attributes from its attributes collection. Multiplying them together creates an item subtotal, which we add to the running total. Alternatively, if the element is one of tax, shippingAndHandling, or totalCost, we prepare to extract a money amount from its text content. All other elements are ignored.

When we receive end element notifications, we only need to process the ones where we expect to extract a money amount from their content. Based on the name of the element, we decide whether to save the amount as the total cost of the invoice or whether to add it to the running total.

When we process character data and we're expecting a dollar value, we extract the element content, convert it to a double value, and save it in the amount class member for use by the endElement() callback.

Note that we could have skipped implementing endElement() if we had also stored the element name as a string member of the class or used an enumerated value. Then, we would have decided how to use the dollar amount inside characters().

That's all there is to it. Of course, this is a simple example. A real application would have done at least two things differently:

- It would have used namespace information and prefixed element names instead of local names.

- It would have defined its own exception type to communicate invoice validation information. It would have also overridden the default callbacks for error() and fatalError() and used these to collect better exception information.

Unfortunately, these extensions fall outside the scope of this chapter. The rest of the book has several examples of building robust XML-processing software.

DOM-Based checkInvoice()

The basic architecture of the JAXP DOM parsing APIs is shown in Figure 2.8. This architecture uses the same factory design pattern as the SAX API. An application uses the javax.xml.parsers.DocumentBuilderFactory class to get a DocumentBuilder object instance, and uses that to produce a document that conforms to the DOM specification. The value of the system property javax.xml.parsers.DocumentBuilderFactory determines which factory implementation produces the builder. This is how JAXP enables applications to work with different DOM parsers.

The important packages for working with JAXP and DOM are as follows:

- org.w3c.dom—Defines the DOM programming interfaces for XML (and, optionally, HTML) documents, as specified by the W3C

- javax.xml.parsers—Defines DocumentBuilder and DocumentBuilderFactory classes

The DOM defines APIs that allow applications to navigate XML documents and to manipulate their content and structure. The DOM defines interfaces, not a particular implementation. These interfaces are specified using the Interface Description Language (IDL) so that any language can define bindings for them. Separate Java bindings are provided to make working with the DOM in Java easy.

The DOM has several levels and various facets within a level. In the fall of 1998, DOM Level 1 was released. It provided the basic functionality to navigate and manipulate XML and HTML documents. DOM Level 2 builds upon Level 1 with more and better-segmented functionality:

- The DOM Level 2 Core APIs build on Level 1, fix some problem spots, and define additional ways to navigate and manipulate the content and structure of documents. These APIs also provide full support for namespaces.

- The DOM Level 2 Views API specifies interfaces that let programmers view alternate presentations of the XML or HTML document.

- The DOM Level 2 Style API specifies interfaces that let programmers dynamically access and manipulate style sheets.

- The DOM Level 2 Events API specifies interfaces that give programmers a generic event system.

- The DOM Level 2 Traversal-Range API specifies interfaces that let programmers traverse a representation of the XML document.

- The DOM Level 2 HTML API specifies interfaces that let programmers work with HTML documents.

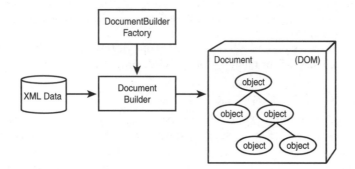

Figure 2.8 DOM parsing architecture

All interfaces (apart from the Core ones) are optional. This is the main reason most applications rely entirely on the DOM Core. You can expect parsers to support more of the DOM soon. In fact, the W3C is currently working on DOM Level 3.

The DOM originated as an API for XML processing at a time when the majority of XML applications were document-centric. As a result, the interfaces in the DOM describe low-level syntax constructs in XML documents. This makes working with the DOM for data-oriented applications somewhat cumbersome and is one of the reasons the Java community is working on the JDOM APIs.

To better understand the XML DOM, you need to be familiar with the core interfaces and their most significant methods. Figure 2.9 shows a Universal Modeling Language (UML) diagram describing some of them.

The root interface is Node. It contains methods for working with the node name (getNodeName()), type (getNodeType()), and attributes (getNodeAttributes()). Node types cover various XML syntax elements: document, element, attribute, character data, text node, comment, processing instruction, and so on. All of these are shown in subclass Node, but not all are shown in Figure 2.9. To traverse the document hierarchy, nodes can access their parent (getParentNode()) as well as their children (getChildNodes()). Node also has several convenience methods for retrieving the first and last child as well as the previous and following sibling.

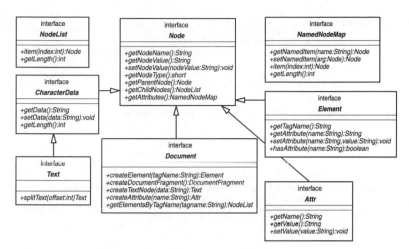

Figure 2.9 Key DOM interfaces and operations

The most important operations in Document involve creating nodes (at least one for every node type); assembling these nodes into the tree (not shown); and locating elements by name, regardless of their location in the DOM (getElementsByTagName()). This last API is convenient because it can save you from having to traverse the tree to get to a particular node.

The rest of the interfaces in the figure are simple. Elements, attributes, and character data each offer a few methods for getting and setting their data members. NodeList and NamedNodeMap are convenience interfaces for dealing with collections of nodes and attributes, respectively.

What Figure 2.9 doesn't show is that DOM Level 2 is fully namespace-aware and that all DOM APIs have versions that take in namespace URIs. Typically, their name is the same as the name of the original API with *NS* appended, such as Element's getAttributeNS(String nsURI, String localName)

With this information in mind, building a class to check invoice totals becomes relatively simple. The DOM implementation of InvoiceChecker is shown in Listing 2.32.

Listing 2.32 **DOM-Based Invoice Checker** (InvoiceCheckerDOM.java)

```
package com.skatestown.invoice;

import java.io.InputStream;
import org.w3c.dom.Node;
import org.w3c.dom.NodeList;
import org.w3c.dom.Document;
import org.w3c.dom.Element;
import org.w3c.dom.CharacterData;
import javax.xml.parsers.DocumentBuilder;
```

Listing 2.32   **Continued**

```java
import javax.xml.parsers.DocumentBuilderFactory;

/**
 * Check SkatesTown invoice totals using a DOM parser.
 */
public class InvoiceCheckerDOM implements InvoiceChecker {
    /**
     * Check invoice totals.
     *
     * @param       invoiceXML Invoice XML document
     * @exception   Exception  Any exception returned during checking
     */
    public void checkInvoice(InputStream invoiceXML)
        throws Exception
    {
        // Invoice running total
        double runningTotal = 0.0;

        // Obtain parser instance and parse the document
        DocumentBuilderFactory factory =
            DocumentBuilderFactory.newInstance();
        DocumentBuilder builder = factory.newDocumentBuilder();
        Document doc = builder.parse(invoiceXML);

        // Calculate order subtotal
        NodeList itemList = doc.getElementsByTagName("item");
        for (int i = 0; i < itemList.getLength(); i++) {
            // Extract quantity and price
            Element item = (Element)itemList.item(i);
            Integer qty = Integer.valueOf(
                item.getAttribute("quantity"));
            Double price = Double.valueOf(
                item.getAttribute("unitPrice"));

            // Add subtotal to running total
            runningTotal += qty.intValue() * price.doubleValue();
        }

        // Add tax
        Node nodeTax = doc.getElementsByTagName("tax").item(0);
        runningTotal += doubleValue(nodeTax);

        // Add shipping and handling
        Node nodeShippingAndHandling =
            doc.getElementsByTagName("shippingAndHandling").item(0);
```

Listing 2.32   **Continued**

```
        runningTotal += doubleValue(nodeShippingAndHandling);

        // Get invoice total
        Node nodeTotalCost =
            doc.getElementsByTagName("totalCost").item(0);
        double total = doubleValue(nodeTotalCost);

        // Use delta equality check to prevent cumulative
        // binary arithmetic errors. In this case, the delta
        // is one half of one cent
        if (Math.abs(runningTotal - total) >= 0.005)
        {
            throw new Exception(
                "Invoice error: total is " + Double.toString(total) +
                " while our calculation shows a total of " +
                Double.toString(Math.round(runningTotal * 100) / 100.0));
        }
    }

    /**
     * Extract a double from the text content of a DOM node.
     *
     * @param       node A DOM node with character content.
     * @return      The double representation of the node's content.
     * @exception   Exception Could be the result of either a node
     *              that doesn't have text content being passed in
     *              or a node whose text content is not a number.
     */
    private double doubleValue(Node node) throws Exception {
        // Get the character data from the node and parse it
        String value = ((CharacterData)node.getFirstChild()).getData();
        return Double.valueOf(value).doubleValue();
    }
}
```

InvoiceCheckerDOM must implement the InvoiceChecker interface in order to provide the checkInvoice() functionality. Apart from this, it's a standalone class. Also, note that the class has no member data, because there is no need to maintain parsing context. The context is implicit in the hierarchy of the DOM tree that will be the result of the parsing process.

The factory pattern used here to parse the invoice is the same as the one from the SAX implementation; it just uses DocumentBuilderFactory and DocumentBuilder. Although the SAX parse method returns no data (it starts firing events instead), the DOM parse() method returns a Document object that holds the complete parse tree of the invoice document.

Within the parse tree, the call to `getElementsByTagName("item")` retrieves a node list of all order items. The loop iterates over the list, extracting the `quantity` and `unitPrice` attributes for every item, obtaining an item subtotal, and adding this to the running total.

The same `getElementsByTagName()` API combined with the utility function `doubleValue()` extracts the amounts of tax, the shipping and handling, and the invoice total cost.

Just as in the SAX example, the code has to use a difference check instead of a direct equality check to guard against inexact decimal-to-binary conversions.

The class also defines a convenient utility function that takes in a DOM node that should have only character content and returns the numeric representation of that content as a double. Any nontrivial DOM processing will typically require these types of utility functions. It goes to prove that the DOM is very syntax-oriented and not concerned about data.

That's all it takes to process the invoice using DOM. Of course, this is a simple example; just as in the SAX example, a real application would have done at least three things differently:

- It would have used namespace information and prefixed element names instead of using local names.

- It would have defined its own exception type to communicate invoice validation information. It would have implemented try-catch logic inside the `checkInvoice()` method in order to report more meaningful errors.

- It would have either explicitly turned on validation of the incoming XML document or traversed the DOM tree step by step from the document root to all the elements of interest. Using `getElementsByTagName()` presumes that the structure of the document (relative positions of elements) has already been validated. If this is the case, it's okay to ask for all item elements regardless of where they are in the document. The example implementation took this approach for code readability purposes.

These changes aren't complex, but they would have increased the size and complexity of the example beyond its goals as a basic introduction to DOM processing.

JAXB-Based `checkInvoice()`

The basic architecture of the JAXB implementation is shown in Figure 2.10. The various components are similar to those described in the general architecture of XML processing using schema compilers in Figure 2.7.

To use JAXB, you first have to invoke the schema compiler that comes with the distribution. The compiler that comes with the Sun distribution used in this example is called `xjc` (XML-to-Java Compiler). The compiler is easy to use: It can produce an initial mapping of a schema to Java classes by looking at an XML schema, without requiring any binding customization. To try this on the invoice schema, we have to execute the command `xjc invoice.xsd`. The output of this command is shown in Listing 2.33.

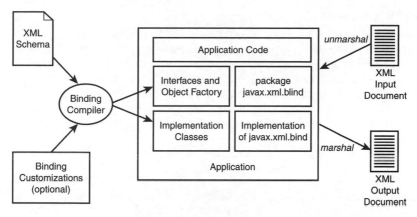

Figure 2.10   JAXB architecture

Listing 2.33   `xjc` Output After Processing the Invoice Schema

```
C:\dev\projects\jaxb>xjc invoice.xsd
parsing a schema...
compiling a schema...
com\skatestown\ns\invoice\impl\InvoiceImpl.java
com\skatestown\ns\invoice\impl\InvoiceTypeImpl.java
com\skatestown\ns\invoice\impl\ItemTypeImpl.java
com\skatestown\ns\invoice\impl\JAXBVersion.java
com\skatestown\ns\invoice\impl\runtime\XMLSerializer.java
com\skatestown\ns\invoice\impl\runtime\SAXUnmarshallerHandler.java
com\skatestown\ns\invoice\impl\runtime\MSVValidator.java
com\skatestown\ns\invoice\impl\runtime\PrefixCallback.java
com\skatestown\ns\invoice\impl\runtime\UnmarshallingEventHandlerAdaptor.java
com\skatestown\ns\invoice\impl\runtime\UnmarshallerImpl.java
com\skatestown\ns\invoice\impl\runtime\Discarder.java
com\skatestown\ns\invoice\impl\runtime\SAXUnmarshallerHandlerImpl.java
com\skatestown\ns\invoice\impl\runtime\ValidatorImpl.java
com\skatestown\ns\invoice\impl\runtime\GrammarInfo.java
com\skatestown\ns\invoice\impl\runtime\DefaultJAXBContextImpl.java
com\skatestown\ns\invoice\impl\runtime\ErrorHandlerAdaptor.java
com\skatestown\ns\invoice\impl\runtime\AbstractUnmarshallingEventHandlerImpl.java
com\skatestown\ns\invoice\impl\runtime\GrammarInfoFacade.java
com\skatestown\ns\invoice\impl\runtime\MarshallerImpl.java
com\skatestown\ns\invoice\impl\runtime\UnmarshallingContext.java
com\skatestown\ns\invoice\impl\runtime\UnmarshallableObject.java
com\skatestown\ns\invoice\impl\runtime\ContentHandlerAdaptor.java
com\skatestown\ns\invoice\impl\runtime\NamespaceContext2.java
com\skatestown\ns\invoice\impl\runtime\ValidatingUnmarshaller.java
com\skatestown\ns\invoice\impl\runtime\SAXMarshaller.java
```

Listing 2.33   **Continued**

```
com\skatestown\ns\invoice\impl\runtime\NamespaceContextImpl.java
com\skatestown\ns\invoice\impl\runtime\Util.java
com\skatestown\ns\invoice\impl\runtime\XMLSerializable.java
com\skatestown\ns\invoice\impl\runtime\ValidatableObject.java
com\skatestown\ns\invoice\impl\runtime\AbstractGrammarInfoImpl.java
com\skatestown\ns\invoice\impl\runtime\ValidationContext.java
com\skatestown\ns\invoice\impl\runtime\UnmarshallingEventHandler.java
com\skatestown\ns\po\impl\AddressTypeImpl.java
com\skatestown\ns\po\impl\ItemTypeImpl.java
com\skatestown\ns\po\impl\JAXBVersion.java
com\skatestown\ns\po\impl\PoImpl.java
com\skatestown\ns\po\impl\PoTypeImpl.java
com\skatestown\ns\invoice\Invoice.java
com\skatestown\ns\invoice\InvoiceType.java
com\skatestown\ns\invoice\ItemType.java
com\skatestown\ns\invoice\ObjectFactory.java
com\skatestown\ns\invoice\bgm.ser
com\skatestown\ns\invoice\jaxb.properties
com\skatestown\ns\po\AddressType.java
com\skatestown\ns\po\ItemType.java
com\skatestown\ns\po\ObjectFactory.java
com\skatestown\ns\po\Po.java
com\skatestown\ns\po\PoType.java
com\skatestown\ns\po\bgm.ser
com\skatestown\ns\po\jaxb.properties
```

After parsing, analyzing, and processing the invoice schema (and the PO schema on which it depends), the compiler outputs 50 (!) files that fall into three categories: interface files, implementation files, and supporting files.

Note that the namespace URIs for the invoice and PO schemas are mapped to the Java package names com.skatestown.ns.po and com.skatestown.ns.invoice. Inside these two packages are the interfaces generated for the schema types. A Java interface is generated for every type and element in the schema. For example, invoiceType in the schema is mapped to InvoiceType.java. The compiler also generates three supporting files:

- ObjectFactory.java—Contains factory methods for each generated Java interface. It allows you to programmatically construct new instances of Java objects representing XML content.

- jaxb.properties—Provides information about the specific JAXB implementation provider.

- bgm.ser—Contains a serialized representation of the schema information that can be used for efficient on-the-fly validation during XML-to-Java and Java-to-XML mapping.

All the files in the . . . \impl packages are specific to the Sun JAXB implementation and can be ignored.

Generated Interfaces

Let's look more closely at the interfaces generated by xjc, in particular the invoice and invoice item types we'll need to work with to check the invoice totals (Listing 2.34). For convenience purposes, we've reformatted the code and removed comments.

Listing 2.34   **Example Generated Interfaces**

```
package com.skatestown.ns.invoice;

public interface InvoiceType {
    java.math.BigDecimal getTotalCost();
    void setTotalCost(java.math.BigDecimal value);

    com.skatestown.ns.invoice.InvoiceType.OrderType getOrder();
    void setOrder(com.skatestown.ns.invoice.InvoiceType.OrderType value);

    java.math.BigInteger getCustomerId();
    void setCustomerId(java.math.BigInteger value);

    java.math.BigDecimal getShippingAndHandling();
    void setShippingAndHandling(java.math.BigDecimal value);

    com.skatestown.ns.po.AddressType getShipTo();
    void setShipTo(com.skatestown.ns.po.AddressType value);

    com.skatestown.ns.po.AddressType getBillTo();
    void setBillTo(com.skatestown.ns.po.AddressType value);

    java.util.Calendar getSubmitted();
    void setSubmitted(java.util.Calendar value);

    java.math.BigInteger getId();
    void setId(java.math.BigInteger value);

    java.math.BigDecimal getTax();
    void setTax(java.math.BigDecimal value);

    public interface OrderType {
        java.util.List getItem();
    }
}

public interface ItemType
    extends com.skatestown.ns.po.ItemType
```

Listing 2.34 **Continued**

```
{
    java.math.BigDecimal getUnitPrice();
    void setUnitPrice(java.math.BigDecimal value);
}


package com.skatestown.ns.po;

public interface ItemType {
    java.lang.String getSku();
    void setSku(java.lang.String value);

    java.lang.String getDescription();
    void setDescription(java.lang.String value);

    java.math.BigInteger getQuantity();
    void setQuantity(java.math.BigInteger value);
}
```

As you can see, the structure of the schema types is directly expressed in the Java classes with the appropriate type information. There is no sign of elements and attributes at the XML syntax level—they become properties of the Java classes. Working with repeated types maps well to Java programming patterns. For example, order items are accessed via java.util.List. We don't need to parse numbers; this is done by the JAXB implementation. It's easy to see why the JAXB implementation of checkInvoice() is likely to be the simplest and most resilient to potential future changes in the XML schema, compared to the SAX and DOM implementations.

JAXB Binding Customization

Only one thing about the default mapping generated by xjc doesn't seem quite right. All numeric values in the schema are mapped to BigInteger and BigDecimal types. The default rules of type mapping are meant to preserve as much information as possible. Therefore, schema types with unbounded precision such as xsd:decimal and xsd:positiveInteger are mapped to BigDecimal and BigInteger. The rules of JAXB name and type mapping are complex, and unfortunately we don't have space to discuss them here. However, we can address the number-mapping issue.

It would be nice to map to int and double in this example, because they're more convenient and efficient to use. To do so, we need to provide a binding customization to the schema compiler (Listing 2.35).

Listing 2.35 **Binding Customization for** xjc (binding.xjb)

```
<jxb:bindings version="1.0"
              xmlns:jxb="http://java.sun.com/xml/ns/jaxb"
              xmlns:xsd="http://www.w3.org/2001/XMLSchema">
```

Listing 2.35   **Continued**

```
    <jxb:bindings schemaLocation="po.xsd" node="/xsd:schema">
        <jxb:bindings node="//xsd:complexType[@name='poType']/
➙xsd:attribute[@name='id']">
            <jxb:javaType name="int"
                parseMethod="javax.xml.bind.DatatypeConverter.parseInt"
                printMethod="javax.xml.bind.DatatypeConverter.printInt"/>
        </jxb:bindings>
        <jxb:bindings node="//xsd:attribute[@name='customerId']">
            <jxb:javaType name="int"
                parseMethod="javax.xml.bind.DatatypeConverter.parseInt"
                printMethod="javax.xml.bind.DatatypeConverter.printInt"/>
        </jxb:bindings>
        <jxb:bindings node="//xsd:attribute[@name='quantity']">
            <jxb:javaType name="int"
                parseMethod="javax.xml.bind.DatatypeConverter.parseInt"
                printMethod="javax.xml.bind.DatatypeConverter.printInt"/>
        </jxb:bindings>
    </jxb:bindings> <!-- schemaLocation="po.xsd" node="/xsd:schema" -->

    <jxb:bindings schemaLocation="invoice.xsd" node="/xsd:schema">
        <jxb:bindings node="//xsd:complexType[@name='invoiceType']/
➙xsd:attribute[@name='id']">
            <jxb:javaType name="int"
                parseMethod="javax.xml.bind.DatatypeConverter.parseInt"
                printMethod="javax.xml.bind.DatatypeConverter.printInt"/>
        </jxb:bindings>
        <jxb:bindings node="//xsd:attribute[@name='customerId']">
            <jxb:javaType name="int"
                parseMethod="javax.xml.bind.DatatypeConverter.parseInt"
                printMethod="javax.xml.bind.DatatypeConverter.printInt"/>
        </jxb:bindings>
        <jxb:bindings node="//xsd:simpleType[@name='priceType']">
            <jxb:javaType name="double"
                parseMethod="javax.xml.bind.DatatypeConverter.parseDouble"
                printMethod="javax.xml.bind.DatatypeConverter.printDouble"/>
        </jxb:bindings>
    </jxb:bindings> <!-- schemaLocation="invoice.xsd" node="/xsd:schema" -->
</jxb:bindings>
```

In JAXB's case, you can insert binding customizations directly in the XML schema using schema extensibility mechanisms or provide them in a separate XML document. The latter is a better practice in that the XML schema is a programming-language-independent representation of data that shouldn't be encumbered by this information.

The basic mechanism of binding customizations involves two parts: identifying the part of the schema where the mapping should be modified and specifying the binding modification. All the customizations in this example are simple type mappings to `int` and `double` performed via the element `jxb:javaType`. The Java type to map to is specified via the `name` attribute. Two other attributes, `parseMethod` and `printMethod`, provide the unmarshalling and marshalling operations. JAXB provides convenience methods in the `javax.xml.bind.DatatypeConverter` class, which we use here.

Identifying the part of the schema to modify is more complicated. We need a mechanism to point to a part of the schema document. This mechanism is a language called *XPath* 📖. XPath is one the XML standards developed by W3C. Think about the directory structure of your computer: The file path mechanism (for example, `C:\dev\projects\jaxb`) gives you a way to navigate that structure. Now think about the structure described by the DOM representation of XML documents: XPath lets you navigate that structure quickly and efficiently. We don't have the space to get into XPath, but here are a few examples taken from the binding customization file:

- `/xsd:schema`—The top-level element in the XML document called `xsd:schema`. The `/` syntax defines a level in the document element hierarchy, beginning from the current node. Initially, the current node is the root of the DOM.

- `//xsd:attribute[@name='quantity']`—An element called `xsd:attribute` (occurring anywhere in the document) whose `name` attribute value is `quantity`. The `//` syntax covers all descendants from the current node.

- `//xsd:complexType[@name='poType']/xsd:attribute[@name='id']`—An `xsd:complexType` element called `poType` (anywhere in the document) that has an `xsd:attribute` child with the name `id`. Note that we can't use the simpler XPath expression `//xsd:attribute[@name='id']` because `AddressType` in the schema also has an `id` attribute. The XPath expression would result in more than one DOM node, and the schema compiler would be unsure where to apply the binding customization.

In the binding customization, these XPath expressions are used within the context of nested `jxb:bindings` elements. The top-level element lets us change global binding rules. It has two children: one for the PO schema and one for the invoice schema. Within those, we modify each attribute with a numeric type. In the invoice schema, we modify the binding of `priceType`, and that modification automatically applies to all uses of that type in `unitPrice`, `tax`, and other attributes.

For `xjc` to take advantage of the binding customization, we need to modify the command line slightly to `xjc -b bindings.xjb invoice.xsd`. The same number of files are generated. This time, however, the `BigInteger` and `BigDecimal` types in Listing 2.34 are replaced with `int` and `double` types.

JAXB Processing Model

Now that the schema compiler is generating the correct Java classes, it's time to look at the JAXB processing model. Working with JAXB involves one main Java package: `javax.xml.bind`. This package provides abstract classes and interfaces for working with the JAXB framework's three operations: marshalling, unmarshalling, and validation. You access these operations via the `Marshaller`, `Unmarshaller`, and `Validator` classes in the package.

The `JAXBContext` class is the entry point into the JAXB framework. It provides support for multiple JAXB implementations, and it also manages the connection between XML elements and the Java classes that represent them. The package also has a rich set of exception classes for marshalling, unmarshalling, and validation events that make working with JAXB much easier and more natural than working with SAX or DOM.

With this information in mind, building a class to check invoice totals becomes relatively simple. The JAXB implementation of `InvoiceChecker` is shown in Listing 2.36.

Listing 2.36   **JAXB-Based Invoice Checker** (`InvoiceCheckerJAXB.java`)

```
package com.skatestown.invoice;

import com.skatestown.ns.invoice.InvoiceType;

import javax.xml.bind.JAXBContext;
import javax.xml.bind.Unmarshaller;
import java.io.InputStream;
import java.util.Iterator;
import java.util.List;

/**
 * InvoiceChecker implementation using JAXB
 */
public class InvoiceCheckerJAXB implements InvoiceChecker
{
    /**
     * Check invoice totals.
     *
     * @param    invoiceXML   Invoice XML document
     * @exception    Exception   Any exception returned during checking
     */
    public void checkInvoice(InputStream invoiceXML)
    throws Exception
    {
        // Create JAXB context + point it to schema types
        JAXBContext jc = JAXBContext.newInstance(
                "com.skatestown.ns.po:com.skatestown.ns.invoice");

        // Create an unmarshaller
        Unmarshaller u = jc.createUnmarshaller();

        // Unmarshall the invoice document
        InvoiceType inv = (InvoiceType)u.unmarshal(invoiceXML);
```

104   Chapter 2 XML Primer

Listing 2.36   **Continued**

```
        double runningTotal = 0.0;

        // Iterate over order items and update the running total
        List items = inv.getOrder().getItem();
        for( Iterator iter = items.iterator(); iter.hasNext(); ) {
            com.skatestown.ns.invoice.ItemType item =
                    (com.skatestown.ns.invoice.ItemType)iter.next();
            runningTotal += item.getQuantity() * item.getUnitPrice();
        }

        // Add tax and shipping and handling
        runningTotal += inv.getShippingAndHandling();
        runningTotal += inv.getTax();

        // Get invoice total
        double total = inv.getTotalCost();

        // Use delta equality check to prevent cumulative
        // binary arithmetic errors. In this case, the delta
        // is one half of one cent
        if (Math.abs(runningTotal - total) >= 0.005) {
            throw new Exception(
                "Invoice error: total is " + Double.toString(total) +
                " while our calculation shows a total of " +
                Double.toString(Math.round(runningTotal * 100) / 100.0));
        }
    }
}
```

`InvoiceCheckerJAXB` must implement the `InvoiceChecker` interface in order to pro-vide the `checkInvoice()` functionality. Apart from this, it's a standalone class. As with DOM, note that the class has no member data, because there's no need to maintain pars-ing context. The context is implicit in the hierarchy of the Java object tree that will be generated during the unmarshalling process.

The JAXB context is initialized with the names of the Java packages we want to work with in the `JAXBContext.newInstance` factory call. This prepares the JAXB framework to deal with PO and invoice XML documents. The next factory pattern call creates an unmarshaller object. Parsing and unmarshalling the invoice document takes one call to `unmarshal()`. We have to cast to the top-level invoice type because the inter-face of the `Unmarshaller` class is generic to JAXB.

The code to recalculate the invoice total is simpler and more Java-friendly than in the SAX and DOM examples. There is no indication of any XML behind the scenes. This is what JAXB does best—it allows you to separate the Java data structures you want to work with from the XML representation of these structures. Just as in the SAX and

DOM examples, the code has to use a difference check instead of a direct equality check to guard against inexact decimal-to-binary conversions.

That completes the JAXB implementation of the invoice checker. Of course, JAXB is much more powerful (and complex), and we don't have space to dig into it here; but you've gotten an idea of why it's the preferred method of working with XML from Java.

Testing the Code

The code to test the three different invoice checker implementations is written using JavaServer Pages (JSP) (Listing 2.37). JSP allows Java code to be mixed with HTML for building Web applications. JSP builds on the Java Servlet standard for building Web components. Java application servers compile JSPs down to servlets.

Listing 2.37 **JSP Page for Checking Invoices**

```
<%@ page import="java.io.*,hws.BookUtil,com.skatestown.invoice.*" %>
<HTML>
<HEAD><TITLE>Invoice Checker</TITLE></HEAD>
<h1>Invoice Checker</h1>

<p>This example implements a web form driver for SkatesTown's invoice
checker. You can modify the invoice on the form if you wish (the
default one is from Chapter 2), select a DOM or SAX parser and perform
 a check on the invoice total.</p>

<FORM action="index.jsp" method="POST">
<%
    String xml = request.getParameter("xml");
    if (xml == null) {
        xml = BookUtil.readResource(application,
                        "/resources/sampleInvoice.xml");
    }
%>
    <TEXTAREA NAME="xml" ROWS="20" COLS="90"><%= xml%></TEXTAREA>
    <P></P>
    Select parser type:
    <INPUT type="RADIO" name="parserType" value="SAX" CHECKED> SAX
    <INPUT type="RADIO" name="parserType" value="DOM"> DOM
    <INPUT type="RADIO" name="parserType" value="JAXB"> JAXB
    <P></P>
    <INPUT type="SUBMIT" value=" Check Invoice ">
</FORM>

<%
    // Check for form submission
    if (request.getParameter("xml") != null) {
        out.println("<HR>");
```

Listing 2.37 **Continued**

```
        // Instantiate appropriate parser type
        InvoiceChecker ic;
        if (request.getParameter("parserType").equals("SAX")) {
            out.print("Using SAX parser...<br>");
            ic = new InvoiceCheckerSAX();
         } else if (request.getParameter("parserType").equals("DOM")) {
            out.print("Using DOM implementation...<br>");
            ic = new InvoiceCheckerDOM();
        } else {
            out.print("Using JAXB implementation...<br>");
            ic = new InvoiceCheckerJAXB();
        }

        // Check the invoice
        try {
            ic.checkInvoice(new StringBufferInputStream(xml));
            out.print("Invoice checks OK.");
        } catch(Exception e) {
            out.print(e.getMessage());
        }
    }
%>

</BODY>
</HTML>
```

JSP uses the `<%@ ... %>` syntax for compile-time directives. The `page import="..."` directive accomplishes the equivalent of a Java `import` statement.

The HTML code sets up a Web form that posts back to the same page. The form contains a text area with the name `xml` that contains the XML of the invoice to be validated.

In JSP, you can use the construct `<% ... %>` to surround arbitrary Java code embedded in the JSP page. The request object is an implicit object on the page associated with the Web request. Implicit objects in JSP are set up by the JSP compiler. They can be used without requiring any type of declaration or setup. One of the most useful methods of the request object is `getParameter()`, which retrieves the value of a parameter passed from the Web such as a form field, or returns null if this parameter didn't come with the request. The code uses `getParameter("xml")` to check whether the form is being displayed (return is null) versus submitted (return is non-null). If the form is displayed for the first time, the page loads the invoice XML from a sample file in `/resources/sampleInvoice.xml`.

The rest of the Java code runs only if the form has been submitted. It uses the implicit `out` object to send output to the resulting Web page. It uses the value of the `parserType` field in the Web page to determine whether to instantiate a SAX, DOM, or

JAXB implementation. It then checks the invoice by passing the value of the xml text area on the page to the checkInvoice() method. If the call is successful, the invoice checks out okay, and an appropriate message is displayed. If checkInvoice() throws an exception, an invoice total discrepancy (or an XML processing error) has been detected, which is output to the browser.

Figure 2.11 shows the Web test client for the invoice checker, ready for submission.

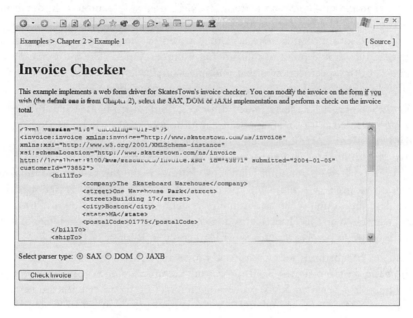

Figure 2.11   Invoice checker Web page

Summary

This chapter has focused on core features of XML and related technologies. The goal was to prepare you for the Web service–related material in the rest of the book, which relies heavily on the concepts presented here. We covered the following topics:

- The origins of XML and the fundamental difference between document- and data-centric XML applications. Web services are an extreme example of data-centric XML use. The material in this chapter purposely ignored some aspects of XML that are more document-oriented.

- The syntax and rules governing the physical structure of XML documents: document prologs, elements, attributes, character content, CDATA sections, and so on. We omitted document-oriented features of XML such as entities and notations due to their infrequent use in the context of Web services. The SkatesTown PO document format made its initial appearance.

- XML Namespaces, the key tool for resolving the problems of name recognition and name collision in XML applications. Namespaces are fundamental to mixing information from multiple schemas into a single document, and all core Web service technologies rely on them. SkatesTown's PO inside an XML message wrapper is an example of a common pattern for XML use; we'll explore it in depth in the next chapter. The namespace mechanism is simple; however, people often try to read more into it than is there, as demonstrated by the debate over whether namespace URIs should point to meaningful resources. One of the more complex aspects of the specification is that multiple namespace defaulting mechanisms simplify document markup while preserving namespace information.

- XML Schema, the de facto standard for describing document structure and XML datatypes for data-oriented applications. Although XML Schema is a recent standard, the XML community defined specifications based on draft versions for nearly two years. The flexible content models, the large number of predefined datatypes, and the powerful extensibility and reuse features make this one of the most important developments in the XML space since XML 1.0. All Web service specifications are described using schemas. Through the definition of SkatesTown's PO and invoice schemas, this chapter introduced enough of the key capabilities of the technology to prepare you for what is to come in the rest of the book.

- The key mechanisms for creating and processing XML with software. Starting with the basic syntax-oriented XML processing architecture, the chapter progressed to define a data-oriented XML processing architecture together with the key concepts of XML data mapping and XML parsing. In the context of SkatesTown's desire to independently validate invoice totals sent to its customers, we used the Java APIs for XML Processing (JAXP), the Simple APIs for XML (SAX), the XML Document Object Model (DOM), and the Java Architecture for XML Binding (JAXB) to build three separate implementations of an invoice checker. A Web-based front end served as the test bed for the code.

This chapter didn't focus on other less relevant XML technologies such as XPointer/XLink, Resource Definition Framework (RDF), XPath, Extensible Stylesheet Language Transformations (XSLT), or XQuery. They're important in their own domains but not commonly used in the context of Web services. Other more technical XML specifications, such as XML Digital Signatures, will be introduced later in the book as part of Web service usage scenarios.

You now know enough about XML to go deep into the world of Web services. Chapter 3 introduces the core Web service messaging technology: SOAP.

Resources

- *DOM Level 1*—"Document Object Model (DOM) Level 1 Specification" (W3C, October 1998), http://www.w3.org/TR/REC-DOM-Level-1

- *DOM Level 2 Core*—"Document Object Model (DOM) Level 2 Core Specification" (W3C, November 2000), http://www.w3.org/TR/DOM-Level-2-Core/

- *JAXB*—"Java Technology and XML Downloads—Java Architecture for XML Binding" (Sun Microsystems, Inc., January 2003), http://java.sun.com/xml/downloads/jaxb.html

- *JAXP 1.2*—"Java API for XML Processing (JAXP)" (Sun Microsystems, Inc., August 2003), http://java.sun.com/xml/xml_jaxp.html

- *JDOM*—http://www.jdom.org/docs/apidocs

- *JSP 1.2*—"JavaServer Pages Technology" (Sun Microsystems, Inc., April 2001), http://java.sun.com/products/jsp

- RFC 2396, "Uniform Resource Identifiers (URI): Generic Syntax" (IETF, August 1998), http://www.ietf.org/rfc/rfc2396.txt

- *SAX*—"Simple API for XML (SAX) 2.0.1" (January 2002), http://www.saxproject.org/

- *Unicode*—"Forms of Unicode" (Mark Davis, September 1999), http://www-106.ibm.com/developerworks/library/utfencodingforms/

- *XML*—"Extensible Markup Language (XML) 1.0 (Second Edition)" (W3C, October 2000), http://www.w3.org/TR/REC-xml

- *XML Namespaces*—"Namespaces in XML" (W3C, January 1999), http://www.w3.org/TR/REC-xml-names/

- *XML Schema*—"XML Schema Part 0: Primer," http://www.w3.org/TR/xmlschema-0/; "XML Schema Part 1: Structures," http://www.w3.org/TR/xmlschema-1/; "XML Schema Part 2: Datatypes," http://www.w3.org/TR/xmlschema-2/ (all W3C, May 2001)

3

The SOAP Protocol

THE WEB SERVICES ARCHITECTURE GROUP AT THE W3C has defined a Web service as follows (italics added):

A Web service is a software system designed to support interoperable machine-to-machine interaction over a network. It has an interface described in a machine-processable format (specifically WSDL). Other systems interact with the Web service in a manner prescribed by its description *using SOAP-messages*, typically conveyed using HTTP with an XML serialization in conjunction with other Web-related standards.

Although our definition (see Chapter 1, "Web Services Overview and Service-Oriented Architectures") may be a bit broader, it's clear that *SOAP* 📖 is at the core of any survey of Web service technology. So just what is SOAP, and why is it often considered the harbinger of a new world of interoperable systems?

The trouble with SOAP is that it's so simple and so flexible that it can be used in many different ways to fit the needs of different Web service scenarios. This is both a blessing and a curse. It's a blessing because chances are, SOAP can fit your needs. It's a curse because you may not know how to make it do what you require. When you're through with this chapter, you'll know not only how to use SOAP straight out of the box but also how to extend SOAP to support your diverse and changing needs. You'll have also followed the development of a meaningful e-commerce Web service for our favorite company, SkatesTown. Last but not least, you'll be ready to handle the rest of the book and climb higher toward the top of the Web services interoperability stack.

The chapter will cover the following topics:

- The evolution of XML protocols and the history and motivation behind SOAP's creation
- The SOAP messaging framework: versioning, the extensibility framework, header-based vertical extensibility, intermediary-based horizontal extensibility, error handling, and bindings to multiple transport protocols

- The various mechanisms for packaging information in SOAP messages, including SOAP's own data encoding rules and heuristics for putting just about any kind of data in SOAP messages
- The use of SOAP within multiple distributed system architectures such as RPC- and messaging-based systems in all their flavors
- A quick introduction to building and consuming Web services using the Java-based Apache Axis Web services engine

So, why SOAP? As this chapter will show, SOAP is simple, flexible, and highly extensible. Since it's XML based, SOAP is programming-language, platform, and hardware neutral. What better choice for the XML protocol that's the foundation of Web services? To prove this point, let's start the chapter by looking at some of the earlier work that inspired SOAP.

SOAP

Microsoft started thinking about XML-based distributed computing in 1997. The goal was to enable applications to communicate via Remote Procedure Calls (RPCs) using a simple network of standard data types on top of XML/HTTP. DevelopMentor (a long-standing Microsoft ally) and Userland (a company that saw the Web as a great publishing platform) joined the discussions. The name SOAP was coined in early 1998.

Things moved forward, but as the group tried to involve wider circles within Microsoft, politics stepped in and the process stalled. The DCOM camp at the company disliked the idea of SOAP and believed that Microsoft should use its dominant position in the market to push the DCOM wire protocol via some form of HTTP tunneling instead of pursuing XML. Some XML-focused folks at Microsoft believed that the SOAP idea was good but had come too early. Perhaps they were looking for some of the advanced facilities that could be provided by XML Schema and Namespaces. Frustrated by the deadlock, Userland went public with a version of the spec published as XML-RPC in the summer of 1998.

In 1999, as Microsoft was working on its version of XML Schema (XML Data) and adding support for namespaces in its XML products, the idea of SOAP gained momentum. It was still an XML-based RPC mechanism, however, which is why it met with resistance from the BizTalk (http://www.biztalk.org) team; the BizTalk model was based more on messaging than RPCs. SOAP 0.9 appeared for public review on September 13, 1999. It was submitted to the IETF as an Internet public draft. With few changes, in December 1999, SOAP 1.0 came to life.

Right before the XTech conference in March 2000, the W3C announced that it was looking into starting an activity in the area of XML protocols. At the conference, there was an exciting breakout session in which a number of industry visionaries argued the finer points of what XML protocols should do and where they were going—but this conversation didn't result in one solid vision of the future.

On May 8, 2000 SOAP 1.1 was submitted as a note to the W3C with IBM as a co-author. IBM's support was an unexpected and refreshing change. In addition, the SOAP 1.1 spec was much more modular and extensible, eliminating some concerns that backing SOAP implied backing a Microsoft proprietary technology. This, and the fact that IBM immediately released a Java SOAP implementation that was subsequently donated to the Apache XML Project (`http://xml.apache.org`) for open source development, convinced even the greatest skeptics that SOAP was something to pay attention to. Sun voiced support for SOAP and started work on integrating Web services into the J2EE platform. Not long after, many vendors and open source projects began working on Web service implementations.

In September 2000, the XML Protocol working group at the W3C was formed to design the XML protocol that was to become the core of XML-based distributed computing in the years to come. The group started with SOAP 1.1 as a foundation and produced the first working draft. After many months of changes, improvements, and difficult decisions about what to include, SOAP 1.2 became a W3C recommendation almost two years after that first draft, in June 2003.

What Is SOAP, Really?

Despite the hype that surrounds it, SOAP is of great importance because it's the industry's best effort to date to standardize on the infrastructure technology for cross-platform XML distributed computing. Above all, SOAP is relatively simple. Historically, simplicity is a key feature of most successful architectures that have achieved mass adoption.

At its heart, SOAP is a specification for a simple yet flexible second-generation XML protocol. Because SOAP is focused on the common aspects of all distributed computing scenarios, it provides the following (covered in greater detail later):

- *A mechanism for defining the unit of communication*—In SOAP, all information is packaged in a clearly identifiable SOAP *message* 📖. This is done via a SOAP *envelope* 📖 that encloses all other information. A message can have a *body* 📖 in which potentially arbitrary XML can be used. It can also have any number of *headers* 📖 that encapsulate information outside the body of the message.

- *A processing model*—This defines a well-known set of rules for dealing with SOAP messages in software. SOAP's processing model is simple; but it's the key to using the protocol successfully, especially when extensions are in play.

- *A mechanism for error handling*—Using SOAP *faults* 📖, you can identify the source and cause of an error and it allows for error diagnostic information to be exchanged between participants of an interaction.

- *An extensibility model*—This uses SOAP headers to implement arbitrary extensions on top of SOAP. Headers contain pieces of extensibility data which travel along with a message and may be *targeted* at particular nodes along the *message path*.

- *A flexible mechanism for data representation*—This mechanism allows for the exchange of data already serialized in some format (text, XML, and so on) as well as a convention for representing abstract data structures such as programming language datatypes in an XML format.

- *A convention for representing Remote Procedure Calls (RPCs) and responses as SOAP messages*—RPCs are a common type of distributed computing interaction, and they map well to procedural programming language constructs.

- *A protocol binding framework*—The framework defines an architecture for building bindings to send and receive SOAP messages over arbitrary underlying transports. This framework is used to supply a binding that moves SOAP messages across HTTP connections, because HTTP is a ubiquitous communication protocol on the Internet.

Before we dive deeper into the SOAP protocol and its specification, let's look at how our example company, SkatesTown, is planning to use SOAP and Web services.

Doing Business with SkatesTown

When Al Rosen of Silver Bullet Consulting first began his engagement with SkatesTown, he focused on understanding the e-commerce practices of the company and its customers. After a series of conversations with SkatesTown's CTO, Dean Caroll, Al concluded the following:

- SkatesTown's manufacturing, inventory management, and supply chain automation systems are in good order. These systems are easily accessible by SkatesTown's Web-centric applications.

- SkatesTown has a solid consumer-oriented online presence. Product and inventory information is fed into an online catalog that is accessible to both direct consumers and SkatesTown's reseller partners via two different sites.

- Although SkatesTown's order-processing system is sophisticated, it's poorly connected to online applications. This is a pain point for the company because SkatesTown's partners are demanding better integration with their supply chain automation systems.

- SkatesTown's internal purchase order system is solid. It accepts purchase orders in XML format and uses XML Schema–based validation to guarantee their correctness. Purchase order item SKUs and quantities are checked against the inventory management system. If all items are available, an invoice is created. SkatesTown charges a uniform 5% tax on purchases and the higher of 5% of purchases or $20 for shipping and handling.

Digging deeper into the order-processing part of the business, Al discovered that it uses a low-tech approach that has a high labor cost and isn't suitable for automation. One area that badly needs automation is the process of purchase order submission. Purchase orders are sent to SkatesTown by email. All emails arrive in a single manager's account in operations. The manager manually distributes the orders to several subordinates. They have to open the email, copy only the XML over to the purchase order system, and enter the order there. The system writes an invoice file in XML format. This file has to be opened, and the XML must be copied and pasted into a reply email message. Simple misspellings of email addresses and cut-and-paste errors are common, and they cost SkatesTown and its partners money and time.

Another area that needs automation is the inventory checking process. SkatesTown's partners used to submit purchase orders without having a clear idea whether all the items were in stock. This often caused problems having to do with delayed order processing. Further, purchasing personnel from the partner companies would engage in long email dialogs with operations people at SkatesTown. To improve the situation, SkatesTown built a simple online application that communicates with the company's inventory management system. Partners can log in, browse SkatesTown's products, and check whether certain items are in stock, all via a standard web browser. This was a good start, but now SkatesTown's partners are demanding the ability to have their purchasing applications directly inquire about order availability.

Looking at the two areas that most needed to be improved, Al chose to focus first on the inventory checking process because the business logic was already present. He just had to enable better automation. To do this, he had to better understand how the application worked.

The logic for interacting with the inventory system is simple. Looking through the JSP pages that made up the online application, Al easily extracted the key business logic operations. Given a SKU and a desired product quantity, an application needs to get an instance of the SkatesTown product database and locate a product with a matching SKU. If such a product is available and if the number of items in stock is greater than or equal to the desired quantity, the inventory check succeeds. Since most of the example in this chapter will talk to the inventory system, let's take a slightly deeper look at its implementation.

> **Note**
>
> A note of caution: this book's example applications demonstrate uses of Java technology and Web services to solve real business problems while at the same time remaining simple enough to fit in the book's scope and size limitations. To keep the code simple, we do as little data validation and error checking as possible without allowing applications to break. We don't define custom exception types or produce long, readable error messages. Also, to get away from the complexities of external system access, we use simple XML files to store data.

SkatesTown's inventory is represented by a simple XML file stored in `/resources/products.xml`. The inventory database XML format is as follows:

```
<?xml version="1.0" encoding="UTF-8"?>
<products>
```

```
<product>
   <sku>947-TI</sku>
   <name>Titanium Glider</name>
   <type>skateboard</type>
   <desc>Street-style titanium skateboard.</desc>
   <price>129.00</price>
   <inStock>36</inStock>
</product>
...
</products>
```

By modifying this file, you can change the behavior of the examples. The Java representation of products in SkatesTown's systems is the com.skatestown.data.Product class; it's a simple bean that has one property for every element under product.

SkatesTown's inventory system is accessible via the ProductDB (for product database) class in package com.skatestown.backend. Listing 3.1 shows the key operations it supports. To construct an instance of the class, you pass an XML DOM Document object representation of products.xml. After that, you can get a listing of all products or search for a product by its SKU.

Listing 3.1   **SkatesTown's Product Database Class**

```
public class ProductDB
{
    private Product[] products;

    public ProductDB(Document doc) throws Exception
    {
        // Load product information
    }

    public Product getBySKU(String sku)
    {
        Product[] list = getProducts();
        for ( int i = 0 ; i < list.length ; i++ )
            if ( sku.equals( list[i].getSKU() ) ) return( list[i] );
        return( null );
    }

    public Product[] getProducts()
    {
        return  products;
    }
}
```

This was all Al Rosen needed to know to move forward with the task of automating the inventory checking process.

Inventory Check Web Service

SkatesTown's inventory check Web service is simple. The interaction model is that of an RPC. There are two input parameters: the product SKU (a string) and the quantity desired (an integer). The result is a simple Boolean value that's true if more than the desired quantity of the product is in stock and false otherwise.

Choosing a Web Service Engine

Al decided to host all of SkatesTown's Web services on the Apache Axis Web service engine for a number of reasons:

- The open source implementation guaranteed that SkatesTown won't experience lock-in by a commercial vendor. Further, if any serious problems were discovered, a programmer could look at the code to see what was going on or fix the issue.

- Axis is one of the best Java-based Web services engines. It's better architected and much faster than its Apache SOAP predecessor. The core Axis team includes Web service gurus from companies such as Macromedia, IBM, Computer Associates, and Sonic Software.

- Axis is also one of the most extensible Web service engines. It can be tuned to support new versions of SOAP as well as the many types of extensions that current versions of SOAP allow for.

- Axis can run on top of a simple servlet engine or a full-blown J2EE application server. SkatesTown could keep its current J2EE application server without having to switch.

SkatesTown's CTO, Dean, agreed to have all Web services developed on top of Axis. Al spent some time on http://ws.apache.org/axis learning more about the technology and its capabilities.

Service Provider View

To expose the inventory check Web service, Al had to do two things: implement the service backend and deploy it into the Web service engine. Building the backend for the inventory check Web service was simple because most of the logic was already available in SkatesTown's JSP pages. You can see the service class in Listing 3.2.

Listing 3.2 **Inventory Check Web Service Implementation**

```
package com.skatestown.services;

import com.skatestown.data.Product;
import com.skatestown.backend.ProductDB;
import com.skatestown.STConstants;
```

Listing 3.2   **Continued**

```java
/**
 * Inventory check Web service
 */
public class InventoryCheck implements STConstants {
    /**
     * Checks inventory availability given a product SKU and
     * a desired product quantity.
     *
     * @param sku          product SKU
     * @param quantity     quantity desired
     * @return             true|false based on product availability
     * @exception Exception most likely a problem accessing the DB
     */
    public static boolean doCheck(String sku, int quantity)
        throws Exception
    {
        // Get the product database, which has been conveniently pre-placed
        // in a well-known place (if you want to see how this works,
        // check out the com.skatestown.GlobalHandler class!).
        ProductDB db = ProductDB.getCurrentDB();

        Product prod = db.getBySKU(sku);
        return (prod != null && prod.getNumInStock() >= quantity);
    }
}
```

The backend code for this service relies on the fact that some other piece of code has already made the appropriate ProductDB available via a static accessor method on the ProductDB class. We'll unearth the provider of ProductDB in Chapter 5, "Implementing Web Services with Apache Axis."

Once we have the ProductDB, the rest of the service code is trivial; we check if the quantity available for a given product is equal to or greater than the quantity requested, and return true if so.

Deploying the Service

To deploy this initial service, Al chose to use the instant deployment feature of Axis: Java Web service (JWS) files. In order to do so, he saved the InventoryCheck.java file as InventoryCheck.jws underneath the Axis webapp, so it's accessible at http://skatestown.com/axis/InventoryCheck.jws.

The Client View

Once the service was deployed, Al wanted some of SkatesTown's partners to test it. To test it himself, he built a simple client using Axis (see Listing 3.3).

Listing 3.3   **The** InventoryCheck **Client Class**

```
package ch3.ex2;

import org.apache.axis.AxisEngine;
import org.apache.axis.client.Call;
import org.apache.axis.soap.SOAPConstants;

/*
 * Inventory check Web service client
 */
public class InventoryCheckClient {
    /** Service URL */
    static String url =
            "http://localhost:8080/axis/InventoryCheck.jws";

    /**
     * Invoke the inventory check Web service
     */
    public static boolean doCheck(String sku, int quantity)
        throws Exception {
        // Set up Call object
        Call call = new Call(url);
        // Use SOAP 1.2 (default is SOAP 1.1)
        call.setSOAPVersion(SOAPConstants.SOAP12_CONSTANTS);
        // Set up parameters for invocation
        Object[] params = new Object[] { sku, new Integer(quantity) };
        // Call it!
        Boolean result = (Boolean)call.invoke("", "doCheck", params);
        return result.booleanValue();
    }

    public static void main(String[] args) throws Exception {
        String sku = args[0];
        int quantity = Integer.parseInt(args[1]);
        System.out.println("Making SOAP call...");
        boolean result = doCheck(sku, quantity);
        if (result) {
            System.out.println(
                "Confirmed - the desired quantity is available");
        } else {
            System.out.println(
                "Sorry, the desired quantity is not available.");
        }
    }
}
```

The client uses Axis's `Call` class, which is the central client-side API. When Al constructs the `Call` class, he passes in the URL of his deployed service so that the `Call` knows where to send SOAP messages. The actual invocation is simple: He knows he's calling the `doCheck()` method, so he passes the method name and an array of arguments (obtained from the command line) to the `invoke()` method on the `Call` object. The results come back as a Boolean object, and when the client is run, it looks like this:

```
% java InventoryCheckClient SKU-56 35
Making SOAP call...
Confirmed - the desired quantity is available.
%
```

A Closer Look at SOAP

The current SOAP specification is version 1.2, which was released as a W3C recommendation in June 2003. At the time of this writing (early 2004), toolkits are just starting to offer complete support for the new version, and most of them still use SOAP 1.1 as a baseline. Since this chapter is primarily about the SOAP protocol, we'll focus on SOAP 1.2—the standard the industry will be using into the future. The 1.1 version is also critically important, so we'll also explain it and use sidebars to call out differences between the versions as we go. (You can find an exhaustive list of differences between SOAP 1.1 and SOAP 1.2 in the SOAP 1.2 Primer: `http://www.w3.org/TR/2003/REC-soap12-part0-20030624/`.) Most of the other examples in this book use SOAP 1.1, but we want you to be a 1.2-ready developer.

The Structure of the Spec

The SOAP 1.2 specification is the ultimate reference to the SOAP protocol; the latest version is at `http://www.w3.org/TR/SOAP`. The spec is divided into two parts:

- *Part 1, the Messaging Framework*—Lays out the central foundation of SOAP, consisting of the processing model, the extensibility model, and the message structure.

- *Part 2, Adjuncts*—Important adjuncts to the core spec defined in Part 1. Although they're extensions (and therefore by definition optional), they serve two critical purposes. First, they act as proofs-of-concept for the modular design of SOAP, demonstrating that it isn't limited, for instance, to only being used over HTTP (a common misconception). Second, the core of SOAP in Part 1 isn't enough to build something usable for functional interoperable services. The extensions in part 2, in particular the HTTP binding, provide a baseline for implementers to use, even though the marketplace may define other components beyond those in the spec as well.

Infosets

The SOAP 1.2 spec has been written in terms of the XML *infoset*, which is an abstract model of all the information in an XML document or document fragment. When the spec talks about "element information items" instead of just elements, it means that what is important is the structure of the information, not necessarily the fact that it's serialized with angle brackets. As you'll see later, this becomes important when we talk about bindings. The key thing to remember is that all the information items are really abstract ways of talking about things like elements and attributes that you see in everyday XML. So this XML

```
<elem attr="foo">
  <childEl>text</childEl>
  Other text
</elem>
```

would abstractly look like the structure in Figure 3.1 (rectangles are elements, rounded rectangles attributes and ovals text).

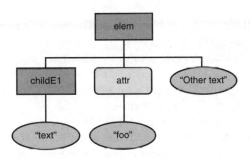

Figure 3.1   A simple XML infoset

The SOAP Messaging Framework

The first part of the SOAP specification is primarily concerned with defining how SOAP messages are structured and the rules processors must abide by when producing and consuming them. Let's look at a sample SOAP message, the inventory check request described in our earlier example:

Note

All the wire examples in this book have been obtained by using the tcpmon tool, which is included in the Axis distribution you can obtain with the example package from the Sams Web site. Tcpmon (short for *TCP monitor*) allows you to record the traffic to and from a particular TCP port, typically HTTP requests and responses. We'll go into detail about this utility in Chapter 5.

```
POST /axis/InventoryCheck.jws HTTP/1.0
Content-Type: application/soap+xml; charset=utf-8

<?xml version="1.0" encoding="UTF-8"?>
<soapenv:Envelope xmlns:soapenv="http://www.w3.org/2003/05/soap-envelope"
                  xmlns:xsd="http://www.w3.org/2001/XMLSchema"
                  xmlns:xsi="http://www.w3.org/2001/XMLSchema-instance">
<soapenv:Body>
  <doCheck soapenv:encodingStyle="http://www.w3.org/2003/05/soap-encoding">
   <arg0 xsi:type="soapenc:string"
         xmlns:soapenc="http://schemas.xmlsoap.org/soap/encoding/">947-TI</arg0>
   <arg1 xsi:type="soapenc:int"
         xmlns:soapenc="http://schemas.xmlsoap.org/soap/encoding/">3</arg1>
  </doCheck>
 </soapenv:Body>
</soapenv:Envelope>
```

This is clearly an XML document (Chapter 2, "XML Primer," covered XML in detail), which has been sent via an HTTP POST. We've removed a few of the nonrelevant HTTP headers from the trace, but we left the content-type header, which indicates that this POST contains a SOAP message (note that this content-type would be different for SOAP 1.1—see the sidebar for details). We'll cover the HTTP-specific parts of SOAP interactions further a bit later in the chapter.

The root element is `soapenv:Envelope`, in the `http://www.w3.org/2003/05/soap-envelope` namespace, which surrounds a `soapenv:Body` containing application-specific content that represents the central purpose of the message. In this case we're asking for an inventory check, so the central purpose is the `doCheck` element. The `Envelope` element has a few useful namespace declarations on it, for the SOAP envelope namespace and the XML Schema data and instance namespaces.

SOAP 1.1 Difference: Identifying SOAP Content

The SOAP 1.1 envelope namespace is `http://schemas.xmlsoap.org/soap/envelope/`, whereas for SOAP 1.2 it has changed to `http://www.w3.org/2003/05/soap-envelope`. This namespace is used for defining the envelope elements and for versioning, which we will explain in more detail in the "Versioning in SOAP" section.

The content-type used when sending SOAP messages across HTTP connections has changed as well—it was `text/xml` for SOAP 1.1 but is now `application/soap+xml` for SOAP 1.2. This is a great improvement, since `text/xml` is a generic indicator for any type of XML content. The content type was so generic that machines had to use the presence of a custom HTTP header called `SOAPAction:` to tell that XML traffic was, in fact, SOAP (see the section on the HTTP binding for more). Now the standard MIME infrastructure handles this for us.

The `doCheck` element represents the remote procedure call to the inventory check service. We'll talk more about using SOAP for RPCs in a while; for now, notice that the

name of the method we're invoking is the name of the element directly inside the
soapenv:Body, and the arguments to the method (in this case, the SKU number and the
quantity desired) are encoded inside the method element as arg0 and arg1. The real
names for these parameters in Java are SKU and quantity; but due to the ad-hoc way
we're calling this method, the client doesn't have any way of knowing that information,
so it uses the generated names arg0 and arg1.

The response to this message, which comes back across in the HTTP response, looks
like this:

```
Content-Type: application/soap+xml; charset=utf-8

<?xml version="1.0" encoding="UTF-8"?>
<soapenv:Envelope
    xmlns:soapenv="http://www.w3.org/2003/05/soap-envelope"
    xmlns:xsd="http://www.w3.org/2001/XMLSchema"
    xmlns:xsi="http://www.w3.org/2001/XMLSchema-instance">
 <soapenv:Body>
  <doCheckResponse
        soapenv:encodingStyle="http://www.w3.org/2003/05/soap-encoding">
   <rpc:result xmlns:rpc="http://www.w3.org/2003/05/soap-rpc">return</rpc:result>
   <return xsi:type="xsd:boolean">true</return>
  </doCheckResponse>
 </soapenv:Body>
</soapenv:Envelope>
```

The response is also a SOAP envelope, and it contains an encoded representation of the
result of the RPC call (in this case, the Boolean value true).

What good is having this envelope structure, when we could send our XML formats
directly over a transport like HTTP without a wrapper? Good question; as we answer it,
we'll examine some more details of the protocol.

Vertical Extensibility

Let's say you want your purchase order to be extensible. Perhaps you want to include
security in the document someday, or you might want to enable a notarization service to
associate a token with a particular purchase order, as a third-party guarantee that the PO
was sent and contained particular items. How might you make that happen?

You could drop extensibility elements directly into your document before sending it.
If we took the purchase order from the last chapter and added a notary token, it might
look something like this:

```
<po id="43871" submitted="2004-01-05" customerId="73852">
  <notary:token xmlns:notary="http://notaries-r-us.com">
    XQ34Z-4G5
  </notary:token>
  <billTo>
```

```
  <company>The Skateboard Warehouse</company>
  ...
 </billTo>
 ...
</po>
```

To do things this way, and make it easy for your partners to use, you'd need to do two things. First, your schema would have to be explicitly extensible at any point in the structure where you might want to add functionality later (this can be accomplished in a number of ways, including the xsd:any/ schema construct); otherwise, documents containing extension elements wouldn't validate. Second, you would need to agree on rules by which those extensibility elements were to be processed—which ones are optional, which ones affect which parts of the document, and so on. Both of these requirements present challenges. Not all schemas have been designed for extensibility, and you may need to extend a document that follows a preexisting standard format that wasn't built that way. Also, processing rules might vary from document type to document type, so it would be challenging to have a uniform model with which to build a common processor. It would be nice to have a standardized framework for implementing arbitrary extensibility in a way that everyone could agree on.

It turns out that the SOAP envelope, in addition to containing a body (which must always be present), may also contain an optional Header element—and the SOAP Header structure gives us just what we want in an XML extensibility system. It's a convenient and well-defined place in which to put our extensibility elements. Headers are just XML elements that live inside the soapenv:Header/soapenv:Header tags in the envelope. The soapenv:Header always appears, incidentally, *before* the soapenv:Body if it's present. (Note that in the SOAP 1.2 spec, the extensibility elements are known as *header blocks*. However, the industry—and the rest of this book—colloquially refers to them simply as *headers*.)

Let's look at the extensibility example recast as a SOAP message with a header:

```
<soapenv:Envelope
   xmlns:soapenv="http://www.w3.org/2003/05/soap-envelope">
 <soapenv:Header>
  <notary:token xmlns:notary="http://notaries-r-us.com">
    XQ34Z-4G5
  </notary:token>
 </soapenv:Header>
 <soapenv:Body>
  <PO>
    ...normal purchase order here...
  </PO>
 </soapenv:Body>
</soapenv:Envelope>
```

Since the SOAP envelope wraps around whatever XML content you want to send in the body (the PO, in this example), you can use the Header to insert extensions (the `notary:token` header) without modifying the central core of the message. This can be compared to a situation in real life where you want to send a document and some auxiliary information, but you don't want to mark up the document—so you put the document inside an envelope and then add another piece of paper or two describing your extra information.

Each individual header represents one piece of extensibility information that travels with your message. A lot of other protocols have this same basic concept—we're all familiar with the email model of headers and body. HTTP also contains headers, and both email and HTTP use the concept of extensible, user-defined headers. However, the headers in protocols like these are simple strings; since SOAP uses XML, you can encode much richer data structures for individual headers. Also, you can use XML's structure to make processing headers much more powerful and flexible than a basic string-based model.

Headers can contain any sort of data imaginable, but typically they're used for two purposes:

- *Extending the messaging infrastructure*—Infrastructure headers are typically processed by middleware. The application doesn't see the headers, just their effects. They could be things like security credentials, correlation IDs for reliable messaging, transaction context identifiers, routing controls, or anything else that provides services to the application.
- *Defining orthogonal data*—The second category of headers is application defined. These contain data that is orthogonal to the body of the message but is still destined for the application on the receiving side. An example might be extra data to accompany nonextensible schemas—if you wanted to add more customer data fields but couldn't change the `billTo` element, for instance.

Using headers to add functionality to messages is known as *vertical* extensibility, because the headers build on top of the message. A little later we'll discuss horizontal extensibility as well.

Now that you know the basics, we'll consider some of the additional framework that SOAP supplies for headers and how to use it. After that, we'll explain the SOAP processing model, which is the key to SOAP's scalability and expressive power.

The `mustUnderstand` Flag

Some extensions might use headers to carry data that's nice to know but not critical to the main purpose of the SOAP message. For instance, you might be invoking a "buy book" operation on a store's Web service. You receive a header in the response confirmation message that contains a list of other books the site thinks you might find interesting. If you know how to process that extension, then you might offer a UI to access those books. But if you don't, it doesn't matter—your original request was still processed successfully. On the other hand, suppose the *request* message of that same "buy book" operation contained private information (such as a credit card number). The sender might want to encrypt the XML in the SOAP body to prevent snooping. To make sure the other side knows what to do with the postencryption data inside the body, the sender inserts a header that describes how to decrypt the message. *That* header is important, and anyone trying to process the message without correctly processing the header and decrypting the body is going to run into trouble.

This is why we have the `mustUnderstand` 📖 attribute, which is always in the SOAP envelope namespace. Here's what our notary header would look like with that attribute:

```
<notary:token xmlns:notary="http://notaries-r-us.com"
    soapenv:mustUnderstand="true">
  XQ34Z-4G5
</notary:token>
```

By marking things `mustUnderstand` (when we refer to headers "marked `mustUnderstand`," we mean having the `soapenv:mustUnderstand` attribute set to true), you're saying that the receiver must agree to all the terms of your extension specification or they can't process the message. If the `mustUnderstand` attribute is set to false or is missing, the header is defined as optional—in this case, processors not familiar with the extension can still safely process the message and ignore the optional header.

> ### SOAP 1.1 Difference: `mustUnderstand`
> In SOAP 1.2, the `mustUnderstand` attribute may have the values 0/false (false) or 1/true (true). In SOAP 1.1, despite the fact that XML allows true and false for Boolean values, the only legal `mustUnderstand` values are 0 and 1.

The `mustUnderstand` attribute is a key part of the SOAP processing model, since it allows you to build extensions that fundamentally change how a given message is processed in a way that is guaranteed to be interoperable. *Interoperable* here means that you can always know how to gracefully fail in the face of extensions that aren't understood.

SOAP Modules

When you implement a semantic using SOAP headers, you typically want other parties to use your extension, unless it's purely for internal use. As such, you typically write a specification that details all the constraints, rules, preconditions, and data formats of your extension. These specifications are known as *SOAP modules* 📖. Modules are named with URIs so they can be referenced, versioned, and reasoned about. We'll talk more about module specifications when we get to the SOAP binding framework a bit later.

SOAP Intermediaries

So far, we've addressed SOAP headers as a means for vertical extensibility within SOAP messages. There is another related notion, however: *horizontal* extensibility. Whereas vertical extensibility is about the ability to introduce new pieces of information within a

SOAP message, horizontal extensibility is about targeting different parts of the same SOAP message to different recipients. Horizontal extensibility is provided by SOAP *intermediaries* 📖.

The Need for Intermediaries

SOAP intermediaries are applications that can process parts of a SOAP message as it travels from its origination point to its final destination point. The route taken by a SOAP message, including all intermediaries it passes through, is called the SOAP *message path* 📖 (see Figure 3.2).

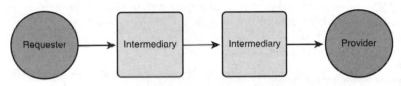

Figure 3.2   The SOAP message path

Intermediaries can both accept and forward SOAP messages, and they usually do some form of message processing as well. Three key use-cases define the need for SOAP intermediaries: crossing trust domains, ensuring scalability, and providing value-added services along the SOAP message path.

Crossing trust domains is a common issue faced while implementing security in distributed systems. Consider the relation between a corporate or departmental network and the Internet. For small organizations, it's likely that the IT department has put most computers on the network within a single trusted security domain. Employees can see their co-workers' computers as well as the IT servers, and they can freely exchange information between them without the need for separate logons. On the other hand, the corporate network probably treats all computers on the Internet as part of a separate security domain that isn't trusted. Before an Internet request reaches the network, it needs to cross from its untrustworthy domain to the trusted domain of the internal network. Corporate firewalls and virtual private network (VPN) gateways guard the network: Their job is to let some requests cross the trust domain boundary and deny access to others.

Another important need for intermediaries arises because of the scalability requirements of distributed systems. A simplistic view of distributed systems could identify two types of entities: those that request work to be done (clients) and those that do the work (servers). Clients send messages directly to the servers they want to communicate with. Servers, in turn, get some work done and respond. In this naïve universe, there is little need for distributed computing infrastructure. However, we can't use this model to build highly scalable distributed systems.

Take email as an example. When someone@company.com sends an email message to myfriend@london.co.uk, it's not the case that their email client locates the mail server london.co.uk and sends the message to it. Instead, the client sends the message to its email server at company.com. Based on the priority of the message and how busy the mail server is, the message will leave either by itself or in a batch of other messages. (Messages are often batched to improve performance.) The message will probably make a few hops through different nodes on the Internet before it gets to the mail server in London.

The lesson from this example is that highly scalable distributed systems (such as email) require flexible buffering of messages and routing based both on message parameters such as origin, destination, and priority, and on the state of the system considering factors such as the availability and load of its nodes as well as network traffic information. Intermediaries hidden from the eyes of the originators and final recipients of messages can perform this work behind the scenes.

Finally, we need intermediaries so that we can provide value-added services in a distributed system. The type of services can vary significantly, and some of them involve the message sender being explicitly aware of the intermediary, unlike our previous examples. Here are a couple of common scenarios:

- *Securing message exchanges, particularly through untrustworthy domains*—You could secure SOAP messages by passing them through an intermediary that first encrypts them and then digitally signs them. On the receiving side an intermediary would perform the inverse operations: checking the digital signature and, if it's valid, decrypting the message.

- *Notarization/nonrepudiation*—when the sender or receiver (or both) desires a third party to make a record of an interaction, a *notarizing intermediary* is a likely solution. Instead of sending the message directly to the receiver, the sender sends to the intermediary, who makes a persistent copy of the request and then sends it to the service provider. The response typically comes back via the intermediary as well, and then both parties are usually given a token they can use to reference the transaction record in the future.

- *Providing message tracing facilities*—Tracing allows the message recipient to find out the path the message followed, complete with detailed timings of arrivals and departures to and from intermediaries. This information is indispensable for tasks such as measuring quality of service (QoS), auditing systems, and identifying scalability bottlenecks.

Transparent and Explicit Intermediaries

Message senders may or may not be aware of intermediaries in the message path. A *transparent intermediary* is one the client knows nothing about—the client believes it's sending messages to the actual service endpoint, and the fact that an intermediary is doing work in the middle is incidental. An *explicit intermediary*, on the other hand, involves specific knowledge on the part of the client—the client knows the message will travel through an intermediary before continuing to its ultimate destination.

The security intermediaries discussed earlier would likely be transparent; the organization providing the service would publish the outward-facing address of the intermediary as the service endpoint. The notarization service described earlier would be an example of an explicit intermediary—the client would know that a notarization step was going on.

Intermediaries in SOAP

SOAP is specifically designed with intermediaries in mind. It has simple yet flexible facilities that address the three key aspects of an intermediary-enabled architecture:

- How do you pass information to intermediaries?
- How do you identify who should process what?
- What happens to information that is processed by intermediaries?

All header elements can optionally have the `soapenv:role` attribute. The value of this attribute is a URI that identifies who should handle the header entry. Essentially, that URI is the name of the intermediary. This URI might mean a particular node (for instance "the Solaris machine on John's desk"), or it might refer to a class of nodes (as in, "any cache manager along the message path"). (This latter case prompted the name change from *actor* to *role* in SOAP 1.2.) Also, a given node can play multiple roles: the Solaris machine on John's desk might also be a cache manager, for instance, so it would recognize either role URI.

The first step any node takes when processing a SOAP message is to collect all the headers that are targeted at the node—this means headers that have a `role` attribute matching *any* of the roles node is playing. It then looks through these nodes for headers marked `mustUnderstand` and confirms that it recognizes each such header and is able to process it in accordance with the rules associated with that SOAP header. If it finds a `mustUnderstand` header that it doesn't recognize, it must immediately stop processing.

There are several special values for the `role` attribute:

- `http://www.w3.org/2003/05/soap-envelope/role/next`—Indicates that the header entry's recipient is the next SOAP node that processes the message. This is useful for hop-by-hop processing required, for example, by message tracing.
- `http://www.w3.org/2003/05/soap-envelope/role/ultimateReceiver`—Refers to the final recipient of the SOAP message. Note that omitting the `role` attribute or using an empty value ("") also implies that the final recipient of the SOAP message should process the header entry. The final recipient of the SOAP message is the same node that processes the body.

- `http://www.w3.org/2003/05/soap-envelope/role/none`—A special role that no SOAP node should ever assume. That means that headers addressed to this role should never be processed; and since no one will ever be in this role, the value of the `mustUnderstand` attribute won't matter for such headers (remember that the first thing a SOAP node does is pick out the headers it can see by virtue of playing the right role, before looking at `mustUnderstand`). Also note that the `relay` attribute (discussed later) never matters on a header addressed to the none role, for the same reason. Even though your SOAP node can't act as the none role, it can still look at the data inside headers marked as none. So, headers marked for the none role can still be used to carry data. (We'll give an example in a bit.)

> **SOAP 1.1 Difference: `actor` versus `role`**
>
> In SOAP 1.1, the attribute used to target headers is called `actor`, not `role`. Also, SOAP 1.1 only specifies a special next actor URI (`http://schemas.xmlsoap.org/soap/actor/next`), not an actor for none or `ultimateRecipient`.

Forwarding and Active Intermediaries

Some intermediaries, like the notarization example discussed earlier, only do processing related to particular headers in the SOAP envelope before forwarding the message to the next node in the message path. In other words, the work of the intermediary is defined by the contents of the incoming messages. These are known as *forwarding* intermediaries.

Other intermediaries do processing and potentially modify the message in ways *not* defined by the message contents. For instance, an intermediary at a company boundary to the outside world might add a digital signature header to every outbound message to ensure that receivers can check the integrity of all messages. No explicit markers in the messages are used to trigger this behavior; the node simply does it. This type of intermediary is known as an *active* intermediary.

Either type of intermediary may do arbitrary work on the message (including the body) based on its internal rules.

Rules for Intermediaries and Headers

By default, all headers targeted at a particular intermediary are removed from the message when it's forwarded on to the next node. This is because the specification tells us that the contract implied by a given header is between the sender of that header and the first node satisfying the role at which it's targeted. Headers that aren't targeted at a particular intermediary should, in general, be forwarded through untouched (see Figure 3.3).

An intermediary removes headers targeted at any role it's playing, regardless of whether they're understood. In Figure 3.4, one header is processed and then removed; another isn't understood, but because it's targeted at our intermediary and not marked `mustUnderstand`, it's still removed.

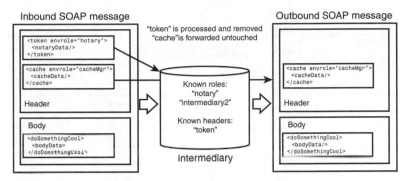

Figure 3.3 Intermediary header removal

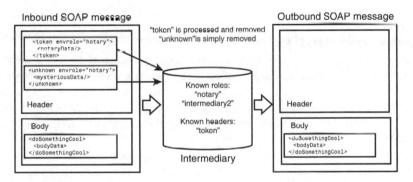

Figure 3.4 Removing optional headers targeted at an intermediary

There are two exceptions to the removal rules. First, the specification for a particular extension may explicitly indicate that an identical copy of a given header from the incoming message is supposed to be placed in the outgoing message. Such headers are known as *reinserted*, and this has the effect of forwarding them through after processing. An example might be a logging extension targeted at a `logManager`. Any log manager receiving it along the message path would make a persistent copy of the message for logging purposes and then reinsert the header so that other log managers later in the chain could do the same.

The second exception is when you want to indicate to intermediaries that extensions targeted at them, but not understood, should still be passed through. SOAP 1.2 introduces the `relay` attribute for this purpose. If the `relay` attribute is present on a header which is targeted at a given intermediary, and it has the value true, the intermediary should forward the header regardless of whether it understands it. Figure 3.5 shows an unknown header arriving at our notary intermediary. Since all nodes must recognize the next role, the unknown header is targeted at the intermediary. Despite the fact that the intermediary doesn't understand the header, it's forwarded because the `relay` attribute is true.

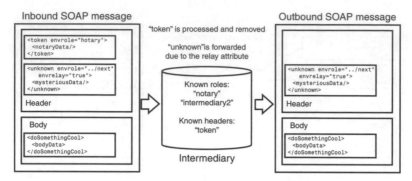

Figure 3.5 Forwarding headers with the `relay` attribute

The SOAP Body

The SOAP `Body` 📖 element immediately surrounds the information that is core to the SOAP message. All immediate children of the `Body` element are body entries (typically referred to as *bodies*). Bodies can contain arbitrary XML. Sometimes, based on the intent of the SOAP message, certain conventions govern the format of the SOAP body (for instance, we discuss the conventions for representing RPCs and communicating error information later).

When a node that identifies itself as the ultimate recipient (the service provider in the case of requests, or the client in the case of responses) receives a message, it's required to process the contents of the body and perform whatever actions are appropriate. The body carries the core of the SOAP message.

The SOAP Processing Model

Now we're ready to finish describing the SOAP 1.2 processing model. Here are the steps a processor must perform when it receives a SOAP message, as described in the spec:

1. Determine the set of roles in which the node is to act. The contents of the SOAP envelope, including any SOAP header blocks and the SOAP body, *may* be inspected in making such determination.

2. Identify all header blocks targeted at the node that are mandatory.

3. If one or more of the SOAP header blocks identified in step 2 aren't understood by the node, then generate a single SOAP fault with the value of `Code` set to `env:mustUnderstand`. If such a fault is generated, any further processing *must not* be done. Faults related to processing the contents of the SOAP body *must not* be generated in this step.

4. Process all mandatory SOAP header blocks targeted at the node and, in the case of an ultimate SOAP receiver, the SOAP body. A SOAP node *may* also choose to process nonmandatory SOAP header blocks targeted at it.

5. In the case of a SOAP intermediary, and where the SOAP message exchange pattern and results of processing (for example, no fault generated) require that the SOAP message be sent further along the SOAP message path, relay the message.

The processing model has been designed to let you use `mustUnderstand` headers to do anything you want. We could imagine a `mustUnderstand` header, for instance, that tells the processor at the next hop to process all headers and ignore the `role` attribute.

Versioning in SOAP

One interesting note about SOAP is that the `Envelope` element doesn't expose any explicit protocol version in the style of other protocols such as HTTP (HTTP/1.0 versus HTTP/1.1) or even XML (`?xml version="1.0"?`). The designers of SOAP explicitly made this choice because experience had shown simple number-based versioning to be fragile. Further, across protocols, there were no consistent rules for determining what changes in major versus minor version numbers mean.

Instead of going this way, SOAP leverages the capabilities of XML namespaces and defines the protocol version to be the URI of the SOAP envelope namespace. As a result, the only meaningful statement you can make about SOAP versions is that they are the same or different. It's no longer possible to talk about compatible versus incompatible changes to the protocol.

This approach gives Web service engines a choice of how to treat SOAP messages that have a version other than the one the engine is best suited for processing. Because an engine supporting a later version of SOAP will know all previous versions of the specification, it has options based on the namespace of the incoming SOAP message:

- If the message version is the same as any version the engine knows how to process, it can process the message.

- If the message version is recognized as older than any version the engine knows how to process, or older than the preferred version, it should generate a `VersionMismatch` fault and attempt to negotiate the protocol version with the client by sending information regarding the versions it can accept. SOAP 1.1 didn't specify how such information might be encoded, but SOAP 1.2 introduces the `soapenv:Upgrade` header for this purpose. (We'll describe it in detail when we cover faults.)

- If the message version is newer than any version the engine knows how to process (in other words, completely unrecognized), it must generate a `VersionMismatch` fault.

The simple versioning based on the namespace URI results in fairly flexible and accommodating behavior of Web service engines.

Processing Headers and Bodies

The SOAP spec has a specific meaning for the word *process*. Essentially, it means to fulfill the contract indicated by a particular piece of a SOAP message (a header or body). Processing a header means following the rules of that extension, and processing the body means performing whatever operation is defined by the service.

SOAP says you don't have to process an element in order to look at it as a part of other processing. So even though an intermediary might, for instance, encrypt the body as a message passes through it, we don't consider this processing in the SOAP sense, because encrypting the body isn't the same as doing what the body requests.

This gets back to the question of why you might use the none role. Imagine that SkatesTown wants to extend its purchase order schema by adding additional customer information. The company didn't design the schema for explicit extensibility, so adding elements in the middle will cause any older systems receiving the new XML to fail validation. SkatesTown can continue to use the old schema in the body but add arbitrary additional information in a SOAP header. That way, newer systems will notice the extensions and use them, but older ones won't be confused. This header would be purely data, without an associated SOAP module specification and processing rules, so it would make sense for SkatesTown to target the header at the none role to make sure no one tries to process it.

Faults: Error Handling in SOAP

When something goes wrong in Java, we expect someone to throw an exception; the exception mechanism gives us a common framework with which to deal with problems. The same is true in the SOAP world. When a problem occurs, the SOAP spec provides a well-known way to indicate what has happened: the SOAP fault. Let's look at an example fault message:

```
<env:Envelope xmlns:env="http://www.w3.org/2003/05/soap-envelope"
              xmlns:st="http://www.skatestown.com/ws">
  <env:Header>
    <st:PublicServiceAnnouncement>
      Skatestown's Web services will be unavailable after 5PM today
      for a two hour maintenance window.
    </st:PublicServiceAnnouncement>
  </env:Header>
  <env:Body>
    <env:Fault>
      <env:Code>
        <env:Value>env:Sender</env:Value>
        <env:Subcode>
          <env:Value>st:InvalidPurchaseOrder</env:Value>
        </env:Subcode>
      </env:Code>
```

```
      <env:Reason>
        <env:Text xml:lang="en-US">
          Your purchase order did not validate!
        </env:Text>
      </env:Reason>
      <env:Detail>
        <st:LineNumber>9</st:LineNumber>
        <st:ColumnNumber>24</st:ColumnNumber>
      </env:Detail>
    </env:Fault>
  </env:Body>
</env:Envelope>
```

Structure of a Fault

A SOAP fault message is a normal SOAP message with a single, well-known element inside the body: soapenv:Fault. The presence of that element acts as a signal to processors to indicate something has gone wrong. Of course, just knowing something is wrong is rarely useful enough; you need a structure to help determine what happened so you can either try again with a better idea of what might work or let the user know the problem. SOAP faults have several components to help in this regard.

Fault Code

The fault code is the first place to look, since it tells you in a general sense what the problem was. Fault codes are QNames, and SOAP defines the set of legal codes as follows (each item is the local part of the QName—the namespace is always the SOAP envelope namespace):

- Sender—The problem was caused by incorrect or missing data from the sender. For instance, if a service required a security header in order to do its work and it was called without one, it would generate a Sender fault. You typically have to make a change to your message before resending it if you hope to be successful.

- Receiver—Something went wrong on the receiver while processing the message, but it wasn't directly attributable to the message contents. For example, a necessary resource like a database was down, a thread wasn't available, and so on. A message causing a Receiver fault might succeed if resent at a later time.

- mustUnderstand—This fault code indicates that a header was received that was targeted at the receiving node, marked mustUnderstand="true", and not understood.

- VersionMismatch—The VersionMismatch code is generated when the namespace on the SOAP envelope that was received isn't compatible with the SOAP version on the receiver. This is the way SOAP handles protocol versioning; we'll talk about it in more detail later.

The fault code resides inside the `Code` element in the fault, in a subelement called `Value`. In the example code, you can see the `Sender` code, meaning something must have been wrong with the request that caused this fault. We have the `Value` element instead of putting the code `qname` directly inside the `Code` element so that we can extend the expressive space of possible fault codes by adding more data inside another element, `Subcode`.

Subcodes

SOAP 1.2 lets you specify an arbitrary hierarchy of fault subcodes, which provide further detail about what went wrong. The syntax is a little verbose, but it works. Here's an example:

```
<env:Code>
   <env:Value>env:Sender</env:Value>
   <env:Subcode>
     <env:Value>st:InvalidPurchaseOrder</env:Value>
   </env:Subcode>
</env:Code>
```

The `Code` element contains an optional `Subcode` element. Just as `Code` contains a mandatory `Value`, so too does each `Subcode`—and each `Subcode` may contain another `Subcode`, to whatever level of nesting is desired. Generally the hierarchy won't go more than about three levels deep. In our example, the subcode tells us that the problem was an invalid purchase order.

Reason

The `Reason` element, also required, contains one or more human-readable descriptions of the fault condition. Typically, the reason text might appear in a dialog box that alerts the user of a problem, or it might be written into a log file. The `Text` element contains the text and there can be one or more such messages. Why would you have more than one? In the increasingly international environment of the Web, you might wish to send the fault description in several languages, as in this example from the SOAP primer:

```
<env:Reason>
 <env:Text xml:lang="en-US">Processing error</env:Text>
 <env:Text xml:lang="cs">Chyba zpracování</env:Text>
</env:Reason>
```

The spec states that if you have multiple `Text` elements, you should have a different value for `xml:lang` in each one—otherwise you might confuse the software that's trying to print out a single coherent message in a given language.

`Node` and `Role`

The optional `Node` element, not shown in our example, tells us which SOAP node (the sender, an intermediary, or the ultimate destination) was processing the message at the time the fault occurred. It contains a URI.

The Role element tells which role the faulting node was playing when the fault occurred. It contains a URI that has exactly the same semantics, and the same values, as the role attribute we described when we were talking about headers. Note the difference between this element and Node—Node tells you *which* SOAP node generated the fault, and Role tells *what* part that node was playing when it happened. The Role element is also optional.

Fault Details

We have a custom fault code and a fault message, both of which can tell a user or software something about the problem; but in many cases, we would also like to pass back some more complex machine-readable data. For example, you might want to include a stack trace while you're developing services to aid with debugging (though you likely wouldn't do this in a production application, since stack traces can sometimes give away information that might be useful to someone trying to compromise your system).

You can place anything you want inside the SOAP fault's Detail element. In our example at the beginning of the section, the line number and column number where the validation error occurred are expressed, so that automated tools might be able to help the user or developer to fix the structure of the transmitted message.

SOAP 1.1 Difference: Handling Faults

Faults in SOAP 1.2 got an overhaul from SOAP 1.1's version. All the subelements of the SOAP Fault element in SOAP 1.1 are unqualified (in no namespace). The Fault subelements in SOAP 1.2 are in the envelope namespace.

In SOAP 1.1, there is no Subcode, only a single faultcode element. The SOAP 1.1 fault code is a QName, but its hierarchy is achieved through dots rather than explicit structure—in other words, whereas in SOAP 1.1 you might have seen

```
<faultcode>env:Sender.Authorization.BadPassword</faultcode>
```

in SOAP 1.2 you see something like:

```
<env:Code>
  <env:Value>env:Sender</env:Value>
  <env:Subcode>
    <env:Value>myNS:Authorization</env:Value>
    <env:Subcode>
      <env:Value>myNS:BadPassword</env:Value>
    </env:Subcode>
  </env:Subcode>
</env:Code>
```

The env:Reason element in SOAP 1.2 is called faultstring in SOAP 1.1. Also, 1.1 only allows a single string inside faultstring, whereas 1.2 allows different env:Text elements inside env:Reason to account for different languages.

> The Client fault code from 1.1 is now Sender, which is less prone to interpretation. Similarly, 1.1's Server fault code is now Receiver.
>
> In SOAP 1.1, the detail element is used only for information pertaining to faults generated when processing the SOAP body. If a fault is generated when processing a header, any machine-readable information about the fault must travel in headers on the fault message. The reasoning for this went something like this: Headers exist so that SOAP can support orthogonal extensibility; that means you want a given message to be able to carry several extensions that might not have been designed by the same people and might have no knowledge of each other. If problems occurred that caused each of these extensions to want to pass back data, they might have to fight for the detail element. The problem with this logic is that the detail element isn't a contended resource, in the same way the soapenv:Header isn't a contended resource. If multiple extensions want to drop their own elements into detail, that works just as well as putting their own headers into the envelope. So this restriction was dropped in SOAP 1.2, and env:Detail can contain anything your application desires—but the rule still must be followed for SOAP 1.1.
>
> SOAP 1.2 introduces the NotUnderstood header and the Upgrade header, both of which exist in order to clarify what went wrong with particular faults (mustUnderstand and VersionMismatch) in a standard way.

Using Headers in Faults

Since a fault is also a SOAP message, it can carry SOAP headers as well as the fault structure. In our example at the beginning of this section, you can see that SkatesTown has included a public service announcement header. This optional information lets anyone who cares know that the Web services will be down for maintenance; and since it isn't marked mustUnderstand, it doesn't affect the processing of the fault message in any way. SOAP defines some headers specifically for use in faults.

The NotUnderstood Header

You'll recall that SOAP processors are forced to fault if they encounter a mustUnderstand header that they should process but don't understand. It's great to know something wasn't understood, but it's more useful if you have an indication of *which* header was the cause of the problem. That way you might be able to try again with a different message if the situation warrants. For example, let's say a message was sent with a routing header marked mustUnderstand="true". The purpose of the routing header is to let the service know that after it finishes processing the message, it's supposed to send a copy to an endpoint whose address is in the contents of the header (probably for logging purposes). If the receiver doesn't understand the header, it sends back a mustUnderstand fault. The sender might then, for instance, ask the user if they would still like to send the message, but without the carbon-copy functionality. If the routing header is the only one in the envelope, then it's easy to know which header the mustUnderstand fault refers to. But what if there are multiple mustUnderstand headers?

SOAP 1.2 introduced a `NotUnderstood` header to deal with this issue. When sending back a `mustUnderstand` fault, SOAP endpoints should include a `NotUnderstood` header for each header in the original message that was not understood. The `NotUnderstood` header (in the SOAP envelope namespace) has a `qname` attribute containing the QName of the header that wasn't understood. For example:

```
<env:Envelope xmlns:env='http://www.w3.org/2003/05/soap-envelope'>
  <env:Header>
    <abc:Extension1
        xmlns:abc='http://example.org/2001/06/ext'
        env:mustUnderstand='true'/>
    <def:Extension2
        xmlns:def='http://example.com/stuff'
        env:mustUnderstand='true' />
  </env:Header>
  <env:Body>
    . . .
  </env:Body>
</env:Envelope>
```

If a processor received this message and didn't understand `Extension1` but did understand `Extension2`, it would return a fault like this:

```
<env:Envelope
   xmlns:env='http://www.w3.org/2003/05/soap-envelope'
   xmlns:xml='http://www.w3.org/XML/1998/namespace'>
 <env:Header>
  <env:NotUnderstood qname='abc:Extension1'
      xmlns:abc='http://example.org/2001/06/ext' />
 </env:Header>
 <env:Body>
  <env:Fault>
   <env:Code>
    <env:Value>env:mustUnderstand</env:Value>
   </env:Code>
   <env:Reason>
     <env:Text xml:lang='en'>One or more mandatory
       SOAP header blocks not understood
     </env:Text>
   </env:Reason>
  </env:Fault>
 </env:Body>
</env:Envelope>
```

This information is handy when you're trying to use the SOAP extensibility mechanism to negotiate QoS or policy agreements between communicating parties.

The `Upgrade` **Header**

Back in the section on versioning, we mentioned the `Upgrade` header, which SOAP 1.2 defines as a standard mechanism for indicating which versions of SOAP are supported by a node generating a `VersionMismatch` fault. This section fully defines this header.

An `Upgrade` header (which actually is a misnomer—it doesn't always imply an upgrade in terms of using a more recent version of the protocol) looks like this in context:

```
<?xml version="1.0" ?>
<env:Envelope
   xmlns:env="http://www.w3.org/2003/05/soap-envelope"
   xmlns:xml="http://www.w3.org/XML/1998/namespace">
 <env:Header>
  <env:Upgrade>
   <env:SupportedEnvelope qname="ns1:Envelope"
    xmlns:ns1="http://www.w3.org/2003/05/soap-envelope"/>
   <env:SupportedEnvelope qname="ns2:Envelope"
    xmlns:ns2="http://schemas.xmlsoap.org/soap/envelope/"/>
  </env:Upgrade>
 </env:Header>
 <env:Body>
  <env:Fault>
   <env:Code>
    <env:Value>env:VersionMismatch</env:Value>
   </env:Code>
   <env:Reason>
    <env:Text xml:lang="en">Version Mismatch</env:Text>
   </env:Reason>
  </env:Fault>
 </env:Body>
</env:Envelope>
```

This fault would be generated by a node that supports both SOAP 1.1 and SOAP 1.2, in response to some envelope in another namespace. The `Upgrade` header, in the SOAP envelope namespace, contains one or more `SupportedEnvelope` elements, each of which indicates the QName of a supported envelope element. The `SupportedEnvelope` elements are ordered by preference, from most preferred to least. Therefore, the previous fault indicates that although this node supports both SOAP 1.1 and 1.2, 1.2 is preferred.

All the `VersionMismatch` faults we've shown so far use SOAP 1.2. However, if a SOAP 1.1 node doesn't understand SOAP 1.2, it won't be able to parse a SOAP 1.2 fault. As such, SOAP 1.2 specifies rules for responding to SOAP 1.1 messages from a node that only supports SOAP 1.2. It's suggested that such nodes recognize the SOAP 1.1 namespace and respond with a SOAP 1.1 version mismatch fault containing an `Upgrade` header as specified earlier. That way, nodes that have the capability to switch to SOAP 1.2 will know to do so, and nodes that can't do so will still be able to understand the fault as a versioning problem.

Objects in XML: The SOAP Data Model

As you saw in Chapter 2, XML has an extremely rich structure—and the possible contents of an XML data model, which include mixed content, substitution groups, and many other concepts, are a lot more complex than the data/objects in most modern programming languages. This means that there isn't always an easy way to map any given XML Schema into familiar structures such as classes in Java. The SOAP authors recognized this problem, so (knowing that programmers would like to send Java/C++/VB objects in SOAP envelopes) they introduced two concepts: the *SOAP data model* and the *SOAP encoding*. The data model is an abstract representation of data structures such as you might find in Java or C#, and the encoding is a set of rules to map that data model into XML so you can send it in SOAP messages.

Object Graphs

The SOAP data model is about representing *graphs* of nodes, each of which may be connected via directional *edges* to other nodes. The nodes are values, and the edges are labels. Figure 3.6 shows a simple example: the data model for a `Product` in SkatesTown's database, which you saw earlier.

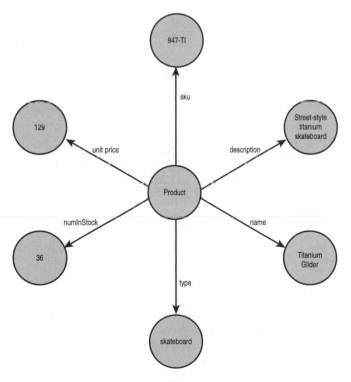

Figure 3.6   An example SOAP data model

In Java, the object representing this structure might look like this:

```
class Product {
    String description;
    String sku;
    double unitPrice;
    String name;
    String type;
    int numInStock;
}
```

Nodes may have outgoing edges, in which case they're known as *compound* values, or only incoming edges, in which case they're *simple* values. All the nodes around the edge of the example are simple values. The one in the middle is a compound value.

When the edges coming out of a compound value node have names, we say the node represents a *structure*. The edge names (also known as *accessors*) are the equivalent of field names in Java, each one pointing to another node which contains the value of the field. The node in the middle is our Product reference, and it has an outgoing edge for each field of the structure.

When a node has outgoing edges that are only distinguished by position (the first edge, the second edge, and so on), the node represents an *array*. A given compound value node may represent either a structure or an array, but not both.

Sometimes it's important for a data model to refer to the same value more than once—in that case, you'll see a node with more than one incoming edge (see Figure 3.7). These values are called multireference values, or *multirefs* 📖.

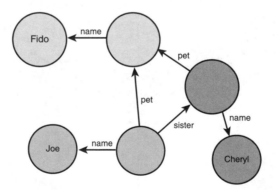

Figure 3.7 Multireference values

The model in this example shows that someone named Joe has a sister named Cheryl, and they both share a pet named Fido. Because the two pet edges both point at the same node, we know it's exactly the same dog, not two different dogs who happen to share the name Fido.

With this simple set of concepts, you can represent most common programming language constructs in languages like C#, JavaScript, Perl, or Java. Of course, the data model isn't very useful until you can read and write it in SOAP messages.

The SOAP Encoding

When you want to take a SOAP data model and write it out as XML (typically in a SOAP message), you use the SOAP *encoding* 📖. Like most things in the Web services world, the SOAP encoding has a URI to identify it, which for SOAP 1.2 is `http://www.w3.org/2003/05/soap-encoding`. When serializing XML using the encoding rules, it's strongly recommended that processors use the special `encodingStyle` attribute (in the SOAP envelope namespace) to indicate that SOAP encoding is in use, by using this URI as the value for the attribute. This attribute can appear on headers or their children, bodies or their children, and any child of the `Detail` element in a fault. When a processor sees this attribute on an element, it knows that the element and all its children follow the encoding rules.

> **SOAP 1.1 Difference: `encodingStyle`**
>
> In SOAP 1.1, the `encodingStyle` attribute could appear anywhere in the message, including on the SOAP envelope elements (`Body`, `Header`, `Envelope`). In SOAP 1.2, it may only appear in the three places mentioned in the text.

The encoding is straightforward: it says when writing out a data model, each outgoing edge becomes an XML element, which contains either a text value (if the edge points to a terminal node) or further subelements (if the edge points to a node which itself has outgoing edges). The earlier product example would look something like this:

```
<product soapenv:encodingStyle="http://www.w3.org/2003/05/soap-encoding">
    <sku>947-TI</sku>
    <name>Titanium Glider</name>
    <type>skateboard</type>
    <desc>Street-style titanium skateboard.</desc>
    <price>129.00</price>
    <inStock>36</inStock>
</product>
```

If you want to encode a graph of objects that might contain multirefs, you can't write the data in the straightforward way we've been using, since you'll have one of two problems: Either you'll lose the information that two or more encoded nodes are identical, or (in the case of circular references) you'll get into an infinite regress. Here's an example: If the structure from Figure 3.7 included an edge called `owner` back from the `pet` to the `person`, we might see a structure like the one in Figure 3.8.

If we tried to encode this with a naïve system that simply followed edges and turned them into elements, we might get something like this:

```
<person soapenv:encodingStyle="http://www.w3.org/2003/05/soap-encoding">
  <name>Joe</name>
  <pet>
    <name>Fido</name>
    <owner>
      <name>Joe</name>
      <pet>
        --uh oh! stack overflow on the way!--
```

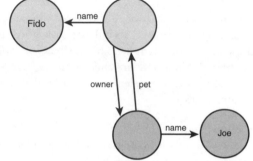

Figure 3.8   An object graph with a loop

Luckily the SOAP encoding has a way to deal with this situation: *multiref encoding*. When you encode an object that you want to refer to elsewhere, you use an ID attribute to give it an anchor. Then, instead of directly encoding the data for a second reference to that object, you can encode a reference to the already-serialized object using the ref attribute. Here's the previous example using multirefs:

```
<person id="1" soapenv:encodingStyle="http://www.w3.org/2003/05/soap-encoding">
  <name>Joe</name>
  <pet id="2">
    <name>Fido</name>
    <owner ref="#1"/> <!-- refer to the person -->
  </pet>
</person>
```

Much nicer. Notice that in this example you see an id of 2 on Fido, even though nothing in this serialization refers to him. This is a common pattern that saves time on processors while they serialize object graphs. If they only put IDs on objects that were referred to multiple times, they would need to walk the entire graph of objects before writing any XML in order to figure that out. Instead, many serializers always put an ID on any object (any nonsimple value) that might potentially be referenced later. If there is no further reference, then you've serialized an extra few bytes—no big deal. If there is, you can notice that the object has been written before and write out a ref attribute instead of reserializing it.

SOAP 1.1 Differences: Multirefs

The `href` attribute that was used to point to the data in SOAP 1.1 has changed to `ref` in SOAP 1.2.

Multirefs in SOAP 1.1 must be serialized as *independent elements*, which means as immediate children of the `SOAP:Body` element. This means that when you receive a SOAP body, it may have multiref serializations either before or after the real `body` element (the one you care about). Here's an example:

```
<soap:Envelope xmlns:soap="http://schemas.xmlsoap.org/soap/envelope"
xmlns:soapenc="http://schemas.xmlsoap.org/soap/encoding">
 <soap:Body>
  <!-- Here is the multiref -->
  <multiRef id="obj0" soapenc:root="0" xsi:type="myNS:Part"
  soapenv:encodingStyle="http://www.w3.org/2003/05/soap-encoding">
   <sku>SJ-47</sku>
  </multiRef>
  <!-- Here is the method element -->
  <myMultirefMethod soapenc:root="1"
                    soapenv:encodingStyle=
                         "http://www.w3.org/2003/05/soap-encoding">
   <arg href="#obj0"/>
  </myMultirefMethod>
  <!-- The multiref could also have appeared here -->
 </soap:Body>
</soap:Envelope>
```

This is the reason for the SOAP 1.1 `root` attribute (which you can see in the example). Multiref serializations typically have the `root` attribute set to 0; the real `body` element has a `root="1"` attribute, meaning it's the root of the serialization tree of the SOAP data model. When serializing a SOAP message 1.1, most processors place the multiref serializations *after* the main `body` element; this makes it much easier for the serialization code to do its work. Each time they encounter a new object to serialize, they automatically encode a forward reference instead (keeping track of which IDs go with which objects), just in case the object was referred to again later in the serialization. Then, after the end of the main `body` element, they write out all the object serializations in a row. This means that *all* objects are written as multirefs whenever multirefs are enabled, which can be expensive (especially if there aren't many multiple references). SOAP 1.2 fixes this problem by allowing *inline multirefs*. When serializing a data model, a SOAP 1.2 engine is allowed to put an ID attribute on an inline serialization, like this:

```
<SOAP:Body>
   <method>
      <arg1 id="1" xsi:type="xsd:string">Foo</arg1>
      <arg2 href="#1"/>
   </method>
</SOAP:Body>
```

Now, making a serialized object available for multireferencing is as easy as dropping an `id` attribute on it. Also, this approach removes the need for the `root` attribute, which is no longer present in SOAP 1.2.

Encoding Arrays

The XML encoding for an array in the SOAP object model looks like this:

```
<myArray soapenc:itemType="xsd:string"
         soapenc:arraySize="3">
 <item>Huey</item>
 <item>Duey</item>
 <item>Louie</item>
</myArray>
```

This represents an array of three strings. The `itemType` attribute on the `array` element tells us what kind of things are inside, and the `arraySize` attribute tells us how many of them to expect. The name of the elements inside the array (`item` in this example) doesn't matter to SOAP processors, since the items in an array are only distinguishable by position. This means that the ordering of items in the XML encoding *is* important.

The `arraySize` attribute defaults to "`*`," a special value indicating an unbounded array (just like `[]` in Java—an `int[]` is an unbounded array of `int`s).

Multidimensional arrays are supported by listing each dimension in the `arraySize` attribute, separated by spaces. So, a 2x2 array has an `arraySize` of "2 x 2." You can use the special "`*`" value to make one dimension of a multidimensional array unbounded, but it may only be the first dimension. In other words, `arraySize="* 3 4"` is OK, but `arraySize="3 * 4"` isn't.

Multidimensional arrays are serialized as a single list of items, in row-major order (across each row and then down). For this two-dimensional array of size 2x2

0	1
Northwest	Northeast
Southwest	Southeast

the serialization would look like this:

```
<myArray soapenc:itemType="xsd:string"
         soapenc:arraySize="2 2">
  <item>Northwest</item>
  <item>Northeast</item>
  <item>Southwest</item>
  <item>Southeast</item>
</myArray>
```

SOAP 1.1 Differences: Arrays

One big difference between the SOAP 1.1 and SOAP 1.2 array encodings is that in SOAP 1.1, the dimensionality and the type of the array are conflated into a single value (`arrayType`), which the processor needs to parse into component pieces. Here are some 1.1 examples:

arrayType Value	Description
xsd:int[5]	An array of five integers
xsd:int[][5]	An array of five integer arrays
xsd:int[,][5]	An array of five two-dimensional arrays of integers
p:Person[5]	An array of five people
xsd:string[2,3]	A 2x3, two-dimensional array of strings

In SOAP 1.2, the itemType attribute contains only the types of the array elements. The dimensions are now in a separate arraySize attribute, and multidimensionality has been simplified.

SOAP 1.1 also supports *sparse arrays* (arrays with missing values, mostly used for certain kinds of database updates) and *partially transmitted arrays* (arrays that are encoded starting at an offset from the beginning of the array). To support sparse arrays, each item within an array encoding can optionally have a position attribute, which indicates the item's position in the array, counting from zero. Here's an example:

```
<myArray soapenc:arrayType="xsd:string[3]">
  <item soapenc:position="[1]">I'm the second element</item>
</myArray>
```

This would represent an array that has no first value, the passed string as the second element, and no third element. The same value can be encoded as a partially transmitted array by using the offset attribute, which indicates the index at which the encoded array begins:

```
<myArray soapenc:arrayType="xsd:string[3]" soapenc:offset="[1]">
  <item>I'm the second element</item>
</myArray>
```

Due to several factors, including not much uptake in usage and interoperability problems when they were used, these complex array encodings were removed from the SOAP 1.2 version.

Encoding-Specific Faults

SOAP 1.2 defines some fault codes specifically for encoding problems. If you use the encoding (which you probably will if you use the RPC conventions, described in the next section), you might run into the faults described in the following list. These all are subcodes to the code env:Sender, since they all relate to problems with the sender's data serialization. These faults aren't guaranteed to be sent—they're recommended, rather than mandated. Since these faults typically indicate problems with the encoding system in a SOAP toolkit, rather than with user code, you likely won't need to deal with them directly unless you're building a SOAP implementation yourself:

- MissingID—Generated when a ref attribute in the received message doesn't correspond to any of the id attributes in the message
- DuplicateID—Generated when more than one element in the message has the same id attribute value
- UntypedValue—Optional; indicates that the type of node in the received message couldn't be determined by the receiver

The SOAP RPC Conventions

Once you have the SOAP data model, it's quite natural to map remote procedure call (RPC) interactions to SOAP by using a struct to represent a call. The best way to describe this is with an example.

Let's say we have this method in Java:

```
public int addFive(int arg);
```

A request message representing a call to this method in SOAP would look something like this:

```
<env:Envelope>
  <env:Body>
    <myNS:addFive xmlns:myNS="http://my-domain.com/"
        enc:encodingStyle="http://">
      <arg xsi:type="xsd:int">33</arg>
    </myNS:addFive>
  </env:Body>
</env:Envelope>
```

Notice that the method name has been translated into XML (the rules by which a name in a language like Java gets turned into an XML name, and vice versa, can be found in part 2 of the SOAP 1.2 spec), and we've put it in a namespace that is specific to our service (this is common practice, but not strictly necessary). The method invocation, as we mentioned, is an encoded struct with one accessor for each argument, so the `arg` element is inside the method element, and the argument contains the value we're passing: 33.

If we pass this message to a service, the response looks something like this:

```
<env:Envelope>
  <env:Body>
    <myNS:addFiveResponse xmlns:myNS="http://my-domain.com/"
              xmlns:rpc="http://www.w3.org/2003/05/soap-rpc"
        enc:encodingStyle="http://">
      <rpc:result>ret</rpc:result>
      <ret xsi:type="xsd:int">38</ret>
    </myNS:addFive>
  </env:Body>
</env:Envelope>
```

The RPC response is also modeled as a struct, and by convention the name of the response struct is the name of the method with *Response* appended to the end. The struct contains accessors for all `inout` and `out` parameters in the method call (see the next section) as well as the return value.

The first accessor in the struct is interesting, and it brings to light another difference between SOAP 1.1 and 1.2: In SOAP 1.1's RPC style, there was no way to tell which accessor in the struct was the return value of the method and which were the `out` parameters. This was a problem unless you had good meta-data, and even then the situation could be confusing. SOAP 1.2 resolves this issue by specifying that an RPC response structure containing a return value must contain an accessor named `result` in the SOAP RPC namespace. The value of this field is a QName that names the accessor containing the return value for the invocation.

`out` and `inout` **Parameters**

In some environments, programmers use *out parameters* 📖 to enable returning multiple values from a given RPC call. For instance, if we wanted to return not only a Boolean yes/no value from our inventory check service but also the actual number of units in stock, we might change our signature to something like this (using pseudocode):

```
boolean doCheck(String SKU,
                int quantity,
                out int numInStock)
```

The idea is that the `numInStock` value is filled in by the service response as well as returning a Boolean true/false. *Inout parameters* 📖 are similar, except that they also get passed in—so we could use an `inout` like this:

```
boolean doCheck(String SKU,
                inout int quantity)
```

In this situation, we'd pass a quantity value in, and then we expect the value of the `quantity` variable to have been updated to the actual quantity available by the service.

Java developers aren't used to the concept of `inout` or `out` parameters because, typically, in Java all objects are automatically passed by reference. When you're using RMI, simple objects may be passed by value, but other objects are still passed by reference. In this sense, any mutable objects (whose state can be modified) are automatically treated as `inout` parameters. If a method changes them, the changes are seen automatically by anyone else.

In Web services, the situation is different: All parameters are passed by value. SOAP has no notion of passing parameters by reference. This design decision was made in order to keep SOAP and its data encoding simple. Passing values by reference in a distributed system requires distributed garbage collection and (potentially) a lot of network round-trips. This not only complicates the design of the system but also imposes restrictions on some possible system architectures and interaction patterns. For example, how can you do distributed garbage collection when the requestor and the provider of a service can both be offline at the same time?

Therefore, for Web services, the notion of `inout` and `out` parameters doesn't involve passing objects by reference and letting the target backend modify their state; instead, copies of the data are exchanged. It's then up to the service client code to create the perception that the state of the object that has been passed in to the client method has been modified. We'll show you what we mean. Let's take the modified `doCheck()` you saw earlier:

```
boolean doCheck(String SKU,
                inout int quantity)
```

When this method is called, the request message looks like this on the wire:

```
<soapenv:Envelope xmlns:soapenv="http://www.w3.org/2003/05/soap-envelope"
xmlns:xsd="http://www.w3.org/2001/XMLSchema"
xmlns:xsi="http://www.w3.org/2001/XMLSchema-instance">
 <soapenv:Body>
  <doCheck soapenv:encodingStyle="http://www.w3.org/2003/05/soap-encoding">
   <SKU>318-BP</SKU>
   <quantity xsi:type="xsd:int">3</quantity>
  </doCheck>
 </soapenv:Body>
</soapenv:Envelope>
```

And here's the response message:

```
<soapenv:Envelope xmlns:soapenv="http://www.w3.org/2003/05/soap-envelope"
                  xmlns:xsd="http://www.w3.org/2001/XMLSchema"
                  xmlns:xsi="http://www.w3.org/2001/XMLSchema-instance">
 <soapenv:Body>
  <doCheckResponse soapenv:encodingStyle=
  "http://www.w3.org/2003/05/soap-encoding">
   <rpc:result xmlns:rpc="http://www.w3.org/2003/05/soap-rpc">return</rpc:result>
   <return>true</return>
   <quantity xsi:type="xsd:int">72</quantity>
  </doCheckResponse>
 </soapenv:Body>
</soapenv:Envelope>
```

This is a request to see if 3 items are available, and the response indicates that not only are there 3 (the true response), but there are in fact 72 (the new quantity value). The endpoint receiving this response should then update the appropriate programming-language construct for the quantity parameter with the new value.

Finally, here's the example that adds an extra out parameter containing the number of items in stock to our doCheck() method:

```
boolean doCheck(in sku, in quantity, out numInStock)
```

If we called this new method, the request would look identical to the one you saw earlier in this chapter, but the response would now look like this:

```
<soapenv:Envelope xmlns:soapenv="http://www.w3.org/2003/05/soap-envelope"
                  xmlns:xsd="http://www.w3.org/2001/XMLSchema"
                  xmlns:xsi="http://www.w3.org/2001/XMLSchema-instance">
 <soapenv:Body>
  <doCheckResponse soapenv:encodingStyle=
  "http://www.w3.org/2003/05/soap-encoding">
   <rpc:result xmlns:rpc="http://www.w3.org/2003/05/soap-rpc">return</rpc:result>
   <return>true</return>
   <numInStock>72</numInStock>
```

```
    </doCheckResponse>
   </soapenv:Body>
  </soapenv:Envelope>
```

Despite the fact that Java doesn't have a native concept of `inout` and `out` parameters, we can still use them with toolkits like Axis—we'll explore how to do this in Chapter 5.

XML, Straight Up: Document-Style SOAP

Although the RPC pattern is a common use case for SOAP, there are no restrictions on the contents of the SOAP body. Typically, sending nonencoded XML content in the body is known as *document-style SOAP*, since it centers around the message as an XML document rather than an abstract data model that happens to be encoded into XML.

Keep in mind that even if you don't explicitly use the SOAP RPC conventions as described, you can still map your document-style XML to and from procedure calls (or use whatever programming paradigm you like, since SOAP is about the structure of messages on the wire). Various toolkits, including .NET and Axis, have been doing this for some time now. When you publish a Visual Basic or C# class as a .NET Web service, the default behavior is to use document-style SOAP to expose the methods. The messages still look similar to the RPC style, but they don't use the SOAP encoding. The only problem with this approach is that there are no standard encodings for things like arrays or structures, and you lose the referential integrity of objects that are referenced multiple times.

When to Use Which Style

As a Java programmer, it might not always be clear which style of SOAP to use. Here are a few rules of thumb you can use when thinking about it:

- If you're starting from code in Java, C#, or another procedural/OO language, and you're trying to expose methods as Web services, the RPC style is a natural fit.

- If you have preexisting XML formats (schemas and so on) that you want to support, using the SOAP encoding would just get in the way. So, document style is preferable.

- If you need to transmit object graphs that must maintain referential integrity (circular lists, for instance, or complex graphs), RPC provides an interoperable way to do it.

- Validating document-style messages is straightforward, because they typically have XML schemas. You can't easily write an XML schema that will correctly validate an encoded SOAP data model, since the model allows for a nondeterministic set of valid serializations—for instance, multiref objects can be serialized in a variety of places (either in-place at any of the references, or as an independent element at the top level), and arrays are still valid regardless of the XML element name of the items. So, if schema validation using standard tools is important, document style is the way to go.

As you'll see in Chapter 13, "Web Services Interoperability," the Web Service Interoperability organization (WS-I) has come down hard against SOAP encoding, and has in fact banned its use in their Basic Profile of SOAP 1.1 (we can only assume they will continue to dislike it for SOAP 1.2).

The jury is definitely still out with respect to the value of the SOAP encoding. A lot of companies seem to be moving away from it; but, on the other hand, it's a developer-friendly technology for people trying to expose preexisting classes and methods as Web services. Despite WS-I's claims, there has been a lot of interoperability work to make sure RPC style works between most implementations of SOAP 1.1 and SOAP 1.2.

We'll talk a lot more about these styles in the next couple of chapters, when we describe them in relationship to WSDL and Axis.

The Transport Binding Framework

The SOAP processing model talks about what a node should do when it processes a SOAP message. As we've discussed, messages are described abstractly in terms of the XML infoset. Now it's time to look more closely at how those infosets are moved from place to place.

A SOAP *protocol binding* 📖 is a set of rules that describes a method of getting a SOAP infoset from one node to another. For instance, you already know that HTTP is a common way to transport SOAP messages. The purpose of the SOAP HTTP binding (which you'll find in part 2 of the spec) is to describe how to take a SOAP infoset at one node and serialize it across an HTTP connection to another node.

Many bindings, including the standard HTTP one, specify that the XML 1.0 serialization for the infoset should be used—that means if you look at the messages on the wire, you'll see angle brackets as in any regular XML document. But the binding's job is really to move the infoset from node to node, and the way the infoset is represented on the wire is up to the binding author. This means bindings have the freedom to specify custom serializations; they might do this to increase efficiency with compression or a binary protocol, or to add security via encryption, among other reasons.

Since bindings determine the concrete structure of the bits on the wire and how they're processed into SOAP messages, it's critical that communicating parties agree on what binding to use—that agreement is just as important as the agreement of what data to send. This is why bindings, like SOAP modules, are named with URIs. The standard SOAP 1.2 HTTP binding, for instance, is identified by the URI `http://www.w3.org/2003/05/soap/bindings/HTTP/`. Note that there can be many different SOAP bindings for a given underlying protocol—agreeing on a binding means not only agreeing to use HTTP to send SOAP messages, but also to follow all the rules of the given binding specification when doing so.

Bindings can be simple or complex, and they can provide a variety of different levels of functionality. A raw UDP binding, for instance, might not provide any guarantee that the messages sent arrive at the other side. On the other hand, a binding to a reliable message queuing system such as the Java Message Service (JMS) might provide guaranteed (eventual) arrival, even in the face of crashes or network failures. We can also imagine bindings to underlying protocols that provide security, such as HTTPS, or with the ability to broadcast messages to a variety of recipients at once, like multicast IP.

Even when the underlying protocol doesn't provide desired functionality directly, it's still possible to write a binding that does fancy things. For instance, you could design a custom HTTP binding specifying that, for security reasons, the XML forming each message should be encrypted before being sent (and decrypted on the receiving side). Such custom bindings are possible, but it's often a better idea to use the extensibility built into the envelope to implement this kind of functionality. Also, bindings only serve to pass messages between adjacent nodes along a SOAP message path. If you need end-to-end functionality in a situation where intermediaries are involved, it's usually better to use in-message extensibility with SOAP headers.

Features and Properties

Bindings can do a huge variety of different things for us—compare this variety to what the SOAP header mechanism can do, and you might notice that the set of possible semantics you can achieve is similar (almost anything, in fact). The designers of SOAP 1.2 noticed the similarity as well, and wanted to write a framework that might help future extension authors describe their semantics in ways that were easy to reason about, compare with each other, and refer to in machine-readable ways.

What was needed was a way to specify that a given semantic could be implemented either by a binding or by using SOAP headers. Nodes might use this information to decide whether to send particular headers—if you're running on top a secure binding, for instance, you might not need to add security headers to your messages, which can save your application effort and time. Also, since a variety of modules might be available to an engine at any given time, it would also be nice to be able to unambiguously indicate that a particular module performed a certain set of desired semantics. To achieve these goals, the first job was to have a standard way to name the semantics in question.

The SOAP authors came up with an extensibility framework that is described in section 3 of part 1 of the SOAP 1.2 spec. The framework revolves around the notion of an abstract *feature* 📖, which is essentially a semantic that has a name (a URI) and a specification explaining what it means. Features can be things like reliability, security, transactions, or anything you might imagine. A feature is typically specified by describing the behavior of each node involved in the interaction, any data that needs to be known before the feature does its thing, and any data that is transferred from node to node as a result. It's generally convenient if the specification of the feature's behavior can be found at the URI naming the feature—so if a user sees a reference to it somewhere, they can easily locate a description of what it does.

The state relevant to a feature is generally described in terms of named *properties* 📖. Properties, in the SOAP 1.2 sense, are pieces of state, named with URIs, which affect the operation of features. For instance, you might describe a "favorite color" feature that involves transferring a hexadecimal color value from one node to another. You would pick a URI for the feature, describe the rules of operation, and name the color property with another URI. Because a feature definition is abstract, you don't say anything about how this color would move across the wire.

Features are *expressed* (turned into reality via some mechanism) by *bindings* and *modules*. We've already described both of these—recall that a binding is a means for performing functions below the SOAP processing model, and a module is a means for performing functions using the SOAP processing model, via headers.

Here's a simple example of how a feature might be expressed by a binding in one case and a module in another. Imagine a "secure channel" feature. The specification for this feature indicates that it has the URI `http://skatestown.com/secureChannel`, and the abstract feature describes a message traveling from node to node in an unsnoopable fashion (to some reasonable level of security). We might then imagine a SOAP binding to the HTTPS protocol, which would specify that it implements the `http://skatestown.com/secureChannel` feature. Since HTTPS meets the security requirements of the abstract feature, the feature would be satisfied by the binding with no extra work, and the binding specification would indicate that it natively supports this feature. We could also imagine a SOAP module (something like WS-Security, which we discuss in Chapter 9, "Securing Web Services") that provides encryption and signing of a SOAP message across any binding. The module specification would also state that it implements the `secureChannel` feature. With this information in hand, it would be possible, in a situation that required a secure channel, to decide to engage our SOAP module in some situations (when using the HTTP binding, for instance) and to not bother in other situations where the HTTPS binding is in use.

Another example of making features concrete could be the color feature discussed earlier. The feature spec describes moving a color value from the sender to the receiver in the abstract. A custom binding over email might define a special SMTP header to carry this color information outside the SOAP envelope. Writing a SOAP module to satisfy the feature would involve defining a SOAP header that carried the value in the envelope.

Message Exchange Patterns

One common type of feature is a *Message Exchange Pattern (MEP)* 📖. An MEP specifies how many messages move around in a given interaction, where they originate, and where they end up. Each binding can (and must) support one or more message exchange patterns. The SOAP 1.2 spec defines two standard MEPs: Request-Response and SOAP Response. Without going into too much detail (you can find the full specifications for these MEPs in the SOAP 1.2 spec, part 2), we'll give you a flavor of what these MEPs are about.

The Request-Response MEP involves a requesting node and a responding node. As you might expect, it has the following semantics: First, the requesting node sends a SOAP message to the responding node. Then the responding node replies with a SOAP message that returns to the requesting node. See Figure 3.9.

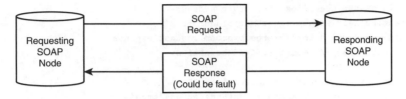

Figure 3.9   The Request-Response MEP

You should note a couple of important things here. First, the response message is correlated to the request message—in other words, the requesting node must be able to figure
out which response goes with which request. Since the MEP is abstract, though, it
doesn't specify *how* this correlation is achieved but leaves that up to implementations.
Second, if a fault is generated at the responding node, the fault is delivered in the
response message.

The SOAP Response MEP is similar to the Request-Response MEP, except for the
fact that the request message is explicitly *not* a SOAP message. In other words, the
request doesn't trigger the execution of the SOAP processing model on the receiving
node. The receiving node responds to the request with a SOAP message, as in the
Request-Response MEP (see Figure 3.10).

Figure 3.10   The SOAP Response MEP

The primary reason for introducing this strange-seeming MEP is to support REST-style
interactions with SOAP (see the sidebar "REST-Style versus Tunneled Web Services").
The SOAP Response MEP allows a request to be something as simple as an HTTP
GET; and since the responding node doesn't have to implement the SOAP processing
model, it can return a SOAP message in any way it deems appropriate. It might, for
instance, be an HTTP server with a variety of SOAP messages in its filesystem.

As you'll see in a moment, the HTTP binding natively supports both of these MEPs.
Of course, MEPs, like other abstract features, can also be implemented via SOAP modules. Here's an example of how the Request-Response MEP might be implemented
using SOAP headers across a transport that only allows one-way messages:

```
<soapenv:Envelope
  xmlns:soapenv="http://www.w3.org/2003/05/soap/envelope">
 <soapenv:Header>
```

```
<!--This header specifies the return address-->
<reqresp:ReplyTo soapenv:mustUnderstand="true"
   xmlns:reqresp="http://skatestown.com/requestResponse">
 <destination>udp://me.com:6666</destination>
</reqresp:ReplyTo>
<!--This header specifies a correlation ID-->
<reqresp:correlationID soapenv:mustUnderstand="true"
   xmlns:reqresp="http://skatestown.com/requestResponse">
   1234
</reqresp:correlationID>
 </soapenv:Header>
 <soapenv:Body>
 <doSomethingCool/>
 </soapenv:Body>
</soapenv:Envelope>
```

This message might have been sent in a UDP datagram, which is a one-way interaction. The receiver would have to understand these headers (since they're marked mustUnderstand) in order to process the message; when it generated a reply, it would follow the rules of the ReplyTo header and send the reply via UDP to port 6666 of host me.com. The reply would contain the same correlationID sent in the request, so that the receiver on me.com would be able to match the response to the pending request. The WS-Addressing spec includes a mechanism a lot like this, which we'll cover in Chapter 8, "Web Services and Stateful Resources."

If your interaction requires the request-response MEP, you might choose to use the HTTP binding (or any binding that implements that MEP natively), *or* you might use a SOAP module that specifies how to implement the MEP across other bindings. The important goal of the framework is to enable *abstractly* defining what functionality you need—then you're free to select appropriate implementations without tying yourself to a particular way of doing things.

REST-Style versus Tunneled Web Services

REpresentational State Transfer (REST) 📖 refers to an architectural style of building software that mirrors what HTTP is built to do: transfer representations of the state of named resources from place to place with a small set of methods (GET, POST, PUT, DELETE). The methods have various semantics associated with them—for instance, a GET is a request for a resource's representation, and by definition GETs should be safe operations. "Safe" in this context means they should have no side effects. So, you do a GET on my bank account URL in order to obtain your current balance, you can repeat that operation many times with no ill effects. However if the GET withdrew funds from your account, , that would clearly be a serious side effect (and therefore illegal in REST).

Another interesting thing to note about GET is that the results are often *cacheable*: If you do a GET on a weather report URL, the results probably won't change much if you do it again in 10 minutes. As a result, the infrastructure can cache the result, and if someone asks for the same GET again before the cache entry expires, you can return the cached data instead of going out over the Net to fetch the same weather again.

The HTTP infrastructure uses this caching style to great effect; most large ISPs or companies have shared caching proxies at the edge of the network that vastly reduce the network bandwidth outside the organization—each time anyone asks for `http://cnn.com`, the cache checks if a local, fresh copy exists before going out across the network.

We bring up REST because it shines light on an interesting controversy. REST advocates (sometimes known as RESTifarians) noticed that SOAP 1.1's HTTP binding mandated using the POST method. Since POSTs are *not* safe or cacheable in the same way GETs are, even simple SOAP requests to obtain data like stock quotes or weather reports had to use a mechanism that prevented the HTTP infrastructure from doing its job. Even though these operations might have been safe, SOAP was ignoring the HTTP semantic for safe operations and losing out on valuable caching behavior as a consequence.

This issue has since been fixed in the SOAP 1.2 HTTP binding, which supports the WebMethod feature. In other words, SOAP 1.2 is a lot more REST-friendly than SOAP 1.1 was, since it includes a specific technique for utilizing HTTP GET, including all that goes along with it in terms of caching support and operation safety. HTTP semantics are respected, and HTTP isn't always used as a tunnel for SOAP messages.

We believe that SOAP's flexible messaging and extensibility model (which supports both semantics provided by the underlying protocol and also those provided by higher-level extensions in the SOAP envelope) offer the right framework for supporting a large variety of architectural approaches. We hope this framework will allow the protocol both good uptake and longevity in the development community.

Features and Properties Redux

The features and properties mechanism in SOAP 1.2 is a powerful and flexible extensibility framework. By naming semantics, as well as the variables used to implement those semantics, we enable referencing those concepts in an unambiguous way. Doing so is useful for a number of reasons—as you'll see in Chapter 4, "Describing Web Services," naming semantics lets you express capabilities and requirements of your services in machine-readable form. This allows software to *reason* about whether a given service is compatible with particular requirements. In addition to the machine-readability aspect, naming features and properties allows multiple specifications to refer to the same concepts when describing functionality. This encourages good composition between extensions, and also allows future extensions to be written that implement identical (but perhaps faster, or more flexible) semantics.

Now that you understand the framework and its components, we'll go into more detail about the SOAP HTTP binding.

The HTTP Binding

You already know the HTTP binding is identified with the URI `http://www.w3.org/2003/05/soap/bindings/HTTP/` and that it supports both the Request-Response and the SOAP Response MEPs. Before we examine the other interesting facets of this binding, let's discuss how those MEPs are realized.

Since HTTP is natively a request/response protocol, when using the Request-Response MEP with the HTTP binding, the request/response semantics map directly to the equivalent HTTP messages. In other words, the SOAP request message travels in the HTTP request, and the SOAP response message is in the HTTP response. This is a great example of utilizing the native capabilities of an underlying protocol to implement an abstract feature.

The SOAP Response MEP is also implemented natively by the HTTP binding and is typically used with the GET Web method to retrieve representations of Web resources expressed as SOAP messages, or to make idempotent (safe) queries. When using this MEP this way, the non-SOAP request is the HTTP GET request, and the SOAP response message (or fault) comes back, as in the Request/Response case, in the HTTP response.

The HTTP binding also specifies how faults during the processing of a message map to particular HTTP status codes and how the semantics of HTTP status codes map to Web service invocations.

SOAP 1.1 Differences: Status Codes

In SOAP 1.1, the HTTP binding specified that if a fault was returned in an HTTP response, the status code had to be 500 (server error). This worked, but it didn't allow systems to use the inherent meaning in the HTTP status codes—400 means a problem with the sender, 500 means a problem with the receiver, and so on. SOAP 1.2 resolves this issue by specifying a richer set of fault codes; for example, if a soapenv:Sender fault is generated, indicating a problem with the request message, the engine should use the 400 HTTP status code when returning the fault. Other faults generate a 500, as in SOAP 1.1.

The HTTP binding also implements two abstract features, which are described next.

The SOAP Action Feature

In the SOAP 1.1 HTTP binding, you were required to send a custom HTTP header called SOAPAction along with SOAP messages. The purpose of this header was twofold: to let any system receiving the message know that the contents were SOAP and to convey the intent of the message via a URI. In SOAP 1.1, the first purpose was necessary because the media type was text/xml; since that media type could carry any XML document, processors needed to look inside the XML (which might involve an expensive parse) to check if it was a SOAP envelope. The SOAPAction header allowed them to realize this was a SOAP message and perhaps make decisions about routing or logging based on that knowledge. The presence of the header was enough to indicate that it was SOAP, but the URI could also convey more specific meaning, abstractly describing the intent of the message. Many implementations use this URI for dispatching to a particular piece of code on the backend, especially when using document-style SOAP. For example, you might send a purchase order as the body contents to two different methods—one called submitPO() and the other called validatePO(). Since the XML is the same in both cases, you could use the value of the SOAPAction URI to differentiate.

SOAP 1.2 uses the `application/soap+xml` media type, and the `SOAPAction` header is no longer needed to differentiate SOAP traffic from other XML documents moving across HTTP connections. But a lot of people still want a standard way to indicate a message's purpose outside of the SOAP envelope. The features and properties mechanism described earlier seemed like a perfect fit for an abstract feature.

The SOAPAction feature can be made available for any binding that uses the `application/soap+xml` media type to send its messages. The definition of that media type (which you can find in the glossary) specifies an optional `action` parameter, which is used in SOAP 1.2 instead of an HTTP-specific header to carry the `SOAPAction` URI. The feature has a single property, `http://www.w3.org/2003/05/soap/features/action/Action`. When this property is given a URI value, the spec indicates that the binding that implements the feature must place the value into the `action` parameter. So, if the property had the value `http://example.com/myAction` at the sender, the message would start like this (assuming the HTTP binding):

```
POST /axis/SomeService.jws
Content-Type: application/soap+xml; charset=utf-8;
➥action="http://example.com/myAction"
...rest of message...
```

On the receiving side, a node receiving a message with an `action` parameter over a binding that supports the SOAP Action feature is required to make the value of the `action` parameter available in the `http://www.w3.org/2003/05/soap/features/action/Action` property.

The Web Method Feature

Normal SOAP exchanges across HTTP use the POST HTTP verb. However, sometimes other HTTP methods are more appropriate for a given situation. For instance, when you use the SOAP Response MEP, you're often making a state query, which in HTTP is modeled with the GET verb. If you only allowed POST, you would be forcing HTTP into a particular limited set of uses (purely as a transport). Therefore, in an effort to allow developers to better integrate the semantics of SOAP with the semantics of HTTP, the Web Method Feature (defined in part 2 of the spec) was born.

This feature defines a single property, `http://www.w3.org/2003/05/soap/features/web-method/Method`, which contains one of the words GET, POST, PUT, or DELETE (although other values may be supported later). When sending a message, the HTTP binding will use the verb specified in this property instead of the default POST. This is most often used in concert with the SOAP Response MEP to implement REST semantics.

Right now this feature is only relevant to HTTP; but if other bindings are developed to underlying protocols with REST-like semantics, it would be available for them as well.

Using SOAP to Send Binary Data

Our example messages to date have been fairly small, but we can easily imagine wanting to use SOAP to send large binary blobs of data. For example, consider an automated insurance claim registry—remote agents might use SOAP-enabled software to submit new claims to a central server, and part of the data associated with a claim might be digital images recording damages or the environment around an accident. Since XML can't directly encode true 8-bit binary data at present, a simple way to do this kind of thing might be to use the XML Schema type `base64binary` and encode your images as base64 text inside the XML:

```
<soap:Envelope
  xmlns:soap="http://www.w3.org/2003/05/soap-envelope"
  xmlns:xsi="http://www.w3.org/2001/XMLSchema-instance">
 <soap:Body>
  <submitClaim>
    <accountNumber>5XJ45-3B2</accountNumber>
    <eventType>accident</eventType>
    <image imageType="jpg" xsi:type="base64binary">
      4f3e9b0...(rest of encoded image)
    </image>
  </submitClaim>
 </soap:Body>
</soap:Envelope>
```

This technique works, but it's not particularly efficient in terms of bandwidth, and it takes processing time to encode and decode bytes to and from base64. Email has been using the Multipurpose Internet Mail Extensions (MIME) standard for some time now to do this job, and MIME allows the encoding of 8-bit binary. MIME is also the basis for some of the data encoding used in HTTP; since HTTP software can usually deal with MIME, it might be nice if there were a way to integrate the SOAP protocol with this standard and a more efficient way of sending binary data.

SOAP with Attachments and DIME

In late 2000, HP and Microsoft released a specification called "SOAP Messages with Attachments." The spec describes a simple way to use the multiref encoding in SOAP 1.1 to reference MIME-encoded attachment parts. We won't go into much detail here; if you want to read the spec, you can find it at `http://www.w3.org/TR/2000/NOTE-SOAP-attachments-20001211`.

The basic idea behind *SOAP with Attachments (SwA)* 📖 is that you use the same HREF trick you saw in the section "Object Graphs" to insert a reference to the data in the SOAP message instead of directly encoding it. In the SwA case, however, you use the content-id (cid) of the MIME part containing the data you're interested in as the reference instead of the ID of some XML. So, the message encoded earlier would look something like this:

```
MIME-Version: 1.0
Content-Type: Multipart/Related; boundary=MIME_boundary;
type=application/soap+xml;start="<claim@insurance.com>"

--MIME_boundary
Content-Type: application/soap+xml; charset=UTF-8
Content-Transfer-Encoding: 8bit
Content-ID: <claim@insurance.com>

<soap:Envelope
  xmlns:soap="http://www.w3.org/2003/05/soap-envelope">
 <soap:Body>
  <submitClaim>
    <accountNumber>5XJ45-3B2</accountNumber>
    <eventType>accident</eventType>
    <image href="cid:image@insurance.com"/>
  </submitClaim>
 </soap:Body>
</soap:Envelope>

--MIME_boundary
Content-Type: image/jpeg
Content-Transfer-Encoding: binary
Content-ID: <image@insurance.com>

...binary JPG image...

--MIME_boundary--
```

Another technology called *Direct Internet Message Encapsulation (DIME)*, from
Microsoft and IBM, used a similar technique, except that the on-the-wire encoding was
smaller and more efficient than MIME. DIME was submitted to the IETF in 2002 but
has since lost the support of even its original authors.

SwA and DIME are great technologies, and they get the job done, but there are a few
problems. The main issue is that both SwA and DIME introduce a data structure that is
explicitly outside the realm of the XML data model. In other words, if an intermediary
received the earlier MIME message and wanted to digitally sign or encrypt the SOAP
body, it would need rules that told it how the content in the MIME attachment was
related to the SOAP envelope. Those rules weren't formalized for SwA/DIME.
Therefore, tools and software that work with the XML data model need to be modified
in order to understand the SwA/DIME packaging structure and have a way to access the
data embedded in the MIME attachments.

Various XML and Web service visionaries began discussing the general issue of merging binary content with the XML data model in earnest. As a result, several proposals are
now evolving to solve this problem in an architecturally cleaner fashion.

PASWA, MTOM, and XOP

In April 2003, the *"Proposed Infoset Addendum to SOAP With Attachments"* (PASWA) 📖 document was released by several companies including Microsoft, AT&T, and SAP. PASWA introduced a logical model for including binary content directly into a SOAP infoset. Physically, the messages that PASWA deals with look almost identical to our two earlier examples (the image encoded first as base64 inline with the XML and then as a MIME attachment)—the difference is in how we think about the attachments. Instead of thinking of the MIME-encoded image as a separate entity that is explicitly referred to in the SOAP envelope, we logically think of it as if it were still inline with the XML. In other words, the MIME packaging is an optimization, and implementations need to ensure that processors looking at the SOAP data model for purposes of encryption or signing still see the actual data as if it were base64-encoded in the XML.

In July 2003, after a long series of conversations between the XML Protocol Group and the PASWA supporters, the *Message Transmission Optimization Mechanism (MTOM)* 📖 was born, owned by the XMLP group. It reframed the ideas in PASWA into an abstract feature to better sync with the SOAP 1.2 extensibility model, and then offered an implementation of that feature over HTTP. The serialization mechanism is called *XML-Binary Optimized Packaging (XOP)* 📖; it was factored into a separate spec so that it could also be used in non-SOAP contexts.

As an example, we slightly modified the earlier insurance claim by augmenting the XML with a content-type attribute (from the XOP spec) that tells us what MIME content type to use when serializing this infoset using XOP. Here's the new version:

```
<soap:Envelope
  xmlns:soap="http://www.w3.org/2003/05/soap-envelope"
  xmlns:xsi="http://www.w3.org/2001/XMLSchema-instance"
  xmlns:xop-mime="http://www.w3.org/2003/12/xop/mime">
 <soap:Body>
  <submitClaim>
    <accountNumber>5XJ45-3B2</accountNumber>
    <eventType>accident</eventType>
    <image xop-mime:content-type="image/jpeg"
           xsi:type="base64binary">
      4f3e9b0...(rest of encoded image)
    </image>
  </submitClaim>
 </soap:Body>
</soap:Envelope>
```

An MTOM/XOP version of our modified insurance claim looks like this:

```
MIME-Version: 1.0
Content-Type: Multipart/Related; boundary=MIME_boundary;
type=application/soap+xml;start="<claim@insurance.com>"
```

```
--MIME_boundary
Content-Type: application/soap+xml; charset=UTF-8
Content-Transfer-Encoding: 8bit
Content-ID: <claim@insurance.com>

<soap:Envelope
  xmlns:soap="http://www.w3.org/2003/05/soap-envelope"
  xmlns:xop='http://www.w3.org/2003/12/xop/include'
  xmlns:xop-mime='http://www.w3.org/2003/12/xop/mime'>
 <soap:Body>
  <submitClaim>
    <accountNumber>5XJ45-3B2</accountNumber>
    <eventType>accident</eventType>
    <image xop-mime:content-type='image/jpeg'>
      <xop:Include href="cid:image@insurance.com"/>
    </image>
  </submitClaim>
 </soap:Body>
</soap:Envelope>

--MIME_boundary
Content-Type: image/jpeg
Content-Transfer-Encoding: binary
Content-ID: <image@insurance.com>

...binary JPG image...

--MIME_boundary--
```

Essentially, it's the same on the wire as the SwA version, but it uses the xop:Include> element instead of just the href attribute. The real difference is architectural, since we imagine tools and APIs will manipulate this message exactly as if it were an XML data model.

MTOM and XOP are on their way to being released by the XML Protocol Working Group some time in 2004, and it remains to be seen how well they will be accepted by the broader user community. Early feedback has been very positive, however, and the authors of this book are behind the idea of a unified data model for XML and binary content.

Small-Scale SOAP, Big-Time SOAP

To finish our coverage of the SOAP protocol in this chapter, we'll briefly examine how the simple rules of SOAP's design allow a lot of flexibility for implementations. Let's consider three different styles of SOAP processors and look at how this one baseline protocol can scale from the very small to the very large.

Imagine that a maker of scientific equipment has just released a new digital thermometer for the home. Being a forward-looking company, it decides to add a SOAP-over-HTTP interface so that other devices plugged into the home network can query the temperature. This thermometer has exactly one method, `getTemperature()`, which returns the current temperature in degrees Celsius. Since it's so simple, the vendor has built a single-purpose SOAP engine into the hardware. This engine doesn't include a full XML processor but instead uses simple pattern-matching with regular expressions to do three simple things:

- Check that the envelope looks right, and return a `VersionMismatch` fault if necessary.
- If any header blocks are targeted for the ultimate destination that are marked `mustUnderstand=true`, return a `mustUnderstand` fault.
- Confirm the `soap:Body` contains exactly one element with the `getTemperature` QName.

Despite its simplicity and extremely limited processing capability, our thermometer is perfectly SOAP 1.2 compliant. That means any other software that speaks SOAP can talk to it.

Our second example is a single-purpose application built to talk to a particular kind of Web service. SkatesTown might have built something like this in order to automate finding the lowest price on parts from its various suppliers (all of whom implement a standard RPC-style price checking service) each day. This sort of system typically has real XML parsing and uses shared libraries to manage the SOAP processing model, so that the developer doesn't have to rewrite the same `mustUnderstand`-checking logic again and again. It might also support one or two built-in extensions, such as a commonly supported security module. However, the capabilities of this system are determined when it's constructed, and it can't be dynamically extended.

Finally, let's consider a general-purpose middleware SOAP solution as you might implement it with a toolkit like Axis. Axis was designed to be a flexible framework that provides as much generic processing capability as possible while letting you build applications and extensions that easily plug in to the framework. It uses full-scale XML parsing, supports schema validation, and has a mechanism for building *handlers*—pieces of extension code that process SOAP messages in order to implement either local functionality (logging, management) or extension semantics (security, correlation).

The system in this example might be for a Grid computing system (see Chapter 8 for more) that needs to be able to talk to an unbounded variety of other services. Our SOAP engine has a variety of extensions for popular security, transactionality, reliability, and management protocols on top of SOAP. When conversations begin, an initial negotiation phase uses SOAP headers to determine which encryption protocols to use, whether the parties are legally allowed to transact business across the network, and what kind of notarization service will be used. Essentially, we use `mustUnderstand` headers to ask for the maximum level of functionality; then, if we receive errors, we back off to lower levels if appropriate. Once the business-level messages start to flow, they will be safely encrypted and contain SOAP headers to manage transactional context, handle routing through intermediaries, and ensure nonrepudiation. The system is also extensible by dropping in new JAR files and tweaking a few deployment descriptors.

So we've gone from a completely static, dumb system like a thermometer all the way to a richly functional B2B fabric—and SOAP's model of simple, well-layered abstractions has been the foundation throughout. Although it's true that the secure Grid client won't be able to make the thermometer talk at its level, the inherent capabilities of the SOAP processing model make it possible for the more functional client to find that out and to scale back (if appropriate) in order to talk to the simpler service.

Of course, wouldn't it be nice if there were standard ways for communicating parties to automatically find out about each other's capabilities *before* any messages even flow over the wire? There is such a way: It's called WSDL, and it's the subject of the next chapter.

Summary

We hope this chapter has demystified what SOAP is about and given you a good grounding in the essentials of the protocol and its behavior. You've seen how vertical (SOAP headers) and horizontal (intermediaries) extensibility, plus the binding framework, can be used to stretch the capabilities of the core in controlled ways. We'll return again and again to these extensibility concepts as we move through the examples in the rest of the book.

Of course, unless you plan to implement a SOAP engine on your own, you'll be using a toolkit to perform SOAP invocations. As such, we've also talked about Apache Axis, the open source SOAP engine that SkatesTown and SBC are using, and you've seen how the HTTP-based purchase order system can be converted into a SOAP Web service. You'll learn a lot more about Axis in Chapter 5, but before that we'll look at the other major pillar that makes up the foundation of Web services: the Web Service Description Language, or WSDL.

Resources

- *XML Protocol Working Group* (home of all SOAP 1.2 information)— http://www.w3.org/2000/xp/Group
- *SOAP 1.2 spec* (latest version)—http://www.w3.org/TR/SOAP
- *SOAP 1.2 Primer*—http://www.w3.org/TR/2003/REC-soap12-part0-20030624/
- *SOAP 1.1 spec*—http://www.w3.org/TR/2000/NOTE-SOAP-20000508/
- *SOAP with Attachments*—http://www.w3.org/TR/SOAP-attachments
- *MTOM*—http://www.w3.org/TR/soap12-mtom/
- *XOP*—http://www.w3.org/TR/xop10/

4

Describing Web Services

To this point, we've described XML and positioned it as the underpinning of the SOAP messaging protocol. Given that XML is a self-describing, human-readable representation of data, isn't that enough to make a SOAP message also self-describing? If so, then why do we need an approach for service descriptions? We'll answer these questions in this chapter.

Why Service Descriptions?

Let's look at this problem from the service requestor's perspective. A customer of SkatesTown wants to invoke the POSubmission service. How does the customer know what kind of message to send? Sure, they probably know to use SOAP, but SOAP is just the format of the envelope; SOAP itself doesn't indicate what message format to put into the envelope. The customer needs to understand what XML to put into the body of the SOAP envelope, whether a particular security SOAP header is required, what format the response message might come in, and whether a response is to be expected at all. The customer also needs to know what messaging protocol to use and where, exactly, to send the message. The customer may even determine that the service supports alternatives to SOAP; perhaps just straight HTTP POST of an XML message is all that is needed to submit the PO.

One way for the customer to determine what message to send is to examine a textual description of the service published on the SkatesTown Web site. Although doing so is simple, it could cause problems. The textual description may not be precise and can allow the customer's developers to misinterpret the specification. This results in too much trial and error on the customer's part to get the message format right.

Another approach is to include sample message formats in the documentation. The developer can then observe the samples and modify them to suit their company's needs. This approach is slightly better in that the developer can probably get the message format correct with fewer iterations, but the customer still must do too much hand-crafted code development. If each Web service required analysis, design, and coding to invoke, the Web services approach would quickly pass into the dustbin of technology history.

To make the job of invoking Web services easier for the service requestor, we need a formal mechanism to describe the service. This formal approach provides unambiguous specification of what the service requestor needs to do in order to invoke the Web service. As a result of the formality of the service description, software tool developers can provide tooling to automate the development of code to invoke Web services. Software tools help developers build Web services quickly from shared, industry-accepted Web service descriptions.

Role of Service Description in a Service-Oriented Architecture

Service description is key within a service-oriented architecture (SOA). A service description is involved in each of the three operations of SOA: publish, find, and bind.

Recall the SOA approach, depicted in Figure 4.1. The service provider publishes a service description to one or more service registries. The description of the service is published in service registries, not the actual code for the Web service itself. The service provider uses a service description to tell the service requestor everything it needs to know in order to properly understand how to invoke the Web service.

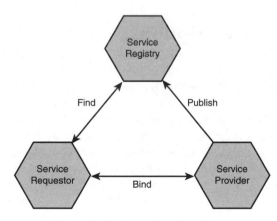

Figure 4.1 Service-oriented architecture

Similarly, the service description is central to the find operation. The service requestor uses aspects of the service description; for example, you might be looking for a Web service that implements a particular purchase order standard, as the basis for the find query to a service registry. In Chapter 6, "Discovering Web Services," we discuss service registries at length and describe the find and publish operations in more detail. The result of the find operation is ultimately a service description made available to the service requestor.

Why does the service provider publish a service description? To communicate to service requestors how to invoke a Web service. Why does a service requestor want to get hold of a service description? Because it describes exactly what needs to happen at the bind operation. Service description is key to the bind operation, describing exactly what message format needs to be delivered to what network address in order to invoke a Web service.

Well-Defined Service

What makes a good service description? What aspects of the Web service must be described in order for the Web service to be considered sufficiently defined?

A service description has two major components: its functional description and its nonfunctional description. The *functional description* defines details of how the Web service is invoked, where it's invoked, and so on. This description is focused on details of the syntax of the message and how to configure the network protocols to deliver the message. The *nonfunctional description* provides other details that are secondary to the message (such as security policy) but instruct the requestor's runtime environment to include additional SOAP headers (for example) or may influence whether a service requestor would choose to invoke the Web service. An example of the latter may be a privacy policy statement.

Functional Description

The functional description of a Web service describes what operations are available on the Web service and the syntax of the message required to invoke them; it defines the *Interface Definition Language (IDL)* 📖 for the Web service description. The IDL for Web services serves the same function as IDLs in other distributed computing approaches (see the section "History of IDLs"). Fundamentally, it's the functional description of the Web service that determines what the service requestor needs to do in order to invoke a Web service.

Like most things in Web services, XML is at the basis of service description. XML is the type system in Web services. As you saw in Chapter 3, "The SOAP Protocol," XML describes the datatypes for the elements that flow within the SOAP message and, in particular, within the SOAP payload. This XML needs to be formatted by the service requestor and interpreted by the service provider. Much of the effort within a Web services infrastructure (like Axis, IBM's WebSphere, or Microsoft's .NET) goes into properly encoding and decoding XML elements to/from native programming language objects.

The functional description can be decomposed into two major pieces: the *service implementation definition* 📖 and the *service interface definition* 📖. Both use the Web Services Description Language (WSDL) standard. We'll describe the WSDL language in more detail later in this chapter in the "Web Services Description Language (WSDL)" section.

The service implementation definition describes *where* the service is located or, more precisely, to which network address messages must be sent in order to invoke the Web service. The service interface definition describes exactly *what* messages need to be sent and *how* to use the various messaging protocols and encoding schemes in order to format messages in a manner acceptable to the service provider.

Nonfunctional Description

The functional description is important, but there is more that should be described about a Web service. Basically, a nonfunctional description can be characterized in contrast to the functional description. Whereas the functional description describes where to send the message, how the core application-specific message syntax needs to appear, and how to use the network transport protocols and message encoding schemes, the nonfunctional description addresses several other things including *why* a service requestor should invoke the Web service—for example, what business function the Web service addresses and how it fits into a broader business process. A nonfunctional description may also give more details about *who* the service provider is. For example, does the service provider provide auditing and ensure privacy? A nonfunctional description may also augment the *how* aspect of the service description, adding details about security and so on that aren't part of the domain-specific or business-process-specific nature of the message.

At the moment, the most widely adopted approach to describing nonfunctional requirements is the combination of two specifications: WS-Policy and WS-PolicyAttachment. Characteristics of the hosting environment could include the security policy in place at the service provider's endpoint, what levels of quality of service (QoS) are available to support Web service invocation, what kind of privacy policy is observed by the service provider, and so on. We go into more detail about these specifications later in the chapter. At one level, you can think of the nonfunctional description as aspects of the Web service that don't affect the shape of the application-specific parts of the message. Nonfunctional descriptions might have some influence on the syntax of the message (for example, adding security-related SOAP headers to the message), but the core, application-specific content of the payload of the message is derived from the functional description.

As we'll examine in Chapter 6, the UDDI service registry also has an impact on certain nonfunctional aspects of the service description. In particular, the taxonomy scheme supported by UDDI is another mechanism by which a service provider can describe what kind of service is being provided, what business function it supports, and what kind of business is providing the service.

Description Summary

Currently, most of the work in the standards community has been devoted to establishing and evolving the functional description of the service. The WSDL approach is well established, is the basis for standardization work in the W3C, is the basis for Web services runtime and tooling support from multiple vendors, and is used by the majority of Web services developers.

The standards related to the nonfunctional description are still being developed. WS-Policy and WS-PolicyAttachment exist, and work is under way to describe how these general frameworks can be used to describe discipline-specific policies such as security, QoS, and so on.

To summarize, a Web service is described using a combination of techniques. A Web service's description is used to unambiguously answer several questions about the Web service. Table 4.1 summarizes these questions and how they're addressed.

Table 4.1   **Roles of Each Layer of the Service Description Stack**

Question	Where Addressed
Who	Nonfunctional description
What	Service interface
Where	Service implementation
Why	Nonfunctional description
How	Service interface and nonfunctional description

For most of the remainder of this chapter, let's focus on the use of the WSDL 1.1 standard as the functional description of a Web service. Toward the end of the chapter, in the WS-Policy section, we'll briefly revisit the nonfunctional layers of the service description. We'll also examine the evolution of the WSDL 2.0 standardization activity within the W3C.

History of Interface Definition Languages (IDLs)

Before we dive into the WSDL discussion, a little background might be helpful. Every distributed computing approach has a mechanism for describing interfaces to components. Let's examine a brief history of IDLs.

IDLs have a long history in distributed computing. The major use of IDL came as part of the Open Software Foundation's Distributed Computing Environment (DCE) in its specification of RPC in 1994. DCE IDL was a breakthrough concept that quickly spread to other distributed computing initiatives, such as Object Management Group's (OMG) CORBA IDL and Microsoft's COM IDL and COM ODL (Object Definition Language). As with most such technologies, the various flavors of IDL are slightly different and, therefore, are more or less incompatible. WSDL brings unity to the Web services brand of distributed computing.

Most people used to developing simple software say, "Why bother defining the interfaces of any software operations? Just get a pointer/reference to an object or a function and make the call." The reason is that if a software system has even the slightest amount of heterogeneity, this simple approach won't work.

The best way to approach these problems is to agree on a bridging strategy. This strategy establishes common ground in the middle (the bridge) without worrying about how the roads at the endpoints are constructed. In distributed computing, a bridging strategy involves two parts:

1. Agreeing on *how* to make an invocation: the mechanics of naming, activation, data encoding, error handling, and so on. This is what distributed computing standards such as DCE, CORBA, and COM do.

2. Specifying *what* to call: the operation names, their signatures, return types, and any exceptions that they might generate. This is the job of IDL.

In a typical distributed computing architecture, a tool called an IDL compiler combines the information in an IDL file together with the conventions on how to make invocations to code-generate the pieces that make the bridge work. The client that wants to invoke operations uses a *client proxy* (sometimes called a *client stub*). The proxy has the same interface as the operation provider. It can be used as a local object on the client. The proxy implementation knows how to encode and marshal the invocation data to the operation provider and how to capture the operation result and return it to the client. The operation provider wraps its implementation inside a *skeleton* (sometimes called a *server stub*). The skeleton knows how to capture the data sent by the proxy and pass it to the implementation. It also knows how to package the result of operations and send it back to the client. Proxies and skeletons are helped by sophisticated distributed computing middleware. A key part of the story is that proxies and skeletons need not be generated by the same IDL compilers, as long as these compilers are following the same distributed computing conventions. This is the power of IDL—it describes everything necessary to make invocation possible in a distributed environment.

DCE IDL specified flat function interfaces. There was no notion of object instance contexts when making calls. CORBA IDL changed that by adding many important extensions to IDL. CORBA's IDL is the de facto IDL standard on non-Microsoft environments. It's also standardized internationally as ISO/IEC 14750.

CORBA's IDL is purely declarative; it provides no implementation details. It defines a remote object API concisely (the spec is less than 40 pages long) and covers key issues such as naming, complex type definition, in/out/in-out parameters, and exceptions. The syntax is reminiscent of C++ with some keywords to cover additional concepts. This IDL supports the notion of inheritance, which makes it convenient to describe object-oriented distributed systems. CORBA IDL even supports the notion of multiple interface inheritance, as in `MyPetTurtle` deriving from both `Pet` and `Animal`.

In a CORBA-enabled environment, the IDL can be used to invoke the CORBA object via dynamic invocation from a scripting language, generate proxies for client access to the object, generate implementation skeletons to be plugged into the CORBA middleware, and store information about the implementation in an *interface repository* (a central store of meta-data about CORBA components' interfaces)—all without being tied to a specific implementation language.

Microsoft's ODL isn't syntax-compatible, or even concept-compatible, with CORBA IDL. However, apart from syntactical differences, COM objects can be used in a fashion similar to CORBA objects.

Programmers working with modern languages, such as Java, C#, and any other .NET Common Language Runtime (CLR) languages can typically engage in distributed computing applications without having to worry much about IDL. Has IDL become irrelevant in these cases? Not at all! IDL isn't present on the surface, but IDL concepts are working behind the scenes.

Both Java and the CLR languages are fully introspectable. This means a compiled language component carries complete meta-data about itself, such as information about its parent class, properties, methods, and any supported interfaces. This information is sufficient to replace the need for an explicit IDL description of the component. That is why, for example, Java developers can invoke the RMI compiler directly on their object without having to generate IDL first.

However, in the cases where these languages need to interoperate with components built using other programming languages, there is no substitute for IDL. Separating interfaces from implementations is the only guaranteed mechanism for ensuring the potential for interoperability across programming languages, platforms, machines, address spaces, memory models, and object versions. On the Web, where heterogeneity is the rule, this is more important than ever.

Web Services Description Language (WSDL)

WSDL is used to describe the message syntax associated with the invocation and response of a Web service. WSDL version 1.1 was submitted to the W3C for standardization by IBM, Microsoft, and a number of other companies in March 2001. The current version of the specification is available at http://www.w3.org/TR/wsdl. WSDL 1.1 forms the basis for the current standards work in this area, WSDL version 2.0. We'll discuss WSDL 2.0 later in this chapter.

A WSDL service description is an XML document conformant to the WSDL schema definition. A WSDL 1.1 document, without any extensions, isn't a complete service description, but rather it covers the functional description of the service. WSDL is the IDL for Web services. Essentially, a WSDL description describes three fundamental properties of a Web service:

- *What* a service does—The operations (methods) the service provides, and the data (arguments and returns) needed to invoke them
- *How* a service is accessed—Details of the data formats and protocols necessary to access the service's operations
- *Where* a service is located—Details of the protocol-specific network address, such as a URL

WSDL Information Model

The WSDL information model takes full advantage of the separation between abstract specifications and concrete implementations of these specifications. This reflects the split between service interface definition (abstract interface) and service implementation definition (concrete implementation at a network endpoint).

Like all good applications of XML, the WSDL schema defines several high-level or major elements in the language. Let's look at Web service description in terms of the major elements in WSDL:

- `portType`—A Web service's abstract interface definition (think Java interface definition) where each child `operation` element defines an abstract *method* signature.

- `message`—Defines the format of the message, or a set of parameters, referred to by the method signatures or operations. A message can be further decomposed into `parts` (think detailed method parameter format definitions).

- `types`—Defines the collection of all the datatypes used in the Web service as referenced by various message part elements (think base datatypes; think XML).

- `binding`—Contains details of how the elements in an abstract interface (`portType`) are converted into a concrete representation in a particular combination of data formats and protocols (think encoding schemes; think SOAP over HTTP).

- `port`—Expresses how a binding is deployed at a particular network endpoint (think details about a particular server on a particular network location; think place where you specify HTTP URL).

- `service`—A poorly named element. A named collection of ports (think arbitrary bag of Web services endpoints).

So the `portType` (with details from the `message` and `type` elements) describes the *what* of the Web service. The `binding` describes the *how*, and WSDL `port` and `service` describe the *where* of the Web service.

Figure 4.2 shows one perspective on the relationships between the elements in WSDL.

The figure shows one possible view of the organization of the WSDL information model. You can see a clear relationship between the abstract and concrete notions of message and operation as contained in the `portType` and `binding`. The words in bold on the diagram signify the terms from the WSDL specification. The element names used in WSDL are somewhat confusing because no consistent naming convention allows you to distinguish between abstract and concrete concepts. For example, `portType` could have been called `AbstractInterface` and binding called `ConcreteInterface`. You have to memorize which elements represent abstract concepts and which elements represent concrete concepts.

At first glance, WSDL seems complicated. Don't worry; we'll explain the components in more detail. Part of this appearance is due to the factoring chosen by the WSDL authors. This complexity feels a lot like the complexity observed with a highly normalized relational data model. WSDL 2.0 reduces some of this complexity (but adds different complexity of its own). Although the same information might be more succinctly expressed, the flexibility that results from the factoring in WSDL is occasionally necessary. So, just as you might have learned to understand highly normalized relational models, practice with reading WSDL documents will help you to focus on the important aspects of a Web service description.

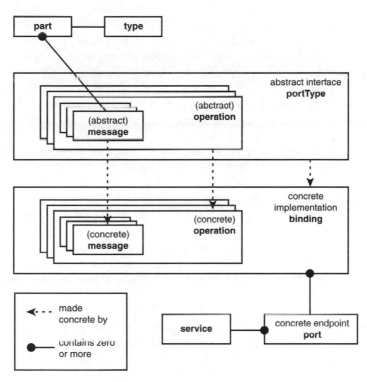

Figure 4.2   The WSDL information model

Origin of WSDL

WSDL wasn't the first IDL language for Web services. IBM developed a language called Network Accessible Service Specification Language (NASSL) to further early internal adoption of SOAP. Meanwhile, Microsoft developed SOAP Contract Language (SCL), which was an evolution of Microsoft's earlier attempt at a SOAP IDL called Service Definition Language.

IBM and Microsoft realized that having competing IDLs would hinder rapid adoption of Web services. WSDL is the result of hard work and compromise in merging NASSL and SCL. As a result of this merger, a single ubiquitous mechanism describes the interface definition of Web services: WSDL.

Parts of the WSDL Language

Let's take a closer look at the parts of a WSDL description. Although we examine these elements in detail, you don't have to become an expert in WSDL; the software industry continues to churn out tools to generate WSDL from existing IT assets like COM objects and Enterprise JavaBeans (EJBs) and to generate client-side stubs or proxies (access mechanism helper classes) from WSDL to ease the burden of invoking Web services by the service requestor. Later in this chapter, we'll sketch how WSDL translates to Java; and in Chapter 5, "Implementing Web Services with Apache Axis," we'll examine the WSDL tooling available in Axis. However, by reviewing WSDL, you will get a good background in case the tools don't generate exactly the WSDL or Java to fit your particular needs. In certain circumstances, WSDL descriptions must be hand crafted, and client and Web service implementation code must be manually developed.

Let's discuss the WSDL language in the context of a WSDL example. We'll start with a simple use of WSDL: SkatesTown's priceCheck service. Later, we'll examine more advanced WSDL concepts by reviewing SkatesTown's StockAvailableNotification service and the POSubmission service. When we review SkatesTown's use of WSDL, we'll comment on various best practices with WSDL design. In particular, we'll comment on various points raised by Web Service Interoperability (WS-I) Organization that clarify how to build interoperable WSDL descriptions of Web services. We cover WS-I in more detail in Chapter 13, "Web Services Interoperability."

This chapter will help get you started understanding WSDL. The best way to learn WSDL is to examine a collection of WSDL documents. You can find an excellent registry of WSDL documents at the SalCentral Web services brokerage (http://www.salcentral.com) or the XMethods Web site (http://www.xmethods.net). After a little practice, reading a WSDL document will become as familiar as reading Java code.

Simple WSDL

The priceCheck service was built in response to growing demand from customers to extend the inventoryCheck Web service to include price information as well as availability. The priceCheck Web service is an extension of the inventoryCheck Web service, allowing a requestor to determine the price of one of SkatesTown's products. It's invoked with a product SKU number, and the response is a price and the number of units of that item currently available from inventory. The entire priceCheck WSDL document is shown in Listing 4.1.

Listing 4.1 **The priceCheck WSDL Document**

```
<?xml version="1.0"?>
<definitions name="PriceCheck"
    targetNamespace="http://www.skatestown.com/services/PriceCheck"
    xmlns:pc="http://www.skatestown.com/services/PriceCheck"
    xmlns:avail="http://www.skatestown.com/ns/availability"
    xmlns:wsi="http://ws-i.org/schemas/conformanceClaim/"
    xmlns:xsd="http://www.w3.org/2001/XMLSchema"
```

Listing 4.1   **Continued**

```
xmlns:soap="http://schemas.xmlsoap.org/wsdl/soap/"
xmlns="http://schemas.xmlsoap.org/wsdl/">

<!-- Type definitions -->
<types>
   <xsd:schema
      targetNamespace="http://www.skatestown.com/ns/availability" >

      <xsd:element name="sku" type="xsd:string" />

      <xsd:complexType name="availabilityType">
         <xsd:sequence>
            <xsd:element ref="avail:sku"/>
            <xsd:element name="price" type="xsd:double"/>
            <xsd:element name="quantityAvailable" type="xsd:integer"/>
         </xsd:sequence>
      </xsd:complexType>

      <xsd:element name="StockAvailability"
                   type="avail:availabilityType" />
   </xsd:schema>
</types>

<!-- Message definitions -->
<!-- A PriceCheckRequest is simply an item code (sku)  -->
<message name="PriceCheckRequest">
   <part name="sku" element="avail:sku"/>
</message>

<!-- A PriceCheckResponse consists of an availability structure,   -->
<!-- defined above in the types element.                           -->
<message name="PriceCheckResponse">
   <part name="result" element="avail:StockAvailability"/>
</message>

<!-- Port type definitions -->
<portType name="PriceCheckPortType">
   <operation name="checkPrice">
      <input message="pc:PriceCheckRequest"/>
      <output message="pc:PriceCheckResponse"/>
   </operation>
</portType>

<!-- Binding definitions -->
<binding name="PriceCheckSOAPBinding" type="pc:PriceCheckPortType">
```

Listing 4.1   **Continued**

```
    <soap:binding
    style="document" transport="http://schemas.xmlsoap.org/soap/http" />
    <operation name="checkPrice">
       <soap:operation
    soapAction="http://www.skatestown.com/services/PriceCheck/checkPrice" />
       <input>
          <soap:body use="literal" />
       </input>
       <output>
          <soap:body use="literal" />
       </output>
    </operation>
  </binding>

  <service name="PriceCheck">
    <port name="PriceCheck" binding="pc:PriceCheckSOAPBinding">
      <soap:address location="http://www.skatestown.com/services/PriceCheck"/>
    </port>
  </service>

</definitions>
```

Structure of a WSDL Document: Definitions

The root element of a WSDL document is a `definitions` element. A WSDL `definitions` contains all the other WSDL elements (we'll examine each element in its own section). A `definitions` element can contain the following (in recommended order of appearance):

- Zero or more `documentation` elements
- Zero or more `import` elements
- Optionally, one `types` element
- Zero or more `message` elements
- Zero or more `portType` elements (usually just one)
- Zero or more `binding` elements (usually just one, for the `portType` element)
- Zero or more `service` elements (again, usually just one)

A WSDL document must conform to the XML Schema defined for the WSDL language and available at `http://schemas.xmlsoap.org/wsdl/2003-02-11.xsd`.

The `definitions` element contains a `name` attribute (the name usually corresponds to the name of the Web service), which is purely for purposes of documentation. The `definitions` element also defines the `targetNamespace` attribute (a namespace URI) for the entire WSDL file. This `targetNamespace` attribute is critical to understanding how to form QNames of `portTypes`, `bindings`, and so on, and how to combine WSDL descriptions that span multiple files. Of course, the usual XML namespace (`xmlns:`) declarations also typically appear in the `definitions` element.

The following is the `definitions` element from the `priceCheck` WSDL:

```
<?xml version="1.0"?>
<definitions name="PriceCheck"
    targetNamespace="http://www.skatestown.com/services/PriceCheck"
    xmlns:pc="http://www.skatestown.com/services/PriceCheck"
    xmlns:avail="http://www.skatestown.com/ns/availability"
    xmlns:wsi="http://ws-i.org/schemas/conformanceClaim/"
    xmlns:xsd="http://www.w3.org/2001/XMLSchema"
    xmlns:soap="http://schemas.xmlsoap.org/wsdl/soap/"
    xmlns="http://schemas.xmlsoap.org/wsdl/">
. . .
</definitions>
```

Except for the value of the `name` attribute `targetNamespace` attribute and the various `xmlns:` declarations, you'll see this pattern at the beginning of every WSDL document.

PortType

The best starting point to understanding a WSDL document is the `portType` element. The `portType` describes the interface to a Web service. Just as a Java interface definition is comprised mainly of method signatures, the interesting part of a `portType` definition is the collection of `operation` elements it contains.

This is the most succinct description of what the service does; understand the `portType`, and you understand what the Web service does. The rest of the elements in the WSDL definition are essentially details that the `portType` depends on; we'll examine them in later sections.

The `portType` in the `priceCheck` service description looks like this:

```
<!-- Port type definitions -->
<portType name="PriceCheckPortType">
    <operation name="checkPrice">
        <input message="pc:PriceCheckRequest"/>
        <output message="pc:PriceCheckResponse"/>
    </operation>
</portType>
```

The `priceCheck` `portType` is about as simple as `portTypes` can get. It defines one operation: `checkPrice`. We'll study the `checkPrice` operation in more detail in the next section, but first, a few more thoughts about `portTypes`.

A WSDL document can contain zero or more `portType` definitions. Typically, WSDL documents contain a single `portType`. Using this convention separates different Web service interface definitions into different documents. This granularity of separation is good for reasons of reuse; when we discuss how UDDI can be used to register WSDL documents (in Chapter 6), it will become apparent why this is a best practice.

A `portType` has a single `name` attribute. In our case, the `priceCheck` Web service contains a `portType` of name `PriceCheckPortType`. Often, you'll see the name of the `portType` follow this pattern: *nameOfWebService*`PortType`. If a WSDL file contains multiple `portTypes`, each `portType` must have a different name. The name of the `portType` together with the namespace of the WSDL document (refer to the discussion of the `definitions` element) define a unique name for the `portType`. This unique name, or QName, is the way the `portType` is referenced by other components of WSDL.

Simple, well-factored Web services often result in simple looking `portTypes`. Much of the detail is in the rest of the elements in the WSDL definition; and as far as the `portType` element is concerned, the detail is in the collection of `operation` child elements.

Operation

An `operation` in WSDL is the equivalent of a method signature in Java. An `operation` defines a method on a Web service, including the name of the method and the input parameters and the output or return type of the method.

The `PriceCheck` `portType` describes one `operation`, named (cleverly) `checkPrice`. The `checkPrice` operation defines an input message and output message. If we invoke the `checkPrice` operation with a `priceCheckRequestMessage` (you'll see what these messages look like in the next section), the Web service returns a `priceCheckResponseMessage`. Note that the input elements and output elements are associated with a `message` and use the QName style of referencing. As it turns out, messages also have QNames.

> **Note**
> When you're designing WSDL `portTypes`, you should be careful with the names of the `portType`'s operations: They should all be different.

The `operation` elements define a combination of input, output, and fault messages. The different combinations are the subject of advanced WSDL concepts covered later in this chapter.

Message

A `message` is a simple concept. It's the construct that describes the abstract form of an input, output, or fault message. The `message` is modeled either as an XML document (document-centric) or as the parameters in a method call (RPC-style messaging).

A WSDL document can contain zero or more `message` elements. Each `message` has a name, which must be unique within the WSDL document, and contains a collection of `part` elements.

Let's look at the `messages` defined in the `priceCheck` WSDL:

```
<!-- Message definitions -->
<!-- A PriceCheckRequest is simply an item code (sku)  -->
<message name="PriceCheckRequest">
   <part name="sku" element="avail:sku"/>
</message>

<!-- A PriceCheckResponse consists of an availability structure,  -->
<!-- defined above in the types element.                          -->
<message name="PriceCheckResponse">
   <part name="result" element="avail:StockAvailability"/>
</message>
```

The first `message`, `PriceCheckRequest`, is a simple message element. Recall that `PriceCheckRequest` is used as the input message to the `checkPrice` operation. The `PriceCheckRequest` message defines one `part` element named `sku`.

Part

`Message` elements aren't terribly interesting; they're just collections of `parts`. However, `parts` are quite interesting. The `parts` mechanism in WSDL allows a `message` to be decomposed into smaller units or parts. Each `part` can be manifested in different ways depending on the network protocol chosen for the Web service. This mapping between `parts` and protocol-specific components is described in the `binding` element. Some `parts` can appear as SOAP `header` elements, some can be mapped to HTTP headers, and some can be used as individual parameters in an RPC message or to form the body of a document-centric message. You can't understand the true use of a `part` until you look at how the abstract notion of the `part` is mapped into a concrete data representation. This mapping is the responsibility of the `binding` element. We'll examine how different `parts` are modeled as different components of a message later in this chapter.

A `part` element is made up of two properties: the name of the `part` and the kind of the `part`. The name property is represented by the `name` attribute, which must be unique among all the `part` child elements of the `message` element. The kind property of the `part` is defined as either a `type` attribute (a `simpleType` or `complexType` from the XSD schema type system) or an `element` attribute (also defined by referring to an `element` defined in XML schema). You choose one of these attributes to represent the kind of `part` being described. You can't use both an `element` attribute and a `type` attribute to define the same part. (We'll examine XML Schema elements and types in more detail in the next section.) Often, the name of the `part` says it all, and you need not dive into the details of how the types associated with the `part` are modeled. As you'll see later, the `sku` part will turn into a method parameter in the service invocation.

The choice of using `element` or `type` when defining the `part` is very important. When you use the `element` attribute, you're specifying that the payload of the message on the wire should be precisely that XML element. For example, the

PriceCheckRequest example (listed earlier) specifies that the XML element named sku
from the http://www.skatestown.com/ns/availability namespace must be used as
the body of the message. Here's an example of what a PriceCheckRequest message
would look like on the wire:

```
<?xml version="1.0" encoding="UTF-8"?>
<soapenv:Envelope
   xmlns:soapenv="http://schemas.xmlsoap.org/soap/envelope/"
   xmlns:xsd="http://www.w3.org/2001/XMLSchema"
   xmlns:xsi="http://www.w3.org/2001/XMLSchema-instance">
   <soapenv:Body>
      <sku xmlns="http://www.skatestown.com/ns/availability">123</sku>
    </soapenv:Body>
</soapenv:Envelope>
```

Note how the body contains exactly the specified sku element. The element attribute
should be used to define the type of the part when the Web service is meant to be document oriented. (We'll discuss how to specify a document-oriented Web service later in
this chapter when we review the WSDL binding element.) Whenever the element
attribute is used, its value must refer to a global XML element declared (or imported) in
an XML schema in the types section.

The only other message element defined in the priceCheck WSDL is
PriceCheckResponse, which describes the format of the output message of the
checkPrice operation. Like its companion message, PriceCheckResponse defines a single part. Here's what a PriceCheckResponse message looks like on the wire:

```
<?xml version="1.0" encoding="UTF-8"?>
<soapenv:Envelope
  xmlns:soapenv=http://schemas.xmlsoap.org/soap/envelope/
  xmlns:xsd="http://www.w3.org/2001/XMLSchema"
  xmlns:xsi="http://www.w3.org/2001/XMLSchema-instance">
 <soapenv:Body>
  <StockAvailability xmlns="http://www.skatestown.com/ns/availability">
   <sku>123</sku>
   <price xmlns="">100.0</price>
   <quantityAvailable xmlns="">12</quantityAvailable>
  </StockAvailability>
 </soapenv:Body>
</soapenv:Envelope>
```

Note how the response message contains exactly what the WSDL message said it would,
an element named StockAvailability from the http://www.skatestown.com/ns/
availability namespace.

The PriceCheckRequest example could have been built differently, using a part
defined with the type attribute, like this:

```
<!-- Message definitions -->
<!-- A PriceCheckRequest is simply an item code (sku)  -->
```

```
<message name="PriceCheckRequest">
   <part name="sku" type="xsd:string"/>
</message>
```

In this case, we don't explicitly indicate that a particular XML element is required to be the sku in the PriceCheckRequest message on the wire. Rather, the element must have xsd:string as its type. As you'll see later, the element is determined by the binding. Here's an example of a valid PriceCheckRequest request message, using the RPC-style suggested by this form of the PriceCheckRequest message:

```
<?xml version="1.0" encoding="UTF-8"?>
<soapenv:Envelope xmlns:soapenv="http://schemas.xmlsoap.org/soap/envelope/"
   xmlns:xsd="http://www.w3.org/2001/XMLSchema"
   xmlns:xsi="http://www.w3.org/2001/XMLSchema-instance">
 <soapenv:Body>
  <ns1:checkPrice soapenv:encodingStyle="http://schemas.xmlsoap.org/soap/encoding/"
      xmlns:ns1="http://www.skatestown.com/services/PriceCheck">
   <sku xsi:type="xsd:string">123</sku>
  </ns1:checkPrice>
 </soapenv:Body>
</soapenv:Envelope>
```

The PriceCheckResponse example could also have been built using a part defined with the type attribute. This form of the message would look like this:

```
<!-- A PriceCheckResponse consists of an availability structure,   -->
<!-- defined above.                                                 -->
<message name="PriceCheckResponse">
   <part name="result" type="avail:availabilityType"/>
</message>
```

The result part is slightly more interesting because its type is any element whose complex type is the availabilityType from the namespace corresponding to the avail: prefix. Here's an example of a valid response message:

```
<?xml version="1.0" encoding="UTF-8"?>
<soapenv:Envelope
   xmlns:soapenv="http://schemas.xmlsoap.org/soap/envelope/"
   xmlns:xsd="http://www.w3.org/2001/XMLSchema"
   xmlns:xsi="http://www.w3.org/2001/XMLSchema-instance">
 <soapenv:Body>
  <ns1:checkPriceResponse
    soapenv:encodingStyle="http://schemas.xmlsoap.org/soap/encoding/"
    xmlns:ns1="http://www.skatestown.com/services/PriceCheck">
     <result href="#id0"/>
  </ns1:checkPriceResponse>
  <multiRef id="id0"
    soapenc:root="0"
```

```
     soapenv:encodingStyle="http://schemas.xmlsoap.org/soap/encoding/"
     xsi:type="ns2:availabilityType"
     xmlns:soapenc="http://schemas.xmlsoap.org/soap/encoding/"
     xmlns:ns2="http://www.skatestown.com/ns/availability">
       <sku xsi:type="xsd:string">123</sku>
       <price xsi:type="xsd:double">100.0</price>
       <quantityAvailable xsi:type="xsd:integer">12</quantityAvailable>
  </multiRef>
 </soapenv:Body>
</soapenv:Envelope>
```

In this case, an element named `result` and the contents of this element are defined using an href to the actual contents.

You can see that the separation of `messages` from the `operation` is well factored, but it's overkill for our simple SkatesTown examples. Many WSDL documents don't require the full power achieved by factoring `messages` from `operations` and decomposing `messages` into `parts`. Some uses of WSDL (for example, those that describe multipart MIME messages) exploit the flexibility of the WSDL part mechanism.

Types

You've seen the `message` element in WSDL and its `parts`. However, some of the types used in these example WSDL documents need further discussion.

The default type system in WSDL is XML Schema (XSD). To build interoperable Web services, the WSDL should only use datatypes defined using XML Schema. XML Schema can be used to describe all the types used in the messages to invoke a Web service.

The `types` element in the `priceCheck` WSDL is typical of the use of this element:

```
<!-- Type definitions -->
<types>
   <xsd:schema
      targetNamespace="http://www.skatestown.com/ns/availability" >

      <xsd:element name="sku" type="xsd:string" />

      <xsd:complexType name="availabilityType">
         <xsd:sequence>
            <xsd:element ref="avail:sku"/>
            <xsd:element name="price" type="xsd:double"/>
            <xsd:element name="quantityAvailable" type="xsd:integer"/>
         </xsd:sequence>
      </xsd:complexType>

      <xsd:element name="StockAvailability"
                   type="avail:availabilityType" />
   </xsd:schema>
</types>
```

The `types` element is essentially a place for the WSDL document to define user-defined XML types and elements for later use in the `parts` elements. A WSDL document can have at most one `types` element. When a `types` element appears in a WSDL document, it typically contains a single `schema` definition element, as you saw with the `priceCheck` WSDL. However, it's legal (but not recommended) to have more than one `schema` element contained by a `types` element.

> **Note**
>
> Many organizations have modeled their data objects as XML schemas. Because WSDL `types` is defined to contain `schema` definition element(s), WSDL can import these definitions, and you don't have to duplicate work already done in XML schema. Business objects already modeled in XML can be imported and then used to define `parts` of `messages` and, therefore, used to define the input and output messages for the Web services `operations`. When you want to use existing XML types and elements in your WSDL, use an XML schema import element within the `types` element.

Many WSDL documents don't include a `types` element with much more than an import statement. Consider the following `types` element from a `POSubmission` Web service:

```
<!-- Type definitions -->
<types>
   <xsd:schema>
   <!-- rest of invoice schema definition from chapter 2
        assumes XSD file is in same directory         -->
   <xsd:import namespace="http://www.skatestown.com/ns/invoice"
               schemaLocation="http://www.skatestown.com/schema/invoice.xsd"/>

   <!-- rest of purchaseOrder schema definition from chapter 2
        assumes XSD file is in same directory         -->
   <xsd:import namespace="http://www.skatestown.com/ns/po"
               schemaLocation="http://www.skatestown.com/schema/po.xsd"/>
   </xsd:schema>
</types>
```

All this schema defines is two `import` statements. Now any of the datatypes and elements defined in the `invoice.xsd` and `po.xsd` XML Schema files can be used to define `parts` in this WSDL file. The `schemaLocation` attribute indicates that these files can be found in the same directory as the WSDL file. Note that unlike the `types` element from the `priceCheck` WSDL, this WSDL doesn't define a `targetNamespace` as part of its schema element. This is good practice *only* when the `schema` element contains just `import` element children. If you use the `schema` element in the `types` part of your WSDL to define XML datatypes or elements, put a `targetNamespace` attribute on it. Many WSDL designers use the same `targetNamespace` for their `schema` element as they do for the entire WSDL `definitions` element.

For the `priceCheck` WSDL, the `availability` type is defined by a `schema` element within a WSDL `types` element. Recall that the `availability` type was used as part of the `PriceCheckResponse message`. This is all standard XML Schema work that we covered in Chapter 2, "XML Primer." You can use any XML Schema construct within the `schema` element defined in a WSDL `types` element.

WSDL is quite flexible in the type system used. Although XML Schema is the predominant type system used, the `types` element allows you the flexibility to describe a completely different type system. WSDL `types` lets you describe another type system, say the Java type system, and define all the messages in terms of this type system. The use of this flexibility is theoretical; it's rare in practice. Consider that deviating from the XML schema type system increases the chances that more service requestors will be unable to invoke your Web service.

> **Note**
>
> There are several variants of XML schema; schema has been under development by the W3C for several years. The XML Schema version referenced in the listings is `http://www.w3.org/2001/XMLSchema`. You might also encounter other versions used in `types` elements such as `http://www.w3.org/2000/10/XMLSchema` and `http://www.w3.org/1999/XMLSchema`. These declarations have subtle implications on some sophisticated use of the XML schema language. Consult advanced resources on XML schema for more detail. As time moves on, uses of these older versions of schema become rarer. To make sure your Web service is maximally interoperable, use the `http://www.w3.org/2001/XMLSchema` version.

Binding

You've seen that a `portType`, like the `PriceCheckPortType`, defines one or more `operations`, and you have some idea about the sorts of XML types and elements these operations need as input and produce for output. However, you still don't know how to format the `message` to invoke these operations. We haven't seen anything in the WSDL description that relates to SOAP headers, SOAP bodies, SOAP encoding, and so on. The `portType`, `message`, and `type` elements define the *abstract* or *reusable* portion of the WSDL definition. Is this service invoked by a SOAP message or a simple HTTP POST of an XML payload? Is this an RPC invocation or a document-centric message invocation? These details are given by one or more `binding` elements associated with the `portType`.

The `binding` element in WSDL tells the service requestor how to format the `message` in a protocol-specific manner. Each `portType` can have one or more `binding` elements associated with it. For a given `portType`, a `binding` element can describe how to invoke operations using a particular messaging/transport protocol, like SOAP over HTTP, SOAP over SMTP, a simple HTTP POST operation, or any other valid combination of networking and messaging protocol standards.

Let's look at the binding element in the priceCheck WSDL:

```
<binding name="PriceCheckSOAPBinding" type="pc:PriceCheckPortType">
    <soap:binding style="document"
        transport="http://schemas.xmlsoap.org/soap/http" />
    <operation name="checkPrice">
        <soap:operation
            soapAction=
                "http://www.skatestown.com/services/PriceCheck/checkPrice" />
        <input>
            <soap:body use="literal" />
        </input>
        <output>
            <soap:body use="literal" />
        </output>
    </operation>
</binding>
```

The name of this binding element is PriceCheckSOAPBinding. The name must be unique among all the binding elements defined in the WSDL document. Conventionally, the name of the binding combines the portType name with the name(s) of the protocol(s) to which the binding maps. You often see the word *binding* appended to the name. The type attribute identifies which portType this binding describes. Because WSDL uses a QName reference to link the binding element to a portType, you can see why portType name uniqueness is so important. You'll see the same is true for binding name uniqueness when we discuss how a port references a binding.

Typically, most WSDL documents contain only a single binding. The reason is similar to why conventional WSDL documents contain a single portType element: convenience of document reuse.

Now, to which protocol is this binding mapping the priceCheck portType? We need to look for clues inside the binding element (besides the naming convention, of course). The first clue is the XML namespace of the first child element (the prefix of the element is soap:). This is a strong hint that this binding is related to the SOAP messaging protocol. So, the PriceCheckSOAPBinding element describes how the priceCheck portType (remember, priceCheck is an abstract service interface definition) is expressed using SOAP. Most Web services you see in practice have at least a SOAP binding defined for them. You can define other bindings in addition to the SOAP/HTTP binding.

WSDL defines a clever extensibility convention that allows the binding to be extended with elements from different XML namespaces to describe bindings to any number of messaging and transport protocols. Pick a messaging/transport protocol set, find the WSDL convention that corresponds to that pair, and fill in the details. The WSDL spec defines three standard binding extensions for SOAP/HTTP, HTTP GET/POST, and SOAP with MIME attachments.

The `PriceCheckSOAPBinding` element shown earlier decorates the `priceCheck` `portType` in four ways (invocation style, `SOAPAction`, input message appearance, and output message appearance), as explained in the following sections. This is a straightforward use of the SOAP binding extension convention defined in the WSDL specification. We'll examine more advanced features of the `binding` element later in this chapter.

Invocation Style

The first use of the SOAP binding extension indicates the style of invocation:

```
<soap:binding style="document"
    transport="http://schemas.xmlsoap.org/soap/http"/>
```

This declaration applies to the entire `binding`. It indicates that all operations for the `priceCheck` `portType` are defined in this binding as SOAP messages. Further, the `style` attribute indicates that operations will follow a document-centric approach, meaning the body of the SOAP message is to be interpreted as straight XML; this is contrasted with the other alternative value for the `style` attribute (`rpc`), which indicates that binding uses the Remote Procedure Call (RPC) conventions for the SOAP body as defined in the SOAP specification. The default `style` for the binding can be explicitly overridden by a `style` declaration in any child `operation` element. However, it's strongly recommended that you don't override the `style` value. Practice has shown that overriding the style of the `binding` leads to interoperability problems.

With the document `style` comes some restrictions. You should only use a document style `binding` for certain kinds of `portTypes`—those that reference `messages` that contain `parts` using the `element` attribute. If a `portType` references a `message` whose `parts` use the `type` attribute, you should define only RPC bindings for it. Note that this is an example where the separation between abstract elements and concrete elements in WSDL isn't clean.

`PriceCheckRequest` and `PriceCheckResponse` messages only use the `element` attribute in their `parts`; this allows SkatesTown to define a document-style binding.

The `transport` attribute tells you that the requestor must send the SOAP message using HTTP. Other possible values for this attribute could include `http://schemas.xmlsoap.org/soap/SMTP/`, `http://schemas.xmlsoap.org/soap/ftp/`, or any other URI. For interoperability reasons, each `portType` should have one SOAP/HTTP binding defined. In the Web services world, almost all clients can participate in a protocol defined by SOAP using HTTP.

SOAPAction

The second use of the SOAP binding extension is

```
<operation name="checkPrice">
  <soap:operation
    soapAction=
      "http://www.skatestown.com/services/PriceCheck/checkPrice" />
```

This declaration indicates the value that should be placed in the SOAPAction HTTP header as part of the HTTP message carrying the priceCheck service invocation message. As we discussed in Chapter 3, the purpose of the SOAPAction header is to describe the intent of the message. In the case of the checkPrice operation, the WSDL tells the service requestor to put exactly the http://www.skatestown.com/services/ PriceCheck/checkPrice string as the value for the SOAPAction header. Here's an example HTTP header for a priceCheckRequest message:

```
POST /pc/services/PriceCheck HTTP/1.0
Content-Type: text/xml; charset=utf-8
Accept: application/soap+xml, application/dime, multipart/related, text/*
User-Agent: Axis/1.0
Host: localhost:9080
Cache-Control: no-cache
Pragma: no-cache
SOAPAction: "http://www.skatestown.com/services/PriceCheck/checkPrice"
Content-Length: 334
```

Note that a SOAPAction header whose value is an empty string indicates that the URI of the request is the place where the intent of the message is to be found. If the SOAPAction value is empty, no intent of the message is to be found. Better conventions with SOAP would require the requestor to put an interesting value as the SOAPAction to help SOAP routers dispatch the message to the appropriate Web service. When binding different operations in the same portType, you can assign different SOAPAction headers for each operation.

Input Message Appearance

The third use of the SOAP binding extension is to describe what the input message should look like, including specifying the SOAP body and SOAP header components of the message. The priceCheck WSDL document describes how the input message to the checkPrice appears in the parts of the SOAP message:

```
<input>
   <soap:body use="literal" />
</input>
```

The entire input message, PriceCheckRequest (from the portType declaration for the checkPrice operation), is declared to have exactly one component (a SOAP body); and the content of that SOAP body is literally a single XML element (there is only one part defined for the PriceCheckRequest message) named sku, from the namespace http://www.skatestown.com/ns/availability. Here's an example PriceCheckRequest message, illustrating this SOAP body:

```
<?xml version="1.0" encoding="UTF-8"?>
<soapenv:Envelope
  xmlns:soapenv="http://schemas.xmlsoap.org/soap/envelope/"
```

```
  xmlns:xsd="http://www.w3.org/2001/XMLSchema"
  xmlns:xsi="http://www.w3.org/2001/XMLSchema-instance">
 <soapenv:Body>
  <sku xmlns="http://www.skatestown.com/ns/availability">123</sku>
 </soapenv:Body>
</soapenv:Envelope>
```

WSDL `bindings` whose style is `document` should contain only `soap:body` elements with a use attribute of `literal`. WSDL `message` elements intended for document-style `bindings` must contain `parts` that only use the `element` attribute to define the type of the part. If a `type` attribute appears on the `part`, it isn't meant for a document-style `binding`.

Output Message Appearance

The fourth use of the SOAP binding extension in our example describes how the output message of `checkPrice` should appear. Nothing new is introduced with this example. For completeness, here's an example response that corresponds to the pattern described in the `binding` element for the output of the `checkPrice` operation:

```
<?xml version="1.0" encoding="UTF-8"?>
<soapenv:Envelope
  xmlns:soapenv="http://schemas.xmlsoap.org/soap/envelope/"
  xmlns:xsd="http://www.w3.org/2001/XMLSchema"
  xmlns:xsi="http://www.w3.org/2001/XMLSchema-instance">
 <soapenv:Body>
  <StockAvailability xmlns="http://www.skatestown.com/ns/availability">
   <sku xsi:type="xsd:string">123</sku>
   <price xmlns="">100.0</price>
   <quantityAvailable xmlns="">12</quantityAvailable>
  </StockAvailability>
 </soapenv:Body>
</soapenv:Envelope>
</SOAP-ENV:Envelope>
```

Just like the `PriceCheckRequest` message, the output message of the `checkPrice` operation (`PriceCheckResponse`) is literal. The contents of the SOAP body is an element corresponding to an XML global element declaration named `StockAvailability` in the namespace identified by `http://www.skatestown.com/ns/availability`.

The only missing piece is the network address: To what URL do we send the message? These details are given in the WSDL `port` and `service`.

Port

The `port` in WSDL is simple. Its only purpose is to specify the network address of the endpoint hosting the Web service. More precisely, the `port` associates a single protocol-specific address to an individual `binding`. `Port` elements are named, and the name must be unique among all the `ports` within a WSDL document. The `port` element for the `priceCheckSOAPBinding` is:

```
<port name="PriceCheck" binding="pc:PriceCheckSOAPBinding">
...
    <soap:address location="http://www.skatestown.com/services/PriceCheck"/>
</port>
```

This `port` indicates the URL to which messages should be sent in order to invoke the `priceCheck` operations over SOAP. Note the `soap:address` element; this is another aspect of the SOAP extension to WSDL. Most of the extension is in the `binding`, and this is the only part of the extension outside the `binding`.

The `port` doesn't stand alone; `port` elements are children of a WSDL `service`.

Service

The purpose of a WSDL `service` is to contain a set of related `ports`—nothing more. Although a WSDL document can contain a collection of `service` elements, conventionally a WSDL document contains a single `service`. Each `service` is named, and each name must be unique among all the `services` in the WSDL document. The following shows the entire `service` for the `priceCheck` Web service:

```
<service name="PriceCheck">
  <port name="Pricecheck" binding="pc:PriceCheckSOAPBinding">
...
    <soap:address location="http://www.skatestown.com/services/PriceCheck"/>
  </port>
</service>
```

It seems like a lot of bother to waste all these elements to express a group of `ports`. Why would you group several `ports` together into a `service`?

One reason is to group the `ports` that are related to the same `service` interface (`portType`) but expressed by different protocols (`bindings`). For example, if the `priceCheck portType` was implemented in two ways, one using SOAP over HTTP and another using SOAP over SMTP, a single `service` could contain the `port` describing the URL for the SOAP/HTTP network endpoint and the `port` describing the email address for the SOAP/SMTP network endpoint. It's a good convention to have a different address for each `port` in a `service`.

Another reason might be to group related but different `portTypes` together. This, however, isn't very interoperable and, as you'll see in our examination of WSDL 2.0, doesn't move forward into the upcoming version of the language.

However, no standard describes or documents the meaning of any aggregation of `ports` within a `service`. Largely for this reason, most `services` contain only one `port`.

That is the bulk of the important elements in a WSDL definition. We'll now examine a few other elements that appear in a WSDL document.

Documentation

The documentation element is used to provide useful, human-readable information about the Web service description. One conventional use is to declare that the WSDL file is an interoperable description (compliant with the WS-I basic profile, as discussed in Chapter 13). This use of the documentation element appears in the priceCheck service element:

```
<service name="PriceCheck">
  <port name="Pricecheck" binding="pc:PriceCheckSOAPBinding">
    <documentation>
      <wsi:Claim
        conformsTo="http://ws-i.org/profiles/basic/1.0" />
    </documentation>
    <soap:address location="http://www.skatestown.com/services/PriceCheck"/>
  </port>
</service>
```

Any other WSDL element can contain a documentation element, usually as the first child element.

Import

WSDL defines an import element that allows WSDL documents to be linked together. The import element lets you reuse WSDL documents, by allowing WSDL elements in one file to reference WSDL elements defined in a different file. Really, an import element binds a network location to an XML namespace. This is similar to the import element in XML Schema; however, don't mix the two. Use WSDL import to import WSDL definitions, and use XML Schema import (within a schema element in the types section) to import other XML Schema type and element definitions.
The following line shows the definition of an import element in WSDL:

```
<import namespace="uri" location="uri"/>
```

Just like similar constructs such as the schemaLocation attribute on the import element in XSD, the location attribute is a hint to the location of the WSDL file. This value should be a URL. The namespace value should be the same as the WSDL definitions file found wherever the location attribute points.

Conventional Use of the Import Element

Many developers split their WSDL designs into two parts, a service interface definition and a service implementation definition, each placed in a separate document. The service interface definition, containing the types, message, portType, and binding elements, appears in one file; it encapsulates the reusable components of a service description. You can then place this file, for example, on a well-known Web site (in an e-marketplace, for example) for everyone to view. Each organization that wants to implement a Web service conformant to that well-known service interface definition would describe a service implementation definition containing the `port` and `service` elements, describing how that common, reusable, service interface definition was, in fact, implemented at the network endpoint hosted by that organization. (You'll see in Chapter 6 that this split is very important for registering WSDL Web service definitions in UDDI.)

When the WSDL definition is split among multiple files, the naming restrictions (for example, `portType` names must be unique) apply across files. Technically, names like `portType`, and so on, must be unique among all files that include a `definitions` element that has the same `targetNamespace`.

The designers at SkatesTown used multiple files for the `poSubmission` WSDL, which is a service description for the `poSubmission` SOAP service you saw in Chapter 3. It uses schema definitions from Chapter 2. The service interface definition for the `poSubmission` service interface definition file is shown in Listing 4.2.

Listing 4.2   `poSubmission` **Service Interface Definition**

```xml
<?xml version="1.0" ?>
<definitions name="poSubmission"
    targetNamespace=
        "http://www.skatestown.com/services/interfaces/poSubmission.wsdl"
    xmlns:xsd="http://www.w3.org/2001/XMLSchema"
    xmlns:po="http://www.skatestown.com/ns/po"
    xmlns:pos="http://www.skatestown.com/services/interfaces/poSubmission.wsdl"
        xmlns:inv="http://www.skatestown.com/ns/invoice"
        xmlns:soap="http://schemas.xmlsoap.org/wsdl/soap/"
        xmlns="http://schemas.xmlsoap.org/wsdl/">

    <!-- Type definitions -->
    <types>
      <xsd:schema>
      <!-- rest of invoice schema definition from chapter 2
           assumes XSD file is in same directory         -->
      <xsd:import namespace="http://www.skatestown.com/ns/invoice"
                  schemaLocation="http://www.skatestown.com/schema/invoice.xsd"/>

      <!-- rest of purchaseOrder schema definition from chapter 2
           assumes XSD file is in same directory         -->
      <xsd:import namespace="http://www.skatestown.com/ns/po"
                  schemaLocation=" http://www.skatestown.com/schema//po.xsd"/>
      </xsd:schema>
    </types>

    <!-- Message definitions -->
    <message name="poSubmissionRequest">
      <part name="purchaseOrder" element="po:po"/>
    </message>
```

Listing 4.2   **Continued**

```xml
<message name="poSubmissionResponse">
   <part name="invoice" element="inv:invoice"/>
</message>

<!-- Port type definitions -->
<portType name="poSubmissionPortType">
   <operation name="doSubmission">
      <input message="pos:poSubmissionRequest"/>
      <output message="pos:poSubmissionResponse"/>
   </operation>
</portType>

<!-- Binding definitions -->
<binding name="poSubmissionSOAPBinding"
   type="pos:poSubmissionPortType">
   <soap:binding style="document"
            transport="http://schemas.xmlsoap.org/soap/http"/>
   <operation name="doSubmission">
      <soap:operation soapAction=
         "http://www.skatestown.com/services/poSubmission/submitPO"/>
      <input>
         <soap:body parts="purchaseOrder" use="literal"/>
      </input>
      <output>
         <soap:body parts="invoice" use="literal"/>
      </output>
   </operation>
</binding>
</definitions>
```

Note the use of the XML Schema `import` element, importing the elements defined in the `po` and `invoice` schema definitions.

This WSDL file is a typical pattern for a simple document-centric SOAP service. The messages are document instances; the SOAP binding indicates the use of literal encoding—no deserialization of the XML message into programming language–specific objects will occur.

This service interface definition can be reused by many organizations. This is especially true if the data formats (the purchase order and invoice schemas) are industry standard.

The information specific to how SkatesTown implements the `poSubmission` service interface is contained in the `poSubmissionService` service implementation definition file (Listing 4.3).

Listing 4.3   poSubmissionService **Service Interface Definition**

```
<?xml version="1.0" ?>
<definitions name="poSubmissionService"
    targetNamespace=
        "http://www.skatestown.com/services/POSubmissionService.wsdl"
    xmlns:xsd="http://www.w3.org/2001/XMLSchema"
    xmlns:pop="http://www.skatestown.com/services/interfaces/poSubmission.wsdl"
        xmlns:soap="http://schemas.xmlsoap.org/wsdl/soap/"
        xmlns="http://schemas.xmlsoap.org/wsdl/">

    <import namespace=
                "http://www.skatestown.com/services/interfaces/poSubmission.wsdl"
        location="./poSubmission.wsdl"/>
                    <!-- assumes interface file in same directory -->

    <!-- Service definition -->
    <service name="poSubmissionService">
        <port name="poSubmissionSOAPPort" binding="pop:poSubmissionSOAPBinding">
            <soap:address
                location="http://www.skatestown.com/services/submitPO"/>
        </port>
    </service>

</definitions>
```

This technique is a nice separation of concerns. The service implementation document is succinct and contains information that is specific to the implementation of this type of service by SkatesTown.

Another convention, sometimes followed by WSDL designers, is to separate the binding from the service interface definition. It remains controversial that the service interface definition includes, by convention, the binding element. After all, the binding element, when used with the SOAP extensions to WSDL, includes the SOAPAction attribute in the operation element. This has more to do with implementation than reusable description. As you'll see in Chapter 6, part of the argument to keep the binding element with the other reusable elements was due to the convention of registering WSDL documents within UDDI.

Exploring More WSDL Features

Let's explore some more sophisticated features of WSDL, including richer details on operation definition and bindings, by examining the StockAvailableNotification WSDL (Listing 4.4). SkatesTown provides the StockAvailableNotification Web service to support product ordering. The RegistrationRequest schema defines the datatypes. In particular, this Web service is used when a customer places an order with SkatesTown but one or more of the items aren't currently available from SkatesTown's inventory. The purpose of this service is to allow customers to register to be notified when all the products in their order are once again available for sale from inventory.

Listing 4.4 **The StockAvailableNotification WSDL Document**

```
<?xml version="1.0" ?>
<definitions name="StockAvailableNotification"
        targetNamespace=
            "http://www.skatestown.com/services/StockAvailableNotification"
        xmlns:tns="http://www.skatestown.com/services/StockAvailableNotification"
        xmlns:xsd="http://www.w3.org/2001/XMLSchema"
        xmlns:reg="http://www.skatestown.com/ns/registrationRequest"
        xmlns:soap="http://schemas.xmlsoap.org/wsdl/soap/"
        xmlns:soapenc="http://schemas.xmlsoap.org/soap/encoding/"
        xmlns:wsdl="http://schemas.xmlsoap.org/wsdl/"
        xmlns="http://schemas.xmlsoap.org/wsdl/">

  <!-- Type definitions from the registration schema-->
  <types>
    <xsd:schema
        targetNamespace="http://www.skatestown.com/ns/registrationRequest" >

        <xsd:import namespace="http://schemas.xmlsoap.org/soap/encoding/"
                    schemaLocation="http://schemas.xmlsoap.org/soap/encoding/"/>

        <xsd:complexType name="ArrayOfItem"
            xmlns:soapenc="http://schemas.xmlsoap.org/soap/encoding/">
          <xsd:complexContent>
            <xsd:restriction base="soapenc:Array">
              <xsd:attribute ref="soapenc:arrayType"
                            wsdl:arrayType="xsd:string[]"/>
            </xsd:restriction>
          </xsd:complexContent>
        </xsd:complexType>

        <xsd:complexType name="registrationRequest">
          <xsd:sequence>
            <xsd:element name="items" type="reg:ArrayOfItem" />

            <xsd:element name="address" type="xsd:string"/>

            <xsd:element name="transport"
                        default="smtp" minOccurs="0" >
              <xsd:simpleType>
                <xsd:restriction base="xsd:string">
                  <xsd:enumeration value="http"/>
                  <xsd:enumeration value="smtp"/>
```

Listing 4.4 **Continued**

```
                </xsd:restriction>
              </xsd:simpleType>
            </xsd:element>
            <xsd:element name="clientArg" type="xsd:string" minOccurs="0"/>
         </xsd:sequence>
      </xsd:complexType>

      <xsd:simpleType name="correlationID">
         <xsd:restriction base="xsd:string">
         <!-- some appropriate restriction -->
         </xsd:restriction>
      </xsd:simpleType>

      <xsd:element name="Expiration" type="xsd:dateTime" />
      <xsd:element name="ErrorString" type="xsd:string" />
   </xsd:schema>
</types>

<!-- Message definitions -->
<message name="StockAvailableRegistrationRequest">
   <part name="registration" type="reg:registrationRequest"/>
   <part name="expiration" element="reg:Expiration"/>
</message>

<message name="StockAvailableRegistrationResponse">
   <part name="correlationID" type="reg:correlationID"/>
</message>

<message name="StockAvailableRegistrationError">
   <part name="errorString" element="reg:ErrorString"/>
</message>

<message name="StockAvailableExpirationError">
   <part name="errorString" element="reg:ErrorString"/>
</message>

<message name="StockAvailableNotification">
   <part name="timeStamp" type="xsd:dateTime"/>
   <part name="correlationID" type="reg:correlationID"/>
   <part name="items" type="reg:ArrayOfItem"/>
   <part name="clientArg" type="xsd:string"/>
</message>

<message name="StockAvailableExpirationNotification">
   <part name="timeStamp" type="xsd:dateTime"/>
```

Listing 4.4 **Continued**

```
        <part name="correlationID" type="reg:correlationID"/>
        <part name="items" type="reg:ArrayOfItem"/>
        <part name="clientArg" type="xsd:string"/>
    </message>

    <message name="StockAvailableCancellation">
        <part name="correlationID" type="reg:correlationID"/>
    </message>

    <!-- Port type definitions -->
    <portType name="StockAvailableNotificationPortType">
        <!--Registration Operation -->
        <!-- Note: the requestor must invoke the registration operation first. -->
        <operation name="registration">
          <input message="tns:StockAvailableRegistrationRequest"/>
          <output message="tns:StockAvailableRegistrationResponse"/>
          <fault message="tns:StockAvailableRegistrationError"
             name="StockAvailableNotificationErrorMessage"/>
          <fault message="tns:StockAvailableExpirationError"
             name="StockAvailableExpirationError"/>
        </operation>

        <!--Notification Operation -->
        <operation name="notification">
          <output message="tns:StockAvailableNotification"/>
        </operation>

        <!--Expiration Notification Operation -->
        <operation name="expirationNotification">
          <output message="tns:StockAvailableExpirationNotification"/>
        </operation>

        <!--Cancellation Operation -->
        <operation name="cancellation">
          <input message="tns:StockAvailableCancellation"/>
        </operation>
    </portType>

    <!-- Binding definitions -->
    <binding name="StockAvailableNotificationSOAPBinding"
       type="tns:StockAvailableNotificationPortType">
       <soap:binding style="rpc"
               transport="http://schemas.xmlsoap.org/soap/http"/>

       <!-- Note: the requestor must invoke the registration operation first. -->
       <operation name="registration">
```

Listing 4.4   **Continued**

```
      <soap:operation
        soapAction=
       "http://www.skatesTown.com/StockAvailableNotification/registration" />
      <input>
        <soap:header message="tns:StockAvailableRegistrationRequest"
              part="expiration" use="literal" >
           <soap:headerfault message="tns:StockAvailableExpirationError"
               part="errorString" use="literal" />
        </soap:header>
        <soap:body parts="registration" use="encoded"
                 namespace="http://www.skatestown.com/ns/registrationRequest"
                 encodingStyle="http://schemas.xmlsoap.org/soap/encoding/" />
      </input>
      <output>
        <soap:body use="encoded"
            namespace="http://www.skatestown.com/ns/registrationRequest"
            encodingStyle="http://schemas.xmlsoap.org/soap/encoding/"/>
      </output>
      <fault name="StockAvailableNotificationErrorMessage">
         <soap:fault name="StockAvailableNotificationErrorMessage"
            namespace="http://www.skatestown.com/ns/registrationRequest"
            encodingStyle="http://schemas.xmlsoap.org/soap/encoding/"/>
      </fault>
  </operation>

  <operation name="notification">
     <output>
        <soap:body use="encoded"
            namespace="http://www.skatestown.com/ns/registrationRequest"
            encodingStyle="http://schemas.xmlsoap.org/soap/encoding/"/>
     </output>
  </operation>

  <operation name="expirationNotification">
     <output>
        <soap:body use="encoded"
            namespace="http://www.skatestown.com/ns/registrationRequest"
            encodingStyle="http://schemas.xmlsoap.org/soap/encoding/"/>
     </output>
  </operation>

  <operation name="cancellation">
     <soap:operation
        soapAction=
```

Listing 4.4   **Continued**

```
                "http://www.skatesTown.com/StockAvailableNotification/cancellation" />
            <input>
              <soap:body use="encoded"
                    namespace="http://www.skatestown.com/ns/registrationRequest"
                    encodingStyle="http://schemas.xmlsoap.org/soap/encoding/"/>
            </input>
          </operation>
        </binding>

        <!-- Service definition -->
        <service name="StockAvailableNotification">
            <port name="StockAvailableNotification"
                  binding="tns:StockAvailableNotificationSOAPBinding">
              <soap:address
                location=
                    "http://www.skatestown.com/services/StockAvailableNotification"/>
            </port>
        </service>

      </definitions>
```

This Web service has four `operations`. The first `operation` allows the customer to register for a notification. This is a request/response `operation`. The customer invokes this
service, passing in a collection of item numbers (for out of stock product numbers), a
network address (default is an email address), an optional transport type (valid values are
`http` and `smtp`), and a `client` argument token of type `string`. The `client` argument
token is opaque to the service; it's a requestor-specific correlation identifier. The `client`
argument is returned by the notification operation.

This operation also includes an expiration time to be included in the message (as a
SOAP header, as you'll discover). This is used to indicate what time in the future this
service will cease issuing notifications.

The *normal* response of this operation is a provider-side *correlation id*   (a string).
The possible fault messages include

- Invalid product number (one of the product numbers doesn't correspond to a
  product in SkatesTown's product catalog)

- Invalid transport (some value other than `smtp` or `http` was specified)

- Invalid expiration (this appears as a `soap:headerfault`   if the original expiration time header was invalid in some way; we'll describe `soap:headerfault` elements in more detail later in this chapter)

The second operation, `notification`, uses the `notification` *transmission primitive*
in WSDL (we'll talk about transmission primitives in more detail later). This message is

sent from SkatesTown to the requestor's address indicated in the `registration` operation. This message indicates a timestamp, the provider-side correlation ID established in the registration message, the item numbers from the registration message, and the requestor-specific correlation ID. (Note that this is a simple notification mechanism and specific to SkatesTown. Standardized Web services notification mechanisms are just beginning to appear; we discuss one such specification in Chapter 8, "Web Services and Stateful Resources.")

The third operation, `expirationNotification`, also uses the `notification` transmission primitive in WSDL. This message is sent from SkatesTown to the requestor's address when the expiration period indicated on the original `registration operation` elapses. This functionality is similar to the soft-state mechanism used in the Open Grid Services Infrastructure (OGSI; see Chapter 8). This message indicates a timestamp, the provider-side correlation ID established in the registration message, the item numbers from the registration message, and the requestor-specific correlation ID.

The fourth `operation` is a one-way `operation` for cancellation of the notification. It allows the requestor to abandon its interest in the notification. The cancellation message is the provider-side correlation ID.

Transmission Primitives

The WSDL specification defines four different combinations of input, output, and fault messages. WSDL 1.1 uses the term *transmission primitive* to describe these combinations. WSDL 1.1 defines four transmission primitives: request-response, one-way, notification, and solicit-response. As you'll see later in the chapter, this concept has been generalized in WSDL 2.0 as *message exchange pattern* 📖. We'll now visit each of these transmission primitives in more detail.

Request-Response `Operations`

The request-response style is the most common form of `operation`. This kind style operation defines an input message (the request) followed by an output message (the response), and an optional collection of fault messages. Because many Web services are deployed using SOAP over HTTP, request-response is the most common form of operation found in WSDL documents.

The `checkPrice` operation from the `priceCheckPortType` is a request-response operation, as is `registration` from the `StockAvailableNotification` service. Request-response messages can retrieve information about some object represented by a Web service (like the `checkPrice` operation); they can also change the state of the service provider and include information about the new state in the response (like the `registration` operation).

Although `checkPrice` doesn't use it, the request-response transmission primitive allows the service provider to list the possible fault messages that can appear in response to a Web service invocation. The `fault` element is used in the `StockAvailableNotificationPortType` as part of the definition of the `registration` operation:

```
<!-- Port type definitions -->
<portType name="StockAvailableNotificationPortType">
   <!--Registration Operation -->
   <operation name="registration">
      <input message="tns:StockAvailableRegistrationRequest"/>
      <output message="tns:StockAvailableRegistrationResponse"/>
      <fault name="StockAvailableNotificationErrorMessage"
         message="tns:StockAvailableRegistrationError" />
      <fault name="StockAvailableExpirationError"
         message="tns:StockAvailableExpirationError" />
   </operation>
```

Fault elements must be named, and the name must be unique among all the fault elements defined for the operation. Like the input and output elements, the fault element refers to a message which describes the data contents of the fault.

One-Way Operations

A one-way operation doesn't have an output element (or a fault element); it has no response message going back to the requestor. A one-way operation is like a data sink. You might use it to change the state of the service provider.

The cancellation operation from the StockAvailableNotification service is a one-way operation:

```
<!--Cancellation Operation -->
<operation name="cancellation">
   <input message="tns:StockAvailableCancellation"/>
</operation>
```

Because many Web services are accessed through SOAP over HTTP, many one-way messages end up being request-response messages at the network transport level, with the response being a simple HTTP-level acknowledgment of the message. This is an interesting point to note: The operation description in WSDL doesn't necessarily model the network transport-level message flow. More precisely, for a one-way operation, the HTTP response must not contain a SOAP envelope—clients won't expect it to be there, and most clients will ignore it if it does appear. If you want an application-level semantic to be transmitted in response to the Web service invocation, you should model the operation using a request-response operation style, not a one-way style.

Notification Operations

A notification operation is like a one-way push from the service provider. Output messages are pushed to the service requestor as the result of an event on the service provider side, such as a time-out or operation completion. The notification operation in the StockAvailableNotification Web service is a notification type of operation;

SkatesTown pushes a message to the requestor when a particular item is once again in stock:

```
<!--Notification Operation -->
<operation name="notification">
   <output message="tns:StockAvailableNotification"/>
</operation>
```

The notification style of interaction is commonly used in systems built around asynchronous messaging. Although systems with asynchronous messaging might be a little harder to conceptualize and implement, they're more loosely coupled and, therefore, are easier to maintain; often this flexibility adds robustness to the system.

Given that notification is a one-way push message, how does SkatesTown know where to push the output messages? Nothing in the WSDL specification describes this directly. This correlation semantic must be described by other means. One mechanism used to address this problem is to have a network address (a URL or email address) as a parameter in another message. Another might be to use a transport binding that takes care of this for you, such as you might find in Message-Oriented Middleware (MOM) solutions—the service address in this case would be something the client would listen to, rather than a place to send messages. This sort of coordination problem, and the vagueness of the WSDL specification of a one-way push message, has limited its use by WSDL designers and has limited support by tooling and middleware vendors.

In the case of the StockAvailableNotification Web service, SkatesTown has created the registration operation to determine where to send a notification message. The service requestor must invoke the registration operation first, and then the notification operation can send a message to the requestor. The ordering requirement of these operations—that is, the fact that the registration operation must be invoked in order to receive notification messages—can't be described in WSDL without extensions. At this point, SkatesTown must describe this semantic using prose. The following comment appears with this portType:

```
<!--Registration Operation -->
<!-- Note: the requestor must invoke the registration operation first. -->
```

The semantics of notification style operations haven't been agreed on in the industry. Therefore, to ensure interoperability of Web services, you shouldn't use this style of operation.

Solicit-Response Operations

A solicit-response operation models a push operation similar to a notification operation. However, unlike the notification style of operation, the solicit-response operation expects an input (response) from the service requestor as the response in a solicit-response exchange. A solicit-response operation could look like this:

```
<portType name="someName">
   <operation name="exampleSolicitResponse">
```

```
        <output message="tns:pushThis"/>
        <input message="tns:responseToPush"/>
        <fault name="someFaultName" message="tns:faultPushedToRequestor"/>
    </operation>
</portType>
```

Output and fault flows are pushed to the service requestor as the result of some event on the service provider side, such as a time out or operation completion. The solicit-response style of operation has the same problem as the notification style of `operation`: It isn't clear how to determine where to push the output/fault messages. Again, one solution is the same as we discussed with the notification style of `operation`.

You can tell the difference between a request-response `operation` and a solicit-response `operation` by looking at the ordering of the input and output elements. In `request-response`, the input child element comes first. In solicit-response, the output child element comes first.

Solicit-response also has uneven interpretation by tooling and middleware vendors, limiting its use by WSDL designers. In fact, the vagueness of the WSDL 1.1 specification in this area motivated the WSDL 2.0 specification team to define the message exchange pattern work. And, as noted with notification style `operations`, interoperable Web services shouldn't use the solicit-response style of `operation`.

Rounding Out WSDL `Operations`

Let's consider a couple of final details related to the `operation` element. The WSDL specification allows the input, output, and fault messages to have a `name` attribute. Typically, the designer doesn't bother to come up with a name for `input` and `output` elements. This detail is often too much clutter in the WSDL document. And besides, WSDL provides default values for these names based on the `operation` name. For example, we repeat our `checkPrice` example, this time filling in the default values WSDL would have supplied:

```
<!-- Port type definitions -->
<portType name="PriceCheckPortType">
    <operation name="checkPrice">
        <input name="checkPriceRequest" message="pc:PriceCheckRequest"/>
        <output name="checkPriceResponse" message="pc:PriceCheckResponse"/>
    </operation>
</portType>
```

Typically, the `name` attribute of the `input` and `output` elements doesn't add much. Further, many WSDL designers encode this information into the names of the message elements they define. If you do add a name to an `input` or `output` element, it must be unique among all the `input` and `output` elements within the `portType`. Table 4.2 describes the default names for `input` and `output` elements, for an operation named xxx.

Table 4.2   **Defaults for** `Input` **and** `Output` **Elements for Operation** `XXX`

	Input	Output
Request–response	XXXRequest	XXXResponse
One–way	XXX	Not applicable
Solicit–response	XXXSolicit	XXXResponse
Notification	Not applicable	XXX

`Fault` elements require a name, because several `fault` elements can be associated with any `operation` and the fault name is used to distinguish among the set of possible faults. This is particularly important in the `binding`, which describes the mapping between the `fault` element and the way the fault is presented in a protocol-specific fashion. It's good design to include as many `faults` as are known when the `portType` is designed. However, this list of `faults` isn't exhaustive, and other `faults` could appear at runtime for any Web service implementing the `portType`.

WSDL also lets you specify a `parameterOrder` attribute on an `operation`, which is used only for RPC-style `operations`. This is a bit of a layering violation in the specification, because the `portType` is abstract, and its nature as an RPC or document-centric message is revealed in the `binding`. Further, this attribute is informational only and is completely optional, even for operations described as RPC within the `binding`. This attribute has two purposes: It provides a mechanism to describe the original parameter ordering of the RPC function as a list of part names separated by spaces, and it disambiguates which of the parameters contain a return value.

Rounding Out WSDL Bindings

The SOAP binding style also specifies the way SOAP headers, SOAP faults, and SOAP header faults should be formatted. These additional aspects of the SOAP binding convention are illustrated in the `StockAvailableNotificationSOAPBinding`.

Binding and RPC

We can explore more sophisticated options with `bindings` and at the same time discuss the other major style of `binding`: RPC. With an RPC-style binding, the way the SOAP body format is specified is quite different. The `binding` for the `StockAvailableNotification` `portType` demonstrates a typical RPC style of `binding`:

```
<binding name="StockAvailableNotificationSOAPBinding"
    type="tns:StockAvailableNotificationPortType">
  <soap:binding style="rpc"
          transport="http://schemas.xmlsoap.org/soap/http"/>
...
```

In addition, this `binding` illustrates how the abstract input and output messages specified by the `portType` can correspond to SOAP body and SOAP header elements on the wire. Let's look at how the binding specifies a SOAP body. (We'll examine how this binding specifies SOAP headers in the next section.) The binding for the `registration` operation illustrates an RPC operation:

```
<!-- Note: the requestor must invoke the registration operation first. -->
<operation name="registration">
  <soap:operation
    soapAction=
    "http://www.skatesTown.com/StockAvailableNotification/registration" />
  <input>
...

    <soap:body parts="registration" use="encoded"
             namespace="http://www.skatestown.com/ns/registrationRequest"
             encodingStyle="http://schemas.xmlsoap.org/soap/encoding/" />
  </input>
```

Recall from the `StockAvailableNotificationPortType` that the input message to the `registration` operation has two parts: `registration` and `expiration`. The previous binding specifies that just the `registration` part goes in the body and, furthermore, that it uses SOAP encoding. The rule here is that the `binding` must map all the `parts` of the `message` to a SOAP body or a SOAP header. The `encodingStyle` causes the binding to specify a SOAP body like the following to appear on the wire:

```
<?xml version="1.0" encoding="UTF-8"?>
<soapenv:Envelope
  xmlns:soapenv="http://schemas.xmlsoap.org/soap/envelope/"
  xmlns:xsd="http://www.w3.org/2001/XMLSchema"
  xmlns:xsi="http://www.w3.org/2001/XMLSchema-instance">
 <soapenv:Header>
  <ns1:Expiration xsi:type="xsd:dateTime"
     xmlns:ns1="http://www.skatestown.com/ns/registrationRequest">
    2004-01-30T05:00:00.000Z
  </ns1:Expiration>
 </soapenv:Header>
 <soapenv:Body>
  <ns2:registration
    soapenv:encodingStyle="http://schemas.xmlsoap.org/soap/encoding/"
    xmlns:ns2="http://www.skatestown.com/ns/registrationRequest">
   <registration href="#id0"/>
  </ns2:registration>
  <multiRef id="id0"
     soapenc:root="0"
     soapenv:encodingStyle="http://schemas.xmlsoap.org/soap/encoding/"
     xsi:type="ns3:registrationRequest"
     xmlns:soapenc="http://schemas.xmlsoap.org/soap/encoding/"
     xmlns:ns3="http://www.skatestown.com/ns/registrationRequest">
   <items xsi:type="soapenc:Array" soapenc:arrayType="xsd:string[2]">
    <item>Skateboard</item>
    <item>Wheels</item>
```

```
    </items>
    <address xsi:type="xsd:string">buyer@customer.com</address>
    <transport href="#id1"/>
    <clientArg xsi:type="xsd:string">RFQ8</clientArg>
  </multiRef>
  <multiRef id="id1"
    soapenc:root="0"
    soapenv:encodingStyle="http://schemas.xmlsoap.org/soap/encoding/"
    xmlns:soapenc="http://schemas.xmlsoap.org/soap/encoding/">
      smtp
  </multiRef>
 </soapenv:Body>
</soapenv:Envelope>
```

The parameter of the message, registration, appears as its own element in the body of the SOAP message.

Note the child element of the SOAP body:

```
<soapenv:Body>
  <ns2:registration
```

With RPC-encoded bindings, the name of child element of the SOAP body is derived from the operation name (in this case, the operation is named registration).

You don't see the namespace or the encodingStyle attribute used with document-literal bindings, just RPC-encoded bindings. Because special encodings are tricky to get right between requestors and providers, they aren't considered a form of interoperable binding. A recommended approach is to use RPC with the value of the use attribute as literal rather than encoded.

SOAP Header and Header Fault Formatting

Now we can examine the other part in the input message to the registration operation. This Web service has been designed to allow the expiration to be carried in the input message as a SOAP header. Here's the part of the input binding for the registration operation that deals with the expiration header:

```
<soap:header message="tns:StockAvailableRegistrationRequest"
    part="expiration" use="literal" >
  <soap:headerfault message="tns:StockAvailableExpirationError"
    part="errorString" use="literal" />
</soap:header>
```

Note that the soap:header extension to the binding can specify a part from messages other than the one associated with the operation's input or output message; this is what the message attribute is used for. The message attribute and the part attribute together identify the header element. Note that best practice is to declare soap:header elements to have the value literal for the use attribute; this is better for interoperability.

This `binding` would cause the input message to the `registration` request to include a SOAP header like the following:

```
<?xml version="1.0" encoding="UTF-8"?>
  <soapenv:Envelope
  xmlns:soapenv="http://schemas.xmlsoap.org/soap/envelope/"
  xmlns:xsd="http://www.w3.org/2001/XMLSchema"
  xmlns:xsi="http://www.w3.org/2001/XMLSchema-instance">
 <soapenv:Header>
  <ns1:Expiration xsi:type="xsd:dateTime"
    xmlns:ns1="http://www.skatestown.com/ns/registrationRequest">
    2004-01-30T05:00:00.000Z
  </ns1:Expiration>
 </soapenv:Header>
 <soapenv:Body>
  <ns2:registration  ...
...
```

Otherwise, the specification for a SOAP header in a binding is similar to that of a SOAP body. Note one interesting distinction: There can be many SOAP headers, and each of these can reference only a single `part`, whereas with the SOAP body there can be only one, but it can reference multiple `parts`.

SOAP Fault and Header Fault Formatting

The `soap:fault` extension is an additional facility described by the `soap:binding` extension that appears in the `StockAvailableNotification` WSDL. The `soap:fault` extension describes how a `fault` element (like the one described in the `registration` operation in the `StockAvailableNotificationPortType`) is mapped in SOAP. A use of this extension is shown here:

```
    <operation name="registration">
.  .  .
        <fault name="StockAvailableNotificationErrorMessage">
          <soap:fault name="StockAvailableNotificationErrorMessage"
              namespace="http://www.skatestown.com/ns/registrationRequest"
              encodingStyle="http://schemas.xmlsoap.org/soap/encoding/"/>
        </fault>
```

The `soap:fault` extension has attributes similar to those of the `soap:body` extension. The fault `message` must have a single `part`.

   SOAP requires that the details of any errors generated by the SOAP engine when processing a SOAP header (rather than the body) must be communicated back to the requestor in the form of SOAP headers, not in the details element of a `fault` message. `MustUnderstand faults` are communicated this way, for example. The SOAP extension in WSDL defines the `soap:headerfault` element for this purpose. A `soap:headerfault` element is used to describe how the `StockAvailableExpirationError` is expressed in

SOAP, as a `fault` header that could potentially flow to communicate errors related to how the requestor formats the expiration header. The following example shows how WSDL models this situation:

```
<operation name="registration">
...

   <input>
      <soap:header message="tns:StockAvailableRegistrationRequest"
           part="expiration" use="literal" >
        <soap:headerfault message="tns:StockAvailableExpirationError"
           part="errorString" use="literal" />
      </soap:header>

. . .
```

The `soap:headerfault` element is associated with the `soap:header` definition that might be in error, not as part of a fault or output message part of the operation.

Example `SMTPBinding`

As a slight variant on the SOAP using HTTP `binding` theme, consider the possibility of sending a `priceCheck` request using email. SkatesTown could provide an additional SOAP over SMTP `binding` to the `priceCheck` `portType`, allowing a customer to email a `priceCheck` request and receive as a reply email the `priceCheck` response message.

Not much changes with this new `binding`. Of course, the `priceCheck` `portType` and the messages and types it references don't change. What does change is additional `binding`, `port`, and `service` elements. The biggest changes include use of a different URI for the `transport` attribute of the `soap:binding` element to indicate SMTP is the transport mechanism:

```
<!-- Binding definitions -->
<binding name="PriceCheckSMTPBinding" type="pc:PriceCheckPortType">
   <soap:binding style="document"
      transport="http://schemas.xmlsoap.org/soap/smtp"/>
   <operation name="checkPrice">
      <input>
         <soap:body use="literal"/>
      </input>
      <output>
         <soap:body use="literal"/>
      </output>
   </operation>
</binding>
```

So, we now know that the only format supported for the `priceCheck` and `StockAvailableNotification` services is SOAP, and we know how the abstract types should be formatted into a concrete message. We now have (almost) all the details

needed to invoke these Web services. At this point, we must use a SOAP message something like the following to invoke the `checkPrice` operation:

```
<?xml version="1.0" encoding="UTF-8"?>
<soapenv:Envelope
  xmlns:soapenv="http://schemas.xmlsoap.org/soap/envelope/"
  xmlns:xsd="http://www.w3.org/2001/XMLSchema"
  xmlns:xsi="http://www.w3.org/2001/XMLSchema-instance">
 <soapenv:Body>
  <sku xmlns="http://www.skatestown.com/ns/availability">123</sku>
 </soapenv:Body>
</soapenv:Envelope>
```

and the response message is formatted as follows:

```
<?xml version="1.0" encoding="UTF-8"?>
<soapenv:Envelope
  xmlns:soapenv="http://schemas.xmlsoap.org/soap/envelope/"
  xmlns:soapenc="http://schemas.xmlsoap.org/soap/encoding/"
  xmlns:xsd="http://www.w3.org/2001/XMLSchema"
  xmlns:xsi="http://www.w3.org/2001/XMLSchema-instance">
  <soapenv:Body>
    <StockAvailability xmlns="http://www.skatestown.com/ns/availability">
      <sku>123</sku>
      <price>100.0</price>
      <quantityAvailable>12</quantityAvailable>
    </StockAvailability>
  </soapenv:Body>
</soapenv:Envelope>
```

WSDL Extension Mechanism

The WSDL language allows most of the WSDL elements to be extended with elements
from other namespaces. The language specification further defines standard extensions for
SOAP, HTTP GET/POST operations, and MIME attachments. You've seen the use of
the SOAP extension extensively in the previous sections of this chapter. We'll briefly
describe the other two extension frameworks here.

WSDL Descriptions of HTTP GET/POST Web Services

Imagine a variant on the `priceCheck` Web service that was tuned to support Web
browsers. It would use URL encoding to include the item number as part of the service
request using HTTP GET. An invocation of this service could look like an HTTP GET
message sent to the following URL:

```
http://www.skatestown.com/checkPrice?item=xxx1234.
```

The `priceCheck` WSDL definition would be extended to include a new `binding`:

```
<!-- Binding definitions -->
. . .
<binding name="PriceCheckHTTPGetBinding" type="pc:PriceCheckPortType">
    <http:binding verb="GET"/>
    <operation name="checkPrice">
        <http:operation location="checkPrice"/>
        <input>
            <http:urlEncoded/>
        </input>
        <output>
            <mime:content type="text/xml"/>
        </output>
    </operation>
</binding>
```

The first HTTP extension is shown as the first child of the `binding`. This element does two things: It tells us that this `binding` is an HTTP binding, and it indicates that the GET verb is used (the other option was the POST verb).

The second HTTP extension is shown as the first child of the `operation`. This element indicates that the service is to be invoked at a relative URI location. This is to be with the absolute URI location indicated in the `port` element.

The third HTTP extension is shown as the first child of the `input`. This element indicates that the parts of the input message are encoded in the request URI as name/value pairs, where the HTTP GET parameter names correspond to the WSDL part names. Recall that the input message to the `checkPrice` operation is the `PriceCheckRequest` message, and it has only one part: a string named `sku`. This means that the value of the input will appear in the URI, following the string `?sku=`.

The fourth HTTP extension is shown as the first child of the `output` element. This element indicates that the `priceCheckResponse` message will appear as XML text in the HTTP response.

The last thing required is to update the `service` of the `priceCheck` WSDL to include a `port` describing the `http:address` of the `priceCheckHTTPGetBinding`. This update is as follows:

```
<!-- Service definition -->
<service name="PriceCheckService">
. . .
    <port name="PriceCheckBrowserPort" binding="pc:PriceCheckHTTPGetBinding">
        <http:address location="http://www.skatestown.com/services/"/>
    </port>
. . .
```

Here the URL of the `priceCheck` service is given using the `http:address` WSDL extension. Just like the SOAP extension, most of the HTTP extension is in the `binding` (where you would expect it), and the only remaining piece is an extension to the port expressing the endpoint network address in a protocol-specific manner.

The HTTP extension also specifies how to express the input message as HTTP POST using FORM-POST and how to express the input using urlReplacement. Refer to the WSDL specification for more detail.

WSDL Descriptions of Web Services Incorporating MIME

WSDL also supports a standard extension to describe message parts as MIME. We covered SOAP with MIME attachments in Chapter 3. This extension would be used if the designers at SkatesTown decided to include (in addition to the normal SOAP response) a GIF or JPEG image of the part queried in a priceCheck service invocation. To support this addition, the following changes would be necessary in the priceCheck WSDL. First, the response message would be updated to include the new part:

```
<message name="PriceCheckResponse">
    <part name="result" type="avail:availability"/>
    <part name="picture" type="xsd:binary"/>
</message>
```

This change doesn't exercise the MIME extension standard, because the MIME extensions are only within the binding. However, the only change necessary in the binding is to indicate that the output is modeled as multipart MIME, with the result part appearing as one MIME part, the SOAP body; the picture appears in another MIME part as GIF or JPEG. The following listing shows the binding element with these changes:

```
<!-- Binding definitions -->
<binding name="PriceCheckSOAPBinding" type="PriceCheckPortType">
  <soap:binding style="rpc"
          transport="http://schemas.xmlsoap.org/soap/http"/>
  <operation name="checkPrice">
    <soap:operation SOAPAction=""/>
    <input>
      <soap:body use="encoded"
          namespace="http://www.skatestown.com/ns/availability"
          encodingStyle="http://schemas.xmlsoap.org/soap/encoding/"/>
    </input>
    <output>
      <mime:multipartRelated>
        <mime:part>
            <soap:body use="encoded"
            namespace="http://www.skatestown.com/services/PriceCheck"
            encodingStyle="http://schemas.xmlsoap.org/soap/encoding/"/>
        </mime:part>
        <mime:part>
          <mime:content part="picture" type="image/gif"/>
```

```
            <mime:content part="picture" type="image/jpeg"/>
        </mime:part>
    </mime:multipartRelated>
</output>
    </operation>
</binding>
```

The only thing that has changed is within the output element (added definitions are in bold). Note the duplicate mime:content elements with the part named picture. When you see them, you are to interpret them as alternative formats, one of which might appear.

A Sketch of How WSDL Maps to Java

We've examined the WSDL standard for service description. Now let's see how it addresses automating the invocation of Web services by the service requestor.

WSDL maps naturally to Java. Many tools automate this mapping, for both the requestor and the service provider. One tool in particular, WSDL2Java (provided by Axis), is examined in more detail in Chapter 5. For now, we'll sketch the mapping from a WSDL definition to Java. There are many possible approaches to mapping Java to WSDL; we'll use the pattern that the Axis WSDL2Java tool uses.

Just as with the examination of WSDL, let's start by looking at the portType. The portType most naturally maps into a Java interface. The name of the interface typically takes on the name of the portType. So, the portType named PriceCheckPortType generates a Java interface named PriceCheckPortType. This file is declared in a package named from the targetNamespace URI of the WSDL definitions element containing the portType. Here's a piece of the Java interface generated for the PriceCheck portType:

```
package com.skatestown.www.services.PriceCheck;

public interface PriceCheckPortType extends java.rmi.Remote {


}
```

For each of the portType's operations, a public method is declared as a part of the interface. The signature of the method is built from the name of the operation; the input and output signatures as defined in the operation and any fault elements associated with the operation are included as exceptions thrown by the method. Here's the method signature generated (as part of the PriceCheckPortType interface) from the checkPrice operation:

```
public com.skatestown.www.ns.availability.AvailabilityType
        checkPrice(java.lang.String sku) throws java.rmi.RemoteException;
```

If the checkPrice operation had a fault element, it would have appeared as an exception thrown by the checkPrice method.

For those messages that are referenced by input, output, and fault elements, a separate class is generated for `complexTypes` (and all faults, regardless of whether they're simple or `complexTypes`) referenced by the parts of those messages. These type-based classes are used as part of the mechanism to deserialize and serialize XML to and from Java. The name of the class is taken from the name of the type or element. The package for the class is taken from the `targetNamespace` URI of the XML schema that defines the type or element. The class to serialize and deserialize the `AvailabilityType` element is an example and is used as part of the signature for the `checkPrice` method.

Each `binding` also generates a separate stub class, again using the name of the binding to name the class and the `targetNamespace` of the definitions element to define the package name. This class is a proxy to the service, in that it encapsulates all the implementation details associated with how a given `portType` is made concrete by the `binding`. This class implements the interface defined by the `portType`. Think of the binding class as a protocol and transport-specific implementation of the interface defined by the `portType`. For convenience, you can also use the `binding` to define a corresponding server-side skeleton to help insulate all the protocol- and transport-specific details from the actual implementation of the business logic associated with the Web service.

Finally, the WSDL `service` also generates an interface and class, which encapsulate details of invoking the service from the client application.

Nonfunctional Descriptions in WSDL

We've described how WSDL is used to describe the functional characteristics of a Web service, but what about the nonfunctional characteristics of a Web service? How can you describe security requirements and transactional capabilities of a Web service? How can a requestor determine whether a Web service invocation will be logged or audited by the service provider? How can the requestor know if their privacy will be respected?

These sorts of nonfunctional characteristics of a Web service can be described using WS-Policy and related specifications. In this section, we'll give an overview of how you can use WS-Policy to describe the requirements, capabilities, and restrictions associated with your Web services and the endpoints in which they execute.

Policies

There are several reasons why you might want to augment your WSDL functional descriptions with policy-based nonfunctional descriptions. First, it's important that a requestor know everything needed in order to invoke a Web service. The WSDL describes the sort of parameters to put into a request message to invoke business logic, but no part of WSDL natively describes things like security headers, reliable messaging capabilities, and so on. To complete a well-defined service, you augment WSDL with extra information.

Another reason to associate a WSDL with this extra information is to help the requestor make an appropriate choice of service. For example, all things being equal, a requestor will prefer to interact with a service that provides a statement of a privacy policy over one that doesn't. So, sometimes, the nonfunctional decorations of a service description have no bearing on the format of the messages going into and out from the Web service and only serve the purpose to help the requestor choose to invoke the Web service.

If nonfunctional information is added to the WSDL in a standard and well-known way, then there is a better chance that client- and server-side tooling will be available to act on these nonfunctional statements about a Web service. WS-Policy is one common way to express policy information in a service description.

The WS-Policy family of specifications has three major components: the framework, the assertions, and the attachment. Let's review how these pieces fit together and then get into details.

The basic component of the policy framework is a *policy assertion* 📖: a concrete statement about the requirement, preference, capability, or other characteristic of a Web service or its operating environment. Policy assertions describe certain qualities of service such as reliability of messaging:

```
<wsrm:DeliveryAssurance Value="wsrm:ExactlyOnce"/>
```

(This is described in more detail in Chapter 10, "Web Services Reliable Messaging.") You'll also see policy assertions in security. For example, the requestor must use digital signatures when invoking a Web service, described as follows:

```
<wsse:Integrity wsp:Usage="wsp:Required">
    <wsse:Algorithm  Type="wsse:AlgCanonicalization"
            URI="http://www.w3.org/Signature/Drafts/xml-exc-c14n"/>
    <wsse:Algorithm Type="wsse:AlgSignature"
                URI=" http://www.w3.org/2000/09/xmldsig#rsa-sha1"/>
    <MessageParts
            Dialect="http://schemas.xmlsoap.org/2002/12/wsse#soap">
        S:Body
    </MessageParts>
    </wsse:Integrity>
    <wsse:SecurityToken>
        <wsse:TokenType>wsse:X509v3</wsse:TokenType>
    </wsse:SecurityToken>
</wsse:Integrity>
```

An entire specification, WS-SecurityPolicy, describes security-related policy assertions. We go into more detail about security policies in Chapter 9, "Securing Web Services."

Sometimes a policy assertion is a simple statement of fact, such as "this Web service uses a certain privacy policy" or "this service uses a certain dialect of SOAP." Sometimes the policy assertion is a complicated statement, indicating possible sets of requestor-specifiable parameters, various optional solutions to a requirement, and so on.

Policy assertions come from various realms, such as security and reliable messaging. WS-Policy itself doesn't define any policy assertions (except a few general-purpose ones we'll describe later, which are defined by a related specification called WS-PolicyAssertions).

Policy assertions are grouped together to form a *policy* 📖. You can think of policy assertions as building blocks, or basic components that are combined in various ways to form an actual policy. The WS-Policy specification defines the associated framework, including a container, grouping elements, and standard attributes.

A policy forms a named collection of policy assertions that can be referenced, using standard XML mechanisms, by other XML and Web services components such as a WSDL definition. One common form of reference mechanism is the way by which a policy is associated (attached) to a *policy subject* 📖. A policy subject can be a Web service, a component of a Web service description, a part of the Web service's operating environment, or various other entities related to a Web service. The specification called WS-PolicyAttachments describes how policies are associated with policy subjects.

WS-Policy

WS-Policy was originally published in December 2002 by BEA, IBM, Microsoft, and SAP. Version 1.1 was published in May 2003, to improve on version 1.0.

WS-Policy defines how to group policy assertions into a named collection that can be referenced by other components. WS-Policy defines the fundamental framework for policies in a Web services world. This framework has three pieces:

- An XML element to act as a container for one or more policy assertions
- A set of XML elements that describe how the policy assertions grouped by the container are to be combined
- A set of standard XML attributes that may be associated with policy assertions

WS-Policy has a frustratingly schizophrenic mechanism to name policies. There is not one, but *two* standard mechanisms by which a policy can be named: by XML QName or by URI. You should choose one form and stick with it for all your policy work. If you're using WS-Policy mostly in conjunction with WSDL, stay with the QName approach used throughout WSDL. (In our opinion, it's unfortunate that the WS-Policy authors couldn't settle on one form.) Throughout the rest of the WS-Policy specification and related specifications, various optional elements and attributes describe how to refer to policies by QName or by URI. You'll need to cope with both forms, since either might be associated with Web services defined by your business partners.

The general form of the `policy` container element appears as follows:

```
<wsp:Policy ((Name=" " TargetNamespace= " "? )| Id= " " )
  <policy specific assertion> *
  <policy-specific security>?
</wsp:Policy>
```

You need to name a policy using the `Name` and `TargetNamespace` attributes (forming the QName of the policy) or using an `Id`, which is a local name and is combined with the XML base of the document containing the policy element to form a URI to the policy. Note that the `TargetNamespace` can also be derived from the context of the policy element (for example, the namespace in which the element is defined, such as defined by an XML schema element or a WSDL `definitions` element).

The container also provides an option to specify security policy assertions specific to this policy element. This is an interesting example of the specification using itself to define itself.

Policy assertions are normally added to the policy container as independent entities. Unless there is some discipline-specific rule about how individual policy assertions interact when they're placed within the same policy container element, we assume they're completely independent. But what are the semantics of this group of individual policy assertions? How should a requestor interpret how the individual assertions are meant to be combined? This is the role of the second component of the WS-Policy framework: the combinatorial elements or operators.

Policy Operators

Four operators are defined by WS-Policy to describe different combinations of policy assertions: `All`, `ExactlyOne`, `OneOrMore`, and the basic `policy` element (which has the same semantic as the `All` operator).

A policy such as

```
<wsp:Policy
    name="PolicyExample1"
    TargetNamespace="http://www.skatestown.com/policies" >
  <wsp:All>
    <Assertion:A />
    <Assertion:B />
    <Assertion:C />
  </wsp:All>
</wsp:Policy>
```

defines a policy named `PolicyExample1` in the `http://www.skatestown.com/policies` namespace. This policy states that all of the assertions A, B, and C are in effect. Of course, what it means for a policy assertion to be *in effect* is entirely dependent on the domain of each policy assertion and the policy subject to which the policy is attached. Some policy assertions, like the assertion of a privacy policy, are in effect because they state an intention of the Web service. Other policy assertions are in effect because they make a statement on required components the requestor needs to include in a message to invoke the Web service.

The `ExactlyOne` operation defines a choice between the component policy assertions, so a policy such as:

```
<wsp:Policy
    name="PolicyExample2"
    TargetNamespace="http://www.skatestown.com/policies" >
```

```
   <wsp:ExactlyOne>
     <Assertion:A />
     <Assertion:B />
     <Assertion:C />
   </wsp:ExactlyOne>
</wsp:Policy>
```

defines a policy named `PolicyExample2` in the `http://www.skatestown.com/policies`
namespace in which only one of the assertions A, B, and C is in effect.

Finally, the operator named `OneOrMore` is a variation of this combination, where some
subset of the policy assertions listed as child elements is in effect.

Note that operators can nest. For example, in the previous examples, any of the
`Assertion` elements can be replaced by an operator, allowing you to form complex,
nested policy expressions that combine policy assertions in arbitrary ways.

Policy Usage and Preference

The third component of WS-Policy is a pair of global XML attributes: `Usage` and
`Preference`. You can add these attributes to the various `policy` assertion child elements
of the policy. The `Usage` attribute describes how the policy assertion is to be interpreted
in the context of the policy; it can take any of the following values:

- `Required`—The assertion must apply, or an error occurs. As an example, this `Usage`
  would be used on a digital signature policy assertion if the Web service provider
  wanted all input messages to be digitally signed.

- `Rejected`—The assertion must not apply, or an error occurs. For example, if you
  explicitly don't want to receive encrypted messages, and you return a fault message
  if one is received, a policy assertion using this `Usage` should be used.

- `Optional`—The assertion may apply, but it doesn't have to apply. This `Usage`
  would be used if you've built a Web service that could accept digitally signed input
  messages but is also willing to accept input messages that aren't signed.

- `Observed`—This `Usage` is informational in nature; it lets the requestor know that a
  particular assertion will be applied. A privacy policy would typically use this
  `Usage`.

- `Ignored`—This `Usage` is also informational, telling the requestor that if something
  happens to cause the policy assertion to be in effect, no error message will be
  emitted, nor will some other action be taken by the Web service.

The other global XML attribute defined by WS-Policy is the `Preference` attribute. This
attribute is usually used in conjunction with the `ExactlyOnce` operator. If there is a
choice between a set of policy assertions, this attribute can act as a hint to the requestor.
The value of the `Preference` attribute is an integer value; the higher the number, the
stronger the preference. So, a policy such as

```
<wsp:Policy
    name="PolicyExample3"
```

```
        TargetNamespace="http://www.skatestown.com/policies" >
  <wsp:ExactlyOne>
    <Assertion:A wsp:Preference="100" />
    <Assertion:B wsp:Preference="50" />
    <Assertion:C wsp:Preference="1" />
  </wsp:ExactlyOne>
</wsp:Policy>
```

suggests to the requestor that it has a choice of assertion A, B, or C, and that the service provider would much prefer the requestor to choose assertion A.

Referencing Policies

The last part of the WS-Policy specification we'll review is the policy referencing capability. WS-Policy defines an element called `PolicyReference` that allows you to include the contents of one policy into another. The `PolicyReference` element can appear anywhere a policy assertion can, and it refers (by QName or URI) to another policy. The meaning of this include function is that the contents of the included policy element are wrapped with an `All` operator element and inserted in place of the `PolicyReference` element. For example, combined with the previous examples, the following policy statement

```
<wsp:Policy
    name="PolicyExample4"
    TargetNamespace="http://www.skatestown.com/policies"
    xmlns:tns="http://www.skatestown.com/policies">
  <wsp:ExactlyOne>
    <wsp:PolicyReference Ref="tns:PolicyExample2" />
    <Assertion:D />
    <Assertion:E />
  </wsp:ExactlyOne>
</wsp:Policy>
```

is equivalent to

```
<wsp:Policy
    name="PolicyExample4"
    TargetNamespace="http://www.skatestown.com/policies" >
  <wsp:ExactlyOne>
    <wsp:All>
      <wsp:ExactlyOne>
        <Assertion:A />
        <Assertion:B />
        <Assertion:C />
      </wsp:ExactlyOne>
    </wsp:All>
    <Assertion:D />
    <Assertion:E />
  </wsp:ExactlyOne>
</wsp:Policy>
```

The WS-Policy framework is simple and powerful. But most of the art of policy design is in the way policy assertions are specified and standardized and then used by Web service designers.

Policy Assertions

As we mentioned earlier, policy assertions are the building blocks for policies. Policy assertions are discipline-specific, such as security policy assertions, reliability policy assertions, and so on. You choose from these standardized policy assertions, configure them, and combine them into a policy document.

WS-Policy includes a separate document, WS-PolicyAssertions, that defines four standard policy assertions describing generic policy statements you should make about a Web service. These assertions are as follows:

- *Text Encoding*—This policy assertion lets you declare which character set is used for text that appears in Web services messages. The possible values are the ones typically associated with XML documents (such as ISO-8859-5) and are defined in the XML Schema documents.

- *Language Assertion*—This policy assertion allows you to declare which human language is expected in messages. These values are the ones that are typically associated with the `xml:lang` attribute in XML.

- *Spec Assertion*—This policy lets you declare which versions of a particular technical specification a Web service is compliant with. For example, you can use this policy assertion to declare exactly which version of a security specification the Web service has been built to accommodate.

- *Message Predicate*—This policy assertion is pretty sophisticated. It lets you be detailed about the exact contents of a message going into or coming out of a Web service. The contents of the message are described using a pattern, typically using the XPath language. Although the WSDL language does a much clearer job of describing the content of Web service messages, this policy assertion can be more detailed in the description of the message. To make the job of specifying the contents of a Web service message easier, WS-PolicyAssertions also defines a function library of XPath functions to reference various parts of a SOAP message.

Policy Attachments

So far, we've discussed policies and policy assertions, but we haven't been clear about how a policy is associated with a policy subject like a WSDL `portType` or a WSDL message. You can even attach policies to UDDI elements. This is the job of the WS-PolicyAttachment specification.

A policy can be associated with a policy subject in one of two ways: as part of the subject's definition (for example, within a WSDL document) or external to the subject's definition. WS-PolicyAttachment standardizes a pair of XML global attribute definitions that can be added to any XML element either explicitly in the element's schema definition or implicitly, if the element is defined with open attribute content (it allows attributes in addition to those declared explicitly in its definition). A pair of global attributes is defined because WS-Policy can be named by URI or by QName. For example, the following policy expression could be included to declare that the language expected with SkatesTown's services can be English, Spanish, or French (to serve the entire North American marketplace for skateboards). The policy itself would be declared as follows:

```
<wsp:Policy name="SkatestownLanguages"
    TargetNamespace="http://www.skatestown.com/policies" >
  <wsp:OneOrMore>
    <wsp:Language Language="en" />
    <wsp:Language Language="es" />
    <wsp:Language Language="fr" />
  </wsp:OneOrMore>
</wsp:Policy>
```

The policy could then be referenced from within the PriceCheck service declaration, using a WS-PolicyAttachment attribute:

```
<service name="PriceCheck"
  wsp:PolicyRefs="stp:SkatestownLanguages"
  xmlns:wsp="http://schemas.xmlsoap.org/ws/2002/12/policy"
  xmlns:stp="http://www.skatestown.com/policies" >
  <port name="PriceCheck" binding="pc:PriceCheckSOAPBinding">
    <documentation>
      <wsi:Claim
          conformsTo="http://ws-i.org/profiles/basic/1.0" />
    </documentation>
    <soap:address location="http://www.skatestown.com/services/PriceCheck"/>
  </port>
</service>
```

The PolicyRefs attribute takes a list of QNames as its value, allowing you to associate a collection of policies to any policy subject. The alternative approach, using PolicyURIs, has a similar function, but it uses the URI mechanism of naming policies. (Don't you wish the designers of WS-Policy had agreed on one naming mechanism rather than two?)

It's worth noting that policies can be inherited with a collection of WSDL elements. WS-PolicyAttachment exploits a natural *inheritance* within WSDL. For example, you would expect that a policy attached to a portType would be inherited by its input, output, and fault child elements. The term *effective policy* 📖 defines the policy associated with a WSDL element. This can be either a policy that is inherited or a policy that is directly attached to a WSDL element, either explicitly, as part of the WSDL document, or using the external policy attachment mechanism we'll discuss shortly. The inheritance of effective policy in WSDL is described in Table 4.3.

Table 4.3 **Policy Inheritance in WSDL**

WSDL Element	Effective Policy
message	Policy associated with the message
message/part	Policy associated with the part, merged with the effective policy of the part's message parent
portType	Policy associated with the portType
portType/operation	Policy associated with the operation merged with the effective policy of the operation's portType parent
portType/operation/input	Policy associated with the input merged with the effective policy of the input's operation parent *and* merged with the effective policy of the message associated with the input element
portType/operation/output	Similar to input
portType/operation/fault	Similar to fault
binding	Policy associated with the binding merged with the effective policy of the associated portType
binding/operation	Policy associated with the operation merged with the effective policy of the operation's binding parent *and* merged with the effective policy of the corresponding portType/operation
binding/operation/input	Policy associated with the input merged with the effective policy of the input's operation parent *and* merged with the effective policy of the corresponding portType/operation/input
binding/operation/output	Similar to input
binding/operation/fault	Similar to fault
service	Policy associated with the service
service/port	Policy associated with the port merged with the effective policy of the port's service parent

Now consider the following problem: what if you don't have the ability to modify a WSDL used to describe one of your Web services? For example, perhaps the portType being used is defined by an industry standards body, and you can't go in and add a PolicyRefs attribute to the WSDL definition of the portType. This is an example of why the WS-PolicyAttachment specification defines an alternate or external means of attaching policy to a policy subject.

The PolicyAttachment element is defined to allow you to express the attachment of one or more policies to a policy subject. The policy subject is identified by a domain-specific expression. For example, the PolicyAttachment can be expressed to attach a policy to "any Server given a range of IP addresses."

That's it for our discussion of WS-Policy. Now, let's look ahead to see how the WSDL language is changing.

Standardizing WSDL: W3C and WSDL 2.0

As we mentioned earlier, WSDL is being standardized within the W3C. This work has been underway since the spring of 2001, and it's continuing at the time this book is being written. This section will use the November 2003 version of the draft specifications that define WSDL 2.0. We'll also sketch out how some of SkatesTown's WSDLs might look using WSDL 2.0.

What's New in WSDL 2.0

WSDL 2.0 represents a formal standardization of WSDL. Although the starting point was WSDL 1.1, the W3C working group has made quite a few changes to the WSDL language. There are so many changes, in fact, that the work that began with the name WSDL 1.2 has been renamed WSDL 2.0.

The Web services community did all this work to standardize WSDL 2.0 for several reasons:

- *Remove ambiguity in WSDL 1.1*—For example, no one could agree on one standard definition for solicit-response style of message exchange (transmission primitive).

- *Align and/or simplify language semantics*—For example, it was confusing to some XML users that the WSDL 1.1 import element wasn't the same semantically as XML Schema's import element.

- *Consistency*—For example, all WSDL elements allow open content (elements from other XML namespaces can be inserted as children).

- *Better naming*—Several elements have new names; for example port and portType have been renamed to the more resonant terms endpoint and interface.

- *Simplification*—Certain complexities that many found confusing (such as WSDL message and WSDL part) have been removed and replaced with straightforward XML constructs.

- *New functionality*—Several important new mechanisms have been introduced into the language, such as interface extension.

- *Removal of functionality*—Some things have been removed. For example, WSDL 1.1 allowed operation overloading (multiple operations with the same name but different input or output messages), but WSDL 2.0 doesn't.

The WSDL 2.0 language is defined by three related specifications:

- Part I, the Core Language
- Part II, Message Patterns
- Part III, Bindings

The language used within the specifications has also been greatly formalized. Although this makes the documents harder to read and understand, it removes ambiguity. Happily,

there will be a primer, which will help people understand how to use WSDL 2.0. Of
course, books like this one will also be of great aid to the Web service designer.

Overview of WSDL 2.0

Let's examine the contents of WSDL 2.0 in roughly the same order we examined the
contents of WSDL 1.1. For each component of WSDL, we'll examine what is new,
sketch out how SkatesTown might use WSDL 2.0, and summarize the changes in a table,
using the following notational convention:

+   Feature added

-    Feature removed

Δ   Feature changed

interface

What we knew as a portType in WSDL 1.1, we'll know as an interface in WSDL 2.0.
This represents more than just a name change, and an intuitive one at that. The interface element introduces an important new concept: *interface extension* 📖. It lets you
build a Web service interface by combining the operations defined in other
interfaces. For example, the StockAvailableNotification interface could be refactored to define a notification interface as follows:

```
    <interface name="Notification" ...>
        <operation name="registration" ...>
...
        <operation name="notification" ...>
...
        <operation name="expirationNotification" ...>
...
        <operation name="cancellation" ...>
...
    </interface>
```

The StockAvailableNotification interface could extend it as follows:

```
    <interface name="StockAvailableNotification"
            extends="sa:NotificationPortType" ...>
        <operation name="xyz" ...>
...
    </interface>
```

In this way, Notification is separated out as an interface that can be utilized by other
business functions besides stock availability. By using the extends attribute, the
StockAvailableNotification interface includes the operations defined in the
Notification interface. In fact, the extends attribute can have a list of QNames;
thereby an interface can extend multiple interfaces. This is similar to interface inheritance in Java.

WSDL 2.0 is also much more consistent with respect to extensibility. All elements, including `interface`, can have child elements from other namespaces. Lack of open content in the WSDL 1.1 `portType` was constraining; for example, it wasn't legal to add elements to describe nonfunctional characteristics of a `portType`. Another extensibility mechanism, called features and properties, can be used, but we'll examine that feature later.

Another thing added to the `interface` component is a `styleDefault` attribute. This optional attribute lets you describe a style of message-exchange pattern that applies to all the child `operations` of the `interface`. WSDL 2.0 defines several `styles`, including RPC style and two attribute-related styles (Get-attribute and Set-attribute) that designate certain operations as getter and setter operations (like the JavaBeans pattern). We'll examine message exchange patterns later, when we look in more detail at WSDL 2.0 operation elements.

WSDL 2.0 includes a new concept called features and properties. This concept is used to describe abstract functionality and associated it with various components of a WSDL 2.0 description. This concept is similar to the corresponding feature and module concept in SOAP 1.2. The notion is that a particular feature name and set of corresponding properties is standardized by a discipline. For example, the security community might standardize authentication, authorization, and other features and corresponding properties. Designers would then include these features in their `interface` definition (and other WSDL 2.0 elements) to specify that their Web service uses the feature and how it constrains the properties associated with that feature. Clearly, the features and properties concept is useful to describe the nonfunctional characteristics of a Web service. Unfortunately, we already have a mechanism called WS-Policy to do this for us. You're advised to examine how the Web services community figures out whether to use WS-Policy or WSDL 2.0 features and properties to describe things like security, reliability, transactionality, and so on. At the moment, specifications such as WS-Security use WS-Policy, not features and properties.

Here's a summary of the changes to the interface:

Δ   Name changed to `interface` from `portType`

+   Interface extension (aggregation of operations from multiple interfaces)

+   Open content

+   `styleDefault` attribute

+   Features and properties

operation

The biggest change to `operation` is the clarification of the transmission primitives. Whereas WSDL 1.1 defined four (in, in-out, notification, and solicit-response) and only the first two were ever properly understood and implemented, WSDL 2.0 defines the concept of a message exchange pattern that allows myriad different patterns to be standardized and therefore allows interoperability between implementations. *Message exchange patterns* 📖 are described in a separate specification for WSDL 2.0 (Part II). They describe abstract templates for a set of messages between senders and receivers. The number (cardinality) of messages, the sequence of messages, the direction in which the messages are sent (relative to the provider of the service being described by the WSDL), and the possible placement of fault messages are codified by a message exchange pattern. WSDL 2.0 Part II replaces the four transmission primitives defined in WSDL 1.1 with nine standard patterns (of which only two are likely to ever be used with any regularity: in-only and in-out).

For any given `operation`, you must specify which message exchange pattern is used. For this, WSDL 2.0 defines the `style` attribute, which takes the URI name of the message exchange pattern as its value. Although there can be many different types of message exchange patterns, you really only have to know two of them: in-out (`http://www.w3.org/2003/11/wsdl/in-out`) and in-only (`http://www.w3.org/2003/11/wsdl/in-only`). The `PriceCheck` interface from SkatesTown demonstrates this:

```
<interface name="PriceCheck">
    <operation name="checkPrice"
               style="http://www.w3.org/2003/11/wsdl/in-out">
...
    </operation>
</interface>
```

A major improvement to WSDL is the elimination of the WSDL `message` and `part` elements. You now use the names of XML element declarations to specify the format of `input`, `output`, and `fault` messages. The `checkPrice` operation has a much simpler and direct-looking signature:

```
<interface name="PriceCheck">
    <operation name="checkPrice">
               style="http://www.w3.org/2003/11/wsdl/in-out">
        <input message="avail:sku"/>
        <output message="avail:StockAvailability"/>
    </operation>
</interface>
```

There is no more indirection to look up, from the `input` element, to the `message` element, to the `part` element, to the actual XML element or type declaration. There is, of course, an additional, optional `messageReference` attribute, which may appear when the message exchange pattern being used may define multiple message components associated with the input or output roles. However, if you stick with the simple message exchange patterns, you don't have to worry about naming your messages.

One aspect of WSDL 2.0 that reduces the flexibility of operations is forbidding operation overloading. If two `operations` have the same QName, then they must be equivalent in structure (same input, output, and fault signature). To minimize the chances of this error, when you're combining interfaces using the interface extension feature, make sure each `operation` defined by any `interface` in a WSDL namespace has a name that is unique among all the operations in that namespace.

WSDL 2.0 also clarifies the role of faults. In conjunction with the formalization of message exchange patterns, the WSDL 1.1 `fault` element has been divided into two elements: `infault` and `outfault`. Other than this clarification and the removal of WSDL `message` and `part`, faults are much the same as in WSDL 1.1.

WSDL 2.0 operations may also include `feature` and `properties` elements.

Here's a summary of changes to `operation` (child of `interface`):

Δ   WSDL 1.1 transmission primitives clarified as message exchange patterns

+   `style` attribute

Δ   Abstract message format specified using XML types and elements; WSDL 1.1 `message` and `part` elements removed

-   Overloading of `operations`

Δ   `fault` element becomes `inFault` and `outFault`

+   Features and properties

types

The major change to the `types` element is that its content has been clarified. Whereas in WSDL 1.1 it was only by convention and profiling that you learned to put XML `schema` elements under a `types` element, WSDL 2.0 clarifies that the content should only be an XML `schema` element or an XML `import` element. Note that WSDL 2.0, like WSDL 1.1, lets you use other type systems besides XML schema.

Here's a summary of changes to `types`:

Δ   Clarifies contents as either an XML `schema` element or XML `import` element

binding

The WSDL 2.0 `binding` is similar to the WSDL 1.1 `binding`. The changes are due to the structural changes within `interface`, particularly the removal of the WSDL `message` and `part`.

The `binding` is also used to bind features and properties that are specified for an `interface`. For example, if an `interface` specifies that an authentication feature is being used, a `binding` can specify that this feature is realized by some form of Kerberos ticket that must be presented as proof of identity to authenticate the requestor.

The other major change is in the set of binding types standardized by WSDL 2.0. WSDL 1.1 standardized a SOAP 1.1, an HTTP, and a MIME binding type. WSDL 2.0 defines an HTTP and a MIME binding, but it defines a SOAP 1.2 binding type instead of a SOAP 1.1 binding type. The details of the SOAP 1.2 binding are similar to the SOAP 1.1 binding; the changes are due to the restructuring of the way `messages` are defined in `operations` at the `interface` level, and additional elements were added, such as a module specification element and a property constraint element, to reflect new

concepts introduced by SOAP 1.2. Here's an example binding of SkatesTown's
`PriceCheck` interface:

```
xmlns:soap="http://www.w3.org/2003/11/wsdl/soap12"
...
   <binding name="PriceCheckSOAPBinding" type="pc:PriceCheck">
     <soap:binding
        protocol="http://www.w3.org/2003/05/soap/bindings/HTTP/" />
   </binding>
```

If you don't need to specify SOAP headers or binding-specific properties and features,
you're done. Note that a lot of the complexity, like document versus RPC and encoded
versus literal, has gone away. Message exchange patterns have addressed document versus
RPC (this is now specified using the `style` attribute).

Here's a summary of changes to `binding`:

Δ   Binding of `operations` changed due to changes in `operations` at the `interface`
    level

+   Features and properties

-   `encodingStyle` and `use` attributes

Δ   SOAP 1.2 binding replaces SOAP 1.1 binding

endpoint

The `endpoint` element is a renaming of the `port` element from WSDL 1.1. Otherwise,
it's the same.

The summary of changes to `endpoint` is simple:

Δ   Change of name from `port` to `endpoint`

service

`Service` has been changed slightly to clarify that the constituent `endpoint` elements
represent alternative implementations of the same `interface`. An `interface` attribute
was added to specify which `interface` is implemented by the `service`. Here's what the
`PriceCheck` service looks like in WSDL 2.0:

```
<service name="PriceCheck" interface="pc:PriceCheck">
  <endpoint name="PriceCheck" binding="pc:PriceCheckSOAPBinding">
    <soap:address location="http://www.skatestown.com/services/PriceCheck"/>
  </endpoint>
</service>
```

As you see, not much has changed in this area that affects SkatesTown.
The summary of changes to `service` is as follows:

+   Added the notion that a service implements a single `interface`

Δ   All `endpoints` (was `port`) child elements must refer (via `binding`) to the same
    `interface`

definitions

The only change to the `definitions` element in WSDL 2.0 is the removal of the `name` attribute. It was at best documentation in WSDL 1.1, and by removing it, WSDL 2.0 is slightly simpler with no loss of function.

Here's a summary of changes to `definitions`:

- The `name` attribute

import **and** include

The way that WSDL documents are linked together has changed in WSDL 2.0. WSDL 1.1 used a single element, `import`, to link any WSDL document, regardless of namespace. WSDL 1.1 also was never clear about which types of documents could legally be imported. WSDL 2.0 clarifies this area. First, it introduces an additional element, `include`, which divides the work between `import` and `include`. The `import` element is used to import WSDL definitions from other WSDL namespaces. The `include` element is used to include elements defined in different documents, but with the same namespace. This semantic is analogous to the way `import` and `include` work in XML schema.

The summary of changes to WSDL document linking is as follows:

Δ   Clarified the content of the `import` element to refer to WSDL documents only

+   `include` element, aligning WSDL document linking with XML schema document linking

A Complete WSDL 2.0 Description

Although we haven't exhaustively reviewed all the details of WSDL 2.0, we have given you an idea of the scope of the changes. We end this section with a sketch of what Skatestown's `PriceCheck` service looks like, in its entirety, in WSDL 2.0 (see Listing 4.5).

Listing 4.5   **PriceCheck Service described in WSDL 2.0**

```
<?xml version="1.0" encoding="UTF-8"?>
<definitions
    targetNamespace="http://www.skatestown.com/services/PriceCheck"
    xmlns:pc="http://www.skatestown.com/services/PriceCheck"
    xmlns:avail="http://www.skatestown.com/ns/availability"
    xmlns:xsd="http://www.w3.org/2001/XMLSchema"
    xmlns:soap="http://www.w3.org/2003/11/wsdl/soap12"
    xmlns:wsdl2="http://www.w3.org/2003/11/wsdl"
    xmlns="http://www.w3.org/2003/11/wsdl">

    <!-- Type definitions -->
    <types>
      <xsd:schema
         targetNamespace="http://www.skatestown.com/ns/availability"
         xmlns:xsd="http://www.w3.org/2001/XMLSchema">
```

Listing 4.5   **Continued**

```xml
        <xsd:element name="sku" type="xsd:string" />

        <xsd:complexType name="availabilityType">
          <xsd:sequence>
             <xsd:element ref="avail:sku"/>
             <xsd:element name="price" type="xsd:double"/>
             <xsd:element name="quantityAvailable" type="xsd:integer"/>
          </xsd:sequence>
        </xsd:complexType>

        <xsd:element name="StockAvailability"
                     type="avail:availabilityType" />
     </xsd:schema>
  </types>

  <interface name="PriceCheck">
     <operation name="checkPrice">
              style="http://www.w3.org/2003/11/wsdl/in-out">
        <input message="avail:sku"/>
        <output message="avail:StockAvailability"/>
     </operation>
  </interface>

  <binding name="PriceCheckSOAPBinding" type="pc:PriceCheck">
     <soap:binding
        protocol="http://www.w3.org/2003/05/soap/bindings/HTTP/" />
  </binding>

  <service name="PriceCheck" interface="pc:PriceCheck">
     <endpoint name="PriceCheck" binding="pc:PriceCheckSOAPBinding">
        <soap:address location="http://www.skatestown.com/services/PriceCheck"/>
     </endpoint>
  </service>

</definitions>
```

Summary

We began this chapter with a question: How does the requestor know what message format should be used to invoke a Web service? We motivated the role of service description within a service-oriented architecture and explained how service description was
the basis for the publish, find, and bind operations. We reviewed the characteristics of a
well-defined service. The basis of a well-defined service is an IDL-level description of its

interface, described using version 1.1 of the Web Services Description Language (WSDL) together with the nonfunctional characteristics of the service described using WS-Policy. We reviewed the WSDL 1.1 language in great detail, using Web service descriptions for several of SkatesTown's services. We also sketched how WSDL relates to Java programming language artifacts, using the mapping implemented by the Axis tooling as an example.

We also discussed nonfunctional descriptions of Web services, focusing on the use of WS-Policy. We concluded this chapter by discussing the current direction of WSDL, the WSDL 2.0 work within the W3C.

In the next chapter, we'll describe the Axis project and how it supports Web services, including how it uses WSDL to generate Java code for the client and the server.

Resources

- *WSDL 1.1*—Web Services Description Language (WSDL) 1.1, (W3C Note 15 March 2001), `http://www.w3.org/TR/wsdl`

- *WSDL 2.0*—Web Services Description Language (WSDL) Version 2.0 Part 1: Core Language (W3C Editors' copy $Date: 2004/03/25 17:03:13 $), `http://www.w3.org/2002/ws/desc/wsdl20`

- *WS-Policy*—Web Services Policy Framework (WSPolicy) (28 May 2003), `http://www-106.ibm.com/developerworks/library/ws-polfram/`

- *WS-PolicyAttachment*—Web Services Policy Attachment (WSPolicyAttachment) (28 May 2003), `http://www-106.ibm.com/developerworks/library/ws-polatt/`

Implementing Web Services with Apache Axis

IN THIS CHAPTER, WE'RE GOING TO DIVE into the Apache Axis package, which we briefly introduced in Chapter 3, "The SOAP Protocol." To whet your appetite before we do, here's a high-level list of what Axis provides, and therefore what we'll be talking about:

- A set of client-side APIs for dynamically invoking SOAP Web services (with or without WSDL descriptions)
- Tools to translate WSDL documents into easy-to-use Java frameworks for either consuming or supplying Web services
- Mechanisms for hosting your Web services either within a servlet container (such as Tomcat, or any J2EE application server) or via a standalone server
- A framework that lets you create and compose message processing components (called *handlers*) into flexible and powerful processing chains
- A set of APIs for manipulating SOAP envelopes, bodies, and headers, and using them inside `Message` objects, which can also contain attachments (pieces of binary data outside the SOAP envelope)
- A transport framework that allows pluggable usage of a variety of underlying transport mechanisms (such as JMS, email, or anything you're inspired to write components for)
- Data binding, which enables mapping Java classes into XML schemas and vice versa

There's a lot to cover, and we don't mean for this chapter to be a complete reference to all the features of Axis (otherwise it might take up half the book!). However, by the end of the chapter, you should be comfortable enough using most of this functionality to build and consume basic Web services on your own, and you'll have a solid base from which to do more advanced work with the help of the Axis resources available through Apache and elsewhere on the Net. Before we get into the architecture and APIs, let's quickly discuss where Axis came from.

A Brief History of Axis

IBM contributed an early implementation of the SOAP protocol to Apache in 1999, which became known as Apache SOAP. This implementation, based on earlier work called SOAP4J, was a very functional library for processing SOAP messages, but it was written in a monolithic style—one code path pretty much did everything. This didn't jibe with the flexibility inherent in the SOAP extensibility model; so the Apache SOAP community decided in 2000 that some major rearchitecting would help, both in terms of extensibility and in hopes of increasing performance. As such, around the time of Apache SOAP version 2.1, the development team started soliciting input on Apache SOAP 3.0, a major refactoring/redesign of the codebase.

There was a lot of interest in the new project. Several proposals, all evincing similar ideas, were submitted to the development list amidst active discussion. A face-to-face design meeting took place at XML2000, including about 15 participants. That meeting in many ways was the real birthplace of Axis.

Axis is short for Apache eXtensible Interaction System. This name was chosen instead of Apache SOAP 3.0 (the original plan) because at that time, the XML Protocol working group at the W3C was just getting underway, and they believed the protocol was going to be called XP rather than SOAP—as such, having *SOAP* in the name seemed retro. As it turned out, SOAP 1.2 is still SOAP, but the Axis name stuck, and it does a good job of signaling the extensibility that was achieved with the new architecture.

The main architectural idea behind Axis is that of *chains of message-processing components* that can be developed separately and assembled at deployment time. These components, called *handlers* 📖, can each process portions of the message or do other custom work and can be combined to generate powerful and flexible systems. Axis also made the decision to switch from Apache SOAP's DOM-based XML processing to a faster (but somewhat more complex) SAX system. We'll get into more detail about these and other elements of the architecture in the rest of the chapter.

JAX-RPC, JAXM/SAAJ, and JAXB

During the Axis development cycle, the Java Community Process (Sun's consortium for defining Java community standards) was working on a couple of JSRs (Java Specification Requests) related to Web services. In particular, JAXM (XML messaging for Java) 📖 and JAX-RPC (XML based RPC for Java) 📖 were created, and JAXB (Java APIs for XML data-binding) 📖 was also in process.

JAX-RPC's charter was to define standard APIs for implementing RPC-style Web services in Java. Several Axis developers were in the JAX-RPC expert group and helped to introduce a handler concept into the JAX-RPC spec (although the JAX-RPC version is different than Axis's handlers, as you'll see later).

JAXM was originally the JSR that defined the `javax.xml.soap` package, which contained the APIs for manipulating the SOAP data structures (envelopes, bodies, and so on), messages, and attachments. Once JAX-RPC realized a need for these same APIs, the JAXM group refactored the SOAP APIs into a separate specification called SAAJ (Soap with Attachments API for Java) 📖. Axis contains SOAP message classes that implement the SAAJ specification, as well as functionality beyond what SAAJ specifies.

Axis 1.2 (the latest version) implements the current JAX-RPC and SAAJ specs, and Axis developers sit on the JAX-RPC 2.0 expert group, who are in the midst of revamping the JAX-RPC specification for greater functionality and ease of use. Later in the chapter we'll point out a few of the differences between what JAX-RPC currently defines and what Axis provides beyond that.

Current State of the Project

The Axis team, which includes several of the authors of this book, brought the project to a 1.0 release in October 2002. Version 1.1, with many improvements, followed in 2003. As this book is going to press, Axis version 1.2 is on its way to release, so the APIs we cover are from the 1.2 beta version. Although there was a lot of API churn during the first few versions of Axis, things have stabilized greatly, and changes are now much slower and more managed. This means you can count on the APIs we cover here to be the way to do things for a while.

While the Axis team is happy with 1.2 and the progress we've made toward making a usable and interoperable package, there is a lot of room for improvement. At the end of this chapter, we'll discuss some of the changes and new features we expect to see in future versions of Axis.

Installing Axis

You can obtain the latest version of Axis by going to `http://ws.apache.org/axis` and clicking on the Downloads link on the left side of the page. Instructions are included with the package in the `docs/` directory.

Installing Axis on most servlet engines is as easy as dropping a Web application into your deployment directory. In the Axis installation, you'll find a webapps directory, underneath which is an `axis/` directory. Copy that directory into your servlet engine's deployed `webapps` directory (for Apache Tomcat, this would be `tomcat/webapps`), and you should be done. Some other servlet engines may have more complex procedures for installing `webapps`; please read the documentation for your particular system (as well as the installation guide from Axis) to make sure you follow the correct steps.

To check that the installation is running correctly, try to access the app with a Web browser. If you're using Tomcat, this will mean pointing the browser at `http://localhost:8080/axis/` (adjust as appropriate for other servlet engines—refer to the documentation for the servlet engine). On the start page, you should see a link to verify your installation's configuration; click it to make sure Axis is finding all the components it needs (see the section "Development/Debugging Tools" for more details on the happyAxis page).

To use the Axis client software we'll be describing, you'll also need to make sure the JARs in the Axis distribution's `lib/` directory are all on your classpath. These include

- `axis.jar`
- `commons-discovery.jar`
- `commons-logging.jar`
- `log4j-1.2.8.jar`
- `wsdl4j.jar`
- `jaxrpc.jar`
- `saaj.jar`

Axis Architecture

Axis was designed to be usable in a wide variety of environments by users of varying skill levels and interests. As such, the system can be considered in a number of chunks, each of which can be used without needing to know much about the others. This section will cover the essential architecture of Axis. We'll give you a 20,000-foot view, and then in the following sections cover each area in more detail.

Handlers and Chains: Concepts

Axis is all about *chains of message processing components* that work together to handle (receive, process, and produce) SOAP messages. These components are called *handlers*, and they are all Java classes based around a simple interface:

```
void invoke(MessageContext context) throws AxisFault;
```

This method, from the `org.apache.axis.Handler` interface, is the central thing that handlers need to implement. When invoked, each handler does whatever it has been built to do. That might involve reading or writing pieces of a SOAP message, logging information to a database, checking a user's authentication credentials, or anything else you might imagine. Axis comes with prebuilt handlers for common tasks such as authorization and session management, and end-users and third parties are building more all the time.

The `MessageContext` 📖 (see Figure 5.1) is even more central to Axis than handlers. This class represents all the information relevant to a particular SOAP interaction—in particular the request message, the response message, and a bag of properties that allow viewing and controlling the behavior of the system. There are also a few other special fields outside the bag. A given `MessageContext` is passed from handler to handler to process a particular interaction (Web service invocation).

Handlers can be combined into *chains* 📖 which, as it turns out, look just like handlers to the system. In other words, the chain classes that group handlers together also implement the Handler interface and can themselves be invoked. This is a classic example of a composable architecture: When a chain's `invoke()` method is called, it calls invoke() on each of its constituent handlers, which themselves might be chains. This method of grouping and composition allows you to build sets of handlers that work together to accomplish a task, and then use the whole set as a pluggable unit.

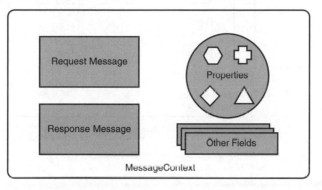

Figure 5.1   The Axis MessageContext

Axis uses two types of chains: *simple* chains 🔖 and *targeted* chains 🔖. A simple chain is a list of handlers that should be invoked in order (see Figure 5.2). A targeted chain (see Figure 5.3) is a little different; instead of a linear list of handlers, a targeted chain has exactly three handlers it cares about: the *request* handler, the *pivot* 🔖 handler, and the *response* handler.

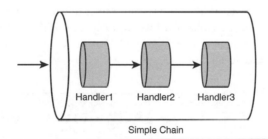

Figure 5.2   A simple chain

Targeted chains are built with the idea that the pivot handler is the place where the real work happens. For instance, deployed services in Axis are targeted chains, and the pivot handler calls the Java class you're exposing as a Web service. Before the pivot, the request handler (which is usually a chain—as such, we'll often refer to the *request chain* and the *response chain*) does preprocessing work. After the pivot, the response handler does post-processing work. On the server side, this means the request chain generally operates on the incoming request message, and the response chain generally operates on the outgoing response message generated by your service.

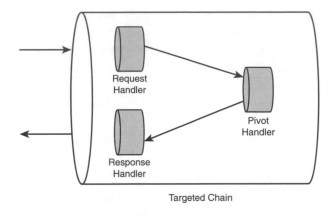

Figure 5.3   A targeted chain

Server-Side Message Processing

Now let's talk about how Axis processes messages. First we'll walk through the message flow on the server side, and then we'll turn our attention to the client.

Look at Figure 5.4, which is a graphical representation of the server-side message flow through Axis. When you use Axis as a SOAP server, the first thing that happens is that a transport listener receives a message. *Transport listener* 📖 is a fancy term for any software that can take input and turn it into something that Axis understands. For example, this might be a servlet, a JMS (Java Message Service) listener, or a class you've written to poll a directory for new files in which you expect to find SOAP messages. The transport listener is the primary piece responsible for implementing the rules of a particular SOAP binding, as described in Chapter 3.

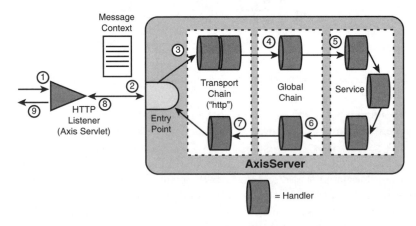

Figure 5.4   Axis server-side message processing

The listener we're most often interested in is the built-in HTTP listener, which is implemented as a servlet (class `org.apache.axis.transport.http.AxisServlet`). This class accepts an HTTP request (step 1 in the diagram), wraps it in an Axis `Message` class, and then puts that `Message` into a `MessageContext` and hands it to an `AxisServer` 📖 (step 2), which is the main server-side processing class.

The transport listener, in addition to the message itself, has loaded up the `MessageContext` with various properties that it thinks might be useful for the engine to know. These properties might include generic things like the time the message was received, and also transport-specific details such as a reference to the HTTP headers in a format that the servlet understands.

One of the special properties the listener must set is the transport name (the `MessageContext` has a specific accessor for this field, instead of carrying it in the property bag). The listener might have a transport name compiled into its code, or it might get the name from a configuration parameter. The transport name allows you to configure different kinds of functionality for different endpoint addresses.

Transport-Specific Message Processing

The first thing the `AxisServer` does when it starts processing the message is to look for a *transport chain* (a targeted chain) whose name matches the transport name in the `MessageContext`. If it finds one, it hands the `MessageContext` to the request handler of that targeted chain before doing anything else. This allows the server to implement *transport-specific* processing.

Transport-specific processing consists of any work that closely relates to the transport over which a message was received. Examples include anything that deals with HTTP headers for an HTTP transport. The general goal of the transport-specific handlers when receiving a message is to take protocol-specific data and make the appropriate parts of that data available in a more general way; ideally, the handlers after the transport-specific chain shouldn't need to access the transport-specific portions of the `MessageContext`.

Here's an example that might make this easier to understand. HTTP has a built-in authentication mechanism that lets you pass a username and password via an HTTP header. Other transport protocols have the same concept of username/password, but they pass that information in different ways. It's also possible to pass a username/password in a SOAP header, which wouldn't be transport-specific. So, because we don't want to have to write three or four different versions of code that checks username/password combinations, we arrange for each transport-specific set of credentials to be turned into a standard username/password pair by handlers specific to that transport. Later handlers can look for the generic version and won't need to worry about the transport-specific one.

Global Message Processing

After the transport-specific request processing completes without error, the server then passes the `MessageContext` on to the *global* request chain (step 4). This chain contains handlers that process *every* message that comes into the system, no matter the transport. You might use the *global chain* 📖 to implement sitewide security policies, for instance, or provide all deployed services with the ability to process a certain set of SOAP extensions in a consistent fashion. Another typical global handler usage is for logging/management.

Service Message Processing

After the global request chain is finished, the server needs to call a service handler that does the real work of processing the message (step 5). Because Axis strives to be flexible, there are a variety of ways the engine might figure out which service to call to process a given message, which might include looking at the endpoint URL or content inside the message. For now, let's assume that we know which service is relevant. (The service, like the transport name, is also one of the special fields in the MessageContext that exist outside the bag of properties.)

The service handler is a special kind of wrapper handler called a SOAPService 📖 (org.apache.axis.handlers.soap.SOAPService). This class is itself a targeted chain, with a request and response chain inside it. This allows you to insert pre- and postprocessing handlers into the flow that are specific to your service, which you might do to implement service-specific extensions or management policies.

Inside the SOAPService is a special handler known as the *provider* 📖 that is responsible for doing the real work of your Web service, including calling your service class. Note that in order to make a successful Java call to a typical back-end Web service, Axis has to use its *type mapping* 📖 system to translate the incoming XML data into Java objects and then again to translate the Java objects in the response back into XML.

The Provider

The provider is the pivot handler for the SOAPService, since it's the point at which you finish processing the request message, turn back toward the other direction, and continue processing with the response message. So the MessageContext, perhaps laden with a response message from your service, passes back out through the service-specific response chain, then the global response chain (step 6), and finally through the transport-specific response chain (step 7). All of these response handlers therefore get a chance to look at or alter the response message as it's on the way out of the system. This is the place you might insert session-management headers, for instance, or encrypt the outgoing body if appropriate.

Once the message comes back out of the AxisServer, the HTTP listener (the servlet) takes the response message out of the MessageContext (step 8) and sends it back to the client as an HTTP response (step 9).

Client-Side Message Processing

The AxisClient 📖 (org.apache.axis.client.AxisClient) is the client-side equivalent of the AxisServer class, and it handles the message flow through the various components on the client. The Call 📖 object (org.apache.axis.client.Call), however, is the main client-side entry point to Axis. Just as on the server side there is always a transport listener that invokes the AxisServer, on the client side you always invoke the

AxisClient by using a Call, or, as you'll see later, by using a custom-built stub that can insulate you from some of the details of using the Call object. In other words, even though the AxisClient does the work of moving the MessageContext through the processing flow, you never call it directly.

Inside the AxisClient (Figure 5.5), the message flow looks similar to that of the server, but the order of the transport/global/service processing flow is reversed. If you think about it a moment, you'll see why this makes sense: On the client, you're making a request to a remote service via a transport such as HTTP. That means the *last* thing that happens to an outgoing message before it gets sent is the transport-specific stuff. Before that, any global request handlers that have been configured for your client get a chance to examine or alter the request message; and before that, any service-specific request handlers get to do the same.

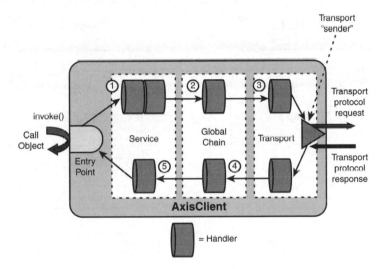

Figure 5.5   Client-side message processing

The transport chain on the client side is a little different than the one on the server. On the server, we only care about the request and response chains inside the transport, and there isn't a specific pivot handler that the engine uses (the same is true of the global handlers, by the way—only the request and response parts are used, not the pivot). On the client, however, the transport targeted chain does have a pivot handler, which is the transport *sender* 📖. The sender is responsible for taking the request message out of the MessageContext and sending it across the wire in a protocol-specific way. Then it retrieves any response message from the other side and, just like the provider on the server side, turns the processing around and lets the response bubble back through the response chains—first transport, then global, then service. At that point, the Call object regains control and takes responsibility for getting the results back to your application code.

The `MessageContext` and Its Many Uses

The `MessageContext`, as you've seen, is a central piece of the Axis architecture. The main reason the `MessageContext` is so important is that it encourages a *loosely coupled* architecture for message-processing components, which is both powerful and flexible. To show you what we mean, let's consider an example.

Imagine that two handlers want to communicate with each other while processing a message. In particular, let's posit a SOAP header that contains a username/password combination. The first handler wants to authenticate that the user checks out against the local user database, with the correct password. It then wants to tell the second handler that the user is OK, after which the second one will (later, on the response chain) include a special header in the response message containing a promotional offer for current customers (see Figure 5.6).

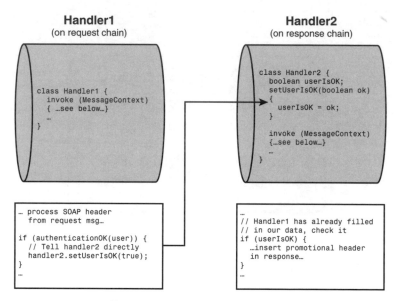

Figure 5.6   Tightly coupled handlers

As you see in the figure, `Handler1` has a reference directly to `Handler2` and sets the `userIsOK` field by calling the appropriate accessor on `Handler2`. This is a fine way to do things—until we encounter a situation that requires us to get at that piece of data from another handler.

For instance, let's say we want to add a logging handler to record the number of authenticated users who have used the service. To do this with the tightly coupled design of Figure 5.6, we'll need to change some code—either `Handler1` will need to also tell the logging Handler about its authentication success/failure, or `Handler2` could do it. In either case, we can't make changes to the system without altering code.

If, instead of communicating directly with the second handler, the first handler takes the value out of the SOAP header and places it in a well-known slot in the MessageContext property bag, it can complete its work without having to know or care about the eventual usage of the data. In particular, this allows us to introduce the logging handler without any code changes—the logging handler pulls the value it's looking for out of the MessageContext (see Figure 5.7). This pattern also allows us to replace the second handler with a new class that does something different with the data without any code changes to the first handler to account for the new class.

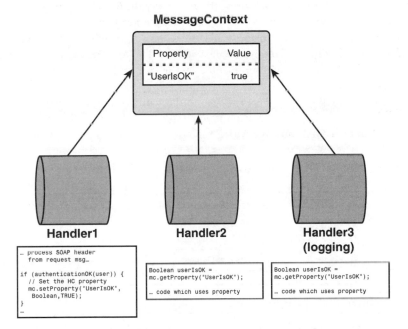

Figure 5.7   Handler collaboration via the MessageContext

This is nothing groundbreaking—it's a lot like the blackboard style of software design from the 1970s, and also somewhat reminiscent of tuple spaces. But it's a simple and potent way to build message-processing systems. Many Web service engines are using or moving toward an architecture like this. You'll see more examples later in the chapter that demonstrate the benefits of this architecture.

The Message APIs and SAAJ

We've talked about handlers processing messages, but we haven't yet shown you what messages look like in Java. Let's remedy that with a brief spin through the Axis message APIs and their parents, the standard SAAJ APIs.

A Message by Any Other Name

If you ask the `MessageContext` for the request or the response message, you get back an object of type `org.apache.axis.Message` (this class extends and makes concrete the abstract `SOAPMessage` class from SAAJ). The main purpose of the `Message` is as a container for two things: a `SOAPPart` 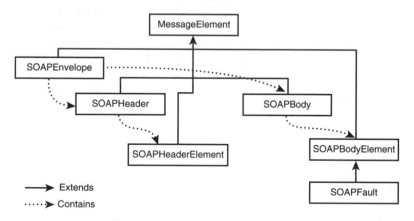 and zero or more `AttachmentParts` . These are called `parts` in order to mirror the WSDL 1.1 specificiation (see Chapter 4, "Describing Web Services").

`Messages` conforming to the simple SOAP HTTP binding will have only a `SOAPPart` and no attachments. If the `Message` uses either SOAP with Attachments or DIME, however, then we expect to find both a `SOAPPart` and some number of `AttachmentParts`. The `SOAPPart` gives you access to the SOAP envelope associated with the message, the form of which we'll discuss more in the next section. The `AttachmentParts` each let you access an abstract attachment represented by the Java Activation Framework's `DataHandler` object.

Dealing with attachments in detail is beyond the scope of this overview chapter, so we refer you to the Axis documentation if you'd like to learn more about it. We'll continue here with the SOAP message APIs.

Accessing the SOAP Envelope, Bodies, and Headers

The `SOAPPart` allows you to get the `SOAPEnvelope`; and for handlers, especially the ones dealing with headers, this is the object that matters. Some important classes involving the SOAP envelope are laid out in Figure 5.8 and defined here:

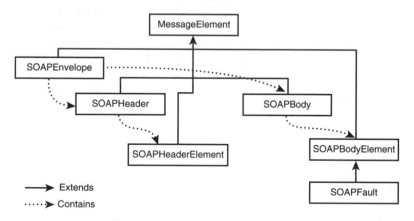

Figure 5.8   The SOAP message classes

- `MessageElement`—All the SOAP element classes in Axis inherit from `org.apache.axis.message.MessageElement` as a common ancestor. `MessageElement` implements the SAAJ `SOAPElement` interface but also lets you do a number of interesting Axis-specific tricks. For instance, `MessageElement` allows you to access the contents of the element in XML-speak by asking for child elements, attribute values, and the like—but it also lets you ask for a Java representation of the deserialized element content. We'll cover this in detail in "Using the MessageElement XML/Object APIs."

- `SOAPEnvelope`—This class represents the SOAP envelope. It directly contains exactly one `SOAPBody` and zero or one `SOAPHeaders`. The Axis version (although not the SAAJ one) has convenience methods that avoid having to deal with the `SOAPBody` and `SOAPHeader` elements directly, so you can add a body element directly to a `SOAPEnvelope` with `envelope.addBodyElement(bodyEl)`, for instance.

- `SOAPBody`—This class represents the `<soap:Body>` element and acts as a container for `SOAPBodyElements`. SAAJ requires using this class explicitly, whereas Axis has usually preferred to let the `<soap:Body>` and `<soap:Header>` elements be managed entirely by the infrastructure.

- `SOAPBodyElement`—These elements live in a SOAP body. They represent RPC calls, SOAP faults, or anything else that goes directly inside `<soap:Body>`.

- `SOAPHeader`—This class represents the `<soap:Header>` element and acts as a container for `SOAPHeaderElements`.

- `SOAPHeaderElement`—This is a SOAP header (in other words, an element living inside the `<soap:Header>` wrapper). A `SOAPHeaderElement` has all the APIs you would expect in order to read and write the SOAP header attributes such as `mustUnderstand` and `actor/role`. Each header also has a `processed` flag, which can be manipulated with the `setProcessed(boolean)` API. This flag determines whether the header has been understood (in the SOAP sense) by the endpoint; so if your handlers process headers, they should remember to call `setProcessed(true)` on them to avoid spurious `MustUnderstand` faults (see Chapter 3).

- `SOAPFault`—This class extends `SOAPBodyElement` and represents a SOAP fault. Accessors are available for all the common fault fields such as `faultString`, `faultCode`, and so on.

To demonstrate the usage of the message APIs, we'll show you a piece of code that you might put in a handler. Its purpose is to print to the console how many headers are in the message, whether a particular header is present, and whether the SOAP body contains a fault:

```
void invoke(MessageContext context) throws AxisFault {
    // Get the SOAP envelope from the request message in the context
    Message requestMsg = context.getRequestMessage();
    SOAPEnvelope env = requestMsg.getSOAPEnvelope();

    // Count the headers
```

```
Vector headers = env.getHeaders();
System.out.println("There are " + headers.size() + " headers.");

// Check if a particular header is present.
SOAPHeaderElement header = env.getHeaderByName("http://example",
                                               "trigger");
if (header != null) {
    System.out.println("Trigger header found.");
}

// Does the body contain a fault?
SOAPBodyElement body = env.getFirstBody();
if (body instanceof SOAPFault) {
    System.out.println("First body element is a fault, code = " +
                ((SOAPFault)body).getFaultCode().toString());
}
}
```

One of the other interesting things to note about these classes is that they all implement (as of SAAJ 1.2) the DOM `Element` APIs as well as their special SOAP-aware APIs. As such, you can take a `SOAPEnvelope` object and feed it into a standard DOM-based tool such as an XSLT engine to get at the data that way.

The Axis Client APIs

The client APIs can broadly be split into two categories: *dynamic invocation* 📖, where you use only preexisting Java classes to do your work, and *stub generation*, where a tool generates code for you from WSDL descriptions. Both are handy, so we'll start with the dynamic invocation interface (DII), which involves using the Axis low-level client objects directly.

The `Service` Object

Although the `Call` object, which you've seen in previous chapters, is the main entry point for invoking services, there is a `Service` 📖 object (`org.apache.axis.client.Service`) that deserves some attention as well.

The `Service` acts as a factory for `Call` objects, and it also stores useful meta-data about the service—for instance, the `Service` object is where the `AxisClient` instance that processes your invocations lives, and it's also where the type mappings for XML↔Java binding are stored. This meta-data lives on the `Service` and not the `Call` itself, because each `Call` object represents a *single* invocation of a service. The `Service` object can generate many `Call` objects, and since all those `Call` objects will talk to the same Web service, it makes sense to keep the common meta-data in a single place instead of repeating it for each `Call`.

A `Service` may or may not be associated with a WSDL description. If it is, you can not only request generic `Call` objects but also `Call`s that have been preconfigured with all the meta-data gleaned from the WSDL; in other words, you can get a `Call` for an operation that knows all the datatypes for the parameters and return values for that operation.

JAX-RPC expects `Service` objects to come from somewhere in the system, usually JNDI, preconfigured with the WSDL. As such, the `Service` API as defined by JAX-RPC has no direct means to access WSDL documents for dynamic invocation. The Axis `Service` object has a couple of constructors that let you do this association in a simple way:

- `Service(URL wsdlLocation, QName serviceName)`—This constructor builds you a `Service` object with meta-data initialized from the WSDL at the specified URL. The second argument is the service QName from the WSDL, as described in Chapter 4.
- `Service(String wsdlLocation, QName serviceName)`—This is just like the previous constructor, except `wsdlLocation` is a string that may be a URL or may also be a filename on the local filesystem, relative to the current directory.

The Axis `Service` object also has a no-argument constructor for use without a WSDL.

Using the `Call` Object for Dynamic Invocation

The `Service` object we just described is the standard JAX-RPC way to get `Call` objects, using the `createCall()` method:

```
import org.apache.axis.client.Service;
import javax.xml.rpc.Call;
...
Service service = new Service();
Call call = service.createCall();
call.setTargetEndpointAddress(url);
```

Here you see the no-argument `Service` constructor that we mentioned earlier, which creates a blank `Service`. Then the `createCall()` factory method, in this case with no arguments (we'll cover other versions in a bit), creates a generic JAX-RPC `Call` object. `CreateCall` returns a `javax.xml.rpc.Call`, but since we're using Axis, we know that this is really an `org.apache.axis.client.Call`—if you need to use any of the Axis-specific methods on the `Call`, you can downcast it to the Axis type.

We called `setTargetEndpointAddress()` after getting the `Call`; this allows us to pass the endpoint URL of the target Web service to the newly created `Call` object. Axis also provides a couple of direct constructors for the `Call` object that allow you to create a `Call` pointing to a particular Web service endpoint:

```
Call(String endpoint)
Call(URL endpoint)
```

These constructors exist as convenience methods to avoid the need to use a `Service` object directly.

What can you do with a Call once you have one? You can explore the full Call API by looking at the JavaDoc included with Axis, but we'll cover a few important pieces here in our overview.

Invoking a Web Service

The main thing you want to do with every Call object is, at some point, invoke a Web service. This is the purpose of the invoke() method, which has several different forms.

The data for any given invocation is typically handed to invoke() as an array of Java objects. For RPC-style services, these objects are parameters for a remote method call, and each one maps to an XML element inside a wrapper method call element on the wire. For document-style services, there is generally only a single object in the array you hand to invoke(), and it maps to the entire SOAP body for your operation.

Let's review an example of an RPC invocation a lot like the one from Chapter 3. It calls the same doCheck() method on the InventoryCheck service, but with hard-coded arguments for simplicity:

```
import org.apache.axis.AxisEngine;
import org.apache.axis.client.Call;
import org.apache.axis.soap.SOAPConstants;

/*
 * Inventory check Web service client
 */
public class InventoryCheckClient {
    /** Service URL */
    static String url =
            "http://localhost:8080/axis/InventoryCheck.jws";

    public static void main(String args[]) {
        // Set up Call object using convenience constructor
        Call call = new Call(url);
        // Use SOAP 1.2 (default is SOAP 1.1)
        call.setSOAPVersion(SOAPConstants.SOAP12_CONSTANTS);
        // Set up parameters for invocation
        Object[] params = new Object[] { "SKU-56", new Integer(25) };
        // Call it!
        Boolean result = (Boolean)call.invoke("", "doCheck", params);
        // ...do something with the result
    }
}
```

This code will end up producing a SOAP message that looks like this:

```
<soapenv:Envelope xmlns:soapenv="http://www.w3.org/2003/05/soap-envelope"
        xmlns:xsd="http://www.w3.org/2001/XMLSchema"
        xmlns:xsi="http://www.w3.org/2001/XMLSchema-instance">
```

```
<soapenv:Body>
  <doCheck soapenv:encodingStyle="http://www.w3.org/2003/05/soap-encoding">
   <arg0 xsi:type="soapenc:string"
         xmlns:soapenc="http://schemas.xmlsoap.org/soap/encoding/">947-TI</arg0>
   <arg1 xsi:type="soapenc:int"
         xmlns:soapenc="http://schemas.xmlsoap.org/soap/encoding/">3</arg1>
  </doCheck>
 </soapenv:Body>
</soapenv:Envelope>
```

Notice that it's a SOAP 1.2 message, because we set the SOAP version using the
`setSOAPVersion()` API (the default is 1.1). It uses the SOAP RPC conventions, including the SOAP encoding, because RPC style is the default for dynamic invocation. The
method name matches the one we passed in, and the parameters have the values we
passed in.

When you use this method of invocation, the arguments are called `arg0`, `arg1`, and so
on, in the generated SOAP message, because we haven't given the engine a reason to call
them anything else. Most of the time, this isn't adequate, because the services you're calling will require the parameters to have certain XML signatures (Axis is a notable exception in that it allows RPC parameters to be referenced by position and not just by
name). As such, you'll need a way to control the names and format of the XML corresponding to your parameters.

Taking Control of Parameters

If you want your parameters to serialize in particular ways instead of the defaults, you
can use the `addParameter()` APIs on the `Call` object to do so. This method also lets
you control the type of the parameter and the parameter mode (`in`, `out`, `inout`). The first
time you call `addParameter()`, you set all this information for the first parameter in the
arguments array that you pass to `invoke()`. The second time, you set it for the second
parameter, and so forth.

There are a number of different signatures for `addParameter()`, but the basic one is

```
addParameter(String paramName, QName xmlType, ParameterMode paramMode)
```

The arguments to this method are as follows:

- `paramName`—The name that should be used when serializing the parameter. A
  quick note here: Then you're using SOAP's RPC conventions, parameters should
  not have namespaces. Therefore this version of `addParameter()` is used. Another
  version of `addParameter()` takes a QName instead of a `String` as the first argument—that's the version to use if you're using document-style services and need
  to control the namespaces of parameter elements.
- `xmlType`—A QName that represents the XML Schema type of the parameter. This
  type is used by the type mapping system so you know how to correctly write and
  read XML for this service.

- paramMode—The parameter mode, which is in, out, or inout (discussed in Chapter 3). JAX-RPC, and therefore Axis, has a ParameterMode class (javax.xml.rpc.ParameterMode) that contains constants for each of the three modes.

Suppose our example changes to this:

```
// Set up Call object
Call call = new Call(url);
// Use SOAP 1.2 (default is SOAP 1.1)
call.setSOAPVersion(SOAPConstants.SOAP12_CONSTANTS);

addParameter("SKU",
             org.apache.axis.Constants.XSD_STRING,
             ParameterMode.IN);
addParameter("quantity",
             org.apache.axis.Constants.XSD_INT,
             ParameterMode.IN);

// Set up parameters for invocation
Object[] params = new Object[] { "SKU-56", new Integer(35) };

// Call it!
Boolean result = (Boolean)call.invoke("", "doCheck", params);
```

Then our SOAP message will change to look like this:

```
<soapenv:Body>
  <doCheck>
    <SKU xsi:type="xsd:string">SKU-56</SKU>
    <quantity xsi:type="xsd:int">35</quantity>
  </doCheck>
</soapenv:Body>
```

The XML has changed to match the parameter names passed to the Call.

Just as you can use addParameter() to set the types for outgoing XML, you can use the setReturnType() API to tell the Call object what XML type to expect as the return value from a Web service invocation. Doing so allows the correct deserialization of XML that lacks xsi:type attributes. The setReturnType() method looks like this:

```
call.setReturnType(qname)
```

The qname argument is an XML type QName. You can find constants for most common schema type QNames in the org.apache.axis.Constants class. For instance, Constants.XSD_STRING is a prebuilt QName object with the namespace http://www.w3.org/2001/XMLSchema and the localPart string. Axis natively supports all the basic XML schema types, and you can see what other types are supported out of the box later in the type mapping section.

NOTE

JAX-RPC is much more stringent than Axis originally was about meta-data requirements for dynamic invo-cation. In particular, JAX-RPC requires you to either specify *all* meta-data (both setReturnType() and addParameter() for each parameter) or *none*. So, if you want to add parameter meta-data but not specify a return type, you're out of luck. The same is true for setting the return type but not adding parame-ter meta-data. The Axis team didn't agree with this restriction (the team thought the engine should be able to work with as much meta-data as it had, since it could generally make good guesses) but needed to implement it to pass the JAX-RPC compatibility tests.

Other invoke()s

The Call object supports a few other invoke() styles, which you can see by investigat-ing the Javadoc or the source. One of note is SOAPEnvelope invoke(SOAPEnvelope env), which allows you to construct your own custom SOAPEnvelope using the message APIs, send it using the Axis framework to a given destination, and then access the SOAP envelope returned from the service (after processing by the appropriate handlers, of course).

Using the Call Object with a WSDL-Enabled Service

When you use one of the WSDL-aware Service() constructors, the Axis framework extracts the same kind of Call meta-data we just spoke about (parameters, endpoint, return types, and so on) from the WSDL description. So if you create Call objects and specify which WSDL ports and operations they correspond to, you don't have to set the meta-data yourself, which can be handy and is less prone to coding mistakes. The APIs for creating Calls this way look like this:

- service.createCall(QName portName)—This accessor returns a Call that has been initialized with the endpoint address referred to by the named port in the WSDL. No other meta-data is set.

- service.createCall(QName portName, QName operation)—This version not only sets the endpoint address but also preconfigures all the parameters and return types for the specified operation. Note that if you try to call addParameter(), setReturnType(), and so on, on the resulting Call object, you'll get an Exception because the configuration is already set.

- service.createCall(QName portName, String operation)—This is just like the previous version, but it accepts the unqualified operation name from the WSDL rather than a full QName.

Type Mapping Using the Call

Axis, as you've seen, has the ability to map XML to Java and vice versa. We'll discuss the type-mapping system in detail later; to control these mappings on the client side, you need to know the following: A type mapping consists of an XML type (a QName), a

Java type (a class), a serializer (to write Java to XML), and a deserializer (to write Java from XML). To map types on the client side, you can use the `Call` object's `registerTypeMapping` API (this API is Axis-specific, it isn't part of JAX-RPC):

```
call.registerTypeMapping(Class javaType,
                         QName xmlType,
                         Class serializerFactoryClass,
                         Class deserializerFactoryClass)
```

If you have a JavaBean class that represents a `Product` (with a name, sku, price, and so on), you can tell Axis how to serialize that type as XML using the default Bean serializer and deserializer that come with Axis:

```
call.registerTypeMapping(Product.class,
                         new QName("http://skatestown.com", "Product"),
                         BeanSerializerFactory.class,
                         BeanDeserializerFactory.class)
```

Setting Properties on the `Call`

The `Call` class has a `setProperty()` API that looks like this:

```
void setProperty(String name, Object value)
```

This method allows you to set properties on the `Call` object, just like you can set properties on the `MessageContext`. All the properties you set on the `Call` will be available to *every* `MessageContext` that is created as a result of using that `Call`. This is an important point, which we'll bring up again when we talk about the server and property scoping. For now, just remember that you can use a `Call` object to make multiple invocations to a given service (although only one at a time)—each time a new `MessageContext` will be created, and all handlers involved in the invocation will have access not only to the `MessageContext` properties for that invocation, but also to the ones you set on the `Call` that persist across invocations.

Using Sessions

As a client, sometimes you're calling services that perform the same functions the same way regardless of who calls them (think `getStockQuote()`). At other times, though, it's important that the server remember who *you* are when you're making multiple service calls—for instance, a shopping cart service needs to keep track of the items in your cart and be able to sell them to you after you finish shopping. To do this, it needs some kind of *session* 📖 that it uses to associate a set of data with your client.

Axis has some simple APIs for session support. The goal of these APIs is to support session maintenance in a pluggable fashion, allowing you to use underlying session mechanisms supplied by application servers to custom sessions implemented as SOAP extensions.

In Axis terms, session maintenance is primarily a server-side concept. The server, by handing the client back some kind of cookie, can then accept the same cookie from the client on subsequent requests and know that the new requests are associated with the same client that made the earlier one. This process enables the server to maintain state on behalf of the client, which is often desirable for interactions that span multiple invocations.

Session Implementations

Axis has two built-in ways to maintain sessions across Web service connections. The first method uses the standard HTTP session mechanism that is built in to any conforming servlet engine; this mechanism uses HTTP cookies to store session state, and the actual session data is kept by the servlet framework. The second method uses a custom implementation to store session data and passes session identifiers via protocol-independent SOAP headers.

To support the first method, you need to use the HTTP transport (the default), and you must call `setMaintainSession(true)` on either the `Call` or the `Service` (either will work fine).

To use the second method, you must deploy the `SimpleSessionHandler` (`org.apache.axis.handlers.SimpleSessionHandler`) that is included with Axis. We'll talk about how to deploy handlers using Web service deployment descriptors (WSDDs) in a little while, but you'll need to deploy this handler on both the global request and response flows of the client in order for it to work.

We'll also cover some other ways of implementing stateful Web services in Chapter 8, "Web Services and Stateful Resources."

Using Stubs and WSDL2Java

As you saw in Chapter 4, WSDL is a great machine-readable way to describe Web services and the operations they can perform for you. To the Java developer, this is a boon because tools can automatically do the kind of work we've been doing by hand with the `Call` object and type mappings. Axis comes with such tools:

- WSDL2Java pulls in WSDL descriptions and generates Java code. It can generate both client stubs, which help call the service, and server-side implementation scaffolding, which makes it easy to build your own implementation of the service.

- Java2WSDL is a command-line tool for taking Java interfaces and generating WSDL.

- At runtime, the Axis engine can automatically generate WSDL for deployed services.

Stubs

A *stub* 📖 is a Java class with a Java-friendly API that closely matches the Web service interface defined in a given WSDL document. In other words, instead of using a generic method like `call.invoke()` and having to typecast return values, you'll see methods like `float getClosingPriceOnDay(String symbol, Date day)`. This is both easier to program and safer, since the compiler can check the types of your arguments and return values instead of using `Object` and casts everywhere. Stubs are built using WSDL2Java.

Here's an example: Let's build a stub from the WSDL for the `InventoryCheck` service from Chapter 3. We can obtain the WSDL by accessing `http://localhost:8080/axis/InventoryCheck.jws?wsdl` (Figure 5.9 shows what this looks like in a browser). Now that we know where the WSDL comes from, we can easily generate a Java client framework to make calling the service extremely simple:

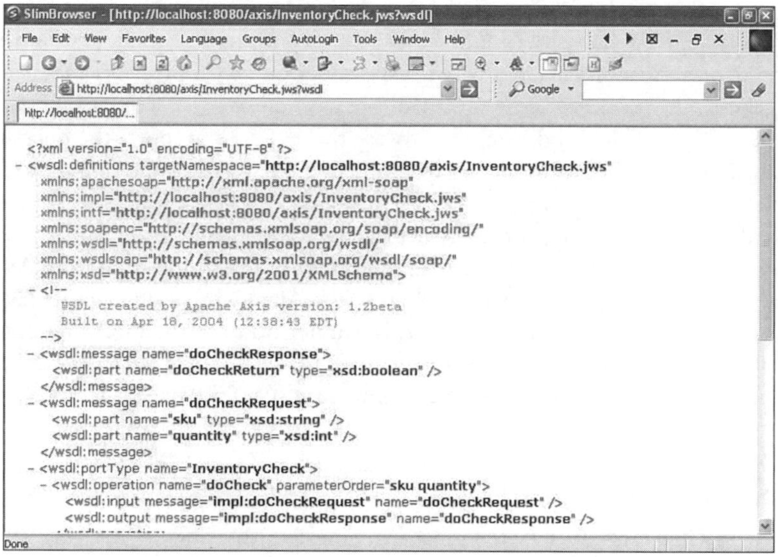

Figure 5.9 Obtaining the WSDL for the `InventoryCheck` service

```
% java org.apache.axis.wsdl.WSDL2Java
Â http://localhost:8080/axis/InventoryCheck.jws?wsdl
```

WSDL2Java will fetch the WSDL, parse it, and generate a Java stub for calling the service in a type-safe, convenient fashion. Let's look at the classes WSDL2Java generates for us:

- `InventoryCheck`—This is the service interface that corresponds to the `portType` in the WSDL. In JAX-RPC terms, this is known as the *Service Endpoint Interface (SEI)* 📖.
- `InventoryCheckService`—This interface is generated as per the JAX-RPC specification and allows type-safe access to the SEI from the locator class below. This interface includes two important methods:
  - `InventoryCheck getInventoryCheck()`
  - `InventoryCheck getInventoryCheck(URL url)`

The first one gets an implementation of the `InventoryCheck` interface that will call the exact endpoint specified in the WSDL. The second one gets an `InventoryCheck` stub that uses the same WSDL interface and binding but points at a different endpoint. This is especially handy when you're using proxies, intermediaries, or test tools.

- `InventoryCheckServiceLocator`—This *locator* class implements the `InventoryCheckService` interface and acts as the factory for stub instances. In a full J2EE environment (as when you're calling Web services from EJBs or servlets), the locator might look in a JNDI repository for pooled stub objects; but the default behavior for Axis is to create stubs as needed.

- `InventoryCheckSoapBindingStub`—This is the real core of our client, the class that implements the `InventoryCheck` interface.

All these classes are in the Java package `localhost.axis.InventoryCheck_jws` because the WSDL `targetNamespace` in this case is the endpoint URL `http://localhost:8080/axis/InventoryCheck.jws`. WSDL2Java maps each XML namespace encountered in a WSDL description into a Java package name (you can even control this mapping with command-line options or a configuration file). The default mapping of a namespace URL like `http://www.skatestown.com/services` would be to the package `com.skatestown.www.services`—in other words, you invert the domain name components as you would for software developed by that company (`com.skatestown.www`) and then add each succeeding component of the URL, changing slashes to dots (`.services`).

WSDL2Java doesn't expect you to edit any of the generated classes yourself, so be careful if you do—if you run the program again on the same WSDL, it will regenerate the Java source files, overwriting anything that might already be there. (There is one exception, when you have WSDL2Java create a service implementation as described later; since those classes are meant for editing, Axis won't overwrite them.)

Using the Generated Stub

Now that we have our stub class, let's test it:

```
import localhost.*;

class Tester {
    public static void main(String args[]) throws Exception {
        // Collect arguments from command line - SKU and quantity
        String sku = args[0];
        int quantity = Integer.parseInt(args[1]);

        // Get our stub from the locator object
        InventoryCheckLocator locator = new InventoryCheckLocator();
        InventoryCheck stub = locator.getInventoryCheck();
```

```
    // Call the Web service
    boolean result = stub.doCheck(sku, quantity);

    if (result) {
        System.out.println(
            "Confirmed - the desired quantity is available.");
    } else {
        System.out.println(
            "Sorry, the desired quantity is not available.");
    }
  }
}
```

When we try it, the result is as follows:

```
% java Tester SKU-56 66
Sorry, the desired quantity is not available.
```

This is nice compared to the dynamic invocation example you saw earlier—instead of having to type the operation name into a string argument of a generic `invoke()` call, we have a `doCheck()` method right on the stub. Likewise, instead of having to pass a generic array of `Objects` as arguments, `doCheck()` takes exactly what we need: a `String` and an `int`.

Generating Test Cases

WSDL2Java can also build a test client for your services, which can be handy especially during the development process. By specifying the `-t` option to the tool, WSDL2Java will generate, in addition to the stub, a file called *<name>*`TestCase.java`, where *<name>* is the name of the service. This file is a *JUnit* 📖 test case skeleton (for more about JUnit, see `http://junit.org`). You'll notice that the generated test templates exercise each of the Web service's operations, but the values that are sent are all zeros and nulls and there is no logic for checking the semantics of the service. As the comments in the generated source indicate, that functionality is up to you to add, since the WSDL doesn't describe the *behavior* of the service—just the data formats that are accepted and returned.

Holders: Mapping `inout`/`out` Parameters to Java

SOAP and WSDL both support the idea of `out` and `inout` parameters for RPCs—values that come back from a service request in addition to the actual return value. Languages with native support for these concepts allow you to pass a variable to a method; then, when the method returns, the variable might have a different value. To support this idea in Java, we need to build something on top of the basic language: a *holder* 📖 class.

A holder class is just what it sounds like: an `Object` that holds a value of a particular type. So an `IntHolder` looks like this:

```
class IntHolder {
    private int value;
```

```
    public int getValue() { return val; }
    public void setValue(int v) { val = v; }
}
```

You can pass one of these objects to a method, and the method code can update the `int` value inside the holder so that the caller can use the new value:

```
void myMethod(IntHolder inOutParam) {
    // Add five to the passed value
    inOutParam.setValue(inOutParam.getValue() + 5);
}
```

When WSDL2Java notices `out` or `inout` parameters in operation descriptions, it automatically generates signatures that include holder classes.

Automatic Type Mapping with WSDL2Java

Most services aren't as simplistic as the examples you've seen so far. In particular, as you've learned in the past few chapters, complex XML datatypes are an important part of most Web services, and these types are typically described using XML schema embedded within, or referenced from, WSDL descriptions. This is why WSDL2Java has been built to help you turn WSDL services into Java stubs and also turn all the XML datatypes referenced by those services into easy-to-use Java classes.

Let's look at an example that uses a slightly modified version of `PriceCheck.wsdl` from Chapter 4. The only change is to replace the `http://www.skatestown.com/services/PriceCheck` endpoint with `http://localhost:8080/axis/services/PriceCheck` so we can access the locally installed service on our machine. Notice that this service uses an `AvailabilityType` complex type as its return value. Pointing WSDL2Java at that file as follows:

```
% java org.apache.axis.wsdl.WSDL2Java PriceCheck2.wsdl
```

results in the following set of files in the package `com.skatestown.www.services.PriceCheck`:

- `PriceCheckPortType.java`—The actual service interface
- `PriceCheck.java`—The locator interface
- `PriceCheckSOAPBindingStub`—The actual stub class
- `PriceCheckLocator`—The locator implementation

Here's the new part: Notice that there is another package, `com.skatestown.www.ns.availability` (because the namespace was `http://www.skatestown.com/ns/availability`), in which we find `AvailabilityType.java`, the Java type corresponding to the XML type `availabilityType`. Taking a look at the new class, we find a JavaBean with data members corresponding to the XML elements inside the `complexType`:

```
public class AvailabilityType  implements java.io.Serializable {
    private java.lang.String sku;
    private double price;
    private java.math.BigInteger quantityAvailable;
    ...
```

Most of the class methods are getters/setters for these fields. There are also prebuilt implementations of the Java `equals()` and `hashCode()` methods, and the class also contains built-in meta-data (a static method called `getTypeDesc()`) for ensuring that the generated Java will always correctly map to the original XML.

Taking a look at the `PriceCheckPortType` interface, you can see the `checkPrice()` method:

```
public interface PriceCheckPortType extends java.rmi.Remote {
    public com.skatestown.www.ns.availability.AvailabilityType
      checkPrice(java.lang.String sku) throws java.rmi.RemoteException;
}
```

Since the WSDL indicates that `checkPrice()` returns an `availabilityType` in the `http://www.skatestown.com/ns/availability` namespace, the Java method therefore returns our `com.skatestown.www.ns.availability.AvailabilityType` class.

Of course, the engine still needs to know how to map the XML type to the Java type—that is accomplished by some generated code in the `Stub` class that ends up calling the `Call.registerTypeMapping()` API we spoke about earlier. It's a lot better than doing all that work manually.

Web Service Deployment Descriptor (WSDD)

How does the engine know where all its handlers come from, in what order to call them, and how to configure them? Not to mention other things like its own configuration options and type mappings? That's where WSDD comes in.

> **NOTE**
>
> All WSDD elements are in the WSDD namespace, `http://xml.apache.org/axis/wsdd/`. When discussing these elements in this chapter, we always assume that the default namespace is the WSDD namespace; so when we say `<deployment>`, it's the same as `<wsdd:deployment xmlns:wsdd="http://xml.apache.org/axis/wsdd/">`.

WSDD is an XML format that Axis uses to store its configuration and deployment information. The Axis server keeps its configuration in a file called `server-config.wsdd`, and the Axis client has an equivalent `client-config.wsdd`. These files both have default versions that are stored in the `axis.jar` itself—this means if there isn't a WSDD file in the appropriate directory, there will always be some reasonable configuration.

When using Axis in a web application, the server looks for a `server-config.wsdd` in the `WEB-INF/` directory of your Web application, and then it looks in the classpath. When using the Axis client code, the client looks for any necessary client configuration in a `client-config.wsdd` file in the directory from which you're running the client and then in the classpath.

The root element of these WSDD files is `<deployment>`. Inside the top-level element is a `<globalConfiguration>` element, which contains options for the Axis engine (client or server) as a whole, plus definitions for the global request and response chains. Here's an example:

```
<globalConfiguration>
  <parameter name="defaultSOAPVersion" value="1.2"/>
  <requestFlow>
    <handler type="java:org.apache.axis.handlers.LogHandler"/>
  </requestFlow>
  <responseFlow>
  </responseFlow>
</globalConfiguration>
```

The `<parameter>` declarations inside `<globalConfiguration>` are for setting options on the `AxisEngine` 📖 object, which is either an `AxisServer` or an `AxisClient`. Particular options allow you to control the default SOAP version (as in our example), whether the engine should default to sending `xsi:type` attributes, and a variety of other things. (See the Axis documentation for more.) Also note that you can set custom options as well as the ones Axis defines.

The `<requestFlow>` and `<responseFlow>` elements define the request and response global chains, as we described earlier. They can contain either `<handler>` elements or `<chain>` elements (both of which are described more fully later). The components inside `<requestFlow>` and `<responseFlow>` are invoked during the processing of a message in exactly the order that they are declared in the XML file. In the previous example, the `LogHandler` will be invoked on the global request chain, and no handlers are defined on the global response chain (we could therefore have omitted the empty `<responseFlow>` element).

Handler Declarations

Handler declarations tell Axis that a given Java class is a handler, configure it with a set of options, and optionally name that configuration so you can easily refer to it later. A handler declaration looks like this:

```
<handler [name="name"] type="type">
  <parameter name="name" value="value"/>
</handler>
```

Handler declarations can appear as immediate children of `<deployment>`, or inside a `<chain>`, `<requestFlow>`, or `<responseFlow>` (all of which you'll see in a moment).

The `type` attribute tells you what kind of handler this is. The value for this attribute is either a QName in a special Java namespace or the name of a previously defined handler/chain.

Axis has a special namespace for Java types, which is usually defined with the prefix `java`, like this:

```
xmlns:java="http://xml.apache.org/axis/wsdd/providers/java"
```

If you use a type value with this namespace, you're declaring a handler based on a Java class. For instance:

```
<handler type="java:org.apache.axis.handlers.LogHandler"/>
```

Sometimes, especially if you'll be using several instances of the same class in a WSDD file, it's nice to have shorthand to avoid typing the whole class name in each handler declaration. If the optional `name` attribute is specified, you're labeling a particular handler configuration that can be used again later by using the name as the value of the `type` attribute in another `<handler>` element.

When you define handlers at the top level (underneath `<deployment>`), you're always doing so for the purpose of referring to those handlers later. Declaring a handler without a `name` attribute at the top level, while technically legal, is useless, since the engine would never invoke such a handler.

You may specify any number of optional `<parameter>` elements inside a handler declaration. These are used to set options for the handler to control its behavior. For instance, if we wanted to specify a particular log file for our `LogHandler` to write to, we would do so like this:

```
<handler name="log" type="java:org.apache.axis.handlers.LogHandler">
  <parameter name="logFile" value="myLog.txt"/>
</handler>
```

Note that we also named this handler `log`. That means in other places in our WSDD, we can refer to it like this, inheriting both the Java class and the option settings with much less typing:

```
<handler type="log"/>
```

The set of options that a given handler supports should be explained in the documentation for that handler. The handler interface includes `getOption()` and `setOption()` APIs that are used to obtain and modify the values of these parameters. To make sure that code never changes the value of your deployed option, you can also specify a `locked="true"` attribute on the `parameter` element. Doing so will prevent any modification to the option value at runtime.

Chain Definitions

You can put a series of handlers together into a chain and give the chain a name. That name can then be used as a handler type just like any other. Here's an example:

```
<chain name="logAndNotify">
  <!-- This chain logs the messages, then also sends an email -->
  <!-- to a specified address.                                 -->
  <handler type="java:org.apache.axis.handlers.LogHandler"/>
  <handler type="java:myPackage.NotificationHandler">
    <parameter name="email" value="admin@skatestown.com"/>
  </handler>
</chain>
```

Now this chain can be used like any other handler. For instance, we could add it to a request flow:

```
<requestFlow>
  <handler type="logAndNotify"/>
  ...more handler declarations...
</requestFlow>
```

Also note that you can parameterize handlers inside chains, as demonstrated by our configuring the NotificationHandler with an email address to which notifications should be sent.

Transports

Transport declarations define a named, targeted chain, which has a requestFlow, a responseFlow, and, on the client, a pivot handler. Remember that on the client, the transport is an *outgoing* concept and the pivot is the sender of the message. On the server, no pivot handler is needed (nor should one be specified). Here's an example of a client transport, from the default client-config.wsdd file:

```
<transport name="http"
           pivot="java:org.apache.axis.transport.http.HTTPSender"/>
```

You define a pivot handler for a transport with the pivot attribute. In this example, there are no other options or request/response handlers.

On the server, the standard HTTP transport declaration looks like this:

```
<handler type="java:org.apache.axis.handlers.http.URLMapper"
         name="URLMapper"/>
<transport name="http">
  <requestFlow>
   <handler type="URLMapper"/>
   <handler type="java:org.apache.axis.handlers.http.HTTPAuthHandler"/>
  </requestFlow>
</transport>
```

We've included the declaration of the URLMapper handler here so you can see another example of referring to a named handler. This transport is named http, and it contains two transport-specific handlers in the request chain. The first is the URLMapper, which sets the Axis service name in the MessageContext based on the HTTP URL; this is the default dispatch mechanism, so that when you access `http://host:8080/axis/ services/POSubmission`, Axis will end up looking for a deployed service named `POSubmission`. The other handler is the HTTP authentication handler, which takes the username and password out of an HTTP Basic authentication header and puts them in the `MessageContext` in a transport-agnostic form.

Type Mappings

Type mappings control how the mapping between Java classes and XML structures works. You can tell the engine to map particular Java classes to particular XML types, and even customize the serializer and deserializer classes that do the translation. Type mappings can be scoped globally (for the whole engine) or per service.

A type mapping in WSDD looks like this:

```
<typeMapping qname="typeQName"
            type="java:classname"
            serializer="Serializer"
            deserializer="DeserializerFactory"
            encodingSytle="uri"/>
```

A type mapping contains the same information you saw earlier in the `Call` API `registerTypeMapping()`: the Java type (class name), the XML schema type (QName), a serializer class, and a deserializer class. The `encodingStyle` attribute also lets you optionally specify a particular encoding style (see Chapter 3) within which you want your type mapping to work. Note that if you fail to specify the encoding style, or you specify "" (the empty string), the type mapping will work for all encoding styles (including literal, or unencoded, use).

Notice the Java type is specified with an attribute called `type`, whose value is a QName in the special WSDD Java namespace (`http://xml.apache.org/axis/wsdd/ providers/java`, here mapped to the prefix `java`). This namespace indicates a Java type, and the local part is the class name. Why a QName instead of just a class name? WSDD is a language-neural deployment mechanism, and doing it this way makes it easier to use the same format for both Java and C++ implementations. This is the same reason we use the java:prefix for handler types as well.

The `<beanMapping>` tag is shorthand for a `<typeMapping>` which uses the `BeanSerializer/BeanDeserializer` classes (in package `org.apache.axis.encoding. ser`) to do Axis's default data-mapping algorithms. In many cases you won't need custom serialization for your JavaBeans, and therefore `beanMappings` are convenient and less cluttered to look at. `BeanMappings` look like this:

```
<beanMapping qname="type QName"
            languageSpecificType="java:classname"
            encodingStyle="url"/>
```

We'll talk more about type mapping after we go over how to write and deploy your own services.

Using Axis with SOAP 1.2

By default, Axis will communicate using SOAP 1.1. However, full support for SOAP 1.2 is built in, and Axis will eventually default to 1.2 in a future release.

To switch an entire Axis engine to use SOAP 1.2, specify the `defaultSOAPVersion` option on the engine's WSDD configuration:

```
<globalConfiguration>
  <option name="defaultSOAPVersion" value="1.2"/>
</globalConfiguration>
```

On the client side, you can also do this dynamically at runtime using the `SOAPConstants` object to set the SOAP version as follows:

```
SOAPConstants constants = SOAPConstants.SOAP12_CONSTANTS;
call.setSOAPVersion(constants);
```

At present, there is no standard WSDL 1.1 binding for SOAP 1.2. The SOAPBuilders group, a grassroots coalition of SOAP developers, has one that a few packages use, but it isn't widely accepted as yet. Axis therefore allows you to build stubs/skeletons from WSDL 1.1 and then use the techniques we've described to switch to SOAP 1.2 after the fact. This issue will be remedied when the community settles on a WSDL 1.1 / SOAP 1.2 binding; the problem will disappear when WSDL 2.0 becomes a W3C Recommendation, because it will have SOAP 1.2 support built in.

Building Services

We've discussed how Axis is architected, how to use the client-side APIs to call services, and how to use WSDD to deploy components like handlers and transports. Now it's time to explore deploying your own Web services using the Axis framework.

Instant Deployment: JWS

You saw how to deploy a *Java Web Service (JWS)* 📖 in Chapter 3, and there's not much else to tell here. JWS services don't require an explicit deployment step aside from copying a `.jws` source file into your Axis-enabled Web application. When a SOAP message arrives destined for a URL ending in `.jws`, Axis automatically notices and compiles the class if necessary before invoking the service.

When you deploy a JWS service, there are a couple of things to note. First, *all* public methods in the class will be exposed as service operations. Second, the only datatypes Axis will know about for your JWS services are the global ones—in other words, if you use Java types in your JWS code that aren't part of the standard type mapping Axis supports, you must declare global type mappings to support those types in your server before the JWS service will function.

WSDD for Services

When you want to deploy a service that uses custom handlers, service-specific type mappings, or any other kind of fine-grained configuration control, you'll discover that JWS isn't adequate because it lacks the ability to use service-specific meta-data. Most of the enterprise-level services you're likely to deal with will use WSDD deployment instead. (This situation may change in the future, due to some soon-to-be-standard ways of embedding the same kind of meta-data you find in WSDD directly into the Java source code of a JWS file.)

The `AxisServer`'s entire configuration is contained in a file usually called `server-config.wsdd`. Each deployed service in the server's world has a `<service>` element in that WSDD file that looks like this (the asterisks mean that element may appear zero or more times, and as usual square brackets around an attribute mean it's optional):

```
<service name="name" [style="rpc|wrapped|document|message"]
        [use="literal|encoded"] [provider="provider"]>
  <operation>* (see below)
  <typeMapping>* / <beanMapping>*
  <namespace>uri</namespace>*
  <wsdlFile>absolute-filename</wsdlFile>
  <endpointURL>uri</endpointURL>
  <handlerInfoChain>
  <parameter name="name" value="value"/>
</service>
```

The `name` attribute is the service's name, which generally appears as the last portion of the endpoint URL to access the service. For a standard installation using HTTP, if a service is called `submitPO`, the URL to access it will be `http://localhost:8080/axis/services/submitPO`, where `localhost` can be replaced with your machine's DNS name. Service names must be unique.

The `style` attribute lets you specify one of several different ways that Axis can map SOAP messages to and from Java method calls: `rpc`, `document`, `wrapped`, or `message`. If you specify a style, you don't need to specify the `use` or `provider` attribute, since they will default based on the style you choose. The default style, if not specified, is `rpc`. Don't worry, we'll fully explain these styles in a later section.

The `provider` attribute allows you to specify a QName that represents the particular provider (see "The Provider" in the "Axis Architecture" section for more about providers) to use for this service. The providers Axis knows about by default are as follows:

- `java:RPC`—The standard RPC provider (`org.apache.axis.providers.java.RPCProvider`), which is used for `rpc`, `document`, and `wrapped` styles. Despite the fact that it also deals with `doc/literal` services, the class name `RPCProvider` is left over from a time when Axis was primarily an RPC toolkit. Note that if you specify `rpc`, `document`, or `wrapped` for the `style` attribute, this provider will be automatically selected.

When using the RPC provider (and it's likely that most of your services will), you have to convey two important pieces of information to the provider: which class you're exposing and which methods are allowed. You do this using service parameters, as follows:

```
<parameter name="className" value="class name"/>
```

This parameter value should be the fully qualified class name of your Web service.

```
<parameter name="allowedMethods" value="methods"/>
```

The value for this parameter is a space-separated list of the methods you want accessible as Web service operations. If you use the special value *, it means that all public methods on your service class will be available.

- java:MSG—The message provider (org.apache.axis.providers.java. MsgProvider), which handles dispatching raw XML to your service. Note that if you specify the java:MSG provider, the service style will automatically be set to message, and vice versa.

- java:EJB—The EJB provider (org.apache.axis.providers.java. EJBProvider), which allows you to use an Enterprise JavaBean as a Web service. See the Axis documentation for more on this.

- Handler—This one is interesting, since it lets you specify your own handler class as the provider for a particular service. For instance, there is a simple handler called org.apache.axis.handlers.EchoHandler, which places a copy of the request message into the response message. You could declare an echo service using the handler like this:

```
<service name="echo" provider="Handler">
  <parameter name="handlerClass"
                    value="org.apache.axis.handlers.EchoHandler"/>
</service>
```

As shown, the handler provider uses the value of the handlerClass variable as the class name of the pivot handler.

Axis also includes providers that bridge to BSF (Bean Scripting Framework), COM (Microsoft's Common Object Model), CORBA, and standard Java RMI. See the Axis documentation for more on these.

The use attribute lets you specify encoded or literal use. This setting will be reflected in WSDL generated from this service (we discuss generating WSDL later) and to control whether the SOAP encoding is used when the service serializes and deserializes XML. You generally won't need to set this yourself, since it defaults correctly based on the style attribute.

If `<typeMapping>` or `<beanMapping>` elements are inside your service deployment, then those XML/Java mappings will hold *only* for that service. This enables multiple services to map the same types in different ways.

You may have zero or more `<namespace>` elements inside your `<service>`. If present, the first one is the default namespace of the service. This namespace is primarily useful for RPC services, and it will determine the namespace of the body elements for the service and the `targetNamespace` of the generated WSDL. Any of the specified name-spaces can also be used by the `axisEngine` to dispatch messages to the service—in other words, the engine can automatically find the correct service if an element in one of the service's namespaces is found in the `<soap:Body>`.

The `<wsdlFile>` element allows you to specify a custom WSDL file that the engine will return when asked about the WSDL for this service. Normally, when someone accesses your service URL plus `?wsdl`, the engine will autogenerate a WSDL description based on your running service. If you want to change this behavior (for example, to add customizations not supported by the autogeneration), you can use this optional WSDD technique to point at a file that will be returned instead.

JAX-RPC Handlers

The `<handlerInfoChain>` element is used to enable deploying JAX-RPC style handlers, which are a little different than Axis handlers. You declare JAX-RPC handlers as follows:

```
<handlerInfoChain>
  <handlerInfo class="className">
    <parameter name="" value=""/>
    <header qname="qname"/>*
    <role soapActorName="uri"/>*
  </handlerInfo>*
</handlerInfoChain>
```

JAX-RPC handlers in this chain will run after the global chain but before the normal `requestFlow` for your service. At that time, each handler in the chain will have its `handleRequest()` method invoked. Then, after the service responseFlow has completed, the handlers on the JAX-RPC chain will have their `handleResponse()` method invoked—but this time the chain will be reversed. This is the main difference: JAX-RPC style handlers have two methods to handle the request and the response separately, whereas Axis handlers use a single `invoke()` method and check the `MessageContext`, if necessary, to figure out whether the current message is the request or the response. Each `<handlerInfo>` defines a single JAX-RPC handler.

The `<header>` and `<role>` elements allow you to specify which header elements should be processed by the handler and which SOAP roles that particular handler is playing. At this time, they aren't implemented in Axis.

The `<operation>` Element

A service can contain zero or more `<operation>` elements. The `<operation>` element is used when you want fine-grained control of the options for a particular operation. In particular, it handles the mapping from arbitrary XML QNames in the SOAP body to arbitrary Java methods, controlling how parameters to those methods map to XML elements and also how the Exceptions that are thrown by the Java methods map to and from SOAP faults. Note that in all but the simplest cases, you won't be writing these yourself—instead they will be generated for you when you use WSDL2Java to create service frameworks from WSDL documents. The element looks like this:

```
<operation name="name" [qname="qname"] [returnQName="qname"]
           [returnType="qname"] [returnHeader="true/false"]>
  <parameter [qname="" | name=""] [mode="in/out/inout"]
             type="qname"
             inHeader="true/false" outHeader="true/false"/>*
  <fault name="name" qname="qname" class="classname" type="qname"/>*
</operation>
```

The operation name is the name of the Java method this Web service operation will invoke. The qname is the QName of the XML element that will map to this operation—for RPC services, there is never a need to specify this because it will always be derived from the operation name.

Inside the operation element are zero or more parameter elements, each of which represents a parameter of the operation. The information in the WSDD parameter element is essentially the same information that would go in the addParameter() call on the client side, with a couple of additions: If the inHeader or outHeader attribute is specified, then the serialization of the parameter in question will be in the SOAP header instead of in the body.

There are also zero or more fault elements inside the operation. These allow particular fault classes to be associated with particular element QNames inside the SOAP fault's <detail> element. In other words, if the faults specified in the <fault> mapping are thrown by your service, Axis will serialize the data inside the fault class as a <detail> element with the specified QName and XML type.

Deploying Services and the AdminClient

You have two choices of how you get the WSDD related to your service (or in fact, any WSDD deployment) into a server's configuration. Either you can directly edit the server-config.wsdd file the server is using (typically in the WEB-INF/ directory of your web application), or you can use the *AdminClient* tool that comes with Axis.

The client is the class org.apache.axis.client.AdminClient, and it works something like this:

```
java org.apache.axis.client.AdminClient [-u{username}] [-w{password}]
➥[-p{port}] [-l{service-url}] {wsdd-file}
```

When you run this from the command line, it reads the specified WSDD file and attempts to deploy it to the Axis engine running at the given URL. The default URL is http://localhost:8080/axis/services/AdminService. If authentication is necessary, the `username` and `password` arguments may be used to send a set of credentials to the deployment service.

If the WSDD has `<deployment>` as its root element, all the components in the WSDD are deployed into the target server. Remember that you need to make sure all the classes referred to in the WSDD (the service class, any data classes, handlers, and so on) are available on the server's classpath before doing the deployment.

If the WSDD has `<undeployment>` as its root, all the referenced components will be *removed* from the running server. When undeploying, you should *only* put the names of the components you want undeployed in the WSDD, not the full configuration. This file would remove a handler and a service:

```
<undeployment xmlns="http://xml.apache.org/axis/wsdd/">
  <handler name="MyHandler"/>
  <service name="MyService"/>
</undeployment>
```

> **NOTE**
>
> By default, the `AdminService` *only* allows deployment from clients on the local machine, for security reasons. If you want to allow remote deployment, you can do so by switching off an option in the server's WSDD. We recommend extreme caution when doing this; please make sure the `AdminService` has been secured to prevent unauthorized users from gaining access to your machine. Remember that deploying a service can make a Java class available for remote access—imagine if someone deployed the `java.lang.System` class, and then called the `exit()` method! Bye-bye app server.
>
> The option for remote deployment, if you wish to enable it, looks like this:
>
> ```
> <service name="AdminService" provider="java:MSG">
> </service>
> ```

Getting at the `MessageContext`

When you're building servlet applications, sometimes you'll want to insulate your application code from the servlet framework, and other times you'll need to use the servlet APIs. In the latter case, you'll put the meat of your functionality into the servlet processing method (`doGet()`, `doPost()`) and utilize the servlet request and response classes directly—your code knows it's running as a servlet, and can use the functionality of the servlet APIs. For the former case, your servlet is really an I/O wrapper for more abstract application code that has no servlet dependence.

The situation is similar in Axis. You can build service methods that perform application logic with no Axis-dependence (if you're exposing prebuilt Java classes as Web services, this will certainly be the case). On the other hand, you can also build service methods that are Axis-aware and thus have access to some of the features of the framework. The main thing such services want access to is the MessageContext, since it contains references to everything you might need regarding the state of Axis: the request and response messages, the type-mapping registry, the engine, the current set of properties, and so on. The only question is how to get at it from your service code.

You can access the current MessageContext from anywhere (including your service code) by using the static method MessageContext.getCurrentContext(). This method uses thread-local storage to make sure each call gets the right context, even if many threads are all calling into your service method at the same time.

Once you have access to the MessageContext, you can get and set properties, examine the messages, find out what transport is in use, and so on. For example, you can easily make your service behave differently based on whether a handler has put, for instance, an authenticated user property into the MessageContext:

```
// Our service method
float getPrice() {
    // Get the regular price
    float result = getNormalPrice();

    // Check if the user has been authenticated by looking in the MC
    // for a User object in a well-known place.
    MessageContext mc = MessageContext.getCurrentContext();
    User user = (User)mc.getProperty("myUserProperty");

    // If an earlier handler dropped a User object in myUserProperty,
    // check if they have priviledges
    if (user != null && user.isGoldMember() == true) {
        // The authenticated user is a member of our
        // Gold Club - give them a discount!
        result = result * 0.85f;
    }
    return result;
}
```

Property Scoping at Runtime

A useful and interesting pattern occurs when you ask for a property value from the MessageContext. Not only will the MessageContext provide you with values that have been directly inserted into its own property bag, but it also makes available options that were configured into the active service and the engine. This allows you to set a configuration option on the axisEngine, which can then be overridden by a particular service, which can be overridden again by handlers in a particular message exchange if appropriate. Let's look at an example. In this example, we use the value SEND_MULTIREFS as a String constant that we assume is defined elsewhere. An Axis server might be configured (by setting the SEND_MULTIREFS option to Boolean.False) to avoid sending multirefs by default, in order to speed up serialization of SOAP 1.1 messages. Active

MessageContexts for that AxisServer that didn't have a value themselves for the property SEND_MULTIREFS would return false if someone called getProperty(SEND_MULTIREFS). A specific service deployed in that engine could set the same parameter to the value true, and for invocations of that service alone, the new value would override the default (see Figure 5.10).

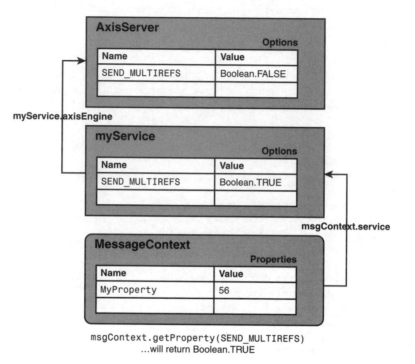

msgContext.getProperty(SEND_MULTIREFS)
...will return Boolean.TRUE

Figure 5.10   Property scoping in Axis

Service Lifecycle and Scopes

When you deploy a service using Axis, you know there is generally a backend Java object that implements the application logic. How is that object created? How many such objects are there? Can they be shared across multiple threads at once? The answers to these questions can be important when deciding how to build your services.

As it turns out, the service deployer has a number of lifecycle choices for service objects, and they're controlled by the scope option on the service in WSDD. Here's an example:

```
<service name="MySingleton">
  ...
  <parameter name="scope" value="application"/>
</service>
```

The valid values for this option are as follows:

- *Application scope* means there will only be a single instance of the service class for the entire AxisEngine. This means that you, the developer of the service class, must make sure all your methods are thread-safe, since there might be many active requests threading their way through the same code in parallel. Any state you keep in your service object will be shared across all invocations for the lifetime of the engine.

- *Request scope* is the opposite of application scope—services configured with request scope will cause a new service object to be created for every SOAP request. If you use request scope, you should try to make sure your service objects don't have slow or expensive initialization code in their constructors, since they'll be created and deleted a lot. Request scope is the default for services without the option specified.

- *Session scope* is somewhere between application and request. Session-scoped service objects are created once per client session (see "Sessions on the Server Side"); once a session has been established with the axisEngine, a given client will use the same service object instance for every request until the session terminates. You can use data fields in your service objects to hold state on a per-session basis. Note that to make session-scoped objects work, your clients must be able to support sessions in a way compatible to the way your server does it—see the next section for more on this.

When a service object is created or destroyed by the Axis runtime, the engine checks to see if that object implements an interface from JAX-RPC called javax.xml.rpc. server.ServiceLifecycle. This interface contains two methods:

```
void init(Object context) throws ServiceException;
void destroy();
```

By implementing these methods, you can do any initialization or cleanup that your service object requires. When the engine creates a new service object, init() is called with a context object that lets the service get at the MessageContext and various servlet-related properties. The object is of type javax.xml.rpc.server. ServletEndpointContext, but we don't recommend using it, since it ties your service object to servlet-specific concepts. You can use the MessageContext.getCurrentContext() API described earlier to get at whatever you need from the environment (this is how the getMessageContext() method on the ServletEndpointContext is implemented).

The Axis engine calls destroy() on your ServiceLifecycle objects when it frees them for garbage collection—either at shutdown (for all objects), when a session expires (for session-scoped objects), or at the end of a request (for request-scoped objects).

Sessions on the Server Side

Sessions, as we mentioned earlier, are about storing data on the server side—data associated with a particular client. Axis has an abstraction for this concept in the `org.apache.axis.session` package.

A given interaction can optionally be associated with a session, and thus the `MessageContext` has a slot in it for the currently active session. You can use the `MessageContext.getSession()` API to get a reference to the active session, if any.

A `Session` object acts much like a `Map`/`Hashtable`, in that it lets you store values in a library indexed by `String` keys. The power of the `Session` lies in the fact that you (that is, handlers or your service object) can put data in the `Session` during one interaction, and then that data will be available again on the next interaction from that same client. This pattern is familiar to anyone who has done web/servlet programming; it lets you do things like remember a user's name, authentication credentials, preferences, and so on.

As with the client, there are two built-in ways of accessing sessions on the Axis server: The first uses the servlet `HttpSession` as its underlying datastore, and the second uses the `SimpleSession`. When using the servlet version, the servlet engine will handle timing out the session for you; when using the SOAP version, the `SimpleSessionHandler` will periodically reap expired sessions. You can set the timeout on a session with `session.setTimeout(int)`; if the number of seconds elapses with no activity on a given session (*activity* is defined as any interaction that uses that session), it expires and all data within it is lost.

The session implementations that Axis includes aren't generally persistent—in other words, the data you store in the session will be lost in case of a server crash/restart. Nothing would prevent you (or a third party) from developing a persistent session implementation, though, and if the `HttpSession` is acting as the storage, it's up to your servlet engine whether to implement persistence.

Using WSDL2Java to Generate Services

Sometimes, instead of starting from Java classes, it's desirable to take a WSDL description of a Web service and create a skeleton implementation of the service described by the WSDL. By specifying the `-s` option to WSDL2Java, you can have the tool generate, in addition to the client and data classes we discussed previously, a framework implementation of the service and associated WSDD deploy and undeploy files.

Let's see what happens with the example from the "Stubs" section:

```
% WSDL2Java -s http://localhost:8080/axis/InventoryCheck.jws?wsdl
```

Now, in addition to the classes we saw previously, we'll find these:

- `InventoryCheckSOAPBindingImpl.java`—The framework implementation of the service
- `deploy.wsdd`—A prebuilt deployment file ready for use by the AdminClient
- `undeploy.wsdd`—A prebuilt undeployment file

If you look inside the `Impl` class, you'll see a method like this:

```
public class InventoryCheckSoapBindingImpl implements
                    localhost.InventoryCheck_jws.InventoryCheck {
   public boolean doCheck(java.lang.String sku, int quantity)
       throws java.rmi.RemoteException {
       return false;
   }
}
```

This is where you'd fill in the logic for your service method and return the real result. Since the framework knows you'll be editing the implementation class, if you run WSDL2Java again in the same directory, it will *not* overwrite what's there (otherwise you might inadvertently lose your work). If you want to make a new version, you should delete or move the `Impl` file before rerunning WSDL2Java.

The steps for deploying a service based on a WSDL are as follows:

1. Use WSDL2Java with the `-s` option to build a Java framework for your service.
2. Open the generated `Impl` class in your favorite editor and actually implement the logic of the methods.
3. Compile all the generated classes and put the `.class` files onto your server's class-path.
4. Either edit the `server-config.wsdd` file for your server and add everything in the generated `deploy.wsdd`, or use the AdminClient tool to deploy the generated `deploy.wsdd` file to the server.
5. The generated `undeploy.wsdd` file can be used as input to the AdminClient and will undeploy the service.

Generating WSDL for Your Services

You know from our earlier discussions that WSDL is a central part of making Web services easy to use. Now that you're deploying Web services with Axis, how do you get the WSDL to give to your prospective users or to publish in directories such as UDDI (discussed in Chapter 6)? Axis provides two ways to generate WSDL from your Java Web services: Java2WSDL and ?wsdl.

Using Java2WSDL

Axis comes with a mirror-image of the WSDL2Java tool called Java2WSDL. Java2WSDL is run from the command line; Axis also includes a custom ant task for using Java2WSDL in Ant builds. Java2WSDL takes a Java class (or interface) and generates a WSDL description of that class as a Web service, including schemas for all the necessary datatypes utilized in the class's methods. Java2WSDL has a lot of options; if you want the lowdown, check out the Axis documentation.

Here's a basic example:

```
java org.apache.axis.wsdl.Java2WSDL -o priceCheck.wsdl
➥ -l"http://localhost:8080/axis/services/priceCheck" -n
➥"http://skatestown.com/com.skatestown.services.PriceCheck
```

The -o option specifies the output WSDL file location. The -l option specifies the end-point URL that will be reflected in the emitted WSDL file. The -n option defines the targetNamespace for the WSDL. Finally, the class name is the Java class that the WSDL emitter will use to generate the WSDL operations.

Java2WSDL is a good tool, but it also has some problems. In particular, it doesn't use the type-mapping configuration for the engine when generating schema types from the Java types in your services. This means that although it will generate schemas from your Java types, it will always use the default mappings, and not necessarily the ones your service uses (as configured in the WSDD for the service). Someday Java2WSDL may be able to read a WSDD file in order to use custom mappings; but for now, if you care about this issue, you might want to consider letting the engine do your WSDL generation for you.

Letting the Engine Do the Work: ?wsdl

The second WSDL-generation technique involves using the Axis server to dynamically generate WSDL from a running deployed service. This technique has a couple of advantages over Java2WSDL. First, it's simpler; there are no command-line tools to learn—you just need to know how to tack ?wsdl onto your normal service URL. As you've already seen, you can get the WSDL for the InventoryCheck service at the URL http://localhost:8080/axis/InventoryCheck.jws?wsdl. For regular services, it's http://*host:port/yourwebapp*/services/*serviceName*?wsdl.

The second advantage of the dynamic ?wsdl technique is that because the WSDL is being generated by a running engine, you can use all the deployment information in the engine. So, you can automatically take advantage of all the active type mappings to generate the right schemas, and you can allow the deployed handler chains to affect the WSDL to insert extensions like SOAP headers.

Handler Framework for Generating WSDL

Each handler has, in addition to the normal invoke API, a method on it that looks like this:

```
void generateWSDL(MessageContext context)
```

Since the provider is the meat of your service, it's the component that is responsible for generating most of the WSDL description. When WSDL is asked for, however, *all* the handlers that would normally be invoked for a service interaction get to participate by adding extensibility elements or documentation or changing things that were generated by the provider. Note that right now, handlers that run *before* the provider can't affect the WSDL much—the provider generates it and then places it (as a DOM document) in a property called "WSDL" in the MessageContext. After the provider, any handler on any of the response chains can then modify the DOM in that property.

We expect this mechanism to change in the future, so that it will be easier for handlers/extensions to contribute to a WSDL model no matter where they are in the deployment order. Also, don't forget that if for some reason the engine isn't doing what you need it to when generating WSDL, you can override the automatic generation and supply a custom WSDL file yourself. We explained how to do this in the "WSDD for Services" section.

SimpleAxisServer: A Lightweight Container for Services

Axis comes with a simple multithreaded HTTP server that can be used to host Web services without the overhead of a servlet engine. The class is called SimpleAxisServer, and it's in org.apache.axis.transport.http.SimpleAxisServer. It supports accessing JWS- and WSDD-deployed services, including handling HTTP GETs to automatically retrieve WSDL.

To start it, execute the class:

```
java org.apache.axis.transport.http.SimpleAxisServer [ p port]
```

The optional port argument lets you select which port the SimpleAxisServer will listen on: the default is 8080.

SimpleAxisServer looks for a server-config.wsdd file in the current directory and, if it finds one, uses that file as its configuration. Note that you must have all the JAR files Axis needs (see the earlier sidebar "Installing Axis") and all the service and data classes that will be used by your deployed services in your classpath.

Although SimpleAxisServer isn't suited for serious high-availability usage, it's a handy tool to have in your toolkit.

A Guide to Web Service Styles

Axis supports four different *styles* of services, which are really just different ways to map Java invocations to Web service invocations. These styles affect things on both the client and the server; in this section we'll explain what they mean, for future reference in the rest of the chapter.

RPC Style

RPC style uses the SOAP RPC conventions and the SOAP data model. In WSDL, this maps directly to the rpc/encoded style we discussed in the last chapter.

On the client, this means that we typically use the invoke(methodName, arguments) API, and that each argument in the passed array turns into a SOAP RPC parameter. On the server, since the RPC conventions explicitly state that the first element in the SOAP body will be the method name, the Axis server can use the QName of that element as a key to dispatch to the correct operation for RPC style services.

Wrapped Style

Wrapped style is a lot like RPC style, except in WSDL terms the messages are document/literal (no SOAP encoding), and they don't use the SOAP RPC conventions. Instead, a wrapper element is defined directly in the schema representing the method name for each operation, and then a series of elements appears inside that, one for each parameter. Once again the engine can use the QName of the body element to figure out which operation to call.

The WSDL for a wrapped operation would look something like this (with details like the binding and the definitions element removed for simplicity):

```
<types>
  <schema targetNamespace="http://skatestown.com/"
        xmlns="http://www.w3.org/2001/XMLSchema">
    <element name="doCheck">
      <complexType>
        <sequence>
          <element name="sku" type="xsd:string"/>
          <element name="quantity" type="xsd:int"/>
        </sequence>
      </complexType>
    </element>

    <element name="doCheckResponse">
      <complexType>
        <sequence>
          <element name="result" type="xsd:boolean"/>
        </sequence>
      </complexType>
    </element>
  </schema>
</types>

<message name="doCheckRequest">
  <part name="part1" element="st:doCheck"
        xmlns:st="http://skatestown.com"/>
</message>
<message name="doCheckResponse">
  <part name="part1" element="st:doCheckResponse"
        xmlns:st="http://skatestown.com"/>
</message>

<interface name="InventoryCheck">
  <operation name="doCheck">
    <input message="doCheckRequest"/>
    <output message="doCheckResponse"/>
  </operation>
</interface>
```

Notice that we've bolded the operation name and the matching element name to indicate that they match. This is how the WSDL processor (and you) can tell that an operation is wrapped.

This pattern of using a wrapper element to represent the method name and the inner elements to represent parameters is ad hoc (several packages support it, but it isn't standard). The downside is that no rules are written down that describe what is allowable and what isn't in terms of message structure, and if such services allow anything that schema allows, we might find ourselves in situations where the XML doesn't cleanly map to Java invocations. The WSDL 2.0 group is remedying this situation by writing clear rules for RPCs specified with schema elements—in other words, they're codifying wrapped operations in a standard and interoperable way.

Document Style

Document style moves further toward generic XML processing but still uses a Java data structure to represent the entire message. In document style, the QName of the first body element in the SOAP message can still be used for dispatching to the right operation on the server, but it's no longer necessarily named the same as the operation. In other words, it's possible to have an operation defined like this in WSDL (again, some details are elided from this example):

```
<types>
  <schema targetNamespace="" xmlns="http://www.w3.org/2001/XMLSchema">
    <element name="theRequest">
      <complexType>
        <sequence>
          <element name="inner" type="string"/>
        </sequence>
      </complexType>
    </element>
  </schema>
</types>

<message name="docRequest">
  <part name="part1" element="theRequest"/>
</message>

<interface name="docInterface">
  <operation name="operation1">
    <input message="docRequest"/>
  </operation>
</interface>
```

Since there is no explicit relationship between the operation name in the WSDL and the element name on the wire, it's possible for a WSDL to define two different operations that use the exact same wire signature. Like many other Web service engines, Axis relies on unique wire signatures to correctly determine which operation to invoke. As long as no other operation in the previous WSDL uses `<theRequest>` as its `body` element, we can safely map any message that arrives with that element to the operation `operation1`. If another operation were using `<theRequest>` as its input, however, dispatch would have to work some other way; this is why the WS-I interoperability group (discussed in Chapter 13, "Web Services Interoperability") restricts document-style operations to having unique element QNames.

To understand the difference between document and wrapped style in terms of Java bindings, let's consider this SOAP message (namespace declarations elided for simplicity):

```
<soap:Envelope>
  <soap:Body>
    <setStockAlert>
      <price xsi:type="xsd:float">50</price>
      <symbol xsi:type="xsd:string">MSFT</symbol>
    </setStockAlert>
  </soap:Body>
</soap:Envelope>
```

If this were dispatched to a document-style service, the appropriate Java service method would be

```
void operation(SetStockAlert body)
```

where `operation` is the operation name. `SetStockAlert` is a JavaBean that represents the entire `<setStockAlert>` element in the SOAP body, something like this:

```
class SetStockAlert {
    float price;
    String symbol;
    ...
}
```

If, on the other hand, this were a wrapped-style service, we would expect the service method like this instead:

```
void setStockAlert(float price, String symbol)
```

Here the method name is the same as the name of the XML `wrapper` element, and the parameters have been unwrapped into individual arguments to the method.

The three styles you've seen so far have one thing in common: the Axis infrastructure handles converting the XML into Java data structures and vice versa.

Message Style

Message style, the fourth option, is used in cases where you want to process the XML yourself, with no data binding. In a message-style service, you don't necessarily have one Java operation per Web service operation—instead it's possible to have, for instance, a single Java method processing any XML that arrives at the service. You'll see how this works later when we discuss deploying services.

Since there are several ways in which you might want to deal with XML, Axis provides several possible signatures for your message-style operations:

```
void method(SOAPEnvelope request, SOAPEnvelope response)
Element [] method(Element [] request)
SOAPBodyElement [] method(SOAPBodyElement [] request)
Document method(Document request)
```

If your service method wants to explicitly look at the whole SOAP envelope, including headers, you probably should use the first method. Note also that the response SOAPEnvelope is passed in to your method, not generated by it—this means there may already be headers in the response that were placed there by earlier handlers (it's up to your code to decide what to do with them, if anything; generally you should leave them alone if possible).

The next two options let you get at all the subelements of <soapenv:Body> (they are arrays, since technically the SOAP spec allows more than one element inside the Body) and return your own collection of elements to go into the response Body. They are identical except for your preference of DOM Elements or SOAPBodyElements.

The last option uses a DOM Document to hold the contents of the <soapenv:Body> and returns a DOM Document for the response body. Note that since a Document can only have a single root element, this method will only give you the first element inside the body; if you expect multiple body elements, use one of the other options.

From XML to Java and Back Again: The Axis Type-Mapping System

We've touched on type mapping a number of times in the chapter; and you already know that you can associate particular Java types with XML Schema types, both by using client-side APIs (manually or as a result of using WSDL2Java) and with server-side metadata (WSDD). This section will duck briefly behind the scenes to describe the type mapping architecture in Axis/JAX-RPC.

Registering Mappings

To make type mapping work, we need a *registry* of mappings, so that when the engine is reading a particular piece of XML and comes across a given element of a given schema type, it can locate an appropriate deserializer in order to convert the XML into Java. The same goes for the other direction, when writing out Java objects as XML. This registry is known as the TypeMappingRegistry. Although you might expect the TypeMappingRegistry to contain the mappings themselves, JAX-RPC decided to introduce another layer called a TypeMapping—so the TypeMappingRegistry (TMR) contains TypeMappings, and then the TypeMappings enable you to map XML and Java types.

For certain encoding styles, the type mappings might be different—in particular, the SOAP encoding defines its own types that won't be understood outside the context of encoded services. As such, the `TypeMappingRegistry` is first indexed by `encodingStyle`. At any given time, there is a `TypeMapping` object for each `encodingStyle`.

The `AxisEngine` has its own `TypeMappingRegistry` to keep track of global type mappings, and each `SOAPService` (on both the client and the server) has its own registry as well, to contain service-specific mappings. The service-specific mapping delegates to the engine global mapping; when it's looking for a particular type from the service-specific mapping, it automatically searches the global mapping if the type isn't found at the service layer. Note that the encoded `TypeMappings` will also search the default `no-encodingStyle` `TypeMapping` if they don't find a given type. This is good because you don't have to store all the default mappings in every `TypeMapping` instance.

An example is shown in Figure 5.11. If you need to deserialize an `xsd:long` with the encoded `TypeMapping`, it will first scan its own table of mappings, notice that the type QName isn't there, and then delegate to the default mapping. There you find a mapping to a Java `long` using the `SimpleDeserializer` (the default deserializer for most simple types).

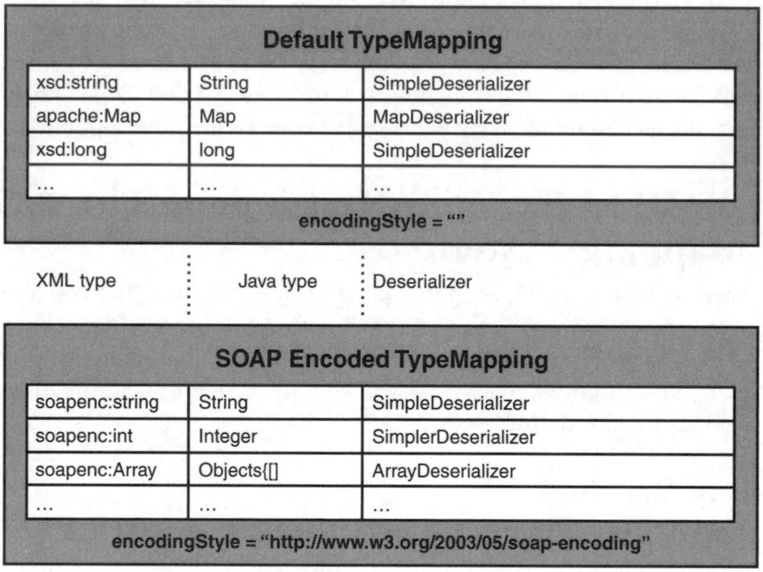

<table>
<tr><td colspan="3">Default TypeMapping</td></tr>
<tr><td>xsd:string</td><td>String</td><td>SimpleDeserializer</td></tr>
<tr><td>apache:Map</td><td>Map</td><td>MapDeserializer</td></tr>
<tr><td>xsd:long</td><td>long</td><td>SimpleDeserializer</td></tr>
<tr><td>...</td><td>...</td><td>...</td></tr>
<tr><td colspan="3">encodingStyle = ""</td></tr>
</table>

XML type	Java type	Deserializer

<table>
<tr><td colspan="3">SOAP Encoded TypeMapping</td></tr>
<tr><td>soapenc:string</td><td>String</td><td>SimpleDeserializer</td></tr>
<tr><td>soapenc:int</td><td>Integer</td><td>SimplerDeserializer</td></tr>
<tr><td>soapenc:Array</td><td>Objects{[]</td><td>ArrayDeserializer</td></tr>
<tr><td>...</td><td>...</td><td>...</td></tr>
<tr><td colspan="3">encodingStyle = "http://www.w3.org/2003/05/soap-encoding"</td></tr>
</table>

Figure 5.11 An example type mapping hierarchy

The `MessageContext` has a special slot for the active `TypeMappingRegistry`, which can be accessed with the `messageContext.getTypeMappingRegistry()` API. The current `TypeMapping` (which also takes into account the active `encodingStyle`) can be obtained with `messageContext.getTypeMapping()`.

When you register a type in WSDD at the global level, the mapping goes into the axisEngine's (either AxisClient or AxisServer) TypeMappingRegistry. Likewise, registering a typeMapping in the <service> will put it into the service-specific TypeMappingRegistry, making it accessible only to that particular service. When you use the registerTypeMapping() method on the Call object on the client side, you're registering types in the AxisClient's global TypeMappingRegistry.

Default Type Mappings

Table 5.1 lists most of the default type mappings supported by Axis. These are the type mappings that are built-in, and if your services use only these types, you won't need to do any custom mappings. The types with the soapenc: prefix are from the SOAP encoding namespace and are described later in this section; their mappings are available only when you're using the SOAP encoding style.

Table 5.1 **Default Axis type mappings**

Schema Type	Java Type
xsd:int	int
xsd:integer	java.math.BigInteger
xsd:long	long
xsd:byte	byte
xsd:float	float
xsd:double	double
xsd:hexBinary	byte[]
xsd:base64Binary	byte[]
xsd:Boolean	boolean
xsd:date	java.util.Date
xsd:decimal	java.math.BigDecimal
xsd:dateTime	java.util.Calendar
xsd:QName	javax.xml.namespace.QName
xsd:string	String
soapenc:int	java.lang.Integer
soapenc:long	java.lang.Long
soapenc:float	java.lang.Float
soapenc:Boolean	java.lang.Boolean
soapenc:short	java.lang.Short
soapenc:double	java.lang.Double
soapenc:integer	java.math.BigInteger
soapenc:decimal	java.math.BigDecimal
xmlsoap:Map	Map (see the next section)

The Apache `Map` Type

One of the problems with XML Schema and SOAP is that no standard type exists for representing the equivalent of a Java `Map` (a simple key/value associative array). As such, the Apache SOAP team came up with a simple serialization that has been adopted by several other toolkits (including Systinet's WASP, WebMethod's GLUE, and Perl's SOAP::Lite). The schema for the `Map` type looks like this:

```
<schema xmlns="http://www.w3.org/2001/XMLSchema"
        xmlns:tns="http://xml.apache.org/xml-soap"
        targetNamespace="http://xml.apache.org/xml-soap">
  <complexType name="Map">
    <sequence>
      <element name="item" type="tns:mapItem"
               minOccurs="0" maxOccurs="unbounded">
    </sequence>
  </complexType>
  <complexType name="mapItem">
    <sequence>
      <element name="key" type="anyType" />
      <element name="value" type="anyType" />
    </sequence>
  </complexType>
</schema>
```

We hope a future version of XML Schema will include built-in support for commonly used types like maps and tabular data sets. But for now the interoperability of these types is somewhat limited due to lack of concerted effort from the greater Web services community.

The SOAP Encoding Datatypes

The SOAP encoding schema, in addition to what we discussed in Chapter 3, also introduced a set of datatypes that mirror most of the XML Schema simple types. These new types enable the `ID` and `href` attributes used for encoding multiref values. In Java, these SOAP encoding types (as you can see in Table 5.1) map to the Java language wrapper types like `Integer`, instead of the simple types like `int`.

Mapping Java Collections to and from XML

Collections are a ubiquitous programming language concept, from simple arrays (a basic type in most languages) to more complex collections like sets. Java supports both basic arrays (`int[]`) and a rich set of collection classes. In XML, collections can be represented in several ways.

When using the SOAP encoding, Java collections and arrays will map to SOAP arrays, with schemas that look like this in WSDL (for a Java `String[]`):

```
<complexType name="ArrayOfString">
  <complexContent>
```

```
    <restriction base="soapenc:Array">
    <attribute ref="soapend:ArrayType"
        wsdlArrayType="xsd:string[]">
    </restriction>
  </complexContent>
</complexType>
```

With typed arrays like `int[]`, `String[]`, and so on, it's easy for the Axis engine to generate specific types like the `ArrayOfString` example. If you use the `Collection` classes (`ArrayList`, `Vector`, and so forth) in your signatures, the WSDL mapping will be a plain SOAP `Array`, since you can put any `Object` in it.

When using literal mode (no encoding), the common XML usage pattern for collections is to use the `maxOccurs` attribute on a schema element declaration:

```
<complexType name="BagOfThings">
  <sequence>
    <element name="things" type="xsd:int"
             minOccurs="0" maxOccurs="unbounded"/>
  </sequence>
</complexType>
```

If we map the `BagOfThings` type to a Java type using the standard mappings, it will look like this:

```
class BagOfThings {
    int [] things;

    ...accessors...
}
```

When elements with `maxOccurs` greater than 1 are fields in a type, they are converted to arrays. The same thing occurs with wrapped mode parameters that have `maxOccurs` greater than 1. We'll give you an example, but we'll do it the other way around this time—if you deploy this Java method as a wrapped service operation:

```
int getAverage(int [] values)
```

you'll see this schema for the operation wrapper element in the generated WSDL:

```
<element name="getAverage">
  <complexType>
    <element name="values" minOccurs="0" maxOccurs="unbounded"/>
  </complexType>
</element>
```

Default Type Mapping and XML/Java Naming

`BeanSerializer` and `BeanDeserializer` are the default classes for reading and writing

Java beans as XML complex types (this is why we have the `<beanMapping>` shorthand element in WSDD). They use the standard JAX-RPC mapping rules, which means that each field in a bean maps to an element or attribute in an XML complex type, and vice versa.

Each class can have meta-data associated with it that tells these default serializers anything special they need to know about how to map the Java fields into XML. You can see examples of this meta-data in the `getTypeDesc()` method of any data class generated by WSDL2Java.

The meta-data mostly serves to map the Java names to XML names, since there are many occasions when an XML name doesn't neatly (and uniquely) map to a Java name. For example, consider this schema snippet for a complex type:

```
<complexType name="NameClash">
  <sequence>
    <element name="name" type="xsd:string"/>
  </sequence>
  <attribute name="name" type="xsd:int"/>
</complexType>
```

Both the element and the attribute associated with this type are called `name`, and therefore they would each individually map to a Java field called name—except this time we can't do that because we can't have two identically named fields. So WSDL2Java would map this class as follows:

```
class NameClash {
    String name;  // element
    int name2;    // attribute
    ...
}
```

Later in the class declaration we would see meta-data that mapped the `name` field to an element called `name` and the `name2` field to an attribute called `name`. The same kind of mapping would need to occur if the XML name of an element or attribute were something like `int` (a Java reserved word) or `456` (an illegal Java identifier).

Since the mapping between the XML data space and the Java data space isn't perfect, without this kind of meta-data to control how individual fields are mapped, we would run into many unworkable situations.

Custom Serializers and Deserializers

As you've already seen, each Java↔XML mapping is associated with particular serializer and deserializer classes; `BeanSerializer`/`BeanDeserializer`, combined with meta-data, take care of most of the complex types you might encounter. You can also build custom serializers and deserializers for tighter control over how your Java classes map to XML or to improve performance over the standard mechanisms. We'll give you a quick overview of doing this here, but we won't go too deeply into the APIs.

Serializers

Just as handlers have the `invoke()` method, serializers have the `serialize()` method as their main focus:

```
void serialize(QName name, Attributes attributes,
               Object value,  context)
```

The point of a serializer is to take the Java object passed in the `value` argument and write it, as XML, to the passed `SerializationContext`. The `SerializationContext` object is the main way Axis writes XML. A `SerializationContext` keeps track of things like which namespace prefix mappings are already in scope, and it can do things like automatically write QNames for you with correct prefixes (including registering new mappings if necessary). It also remembers which Java objects have already been written, in order to correctly implement multiref serialization. If you look at some of the serializer classes in the `org.apache.axis.encoding.ser` package, you'll see a lot of uses of this class.

The code inside serializers is the main arbiter of how particular Java types are turned into XML serializations. So, the knowledge of how to describe what the XML looks like for a particular serializer should also reside in the serializer. As such, the `Serializer` interface has one more method on it, whose purpose is to allow the serializer to generate a schema description of the XML it will write:

```
Element writeSchema(Class javaType, Types types) throws Exception
```

The Axis engine will call this method during WSDL generation when it needs the schema for a Java type that has been mapped to your custom serializer. When implementing this method, your serializer should return a DOM element representing a `<simpleType>` or a `<complexType>` schema element that describes the XML that will be generated when serializing the Java type in the `javaType` argument. The `Types` reference that is also passed to the method allows your code access to the types that have already been written and a few other convenience APIs for situations when your type definition needs to reference other types.

Let's review: You have a Java datatype and wish to write it to XML in some custom way. So, you do the following:

1. Write a `Serializer` implementation that takes an object of your Java type and writes the XML the way you like it using a `SerializationContext`.

2. Make sure the serializer writes a correct schema for the generated XML.

3. Write a simple factory implementation so that the engine can create instances of your serializer. Look at any of the serializer factories in the `org.apache.axis.encoding.ser` package for examples. The `SerializerFactory` you build will be the class you refer to as the serializer component in WSDD type mappings and in the `Call.registerTypeMapping()` client APIs.

Deserializers

The main purpose of a deserializer is to process XML and then end up with a Java object as its value. Since Axis is a SAX-based system, the deserialization framework works by processing SAX events. Deserializers (classes that implement the `org.apache.axis.encoding.Deserializer` interface) have several SAX-like methods, but all of them have an extra argument beyond that supplied by SAX in order to pass the Axis-specific deserialization context. Here's an example:

```
public void startElement(String namespace, String localName,
                         String qName, Attributes attributes,
                         DeserializationContext context)
        throws SAXException;
```

The `DeserializationContext` in a way mirrors the `SerializationContext` we discussed earlier. It enables the deserializer code to get at the current `MessageContext`, the current `TypeMappingRegistry`, the mapping of multiref objects (which IDs map to which objects), and other state for the active deserialization.

All Axis deserializers extend the class `org.apache.axis.encoding.DeserializerImpl`, which contains a lot of boilerplate code to handle common tasks. As with serializers, in order to register deserializers, you also need a factory class, which should implement `org.apache.axis.encoding.DeserializerFactory`.

Look at the Axis source for many examples of writing custom serializers and deserializers.

Using the `MessageElement` XML/Object APIs

The `MessageElement` class in Axis and all its subclasses (which we covered in "The Message APIs and SAAJ") provide some nice extras over the standard JAX-RPC `SOAPElement` class. One of these features is the ability to use the `MessageElement` to easily convert XML to Java and vice versa using the type-mapping infrastructure.

Suppose you have a header like this:

```
<soap:Header>
  <ns:RetryCount xmlns:ns="myNS" xsi:type="xsd:int">5</ns:RetryCount>
</soap:Header>
```

You can ask for its value (assuming you already have a reference to the enclosing `SOAPEnvelope`) by doing the following:

```
SOAPHeaderElement retryHeader =
                      envelope.getHeaderByName("myNS", "RetryCount");
Integer retryCount = (Integer)retryHeader.getObjectValue();
```

The engine knows how to deserialize this particular header as an `Integer` because it has an `xsi:type` attribute that refers to a type that's understood. If the `xsi:type` were not present, `getObjectValue()` as demonstrated here wouldn't work (you'd get an error).

Does this mean you can't rely on this deserialization mechanism if there isn't type data on every element? Not at all.

You can use two other similar APIs to give the engine the necessary hint about what type to use if it doesn't know from the XML. The first is getObjectValue() again, but you can call it and also pass a Class object that is the Java class into which you'd like the element to deserialize:

```
Integer val = (Integer)retryHeader.getObjectValue(Integer.class);
```

If there is an active type mapping in scope for that Java class, the engine will try to deserialize the XML with the appropriate deserializer. Note also that if you use this form of the API and there *is* an xsi:type on the MessageElement, Axis will make sure there is a valid mapping from that particular xsi:type to the Java class you passed—if not, you'll get a fault.

You can also use the getValueAsType() API, which looks like this:

```
element.getValueAsType(Constants.QNAME_XSD_STRING)
element.getValueAsType(xmlType, javaType)
```

This is basically the same idea as getObjectValue(Class) except that instead of passing the Java class, you tell Axis the XML type (a QName). The first version makes Axis behave as if the QName you passed was present in the xsi:type attribute of the XML element. The second one does the same but also suggests a particular Java class to target for deserialization.

Creating MessageElements from Java Objects

Just as you can easily deserialize Java objects from MessageElements you receive, you can also build MessageElements from Java objects when you're writing messages. Consider a handler whose job is to insert a SOAP header that maps to a complex Java data object. You could write the code to generate the Header XML manually, but that would be essentially writing a serializer. Instead, you can allow the serialization framework to do the work for you, like so:

```
SOAPHeaderElement myHeader = new SOAPHeaderElement(myQName, myObject);
```

SOAPHeaderElement borrows this constructor from MessageElement, which has the same form. So we could imagine mixing the two, adding a header like this:

```
<myHeader>
  <myObj>
    <!-- serialized object data here -->
  </myObj>
</myHeader>
```

with the following API call:

```
myHeader = new SOAPHeaderElement(myHeaderQName);
MessageElement myEl = new MessageElement(myObjQName, myObject);
```

This technique can be handy when you're writing both message-style services and handlers.

When Things Go Wrong: Faults and Exceptions

If your service throws an exception, Axis will automatically turn that exception into a SOAP fault on the wire. If you wish to have more direct control over the SOAP fault data (such as the `faultCode` and the `faultRole`, for instance), you can choose to throw an `AxisFault` or any exception derived from `AxisFault`, instead.

You learned in Chapter 3 that when SOAP errors occur, they are serialized as SOAP faults. In the Java world, when things go wrong, `Exceptions` are thrown. What seems logical, then, would be if our Java SOAP framework would translate SOAP faults we receive on the client into thrown `Exceptions`, and `Exceptions` that get thrown on the server into SOAP faults on the wire. As you might surmise, this is exactly what Axis does.

The `AxisFault` Class

`AxisFault` is a base exception class that includes explicit fields to carry the structural items in a SOAP fault (discussed in the last chapter). Here's what some of the interface looks like:

```
class AxisFault {
    // Fault code accessors
    QName getFaultCode();
    void setFaultCode(QName code);

    // Fault string accessors
    String getFaultString();
    void setFaultString(String faultString);

    // Support adding custom headers to a fault message
    ArrayList getHeaders();
    void addHeader(SOAPHeaderElement header);
    ...
}
```

On the server side, if your class throws an `AxisFault`, the resulting wire-level SOAP fault will reflect the values set in the `AxisFault` class. For instance, if a handler did this:

```
AxisFault fault = new AxisFault();
fault.setFaultCode(new QName("", "Server.NoProduct"));
fault.setFaultString("No such product");
fault.addHeader(new SOAPHeaderElement("", "PhoneNumber", "867-5309"));
throw fault;
```

it would turn into this on the wire:

```
<soap:Envelope xmlns:soap="http://www.w3.org/2003/05/soap-envelope"
     xmlns:xsi="http://www.w3.org/2001/XMLSchema-instance"
     xmlns:xsd="http://www.w3.org/2001/XMLSchema">
 <soap:Header>
  <PhoneNumber xsi:type="xsd:string">867-5309</PhoneNumber>
 </soap:Header>
 <soap:Body>
  <soap:Fault>
   <faultcode>Server.NoProduct</faultcode>
   <faultstring>No such product</faultstring>
  </soap:Fault>
 </soap:Body>
</soap:Envelope>
```

Notice that because we set a header on the thrown fault object, it turned into a
PhoneNumber header in the serialized SOAP fault, as expected.

Using Typed Exceptions

AxisFaults work great, but what if you want to include more fault-specific information? You can get at the details with an AxisFault's getFaultDetails() method, which
returns DOM elements, but that isn't very programmer friendly. We'd like to use Java's
structured exception-handling system for returning specific exception types—so that
when the server throws, for instance, a BadPartNumber fault, we can get that same
exception on the client, including any data that the server included in the thrown
exception. We can do this by using the WSDL fault construct.

Faults and WSDL

A fault in WSDL 1.1, as you saw in the last chapter, is defined with a name and an XML
structure that usually ends up in the <detail> element of a SOAP fault. Here's an
example. Let's imagine the WSDL for a modified version of our inventory checker that
throws a specific fault if the client sends a bad SKU. We'll just show some of the changes
here, not reproduce the whole WSDL (we assume the prefix sf is mapped to
http://skatestown.com/faults):

```
<types>
  <schema targetNamespace="http://skatestown.com/faults">
    <element name="BadPart">
      <complexType>
        <sequence>
          <element name="partNumber" type="xsd:int"/>
        </sequence>
      </complexType>
    </element>
```

```
    </schema>
  </types>
<message name="BadPartMsg">
  <part name="thePart" element="sf:BadPart"/>
</message>
...
<portType name="InventoryCheck">
  <operation name="doCheck">
    <input name="doCheckRequest" message="tns:doCheckRequest"/>
    <output name="doCheckResponse" message="tns:doCheckResponse"/>
    <fault name="BadPartFault" message="sf:BadPartMsg"/>
  </operation>
</portType>
```

This would cause WSDL2Java to generate the following class for the fault:

```
class BadPartNumberFault extends AxisFault {
    int partNumber;
    ...
}
```

The element complexType, including all its data (the part number), has been mapped to a Java type that extends AxisFault.

The generated Java interface for the InventoryCheck portType would now contain a method that looked like this:

```
public boolean doCheck(java.lang.String sku, int quantity)
      throws java.rmi.RemoteException, BadPartNumberFault
```

As expected, the method throws the generated fault type. On the wire, a BadPartFault would look like this:

```
<soapenv:Fault>
  <soapenv:Code>
    <soapenv:Value>soapenv:Sender</Value>
  </soapenv:Code>
  <soapenv:detail>
    <sf:BadPart>
      <partNumber>0</partNumber>
    </sf:BadPart>
  </soapenv:detail>
</soapenv:Fault>
```

If the Axis client received a message containing this fault in the SOAP body, it would deserialize the XML to a BadPartNumberFault. Then, the stub would throw that exception.

Note that Axis does this work both ways: If your Java services throw particular faults, and you've mapped them with the correct type mappings and WSDD <fault> declarations, Axis will generate WSDL containing the correct fault descriptions. Naturally, if you build your services with WSDL2Java, all the faults will be correctly generated and mapped in the WSDD automatically.

Axis as an Intermediary

In this section, we'll talk about how to use Axis as a SOAP intermediary. Intermediaries, as explained in Chapter 3, can be useful for a variety of reasons. Axis has been built to take advantage of the SOAP infrastructure for processing messages based on *roles*: URIs that represent classes of processing that a SOAP node might fulfill. By default, every Axis client and server application always fulfills the next and ultimateDestination roles. You can also configure other roles using WSDD as follows:

```
<role>http://skatestown.com/roles/manufacturer</role>
```

The `<role>` element (of which there can be zero or more) can be used either inside the `<globalConfiguration>`, in which case the roles become active for the entire axisEngine, or inside a `<service>` as in our example, which activates those roles only for that particular service.

Reasons for Roles

There are two primary purposes to keeping track of what roles you play. First, doing so enables easy access to all the headers targeted at the current node. The Axis message APIs we discussed earlier automatically filter the headers based on the active roles for the current AxisEngine service, so when your handler calls soapEnvelope.getHeadersByName(namespace, localPart), you will by default see *only* headers targeted at one of the active roles. This allows you to avoid doing this common logic yourself. If you really need to access all the headers when searching for a particular one, you can either do the search yourself by calling envelope.getHeaders() (which returns the entire unfiltered list) or use the secondary form of getHeader(s)ByName(), which includes an extra Boolean argument that indicates whether to search the entire headers list without role filtering (envelope.getHeaderByName(namespace, localPart, searchAllHeaders)).

The second purpose to keeping track of roles is MustUnderstand checking. Before the SOAPService calls the provider to execute the back-end Web service, a MustUnderstandChecker runs to make sure all mandatory headers that were targeted at the current node have been marked as processed. If a MustUnderstand header targeted at the current node is found and it isn't marked processed, the engine will automatically generate a MustUnderstand fault as per the SOAP spec, and your service method will never be called. So it's critical to remember to call setProcessed(true) on headers that your handlers process.

Aside from dealing with roles, using Axis as an intermediary is fairly simple. You have your service objects use the Axis client APIs to send the request message on to its next destination after processing and then, if appropriate, collect the response and run response processing on it before it goes back to the original client.

In the future, Axis may have more explicit support built in for intermediary design patterns. For instance, it may be able to specify an intermediary service in WSDL with a standard place to configure a forwarding address for the next hop.

How to Write a Handler

The main thing you need to do when writing a handler class is to implement the `invoke()` method, which is passed a `MessageContext`. Handlers are defined by the `org.apache.axis.Handler` interface, which in addition to the `invoke()` method contains methods for managing handler options and obtaining meta-data about the handler's deployment options, as well as a hook for participating in the generation of WSDL. We've talked about most of this already, and also how to deploy handlers with WSDD; in this section, we'll present a couple of examples of handler design and show you a few APIs that can come in handy.

The SkatesTown `EmailHandler`

As SkatesTown's business has continued to flourish, it now finds that it wants more visibility into all the Web service calls customers are making to the company's services. In particular, SkatesTown is interested in finding out how often customers are checking for more inventory than the warehouse currently holds; if this is happening a lot, the company might want to start keeping more of particular items in stock.

Al Rosen decided to use the Axis extensibility model to add this functionality to the `InventoryCheck` service without any modifications to the existing code. To do so, he created a handler that will sit on the response chain of the `InventoryCheck` service (keep in mind this is the WSDD version of the service, not the JWS one—JWS services can't have service-specific handlers). The handler is shown in Listing 5.1.

Listing 5.1   **The** `EmailHandler`

```
package com.skatestown.handlers;

import org.apache.axis.AxisFault;
import org.apache.axis.MessageContext;
import org.apache.axis.handlers.BasicHandler;
import org.apache.axis.message.SOAPEnvelope;
import org.apache.axis.message.RPCElement;
import org.apache.axis.message.RPCParam;
import org.xml.sax.SAXException;

import java.util.Vector;

public class EmailHandler extends BasicHandler {
    public EmailHandler() {
    }
```

Listing 5.1   **Continued**

```java
public void invoke(MessageContext context) throws AxisFault {
    try {
        // Get the SOAPEnvelope
        SOAPEnvelope env;
        env = context.getRequestMessage().getSOAPEnvelope();

        // The first body element will be an RPCElement
        RPCElement rpcEl = (RPCElement)env.getFirstBody();
        // Fetch the parameters
        Vector params = rpcEl.getParams();
        // First one is the SKU
        RPCParam param = (RPCParam)params.get(0);
        String sku = (String)(param.getValue());

        // Second is quantity requested
        param = (RPCParam)params.get(1);
        Integer quantity = (Integer)(param.getValue());

        // Now check the response for failures
        env = context.getResponseMessage().getSOAPEnvelope();
        RPCElement resEl = (RPCElement)env.getFirstBody();
        param = resEl.getParam("doCheckReturn");
        Boolean result = (Boolean)(param.getValue());

        // Did we fail?
        if (result.booleanValue() == false) {
            // YES - email the configured address
            String address = (String)getOption("emailAddress");
            // Safety first - use default if no address configured
            if (address == null)
                address = "manager@skatestown.com";

            String content = "A request for " + quantity + " items ";
            content += "of type " + sku + " failed.";

            sendEmail(address, content);
        }

        // The request succeeded, so just return
    } catch (SAXException e) {
        // Catch SAXExceptions and rethrow as AxisFaults
        throw AxisFault.makeFault(e);
    }
}
```

Listing 5.1 **Continued**

```
public void sendEmail(String address, String content) {
    // Fake email sending routine for demonstration. This would be
    // where your real emailing code would go.
    System.out.println("EmailHandler sending mail...");
    System.out.println("EmailHandler : TO " + address);
    System.out.println("EmailHandler : Begin Message");
    System.out.println(content);
    System.out.println("EmailHandler : End Message");
}
}
```

You should notice a few things. First, Al wanted the code to be easily configurable with new email addresses without any code changes. As such, he made the email address a handler parameter and used the `getOption()` API to get the value. This means each time this handler is deployed, the email address for that instance can be controlled like this (in WSDD):

```
<handler type="java:com.skatestown.handlers.EmailHandler">
    <parameter name="emailAddress" value="operations@skatestown.com"/>
</handler>
```

If no `emailAddress` parameter is configured in the WSDD, a default address is hard-coded.

Second, the `RPCElement` and `RPCParam` classes are used here. `RPCElement` is a subclass of `SOAPBodyElement` that represents an Axis method invocation of an operation with parameters. It's used for RPC, document, and wrapped style services, despite the name (a holdover from Axis's original RPC focus). The primary purpose of the class is to make it easy to map an operation invocation and its XML representation, and to get at the individual parameters of such an invocation. As you see here, we can get a `Vector` of the parameters for a given `RPCElement` and then query the value of each one. We know in the case of the request message that the first parameter is the `sku` and the second is the `quantity`, so we get them by position. For the response message, we know the return value will be called `doCheckReturn` (Axis always names return elements {*methodName*}Return by default), so we ask for that `RPCParam` by name.

Finally, notice that the code is surrounded with a `try/catch` for `SAXExceptions`. We do this because accessing the parameters of an `RPCElement` might require XML parsing in some situations, and so methods like `RPCElement.getParam()` throw `SAXExceptions`. Since the `invoke()` method only throws `AxisFaults`, we need to wrap any thrown `SAXExceptions` as `AxisFaults` for this code to work. We do this with the static `AxisFault.makeFault()` API, which takes any `Exception` and wraps an `AxisFault` around it.

The SkatesTown `GlobalHandler`

Our second example will demonstrate how the `InventoryCheck` service we introduced in Chapter 3 obtains its reference to the Product database (`ProductDB`). Listing 5.2 shows you the `GlobalHandler`, which is deployed on the global request chain of the SkatesTown `AxisServer`. Its purpose is to store a `ProductDB` reference in the active `MessageContext`, as the property `PRODUCT_DB` (a `String` constant defined in the interface `STConstants` so that it can be easily shared).

Listing 5.2   **The** `GlobalHandler`

```
package com.skatestown.handlers;

// imports elided

public class GlobalHandler extends BasicHandler implements STConstants {
    /**
     * Set up commonly used MessageContext properties
     */
    public void invoke(MessageContext msgContext) throws AxisFault {
        try {
            // First get the AxisEngine's "application scope" session.
            // This allows us to store things persistently throughout the
            // lifetime of the engine.
            AxisEngine engine = msgContext.getAxisEngine();
            Session appContext = engine.getApplicationSession();

            // Now check if we've already stored the product database in
            // here.
            ProductDB productDB = (ProductDB)appContext.get(PRODUCT_DB);

            if (productDB == null) {
                // No cached productDB - so we'll have to read the XML file
                // and parse it.  Then we store it away in the application
                // session so we only have to do this once.  NOTE : in the
                // real world we'd be watching a database for changes
                // and reloading the cache appropriately, but in this example
                // we're not concerning ourselves with that.
                String path = msgContext.getStrProp(Constants.MC_HOME_DIR);
                path += "/resources/products.xml";
                InputStream inStream =
                        new BufferedInputStream(new FileInputStream(path));
                Document doc = XMLUtils.newDocument(inStream);
                productDB = new ProductDB(doc);
                appContext.set(PRODUCT_DB, productDB);
```

Listing 5.2   **Contiued**

```
        }

        msgContext.setProperty(PRODUCT_DB, productDB);

    } catch (Exception e) {
        // If anything goes wrong above, wrap the exception in an AxisFault
        // and throw it.
        throw AxisFault.makeFault(e);
    }
  }
}
```

Notice the getApplicationSession() API on the AxisServer: This call gets us a Session object that is global to the entire server. Essentially, this is a persistent Map that we can use to store state as long as the AxisServer is running. In this case, we keep a reference to this Session as appContext.

First we check to see if there is already a ProductDB instance in appContext under the key PRODUCT_DB. If there is, we put it in the MesssageContext property of the same name and return. If not, however, we go and initialize the ProductDB object using a DOM Document that we obtain by reading the file product.xml from the resources/ directory underneath the AxisServer's home directory. Two handy things here: Axis always keeps the server's home directory in the MessageContext property MC_HOME_DIR (a constant from org.apache.axis.Constants); and you can use the XMLUtils class (org.apache.axis.utils.XMLUtils) to easily parse XML documents.

Back in Chapter 3, you saw that the ProductDB was obtained by a static call to ProductDB.getCurrentDB(). To finish this example, we'll show you the implementation of that method:

```
class ProductDB implements STConstants {
    static ProductDB.getCurrentDB() {
        MessageContext mc = MessageContext.getCurrentContext();
        return mc.getProperty(PRODUCT_DB);
    }
    ... rest of class ...
}
```

This method, which serves to insulate code like our InventoryCheck class from the details of Axis, gets the value of the PRODUCT_DB property from the current MessageContext. Since the GlobalHandler will have already run by the time we call this method in the service, we'll find the ProductDB waiting there for us, ready to use.

Now that you've seen a couple of handler examples, we'll finish the chapter with a few more important areas you might want to explore about Axis, starting with security.

Built-in Security

Axis includes a few basic security features, and the extensibility mechanism allows you to add more. We'll give you a quick overview of the authentication and authorization mechanisms in this section, but again we refer you to the Axis documentation for more details.

Using the Authentication/Authorization Handlers

To control access to services by username or role using the standard Axis infrastructure, you must deploy two handlers into your system, either in the global request chain or the service-specific request chain:

- `SimpleAuthenticationHandler` serves to confirm at runtime that there is an authenticated user associated with the current request.
- `SimpleAuthorizationHandler` does the work of managing access control lists for particular services.

Both of these handlers are in the package `org.apache.axis.handlers`.

Once you've deployed these two handlers, you can control which users are allowed to use a given service by specifying the `allowedRoles` parameter on the service like so:

```
<service name="MySecureService">
  ...
  <parameter name="allowedRoles" value="manager,jim"/>
</service>
```

The value of the parameter is a comma-separated list of the roles that are allowed to access this service. Roles may be exact usernames (such as `jim`) or groups (`manager`).

The `SimpleAuthenticationHandler` relies on a `SecurityProvider` (`org.apache.axis.security.SecurityProvider`), which is an interface that insulates Axis from all the details of a given security system. Axis provides two implementations:

- `SimpleSecurityProvider` uses a simple text file to store usernames and passwords. The `SimpleSecurityProvider` is provided for demonstration only; it wouldn't be used in any situation where security was a real concern.
- `ServletSecurityProvider` uses the built-in security of the servlet engine into which Axis is deployed.

To use the `ServletSecurityProvider`, you have to tell the `AxisServlet` to enable it. You do so via a servlet init-parameter (this goes inside the `<servlet>` definition for the `AxisServlet` in your `web.xml`):

```
<init-param>
  <param-name>use-servlet-security</param-name>
  <param-value>true</param-value>
</init-param>
```

This parameter causes the `AxisServlet` to automatically set up a `ServletSecurityProvider` in the `MessageContext`, which handlers such as the `SimpleAuthenticationHandler` can utilize without caring about the specific implementation.

Of course, you can define your own `SecurityProvider` subclasses, as you might do to enable other transport-specific security mechanisms. As you've seen, Axis has a flexible notion of underlying transports, which we'll cover a bit more in the next section.

Understanding Axis Transports

Axis has been designed to be a *transport-independent* SOAP engine. As such, despite the fact that most messages that enter and leave the system do so via HTTP, the HTTP-ness is split into HTTP-specific components. In this section, we'll describe the other transports included with Axis and touch on how you can build your own.

Client Transports

On the client side, a new transport requires a class that inherits from the `org.apache.axis.client.Transport` class. You can make sure your calls use the desired transport in one of two ways. First you can directly call `setTransport()` on the `Call` object:

```
call.setTransport(myTransportObject);
```

Second, you can register a `Transport` as the default handler for particular URL protocols, so if you want to register a `Transport` to handle all mail: URLs, you can do that. (See the Axis docs for information.)

The `Transport` object is the client-side equivalent of the transport listener on the server side. It's responsible for setting the transport name in the `MessageContext` and setting up any `MessageContext` properties that should be ready to go before the engine (the `AxisClient` in this case) begins its processing. Just before each outgoing invocation is passed to the `AxisClient`, the `Call` object calls the `setupMessageContext()` method on the current `Transport` object. This lets the `Transport` object set any specific `MessageContext` properties it desires.

When the engine returns, the `Transport` object gets another chance to do some work before the `Call` object returns control to the caller. The `processReturnedMessageContext()` method is invoked to enable any transport-specific processing that might be necessary on the response. Since the `Transport` object survives across invocations, this can be used in order to hold transport-specific values (the `HTTPTransport` uses this technique to hold cookie values so they can be returned on subsequent invocations). You can see examples of these methods in the source code for the various transports we'll describe.

The `Transport` object is the portion of the client transport that is *outside* the `AxisClient`—in other words, it runs before (on the request) and after (on the response) the engine has done its magic with the `MessageContext`. There is also a transport component inside the `AxisClient`, which is the named targeted chain in the WSDD that we spoke about early in this chapter, and the associated transport handlers.

Server Transports

There are two interlinked pieces to transports on the server as well. First is the transport *listener*, which is the piece of code responsible for pulling a transport-specific message from somewhere and invoking Axis. The second piece is the handlers associated with the transport name passed in by the listener.

Since the listener is, by definition, outside the Axis engine, you need a framework to run it. For HTTP, a servlet engine does this for you. For other transports, the listener might be anything from a simple class with a `main()` that polls for messages, to a multi-transport server framework. They all take in messages in some form, generate `MessageContexts`, and deliver them to an `AxisServer` with the transport name field set in a way that enables the server to find the correct targeted chain of handlers to perform transport-specific processing.

Transports Included with Axis

The following transports are included with the Axis distribution.

JMS

Axis includes a JMS (Java Message Service) transport (`org.apache.axis.transport.jms`), which was originally designed and implemented by contributors from Sonic Software, a leading JMS vendor. This transport lets you send messages over the reliable JMS infrastructure and control JMS behavior in convenient ways. See the JMS sample in `samples.jms` for details.

Mail

The mail transport (`org.apache.axis.transport.mail`) lets Axis communicate using SOAP over email connections. Typically you wouldn't use email as a transport for any kind of time-critical interaction, but the email infrastructure does have some nice features. Once your outgoing mail has been accepted by an SMTP server, the server will handle retrying the send in case of any connectivity problems to the destination. On the inbound side, the mail transport uses POP3 to pull SOAP emails from a particular mailbox.

The mail transport requires the Jakarta `commons.net` package, which is available at `apache.org`.

Local

The local transport (`org.apache.axis.transport.local`) is an in-process transport designed mostly for testing. It essentially instantiates an `AxisServer` inside the transport itself and uses that server to handle the request. You can see many examples of its use in the Axis tests (for example, `test.wsdd.TestAdminService` or `test.GenericLocalTest`).

Java

This transport (`org.apache.axis.transport.java`) lets you invoke Java methods directly without deploying service classes. You can access a URL like `java:mypackage.MyClass`, and the transport will call methods of a `MyClass` object as if it had been deployed as an RPC service.

Custom Transports

You'll find a couple of examples of building custom server-side transports in `samples/transport` in the Axis distribution. There is a custom TCP transport, and also a file-based transport that monitors a given directory for new XML files containing SOAP requests. Since these are transport listeners, they are, in a sense, outside of Axis proper. It's their responsibility to accept incoming messages and then call the Axis engine. As such, the `TCPListener` class has a `main()` method and can be run from the command line much like `SimpleAxisServer`. The `FileReader` class doesn't have a `main()`; but it's a `Thread` subclass, so the `FileTest` handles spinning off the listener.

To make any of the optional transports we discussed work, you typically need to make sure the appropriate classes/JAR files are in your classpath. The next section covers some of the other software Axis collaborates with in order to better do its job.

No API Is an Island: Axis and Its Environment

Axis, like many kinds of toolkit software, has some fairly deep relationships with its environment. Depending on the tools available in the environment, Axis can utilize plug-in functionality that people have built as options, and Axis also tries not to reinvent the wheel where possible—it utilizes other libraries for common functions. We'll touch on some of these in this section.

`Commons-Discovery` and Obtaining Resources

The framework Axis uses to get several of its pluggable resources is called the `commons-discovery` library. This library lets you search for configurable implementations of particular interfaces. For instance, you could ask the discovery library to find an appropriate JMS implementation. It would check various configuration options, including system properties and local properties (such as properties of an `AxisEngine`), to find a concrete class implementing the desired interface.

Logging Infrastructure

Axis uses another Jakarta commons library for its logging functionality. The `commons-logging` library was developed because the Java world had at least three commonly used logging systems: log4j, jlog, and the native logging in JDK 1.4. A need was felt for a thin infrastructure layer that insulated the developer from the details of these systems in order to provide a unified API.

Security Providers

A variety of secure socket factory classes are available in the `org.apache.axis.components.net` package. You can select them for use by setting the system property `org.apache.axis.components.net.SecureSocketFactory` to the desired `SecureSocketFactory` class; doing so engages the discovery mechanism described earlier.

Compilers

When Axis needs to compile a JWS file, it uses either the standard javac compiler (the default) or another compiler such as Jikes (a Java compiler from IBM). Again, discovery is used to find a component implementing the `org.apache.axis.components.Compiler` interface.

Especially with all these optional dependencies on other libraries/classes, it can sometimes be a challenge to make sure everything is working correctly when trying to build and deploy your Web service requesters and providers. The next section covers some of the tools Axis includes to help you make sure the system is working the way you want it to, both at deployment time and at runtime.

Development/Debugging Tools

Axis comes with several aids to developing and debugging the installation and your individual clients and services.

The happyAxis Page

As we discussed in the previous section, Axis has dependencies on other libraries, which is the usual case in well-componentized software. Some of those libraries, like the JMS transport or the Castor XML/Java binding system, are optional—Axis runs fine without them. Other pieces, though, need to be present and installed/configured correctly in order for Axis to work. The `commons-discovery` library and an XML parser are both examples.

When the first few versions of Axis came out, it was tricky to figure out what was wrong if your installation wasn't working. As a result, Axis provides a page called `happyAxis.jsp`, whose purpose is to confirm that all the necessary componentry is available and to give clear and user-readable errors if the environment isn't set up correctly.

The happyAxis page looks like Figure 5.12 in a browser when things are set up right. The message "The core Axis libraries are present" appears if everything looks good.

Configuring Logging

Axis uses the Jakarta `commons-logging` package, as mentioned earlier. By default, the `commons-logging` package looks for a log4j installation and uses that as its concrete logger, although you can configure it to use other loggers as well. Logging is a common way to diagnose and debug problems, so you might want to learn a bit about using log4j and commons-logging. Again, we won't cover the details here, but we'll tell you the basics.

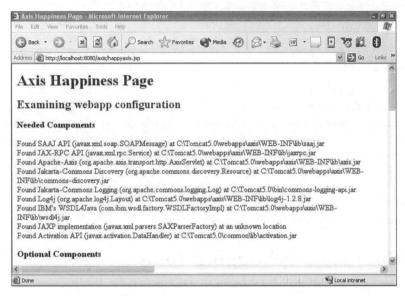

Figure 5.12   The happyAxis page

Commons-logging and log4j both define several levels of severity for each event that might be logged. These include DEBUG (only interesting if you're really debugging, tending toward verbosity), INFO (informative messages that can be nice to see but aren't critical), ERROR (problem tracking), and FATAL (serious problems). These events are logged with loggers that correspond to particular areas of the system—for instance, there is generally a logger associated with each class. You can configure various log destinations like the console and log files, and then control which events from which loggers go to which destinations.

Log4j looks for a file called log4j.properties in one of the directories on your classpath. You'll find a default version of this configuration file in the Axis distribution, which defines a couple of *appenders* (log4j's word for destinations): one for the console and one for a log file called axis.log. By default, all messages of INFO or higher priority are sent to the console logger as a result of this line:

```
# Set root category priority to INFO and its only appender to CONSOLE.
log4j.rootCategory=INFO, CONSOLE
```

The root category is the base from which all the loggers in the system inherit. You can change this to reduce the verbosity (fewer messages) by changing INFO to either ERROR or FATAL, or get more detailed messages by changing INFO to DEBUG. You can opt to log to a file instead of the console by changing CONSOLE to LOGFILE.

Often you don't want to get all the messages that setting the root category to DEBUG produces, but you do want to debug a portion of the system, like the `AxisServlet`. This can be done with a line like the following:

```
log4j.logger.org.apache.axis.transport.http.AxisServlet=DEBUG, CONSOLE
```

This line sets the `AxisServlet` logger to print DEBUG messages, leaving the rest of the system alone.

Using `tcpmon` and `SOAPMonitor`

When you're trying to deploy and use successful Web services, it's often critical to be able to see the SOAP messages on the wire in order to understand what is being produced and consumed by clients and servers. Axis includes two ways to do this: the `tcpmon` application and the `SOAPMonitor` servlet.

`tcpmon`

You can start `tcpmon` as follows:

```
java org.apache.axis.utils.tcpmon <localPort> <remoteHost> <remotePort>
```

Specifying a local port, a remote host, and a remote port (either none or all three must be used) tells the TCP monitor which local port to listen on and where messages received by that port should be forwarded.

If you don't use the command-line options, you'll see a screen like that shown in Figure 5.13. This UI allows you to start new monitor windows, each of which will listen on the given local port and forward messages to and from the desired remote host/port.

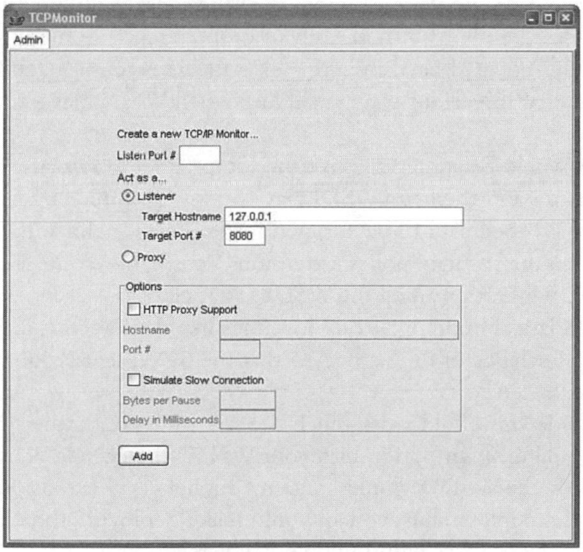

Figure 5.13   The `tcpmon` UI

If you select Proxy, then `tcpmon` will expect to be used as an HTTP proxy, which means clients will send special HTTP headers to tell `tcpmon` where to forward each message. If you select Listener, then as far as the client is concerned, `tcpmon` *is* the endpoint. As such, you'll need to configure in the real endpoint's hostname and port number.

While `tcpmon` is running, it forwards messages back and forth to the real endpoint and displays the message contents so that you can see what's going on. This is an invaluable tool for developing and debugging Web services, and you can also use it to monitor regular non-SOAP HTTP traffic.

SOAPMonitor

`SOAPMonitor` provides essentially the same functionality as `tcpmon`, except that it works within the Axis server. Instead of running a separate application, to use `SOAPMonitor` you deploy a handler in both the request and response flows (either the global ones or for each service you wish to monitor).

The default `server-config.wsdd` that comes with Axis includes commented-out deployments of the `SOAPMonitor` servlet, so all you need to do is uncomment them to use it. The handler watches the request and response messages as they go by and sends copies of them to an applet, so that you can watch the traffic in a Web browser by accessing `http://hostname/axis/SOAPMonitor`. See the Axis user guide for more details on using `SOAPMonitor`.

Axis Futures: A Quick Tour

To close out this chapter, we'll mention a few things that are on the drawing board for Axis 2.0. First and probably foremost, we envision an extensibility architecture that allows new features (implementations for some of the specs we'll discuss later in this book, for example) to be plugged in as easily as dropping a `.jar` file into an `extensions` directory. Essentially, Axis will have a registry of available extensions, and each one can register to be triggered in various ways, including when WSDL2Java sees particular WSDL extensions.

The end result would be something like this: drop `wssecurity.jar` into your Axis `extensions` directory, and then run WSDL2Java on a WSDL file containing policy statements that require WS-Security to be engaged for the service. Since the extension has registered interest in the security policy extensions, Axis hands control over to a class in the extension JAR while it's reading the WSDL. That class has access to the meta-data model that WSDL2Java is building; it can do things like deploy custom handlers into the request and response chains of the service, so that the SOAP extensions can be successfully generated and received.

On the server side, this could work much the same way; but rather than use WSDL as the trigger, you could drop an option into your WSDD that would activate the extension. In other words, the WSDD would contain a higher-level extension marker instead of individual handler deployments, which would make deploying the extension correctly much easier (especially in cases with multiple handlers).

Here are some other directions the Axis team has discussed or intends to investigate:

- A pull-based parser model instead of SAX
- Support for JAX-RPC 2.0 / JAXB 2.0
- Early support for WSDL 2.0
- A rearchitecture of the WSDL processing code for cleanliness, functionality, and speed
- A performance pass to speed up the system in general
- Defaulting to SOAP 1.2 instead of SOAP 1.1
- Real remote deployment, allowing remote administrators to upload JAR files containing service and data classes

Participating in the Axis Community

Axis, as we've mentioned, is an open source project. So, you're welcome to download the source code any time you want. This is great when you want to figure out how something works underneath the APIs. It also means the Axis team welcomes new developers into the community, especially if you're enthusiastic and ready to roll up your sleeves to help. The package is functional, but there are still problems to be solved and a few places where subsystems could use some careful refactoring.

If you might like to participate in this work, you can start by looking at the open bugs list (which you can find off the main Axis Web page,
http://ws.apache.org/axis). If something in there seems like an interesting and reasonably small piece of work, dive in and fix it, feeling free to ask questions on the Axis developers mailing list axis-dev. The same is true if you have a great idea for a way to improve the system.

When you're happy with your changes, submit a patch to the axis-dev mailing list, and one of the team members will review and commit it for you. After you submit a few patches for bug fixes or enhancements and have demonstrated both ability and commitment to the project, you can be granted committer status yourself and become a full-fledged member of the team.

If you aren't necessarily interested in contributing to the project, but you have questions about using Axis, the axis-user mailing list is the place to go. It's an active forum of Axis users, from beginner to advanced, trading information and tips.

Summary

We hope you've enjoyed this whirlwind tour through the Apache Axis SOAP engine. By now you should feel comfortable building and consuming Web services, whether you're starting from Java code or from WSDL descriptions. You understand the basics of the type-mapping system, how to use WSDD to control meta-data and deploy components (services, mappings, and handlers), and what it takes to extend Axis in useful ways. Perhaps you're even inspired to look at the Axis source code, and maybe even join the team.

In the next chapter, we'll look at how services and users find each other using registries like UDDI.

Resources

- *Apache Axis*—http://ws.apache.org/axis
- *log4j*—http://logging.apache.org/log4j/docs/
- *Jakarta Discovery Library*—http://jakarta.apache.org/commons/discovery/
- *Jakarta Commons Network Library*—http://jakarta.apache.org/commons/net/
- *JUnit*—http://junit.org/
- *SOAPBuilders*—http://groups.yahoo.com/group/soapbuilders
- *Axis-user mailing list*, for questions and tips about using Axis—axis-user-request@ws.apache.org
- *Axis-dev mailing list*, for development discussion and serious technical issues—axis-dev-request@ws.apache.org

Discovering Web Services

THIS CHAPTER INTRODUCES THE TOPIC of discovering Web services and the role of a service registry 📖 in a service-oriented architecture. We'll discuss several alternatives to service registries, but focus on the Universal Description, Discovery, and Integration (UDDI) 📖 standard. In addition to describing how a UDDI registry is used, we'll describe how to use Web Services Definition Language (WSDL) in a UDDI registry.

We'll also introduce some business partners of SkatesTown and discuss how a service registry such as UDDI can be used to help integrate their Web services. Throughout this chapter, we'll introduce sample Java code that gives examples of how to use a UDDI registry.

What Is Service Discovery?

In the previous chapters, we explained how to describe and use a Web service. But before you can use a Web service, you must discover its description and location. The service discovery process establishes the relationship between the service requestor and the service provider. Service discovery 📖 defines a process for locating service providers and retrieving service description documents that have been published; it's an important aspect of a service-oriented architecture.

Role of Service Discovery in a Service-Oriented Architecture

Recall the service-oriented architecture approach from Chapter 1, "Web Services Overview and Service-Oriented Architectures" (shown in Figure 6.1). A service-oriented architecture is based on the interactions between three primary roles: service provider, service registry, and service requestor. These roles interact using publish, find, and bind operations. The service provider is the business that provides access to the Web service and publishes the service description in a service registry. The service requestor finds the service description in a service registry and uses the information in the description to bind to a service.

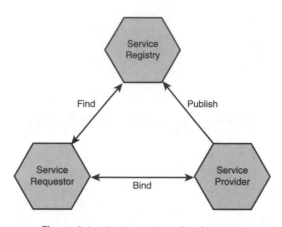

Figure 6.1   Service-oriented architecture

In this view of the service-oriented architecture, the service registry is a logical concept. In addition to representing the publication process, it also represents the service discovery method used to locate information about the service provider and obtain the Web service description.

Service Discovery Mechanisms

The role of the service registry in a service-oriented architecture can be fulfilled using several different mechanisms. Figure 6.2 illustrates a continuum of service discovery techniques.

There is a trade-off between the simplicity of the registry mechanism and the sophistication of the publishing and searching techniques. Let's briefly discuss each of these points on the continuum.

The simplest form of publication and service discovery is to request a copy of a service description directly from a service provider. After receiving the request, the service provider can email the service description as an attachment or provide it to the service requestor on a transferable media, such as a diskette. Although this type of service discovery is simple, it isn't very efficient or dynamic since it requires prior knowledge of the Web service as well as the contact information for the service provider.

At the other end of the spectrum, publication and service discovery use a centralized service registry. Service providers can use a registry to advertise their businesses and the Web services they offer. UDDI is an example of this type of service registry. UDDI allows definitions of businesses and services, detailed binding information, and constructs to support referential categorization, identification, and indication of adherence to technical specifications. This level of function provides the basis for supporting a service requestor when it wants to find a Web service dynamically.

Between these two extremes, there can be other publication and discovery methods. As an example, a distributed publication and discovery method could provide references to service descriptions at the service provider's point of offering. The Web Services

Inspection Language (WS-Inspection) provides this type of distributed support by specifying how to inspect a Web site for available Web services. The WS-Inspection specification (`http://www-106.ibm.com/developerworks/webservices/library/ws-wsilspec.html`) defines the locations on a Web site where you can look for Web service descriptions.

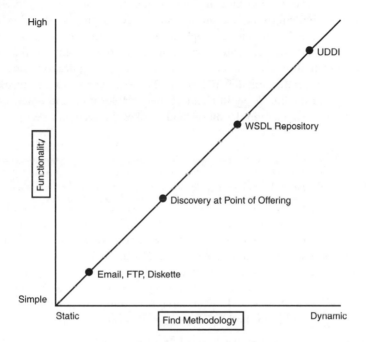

Figure 6.2   Types of service registries

Another approach is a repository of WSDL documents. This is similar in spirit to discovery at the point of offering, since it uses HTTP GET as the primary means by which the service requestor retrieves the service description. A WSDL repository may also provide additional features. For example, SalCentral (`http://www.salcentral.com`) offers features such as notification when a service description has changed, searching tools, and a basic categorization scheme. XMethods (`http://www.xmethods.com`) is another example of a public repository of WSDL documents.

Service Discovery at Design Time and Runtime

There are two basic types of service discovery: static and dynamic. Static service discovery generally occurs at application design time, whereas dynamic discovery occurs at runtime. At application design time, a human designer uses a browser or other user interface to perform a find operation on a service registry. The results of this operation are examined, and the service description returned by the find operation is incorporated into the application logic. In Chapter 5, " Implementing Web Services with Apache Axis," we discussed some of the tooling that can consume WSDL service descriptions and generate code for integration with the application.

In many cases, the service interface definition is used to build a proxy that the application logic uses to invoke the Web service and consume its response. When you're using dynamic service discovery, the service implementation details, such as the network location and network protocol to use, are left unbound at design time so that they can be determined at runtime. At runtime, the application issues a find operation against the service registry to locate one or more service implementation definitions that match the service interface definition used by the application. Based on application logic such as best price, best terms, and so on, the application chooses a Web service to invoke from among the results of the find operation, extracts network location and other information from the service implementation definition, and invokes the Web service.

Scenario Updates

As SkatesTown sells more skateboards, its network of suppliers expands. Let's examine some of the new partners SkatesTown now deals with:

- WeMakeIt Inc. is a large manufacturer of industrial components. Its business is to be a components supplier to a wide variety of different finished goods manufacturers. WeMakeIt manufactures a wide range of components at its manufacturing sites in the USA, Europe, and Asia. Of particular interest to SkatesTown, WeMakeIt manufactures a line of small nylon wheels and wheel bearings ideal for skateboards. Joanna Pravard is the lead Web services developer for WeMakeIt. She is responsible for all of WeMakeIt's Web services technologies, including its UDDI registries and its entry in the UDDI Business Registry.

- A recently created e-marketplace called e-Torus has formed to facilitate efficient buying and selling of wheels and wheel bearing components to finished goods manufacturers. As part of the e-marketplace, e-Torus runs a private UDDI registry listing all the manufacturers of wheels, bearings, and related components. This private UDDI registry is also a place where service interface standards are established for the marketplace, making B2B buying and selling of these components more efficient and less error prone.

- Al Rosen of Silver Bullet Consulting discovered e-Torus and got SkatesTown to use its e-marketplace services. Through e-Torus, SkatesTown established its business relationship with WeMakeIt Inc.

UDDI (Universal Description, Discovery, and Integration)

The UDDI initiative was first announced on September 6, 2000. The first three UDDI versions were developed with UDDI.org as the sponsoring organization. When UDDI version 3.0 was completed, UDDI.org submitted the specifications to the Organization for the Advancement of Structured Information Standards (OASIS) so that they could evolve into formal standards. All the UDDI work is now done through the OASIS UDDI Specification Technical Committee (`http://www.oasis-open.org/committees/tc_home.php?wg_abbrev=uddi-spec`). In April 2003, the UDDI version 2.0 specifications were approved as a formal OASIS standard. At the time this book was written, the UDDI version 3.0 specifications have been published as OASIS committee specifications. Both specifications can be found at `http://www.oasis-open.org/committees/uddi-spec/doc/tcspecs.htm`. This chapter will focus primarily on UDDI version 2.0.

The purpose of UDDI is to facilitate service discovery both at design time and dynamically at runtime. In typical Web services scenarios, service providers want to publish their service descriptions to a registry, and service requestors at either design time or runtime want to query the registry for service descriptions. One important point about a UDDI registry is that it isn't a repository—the entries in a UDDI registry contain references to other data (for example, a WSDL service description document).

There are two primary types of UDDI registries: public and private. The public registry is referred to as the UDDI Business Registry (UBR). The UBR is hosted by a small number of companies (such as IBM and Microsoft), and each company hosts one UDDI node that is replicated with the other UDDI nodes. This means you could find the data published at the site hosted by IBM while searching through the site hosted by Microsoft. Although the concept of a public registry was highly touted when UDDI was first announced, this type of registry hasn't been widely used. A public registry doesn't provide the level of trust that is required to allow a service requestor to select and use any service provider listed in the registry.

Most of the interest in UDDI has been focused on private registries. A private registry can be hosted on the Internet or an intranet, but it usually has a specific purpose. For example, a single enterprise may host a UDDI registry for the Web services it uses internally, or a consortium such as e-Torus may host a registry that is used only by its members.

UDDI Datatypes

Information in a UDDI version 2.0 registry is modeled using five datatypes: `businessEntity`, `businessService`, `bindingTemplate`, `tModel`, and `publisherAssertion`.

Figure 6.3 shows the relationship between these datatypes. To summarize this relationship, the `businessEntity` 📖 element provides information about a business and can contain references to one or more `businessService` 📖 elements. The business is the service provider. The technical and business descriptions for a Web service are defined in a `businessService` and its `bindingTemplate` 📖 elements. Each `bindingTemplate` element contains a reference to one or more `tModels`. A `tModel` 📖 element is used to define the technical specification for a service. A `publisherAssertion` 📖 element is used to define a relationship between two or more `businessEntity` elements.

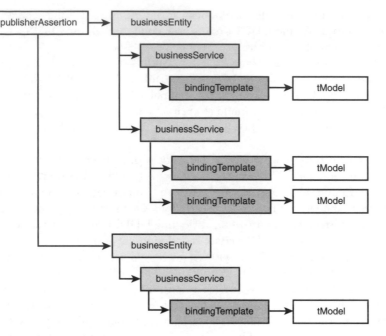

Figure 6.3   UDDI datatypes

Let's look at some examples of these UDDI datatypes that will be described in the following sections of this chapter. Listing 6.1 presents a businessEntity element that contains one businessService element; that businessService element contains two bindingTemplate elements.

Listing 6.1   **UDDI Business, Service, and Binding Definition**

```
<businessEntity businessKey="54438690-573E-11D8-B936-000629DC0A53">
  <name>SkatesTown</name>
  <description>UDDI businessEntity for SkatesTown.</description>
  <contacts>
    <contact useType="Technical Information">
      <description xml:lang="en">CTO for technical information</description>
      <personName>Dean Carroll</personName>
      <phone useType="Main Office">1.212.555.0001</phone>
      <email useType="CTO">dean.carroll@SkatesTown.com</email>
      <email useType="General Information">info@SkatesTown.com</email>
      <address useType="Main Office" sortCode="10001">
        <addressLine>2001 Skate Services Lane</addressLine>
        <addressLine>New York, NY 10001</addressLine>
        <addressLine>USA</addressLine>
      </address>
    </contact>
```

Listing 6.1   **Continued**

```
  <contact useType="Sales Information">
    <description xml:lang="en">VP Sales</description>
    <personName>Sandy Smith</personName>
    <phone useType="Main Office">1.212.555.0001</phone>
    <phone useType="Mobile">1.212.555.8888</phone>
    <email useType="VP Sales">sandy.smith@SkatesTown.com</email>
    <email useType="Sales Information">sales@SkatesTown.com</email>
    <address useType="Main Office" sortCode="10001">
      <addressLine>2001 Skate Services Lane</addressLine>
      <addressLine>New York, NY 10001</addressLine>
      <addressLine>USA</addressLine>
    </address>
  </contact>
</contacts>

<businessServices>
  <businessService serivceKey="4C379407-3E1E-DC97-B1C7-F68597DA4ADB"
      businessKey="55BB30D8-565A-4EF9-BA2E-83118AED644D">
    <name>Purchase Order Submission</name>
    <description>SkatesTown purchase order submission service.</description>

    <bindingTemplates>
      <bindingTemplate bindingKey="2E6BAE12-04E3-DBC2-90DB-A96E21406F79 "
          serviceKey="4C379407-3E1E-DC97-B1C7-F68597DA4ADB">
        <description>
          Web based (HTTP) purchase order submission service.
        </description>
        <accessPoint URLType="http">
          http://www.skatestown.com/services/poSubmission.html
        </accessPoint>
        <tModelInstanceDetails>
          <tModelInstanceInfo
              tModelKey="uuid:68DE9E80-AD09-469D-8A37-088422BFBC36D">
            <description>HTTP address</description>
          </tModelInstanceInfo>
        </tModelInstanceDetails>
      </bindingTemplate>
      <bindingTemplate bindingKey="3F7ABC88-14F2-AEF2-41AE-F86E52908A11"
          serviceKey="4C379407-3E1E-DC97-B1C7-F68597DA4ADB">
        <description>SOAP based purchase order submission service.</description>
        <accessPoint URLType="http">
          http://www.skatestown.com/services/poSubmission
        </accessPoint>
        <tModelInstanceDetails>
          <tModelInstanceInfo
              tModelKey="uuid:7B581129-7926-5202-AB17-74A234F21BA5">
```

Listing 6.1 **Continued**

```
                <description>
                  Reference to tModel Web service interface definition
                </description>
              </tModelInstanceInfo>
            </tModelInstanceDetails>
          </bindingTemplate>
        </bindingTemplates>

        <categoryBag>
          <keyedReference keyName="Sports equipment and accessories"
              keyValue="49221500"
              tModelKey="uuid:CD153257-086A-4237-B336-6BDCBDCC6634"/>
        </categoryBag>
      </businessService>
    </businessServices>

    <identifierBag>
      <keyedReference keyName="DUNS"
          keyValue="00-111-1111"
          tModelKey="uuid:8609C81E-EE1F-4D5A-B202-3EB13AD01823"/>
    </identifierBag>

    <categoryBag>
      <keyedReference keyName="Sporting and Athletic Goods Manufacturing"
          keyValue="33992"
          tModelKey="uuid:C0B9FE13-179F-413D-8A5B-5004DB8E5BB2"/>
      <keyedReference keyName="New York"
          keyValue="US-NY"
          tModelKey="uuid:4E49A8D6-D5A2-4FC2-93A0-0411D8D19E88"/>
    </categoryBag>
</businessEntity>
```

Listing 6.2 contains the tModel elements that are referenced by the bindingTemplate element in Listing 6.1, which defines a SOAP binding for the poSubmission Web service. This tModel references the location of the WSDL document that contains the technical specification for this service. It's important to note that the actual service description isn't stored in a UDDI registry. The section "Using WSDL with UDDI" later in this chapter describes how WSDL relates to UDDI entries.

Listing 6.2 **UDDI** tModel

```
<tModel tModelKey="uuid:7B581129-7926-5202-AB17-74A234F21BA5">
  <name>Purchase order submission service</name>
  <description xml:lang="en">
    Service interface definition for purchase order submission service.
```

Listing 6.2 **Continued**

```
    </description>
    <overviewDoc>
      <description xml:lang="en">
        Reference to the WSDL document that contains the service
        interface definition for the purchase order submission service.
      </description>
      <overviewURL>
        http://www.skatestown.com/services/poSubmissionInterface.wsdl
      </overviewURL>
    </overviewDoc>

    <identifierBag>
      <keyedReference keyName="DUNS"
          keyValue="00-111 1111"
          tModelKey="uuid:8609C81E-EE1F-4D5A-B202-3EB13AD01823"/>
    </identifierBag>

    <categoryBag>
      <keyedReference keyName="uddi-org:types"
          keyValue="soapSpec"
          tModelKey="uuid:C1ACF26D-9672-4404-9D70-39B756E62AB4"/>
      <keyedReference keyName="uddi-org:types"
          keyValue="wsdlSpec"
          tModelKey="uuid:C1ACF26D-9672-4404 9D70-39B756E62AB4"/>
      <keyedReference keyName="Sports equipment and accessories"
          keyValue="49221500"
          tModelKey="uuid:CD153257-086A-4237-B336-6BDCBDCC6634"/>
    </categoryBag>
</tModel>
```

The `publisherAssertion` provides a method to link together two or more businesses that are related to each other. The businesses could be subsidiaries of a larger enterprise, or they could be members of the same industry consortium. As an example, a `publisherAssertion` can be used to model the relationship between WeMakeIt Inc. and its subsidiaries in Asia and Europe. Listing 6.3 contains the publisher assertion for WeMakeIt and its Asian subsidiary.

Listing 6.3 **UDDI** `publisherAssertion`

```
<publisherAssertion>
  <fromKey>
    76CA56B2-789A-1AE8-AB3F-95239FBC235E
  </fromKey>
  <toKey>
    ACFE42A4-77C2-8BE3-BA2E-83118AED644D
```

Listing 6.3   **Continued**

```
  </toKey>
  <keyedReference keyName="subsidiary"
    keyValue="parent-child"
    tModelKey="uuid:807A2C6A-EE22-470D-ADC7-E0424A337C03"/>
</publisherAssertion>
```

In this example, the `fromKey` element contains a reference to WeMakeIt, the `toKey` element references the `businessEntity` for WeMakeIt Asia Inc., and the `keyedReference` element indicates the type of relationship between the two entities. For those service requestors that use the services provided by WeMakeIt, this publisher assertion could be used to find another service provider that may provide the same type of services.

What Is a `tModel`?

There are two primary uses for UDDI `tModel`s. First, they're used to define the *technical fingerprint* for a Web service. This refers to any technical specifications or prearranged agreements on how to conduct business. Second, a `tModel` can define a namespace that is used to identify business entities or classify business entities, business services, and `tModel`s. These namespaces are used in the `identifierBag` and `categoryBag` elements; their use is described in more detail in the next section "Categorization and Identification of Information."

Before you can invoke (or bind to) a Web service, you need to know the service's technical details, including information such as the message formats and transport protocols that must be used to invoke the service. These details are supplied in the description of the service. In Chapter 4, Listing 4.2, you saw an example of a WSDL service interface definition for the `poSubmission` Web service. That definition contained the abstract reusable service specification. Listing 4.2 contains the concrete implementation information (the service implementation definition). By separating these two types of information, you can reuse the abstract definition of the service.

For example, consider the situation where both SkatesTown and another member of the e-Torus marketplace implement the same type of purchase order submission service. The only difference between the two services is the location for the implementation of the service. Would it make sense for both companies to publish the same service interface definition? In a situation like this, e-Torus could abstract the service interface definition and publish it as a consortium standard. This would enable both companies (and any other company in the consortium) to reference the service interface definition; they would only have to publish the service implementation details. This would also help service requestors for this type of service, since they could search the UDDI registry to find implementations of the standard service interface definition. The service interface definition is a perfect example of a `tModel`.

Service definitions that will be reused can be specified by different entities, such as an industry consortium, a standards body, or a large corporation (for use by its suppliers). When you're using one of these types of service definitions, it's important to conform to a known and predefined set of specifications. The tModel concept is the mechanism for achieving this goal. It allows various entities (such as industry groups, standards bodies, and businesses) to publish abstract service specifications that can then be used by other entities that implement services. Using the previous example, e-Torus would register its http://www.e-Torus.org/services/poSubmission.wsdl specification as a tModel. This tModel would be referenced by all businesses in the consortium (such as SkatesTown) that implemented the service interface. In this way, any service requestor that wanted to find services that conform to the e-Torus service specification could query the UDDI registry for services that reference that tModel.

Here's the tModel the e-Torus would publish:

```
<tModel tModelKey="uuid:5492ACB9-8812-6673-EF45-23C421C4A5C1">
  <name>e-Torus purchase order submission service</name>
  <description xml:lang="en">
    This is the standard service interface definition for purchase
    order submission service.
  </description>
  <overviewDoc>
    <description xml:lang="en">
      Reference to the WSDL document that contains the e-Torus standard
      service interface definition for the purchase order submission service.
    </description>
    <overviewURL>
      http://www.e-Torus.com/services/poSubmission.wsdl
    </overviewURL>
  </overviewDoc>

  <identifierBag>
    <keyedReference keyName="DUNS"
        keyValue="00-222-2222"
        tModelKey="uuid:8609C81E-EE1F-4D5A-B202-3EB13AD01823"/>
  </identifierBag>

  <categoryBag>
    <keyedReference keyName="uddi-org:types"
        keyValue="soapSpec"
        tModelKey="uuid:C1ACF26D-9672-4404-9D70-39B756E62AB4"/>
    <keyedReference keyName="uddi-org:types"
        keyValue="wsdlSpec"
        tModelKey="uuid:C1ACF26D-9672-4404-9D70-39B756E62AB4"/>
    <keyedReference keyName="Sports equipment and accessories"
        keyValue="49221500"
        tModelKey="uuid:CD153257-086A-4237-B336-6BDCBDCC6634"/>
  </categoryBag>
</tModel>
```

The only change SkatesTown would make is in the `bindingTemplate` for the SOAP-based Web service binding. The `tModelInstanceInfo` element must be updated to reference the e-Torus `tModel` listed previously:

```
<bindingTemplate bindingKey="3F7ABC88-14F2-AEF2-41AE-F86E52908A11"
    serviceKey="4C379407-3E1E-DC97-B1C7-F68597DA4ADB">
  <description>SOAP based purchase order submission service.</description>
  <accessPoint URLType="http">
    http://www.skatestown.com/services/poSubmission
  </accessPoint>
  <tModelInstanceDetails>
    <tModelInstanceInfo tModelKey="uuid:5492ACB9-8812-6673-EF45-
23C421C4A5C1">
      <description>Reference to tModel Web service interface
definition</description>
    </tModelInstanceInfo>
  </tModelInstanceDetails>
</bindingTemplate>
```

Categorization and Identification of Information

As we stated previously, one of the main uses of a UDDI registry is for static or dynamic discovery of services. This is done by searching the entries in a registry at design time or runtime. Depending on the number of entries in the registry and the type of search criteria, the search result could be a large set of entries. To narrow the result set, UDDI provides a method to perform intelligent searches through taxonomic categorization and classification.

Categorization is the process of creating categories, whereas *classification* is the process of assigning objects to these predefined categories. There are several types of classification schemes, such as the Library of Congress Classification used in most libraries. For a large space such as businesses and services, the most useful ones are hierarchical in nature. One example is the classification scheme used by Yahoo! To find manufacturers of skateboards, you would traverse the Yahoo! classification tree to get to `Business_and_Economy/` `Shopping_and_Services/Sports/Skateboarding/Deck_and_Truck_Makers/`. UDDI defines a set of built-in classification schemes (or taxonomies):

- The North American Industry Classification System (NAICS) 📖 for classifying businesses by industry (`http://www.census.gov/epcd/www/naics.html`)
- The Universal Standard Products and Services Classification (UNSPSC) 📖 for product and service classifications (`http://eccma.org/unspsc`)
- The ISO 3166 📖 standard for geographic location classifications (`http://www.din.de/gremien/nas/nabd/iso3166ma`)

Each of these taxonomies is identified and referenced using a predefined `tModel` key. Table 6.1 lists the `tModel` keys for each of these classification schemes.

Table 6.1   **UDDI Built-in Classification Schemes**

Name	Type	tModel Key
NAICS	Business	uuid:C0B9FE13-179F-413D-8A5B-5004DB8E5BB2
UNSPSC	Product and Services	uuid:CD153257-086A-4237-B336-6BDCBDCC6634
ISO 3166	Geographic	uuid:4E49A8D6-D5A2-4FC2-93A0-0411D8D19E88

In order to take advantage of these classification schemes, businesses need to provide the relevant classification information as they publish their entries. This is done using the categoryBag element. This element contains a set of keyedReference elements, each of which has three attributes: tModelKey, keyName, and keyValue.

The tModelKey attribute is a simple but powerful extension mechanism that acts as a namespace qualifier for the values specified in the other two attributes. For example, if SkatesTown wanted to classify its business using the NAICS and ISO 3166 taxonomy, the following categoryBag element would be used:

```
<categoryBag>
  <keyedReference keyName="Sporting and Athletic Goods Manufacturing"
      keyValue="33992"
      tModelKey="uuid:C0B9FE13-179F-413D-8A5B-5004DB8E5BB2"/>
  <keyedReference keyName="New York"
      keyValue="US-NY"
      tModelKey="uuid:4E49A8D6-D5A2-4FC2-93A0-0411D8D19E88"/>
</categoryBag>
```

In this example, the business definition for SkatesTown is categorized as a Sporting and Athletic Goods Manufacturing business with a key value of 33992 using the NAICS taxonomy. The business location is defined as New York with a key value of US-NY using the ISO 3166 geographical categorization scheme.

Other categorization schemes can be added to a UDDI registry. For example, the Yahoo! classification scheme can be defined as a categorization type of tModel. It establishes a namespace that can be referenced by keyedReference elements within the categoryBag element:

```
<tModel tModelKey="uuid:3D4EC875-E54F-4D8D-9CBF-346D48BCAD9C">
  <name>Yahoo! Business Taxonomy</name>
  <description xml:lang="en">Yahoo! Business Taxonomy</description>
  <categoryBag>
    <keyedReference keyName="Yahoo! Category"
        keyValue="categorization"
        tModelKey="uuid:C1ACF26D-9672-4404-9D70-39B756E62AB4"/>
  </categoryBag>
</tModel>
```

After this tModel is published, another keyedReference element could be added to the categoryBag element within the SkatesTown businessEntity element to indicate the Yahoo! category associated with this business definition:

```
<categoryBag>
  <keyedReference keyName="Sporting and Athletic Goods Manufacturing"
      keyValue="33992"
      tModelKey="uuid:C0B9FE13-179F-413D-8A5B-5004DB8E5BB2"/>
  <keyedReference keyName="New York"
      keyValue="US-NY"
      tModelKey="uuid:4E49A8D6-D5A2-4FC2-93A0-0411D8D19E88"/>
  <keyedReference keyName="Yahoo Business Taxonomy"
      keyValue="Business_and_Economy/Shopping_and_Services/Sports/
➥Skateboarding/Deck_and_Truck_Makers/"
      tModelKey="uuid:3D4EC875-E54F-4D8D-9CBF-346D48BCAD9C"/>
</categoryBag>
```

In addition to specifying categorization information, *identification* information may also
be provided through the identifierBag element. This type of information allows businesses or tModels to be associated with a declared identification scheme, such as a tax ID
or an industry group ID.

As an example, the D-U-N-S number (http://www.dnb.com) is defined as a taxonomy tModel. SkatesTown can identify itself with a D-U-N-S number by using the following identifierBag element:

```
<identifierBag>
  <keyedReference keyName="DUNS"
      keyValue="00-111-1111"
      tModelKey="uuid:8609C81E-EE1F-4D5A-B202-3EB13AD01823"/>
</identifierBag>
```

Since any type of identification information scheme can be registered in a UDDI registry, e-Torus can define its own business identification scheme using this model.
Businesses in the e-Torus marketplace can identify themselves using that e-Torus identification tModel as a namespace. The details of the e-Torus Registry Number tModel
look like this:

```
<tModel tModelKey="uuid:F2390501-A240-4470-8A5A-6088EE5B1A14">
  <name>e-Torus Registry</name>
  <description xml:lang="en">e-Torus Registry Number</description>
  <categoryBag>
    <keyedReference keyName="Unique identifiers for member companies"
        keyValue="identifier"
        tModelKey="uuid:C1ACF26D-9672-4404-9D70-39B756E62AB4"/>
  </categoryBag>
</tModel>
```

To reference this identification scheme, the identifierBag element must be updated to
include an additional keyedReference element, where "12345" is the member number
for SkatesTown:

```
<identifierBag>
  <keyedReference keyName="DUNS"
```

```
      keyValue="00-111-1111"
      tModelKey="uuid:8609C81E-EE1F-4D5A-B202-3EB13AD01823"/>
   <keyedReference keyName="eTorus Registry"
      keyValue="12345"
      tModelKey="uuid:F2390501-A240-4470-8A5A-6088EE5B1A14"/>
 </identifierBag>
```

Business Entity

The businessEntity element is the top-level element in the UDDI information data structure. The structure is used to represent information about an entity or a business. It's also used as a container for the businessService element and indirectly for the corresponding implementation and binding details of all the services that an entity provides.

Business entity information is conceptually divided into three categories, referred to as white pages, yellow pages, and green pages:

- *White pages*—Contain general contact information about the entity. The SkatesTown entry would contain its name, address, and contact information such as phone, fax, and email.

- *Yellow pages*—Contain classification information about the types and location of the services the business entity offers. Again, for SkatesTown, this could be its classification as a sports equipment manufacturer and retailer, and more specifically as a skateboard manufacturer and retailer.

- *Green pages*—Contain information about the details of how to invoke the offered services. If SkatesTown were to offer its catalog online, its green pages entry would have a reference to its catalog URL.

Listing 6.4 presents an example of a businessEntity definition for SkatesTown. This businessEntity definition contains a business name, a human-readable description, and contact information. It also contains a reference to the services it provides through the businessServices element, business identification through the identifierBag element, and business and geographical categorization though the categoryBag element.

Listing 6.4 **UDDI** businessEntity **for SkatesTown**

```
<businessEntity businessKey="54438690-573E-11D8-B936-000629DC0A53">
  <name>SkatesTown</name>
  <description xml:lang="en">UDDI businessEntity for SkatesTown.</description>
  <contacts>
    <contact useType="Technical Information">
      <description>CTP for technical information</description>
      <personName>Dean Carroll</personName>
      <phone useType="Main Office">1.212.555.0001</phone>
      <email useType="CTO">dean.carroll@SkatesTown.com</email>
      <email useType="General Information">info@SkatesTown.com</email>
      <address useType="Main Office" sortCode="10001">
```

Listing 6.4   **Continued**

```
            <addressLine>2001 Skate Services Lane</addressLine>
            <addressLine>New York, NY 10001</addressLine>
            <addressLine>USA</addressLine>
        </address>
    </contact>
    <contact useType="Sales Information">
        <description xml:lang="en">VP Sales</description>
        <personName>Sandy Smith</personName>
        <phone useType="Main Office">1.212.555.0001</phone>
        <phone useType="Mobile">1.212.555.8888</phone>
        <email useType="VP Sales">sandy.smith@SkatesTown.com</email>
        <email useType="Sales Information">sales@SkatesTown.com</email>
        <address useType="Main Office" sortCode="10001">
            <addressLine>2001 Skate Services Lane</addressLine>
            <addressLine>New York, NY 10001</addressLine>
            <addressLine>USA</addressLine>
        </address>
    </contact>
</contacts>

<businessServices>
    <!-- List of businessService elements go here -->
    ...
</businessServices>

<identifierBag>
    <keyedReference keyName="DUNS"
        keyValue="00-111-1111"
        tModelKey="uuid:8609C81E-EE1F-4D5A-B202-3EB13AD01823"/>
</identifierBag>

<categoryBag>
    <keyedReference keyName="Sporting and Athletic Goods Manufacturing"
        keyValue="33992"
        tModelKey="uuid:C0B9FE13-179F-413D-8A5B-5004DB8E5BB2"/>
    <keyedReference keyName="New York"
        keyValue="US-NY"
        tModelKey="uuid:4E49A8D6-D5A2-4FC2-93A0-0411D8D19E88"/>
</categoryBag>
</businessEntity>
```

Business Service

The businessService element is the root element for describing a logical business service, such as the services provided by SkatesTown. The different implementation

details and bindings for the same logical service are grouped under the same
businessService element by using the bindingTemplate element.

The following example shows a businessService element that contains the definition for the SkatesTown purchase order submission service:

```
<businessService serivceKey="4C379407-3E1E-DC97-B1C7-F68597DA4ADB"
    businessKey="55BB30D8-565A-4EF9-BA2E-83118AED644D">
  <name>Purchase Order Submission</name>
  <description>SkatesTown purchase order submission service.</description>

  <bindingTemplates>
    <!-- List of bindingTemplate elements go here -->
    ...
  </bindingTemplates>

  <categoryBag>
    <keyedReference keyName="Sports equipment and accessories"
        keyValue="49221500"
        tModelKey="uuid:CD153257-086A-4237-B336-6BDCBDCC6634"/>
  </categoryBag>
</businessService>
```

A businessService entry must contain a direct reference to the businessEntity entry
that it's associated with. This is done using the businessKey attribute on the
businessService element.

Binding Template

The bindingTemplate element contains the technical information necessary to invoke a
specific Web service. The same logical service may have more than one type of binding.
For example, one service could have a SOAP-based HTTP binding, a HTTP browser-
based binding, or an email SMTP binding. Each of these bindings is described in a
separate bindingTemplate element that generally has a combination of access point
information and tModel references.

The following bindingTemplate element is the browser-based binding for the
SkatesTown purchase order submission service:

```
<bindingTemplate bindingKey="2E6BAE12-04E3-DBC2-90DB-A96E21406F79 "
    serviceKey="4C379407-3E1E-DC97-B1C7-F68597DA4ADB">
  <description>
    Web based (HTTP) purchase order submission service.
  </description>
  <accessPoint URLType="http">
    http://www.skatestown.com/services/poSubmission.html
  </accessPoint>
  <tModelInstanceDetails>
    <tModelInstanceInfo
```

```
                tModelKey="uuid:68DE9E80-AD09-469D-8A37-088422BFBC36D">
            <description>HTTP address</description>
          </tModelInstanceInfo>
        </tModelInstanceDetails>
      </bindingTemplate>
```

The `accessPoint` element contains the location where the Web browser interface to the purchase order submission service can be accessed (`http://www.skatestown.com/ services/poSubmission.html`). The `tModel` referenced by the `tModelInstanceInfo` element indicates that the binding is classified as an HTTP or Web browser–based Web service.

In addition to providing a Web browser interface to the purchase order submission service, SkatesTown has a SOAP-based service interface. This interface is defined as a second `bindingTemplate` element:

```
<bindingTemplate bindingKey="3F7ABC88-14F2-AEF2-41AE-F86E52908A11"
    serviceKey="4C379407-3E1E-DC97-B1C7-F68597DA4ADB">
  <description>SOAP based purchase order submission service.</description>
  <accessPoint URLType="http">
    http://www.skatestown.com/services/poSubmission
  </accessPoint>
  <tModelInstanceDetails>
    <tModelInstanceInfo
        tModelKey="uuid:7B581129-7926-5202-AB17-74A234F21BA5">
      <description>Web service interface definition</description>
    </tModelInstanceInfo>
  </tModelInstanceDetails>
</bindingTemplate>
```

The `bindingTemplate` contains a reference to the `tModel` that contains the technical fingerprint (service interface definition) for the purchase order submission service.

Publisher Assertion

A `publisherAssertion` is used to model business relationships. This feature was introduced in UDDI version 2.0 to address the publication needs of large, complex organizations. Any pair of `businessEntity` entries can be associated in some fashion, reflecting their business relationship.

An assertion is made between two `businessEntity` entries: The `fromKey` element contains the first `businessEntity` for the type of relationship, and the `toKey` element contains the second `businessEntity`. The type of relationship is defined using the `keyedReference` element. Within the `keyedReference` element, the `tModelKey` references the relationship type system, and the `keyName` and `keyValue` attributes are used to indicate the specific type of relationship.

When you're using the relationship type system defined in the UDDI specification, you can use the following values for the `keyValue` attribute:

- parent-child—The businessEntity referenced by the fromKey is the parent of businessEntity referenced by the toKey.

- peer-peer—The businessEntity referenced by the fromKey is a peer of the businessEntity referenced by the toKey.

- identity—The businessEntity referenced by the fromKey is the same organization as the one referenced by the toKey.

The example in Listing 6.3, the UDDI publisherAssertion, modeled the relationship between WeMakeIt Inc. and its subsidiary in Asia. For this type of publisherAssertion, the keyValue attribute would be parent-child, since WeMakeIt Inc. is the parent company for WeMakeIt Asia Inc.

Using a UDDI Registry

A UDDI registry is itself an instance of a Web service. Entries in the registry can be published and queried using a SOAP-based service interface. This means that a SOAP-based message is used for all publish and inquiry operations. The WSDL service interface definitions for a UDDI registry can be found at the following locations:

- *UDDI Inquiry API V2.0*—http://uddi.org/wsdl/inquire_v2.wsdl

- *UDDI Publication API V2.0*—http://uddi.org/wsdl/publish_v2.wsdl

- *UDDI API V3.0 portTypes*—
  http://uddi.org/wsdl/uddi_api_v3_portType.wsdl

- *UDDI API V3.0 Bindings*—http://uddi.org/wsdl/uddi_api_v3_binding.wsdl

You can use a few Java programming interfaces to build client applications that use a UDDI registry:

- *UDDI4J*—The UDDI for Java (UDDI4J) API provides a UDDI-specific Java programming model. When you're using UDDI4J, each UDDI datatype is represented by a separate Java class, and the UDDIProxy class is used to interact with any UDDI registry. UDDI4J is an open source project located at http://www.uddi4j.org.

- *JAXR*—The Java API for XML Registries (JAXR) provides an API that can be used to build Java applications that use business registries based on open standards, such as ebXML and UDDI. The documentation for JAXR and a reference implementation are available at http://java.sun.com/xml/jaxr/.

- *JAX-RPC*—The Java API for XML-based RPC (JAX-RPC) can be used to build client applications that use Web services. It doesn't provide direct support for a UDDI registry; but, as previously mentioned, a UDDI registry is a Web service. This means JAX-RPC could be used to build a client application that uses a UDDI registry. Work is going on in OASIS to enable a standard JAX-RPC programming model to be generated from the WSDL and XML schema documents for UDDI version 3.0. Information on JAX-RPC is located at http://java.sun.com/xml/jaxrpc/.

At the time this book was written, both UDDI4J and JAXR were designed to be used with UDDI version 2.0 registries. Both programming interfaces can be used with UDDI version 3.0, but the functionality is limited to that which is available in UDDI version 2.0.

Throughout the rest of this chapter, all the programming examples will use UDDI4J version 2.0.2.

Publishing Service Descriptions

Most UDDI registries require you to register before you can publish any UDDI entries. The registration process provides you with a publisher account (generally with a user ID and password) that you can use to create entries in the registry. Entries in the registry are owned by the publisher who created them, and only the owner can update or delete a registry entry. The UDDI publication APIs provide support for creating, updating, and deleting `businessEntity`, `businessService`, `bindingTemplate`, `tModel`, and `publisherAssertion` entries.

To use a publication API call that creates, updates, or deletes entries in the UDDI registry, you must first obtain an authentication token using the `get_authToken` API call. *Authentication tokens* are opaque values required for all other publication API calls; they represent an active session with the registry. This API call has the following format, where the `userID` attribute contains the user ID obtained during registration, and the `cred` attribute contains the password:

```
<get_authToken generic="2.0" xmlns="urn:uddi-org:api_v2"
    userID="userid"
    cred="password"/>
```

Authentication tokens are typically valid only for a period of time defined by the registry. If an authentication token is no longer valid and you use a publication API, a message is returned indicating that the token has expired. When an authentication token is no longer needed, you can use the `discard_authToken` message to inform that registry that it can be discarded. Doing so terminates any session state that was associated with the token.

Table 6.2 gives a summary of the publishing APIs for the four primary datatypes.

Table 6.2 **UDDI Publish APIs**

Datatype	Save API	Delete API
bindingTemplate	save_binding	delete_binding
businessEntity	save_business	delete_business
serviceBusiness	save_service	delete_service
tModel	save_tModel	delete_tModel

The save APIs are used to create a new entry in the registry or update an existing entry. The delete APIs are used to remove a UDDI entry from the registry. As an example, here's the message that would be sent to publish (or save) the businessEntity for SkatesTown:

```
<save_business generic="2.0" xmlns="urn:uddi-org:api_v2">
  <authInfo>[authInfo value]</authInfo>
  <businessEntity businessKey="55BB30D8-565A-4EF9-BA2E-83118AED644D">
    <name>SkatesTown</name>
    <description>UDDI business entity  for SkatesTown</description>
    <contacts>
      ...
    </contacts>

    <identifierBag>
      <keyedReference keyName="DUNS"
          keyValue="00-111-1111"
          tModelKey="uuid:0609C01E-EE1F-4D5A-D202-3ED13AD01823"/>
    </identifierBag>

    <categoryBag>
      <keyedReference keyName="Sporting and Athletic Goods Manufacturing"
          keyValue="33992"
          tModelKey="uuid:C0B9FE13-179F-413D-8A5B-5004DB8E5BB2"/>
      <keyedReference keyName="New York"
          keyValue="US-NY"
          tModelKey="uuid:4E49A8D6-D5A2-4FC2-93A0-0411D8D19E88"/>
    </categoryBag>
  </businessEntity>
</save_business>
```

Listing 6.5 provides an example of how to use UDDI4J to process the preceding save_business operation.

Listing 6.5   **Publish** BusinessEntity **Example**

```
import org.uddi4j.client.*;
import org.uddi4j.datatype.*;
import org.uddi4j.datatype.business.*;
import org.uddi4j.datatype.tmodel.*;
import org.uddi4j.response.*;
import org.uddi4j.util.*;

import java.util.*;

/**
 * Chapter 6 - Publish BusinessEntity Example
 *
 * This example shows how to publish the businessEntity
 * that represents SkatesTown.
```

Listing 6.5   **Continued**

```
*/
public class PublishBusinessEntity {
  // Location of UDDI registry
  String publishURL = "https://uddi.ibm.com/testregistry/publishapi";

  /**
   * Create the businessEntity and then process the save_business operation.
   */
  protected void saveBusiness(String userid, String password) throws Exception {
    UDDIProxy uddiProxy = null;

    // Add SSL support (this is IBM's SSL support but it can be replaced
    // with other implementations)
    System.setProperty("java.protocol.handler.pkgs",
      "com.ibm.net.ssl.internal.www.protocol");
    java.security.Security.addProvider(new com.ibm.jsse.JSSEProvider());

    // Create UDDI proxy
    uddiProxy = new UDDIProxy();
    uddiProxy.setPublishURL(publishURL);

    // Create businessEntity
    BusinessEntity businessEntity = new BusinessEntity();
    businessEntity.setBusinessKey("");

    // Set name and description
    businessEntity.setDefaultNameString("SkatesTown", "en");
    Vector description = new Vector();
    description.add(new Description("UDDI businessEntity for SkatesTown.", "en"));
    businessEntity.setDescriptionVector(description);

    // Create first contact
    Contact ctoContact = new Contact("Dean Carroll");
    ctoContact.setUseType("Technical Information");
    ctoContact.setDefaultDescriptionString("CTO for technical information");
    Vector phoneList = new Vector();
    Phone mainPhone = new Phone("1.212.555.0001");
    mainPhone.setUseType("Main Office");
    phoneList.add(mainPhone);
    ctoContact.setPhoneVector(phoneList);
    Vector emailList = new Vector();
    Email email = new Email("dean.carroll@SkatesTown.com");
    email.setUseType("CTO");
    emailList.add(email);
    email = new Email("info@SkatesTown.com");
```

Listing 6.5 **Continued**

```
email.setUseType("General Information");
emailList.add(email);
ctoContact.setEmailVector(emailList);
Vector skatesTownAddress = new Vector();
Address address = new Address();
address.setSortCode("10001");
address.setUseType("Main Office");
Vector addressLineList = new Vector();
addressLineList.add("2001 Skate Services Lane");
addressLineList.add("New York, NY 10001");
addressLineList.add("USA");
address.setAddressLineStrings(addressLineList);
skatesTownAddress.add(address);
ctoContact.setAddressVector(skatesTownAddress);

// Create second contact
Contact salesContact = new Contact("Sandy Smith");
salesContact.setUseType("Sales Information");
salesContact.setDefaultDescriptionString("VP Sales");
phoneList = new Vector();
phoneList.add(mainPhone);
Phone mobilePhone = new Phone("1.212.555.8888");
mobilePhone.setUseType("Mobile");
phoneList.add(mobilePhone);
salesContact.setPhoneVector(phoneList);
emailList = new Vector();
email = new Email("sandy.smith@SkatesTown.com");
email.setUseType("VP Sales");
emailList.add(email);
email = new Email("sales@SkatesTown.com");
email.setUseType("Sales Information");
emailList.add(email);
salesContact.setEmailVector(emailList);
salesContact.setAddressVector(skatesTownAddress);

// Set contacts
Contacts contacts = new Contacts();
contacts.add(ctoContact);
contacts.add(salesContact);
businessEntity.setContacts(contacts);

// Set identifierBag
IdentifierBag identifierBag = new IdentifierBag();
Vector keyedReferenceList = new Vector();
keyedReferenceList.add(new KeyedReference("DUNS", "00-111-1111",
```

Listing 6.5   **Continued**

```
      "uuid:8609C81E-EE1F-4D5A-B202-3EB13AD01823"));
    identifierBag.setKeyedReferenceVector(keyedReferenceList);
    businessEntity.setIdentifierBag(identifierBag);

    // Set categoryBag
    CategoryBag categoryBag = new CategoryBag();
    keyedReferenceList = new Vector();
    keyedReferenceList.add(new KeyedReference(
      "Sporting and Athletic Goods Manufacturing", "33992",
      "uuid:C0B9FE13-179F-413D-8A5B-5004DB8E5BB2"));
    keyedReferenceList.add(new KeyedReference("New York", "US-NY",
      "uuid:4E49A8D6-D5A2-4FC2-93A0-0411D8D19E88"));
    categoryBag.setKeyedReferenceVector(keyedReferenceList);
    businessEntity.setCategoryBag(categoryBag);

    // Obtain authToken using get_authToken UDDI API
    AuthToken authToken = uddiProxy.get_authToken(userid, password);

    // Save businessEntity
    Vector businessEntityList = new Vector();
    businessEntityList.add(businessEntity);
    BusinessDetail businessDetail =
      uddiProxy.save_business(authToken.getAuthInfoString(), businessEntityList);

    // Get businessKey for published businessEntity
    String businessKey = ((BusinessEntity)
      businessDetail.getBusinessEntityVector().elementAt(0)).getBusinessKey();

    // Display businessKey
    System.out.println("Published businessEntity key: " + businessKey + ".");
  }

  public static void main(String[] args) {
    try {
      PublishBusinessEntity publishBusinessEntity = new PublishBusinessEntity();
      publishBusinessEntity.saveBusiness(args[0], args[1]);
    }

    catch (Exception e) {
      System.out.println("EXCEPTION: " + e.toString());
    }

    System.exit(0);
  }
}
```

As previously mentioned, a publisher assertion is used to associate a pair of existing businessEntity entries. An assertion isn't complete until the publishers of both businessEntity entries have made the same assertion. Five APIs are used to process publisher assertions:

- add_publisherAssertions—Adds one or more publisherAssertions to the publisher's assertion collection.
- delete_publisherAssertions—Deletes one or more publisherAssertions from the publisher's assertion collection.
- get_publisherAssertions—Gets the full list of publisherAssertions associated with a publisher's assertion collection.
- get_assertionStatusReport—Determines the status of current and outstanding assertions.
- set_publisherAssertions—Adds new assertions or updates existing assertions. The call operates on the entire set of assertions for a publisher.

The final publication API call is get_registeredInfo. This message is used to obtain a complete list of businessEntity and tModel entries that are owned by the publisher associated with the provided authentication token.

Finding Service Descriptions

When you're finding a service description, you can use two types of inquiry APIs: the find APIs and the get APIs. Except for the find_binding API, the find APIs for the primary datatypes are used to retrieve a list of references (UDDI keys) to UDDI data entries using specified search criteria. The find_binding API returns the contents of a bindingTemplate. The get APIs are used to return the actual contents of a data entity.

Table 6.3 summarizes the inquiry APIs for the primary datatypes.

Table 6.3 **UDDI Inquiry APIs**

Datatype	Find API	Get API
bindingTemplate	find_binding	get_bindingDetail
businessEntity	find_business	get_businessDetail
serviceBusiness	find_service	get_serviceDetail
tModel	find_tModel	get_tModelDetail

Here's an example of the message that would be sent to find the businessEntity for SkatesTown, using just identifier and categorization information:

```
<find_business maxRows="10" generic="2.0" xmlns="urn:uddi-org:api_v2">
  <identifierBag>
    <keyedReference keyName="DUNS"
        keyValue="00-111-1111"
        tModelKey="uuid:8609C81E-EE1F-4D5A-B202-3EB13AD01823"/>
```

```
    </identifierBag>

    <categoryBag>
      <keyedReference keyName="Sporting and Athletic Goods Manufacturing"
          keyValue="33992"
          tModelKey="uuid:C0B9FE13-179F-413D-8A5B-5004DB8E5BB2"/>
      <keyedReference keyName="New York"
          keyValue="US-NY"
          tModelKey="uuid:4E49A8D6-D5A2-4FC2-93A0-0411D8D19E88"/>
    </categoryBag>
</find_business>
```

The response to this message contains a list of businessInfo elements, each of which contains a reference to a businessEntity that matched the find criteria:

```
<?xml version="1.0" encoding="UTF-8"?>
<businessList generic="2.0"  xmlns="urn:uddi-org:api_v2"
    operator="operatorName" truncated="false">
  <businessInfos>
    <businessInfo businessKey="54438690-573E-11D8-B936-000629DC0A53">
      <name>SkatesTown</name>
      <serviceInfos>
        ...
      </serviceInfos>
    </businessInfo>
  </businessInfos>
</businessList>
```

Each businessEntity is referenced by its businessKey. The businessKey can be used to retrieve the actual contents of the businessEntity. The following message would be used to retrieve the full contents of the businessEntity (which appears in Listing 6.4):

```
<?xml version="1.0" encoding="UTF-8"?>
<get_businessDetail generic="2.0" xmlns="urn:uddi-org:api_v2">
  <businessKey>54438690-573E-11D8-B936-000629DC0A53</businessKey>
</get_businessDetail>
```

Listing 6.6 provides an example of how to use UDDI4J to process the preceding find_business and get_businessDetail operations.

Listing 6.6   **Find** BusinessEntity **Example**

```
import org.uddi4j.client.*;
import org.uddi4j.datatype.*;
import org.uddi4j.datatype.business.*;
import org.uddi4j.datatype.tmodel.*;
import org.uddi4j.response.*;
import org.uddi4j.util.*;
```

Listing 6.6   **Continued**

```java
import java.util.*;

/**
 * Chapter 6 - Find BusinessEntity Example
 *
 * This example shows how to find the businessEntity
 * that represents SkatesTown.
 */
public class FindBusinessEntity {
  // Location of UDDI registry
  String inquiryURL = "http://uddi.ibm.com/testregistry/inquiryapi";

  /**
   * Find the businessEntity and then get its details.
   */
  protected void getBusinessDetail() throws Exception {
    UDDIProxy uddiProxy = null;

    // Create UDDI proxy
    uddiProxy = new UDDIProxy();
    uddiProxy.setInquiryURL(inquiryURL);

    // Create identifierBag
    IdentifierBag identifierBag = new IdentifierBag();
    Vector keyedReferenceList = new Vector();
    keyedReferenceList.add(new KeyedReference("DUNS", "00-111-1111",
      "uuid:8609C81E-EE1F-4D5A-B202-3EB13AD01823"));
    identifierBag.setKeyedReferenceVector(keyedReferenceList);

    // Create categoryBag
    CategoryBag categoryBag = new CategoryBag();
    keyedReferenceList = new Vector();
    keyedReferenceList.add(new KeyedReference(
      "Sporting and Athletic Goods Manufacturing", "33992",
      "uuid:C0B9FE13-179F-413D-8A5B-5004DB8E5BB2"));
    keyedReferenceList.add(new KeyedReference("New York", "US-NY",
      "uuid:4E49A8D6-D5A2-4FC2-93A0-0411D8D19E88"));
    categoryBag.setKeyedReferenceVector(keyedReferenceList);

    // Find the businessEntity using just the identifierBag
    // and categoryBag as a search criteria
    BusinessList businessList = uddiProxy.find_business((Vector) null,
        (DiscoveryURLs) null,
        identifierBag, categoryBag,
        (TModelBag) null, (FindQualifiers) null, 10);
```

Listing 6.6   **Continued**

```java
    // Get businessKey for the first businessEntity found
    String businessKey =
      ((BusinessInfo) businessList.getBusinessInfos().get(0)).getBusinessKey();

    // Display businessKey
    System.out.println("Key for businessEntity found: " + businessKey + ".");

    // Get the businessEntity details
    BusinessDetail businessDetail = uddiProxy.get_businessDetail(businessKey);

    // Get first business name
    Name businessName = (Name) ((BusinessEntity)
    businessDetail.getBusinessEntityVector().elementAt(0)).getNameVector().get(0);

    // Display business name
    System.out.println("Name of businessEntity found: " +
      businessName.getText() + ".");
  }

  public static void main(String[] args) {
    try {
      FindBusinessEntity findBusinessEntity = new FindBusinessEntity();
      findBusinessEntity.getBusinessDetail();
    }

    catch (Exception e) {
      System.out.println("EXCEPTION: " + e.toString());
    }

    System.exit(0);
  }
}
```

In addition to the find and get APIs for the primary UDDI datatypes, the following APIs are also available:

- find_relatedBusinesses—Used to find all the businesses affiliated with a specified business type. The affiliation would have been defined previously using the save_publisherAssertion call.

- get_businessDetailExt—Returns extended businessEntity information for one or more specified businessEntity entries. This message returns the same information as the get_businessDetail message, but it may contain additional information.

What's New in UDDI Version 3.0

UDDI version 3.0 provides a significant set of improvements over UDDI version 2.0. The major enhancements are described in this section.

Policy

Polices are used to define the specific operational behavior for a UDDI registry. This feature was added to make it easier to use a UDDI registry in environments that have different operational characteristics (for example, a test registry versus a production registry).

A registry can set the following types of policies:

- *Policy delegation*—Defines the set of policies that can be delegated to nodes.
- *Keying*—Defines the policies that affect key generation and format. As an example, these policies could be set to allow publisher-assigned keys (described later).
- *APIs*—Describes policies for the data confidentiality of the different sets of APIs.
- *Time policies*—Defines how nodes in a registry synchronize their clocks.
- *User policies*—Defines the policies for publication limits and transferring ownership of UDDI data entities.
- *Data custody*—Defines the policy for custody transfer between nodes. Custody indicates the node where changes must be made to a data entity.
- *Replication*—Defines whether replication is supported, and what protocol should be used.
- *Subscription*—Defines whether subscription is supported, as well as aspects such as conditions for renewal and volume limits.
- *Value set policy*— Describes policies related to the external validation of values and the associated caching behavior.

Security

Starting with UDDI version 3.0, entities published to a UDDI registry can be digitally signed, providing a way to ensure the authenticity and integrity of data in the registry. All five of the primary UDDI datatypes can be signed using XML digital signatures. You can learn more about digital signatures in Chapter 9, "Securing Web Services."

When publishing an entity in a UDDI registry, the publisher digitally signs the content of the entity and provides the digital signature as an element within the entity. When a service requestor searches the registry, it may specify that its query should only return entities that have been signed.

When SkatesTown starts using UDDI version 3.0 registries, the company will sign all the entities it publishes. By doing so, SkatesTown assures its customers and business partners that the data represented by those entities are valid.

Support for Multi-Registry Environments

UDDI version 3.0 introduces the concepts of root and affiliate registries. Affiliate registries rely on the root registry to ensure that key values are unique across both types of registries. An example of a root registry is the UDDI Business Registry. Since the root registry ensures unique key values, data can be easily shared between root and affiliate registries. This support has helped enable two other new functions: subscription and publisher-assigned keys.

In SkatesTown's environment, the UDDI registry hosted by e-Torus could be the root registry, and the affiliate registries could be hosted by the members for the e-Torus marketplace.

Subscription

You can use the new subscription function to receive notification when changes occur in a registry. There are two types of subscriptions: entity-based and query-based. An entity-based subscription notifies the subscriber when one or more entities have changed. When using a query-based subscription, the subscriber is notified when the result set for the query changes within a specified time period.

SkatesTown can use the subscription feature to track the services its competitors add, or to track the services that are added to the e-marketplace registry. This mechanism can also be used to keep the contents of two or more registries synchronized.

Publisher-Assigned Keys

When an entity is added to a UDDI registry, it's assigned a unique key that is a URI. This key is used to identify the entity in much the same way that a primary key is used in a relational database. In version 3.0, assigning keys to an entity is controlled by policy, and the policy can be defined to allow the publisher to specify the key for an entity when it's published.

This feature provides two benefits. First, it provides a method to move entities between UDDI registries without having to create new keys. As an example, if you have a test registry and a production registry, you can move a businessEntity from one to the other without changing its business key. Second, the keys may contain values that make them easier to use.

There are three types of keys: uuidKey, domainKey, and derivedKey. All the keys use the format "scheme : value", where the scheme is always "uddi". The uuidKey is the same as the UDDI version 2.0 (and version 1.0) keys. These keys contain a UUID (Universally Unique Identifier) as a value. The domainKey has a valid hostname as a value, and the derivedKey is a UDDI key with a key-specific string appended to it.

Here are some examples of these keys and how SkatesTown could use the domainKey and derivedKey:

- uuidKey—uddi:4CD7E4BC-648B-426D-9936-443EAAC8AE23
- domainKey—uddi:www.SkatesTown.com
- derivedKey—uddi:www.SkatesTown.com:PriceCheck,
  uddi:www.SkatesTown.com:PurchaseOrderSubmission

Using WSDL with UDDI

UDDI provides a method for publishing and finding service descriptions. The UDDI data entities provide support for defining both business and service information. The service description information defined in WSDL is complementary to the information found in a UDDI registry.

UDDI provides support for many different types of service descriptions. A Web service, registered in UDDI as a businessService, can be described using WSDL, a plain ASCII text document, a RosettaNet pip, RDF, or any other type of description mechanism. As a result, UDDI has no direct support for WSDL or any other service description mechanism. In this section, we explore how to publish in a UDDI registry Web services that are described using WSDL.

How to Publish WSDL-Based Service Descriptions

The UDDI organization has published two best-practices documents that describe how to publish WSDL-based service descriptions in a UDDI registry:

- *Using WSDL in a UDDI Registry 1.08* http.//www.oasis open.org/
  committees/uddi-spec/doc/bp/uddi-spec-tc-bp-using-wsdl-v108-
  20021110.htm
- *Using WSDL in a UDDI Registry, Version 2.0*—http://www.oasis-open.org/
  committees/uddi-spec/doc/tn/uddi-spec-tc-tn-wsdl-v200-20031104.htm

The second document supplements the information in the first. The primary difference is that the second document provides a method to model and represents individual Web service artifacts. Since the first document is referenced by the WS-I Basic Profile (see Chapter 13, "Web Services Interoperability," for more details), Al Rosen has decided to use these conventions as the process for publishing the SkatesTown WSDL service descriptions in a UDDI registry.

Mapping from WSDL to UDDI

A WSDL service description contains an abstract definition for a set of operations and messages, a concrete protocol binding for these operations and messages, and a network endpoint specification for the binding. Figure 6.4 outlines how the major WSDL elements map into UDDI elements. Since the service interface represents a reusable definition of a service, a reference to it is published in a UDDI registry as a tModel. If the service interface definition contains more than one binding element, the reference to the service interface may include a pointer to a specific WSDL binding element. The service implementation describes an instance of a service, and each instance is defined using a WSDL service element. Each service element in a service implementation document corresponds to a UDDI businessService element. In particular, the Web service location (address) listed in a WSDL port element must be the same as the value in the UDDI accessPoint element.

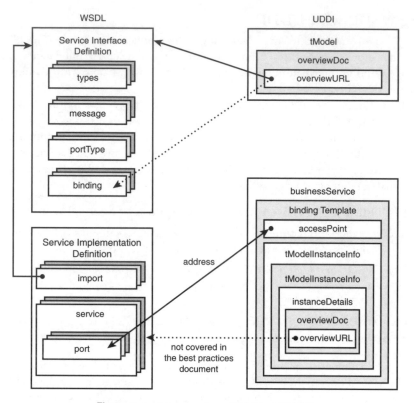

Figure 6.4   Mapping from WSDL to UDDI

How to Publish the Purchase Order Submission Service

Based on this overview, let's examine the steps that Al Rosen needs to follow in order to publish the SkatesTown poSubmission Web service. First, the best-practices document for using WSDL in a UDDI registry describes how to represent the service interface definition as a tModel. The following tModel is replicated from Listing 6.2 with the relevant elements highlighted:

```
<tModel tModelKey="uuid:7B581129-7926-5202-AB17-74A234F21BA5">
  ...
  <overviewDoc>
    <description xml:lang="en">
      Reference to the WSDL document that contains the service
      interface definition for the purchase order submission service.
    </description>
    <overviewURL>
      http://www.skatestown.com/services/poSubmissionInterface.wsdl
```

```
      </overviewURL>
    </overviewDoc>

...

    <categoryBag>
      ...
      <keyedReference keyName="uddi-org:types"
          keyValue="wsdlSpec"
          tModelKey="uuid:C1ACF26D-9672-4404-9D70-39B756E62AB4"/>
      ...
    </categoryBag>
  </tModel>
```

For a `tModel`, the mapping from WSDL to UDDI is the following:

- The overviewURL element must contain a reference to the WSDL binding element in the poSubmission Web service interface definition. Since the poSubmission.wsdl document contains only one binding element in it, there is no need to directly reference the binding definition.

- The keyedReference element in the categoryBag is used to indicate that this tModel is categorized as a WSDL specification. This means the document referenced by the overviewURL must be a WSDL document.

- The value of the tModelKey attribute must be referenced by the bindingTemplate that's created next.

After the `tModel` is published, Al can publish the following `businessService` for the poSubmission Web service:

```
<businessService serivceKey="4C379407-3E1E-DC97-B1C7-F68597DA4ADB"
    businessKey="55BB30D8-565A-4EF9-BA2E-83118AED644D">
  <name>Purchase Order Submission</name>
  <description>SkatesTown purchase order submission service.</description>

  <bindingTemplates>
    ..
    <bindingTemplate bindingKey="3F7ABC88-14F2-AEF2-41AE-F86E52908A11"
        serviceKey="4C379407-3E1E-DC97-B1C7-F68597DA4ADB">
      <description>SOAP based purchase order submission service.</description>
      <accessPoint URLType="http">
        http://www.skatestown.com/services/poSubmission
      </accessPoint>
      <tModelInstanceDetails>
        <tModelInstanceInfo
            tModelKey="uuid:7B581129-7926-5202-AB17-74A234F21BA5">
          <description>
```

```
               Reference to tModel with Web service interface definition
          </description>
          <instanceDetails>
            <overviewDoc>
              <description>
                Reference to WSDL service implementation document.
              </description>
              <overviewURL>
                http://www.skatestown.com/services/
➥poSubmissionImplementation.wsdl
              </overviewURL>
            </overviewDoc>
          </instanceDetails>
        </tModelInstanceInfo>
      </tModelInstanceDetails>
    </bindingTemplate>
  </bindingTemplates>


    ...

  </businessService>
</businessServices>
```

The important content within the `bindingTemplate` element is as follows:

- The `accessPoint` element contains the URL at which the Web service can be invoked. This value must be the same as the address value from the `port` element in the WSDL service implementation document.

- The `tModel` referenced by the `tModelInstanceInfo` element must be the `tModel` that contains the reference to the service interface definition for this service.

- Al followed an extended convention that defined how to reference the service implementation document from the `bindingTemplate` element. The `overviewURL` element contains a reference to the WSDL service implementation document. Although this isn't defined in the best-practices document, it does provide a way for the service requestor to obtain additional WSDL-based information for this service.

Publishing a Service Definition with Multiple Bindings

Let's look at another example that requires us to reference a single binding within a WSDL service interface definition that contains multiple bindings (see Listing 6.7). The e-Torus marketplace has decided to publish a standard version of both the `PriceCheck` and `poSubmission` Web service definitions. It combined both service interface definitions into one physical file, which is located on the e-Torus Web site:
`http://www.etorus.com/services/OrderInterface.wsdl`

Listing 6.7 **e-Torus Order Service Definition**

```
<definitions name="e-Torus Order Services Interface"
  targetNamespace="http://www.e-Torus.com/services/OrderInterfaces" ...>
  ...
  <!-- Port type definitions -->
  <portType name="PriceCheckPortType">
    <operation name="checkPrice">
      <input message="pc:PriceCheckRequest"/>
      <output message="pc:PriceCheckResponse"/>
    </operation>
  </portType>

  <portType name="poSubmissionPortType">
    <operation name="doSubmission">
      <input message="pos:poSubmissionRequest"/>
      <output message="pos:poSubmissionResponse"/>
    </operation>
  </portType>

  <!-- Binding definitions -->
  <binding name="PriceCheckSOAPBinding" type="pc:PriceCheckPortType">
    <soap:binding style="document"
      transport="http://schemas.xmlsoap.org/soap/http" />
    <operation name="checkPrice">
      <soap:operation
        soapAction="http://www.skatestown.com/services/PriceCheck/checkPrice" />
      <input>
        <soap:body use="literal" />
      </input>
      <output>
        <soap:body use="literal" />
      </output>
    </operation>
  </binding>

  <binding name="poSubmissionSOAPBinding"
      type="pos:poSubmissionPortType">
    <soap:binding style="document"
        transport="http://schemas.xmlsoap.org/soap/http"/>
    <operation name="doSubmission">
      <soap:operation
        soapAction="http://www.skatestown.com/services/poSubmission/submitPO"/>
      <input>
        <soap:body parts="purchaseOrder" use="literal"/>
      </input>
      <output>
```

Listing 6.7   **Continued**

```
        <soap:body parts="invoice" use="literal"/>
      </output>
    </operation>
  </binding>
</definitions>
```

When e-Torus publishes this service interface, it will create two tModel entries (one for each binding definition). Here is the tModel for the binding named poSubmissionSOAPBinding:

```
<tModel tModelKey="uuid:6783FF9C-1277-7823-BA89-34A976B1E6D2">
  <name>e-Torus purchase order submission service</name>
  <description xml:lang="en">
    This is the standard service interface definition for purchase order
    submission service.
  </description>
  <overviewDoc>
    <description xml:lang="en">
      Reference to the WSDL document that contains the e-Torus standard
      service interface definition for the purchase order submission service.
    </description>
    <overviewURL>
      http://www.e-Torus.com/services/OrderInterface.wsdl#
➥xmlns(wsdl=http://schemas.xmlsoap.org/wsdl/)
➥xpointer(//wsdl:binding[@name='poSubmissionSOAPBinding'])
    </overviewURL>
  </overviewDoc>

  ...

  <categoryBag>
    <keyedReference keyName="uddi-org:types"
        keyValue="wsdlSpec"
        tModelKey="uuid:C1ACF26D-9672-4404-9D70-39B756E62AB4"/>
    ...
  </categoryBag>
</tModel>
```

The contents of this tModel are similar to the one that SkatesTown published. The primary difference is that the overviewURL contains an XPointer (http://www.w3.org/TR/WD-xptr) reference to the binding named poSubmissionSOAPBinding. To use this tModel, SkatesTown would have to update the bindingTemplate in its businessService element to reference tModelKey: uuid:6783FF9C-1277-7823-BA89-34A976B1E6D2.

Other Service Discovery Methods

There have been other attempts to define specifications for Web service discovery. Two specifications that we review here are the Web Service Inspection Language (WS-Inspection) and WS-ServiceGroup.

WS-Inspection

The Web Services Inspection Language   (WS-Inspection) defines a method to discover service descriptions at the service provider's point of offering (http://www-106.ibm.com/developerworks/webservices/library/ws-wsilspec.html). The WS-Inspection specification defines two primary functions:

- *The XML format used to list references to existing Web services*—A WS-Inspection document can reference a WSDL service description directly, and it can also reference UDDI entries.

- *The set of conventions for locating WS-Inspection documents on a Web site*—WS-Inspection documents can be placed at common entry points for a Web site, or references to WS-Inspection documents can appear within Web content documents, such as HTML pages.

WS-Inspection provides a basic method for service discovery, but it requires you to know the location of a service provider so that you can inspect its Web site. Although WS-Inspection provides a service-discovery methodology that's complementary to UDDI (distributed versus centralized service discovery), it isn't being pursued as a Web service standard because it didn't gain enough support.

WS-ServiceGroup

The WS-ServiceGroup specification is one of the WS-Resource Framework specifications (http://www.globus.org/wsrf). These specifications provide the basis for convergence of the Grid and Web services worlds. The WS-ServiceGroup specification was derived from the ServiceGroup portType in the OGSI 1.0 specification (http://www.globus.org/research/papers/Final_OGSI_Specification_V1.0.pdf). WS-ServiceGroup defines a method for grouping together Web services and WS-Resources (a Web service that is associated with a stateful resource). A Web service that belongs to a ServiceGroup is a Member, and each Member is associated with the ServiceGroup through a ServiceGroupEntry. Members of a ServiceGroup must conform to the membership rules and constraints for the ServiceGroup, so that meaningful queries can be processed to locate entries in the ServiceGroup. The concept of a ServiceGroup could be used to define an aggregation of Web services that form a basic service registry. The queries that are processed against a ServiceGroup could be used to discover Web services that are defined as Members of the ServiceGroup.

Summary

In this chapter, we've described the role of service registries such as UDDI within a service-oriented architecture. We examined UDDI datatypes and APIs in some depth, reviewed the use of UDDI for private service registries, and discussed the new features that will be available in UDDI version 3.0. Finally, we examined the convention for publishing WSDL-based Web services in a UDDI registry and how that convention can make UDDI effective for doing dynamic discovery of Web services at runtime.

Resources

- *UDDI specifications*—http://www.oasis-open.org/committees/uddi-spec/doc/tcspecs.htm
- *UDDI best practices*—http://www.oasis-open.org/committees/uddi-spec/doc/bps.htm
- *UDDI technical notes*—http://www.oasis-open.org/committees/uddi-spec/doc/tns.htm
- *Web Service Inspection Language (WS-Inspection)*—http://www-106.ibm.com/developerworks/webservices/library/ws-wsilspec.html

II

Enterprise Web Services

7

Web Services and J2EE

THIS CHAPTER INTRODUCES THE CONCEPTS of using SOAP, WSDL, and the Web services stack with *Java 2 Enterprise Edition (J2EE)* 📖. Although a single chapter can't do justice to a wide-ranging development platform, we'll show you how to enable *Enterprise JavaBean* 📖 components as Web services using Axis and the *JSR109* 📖 JCP proposal.

Continuing our example scenario, the SkatesTown technical team has been working in Java for a while and recently has been looking at moving some of the Java applications that run on their server into the J2EE platform. They've heard that it's secure, transactional, managed, scalable, and robust—all the things they want for their business applications. But they're also interested in Web services, and they want to be able to create services easily. So, they've decided to build a sample application called SkatesEJB, which will be a pilot project to determine the value in using J2EE to implement their Web services.

J2EE Overview

Java 2 Enterprise Edition (J2EE) is the platform for building enterprise applications in Java. J2EE standardizes the services, programming model, and deployment for applications so that developers can build solutions that can be used on a variety of application servers. J2EE has a number of application models:

- Thin-client/browser-based applications use servlets and *JavaServer Pages* 📖 (JSPs).
- Thick/managed application clients use *RMI-IIOP* 📖 to communicate with server-based Enterprise JavaBeans (EJB) components.
- Messaging applications use the Java Message Service to act on messages in queues or from subscriptions.

To this list we can now add service-based applications, which offer services over SOAP/HTTP to clients.

J2EE provides a framework that supports high quality of service (QoS). In other words, J2EE lets you build transactional, secure, reliable applications that are available across a cluster of highly available servers. A J2EE application server provides a wide variety of capabilities including the following:

- *Workload and performance management*—Thread management, pooling, caching, and cluster support
- *Security management*—Password and certificate management and validation, authentication, and access control
- *Resource management*—Access to relational databases, transactional management systems, connectors to Enterprise Resource Planning (ERP) systems, and messaging systems
- *Transaction management*—Two-phase commit support, transactional access to databases, and distributed transactions
- *Management, configuration, and administration*—Deployment, configuration, and administration tools

These services are provided through the concept of a *container*.

Containers

A container is a logical entity in a J2EE server. Containers are entities that have contracts with the components that are deployed into a server—but they also help you understand the way a J2EE system works. Components are deployed to a container, and the container manages the execution of those components as needed. The container provides *isolation* by intercepting calls to the EJBs, allowing the container to manage aspects such as threads, security, and transactions between components. The container also provides a useful abstraction between components and the resources they use.

For example, when one component uses a database, the programmer uses a *resource reference* 📖 (resource ref) to link to the database. Then the deployment engineer can configure the actual database that maps to the reference. So, the code that is written and compiled isn't hard-coded to a specific database.

This approach is also used for JMS destinations, URLs and URIs, and other EJB components in the same or different applications. Later in the chapter, you'll see an example of an `ejb-ref` 📖 that virtualizes access to another EJB.

Enterprise JavaBeans

The core of J2EE is the EJB component. This is the programming model for writing and deploying business logic into an application server. EJBs provide a component model for creating business applications. EJB components are mainly focused on aspects such as business logic, as well as database and legacy server access, transactions, security, and threading—in other words, how you build core business services in a Java environment.

EJBs initially look complex because they were designed to layer over ordinary Java. For each component, there are multiple `.java` files. Ideally, the user has an Integrated Development Environment (IDE) that shows each component as a whole as well as the individual class files for that component. However, in the examples later in this book, we simply use a text editor and basic tools for portability.

The EJB component model allows you to structure the business logic into discrete connected components. EJB applications are loosely coupled, with well-defined interfaces.

EJBs come in a variety of styles:

- *Session beans* 📖 are business logic components that are instantiated on behalf of a user and last no longer than the time the client program remains active and running (a session).

- *Entity beans* 📖 are components that are mapped into an underlying database or *persistent store* (for example, a bank account, purchase order, telephone number, or email address). Each instance must have a unique key under which it is stored and retrieved.

- *Message-driven beans (MDBs)* 📖 are executed in response to a message at the server, usually a one-way, asynchronous *JMS* 📖 message, but also including messages from other systems such as SAP R/3 or PeopleSoft coming through a connector.

There is another distinction: between local and remote EJBs. Local EJBs can only be called from within the same container, whereas remote EJBs are callable across a network over distributed networking protocols (such as RMI-IIOP).

An application can be thought of as having distinct parts—for example:

- The part that deals with the long-term storage of data in a database or other persistent backend (local entity beans)

- The part that provides business logic (stateless local session beans)

- The part that provides the interface with thick clients or a graphical interface layer (stateless or stateful remote session beans)

- The graphical Web interface (servlets and JSPs)

- The part that deals with messaging—sending and receiving messages from other systems (message-driven beans)

As you can see, the J2EE application model is a component model that provides the right component types to support solid business applications.

EJB Lifecycle

Another aspect of J2EE that's very important to Web services is the lifecycle of an EJB. Components have well-defined lifecycles—they're instantiated, persisted, and destroyed. EJBs define a "home" factory for creating and managing the lifecycle of components. EJBs can be divided into those with no real lifecycle and those with a lifecycle.

> **Note**
>
> The Open Grid Services Infrastructure (OGSI) offers a model of services that have lifecycles. This is a point of debate around Service-Oriented Architecture—whether services have lifecycles like objects or whether they're stateless.

Stateless session beans are session beans with no real lifecycle—the container instantiates a pool of these as needed. Although there are multiple instances of the component, each instance is interchangeable with any other, because they have no state that differs from method call to method call.

Message-driven beans (MDBs) have no lifecycle either. They are instantiated and pooled by the container—so they are always available.

Stateful session beans (SFSBs) are explicitly created by an application, with parameters in the `create()` method (part of the home interface). The instance of an SFSB contains state information specific to that client, and therefore it must either be explicitly destroyed or timed out by the container (otherwise the number would grow until the system's capacity was used up).

Entity beans are stateful and have attributes that are stored in a database, file system, or other persistent storage. They must be either created or found using a key. Because they're kept in a persistent datastore, the objects have a very extended lifetime—unlike SFSBs, which last as long as the client code is running, these object instances remain available until they're explicitly deleted, surviving reboots, crashes, system migrations, and so on. Another difference with SFSBs is that many clients can talk to one entity bean instance.

The lifecycle-free model of services matches the model of stateless session beans and MDBs. In fact, a common design pattern in EJB programming involves all distributed interaction with the EJB application taking place through a façade of stateless session beans and MDBs. This model most closely fits today's services infrastructure.

Initiatives such as WS-Addressing (`http://www-106.ibm.com/developerworks/library/specification/ws-add/`) and the WS-Resource Framework (WSRF; `http://www.globus.org/wsrf/default.asp`) allow stateful components to be addressed as services. There are ways of doing it without these technologies (such as adding a key to the end of the address URL), but they aren't standardized. Apache Axis has recently added support for WS-Addressing, but it isn't supported in Apache Axis or in the J2EE specification at the time of this writing.

Note

Apache SOAP supports this approach. See `http://ws.apache.org/soap/`.

As you'll see when we dive deeper into J2EE support for Web services, the only supported components that can be accessed as Web services are servlets, stateless session beans, and MDBs. For more information about stateful services, see Chapter 8, "Web Services and Stateful Resources."

Roles: Development, Assembly, and Deployment

One of the most useful aspects of J2EE is the way the architecture was designed from the start with ordinary people in mind. Early Web systems were often created from many different technologies, so the developer had to be good at programming in multiple languages and systems as well as understand the network, the database connections, system administration, and so on. For example, many of the early dynamic Web technologies mixed HTML with the programming language in a single file. This meant that a graphic designer couldn't modify the look and feel without risking breaking the logic—with the result the programmer frequently did the layout and HTML/Web design, or spent valuable time cutting and pasting HTML into their code.

The J2EE model clearly separates *roles* such as Web programmer, business logic programmer, deployment engineer, and administrator. To achieve this separation, there are clear contracts between the components and the infrastructure. For example, JSPs allow the HTML and page design to be separate from the business logic.

There are two important roles: the assembler and the deployment engineer. Both are like systems integrators. Like a brick layer, the assembler pulls together a set of components to create an application. Then the deployment engineer comes and wires and connects everything, like an electrician and plumber rolled into one. The mortar, solder, and cabling that keep it all together are called *deployment descriptors*.

Deployment descriptors (DDs) are XML files that capture information about components and applications. They help resolve aspects left undefined by the programmer, such as resolving references, setting policies, and linking to other components.

The following snippet shows a sample DD for an EJB:

```
<?xml version="1.0"?>
<ejb-jar>
    <description>Simple Application</description>
    <display-name>Simple</display-name>
    <enterprise-beans>
      <session>
        <ejb-name>StockQuote</ejb-name>
        <home>com.skatestown.StockQHome</home>
        <remote>com.skatestown.StockQ</remote>
        <ejb-class>
            com.skatestown.StockQHome
        </ejb-class>
        <session-type>Stateless</session-type>
        <transaction-type>Bean</transaction-type>
      </session>
    </enterprise-beans>
</ejb-jar>
```

As you'll see later, the same approach has been applied to the Web services support in J2EE 1.4, where a new DD—webservices.xml—has been added. This file is effectively the Java Standards version of the Axis WSDD file.

Benefits of Using Web Services with J2EE

J2EE is a high-quality, reliable, secure infrastructure for building complex Web and business applications. Web services started more simply with no inherent security, reliability, or transactions, but these are now being added using the open and flexible model that SOAP and Web services offer.

Many businesses are using Web services with J2EE to provide simple interoperable access to existing J2EE applications—for example, creating a C/C++/C# or VB.NET client to an EJB application. Before SOAP and Web services, this was possible but very complex. J2EE uses a distributed object model called RMI-IIOP, which bridges the Java object model and the CORBA (IIOP) protocol. Accessing J2EE components from outside Java used to require either bridge technology or complicated logic to access the components using IIOP from C or C++. This was typically a painful process. SOAP and Web services make this scenario much more appealing, and a number of companies are using the SOAP approach in their systems today.

Why use J2EE with Web services? In other words, why would you write a J2EE application and EJBs if you could simply deploy Java classes into an Axis server to create Web services? The answer, as usual, depends on the individual circumstances. Many small applications will work fine with the Java Axis approach. As the complexity and requirements on the application scale up, having a managed J2EE environment in which to run components becomes more appropriate. In particular, the benefits increase as you start to connect to databases, messaging systems, and other enterprise systems.

Security

The first benefit that a J2EE application server brings is security. Because the individual methods (operations) of an EJB can be secured, and because J2EE has end-to-end security, you can use either HTTPS or WS-Security to authenticate users and then offer them services and/or operations with fine-grained access control. For example, a single service may have *bid* and *cancel* operations, and a J2EE application server can be configured with one group of ordinary users who can bid, and then another group of superusers who can cancel. Because security in J2EE is tightly integrated into the Java runtime, these security models extend to the Web services space, and so the access controls are applied to incoming SOAP requests as well, based on the configuration and administration of the EJBs. (For more details, see Chapter 9, "Securing Web Services.")

Transaction Control Across Distributed Resources

The second benefit a J2EE application server offers is transaction control across distributed resources. Even if you aren't using WS-AtomicTransaction and WS-Coordination (see Chapter 11, "Web Services Transactions"), you may wish to ensure that the backend resources you're communicating with are kept in sync with each other and are transactional. For example, you may wish to have a database log of Web service transactions held in an Oracle or DB2 RDB and then use a JMS system to send messages internally to a legacy system. The J2EE server can make the database log entry and send the message in the same unit of work. That way, even if the HTTP connection fails and the SOAP response message sent to the client fails, your server has a log of what happened. Although it doesn't offer full end-to-end transactionality, this type of architecture has been used extensively in Web-based systems to provide a higher level of robustness at the application level.

Container Managed Persistence

J2EE offers both a programming model for building business applications—including the tools and technology to map your objects into databases (entity beans)—and a reliable, scalable infrastructure for running those applications. As soon as the application moves beyond the simplicity of a sample or first proof of concept, users find that the learning curve and extra complexity of a J2EE solution is repaid in the savings in time and effort that the model offers.

For example, in our sample application, the J2EE application server will automatically save the state of the objects we create using a feature called *Container Managed Persistence* (CMP). This means that instead of having to write database logic and SQL statements, we can write fairly straightforward Java objects and have the container generate the SQL and take care of all the database reads, writes, and updates. This approach makes it quick and easy to build a Web service application with a database at its heart. And, this support is independent of which database server is used.

J2EE Versions

A word about versions: While J2EE 1.4 has just been released, J2EE 1.3 is still the more commonly used version in real systems at the time of this writing. J2EE 1.4 includes significant Web services support, especially the standards JAX-RPC, JAX-R, and JSR 109 ("Implementing Enterprise Web Services"), as well as improvements specifically targeted at producing *WS-I Basic Profile* 🔖 compliance (`http://ws-i.org/Profiles/Basic/2003-08/BasicProfile-1.0a.html`).

As a result, every J2EE application server will support the following:

- A UDDI registry
- Calling out to external Web services through JAX-RPC
- Hosting Web services using EJBs and servlets
- Calling out to UDDI servers

The rest of this chapter is split into three parts. First, we create the EJBs that form the core of the application. This isn't a full tutorial on EJBs, but just a simple EJB application that allows SkatesTown to get going.

Next, we investigate using Web services with an existing J2EE server by using the Apache Axis toolkit. In this section, we assume that there is a running J2EE server such as BEA WebLogic, JBOSS, or IBM WebSphere, and we look at using the Apache Axis framework to connect to EJBs. We're doing this because the SkatesTown developers are familiar with Axis and would like to understand how EJBs fit into the model they already have; and although this is more difficult than the approach in the last part of the chapter, not all application servers support that approach yet.

Finally, we look at how this model is simplified and updated when we utilize new support from J2EE 1.4 to deploy a service directly into an enabled J2EE container. This support (called JSR109) simplifies the model considerably. In this part, we'll use IBM WebSphere as the container, and we'll clearly call out the standard aspects versus the application server–specific aspects. Once J2EE 1.4 is widespread, this will be the standardized approach to using Web services with J2EE, and all J2EE 1.4 application servers will need to support this model.

This last approach is much less work than using Axis, because the tooling and container do much of the work for you; so, if you have a JSR109-enabled container, you may wish to skip trying the Axis approach. However, we recommend reading the section in order to understand the differences between the two approaches and how EJBs fit into the Axis approach.

Using EJBs from Axis

Apache Axis (and its predecessor, Apache SOAP) supports using a stateless session bean as the implementation of a service. One of the benefits of EJBs is the automatic persistence mapping layer for entity beans. To demonstrate, we're going to create a simple entity bean for SkatesTown, to capture prices of products. In order to expose this as a Web service, we'll create a front-end using a stateless session bean. This is shown in Figure 7.1.

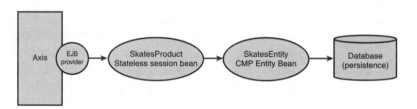

Figure 7.1 High-level overview of the components

The stateless session bean offers a stateless interface to the entity bean and allows it to be easily mapped into a SOAP service via Axis.

This particular entity bean contains no business logic and simply acts as a mapping between the database and the object model. However, in other models, the entity bean could be mapped to more complex databases and could perform more logic. Alternatively (or in addition), there could be more logic in the session bean. However, this scenario demonstrates the aspects of EJBs simply.

Figure 7.2 shows the two components in our application graphically:

- The `Entity` component has three properties: the `productCode`, which is the key field, `description`, and `price`. There are also two home methods that allow the creation and location of instances.

- The front-end session bean represents the service interface to the entity bean. It references the entity bean locally and provides two main business methods to add or view product details.

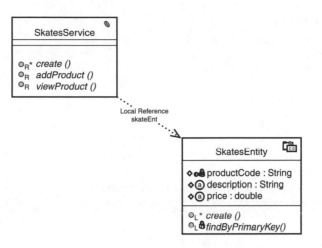

Figure 7.2　Component diagram showing the two EJBs in our sample
application

The Entity Bean

Remember that each EJB component has several files. The key files are the interface and
implementation classes, and of course the DD that ties all this together.

The entity bean interface is as follows:

```
package com.skatestown.ejb;
import javax.ejb.EJBLocalObject;
public interface SkatesEntity extends EJBLocalObject {
    public void setProductCode(String productCode);
    public String getProductCode() ;
    public  void setDescription(String Description) ;
    public  String getDescription() ;
    public  void setPrice(double Price) ;
    public  double getPrice();
```

```
}
```

Listing 7.1 shows the implementation class.

Listing 7.1　**Entity Bean Implementation Class**

```
package com.skatestown.ejb;
import javax.ejb.EntityBean;
public abstract class SkatesEntityBean implements EntityBean {
    private javax.ejb.EntityContext entityContext;

    public SkatesEntityBean() {    }
```

Listing 7.1 **Continued**

```
    public void ejbActivate() {     }

    public void ejbPassivate() {}

    public void ejbRemove() {}

    public void ejbLoad() {}

    public void ejbStore() {}

    public javax.ejb.EntityContext getEntityContext() {
        return entityContext;
    }

    public void
setEntityContext(javax.ejb.EntityContext entityContext) {
        this.entityContext = entityContext;
    }

    public void unsetEntityContext() {
    }

    public String
ejbCreate(String pc) throws javax.ejb.CreateException {
        this.setProductCode(pc);
        this.setDescription(null);
        this.setPrice(0.0D);
        return null;
    }

    public void ejbPostCreate(String pc) {}

    public abstract void
setProductCode(java.lang.String productCode);
    public abstract java.lang.String getProductCode();
    public abstract void
setDescription(java.lang.String Description);
    public abstract java.lang.String getDescription();
    public abstract void setPrice(double Price);
    public abstract double getPrice();
}
```

If you aren't an EJB programmer, you're probably wondering at this point—where's the actual code? Although this code is effectively performing database lookups and inserts, you might expect that it would include SQL or other database query statements. There is no database code because the J2EE application server (and the deployment tools that ship with it) uses the DD and the interface to generate and run the code that implements the database logic. This CMP means the EJB container will manage the mapping of the *properties* of the entity bean component into the *fields* of the database table.

There are different possible mappings:

- *Bottom-up*—The objects are created from a database schema.
- *Meet-in-the-middle*—A set of existing objects is mapped to an existing database schema.
- *Top-down*—The database tables are created from the object definitions.

In this case, we'll use top-down to automatically create a table in which to store our data.

Of equal importance to the classes that make up the EJB is the DD for the bean:

```
<persistence-type>Container</persistence-type>
<prim-key-class>
java.lang.String
</prim-key-class>
<primkey-field>productCode</primkey-field>
<cmp-version>2.x</cmp-version>
<abstract-schema-name>
Skates
</abstract-schema-name>
<cmp-field id="PRICE">
<field-name>price</field-name>
</cmp-field>
<cmp-field id="DESC">
<field-name>description</field-name>
</cmp-field>
<cmp-field id="PRODCODE">
<field-name>productCode</field-name>
</cmp-field>
```

As you'll see later, the DD will be packaged together with the code into a JAR file, which the application server will use to configure the component and code.

In this fragment, the first tag, `persistence-type Container`, says that the programmer will delegate the storage of the object instances to the container. The other type, `Bean Managed`, requires the programmer to write logic to store the instance data in some form of database. The EJB 2.0 specification updated the object to relational mapping style. Generally speaking, new projects should use the new 2.x CMP version as defined by the `<cmp-version>` tag.

Each entity bean must specify a primary (or unique) key by which instances will be known. The rest of the tags identify database names for the schema and the columns of data.

The session bean won't have much more business logic in it, but it forms the place where the service interface is mapped into the data stored in the database.

The Session Bean

The session bean has similar interface and implementation classes (see Listings 7.2 and 7.3).

Listing 7.2   `SkatesProducts.java` **Session Bean Interface**

```
public interface SkatesProducts extends javax.ejb.EJBObject {
public void addProduct(Product prod)
throws java.rmi.RemoteException;
    public Product viewProduct(String prodcode)
throws java.rmi.RemoteException;
}
```

Listing 7.3   `SkatesProductsBean.java` **Session Bean Implementation**

```
import javax.ejb.CreateException;
import javax.ejb.FinderException;
import javax.naming.InitialContext;
import javax.naming.NamingException;
public class SkatesProductsBean implements javax.ejb.SessionBean {
    private javax.ejb.SessionContext mySessionCtx;
    public javax.ejb.SessionContext getSessionContext() {
        return mySessionCtx;      }
    public void setSessionContext(javax.ejb.SessionContext ctx) {
        mySessionCtx = ctx;      }
    public void ejbCreate() throws javax.ejb.CreateException {}
    public void ejbActivate() {}
    public void ejbPassivate() {}
    public void ejbRemove() {}

    public void addProduct(Product prod) {
        try {

            InitialContext ic = new InitialContext();
            SkatesEntityLocalHome selh =
(SkatesEntityLocalHome)
ic.lookup("java:comp/env/skateEnt");
SkatesEntityLocal skent =
selh.create(prod.getProductCode());
            skent.setDescription(prod.getDescription());
            skent.setPrice(prod.getPrice());
        } catch (NamingException ne) { // handle naming
```

Listing 7.3 **Continued**

```
        } catch (CreateException ce) { // handle create
        }
    }
    // viewProduct goes here
}
```

Because the entity is simply a view on the persistence layer, it utilizes the underlying semantics of a data element (create, read, update, delete). The session bean has the interface we wish to offer to the service requestor. We want to expose two "verbs" *add* and *view* to the service requestor. Because the service interface we're designing is stateless, we need to map one (or more) of the parameters of the service request into the unique primary key the entity bean needs.

The implementation code shows some standard code—that is, it's the same in most EJBs. The `ejbXXXXXX()` methods, such as `ejbCreate()`, let you override methods that are called by the container during the component's event lifecycle. A more intelligently designed bean would get a reference to the entity at component creation time, reuse it, and therefore be more efficient. However, for this simple example it's easier to get the reference as needed.

In the `addProduct()` method shown, the logic gets a reference to the entity bean using a local ejb-ref (local name for the entity bean) `"java:comp/env/skateEnt"`. The `"java:comp/env/"` piece is predefined (it's the J2EE way of saying *environment*). `"skateEnt"` is a name we chose to identify the entity bean. This reference is then defined in the DD to point to the real internal name of the entity bean. This capability allows EJBs to be wired together, so a different entity bean (perhaps with a different persistence method) that implemented the same interface contract could be used without recoding our session bean.

The code then calls the `create()` method on the entity to create a new product instance, using the product code as the primary key. At this point, if there is already a product in the database that has the same key, a `createException` will be thrown, which will cause a fault in the Web service response.

There is similar code in the `viewProduct()` method shown here:

```
public Product viewProduct(String prodcode) {
    Product prod = new ProductImpl();
    try {
        InitialContext ic = new InitialContext();
        SkatesEntityHome home =
(SkatesEntityHome)
ic.lookup("java:comp/env/skatesEntity");
SkatesEntity skent =
home.findByPrimaryKey(prodcode);
        prod.setProductCode(prodcode);
        prod.setPrice(skent.getPrice());
```

```
        prod.setDescription(skent.getDescription());
    }
    catch (NamingException ne) { /* deal with exc */}
    catch (FinderException fe) { /* deal with exc */}
    return prod;
}
```

This code looks up the existing product instance and then returns the information as a new `Product` object.

The Deployment Unit

Once the EJBs are written, you should deploy and test them before attempting to Web service–enable them. Typically, the EJBs might already exist. In some circumstances, the EJBs may not offer the right service interface, in which case a layer of stateless session beans can be implemented to offer a clean interface that can then be Web service enabled. The EJBs are packaged in an EJB JAR, which is then packaged in an *Enterprise Application aRchive (EAR file)* 📖.

The EJBs must have appropriate XML DDs. The tags containing the deployment information for each bean are shown in the following snippets. Here's the DD fragment for the entity bean:

```
<entity id="SkatesEntity">
    <ejb-name>SkatesEntity</ejb-name>
    <local-home>
com.skatestown.ejb.SkatesEntityLocalHome
</local-home>
    <local>com.skatestown.ejb.SkatesEntityLocal</local>
    <ejb-class>
com.skatestown.ejb.SkatesEntityBean
</ejb-class>
    <persistence-type>Container</persistence-type>
    <prim-key-class>java.lang.String</prim-key-class>
    <reentrant>False</reentrant>
    <cmp-version>2.x</cmp-version>
    <abstract-schema-name>SKATES</abstract-schema-name>
    <cmp-field id="pc">
        <field-name>productCode</field-name>
    </cmp-field>
    <cmp-field id="desc">
        <field-name>description</field-name>
    </cmp-field>
    <cmp-field id="prc">
        <field-name>price</field-name>
    </cmp-field>
    <primkey-field>productCode</primkey-field>
</entity>
```

And here's the session bean fragment from the DD:

```
<session id="SkatesService">
    <ejb-name>SkatesService</ejb-name>
    <home>com.skatestown.ejb.SkatesServiceHome</home>
    <remote>com.skatestown.ejb.SkatesService</remote>
    <ejb-class>
com.skatestown.ejb.SkatesServiceBean
</ejb-class>
    <session-type>Stateless</session-type>
    <transaction-type>Container</transaction-type>
    <ejb-local-ref id="entref">
        <description>
Reference to SkatesEntity
</description>
        <ejb-ref-name>skateEnt</ejb-ref-name>
        <ejb-ref-type>Entity</ejb-ref-type>
        <local-home>
com.skatestown.ejb.SkatesEntityLocalHome
</local-home>
        <local>com.skatestown.ejb.SkatesEntityLocal</local>
        <ejb-link>SkatesEntity</ejb-link>
    </ejb-local-ref>
</session>
```

As you'll see from looking at the session bean DD, it includes a reference from the session bean to the entity bean. This is the point at which the `"java:comp/env/skateEnt"` is defined.

The EJBs are now packaged into a JAR file together with the DD. The JAR contents are as follows:

```
>jar tf skatesejb.jar

META-INF/ejb-jar.xml
com/skatestown/ejb/Product.class
com/skatestown/ejb/SkatesEntityBean.class
com/skatestown/ejb/SkatesEntityLocal.class
com/skatestown/ejb/SkatesEntityLocalHome.class
com/skatestown/ejb/SkatesService.class
com/skatestown/ejb/SkatesServiceBean.class
com/skatestown/ejb/SkatesServiceHome.class
META-INF/MANIFEST.MF
```

Exposing the EJBs via Axis

This EJB JAR can now be packaged together with Axis into an EAR application. Then the whole can be deployed and the resulting application will let you access these EJBs using SOAP/HTTP via Axis.

The first task is to package the Axis Web application as a WAR file:

```
cd axis11\webapps
    <java_home>\bin\jar cf axis.war *.*
```

Doing so creates a Web Application aRchive (WAR) file containing the Axis code.

The next step is to create an application DD that packages `Axis.WAR` and the `SkatesEJB.jar` together into a single application, as shown here:

```
<?xml version="1.0" encoding="UTF-8"?>
<!DOCTYPE application PUBLIC
➡ "-//Sun Microsystems, Inc.//DTD J2EE Application 1.3//EN"
➡ "http://java.sun.com/dtd/application_1_3.dtd">
<application id="SkatesTownEJBWS">
    <display-name>Skates</display-name>
    <module id="EjbModule_skates">
        <ejb>skatesejb.jar</ejb>
    </module>
    <module id="WebModule_Axis">
        <web>
            <web-uri>axis.war</web-uri>
            <context-root>axis</context-root>
        </web>
    </module>
</application>
```

Usually you'd use a tool from the application server to do this and package the resulting EAR file. The EAR file now contains the following:

- `skates.ear`
- `axis.war`
- `skatesejb.jar`
- `META-INF/MANIFEST.MF`
- `META-INF/application.xml`

At this point we move away from pure interoperable J2EE and into the realm of a specific application server. The *deployment tooling* will augment `skates.ear` with server-specific files. For example, WebSphere Application Server will generate a number of additional classes and XML files that bind the EJBs we've written into the container. For the examples in this book, we used the latest available WebSphere Application Server—version 5.1, which is available for trial download on the Web (`http://www-106.ibm.com/developerworks/websphere/downloads/WASsupport.html`).

WebSphere allows you to do this outside the runtime using the application assembly tool, and also from the administration console. Other application servers have appropriate methods (for example, BEA WebLogic server has an `ejbdeploy` tool).

WebSphere Deployment Process

In order to deploy this as an EJB application, you need to go through a server-specific *deployment* process that configures the application to run on a given server. As an example, we'll show you how to deploy this EAR file into WebSphere Application Server. However, the sample code is pure J2EE and so will deploy in any EJB2.0 server.

The process followed in this book is simple; we use command-line tools and the Web console. However, as of this version of WebSphere, a new tool called the Application Server Toolkit (ASTK) is available, which makes the procedure considerably easier.

If you have a different J2EE application server, then follow the guidelines appropriate to that server. The deployment options should be standard and easily managed. For more information, you may wish to see the settings that were configured in WebSphere to deploy the application.

> ### A Simple View of the Deployment Process
>
> The next stages may seem complicated, so here's a heads-up of what we're about to do. You can think of this process as wiring everything together:
>
> 1. Create a database.
> 2. Wire that to your application server.
> 3. Wire the entity bean to the database.
> 4. Wire the session bean to the entity bean.
> 5. Switch to Axis and create a WSDL file.
> 6. Wire the Axis service to the session bean.
>
> Once you've completed these steps, everything should work!

In order to deploy into WebSphere, the Axis application must be modified to be a Servlet 2.3 application (the default was 2.2). Doing so involves changing the !DOCTYPE line of the web.xml file as follows:

```
<!DOCTYPE web-app PUBLIC
➥ "-//Sun Microsystems, Inc.//DTD Web Application 2.3//EN"
➥"http://java.sun.com/dtd/web-app_2_3.dtd">
```

This is the only change required to convert it into a Servlet 2.3 Web application.

EJB Deployment

The major item that's completely server specific for this application is the database that backs up the CMP entity bean. In order to enable it, you need to configure a new database in your database server and create a new datasource in your application server to manage connections to it.

WebSphere comes with a lightweight database system called Cloudscape. The first step is to create a new Cloudscape database in which to store the data from the CMP entity bean in. Follow these steps:

1. Make a directory to store the database in:

   ```
   >mkdir \db2j\databases\
   ```

2. Create a database. The easiest way to do so is to use the supplied `ij` utility. It's in the `<websphere>\cloudscape\bin\embedded` directory. Start it with the `ij` command line:

   ```
   C:\as51\cloudscape\bin\embedded>echo off
   ij version 5.1 (c) 2001 IBM Corp.
   ij>
   ```

3. Type the following line:

   ```
   connect 'jdbc:db2j:c:\db2j\databases\skatesdb;create=true';
   ```

   Then type

   ```
   exit;
   ```

   to quit `ij`. You'll need to come back to `ij` later to create the table.

You should now have a local database. The next step is to link it to WebSphere by creating a *datasource*: the virtualization of the database that allows your code to be linked to the database without your having coded any DB-specific commands in the application.

To create a new datasource in WebSphere, you must first create a JDBC Provider. This is a configuration that tells WebSphere about a given JDBC database and classes. Luckily, Cloudscape is preconfigured into WebSphere, so you don't need to do much (see Figure 7.3).

Creating a default Cloudscape provider works just fine:

1. In the left-hand pane, select Resources and then, under it, JDBC Providers. Click New.

2. Select Cloudscape JDBC Provider.

Now that you have a JDBC Provider, you can add a datasource. This tells WebSphere about the newly created SKATESDB database. Follow these steps:

1. Go into the new Cloudscape entry and select Data Sources. Click New.

2. Give the datasource the name `SkatesDataSource`, which automatically gives it a JNDI name: `jdbc/SkatesDataSource`.

3. Check the box that says Use This Data Source In Container Managed Persistence (CMP). If you don't, it won't work.

4. Go into Custom Properties at the bottom of the configuration page for `SkatesDataSource`. In the custom entry `databaseName`, change the value to match the new directory you created earlier: `c:/db2j/databases/SkatesDB`.

5. Save your configuration. (For more information, see the WebSphere docs:
`http://publib.boulder.ibm.com/infocenter/wsphelp/topic/`
`com.ibm.websphere.nd.doc/info/ae/ae/tdat_ccrtpds.html`.)

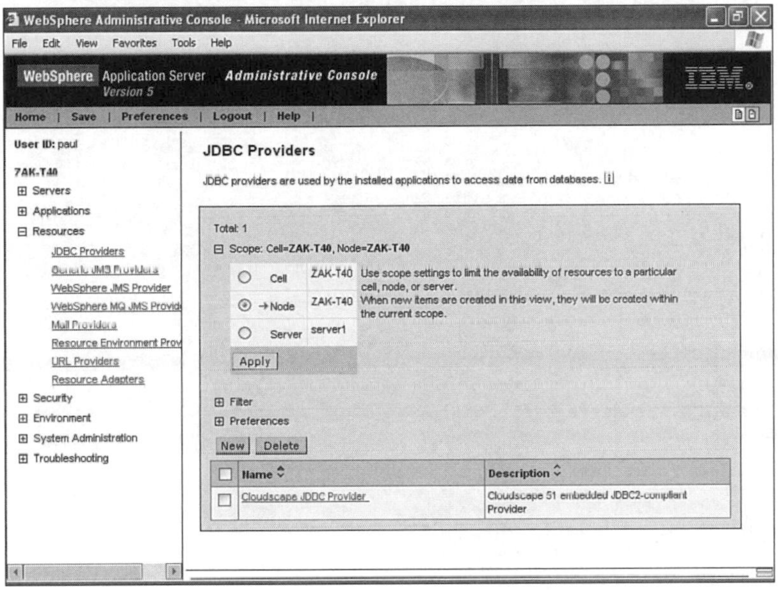

Figure 7.3 The WebSphere Admin console

Now that your database resource is defined, you can configure and deploy the application:

1. From the console, choose Applications and then choose Install New Application.
2. Browse to the `Skates.ear` file.
3. The wizard will take you through a number of steps; in most of them, you can accept the default values. The ones you need to change are listed here:
   - In Deploy EJBs Option, the Database Type is CLOUDSCAPE_V5 and the Database Schema is SKATES.
   - In JNDI Names for Beans, the value for `SkatesEntity` is `ejb/skates/SkatesEntityHome` and the value for `SkatesProduct` is `ejb/skates/SkatesProductHome`.
   - In Provide Default Datasource Mapping For Modules Containing 2.0 Entity Beans, the value for `Skatesejb.jar` is `jdbc/SkatesDataSource`.
   - In Map EJB References To Beans, the value for `SkatesProduct` and `SkatesEntity` is `ejb/skates/SkatesEntityHome`.

4. Click Finish. You should see the following output:

```
ADMA5016I: Installation of Skates started.

ADMA5018I: Starting EJBDeploy on ear
➥ c:\as51\wstemp\3433544\upload\skates4.ear..

Starting workbench.

Creating the project.

Building: /skatesejb.

Deploying jar skatesejb

Creating Top Down Map

Generating deployment code

Refreshing: /skatesejb/ejbModule.

Building: /skatesejb.

Invoking RMIC.

Generating DDL

Generating DDL

Writing output file

Shutting down workbench.

0 Errors, 0 Warnings, 0 Informational Messages

ADMA5007I: EJBDeploy completed on
➥C:\DOCUME~1\paul\LOCALS~1\Temp\app_fa7b3c6751\dpl\dpl_Skates.ear

ADMA5005I: Application Skates configured in WebSphere repository

ADMA5001I: Application binaries saved in
➥c:\as51\wstemp\3433544\workspace\cells
➥\ZAK-T40\applications\Skates.ear\Skates.ear

ADMA5011I: Cleanup of temp dir for app Skates done.
```

```
ADMA5013I: Application Skates installed successfully.

Application Skates installed successfully.
```

5. Choose Save To The Master Configuration and restart the server.

This process creates the DDL database table definition SQL, which you'll use to create the Cloudscape tables:

1. In the Enterprise Applications pane, select the Skates application and click the Export DDL button.

2. Save the file as skates.ddl in a temporary directory.

3. Back to ij—follow the bold steps shown here:

```
ij version 5.1 (c) 2001 IBM Corp.
ij> connect 'jdbc:db2j:c:\db2j\databases\skatesdb';
ij> run '\temp\skates.ddl';
ij> -- Generated by Relational Schema Center on
➥Tue Feb 03 13:47:07 GMT 2004


CREATE SCHEMA SKATES;
0 rows inserted/updated/deleted
ij> CREATE TABLE SKATES.SKATESENTITY
   (PRICE DOUBLE PRECISION NOT NULL,
    DESCRIPTION VARCHAR(250) NULL,
    PRODUCTCODE VARCHAR(250) NOT NULL);
0 rows inserted/updated/deleted
ij> ALTER TABLE SKATES.SKATESENTITY
    ADD CONSTRAINT PK_SKATESENTITY PRIMARY KEY (PRODUCTCODE);
0 rows inserted/updated/deleted
ij>
```

Once you have Axis and SkatesEJB deployed and running in a server, you need to test that Axis is running in the new server. You can use the Enterprise Applications panel to test by browsing http://server:port/axis and seeing whether you get an Axis Web page (see Figure 7.4).

Click the Validate link and receive Axis happiness, as shown in Figure 7.5.

If both of those steps work, then the next task is to create a DD and deploy the SkatesService service.

Configuring Axis to Invoke the SkatesService Session Bean

In this section, we describe how to configure the Axis server to enable Web service access to your application. Having deployed the application, you need to set up the EJB provider to be able to invoke the SkatesService bean. This means creating a WSDD that contains the relevant information.

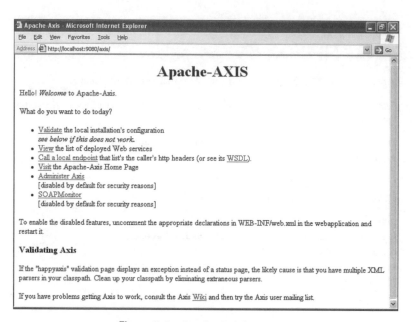

Figure 7.4   Apache Axis homepage

Figure 7.5   Axis Happiness page

If Axis was running on a separate server, you would also need to ensure that the J2EE.JAR library and the client stubs for the SkatesService bean were in the Axis classpath. The client stubs are produced as part of the deployment process; usually, the deployed EJB JAR file will contain them. However, by deploying Axis and the EJBs as part of the same enterprise application, the J2EE application server ensures that the EJB client code is available to the Axis Web application. This makes life much easier.

Before running the following commands, create and move to a new directory. The first aim is to create a WSDL file from the SkatesService remote interface. In order to do this, you must run the Apache Java2WSDL tool. It needs both the EJB-JAR file (skatesejb.jar) and the J2EE class library (j2ee.jar):

```
>set classpath=%axiscp%;.\skatesejb.jar;<appserv>\lib\j2ee.jar
>java org.apache.axis.wsdl.Java2WSDL
-lhttp://server:port/axis/services/SkatesService
com.skatestown.ejb.SkatesProducts
```

For this to work, you first need to set the right Axis classpath into the environment variable axiscp. In particular, you need the following files in your classpath:

- axis.jar
- commons-discovery.jar
- commons-logging.jar
- jaxrpc.jar
- saaj.jar
- wsdl4j.jar

You also need to find the J2EE.JAR library, which will be in your J2EE app server's classpath. You should also set the correct servername and port for your server in the URL.

If this works, you now have a SkatesService.wsdl file, as shown in Listing 7.4.

Listing 7.4   SkatesService.wsdl

```
<?xml version="1.0" encoding="UTF-8"?>
<wsdl:definitions
 targetNamespace="http://ejb.skatestown.com"
 xmlns="http://schemas.xmlsoap.org/wsdl/"
 xmlns:apachesoap="http://xml.apache.org/xml-soap"
 xmlns:impl="http://ejb.skatestown.com"
 xmlns:intf="http://ejb.skatestown.com"
 xmlns:soapenc="http://schemas.xmlsoap.org/soap/encoding/"
 xmlns:wsdl="http://schemas.xmlsoap.org/wsdl/"
 xmlns:wsdlsoap="http://schemas.xmlsoap.org/wsdl/soap/"
 xmlns:xsd="http://www.w3.org/2001/XMLSchema">
 <wsdl:types>
  <schema targetNamespace="http://ejb.skatestown.com"
          xmlns="http://www.w3.org/2001/XMLSchema">
```

Listing 7.4 **Continued**

```
  <import namespace="http://schemas.xmlsoap.org/soap/encoding/"/>
  <complexType name="Product">
   <sequence>
    <element name="description" nillable="true" type="xsd:string"/>
    <element name="price" type="xsd:double"/>
    <element name="productCode" nillable="true" type="xsd:string"/>
   </sequence>
  </complexType>
 </schema>
</wsdl:types>
  <wsdl:message name="addProductResponse">
  </wsdl:message>
  <wsdl:message name="viewProductRequest">
    <wsdl:part name="in0" type="xsd:string"/>
  </wsdl:message>
  <wsdl:message name="viewProductResponse">
    <wsdl:part name="viewProductReturn" type="impl:Product"/>
  </wsdl:message>
  <wsdl:message name="addProductRequest">
    <wsdl:part name="in0" type="impl:Product"/>
  </wsdl:message>
  <wsdl:portType name="SkatesProducts">
    <wsdl:operation name="addProduct" parameterOrder="in0">
       <wsdl:input message="impl:addProductRequest" name="addProductRequest"/>
       <wsdl:output message="impl:addProductResponse"
                    name="addProductResponse"/>
    </wsdl:operation>
    <wsdl:operation name="viewProduct" parameterOrder="in0">
       <wsdl:input message="impl:viewProductRequest" name="viewProductRequest"/>
       <wsdl:output message="impl:viewProductResponse"
                    name="viewProductResponse"/>
    </wsdl:operation>
  </wsdl:portType>

  <wsdl:binding name="SkatesServiceSoapBinding" type="impl:SkatesProducts">
    <wsdlsoap:binding style="rpc"
                      transport="http://schemas.xmlsoap.org/soap/http"/>
    <wsdl:operation name="addProduct">
       <wsdlsoap:operation soapAction=""/>
       <wsdl:input name="addProductRequest">
         <wsdlsoap:body
           encodingStyle="http://schemas.xmlsoap.org/soap/encoding/"
           namespace="http://ejb.skatestown.com" use="encoded"/>
       </wsdl:input>
       <wsdl:output name="addProductResponse">
         <wsdlsoap:body
```

Listing 7.4   **Continued**

```
                encodingStyle="http://schemas.xmlsoap.org/soap/encoding/"
                namespace="http://ejb.skatestown.com" use="encoded"/>
        </wsdl:output>
    </wsdl:operation>
    <wsdl:operation name="viewProduct">
        <wsdlsoap:operation soapAction=""/>
        <wsdl:input name="viewProductRequest">
            <wsdlsoap:body
                encodingStyle="http://schemas.xmlsoap.org/soap/encoding/"
                namespace="http://ejb.skatestown.com" use="encoded"/>
        </wsdl:input>
        <wsdl:output name="viewProductResponse">
            <wsdlsoap:body
                encodingStyle="http://schemas.xmlsoap.org/soap/encoding/"
                namespace="http://ejb.skatestown.com" use="encoded"/>
        </wsdl:output>
    </wsdl:operation>
  </wsdl:binding>
  <wsdl:service name="SkatesProductsService">
    <wsdl:port binding="impl:SkatesServiceSoapBinding" name="SkatesService">
        <wsdlsoap:address
            location="http://localhost:9080/axis/services/SkatesService"/>
    </wsdl:port>
  </wsdl:service>
</wsdl:definitions>
```

In order to help deploy this file, you can now run the WSDL2Java tool. This tool creates a deploy.wsdd deployment XML file for Axis that will act as a good starting point; it also creates code with which to call the service. However, the deploy.wsdd file is designed for use with a standard Java class, so you must modify it to work with your EJB application:

```
>java org.apache.axis.wsdl.WSDL2Java \
SkatesService.wsdl --server-side
```

The deploy.wsdd file shown in Listing 7.5 is now located in com\skatestown\ejb\deploy.wsdd.

Listing 7.5   **Generated** deploy.wsdd **File**

```
<deployment
    xmlns="http://xml.apache.org/axis/wsdd/"
    xmlns:java="http://xml.apache.org/axis/wsdd/providers/java">

  <!-- Services from SkatesServiceService WSDL service -->

  <service name="SkatesService"
```

Listing 7.5 **Continued**

```
              provider="java:RPC" style="rpc" use="encoded">
    <parameter name="wsdlTargetNamespace"
              value="http://ejb.skatestown.com"/>
    <parameter name="wsdlServiceElement"
              value="SkatesServiceService"/>
    <parameter name="wsdlServicePort"
              value="SkatesService"/>
    <parameter name="className"
              value="com.skatestown.ejb.SkatesServiceSoapBindingImpl"/>
    <parameter name="wsdlPortType"
              value="SkatesService"/>
    <operation name="addProduct"
              qname="operNS:addProduct"
              xmlns:operNS="http://ejb.skatestown.com" >
      <parameter name="in0"
                type="tns:Product"
                xmlns:tns="http://ejb.skatestown.com"/>
    </operation>
    <operation name="viewProduct"
              qname="operNS:viewProduct"
              xmlns:operNS="http://ejb.skatestown.com"
              returnQName="viewProductReturn"
              returnType="rtns:Product"
              xmlns:rtns="http://ejb.skatestown.com" >
      <parameter name="in0"
                type="tns:string"
                xmlns:tns="http://www.w3.org/2001/XMLSchema"/>
    </operation>
    <parameter
       name="allowedMethods"
       value="addProduct viewProduct"/>
    <typeMapping
       xmlns:ns="http://ejb.skatestown.com"
       qname="ns:Product"
       type="java:com.skatestown.ejb.Product"
       serializer=
       ➥"org.apache.axis.encoding.ser.BeanSerializerFactory"
       deserializer=
       ➥"org.apache.axis.encoding.ser.BeanDeserializerFactory"
       encodingStyle=
       ➥"http://schemas.xmlsoap.org/soap/encoding/"/>
  </service>
</deployment>
```

The bold sections in Listing 7.5 indicate the incorrect parts of the generated WSDD file. The provider type is java:EJB instead of Java:RPC, and instead of a className parameter, the provider requires `beanJndiName` and `homeInterfaceName` parameters, as shown here:

```
<service name="SkateService" provider="java:EJB">
  <parameter name="beanJndiName"
             value="ejb/skates/SkatesProductHome"/>
  <parameter name="homeInterfaceName"
             value="com.skatestown.ejb.SkatesProductsHome"/>
...

</service>
```

With this file, you can now deploy the service to Axis:

```
>java org.apache.axis.client.AdminClient
com\skatestown\ejb\deploy.wsdd
-lhttp://server:port/axis/servlet/AxisServlet
```

The response should be

```
Processing file skate.wsdd
<Admin>Done processing</Admin>
```

If you pull up a browser and browse the same servlet at `http://server:port/axis/servlet/AxisServlet`, you should see the `SkatesService` listed, as shown in Figure 7.6. You can click *(wsdl)* to view the WSDL.

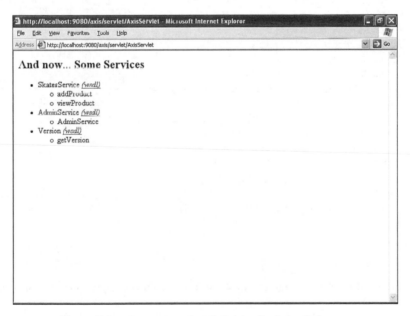

Figure 7.6 `SkatesService` listing in the Axis admin page

To test the service, you need to generate a simple command-line client. To do so, create a new directory and rerun WSDL2Java, but this time to generate client objects:

```
>java org.apache.axis.wsdl.WSDL2Java \
    http://localhost:9080/axis/services/SkatesService?wsdl
```

Now test the service application using a simple test application like that shown in Listing 7.6. Use this command to run the test:

```
    >javac com\skatestown\ejb\*.java
>java com.skatestown.ejb.SkatesTest
```

Listing 7.6 **Test Application**

```
package com.skatestown.ejb;

import java.net.URL;
public class SkatesTest
{

    public static void main(String args[])
        throws Exception
    {
        SkatesProductsService sps = new SkatesProductsServiceLocator();
        SkatesProducts sp =
        sps.getSkatesService(
➥new URL("http://zak:9080/axis/services/SkatesService"));
        Product p = new Product();
        p.setProductCode("Supertastix58s");
        p.setPrice(199.0);
        p.setDescription
➥("The latest inlines from Supertastix—are worth every penny!");
        sp.addProduct(p);
        Product p2 = sp.viewProduct(p.getProductCode());
        System.out.println("\nProduct code = ");
        System.out.println(p2.getProductCode());
        System.out.println("\nPrice = ");
        System.out.println(p2.getPrice());
        System.out.println("\nDescription = ");
        System.out.println(p2.getDescription());
    }

}
```

Note that you'll need to change the host and port in this example in order for it to work.

The results of running the test application are as follows:

```
C:\book\axis>java com.skatestown.ejb.SkatesTest

Product code =
Supertastix58s

Price =
199.0

Description =
The latest inlines from Supertastix—these are worth every penny!
```

EJB Wrap-Up

This section has been long and a little complicated. The overheads of using EJBs aren't completely clear in such a small example, and we've also done many steps by hand that would usually be done by a specialized J2EE tool—and also by the JSR109 support we're about to look at. The main aspect that's complicated is the packaging of applications into EAR files. The imposed discipline is excellent in situations where careful control, versioning of applications, and staging are required—usually in enterprise Web systems. For our smaller scenario, this is probably overkill. The other complexity is understanding the code structure and the linkages and references. These have a great benefit in separating the application from the infrastructure, but at the cost of complexity.

Finally, you can avoid much of the hard work described here by using a well-integrated J2EE development environment. However, because this book isn't designed to be tied to any given system, we've shown you the basic steps using command-line tools and kept the vendor-specific aspects to a minimum.

Using JSR109: Implementing Enterprise Web Services

The JSR109 specification (http://www.jcp.org/en/jsr/detail?id=109) is the way that J2EE embraces Web services much more closely. JSR109 addresses the following aspects of Web services and J2EE:

- Implementation and deployment of Web services using J2EE
- Client access to Web services from a J2EE application
- Service publication
- Security for Web services and mapping to J2EE security

But for SkatesTown, it means something even more useful. The steps to create and deploy a Web service into an application server are reduced. There are still a number of steps, but because the entire Axis part of this model is effectively included into the application server, the result is less work.

The steps required are as follows:

1. Create a WSDL file.
2. Create the DDs for the service.
3. Assemble the EJB JAR and EAR files.
4. Enable the EAR file for Web services (doing so automatically adds a generated Web application to support the Web service endpoint).
5. Deploy the application.

We'll guide you through each of these steps in the following sections. First, create a new working directory, J109, to contain the updated code. Copy the skatesejb.jar file into the directory, and unjar it:

```
>jar xvf skatesejb.jar
```

You'll use the WebSphere tools, which will replace the Axis WSDL2Java and Java2WSDL. To do this, add the <websphere>\bin directory to your path.

Step 1: Creating the WSDL File

Run Java2WSDL on the SkatesProduct interface:

```
>set classpath=skatesejb.jar
>Java2WSDL
➥-implClass com.skatestown.ejb.SkatesProductsBean
➥com.skatestown.ejb.SkatesProducts
```

The -implClass is optional; it uses the implementation class to find the names of the arguments to create nicer-looking WSDL. Axis supports this as well, so we could have used it in the previous part of the chapter. (This only works if you compile the code with the -g option, which adds debug information to the class files).

Now, create the WSDL file. For this project, we need to move it to META-INF\WSDL:

```
>mkdir META-INF
>mkdir META-INF\wsdl
>move SkatesProducts.wsdl META-INF\WSDL\
```

Step 2: Creating the Deployment Descriptors

The extended options for the WebSphere Java2WSDL command are as follows:

```
> WSDL2Java \
-verbose \
-role develop-server \
-container ejb \
-genJava no
META-INF\WSDL\SkatesProducts.wsdl
```

```
WSWS3185I: Info: Parsing XML file:  META-INF\WSDL\SkatesProducts.wsdl
WSWS3282I: Info: Generating META-INF\webservices.xml.
WSWS3282I: Info: Generating META-INF\ibm-webservices-bnd.xmi.
WSWS3282I: Info: Generating META-INF\ibm-webservices-ext.xmi.
WSWS3282I: Info: Generating META-INF\SkatesProducts_mapping.xml.
```

The options disable the generation of any Java classes, say that you're using an EJB as the implementation of the service (JSR109 also allows servlets), and say that you're developing the server-side artifacts.

When this command is run, it creates four new files:

- The `webservices.xml` file is the overall DD that configures the application server to use this bean as the service.

- Two `.xmi` files are additional bindings files, which contain additional information that WebSphere needs to use the EJB as a service.

- `SkatesProducts_mapping.xml` is a JAX-RPC mapping file that contains the mapping between XML Schema types and Java types that is used in this instance.

We now need to edit `webservices.xml` and set the `ejb-name` of the session bean to `SkatesProduct`:

```
<?xml version="1.0" encoding="UTF-8"?>
<!DOCTYPE webservices
➥PUBLIC "-//IBM Corporation, Inc.//DTD J2EE Web services 1.0//EN"
➥"http://www.ibm.com/webservices/dtd/j2ee_web_services_1_0.dtd">
<webservices>
  <webservice-description>
    <webservice-description-name>
      SkatesProductsService
    </webservice-description-name>
    <wsdl-file>META-INF/wsdl/SkatesProducts.wsdl</wsdl-file>
    <jaxrpc-mapping-file>META-INF/SkatesProducts_mapping.xml</jaxrpc-mapping-file>
    <port-component>
      <port-component-name>SkatesProducts</port-component-name>
      <wsdl-port>
        <namespaceURI>http://ejb.skatestown.com</namespaceURI>
        <localpart>SkatesProducts</localpart>
      </wsdl-port>
      <service-endpoint-interface>
      com.skatestown.ejb.SkatesProducts
      </service-endpoint-interface>
      <service-impl-bean>
        <ejb-link>SkatesProduct</ejb-link>
      </service-impl-bean>
    </port-component>
  </webservice-description>
</webservices>
```

As you can see, this is much more like an Axis WSDD file than a WSDL file, in that it configures the server to expose this service.

The descriptor does a number of things. For each service, it defines the following:

- The service description name
- The WSDL file associated with the service
- A JAX-RPC type-mapping file that associates Java types with XML Schema types
- One or more port components, each defining a QName, a service endpoint (business) interface, the EJB which implements the interface, and (optionally) any JAX-RPC handlers to run for that port

The JAX-RPC mapping file is pointless in this instance because we didn't specify any mapping! It's pretty much mechanical. It's a big file, so we'll just show a snippet:

```
?xml version="1.0" encoding="UTF-8"?>
<!DOCTYPE java-wsdl-mapping
➥PUBLIC "-//IBM Corporation, Inc.//DTD J2EE JAX-RPC mapping 1.0//EN"
➥"http://www.ibm.com/webservices/dtd/j2ee_jaxrpc_mapping_1_0.dtd">

<java-wsdl-mapping id="JavaWSDLMapping_1075832345810">
  <package-mapping id="PackageMapping_1075832345820">
    <package-type>com.skatestown.ejb</package-type>
    <namespaceURI>http://ejb.skatestown.com</namespaceURI>
  </package-mapping>
  <java-xml-type-mapping
     id="JavaXMLTypeMapping_1075832345820">
  <class-type>double</class-type>
    <root-type-qname
       id="RootTypeQname_1075832345820">
      <namespaceURI>http://www.w3.org/2001/XMLSchema</namespaceURI>
      <localpart>double</localpart>
    </root-type-qname>
    <qname-scope>simpleType</qname-scope>
  </java-xml-type-mapping>
</java-wsdl-mapping>
```

We've now created the required files for the EJB JAR.

Step 3: Assembling the Application Files

Let's create the EJB JAR file:

```
>jar cvf skates109.jar META-INF\* com\skatestown\ejb\*.class
```

Now we need a new `application.xml` file to create the EAR file. It's shown here:

```
<?xml version="1.0" encoding="UTF-8"?>
<!DOCTYPE application
➥PUBLIC "-//Sun Microsystems, Inc.//DTD J2EE Application 1.3//EN"
➥"http://java.sun.com/dtd/application_1_3.dtd">
```

```
<application id="SkatesTown109">
    <display-name>Skates109</display-name>
    <module id="EjbModule_skates">
        <ejb>skates109.jar</ejb>
    </module>
</application>
```

This is just like the last one, except we only need the EJB JAR—the tooling is about to add the Web router for us. The tool that does this is called the *endpoint enabler* (endptEnabler).

Step 4: Enabling the EAR File for Web Services

We run the endpoint enabler tool as follows:

```
>endptEnabler skates109.ear

WSWS2004I: IBM WebSphere Application Server Release 5
WSWS2005I: Web services Enterprise Archive Endpoint Enabler Tool.
WSWS2007I: (C) COPYRIGHT International Business Machines Corp. 1997, 2003.

WSWS2003I: Backing up EAR file to: skates109.ear~

WSWS2016I: Loading EAR file: skates109.ear
WSWS2017I: Found EJB Module: skates109.jar
WSWS2024I: Adding http router for EJB Module skates109.jar.
WSWS2036I: Saving EAR file skates109.ear...
WSWS2037I: Finished saving the EAR file.
WSWS2018I: Finished processing EAR file skates109.ear.
```

It automatically adds a new Web application into the EAR file.

Step 5: Deploying the Application

This process is just as before, except we'll choose different JNDI names so the application doesn't clash with the other one. Follow these steps:

1. From the console, choose Applications and then Install New Application.

2. Browse to the Skates.ear file.

3. The wizard will take you through a number of steps, and in most of them you can accept the default values. The ones you need to change are as follows:

   - In Deploy EJBs Option, the Database Type is CLOUDSCAPE_V5 and the Database Schema is SKATES.

   - In JNDI Names For Beans, the value for SkatesEntity is ejb/skates109/SkatesEntityHome and the value for SkatesProduct is ejb/skates109/SkatesProductHome.

- In Provide Default Datasource Mapping For Modules Containing 2.0 Entity Beans, the value for `Skatesejb.jar` is `jdbc/SkatesDataSource`.
- In Map EJB References To Beans, the value for `SkatesProduct` and `SkatesEntity` is `ejb/skates109/SkatesEntityHome`.

4. Click Finish.

Start the application, and then browse the WSDL file to see if it's working:

```
http://localhost:9080/skates109/services/SkatesProducts/wsdl/SkatesProducts.wsdl
```

To test it, we can modify the URL in the test client we wrote earlier:

```
....
SkatesProductsService sps = new SkatesProductsServiceLocator();
SkatesProducts sp = sps.getSkatesService(
new URL(
"http://localhost:9080/skates109/services/SkatesProducts"));
....
```

Then run it. This time, we get a failure on the `addProduct`:

```
C:\book\axis>java com.skatestown.ejb.SkatesTest
Fault in adding product

Product code =
Supertastix58s

Price =
199.0

Description =
The latest inlines from Supertastix—these are worth every penny!
```

This, with a little thought, should be expected. The product entry Supertastix58s is already in the database table—we used the same datasource, and therefore the same database, as the original installation. Since we ran this client before, it created the entry, and the code in the EJB fails with an exception if there is an existing entry with the same product code. This isn't actually a bug! Enterprising readers may wish to modify the sample application to offer a choice between adding or viewing products.

JSR109 Client Code

Another aspect of JSR109 is the support for managing clients, which would have helped with the test client we wrote earlier. JSR109 allows any *managed* Web service client to be configured outside the code. In the same way that references to datasources, EJBs, URLs, and so on can be managed by the container, 109 also supports this for *service-refs* 📖 (resource refs to Web services). This works for EJBs, servlets, or J2EE application clients (known as *thick* or *managed clients*) making calls to Web services. The benefit is that a reconfiguration of the application can retarget the Web service—including changing the WSDL and the list of *JAX-RPC handlers* 📖 to be called (JAX-RPC handlers are components that are run outside the application logic and can modify or look at the SOAP message).

In this model, the client code would look like:

```
Service sps = ic.lookup("java:comp/env/skatesProductsRef");
SkatesProducts sp = sps.getPort(SkatesProducts.class);
sp.addProduct(...)
```

JSR109 Wrap-Up

JSR109/WSEE offers a well-defined way to deploy Web services into an application server. Effectively, it standardizes much of what Axis does in a J2EE environment. The benefits to the developer and deployment engineer are knowing that the applications and deployment will be portable across application servers, and some simplification—for example, the requirement to package and deploy Axis as a Web application is removed. JSR109 also offers a managed client environment that allows Web services to be referred to logically using the service-ref capability. In the future, these facilities will be enhanced by the Web Services Meta-data for Java standard (JSR181). JSR181 allows programmers to annotate their code with meta-data tags that define how the code will be deployed as a service, or use Web services.

Summary

In this chapter, we've shown how Enterprise JavaBeans can be exposed as Web services. The two approaches show that Axis can be used to expose EJBs as services, providing a way of exposing existing or newly created EJB business objects over SOAP; and that JSR109 provides a simpler, more integrated approach to exposing stateless session beans as Web services, using a DD and inbuilt J2EE 1.4 capabilities.

Using J2EE as a development environment for services adds both standardization and enhanced quality of service. However, the real benefit comes when you're building complex applications that integrate across reliable, transactional, and secure environments.

Resources

- *J2EE*—http://java.sun.com/j2ee
- *JSR109*—http://www.jcp.org/en/jsr/detail?id=109

8

Web Services and
Stateful Resources

ALMOST EVERY COMPUTER SYSTEM HAS SOME form of *state* or state management. By *state*, we mean a set of persistent data or information items that have a lifetime longer than a single request/response message exchange between a requestor and the Web service. An airline reservation system manages the current state of flights, reservations, airplane capacity, seating arrangements, and so on. This state lasts much longer than the duration of a particular set of message exchanges to create a reservation or cancel a reservation. In a supply chain, the current state of the request for quotes (RFQs), purchase orders, invoices and so on is managed. Most systems of any consequence have some form of state. Many Web service interfaces allow for the manipulation of state; that is, the existence of state is implied by the Web service interface. For example, a purchase order Web service implies the presence of the "purchase order" state associated with the various operations defined on the interface. Because these kinds of interfaces are common, it's important to understand the relationship between Web services and state.

To this point in the evolution of Web services technology, no formal mechanism has been proposed to represent the relationship between Web services and state. Currently, each application deals with stateful resources in a slightly (and occasionally radically) different manner. The lack of a standard convention means there is limited motivation for the industry to produce hardened, reusable middleware, tooling, design practices, and experiences upon which Web services applications can be built. This results in increased integration cost between systems that deal with stateful resources in different ways.

This chapter discusses a recent set of proposed standards that formalize the relationship between Web services and state: WS-Resource Framework. The WS-Resource Framework was developed by Computer Associates, Fujitsu, Globus (a major open-source provider of Grid middleware), Hewlett-Packard, and IBM and has been submitted to the OASIS standards organization. A set of five specifications and a white paper outline an approach to modeling stateful resources using Web services. The five specifications are WS-ResourceProperties, WS-ResourceLifetime, WS-ServiceGroup,

WS-RenewableReferences, and WS-BaseFaults. We'll examine these specifications in more detail later in this chapter.

Built on top of the WS-Resource Framework is a family of specifications called WS-Notification, which defines a Web services standard approach to asynchronous notification message delivery, or the so-called *publish/subscribe* (pub/sub) pattern. We'll also review the WS-Notification specifications in this chapter.

Web Services and State

Fundamentally, Web services are best modeled as stateless message processors that accept request messages, process them in some fashion, and (usually) formulate a response to return to the requestor. Web services are typically implemented by stateless components such as Java servlets or EJB stateless session beans. It's left to the implementation to figure out how (or if) any information about the request needs to be stored more permanently (such as in a database) or whether additional information needs to be acquired (such as a lookup into a file in the filesystem) in order to properly process the Web service message.

Therefore, a Web service (a stateless entity) is separate from any persistent state that it might need in order to complete the processing of request messages. This notion of the separation of Web service and state (a so-called "first amendment of the Web services constitution," to make a poor attempt at humor by historical and political analogy) is at the heart of the WS-Resource Framework.

Aspects of State

State is essentially any piece of information, outside the contents of a Web services request message, that a Web service needs in order to properly process the request. The information that forms the state is often bundled together into a "bag of state" called a *stateful resource.*

Several aspects of stateful resources are of interest to applications that wish to reason about state. These include:

- How a stateful resource is identified and referenced by other components in the system
- How messages can be sent to the stateful resource in order to act upon or query its state values
- How the stateful resource is created, either by an explicit Factory pattern operation (`createResource`) or an operation within the application such as `doSubmission` from the purchase order application
- How the stateful resource is terminated
- How the elements of the resource's state can be modified

All of these aspects are addressed by various aspects of the WS-Resource Framework.

SkatesTown Scenario

We'll examine the WS-Resource Framework in the context of an example from SkatesTown. Recall that in Chapter 4, "Describing Web Services," we described two services: `StockAvailableNotification` and `POSubmission`. These services manipulated stateful resources (purchase orders), although they did so in a very SkatesTown-proprietary fashion. The proprietary nature of SkatesTown's implementation meant that all of SkatesTown's business partners needed to build custom application interfaces to deal just with SkatesTown. Consider the case of one of SkatesTown's customers, the SkateBoard Warehouse. If this company uses Web services to deal with all of its suppliers, not just SkatesTown, it will likely end up with proprietary interfaces to each of its suppliers. This increases the integration costs of using Web services—although the systems are still cheaper to integrate using Web services than at the platform or programming-language level.

However, when SkatesTown updates its purchase order system to take advantage of the industry standards proposed by the WS-Resource Framework, it suddenly uses much more common approaches to many facets of its purchase order system. By adopting these common approaches, SkatesTown can take advantage of middleware and tooling products; but, more importantly, SkatesTown and its business partners can integrate their systems in a more standards-based and therefore cost-effective fashion.

The following list outlines the changes that SkatesTown needs to make to its existing Web services–based purchase order system. These changes are detailed in the remainder of this chapter:

- The `doSubmission` operation of the `POSubmission` portType is updated to create a `PurchaseOrder` stateful resource (as you'll see in the next section, these are called WS-Resources) and return a WS-Addressing endpoint reference to "point to" the newly created `PurchaseOrder` resource and the Web service that allows requestors to manipulate it.

- A `POPortType` is introduced to model the operations that can be executed on a `PurchaseOrder` resource. This `PurchaseOrder` service replaces the functionality that was available in the `StockAvailableNotification` service.

- The notifications that used to be available via registering with the `StockAvailableNotification` are replaced by the way WS-Notification is used.

- WS-ResourceLifetime is used to allow requestors to cancel `PurchaseOrders` and to receive notifications when a `PurchaseOrder` expires.

- WS-ResourceProperties is used to allow requestors to read the details on the `PurchaseOrder` and update certain properties of the `PurchaseOrder`.

WS-Resources

At the heart of the WS-Resource Framework is the way that stateful resources are related to Web services. As mentioned earlier, Web services and the stateful resources they act upon are separate entities. We've described many things about Web services, including how to send messages to them (using SOAP), how to describe them (using WSDL), and how to discover them (using UDDI, for example). However, we haven't described how a Web service relates to stateful resources.

A *WS-Resource* 📖 is the combination of a Web service and a stateful resource. The Web service provides a platform and programming-language-neutral means of sending messages to the stateful resource; the stateful resource represents an identifiable unit of state information.

The WS-Resource Framework doesn't dictate exactly how the stateful resource is implemented; as is typical with Web services technologies, this sort of implementation detail is hidden. The stateful resource associated with a Web service could be implemented as a file in the filesystem, an XML document within an XML-enabled database, or a private communication channel between the Web service and the native implementation of a stateful resource in an operating system.

History: Open Grid Services Infrastructure (OGSI) 1.0

There was one other attempt to model the association between Web services and state. The Open Grid Services Infrastructure (OGSI) was developed by the Global Grid Forum (GGF) between 2002 and 2004. The OGSI standard represented a set of conventions on Web services, particularly WSDL and a collection of portTypes to define the notion of stateful resources.

OGSI was developed as a result of the Grid community's desire to adopt and exploit the emerging phenomenon of Web services. Back in 2002, Web services was very early in its evolution, and many facilities needed by Grid computing (such as the ability to represent a system resource and reason about its properties and lifetime) were missing from Web services.

OGSI introduced the notion of a *Grid Service* as a variant on the Web service concept. The Grid Service was an attempt at a component model for Web services, defining a standard set of operations that can be performed on any Grid Service. This is analogous to an `Object` class in object-oriented languages.

OGSI introduced many concepts that appear in WS-Resource Framework and WS-Notification:

- *ServiceData*—The means to represent state data and mega data
- *GWSDL*—An extension to WSDL 1.1 to allow for `portType` inheritance
- *Grid Service References* (GSRS)—A referencing mechanism similar to WS-Addressing
- *Notification*—A simple point-to-point asynchronous messaging mechanism
- *ServiceGroups*—A grouping mechanism for services

OGSI, however, had some significant short comings that impeded more widespread adoption. Chief among them was the aggressive use of WSDL and XML. GWSDL extended WSDL and therefore didn't allow generic WSDL tooling to be exploited to build OGSI systems. Furthermore, the service data concept used facilities from XML Schema that were beyond the current state of the art of most XML tools.

Another concern was that OGSI blurred the notion between stateless Web services and stateful resources. Although with proper use of URL encoding of resource identity this distinction is immaterial, many in the industry continued to be confused by this point, and with their confusion came the refusal to adopt OGSI.

In addition, the OGSI specification defined too many concepts in a single specification. It's more typical in the Web services community to define smaller specifications and then propose composability between those specifications.

WS-Resource Framework was introduced to provide solutions to the requirements addressed by OGSI in a fashion that was a much better fit with the broader Web services community.

Stateful Resources

Stateful resources appear in several computing contexts. As seen in the sidebar "History: Open Grid Services Infrastructure (OGSI) 1.0," stateful resources are a major focus of Grid computing. In Grid computing, a major focus is effectively managing the allocation of system resources (such as CPUs and disk storage) among a competing set of computational tasks or jobs. These tasks are typically compute-intensive, scientific, and technical computer programs such as the calculations involved in determining the folding patterns of a protein molecule. Although this sort of workload management problem has been around for many years, Grid computing proposes solutions in a distributed heterogeneous environment that typically lacks a central point of administration. Furthermore, Grid computing is typically associated with distributed, heterogeneous resource allocation that includes a means to estimate and deliver a certain level of quality of service. Because of the distributed nature of the Grid computing problem, Web services was a natural base of technology upon which to build Grid computing standards and solutions.

Similarly, the systems management community is beginning to adopt Web services technologies. Recently, the Web Services Distributed Management (WSDM) group (http://www.oasis-open.org/committees/tc_home.php?wg_abbrev=wsdm) within the OASIS standards organization was formed to develop standard means of using Web services to manage systems resources as well as standard means of managing Web services themselves. The WSDM group recognized the importance of modeling state in Web services, and for some time considered adopting OGSI as the basis of its technology. With the advent of the WS-Resource Framework, the WSDM community now has a more natural Web services standard to adopt.

Finally, as we'll illustrate in the examples in this chapter, stateful resources exist in business-oriented applications of Web services. Because of the diverse set of applications using Web services in a business computing context, the need for standardization of representing and manipulating state using Web services is even more crucial.

You can regard the WS-Resource Framework as a set of standards that are intended to unite the way Grid computing, systems management, and business computing use Web services. With a common base of Web services technologies, it becomes possible to build the sort of dynamic, flexible systems needed by On Demand businesses.

Cardinality of Web Services and WS-Resources

To this point, we've described the notion of a WS-Resource, a stateful resource that is associated with a Web service. This relationship deserves more discussion.

In a typical situation, a particular Web service, deployed at a particular endpoint (such as http://www.skatestown.com/services/PO) can be responsible for processing messages related to many different WS-Resources. As you'll see in the section "Implied Resource Pattern," the WS-Resource Framework specifies how to form a SOAP message in order to make sure the correct WS-Resource processes the message.

In certain situations, a stronger encapsulation exists between the Web service and the stateful resource, forming a one-to-one relationship between them. We call this a *singleton pattern* of WS-Resource. In this case, the Web service and the stateful resource appear inseparable to the requestor and appear to have the same lifetime. This is in contrast with the more typical one-to-many situation described previously, wherein the Web service has a different lifecycle (it's deployed, running, and then undeployed) than the associated WS-Resources, which are created and destroyed during the lifetime of the Web service.

In many circumstances, a particular WS-Resource is associated with multiple Web services. This situation may occur when there are Web services deployed on multiple endpoints that allow access to the same stateful resource. This is a typical load-balancing technique for scaling Web services to handle a large volume of incoming messages. Multiple Web services may also be used to provide different Web services interfaces onto the same stateful resource.

Role of WS-Addressing

We'll now describe the role WS-Addressing plays in the WS-Resource Framework, leading up to the concept of the implied resource pattern that codifies how stateful resources are used as context in the processing of Web services requests. WS-Addressing was introduced by BEA, IBM, and Microsoft in March 2003 in order to standardize the notion of a *pointer* to a Web service. WS-Addressing is an XML representation of such a pointer together with a specified SOAP binding that describes how WS-Addressing is to be used by applications. By standardizing the mechanism of a pointer to a Web service, applications can share references to a Web service, including passing a Web service pointer as part of a Web service request message.

For example, in SkatesTown's StockAvailableNotification Web service, the registrationRequest message contains an application-specific means to identify the Web service to be notified when currently out-of-stock items become available. This is a significant interoperability issue for SkatesTown's customers. If each vendor has its own XML representation of a pointer to a Web service for notification, it becomes expensive for a customer to interoperate with each vendor. The solution is to establish a standard XML representation of a pointer to a Web service and have all vendors and customers adopt the standard. WS-Addressing provides this standard to SkatesTown and its customers.

WS-Addressing Endpoint Reference

In WS-Addressing, the XML representation of a Web service pointer is called an *endpoint reference* 📖. A WS-Addressing endpoint reference contains a transport-specific network address to a Web service and an optional set of additional meta-data about the Web service. Let's examine a WS-Address endpoint reference used by SkatesTown:

```
<wsa:EndpointReference
      xmlns:wsa="http://schemas.xmlsoap.org/ws/2003/03/addressing"
      xmlns:wsp="http://schemas.xmlsoap.org/ws/2002/12/policy"
      xmlns:tns="http://www.skatestown.com/services/StockAvailableNotification">
   <wsa:Address>
      http://www.skatestown.com/services/StockAvailableNotification
   </wsa:Address>
   <wsa:PortType>tns:StockAvailableNotificationPortType</wsa:PortType>
   <wsa:ServiceName PortName="StockAvailableNotification">
      tns:StockAvailableNotification
   </wsa:ServiceName>
   <wsp:Policy ...
   <wsa:ReferenceProperties>
      <tns:someProperty> ABC 123 </tns:someProperty>
   </wsa:ReferenceProperties>
</wsa:EndpointReference>
```

This endpoint reference points to the `StockAvailableNotification` service from Chapter 4. The only required element of an endpoint reference is `Address`; all the others are optional. Note the similarity between an endpoint reference and a WSDL 1.1 service element. The `Address` element contains the transport-specific address of the Web service (in this case, an HTTP URL). The `PortType` element gives the name of the `portType` implemented by the Web service located at `http://www.skatestown.com/services/StockAvailableNotification`—that is, `StockAvailableNotificationPortType`. Note that the application examining the endpoint reference could retrieve the actual WSDL definition of the `portType` by querying an XML registry repository, trying to resolve the namespace URI, or some other means. The `ServiceName` element explicitly identifies the WSDL service element that this endpoint reference is equivalent to. The `Policy` element contains a `Policy` expression associated with this Web service. Recall from Chapter 4 that WS-Policy is the language that specifies various nonfunctional characteristics of the Web service, such as security requirements, quality of service guarantees, and so on. We'll discuss the other element, `ReferenceProperties`, in more detail in the next section.

Given there is so much overlap with the WSDL 1.1 service element, why do we need an endpoint reference? The major reason is that WSDL 1.1 has very limited extensibility; the roles of the service and port are fixed and don't allow sufficient extensibility to support environments such as dynamic generation of new Web services and environments where specific shared understanding exists between requestors and providers. And as you'll see later in this chapter, the endpoint reference is handy when you're referring to the combination of a Web service and a stateful resource.

When a requestor receives an endpoint reference as part of an input message request, or perhaps as part of a response message, the requestor's middleware typically forms a software component called a `proxy` to the Web service referenced by the endpoint reference. This proxy typically encapsulates the requestor's application from the binding and policy details associated with the Web service.

Using the Endpoint Reference

The other important part of the WS-Addressing specification is the way in which the endpoint reference is used by requestors to form Web service messages. The WS-Addressing specification requires that each binding type associated with the Web service define a set of rules that dictate how the components of the endpoint reference must be used to form request messages to the Web service pointed to by the endpoint reference. The specification itself defines only the rules specific to SOAP binding.

The SOAP rules are simple: The contents of the `Address` field must appear in the SOAP message's To header, and the contents of the reference properties element must appear as headers in the SOAP message. Here's an example SOAP message that represents a registration request (see Chapter 4 for more details) to a `StockAvailableNotification` service, as pointed to by the endpoint reference we showed earlier:

```
<soap12:Envelope
    xmlns:soap12="http://www.w3.org/2002/12/soap-envelope"
    xmlns:wsa="http://schemas.xmlsoap.org/ws/2003/03/addressing"
    xmlns:tns="http://www.skatestown.com/services/StockAvailableNotification">
  <soap12:Header>
    <wsa:To>
       http://www.skatestown.com/services/StockAvailableNotification
    </wsa:To>
    <wsa:Action>
   http://www.skatestown.com/services/StockAvailableNotification#registration
    <wsa:Action>
    <tns:someProperty> ABC 123 </tns:someProperty>
    <ns1:Expiration xsi:type="xsd:dateTime"
        xmlns:ns1="http://www.skatestown.com/ns/registrationRequest">
      2004-01-30T05:00:00.000Z
    </ns1:Expiration>
  </soap12:Header>
  <soap12:Body>
    <ns2:registration  ...
  </soap12:Body>
</soap12:Envelope>
```

The way the reference properties flow (as SOAP header elements of the message) is important to establish context for processing the message. The WS-Resource Framework exploits this feature, as you'll see later in this chapter.

SOAP Headers Defined by WS-Addressing

WS-Addressing also standardizes a collection of SOAP headers. You saw one of these SOAP headers in the previous example: the To header. The other headers are summarized in the Table 8.1.

Table 8.1   **SOAP Headers Standardized by WS-Addressing**

WS-Addressing SOAP Header	Description
To	The destination header. WS-Addressing requires this header to appear on messages sent to a Web service pointed to by an endpoint reference. Its content is a copy of the contents of the Address element in the endpoint reference.
Recipient	An optional header. It contains a copy of the endpoint reference of the Web service that is the intended recipient of the message. If this header appears, it may help middleware intermediaries to process and route the message.
From	An optional header that contains an endpoint reference of the Web service that created the message.
ReplyTo	An optional header that contains an endpoint reference of a Web service to which any reply to the message should be sent. If this header doesn't appear, the receiver of the message can use the From element to send reply messages. This aspect of WS-Addressing is useful for asynchronous messaging situations where the network transport protocol can't be relied on to target the response message.
FaultTo	An optional header that contains an endpoint reference of a Web service to which any fault messages should be sent. If this header doesn't appear, the receiver of the message can use the ReplyTo or From element to send fault messages.
Action	A mandatory element that contains a URI indicating the intent of the message.
MessageID	An optional URI that uniquely identifies this message.
RelatesTo	An optional collection of QName, URI pairs. This allows you to specify the relationship between this message and other messages in a domain-specific way.

We consistently use only two of these headers: To and Action; the others are optional. For more information on the use of the headers specified by WS-Addressing, refer to the WS-Addressing spec at http://www.ibm.com/developerworks/webservices/library/ws-add/.

Implied Resource Pattern

How is WS-Addressing used to define the relationship between Web services and stateful resources? This is the core of the WS-Resource Framework. The WS-Resource

Framework defines the concept of an *implied resource pattern* 📖. The implied resource
pattern is a convention on XML, WSDL, and WS-Addressing that defines how a particular WS-Resource is referred to as a context for processing a Web service message. We use
the term *implied* because the identity of the resource isn't part of the request message, but
rather is specified using the reference properties feature of WS-Addressing. The identity
of the resource is implied by the context of the message and its association with an endpoint reference, not directly in the signature of the message.

As an example, a purchase order Web service could be created to identify a purchase
order by passing the purchase order number as a parameter of each request message.
Alternatively, the purchase order number could be used as a reference property of an
endpoint reference the Web service creates to point to an individual purchase order WS-
Resource. An endpoint reference that identifies not only the Web service target of the
request message but also the identity of a stateful resource as context for processing the
message is referred to as a *WS-Resource qualified endpoint reference* 📖.

The key to the entire WS-Resource Framework is the use of the WS-Addressing to
identify the stateful resource to be used to process the Web service message. The endpoint reference provides means to point to both the Web service and the stateful
resource in one convenient XML element. You can think of a WS-Resource qualified
endpoint reference as a pointer to a specific WS-Resource.

There are two approaches to identifying the WS-Resource in an endpoint reference:
URI encoding and reference properties. The first approach involves appending some
identifying within the address component of the endpoint reference. This approach
works well in certain circumstances: for example, when a URI scheme is used and the
WS-Resource can be identified by a simple type.

Another approach exploits the reference properties feature of WS-Addressing we
described in the previous section. An endpoint reference may include a reference properties element; if it's included, then the contents of that element must appear in a binding-
specific manner on any Web services request sent to the Web service referred to by that
endpoint reference (for example, in a SOAP binding, the reference property element
must appear as a SOAP header). An endpoint reference can be formed that refers to a
Web service and specifically identifies that a particular stateful resource (for example, a
customer's specific purchase order) must be used as context to processing Web services
messages. The types of messages that can be sent to that WS-Resource are defined by the
`portType` of the Web service identified by the `Address` element of the endpoint reference.

Consider the following example. SkatesTown wishes to model its purchase orders as
WS-Resources that maintain the state associated with the processing of a purchase order
request sent to SkatesTown. This design approach is somewhat analogous to modeling a
purchase order as an Entity EJB. SkatesTown uses the implied resource pattern because
the purchase order is a stateful entity; SkatesTown wishes to allow customers to access
their purchase orders using Web services technologies; and SkatesTown wishes to use
standard, interoperable means of exposing a purchase order as a stateful resource using
Web services.

In order to use the implied resource pattern, the POSubmission service needs some changes. First, let's examine the doSubmission operation. From Chapter 4, the doSubmission operation and related messages appear as follows:

```
<!-- Message definitions -->
<message name="poSubmissionRequest">
    <part name="purchaseOrder" element="po:po"/>
</message>

<message name="poSubmissionResponse">
    <part name="invoice" element="inv:invoice"/>
</message>

<!-- Port type definitions -->
<portType name="poSubmissionPortType">
    <operation name="doSubmission">
        <input message="pos:poSubmissionRequest"/>
        <output message="pos:poSubmissionResponse"/>
    </operation>
</portType>
```

With the implied resource pattern, the purchase order can be treated as a WS-Resource. The doSubmission operation then becomes a factory operation to create new purchase order WS-Resources. The response should no longer be an invoice, as you saw in Chapter 4, but rather an endpoint reference pointing to a PurchaseOrder WS-Resource created as a result of the doSubmission request from the customer. This allows us to implement this Web service using the implied resource pattern by changing just the response message:

```
<message name="poSubmissionResponse">
    <part name="poEPR" element="pos:POReference"/>
</message>
```

In the types element of the WSDL definition, the POEndpointReference element is defined as follows:

```
<xsd:element name="POReference"
             type="wsa:EndpointReferenceType" />
```

We'll examine the portType responsible for PurchaseOrder WS-Resources in more detail throughout this chapter. The name of this portType is the POPortType. For now, consider that this POPortType provides operations to allow a customer to query the contents of a purchase order they submitted, make certain modifications on the PurchaseOrder WS-Resource, query status on the processing of the PurchaseOrder, cancel a PurchaseOrder, receive notification when a PurchaseOrder is fully processed, and so on.

Now, the response to a doSubmission operation contains a WS-Resource qualified endpoint reference to a PurchaseOrder WS-Resource:

```
<soap:Envelope
    xmlns:soap= ...
    xmlns:poRP= ...
    xmlns:wsa= ...
... >
    <soap:Header> ...
    <soap:Body>
        <poRP:POReference>
            <wsa:Address>http://www.skatestown.com/services/PO</wsa:Address>
            <wsa:ReferenceProperties>
                <poRP:POResourceID>43871</poRP:POResourceID>
            </wsa:ReferenceProperties>
            <wsa:PortType>poRP:POPortType</wsa:PortType>
            <wsp:Policy>...
        </poRP:POReference>
    </soap:Body>
</soap:Envelope>
```

Let's take a closer look at this response message. The content of the response message is a WS-Resource qualified endpoint reference identifying a PurchaseOrder WS-Resource. The interface of the Web service is described by the POPortType (we'll examine this interface in more detail later). Figure 8.1 outlines the components of the endpoint reference referring to a PurchaseOrder created as a result of processing a doSubmission operation.

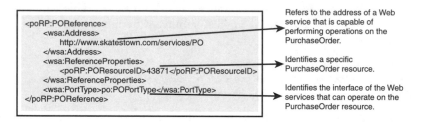

Figure 8.1   An endpoint reference to a PurchaseOrder WS-Resource

There are three important components of the endpoint reference to the PurchaseOrder WS-Resource:

- The required Address element identifies a URL to a Web service that can perform operations on the PurchaseOrder WS-Resource.

- The reference properties element contains the identifier of the PurchaseOrder stateful resource created by the processing of the doSubmission operation. This identifier is meaningful only to the Web service identified by the Address element. The only thing the customer's application should do with this element is include it in any message it sends to the Web service identified by the Address element, following the binding-specific rules defined by WS-Addressing that we discussed previously. The customer's application shouldn't use this identifier for any other reason; it should be treated as an opaque piece of information.

- The `PortType` element indicates that the interface to the Web service identified by the `Address` element is the `POPortType` portType defined by SkatesTown.

Modeling Resource Properties

As part of the WS-Resource Framework's model of stateful resources, the WS-Resource Properties specification outlines how elements of a WS-Resource's state are modeled in XML and accessed through Web services.

What Is a Resource Property?

The idea is that a WS-Resource represents state in a Web services context. This state has components, called *resource property elements*, which represent atomic elements of state that can be read and written. A set of resource property elements are gathered together into a *resource property document*: an XML document that can be queried by client applications using XPath or other query languages. Note that in many cases, a designer chooses to expose only a portion of the resource's state as resource properties.

The metaphor presented to the client application is that the WS-Resource's state is accessed by manipulating an XML document through some operations standardized by WS-ResourceProperties and provided by a Web service. Of course, the actual implementation doesn't have to store the values of the WS-Resource's state as XML. It's valid for a Web service implementation that is compatible with WS-ResourceProperties to use EJBs, simple Java classes, JDBC to a row in a database table, JNI to a physical resource, and so on. SkatesTown, for example, may choose to implement the `PurchaseOrder` WS-Resource as an Entity EJB. Regardless of the physical representation of the WS-Resource's state, the work to be done is to transform that state into an XML representation so that it can participate in the WS-ResourceProperties façade expected by client applications.

Resource Property Documents

Since WS-Resources are accessed through Web services, it makes sense to describe the resource property document and the operations that read and write resource properties through a WSDL `portType`. WS-ResourceProperties defines an XML attribute named `ResourceProperties`, which designers include on their WSDL 1.1 `portTypes` to declare the XML definition of a WS-Resource's state and that the design is following the WS-ResourceProperties standard. Using this approach, SkatesTown declares that the format of the `PurchaseOrder` resource properties document is an XML element of type `poResourceProperties`. The following snippet shows the updated WSDL `portType` for the `POPortType` portType, adding the `ResourceProperties` attribute:

```
...
    xmlns:wsrp= URI of the WS-ResourceProperties specification namespace
    xmlns:poRP="http://www.skatestown.com/ns/poResourceProperties"
...
    <!-- Port type definitions -->
    <wsdl:portType name="POPortType"
              wsrp:ResourceProperties="poRP:poResourceProperties">
    <wsdl:operation name="getInvoice">
...
    </wsdl:portType>
```

The inclusion of the ResourceProperties attribute on the portType indicates a couple
of important things about the POPortType. First, this attribute indicates that any Web
service that implements the POPortType will support any WS-Resource whose state is
modeled by the XML schema element named poResourceProperties. Second, the
portType will include one or more operations as defined in the WS-ResourceProperties
specification (we'll examine these operations in more detail later in the chapter). Because
SkatesTown is using WSDL 1.1, and WSDL 1.1 doesn't have a mechanism to build
portTypes by extending other portTypes, operations from WS-ResourceProperties are
included in the POPortType by copying the operation elements from the WS-
ResourceProperties WSDL.

A closer examination of the poResourceProperties shows the following definition:

```
<?xml version="1.0" encoding="UTF-8"?>
  <xsd:schema xmlns:xsd="http://www.w3.org/2001/XMLSchema"
  targetNamespace="http://www.skatestown.com/ns/poResourceProperties"
  xmlns:po="http://www.skatestown.com/ns/po"
  xmlns:poRP="http://www.skatestown.com/ns/poResourceProperties">

  <xsd:import namespace="http://www.skatestown.com/ns/po"
              schemaLocation="./po.xsd"/>

  <xsd:element name="dateReceived" type="xsd:dateTime" />
  <xsd:element name="status" >
    <xsd:simpleType>
      <xsd:restriction base="xsd:string">
        <xsd:enumeration value="received" />
        <xsd:enumeration value="posted" />
        <xsd:enumeration value="pending" />
        <xsd:enumeration value="invoiced" />
        <xsd:enumeration value="completed" />
      </xsd:restriction>
    </xsd:simpleType>
  </xsd:element>

  <xsd:element name="statusDate" type="xsd:dateTime" />
  <xsd:element name="contactPerson" type="xsd:string" />
```

```
  <xsd:element name="poResourceProperties">
    <xsd:complexType>
      <xsd:sequence>
...
<!-- ========= Purchase Order specific Resource Properties ======== -->
        <xsd:element ref="po:po" minOccurs="1" maxOccurs="1"/>
        <xsd:element ref="poRP:dateReceived" minOccurs="1" maxOccurs="1"/>
        <xsd:element ref="poRP:status" minOccurs="1" maxOccurs="1"/>
        <xsd:element ref="poRP:statusDate" minOccurs="1" maxOccurs="1"/>
        <xsd:element ref="poRP:contactPerson" minOccurs="0" maxOccurs="unbounded"
/>
      </xsd:sequence>
    </xsd:complexType>
  </xsd:element>

</xsd:schema>
```

The actual definition of the poResourceProperties element appears at the bottom of
the listing. The resource properties document was designed to contain the following five
important resource properties associated with a purchase order WS-Resource:

- po:po—The original PO element submitted by the customer that initiated the
  creation of the purchase order resource property.

- poRP:dateReceived—The date and time when the original PO was submitted by
  the customer.

- poRP:status—The current processing status of the purchase order, which has one
  of the following values: received, posted, pending, invoiced, or completed.

- poRP:statusDate—The date and time when the purchase order resource was
  placed into the status indicated by the poRP:status resource property element.

- poRP:contactPerson—The name of the current person in SkatesTown to be
  contacted for further information about the purchase order resource. There can be
  multiple contact person elements associated with a resource.

The complete definition of the resource properties document has a few more elements,
but we'll introduce these later in this chapter.

The construction of the resource property document schema definition is important.
The child elements of the document must be declared using the xsd:ref attribute as
shown. This allows each resource property element to be referred to by QName. You'll
see how we use this facility in the next section.

Finally, Listing 8.1 shows an example resource property document.

Listing 8.1   **Example Resource Properties Document**

```
<?xml version="1.0" encoding="UTF-8"?>
<poRP:poResourceProperties
  xmlns:po="http://www.skatestown.com/ns/po"
```

Listing 8.1 **Continued**

```
  xmlns:poRP="http://www.skatestown.com/ns/poResourceProperties"
  xmlns:xsi="http://www.w3.org/2001/XMLSchema-instance"
  xsi:schemaLocation=
   "http://www.skatestown.com/ns/poResourceProperties POResourceProperties.xsd
    http://www.skatestown.com/ns/po ./po.xsd ">
  <po:po id="43871" submitted="2004-01-05" customerId="73852">
...
    <billTo>
      <company>The Skateboard Warehouse</company>
      <street>One Warehouse Park</street>
      <street>Building 17</street>
      <city>Boston</city>
      <state>MA</state>
      <postalCode>01775</postalCode>
    </billTo>
    <shipTo>
      <company>The Skateboard Warehouse</company>
      <street>One Warehouse Park</street>
      <street>Building 17</street>
      <city>Boston</city>
      <state>MA</state>
      <postalCode>01775</postalCode>
    </shipTo>
    <order>
      <item sku="318-BP" quantity="5">
         <description>Skateboard backpack; five pockets</description>
      </item>
      <item sku="947-TI" quantity="12">
         <description>Street-style titanium skateboard</description>
      </item>
      <item sku="008-PR" quantity="1000"/>
    </order>
  </po:po>
...
  <poRP:dateReceived>2003-12-31T12:00:00</poRP:dateReceived>
  <poRP:status>received</poRP:status>
  <poRP:statusDate>2003-12-31T12:00:00</poRP:statusDate>
  <poRP:contactPerson>Jane Smith</poRP:contactPerson>
  <poRP:contactPerson>Alex Jones</poRP:contactPerson>
</poRP:poResourceProperties>
```

This resource property document represents the resource properties (and their values) of a WS-Resource created when a customer (The Skateboard Warehouse) invoked the doSubmission operation on SkatesTown's POSubmission service.

WS-Resource Factory

The notion of a WS-Resource factory is defined within the WS-Resource Framework. This factory pattern is well understood in computer science: the notion of an entity that is capable of creating new instances of some component. This pattern is called out in the WS-Resource Framework and illustrated by the relationship between the POSubmission portType and the POPortType. In WS-Resource Framework, a WS-Resource factory is any service that is capable of creating a new WS-Resource, assigning it an identity, and creating a WS-Resource qualified endpoint reference to point to it. In the example illustrated in the previous section, the POSubmission service acts as a factory, creating new PurchaseOrder WS-Resources.

Resource Property Operations

WS-ResourceProperties defines four operations related to querying and updating resource properties values: GetResourceProperty, GetMultipleResourceProperties, QueryResourceProperties, and SetResourceProperties. These provide simple, standardized access to the resource properties values of a WS-Resource. Nothing prevents the designer from specifying additional operations that also read or change the WS-Resource's state. However, by defining simple, standardized access, WS-ResourceProperties enables common tooling and better composability of Web services. Let's examine how SkatesTown uses these operations.

Although these operations are defined in the WS-ResourceProperties specifications, SkatesTown includes them in its WSDL definition of its POPortType definition by copying and pasting the WSDL operations. Of course, SkatesTown uses the WSDL import element to allow these copied operations to refer to the WSDL messages and other WSDL elements defined by WS-ResourceProperties. Listing 8.2 shows the new POSubmission WSDL, which incorporates the WS-ResourceProperties concepts.

Listing 8.2 ResourceProperties **Operations in the** POPortType

```xml
<?xml version="1.0" ?>
<wsdl:definitions name="PurchaseOrder"
    targetNamespace=
        "http://www.skatestown.com/services/interfaces/poResource.wsdl"
    xmlns:xsd="http://www.w3.org/2001/XMLSchema"
    xmlns:po="http://www.skatestown.com/ns/po"
    xmlns:poR="http://www.skatestown.com/services/interfaces/poResource.wsdl"
    xmlns:poRP="http://www.skatestown.com/ns/poResourceProperties"
    xmlns:inv="http://www.skatestown.com/ns/invoice"
    xmlns:wsrp="http://www.ibm.com/xmlns/stdwip/web-services/WS-ResourceProperties"
    xmlns:wsrl="http://www.ibm.com/xmlns/stdwip/web-services/WS-ResourceLifetime"
    xmlns:soap="http://schemas.xmlsoap.org/wsdl/soap/"
    xmlns:wsdl="http://schemas.xmlsoap.org/wsdl/"
    xmlns="http://schemas.xmlsoap.org/wsdl/">
```

Listing 8.2   Continued

```
<wsdl:import
      namespace=
 "http://www.ibm.com/xmlns/stdwip/web-services/WS-ResourceProperties"
.../>

  <wsdl:import
      namespace=
 "http://www.ibm.com/xmlns/stdwip/web-services/WS-ResourceLifetime"
... />

  <!-- Type definitions -->
  <wsdl:types>
    <xsd:schema
       targetNamespace=
         "http://www.skatestown.com/services/interfaces/poResource.wsdl">
...

    <xsd:element name="ErrorMessage" type="xsd:string" />
    <xsd:element name="POResourceID" type="xsd:positiveInteger" />

    </xsd:schema>
  </wsdl:types>

  <!-- Message definitions -->
  <wsdl:message name="ErrorMessage">
    <wsdl:part name="ErrorMessage" element="poR:ErrorMessage"/>
  </wsdl:message>

  <wsdl:message name="GetInvoiceRequest" />
  <wsdl:message name="GetInvoiceResponse" >
    <wsdl:part name="GetInvoiceRequest" element="inv:invoice" />
  </wsdl:message>

  <!-- Port type definitions -->
  <wsdl:portType name="POPortType"
          wsrp:ResourceProperties="poRP:poResourceProperties">
    <wsdl:operation name="getInvoice">
      <wsdl:input name="GetInvoiceRequest"
                  message="poR:GetInvoiceRequest" />
      <wsdl:output name="GetInvoiceResponse"
                   message="poR:GetInvoiceResponse" />
      <wsdl:fault name="NoInvoiceFault"
                  message="poR:ErrorMessage" />
    </wsdl:operation>
```

Listing 8.2   Continued

```
  <!-- ========== extends wsrp:GetResourceProperty ============ -->
    <wsdl:operation name="GetResourceProperty">
      <wsdl:input   name="GetResourcePropertyRequest"
...
    </wsdl:operation>

  <!-- ===== extends wsrp:GetMultipleResourceProperties ======= -->
    <wsdl:operation name="GetMultipleResourceProperties">
      <wsdl:input   name="GetMultipleResourcePropertiesRequest"
...
    </wsdl:operation>

  <!-- ======== extends wsrp:SetResourceProperties ============ -->
    <wsdl:operation name="SetResourceProperties">
      <wsdl:input    name="SetResourcePropertiesRequest"
...
  </wsdl:operation>

  <!-- ======= extends wsrp:QueryResourceProperties =========== -->
    <wsdl:operation name="QueryResourceProperties">
...
    </wsdl:operation>

  </wsdl:portType>
</wsdl:definitions>
```

This WSDL shows the definition for the `POPortType`. This definition combines an application-specific operation (`GetInvoice`) with WS-ResourceProperties–specific operations copied from the WS-ResourceProperties WSDL.

We can examine the details of the WS-ResourceProperties operations in the context of a `PurchaseOrder` WS-Resource instance. In particular, we can examine the situation where the client, The Skateboard Warehouse, has a WS-Resource–qualified endpoint reference, as shown in Figure 8.1, that it got in response to an invocation of SkatesTown's `POSubmission` service. The WS-Resource pointed to by that endpoint reference has resource property values as shown in Listing 8.1.

GetResourceProperty

WS-ResourceProperties defines a simple "get by name" method to retrieve a WS-Resource's resource property values in a standard way. You can think of this operation as a simple, straightforward getter method. WS-ResourceProperties requires that this operation appear on any `portType` that supports access to a WS-Resource. In fact, it's a rule that any `portType` that includes the `resourceProperties` attribute in its definition must include this operation. The other operations defined by WS-ResourceProperties are optional.

In our situation, the customer is interested in examining the status of the purchase order. Given that SkatesTown didn't define an application-specific operation to retrieve the status of the `PurchaseOrder` WS-Resource, the customer needs to use the `GetResourceProperty` operation.

To retrieve the value of the `poRP:status` resource property, the customer would need to send the following message to the WS-Resource. Recall that in the WS-Resource Framework, a particular WS-Resource is targeted by sending a message to a Web service (as indicated by the `Address` element of an endpoint reference) and including the identity of the WS-Resource (as indicated by the `referenceProperties` element of the endpoint reference). Here is an example SOAP request message to retrieve the status of the `PurchaseOrder`:

```
<soap:Envelope
    xmlns:soap="http://www.w3.org/2003/05/soap-envelope"
    xmlns:wsa="http://schemas.xmlsoap.org/ws/2003/03/addressing"
    xmlns:wsrp=
  "http://www.ibm.com/xmlns/stdwip/web-services/WS-ResourceProperties"
   xmlns:poRP="http://www.skatestown.com/ns/poResourceProperties">
  <soap:Header>
   <wsa:Action>
  http://www.ibm.com/xmlns/stdwip/web-services/WS-ResourceProperties/
➥GetResourceProperty
   </wsa:Action>
   <wsa:To soap:mustUnderstand="1">
       http://www.skatestown.com/services/PO
   </wsa:To>
   <poRP:POResourceID>43871</poRP:POResourceID>
  </soap:Header>
  <soap:Body>
   <wsrp:GetResourceProperty>
      poRP:status
   </wsrp:GetResourceProperty>
  </soap:Body>
</soap:Envelope>
```

Note the use of the implied resource pattern in the request message. The `wsa:To` element and the reference property (`poRP:POResourceID`) are derived from the endpoint reference.

The response message is straightforward; it contains the value of the status resource property for the WS-Resource targeted in the request message:

```
<soap:Envelope
    xmlns:soap="http://www.w3.org/2003/05/soap-envelope"
    xmlns:wsa="http://schemas.xmlsoap.org/ws/2003/03/addressing"
    xmlns:wsrp=
  "http://www.ibm.com/xmlns/stdwip/web-services/WS-ResourceProperties"
```

```
    xmlns:poRP="http://www.skatestown.com/ns/poResourceProperties">
  <soap:Header>
    <wsa:Action>
        http://www.ibm.com/xmlns/stdwip/web-services/WS-ResourceProperties/
➥GetResourceProperty
    </wsa:Action>
    <wsa:To soap:mustUnderstand="1">
        http://www.skateWarehouse.com/someEndpoint
    </wsa:To>
  </soap:Header>
  <soap:Body>
    <wsrp:GetResourcePropertyResponse>
      <poRP:status>received</poRP:status>
    </wsrp:GetResourcePropertyResponse>
  </soap:Body>
</soap:Envelope>
```

The Skateboard Warehouse could use the simple GetResourceProperty operation to retrieve single resource property values. However, if its application needs to frequently retrieve the value of multiple resource properties, it's better off using the operation we describe in the next section.

GetMultipleResourceProperties

The designers of WS-ResourceProperties included another get operation, GetMultipleResourceProperties, that looks similar to the GetResourceProperty operation. Although both operations allow a requestor to retrieve values of resource properties, GetMultipleResourceProperties allows the requestor to retrieve the values of multiple resource properties with a single message exchange by including a list of resource property QNames in the request message. Although there is overlap between the two operations, they address different usage scenarios:

- The GetResourceProperty operation is a required operation. It's the minimal, simple operation to allow resource-constrained Web services to participate in WS-ResourceProperties.

- The GetMultipleResourceProperties operation allows requestors to avoid multiple round trips to retrieve the value of multiple resource property elements. This avoids applications doing too many fine-grained network accesses to retrieve resource property information, which yields poor application performance and inefficient use of the network.

In our running example with the SkatesTown purchase order WS-Resource, if The Skateboard Warehouse wanted to examine the values of several resource properties of their PurchaseOrder WS-Resource—say, status, status date, and contact person—then it could retrieve this information with a single GetMultipleResourceProperties operation:

```
<soap:Envelope
    xmlns:soap="http://www.w3.org/2003/05/soap-envelope"
    xmlns:wsa="http://schemas.xmlsoap.org/ws/2003/03/addressing"
    xmlns:wsrp=
  "http://www.ibm.com/xmlns/stdwip/web-services/WS-ResourceProperties"
   xmlns:poRP="http://www.skatestown.com/ns/poResourceProperties">
  <soap:Header>
    <wsa:Action>
      http://www.ibm.com/xmlns/stdwip/web-services/WS-ResourceProperties/
➥GetResourceProperty
    </wsa:Action>
    <wsa:To soap:mustUnderstand="1">
        http://www.skatestown.com/services/PO
    </wsa:To>
    <poRP:POResourceID>43871</poRP:POResourceID>
  </soap:Header>
  <soap:Body>
    <wsrp:GetMultipleResourceProperties>
      <wsrp:ResourceProperty>poRP:status</wsrp:ResourceProperty>
      <wsrp:ResourceProperty>poRP:statusDate</wsrp:ResourceProperty>
      <wsrp:ResourceProperty>poRP:contactPerson</wsrp:ResourceProperty>
    </wsrp:GetMultipleResourceProperties>
  </soap:Body>
</soap:Envelope>
```

Again, remember that the implied resource pattern is used to target the correct
PurchaseOrder WS-Resource. The response message contains the values of the resource
properties identified by QName:

```
<soap:Envelope
    xmlns:soap="http://www.w3.org/2003/05/soap-envelope"
    xmlns:wsa="http://schemas.xmlsoap.org/ws/2003/03/addressing"
    xmlns:wsrp=
  "http://www.ibm.com/xmlns/stdwip/web-services/WS-ResourceProperties"
   xmlns:poRP="http://www.skatestown.com/ns/poResourceProperties">
  <soap:Header>
    <wsa:Action>
      http://www.ibm.com/xmlns/stdwip/web-services/WS-ResourceProperties/
➥GetResourceProperty
    </wsa:Action>
    <wsa:To soap:mustUnderstand="1">
        http://www.skateWarehouse.com/someEndpoint
    </wsa:To>
  </soap:Header>
  <soap:Body>
    <wsrp:GetMultipleResourcePropertiesResponse>
      <poRP:status>received</poRP:status>
```

```
        <poRP:statusDate>2004-03-01T12:00:00</poRP:statusDate>
        <poRP:contactPerson>Jane Smith</poRP:contactPerson>
        <poRP:contactPerson>Alex Jones</poRP:contactPerson>
      </wsrp:GetMultipleResourcePropertiesResponse>
    </soap:Body>
</soap:Envelope>
```

It's up to the requestor's application to correlate which elements in the response message correspond to which resource properties listed in the request message. Because this is all XML, the correlation is simple: the values of the resource property named poRP:status are identified by elements whose tag is poRP:status.

Note that one of the resource properties, poRP:contactPerson, has multiple values. The cardinality of the resource property is determined by the minOccurs and maxOccurs attributes in the resource property document declaration. Whereas many resource properties will have minOccurs and maxOccurs values of 1, an optional resource property is indicated by a minOccurs value of 0; and a resource property with possibly multiple values is indicated by a maxOccurs value greater than 1.

QueryResourceProperties

The QueryResourceProperties operation was designed to allow applications to issue query expressions, like XPath, against the content of a WS-Resource's resource property document. Although the syntax of QueryResourceProperties allows for any type of query expression, the normal usage is for an XPath version 1.0 expression to be evaluated on the resource properties document. The form of the query element is

```
<wsrp:QueryExpression dialect="URI">
  xsd:any
</wsrp:QueryExpression>
```

And the language used in the content of the query is indicated by the URI value of the dialect attribute. The WS-ResourceProperties specification defines two expression dialect URIs: XPath 1.0 (http://www.w3.org/TR/1999/REC-xpath-19991116) and XPath 2.0 (http://www.w3.org/TR/2003/WD-xpath20-20031112).

Imagine if The Skateboard Warehouse had a collection of outstanding PurchaseOrder WS-Resources, some with SkatesTown and some with other vendors. Although it could group these WS-Resource references together into a collection (such as a ServiceGroup that we'll briefly discuss toward the end of this chapter), imagine for now that the reorder application simply keeps an array of WS-Resource endpoint references to these PurchaseOrder WS-Resources. Now, consider the case where a decision maker wants to get a list of all the pending PurchaseOrders. The application could iterate through the array of endpoint references, issuing the following XPath 1.0 Query:

```
<soap:Envelope>
...
    <!--identify the resource from the EPR -->
    <poRP:POResourceID>XXXXX</poRP:POResourceID>
```

```
   </soap:Header>
   <soap:Body>
     <wsrp:QueryResourcePropertiesRequest>
       <wsrp:QueryExpression
         dialect="http://www.w3.org/TR/1999/REC-xpath-19991116">
         ./poRP:status="pending"
       </wsrp:QueryExpression>
     </wsrp:GetMultipleResourcePropertiesRequest>
   </soap:Body>
</soap:Envelope>
```

The application would then aggregate the responses from the query evaluation on each `PurchaseOrder` WS-Resource. In the case of the `PurchaseOrder` we've been examining in this section, the status is `received`, not `pending`; therefore the response will be

```
<soap:Envelope
...
     <poRP:POResourceID>43871</poRP:POResourceID>
   </soap:Header>
   <soap:Body>
     <wsrp:QueryResourcePropertiesResponse>
       false
     </wsrp:QueryResourcePropertiesResponse>
   </soap:Body>
</soap:Envelope>
```

Currently, there is no way for the Web service to communicate which query languages it supports. It would need to be declared using some WS-Policy assertion, but WS-ResourceProperties doesn't specify this WS-Policy grammar.

SetResourceProperties

So far, we've examined the operations defined by WS-ResourceProperties to retrieve or get values of resource properties. WS-ResourceProperties also defines an additional operation, `SetResourceProperties`, which allows a requestor to insert, update, and delete values of resource properties. The *SetResourceProperties* message request consists of a collection of components (`Insert`, `Update`, or `Delete` components); so, you can think of this operation as a simple script that can be executed against the WS-Resource, making multiple change operations happen with a single Web service invocation. Many uses of `SetResourceProperties` involve a single change, like "change the value of ResourceProperty tns:XYZ to 7." Other applications, such as in a systems-management domain, may involve a sophisticated collection of inserts, updates, and deletes in a single `SetResourceProperties` invocation.

Let's examine each type of set component (`Insert`, `Update`, and `Delete`) individually. Then we'll summarize their use with an example that combines all three components.

`SetResourceProperties Insert` *Component*

The `Insert` component can be used to insert new values for a resource property. For example, if The Skateboard Warehouse wishes to add another contact person to its `PurchaseOrder` WS-Resource, it sends the following message:

```
<soap:Envelope>
...
    <poRP:POResourceID>43871</poRP:POResourceID>
  </soap:Header>
  <soap:Body>
    <wsrp:SetResourceProperties
      <wsrp:Insert>
        <poRP:contactPerson>Laura Tang</poRP:contactPerson>
      </wsrp:Insert>
    </wsrp:SetResourceProperties>
  </soap:Body>
</soap:Envelope>
```

This causes the resource properties document to include a new value for the `poRP:contactPerson` resource property. The exact resource property that is modified is identified by the tag of the child of the `Insert` element. In this case, it's `poRP:contactPerson`, indicating that the `poRP:contactPerson` resource property is the target of this modification.

After this request is successfully executed, the response message is returned:

```
<soap:Envelope
...
  </soap:Header>
  <soap:Body>
    <wsrp:SetResourcePropertiesResponse>
    </wsrp:SetResourcePropertiesResponse>
  </soap:Body>
</soap:Envelope>
```

The response message isn't terribly interesting. Essentially, it appears to indicate that no error was detected when processing the `SetResourcePropertiesRequest`. We won't repeat the response message again in the rest of our discussion of `SetResourceProperties`.

As a result of the successful insertion of the new contact person, the resource properties document now looks like this:

```
<?xml version="1.0" encoding="UTF-8"?>
<poRP:poResourceProperties xmlns:po="http://www.skatestown.com/ns/po"
...

  <po:po id="43871" submitted="2004-01-05" customerId="73852">
...
```

```
  </po:po>
...
  <poRP:dateReceived>2003-12-31T12:00:00</poRP:dateReceived>
  <poRP:status>received</poRP:status>
  <poRP:statusDate>2003-12-31T12:00:00</poRP:statusDate>
  <poRP:contactPerson>Jane Smith</poRP:contactPerson>
  <poRP:contactPerson>Alex Jones</poRP:contactPerson>
  <poRP:contactPerson>Laura Tang</poRP:contactPerson>
</poRP:poResourceProperties>
```

Note that it's up to the implementation to determine where the new contact person is inserted. It could appear at the beginning, in the middle, or at the end of the list of existing contact person elements. The only requirement is that the insertion allow the resource properties document to still be validatable against its schema. So, had the implementation inserted the contact person before the status element, the document would not be valid with respect to its schema, and we would consider the implementation to be not in compliance with WS-ResourceProperties.

It's important to be careful with any of these components. It's easy to issue a SetResourceProperties request that would render the resource properties document unable to validate. You need to pay close attention to the definition of the resource properties elements and make sure that the minOccurs and maxOccurs cardinality properties aren't violated. For example, for the status resource property, the maxOccurs is equal to 1, meaning it can have at most one value. Given that there is already a value for the status resource property in our example's resource properties document, the following insertion request would fail:

```
<soap:Envelope>
...
    <poRP:POResourceID>43871</poRP:POResourceID>
  </soap:Header>
  <soap:Body>
    <wsrp:SetResourceProperties>
      <wsrp:Insert>
        <poRP:status>posted</poRP:status>
      </wsrp:Insert>
    </wsrp:SetResourceProperties>
  </soap:Body>
</soap:Envelope>
```

It isn't valid for there to be two values of poRP:status in the resource properties document (because maxOccurs is set to 1).

SetResourceProperties Update *Component*

The Update component is similar to the Insert component, in that new values are added to the resource properties document. However, unlike the Insert component, which only inserts new values in addition to the existing values of a resource property, the update operation replaces all existing values with the contents of the request. So, to change the value of the status resource property to posted, the following update operation is used:

```
<soap:Envelope>
...
    <poRP:POResourceID>43871</poRP:POResourceID>
  </soap:Header>
  <soap:Body>
    <wsrp:SetResourceProperties
      <wsrp:Update>
        <poRP:status>posted</poRP:status>
      </wsrp:Update>
    </wsrp:SetResourceProperties>
  </soap:Body>
</soap:Envelope>
```

The effect of an update operation is that all the values for the resource property identified by the ResourceProperty attribute of the Update component are deleted, and then the contents of the Update component are inserted in their place. Note that the QName of the child element must match the value of the ResourceProperty attribute (in this case, they're both poRP:status).

SetResourceProperties Delete *Component*

The last type of component in a SetResourceProperties element is the Delete component. With the Delete component, all the values associated with the resource property identified (by QName) in the Delete component are removed from the resource properties document. Again, you need to be aware of the resource property's minOccurs attribute. If the value of minOccurs isn't 0, the Delete component will fail.

Because most of the resource properties associated with our PurchaseOrder WS-Resource example have minOccurs greater than 0, the only possible legal delete operation involves the contact person resource property. Here's a request that deletes all the values of the contact person resource property:

```
<soap:Envelope>
...
    <poRP:POResourceID>43871</poRP:POResourceID>
  </soap:Header>
  <soap:Body>
    <wsrp:SetResourceProperties
      <wsrp:Delete ResourceProperty="poRP:contactPerson">
      </wsrp:Delete>
    </wsrp:SetResourceProperties>
  </soap:Body>
</soap:Envelope>
```

The resource properties document will still validate.

Combining the `SetResourceProperties` *Components*

The operations we've discussed can be used separately, with individual request/response message exchanges; or they can be combined, for efficiency reasons, into a single request/response. Let's apply the following `SetResourceProperties` request to the original resource properties document (shown in Listing 8.1):

```
<soap:Envelope>
...

    <poRP:POResourceID>43871</poRP:POResourceID>
  </soap:Header>
  <soap:Body>
    <wsrp:SetResourceProperties>
      <wsrp:Update>
        <poRP:status>posted</poRP:status>
      </wsrp:Update>
      <wsrp:Delete ResourceProperty="poRP:contactPerson">
      </wsrp:Delete>
      <wsrp:Insert>
        <poRP:contactPerson>Laura Tang</poRP:contactPerson>
      </wsrp:Insert>
      <wsrp:Update>
        <poRP:statusDate>2004-1-05T1:35:27</poRP:statusDate>
      </wsrp:Update>
    </wsrp:SetResourceProperties>
  </soap:Body>
</soap:Envelope>
```

Note the order of operations:

1. The value of the status resource property is updated.
2. The values of the `poRP:contactPerson` resource property are deleted.
3. A new value for `contactPerson` is inserted.
4. The value of the `statusDate` is updated.

It's important to understand that the components of the `SetResourceProperties` request are processed in the order they appear in the message. Furthermore, the results of processing a component are visible to the processing of subsequent components.

The resulting resource properties document looks like this:

```
<?xml version="1.0" encoding="UTF-8"?>
<poRP:poResourceProperties xmlns:po="http://www.skatestown.com/ns/po"
...

  <po:po id="43871" submitted="2004-01-05" customerId="73852">
...
  </po:po>
...
  <poRP:dateReceived>2003-12-31T12:00:00</poRP:dateReceived>
```

```
    <poRP:status>posted</poRP:status>
    <poRP:statusDate>2004-1-05T1:35:27</poRP:statusDate>
    <poRP:contactPerson>Laura Tang</poRP:contactPerson>
</poRP:poResourceProperties>
```

Rounding Out SetResourceProperties

We need to add a few more comments about the SetResourceProperties operation.
Errors are handled in a normal Web services way. Faults are listed on the
SetResourceProperties operation definition in the WSDL. Errors flow back to the
requestor's application instead of a normal SetResourcePropertiesResponse message.
The sorts of errors that can occur include:

- "The resource identified by the request was unknown to the Web service" (you see
  this sort of error message with most of the WS-Resource Framework operations).
- "The request was rejected because it would render the resource properties docu-
  ment no longer able to validate."
- "The resource property could not be modified because it's read-only."
- "The resource property identified was unknown to the resource."
- "The request failed for some reason."

So, much of the error-checking is done to make sure the resource properties document
remains validatable with respect to its schema. Of course, other errors, which are application specific, can be detected. Many aspects of a resource property element, such as
whether it's read-only, or whether there is some sort of complicated, algorithmic constraint on its value, can't be expressed in XML Schema.

The actual failure recovery is implementation dependent. Some implementations may
restore the resource property values to where they were prior to the attempt to process
the failed component; some may restore the entire resource property document to the
state prior to processing any component in the entire SetResourceProperties request.
Outside of an application-specific WS-Policy assertion, there is no way for the requestor
to determine the expected failure semantic. However, if the SetResourceProperties
request is executed under a transaction semantic (such as we'll discuss in Chapter 11,
"Web Services Transactions"), the failure semantics of the entire
SetResourceProperties request will be clear to the requestor.

You may have noticed the granularity of all the WS-ResourceProperties operations:
Things work only at the resource property level. If an application needs finer-grained
update capability, it needs to use other means. For example, if The Skateboard Warehouse
wants to make a change to the shipTo part of the po:PO resource property of its
PurchaseOrder WS-Resource, it could do an update, replacing the entire value of the
po:PO with a new one that differs only in the shipTo element. More sophisticated
mechanisms, such as an update language associated with XQuery, aren't currently well
specified. At this point, XQuery is still read-only.

Of course, security is an important consideration with WS-ResourceProperties. However, WS-ResourceProperties, like most WS-* specifications, doesn't define a separate, domain-specific security mechanism. Rather, WS-ResourceProperties exploits the feature of Web services known as *composability*—that is, WS-* specifications are designed to be composed together to create an overall solution. WS-ResourceProperties, like the rest of the WS-Resource Framework, relies on WS-Security (see Chapter 9, "Securing Web Services") for its security needs.

Rounding Out the `POPortType`

The `POPortType` includes one additional operation that we haven't discussed to this point. The `getInvoice` operation provides a simple mechanism for the requestor to retrieve an invoice (if it exists) that corresponds to the `PurchaseOrder` WS-Resource. This is an example of an application-specific operation that is composed with the operations from other WS-Resource Framework specifications. It also illustrates the notion that not all pieces of information associated with a WS-Resource are modeled as resource properties. It would have been perfectly valid for the designer of the `POPortType` to make `invoice` a resource property. There could have been application-specific or implementation issues that drove the designer to make retrieval of an invoice an operation as opposed to modeling an invoice as a resource property.

Deciding what is a resource property boils down to application design. If in doubt about whether to make something a resource property, consider the following reasoning by analogy. If you were designing a Java class to model the resource, would you choose an instance variable (public or private) to model the property? Or would it be better to build an application-specific method to access the property? Of course, sometimes you do neither; some aspects of a business object aren't modeled by software.

Using Notifications

Recall the `StockAvailableNotification` service from Chapter 4. SkatesTown introduces this service to notify customers when back-ordered stock became available. We discussed how the customers would use the registration operation to express their interest in receiving notification when certain part numbers (SKUs) were available. This service also provided a means by which stock-available notification messages were delivered (an out-only notification operation) and a means by which the customer could cancel its interest in receiving notifications.

Associated with the WS-Resource Framework, IBM, Sonic, and other companies introduced a family of related specifications called WS-Notification. WS-Notification describes the sort of publish/subscribe/notification pattern that you saw with `StockAvailableNotification` service and many other business processes. The specifications within the WS-Notification family include a standard set of message exchanges that provides a level of interoperability between companies involved in this sort of business process.

Now that WS-Notification is available, SkatesTown can refactor its `StockAvailableNotification` service to take advantage of this standardization opportunity. The benefit to SkatesTown is that it can use more common tooling and infrastructure that often follows the establishment of industry-accepted specifications. The advantage to SkatesTown's customers is that they don't have to build custom application infrastructure to deal with the way that each of their vendors (including SkatesTown) implements this style of notification-based business processes. The net benefit to the industry is that Web services can be used to build more interoperable business processes between suppliers and vendors, yielding reduced operating costs through less expensive and more effective computer systems integration.

The WS-Notification family is made up of the following four components:

- *Publish-Subscribe Notification for Web Services*—A whitepaper that defines the base concepts, roles, and so forth within the WS-Notification set of specifications.
- *WS BaseNotification*—A specification that defines the basic interfaces in WS- ...ification. These include Web service interfaces to describe the behavior of ...ducers of notification messages, consumers of notification messages, and sub ...ptions that relate producers with consumers.

...-Topics—A specification that defines *topics*, a means to categorize notifications.

...-BrokeredNotification—A specification that defines the Web service interface to ...ntermediary or message broker Web service.

...nine WS-Notification in the context of refactoring the facilities from the ...vn-specific `StockAvailableNotification portType` into the WS- ...ion-based operations added to `POPortType`.

Base Notification Concepts and Roles

The basic idea behind WS-Notification is to standardize the way that a Web service can notify interested parties (other Web services) that something of interest has happened. WS-Notification uses the term *situation*  to refer to the thing of interest that has happened. There are many types of situations (situations can be literally anything): a change of state such as the status of a `PurchaseOrder` going from pending to invoiced, a time-based event such as the expiry of a timer, or a system resource like a server going offline. Some similar notification systems use the term *event* to mean a situation; however, the term *event* is also used to describe the message documenting the situation. WS-Notification avoided using the term *event* precisely because of this double meaning.

WS-Notification doesn't define what can or can't be a situation; it simply says that situations exist, and there are entities in the system that are interested in getting a message when a situation occurs. WS-Notification distinguishes between a situation and a *notification message* . A notification message is an XML artifact that captures important details about a situation. When did the `PurchaseOrder` status go from pending to invoiced? Who initiated that transition? What reason was given for the transformation? These are the sorts of information that are usually captured about a situation and made part of the notification message that documents that the situation occurred.

A *notification producer* 📖 is a Web service that is capable of detecting that a situation has occurred and creating an XML artifact (a notification message) that captures important details of that occurrence. In the case of SkatesTown, the `PurchaseOrder` WS-Resource is the entity that can detect situations related to a `PurchaseOrder` and generate related notification messages.

Certain parties are interested in a given situation and want to receive a notification message when that situation occurs. WS-Notification calls those parties *notification consumers* 📖. The purpose of a notification consumer is to receive notification messages. In our running example, we'll make one of the Web services deployed by The Skateboard Warehouse a notification consumer.

A notification consumer is registered with a notification producer to receive notifications. When situations are detected, the notification producer is responsible for sending a notification message to the notification consumer. The basic roles and message exchanges are described in Figure 8.2.

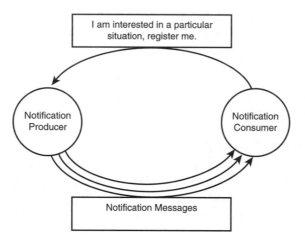

Figure 8.2 Basic notification roles

The notification producer behavior is added to the `PurchaseOrder` by copying the operations defined in WS-BaseNotification's `NotificationProducer` portType into the `POPortType` definition. Two operations are defined by the `NotificationProducer` portType: `Subscribe` and `GetCurrentMessage`. Here is what the `POPortType` looks like with these added operations:

```
<?xml version="1.0" ?>
<wsdl:definitions name="PurchaseOrder"
...
```

```
      xmlns:wsnt="http://www.ibm.com/xmlns/stdwip/web-services/WS-Notification"
...
   <!-- Port type definitions -->
   <wsdl:portType name="POPortType"
             wsrp:ResourceProperties="poRP:poResourceProperties">
      <wsdl:operation name="getInvoice"> ...
      <wsdl:operation name="cancelPO"> ...

    <!-- ========= extends wsrp:GetResourceProperty =========== -->
      <wsdl:operation name="GetResourceProperty"> ...
    <!-- ===== extends wsrp:GetMultipleResourceProperties ======= -->
      <wsdl:operation name="GetMultipleResourceProperties"> ...
    <!-- ======= extends wsrp:SetResourceProperties =========== -->
      <wsdl:operation name="SetResourceProperties"> ...
    <!-- ------- extends wsrp:QueryResourceProperties =========== -->
     <wsdl:operation name="QueryResourceProperties"> ...

    <!-- ======= extends wsnt:NotificationProducer ============= --->
    <wsdl:operation name="Subscribe"> ...
    <wsdl:operation name="GetCurrentMessage"> ...
...
   </wsdl:portType>
</wsdl:definitions>
```

We'll discuss how these two additional operations are used by requestors like The Skateboard Warehouse in the following sections. We'll also discuss the additional resource properties that are added to the PurchaseOrder resource properties document as a result of mixing notification producer behavior into the POPortType. But first, let's examine the subscribe operation in more detail.

Subscribing for Notification

When we reviewed the basic notification consumer and notification producer roles, we explained that notification consumers register their interest in receiving notifications. This is done with a *subscribe operation*. The subscribe operation is provided by any notification producer to allow other entities to register interest in receiving notifications it produces.

There is an additional subtlety that we haven't yet described. WS-Notification defines an additional role: a *subscriber* 📖. A subscriber is an entity that actually does the registration—that is, it invokes the subscribe operation. Many times, the subscriber and the notification consumer are the same entity. However, in many situations the subscriber role and the notification role are played by different entities. For example, the Web service that places a PurchaseOrder (by invoking the doSubmission operation on the POSubmission portType) might subscribe for changes in the status of the PurchaseOrder (because it has the relationship with the Purchase Order service), but it may indicate that a separate inventory management system is the notification consumer.

The most general form of the roles related to notification registration is depicted in Figure 8.3.

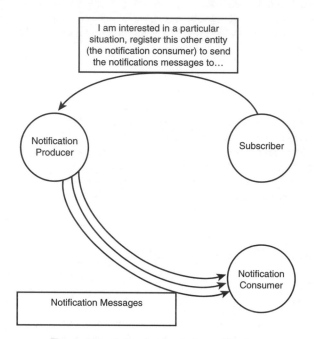

Figure 8.3 Subscriber's role in notification

Four types of information can be found within a subscribe request:

- Where is the location of the notification consumer that will receive the notification messages?
- What is the situation of interest?
- Should all the related notification messages be sent, or just a subset of them?
- Do any other constraints or policies govern the circumstances under which notification messages should be sent to the notification consumer?

Let's examine these components of a subscribe request that The Skateboard Warehouse might send to a `PurchaseOrder` WS-Resource. In this case, The Skateboard Warehouse is interested in receiving notification when the status resource property of the `PurchaseOrder` changes. Because the `POPortType` (the interface of the Web service that SkatesTown provides for customers to access `PurchaseOrder` WS-Resources) has been extended with the notification producer operations, The Skateboard Warehouse can use the endpoint reference to its `PurchaseOrder` WS-Resource to subscribe for changes on that `PurchaseOrder`. Here is an example SOAP message to subscribe one of The Skateboard Warehouse's Web services to receive notification messages:

```
<soap:Envelope
    xmlns:wsnt=
      "http://www.ibm.com/xmlns/stdwip/web-services/WS-BaseNotification"
...
  <soap:Header>
    <wsa:Action>
      http://www.ibm.com/xmlns/stdwip/web-services/WS-BaseNotification/Subscribe
    </wsa:Action>
...
      <poRP:POResourceID>43871</poRP:POResourceID>

  </soap:Header>
  <soap:Body>
    <wsnt:Subscribe>
      <wsnt:ConsumerReference>
        <wsa:Address>
          http://www.skateboardwarehouse.com/services/inventoryManagement
        </wsa:Address>
      </wsnt:ConsumerReference>
      <wsnt:TopicExpression
        dialect=
"http://www.ibm.com/xmlns/stdwip/web-services/WS-Topics/TopicExpression/simple">
        poRP:status
      </wsnt:TopicExpression>
...
    </wsnt: Subscribe>
  </soap:Body>
</soap:Envelope>
```

This example subscribe request registers a service available at http://
www.skateboardwarehouse.com/services/inventoryManagement to be a notification
consumer for notification messages produced by the Purchase Order service, related to
the PurchaseOrder WS-Resource indicated in the poRP:POResourceID SOAP header
(following the implied resource pattern).

The actual location of the notification consumer is identified by the
ConsumerReference element in the subscribe request message. This component is an
endpoint reference; it could be a WS-Resource–qualified endpoint reference or any
other kind of endpoint reference. In this case, the lack of a ReferenceProperties element indicates that it isn't a WS-Resource–qualified endpoint reference. This component
addresses the first kind of subscription information: Where is the notification consumer?

The second component, TopicPathExpression, indicates the situation of interest.
The topic expression is the heart of the subscription; it specifies which subset of all the
notification messages produced by the notification producer is of interest to the subscriber. This component can come in different dialects that can be as simple as a qualified
name (as shown in this example) or as complex as a path-based expression language that

includes subtopics, wildcards, and so on. (We'll examine the topic expression dialects a little later, in the section "Topics and Topic Spaces.")

In this particular example, the subscriber is indicating that the topic named `poPR:status` is of interest to this subscription. Any message associated with that topic should be forwarded to the notification consumer. How does a subscriber know which topics are supported by a given notification producer? The subscriber can examine the `topics` resource property of the notification producer, as we'll describe in the section "Resource Properties of a Notification Producer."

A subscription request can have components in addition to the ones we've shown in this example. These components are summarized in the following list:

- `ConsumerReference`—Identifies the notification consumer: the Web service that will receive the notification message associated with the situations of interest described by the subscription.

- `TopicExpression`—Identifies which topic or topics are of interest to the subscriber. The topic expression is associated with a dialect that describes the contents of the topic expression. The purpose of a `TopicExpression` is to describe a collection of zero or more topics. Each notification message associated with topic(s) identified by this expression will potentially be sent to the notification consumer.

- `UseNotify`—Specifies whether the "raw" notification message is sent to the notification consumer, or whether the message is wrapped in such a way as to invoke the `Notify` operation of the notification consumer. If this component is absent, the notification producer will invoke the `Notify` operation on the notification consumer.

- `Precondition`—An expression that is evaluated *against the notification producer*. This condition must be true before notification messages on this subscription are sent to the notification consumer. One example use of this component is to specify a Boolean XPath expression to be evaluated against the resource properties of the notification producer. This is one way of subsetting the notification messages to be sent to the notification consumer.

- `Selector`—An expression that is evaluated *against each notification message associated with the subscription*. This expression acts like a filter; when the expression is evaluated against a notification message and the evaluation results in a Boolean false, then that notification message isn't sent to the notification consumer.

- `SubscriptionPolicy`—A policy statement, such as a WS-Policy element, that allows the subscriber to associate policies to govern the subscription. This element could be used to specify that notification messages should be batched (in groups of five messages for example) and sent in bulk. Other sorts of policy assertions could include a message rate (no more than five messages per second, for example). There is work to be done by the WS-Notification policy team to specify a notification discipline–specific policy grammar.

- `InitialTerminationTime`—An initial request for how long the subscription should last. This component requests the initial setting of the `TerminationTime` resource property defined in the WS-ResourceLifetime specification (see the section "Resource Lifetime").

If the subscribe request is accepted by the notification consumer, a subscription is set up that associates the notification producer and the notification consumer under the conditions specified by the components of the subscribe request. To record this association, a new WS-Resource is created: a `Subscription` WS-Resource. A WS-Resource–qualified endpoint reference to the subscription resource is returned to the subscriber in response to the subscribe request. Therefore, you can regard the subscribe request as a WS-Resource factory.

As you'll see when we examine the `Subscription` WS-Resource in more detail in the next section, the `Subscription` WS-Resource allows the subscriber to manage the subscription, including making modifications to the components of the subscription and maintaining the lifetime of the subscription.

The `Subscription` **WS-Resource**

WS-Notification models a subscription as a WS-Resource. The subscription is a stateful resource that is created by a subscribe request and that uses operations defined by WS-ResourceLifetime (see the section "Resource Lifetime") to manage the lifetime of the subscription.

The `Subscription` WS-Resource is associated with a Web service implementing the `SubscriptionManager` `portType`. This `portType` defines a collection of resource properties corresponding to the components in the subscribe request, allowing the requestor to use WS-ResourceProperties operations to read and write the values of subscription-related resource properties. This `portType` also defines a `creationTime` resource property that records when the subscription was created.

The `SubscriptionManager` also supports operations defined by WS-ResourceLifetime, to give requestors the ability to terminate the resource. So, for example, if The Skateboard Warehouse was no longer interested in notifications associated with their `PurchaseOrder` WS-Resource, they could send a destroy operation to the `SubscriptionManager` (remembering to use the implied resource pattern to identify the subscription WS-Resource). Of course, the requestor may also use the time-based or scheduled termination mechanism specified by WS-ResourceLifetime to manage the lifetime of the subscription resource.

The complete collection of resource properties defined by a `Subscription` WS-Resource is as follows:

- `ConsumerReference`—The EPR to the consumer that receives notification messages associated with this subscription.

- `TopicExpression`—The expression that indicates the set of topics associated with this subscription.

- `UseNotify`—Determines if the notification message is sent with additional meta-data.

- `Precondition`—The precondition associated with the subscription.

- `Selector`—The selector or filter associated with the subscription.

- `SubscriptionPolicy`—The policies associated with the subscription.

- `CreationTime`—The time the subscription was created.

- `CurrentTime`, `TerminationTime`—Defined by WS-ResourceLifetime. These resource properties describe the lifetime of a subscription.

Note that most of the values of these resource properties are derived from the subscribe request message. A requestor would use operations defined by WS-ResourceProperties (included as part of the `SubscriptionManager` portType) to read and write the values of these resource properties.

The `SubscriptionManager` portType also defines a `pauseSubscription` operation and a `resumeSubscription` operation. These operations work to stop and restart the process of sending notification messages to the notification consumer based on this subscription. If a requestor wishes to temporarily halt the sending of notification messages based on this subscription, it sends a `pauseSubscription` request message to the `SubscriptionManager` Web service associated with the subscription. To resume sending messages, the requestor sends a `resumeSubscription` request.

Topics and Topic Spaces

As we mentioned earlier, a notification producer organizes the situations and associated notification messages into a collection of *topics* 📖. Subscribers use a topic expression to indicate which topic or set of topics they're interested in subscribing to. Because topics are central to the way situations and notification messages are associated, the WS-Topics specification of WS-Notification defines an XML model for topics.

Topics

A *topic* is a category of notification message; it's an organizational structure superimposed on all the notification messages produced by a notification producer. This organization allows the notification producer to declare the kinds of situations for which it produces notification messages, and therefore allows the requestor to understand what it can subscribe for. So, you can think of a topic as a channel associated with a particular kind of notification message. Subscribers can tune into this channel by subscribing to that topic. When a notification message is published on the topic, any notification consumer subscribed to that topic will receive a copy of that notification message.

Topics are organized hierarchically, forming a *topic tree*. A topic tree organizes a family of related topics and child topics. Each topic tree has a *root topic*.

Consider the following example from a customer-relationship management (CRM) system using WS-Notification. The system is responsible for detecting various customer contact situations (customer calls to complain or make an inquiry, customer is contacted by a sales person, customer uses a Web service to place an order, and so on). Various other applications are interested in receiving notifications when certain situations occur, such as a VIP customer calling with a complaint. Topics are used to organize these situations into recognizable categories, making the job of subscribing for particular situations easier.

As part of our CRM topics, we can model a `telephoneContact` topic that is the root topic for all topics related to telephone contacts. There might be several subcategories of telephone contact that we can model as child topics, including `inquiry`, `complaint`, and `orderPlacement`. These subtopics are organized as child topics of the `telephoneContact` root topic as depicted in Figure 8.4.

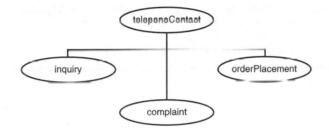

Figure 8.4 An example topic tree

The hierarchical relationship among the topics is represented by the following XML:

```
<wstop:Topic name="telephoneContact">
   <wstop:Topic name="inquiry" .../>
   <wstop:Topic name="complaint" ... />
   <wstop:Topic name="orderPlacement" ... />
</wstop:Topic>
```

The topic named `telephoneContact` has three child topics, each represented by a child topic element. Any of these child topics can have child topics, and so on. The only restriction is that child topic elements must have different names. The names don't have to be unique within the topic tree—they just have to be unique among sibling topics (topics that share the same parent topic). Typically, you don't see more than three or four levels of nesting; many topic trees are made up of the root topic and nothing more.

The XML model for topics is more than just the hierarchical relationship between topics—each topic can be described with additional information. This additional information allows the user of the topic XML to understand more about the topic. The XML model for topics is used by notification designers to communicate a set of topics and the meta-data associated with them. Designers of applications that are WS-Notification subscribers or consumers use the XML model of topics to help determine what are reasonable topic expressions to include in subscribe operations.

The following XML is a more richly detailed topic description for our CRM application:

```
<wstop:topic name="telephoneContact">
   <wstop:topic name="inquiry"
               messageTypes="crm:inquiryNotification"/>
   <wstop:topic name="complaint"
               messageTypes="crm:complaintNotification" final="false">
      <wstop:documentation>
         Note: all complaints, including VIP customer complaints appear
         on this topic.
      </wstop:documentation>
      <wstop:topic name="VIPComplaint"
               messageTypes="crm:complaintNotification" final="false">
      <wsrp:QueryExpression
         dialect="http://www.w3.org/TR/1999/REC-xpath-19991116" >
            boolean(/*/customer/@customerStatus="vip")
      </wsrp:QueryExpression>
      <tns:VIPHotline>555-1212</tns:VIPHotline>
      </wstop:topic>
   </wstop:topic>

   <wstop:topic name="orderPlacement">
      <wstop:AliasRef dialect=
"http://www.ibm.com/xmlns/stdwip/web-services/WS-Topics/TopicExpression/
↪concreteTopicPath" >
            crm:orderContact
      </wstop:AliasRef>
   </wstop:topic>
...
```

The topics modeled here show most of the facilities available in the WS-Topics XML
model of topics. The topic named complaint has two attributes, messageTypes and
final. The messageTypes attribute describes the kind of message that is associated with
this topic. The value of this attribute can be a list of QNames, each corresponding to a
global XML element declaration. The purpose of this attribute is to scope the contents
of notification messages associated with the topic. Each message associated with this
topic must be an element corresponding to a global XML element identified by one of
those QNames. This example includes only one QName, indicating that all notification
messages associated with the complaint topic are crm:complaintNotification messages. Designers that have access to the XML Schema declaration for the namespace
identified by the crm prefix will understand the contents of messages on the complaint
topic. (It's okay that the topic space and the XSD share the same namespace; it's common for a WSDL definition and an XSD definition to share the same namespace.) The
messageTypes information is extremely helpful to design the proper selector expressions
to filter messages on a subscribe request. The final attribute indicates whether it's possible to add topic children to the topic that aren't already defined by the topic XML
model. In this case, the value of final is false, meaning that it's possible to add child topics dynamically to the complaint topic.

The topic model allows topics to contain documentation elements. This allows designers of topics to describe, using human languages like English, extra information to be interpreted by other developers. You see this used in the `complaint` topic to give extra details about the relationship between the `complaint` topic and its child topic named `VIPComplaint`.

The child topic `VIPComplaint` demonstrates two additional features of the XML model of topics in WS-Notification: open content and message patterns. The `messageTypes` attribute and the `final` attribute are repeated. There is no model of attribute inheritance from parent topic to child topic in this model. If the `messageTypes` attribute doesn't appear in the `VIPComplaint` topic, then the value `xsd:any` is assumed (the developer should expect that any kind of XML notification message may appear on that topic). Similarly, if the `final` attribute is missing, the default value is false.

The `QueryExpression` child element is used to describe a message pattern or further constraints on the type of message associated with the topic. Although the `messageTypes` attribute helps define constraints on the message, sometimes it's too coarse grained. In many circumstances, a pattern on the content (not just the type) of message should be further described. In the example of `VIPComplaint`, the designer can be more precise in describing the messages associated with the topic. In this case, the message is a `crm:complaintNotification` message but further constrained to guarantee to the subscriber that the value of the `customerStatus` attribute of the `customer` element of the `crm:complaintNotification` message contains the value `vip`. The message pattern is expressed by a `QueryExpression` from the WS-ResourceProperties specification described earlier.

The XML model for topics also allows the `topic` element to contain attributes from other XML namespaces and elements defined in other namespaces. This is typical open content that you see used in many places in Web services (WSDL, for example). The `VIPComplaint` topic uses this to associate a `VIPHotline` piece of information with this topic. The meaning of this element is dependent on the application for which the topic is defined.

Topic Spaces

We mentioned that topics are organized into topic trees, each topic tree having a root topic and many topic trees having a rich hierarchy of child topics. Topic trees are also organized into *topic spaces* 📖. A topic space works in a way similar to namespaces in XML Schema. A topic space associates topic trees with a namespace; that way, each topic tree can be uniquely identified by the QName of the root of the topic tree.

A topic space document for the CRM example we've been describing appears as follows:

```
<?xml version="1.0" encoding="UTF-8"?>
<wstop:TopicSpace name="CRMTopicSpace"
    targetNamespace="http://.../CRMexample"
    xmlns:crm="http://.../CRMexample"
    xmlns:tns="http://.../AnotherNamespace"
```

```
xmlns:wstop=
    "http://www.ibm.com/xmlns/stdwip/web-services/WS-Topics"
xmlns:wsrp=
    "http://www.ibm.com/xmlns/stdwip/web-services/WS-ResourceProperties" >

<wstop:documentation>
  This is an example TopicSpace definition for a CRM
  (customer relationship management) application.
</wstop:documentation>

<wstop:Topic name="telephoneContact">
  <wstop:Topic name="inquiry" .../>
  <wstop:Topic name="complaint" ... />
  <wstop:Topic name="orderPlacement" ... />
</wstop:Topic>

<wstop:Topic name="emailContact">
...

<wstop:Topic name="orderContact">
...


</wstop:TopicSpace>
```

In this case, the topic space is named CRMTopicSpace and is associated with the namespace http://.../CRMexample. This is much like an XSD file associating a collection of XML Schema element and type definitions with a target namespace or a WSDL document associating WSDL definitions with a target namespace. Don't worry about the name of the topic space; that's just documentation. The important part is the target namespace. All the topics defined in this document will be associated with the namespace identified by the target namespace attribute.

This topic space document defines three topic trees, rooted by telephoneContact, emailContact, and orderContact. Root topics appear as child elements of the topic space element. And just like child topics, each root topic must have a unique name within the namespace. Because root topic names are unique within a topic space, root topics can be identified uniquely by QName. So, the QName crm:telephoneContact uniquely identifies the telephoneContact root topic within the namespace corresponding to the crm prefix. Similarly, crm:emailContact and crm:orderContact can be used to reference the other topic trees in this topic space. All topics are identified relative to their root topic, using hierarchical path syntax. The VIPComplaint topic is identified by the following path: crm:telephoneContact/complaint/VIPComplaint.

Topic spaces can also have documentation elements, and they can contain attributes and elements from other namespaces.

The final topic space document for the CRM example appears as follows:

```xml
<?xml version="1.0" encoding="UTF-8"?>
<wstop:TopicSpace name="CRMTopicSpace"
   targetNamespace="http://.../CRMexample"
   xmlns:crm="http://.../CRMexample"
   xmlns:tns="http://.../AnotherNamespace"
   xmlns:wsnt=
      "http://www.ibm.com/xmlns/stdwip/web-services/WS-BaseNotification"
   xmlns:wsrp=
      "http://www.ibm.com/xmlns/stdwip/web-services/WS-ResourceProperties" >
   <wstop:documentation>
     This is an example TopicSpace definition for a CRM
     (customer relationship management) application.
   </wstop:documentation>

   <wstop:Topic name="telephoneContact">
      <wstop:Topic name="inquiry"
               messageTypes="crm:inquiryNotification"/>
      <wstop.Topic name="complaint"
               messageTypes="crm:complaintNotification" final="false">
        <wstop:documentation>
           Note: all complaints, including VIP customer complaints appear
           on this topic.
        </wstop:documentation>
        <wstop:Topic name="VIPComplaint"
               messageTypes="crm:complaintNotification" final="false">
          <wsrp:QueryExpression
            dialect="http://www.w3.org/TR/1999/REC-xpath-19991116" >
              boolean(/*/customer/@customerStatus="vip")
          </wsrp:QueryExpression>
          <tns:VIPHotline>555-1212</tns:VIPHotline>
        </wstop:Topic>
      </wstop:Topic>

      <wotop:Topic name="orderPlacement" aliasRef="crm:orderContact" />
   </wstop:Topic>

   <wstop:Topic name="emailContact" messageTypes="crm:emailContact" />

    <wstop:Topic name="orderPlacement">
       <wstop:AliasRef dialect=
"http://www.ibm.com/xmlns/stdwip/web-services/WS-Topics/TopicExpression/
➥concreteTopicPath" >
          crm:orderContact
       </wstop:AliasRef>
    </wstop:Topic>
</wstop:TopicSpace>
```

Who creates a topic space definition? Normally, whatever authority owns or defines the target namespace. This is similar to the question of who defines an XML Schema definition (XSD) for a namespace. Sometimes it's a standards organization or an industry association; sometimes it's an organization that wants to put a stake in the ground and establish some sort of interoperability.

But the question still remains, where does the requestor find this topic space document? WS-Notification doesn't specify how this is done. Sometimes the document is published on the Web site of the organization controlling the namespace. Sometimes the topic space document is available in an XML registry or repository. Sometimes the topic space is available as a result of a Web service request, such as a variant on the WS-MetadataExchange operation, or perhaps made available as a resource property of a notification producer.

WS-Notification also defines an ad hoc topic space to allow dynamic, on-the-fly topics to be described without modeling them explicitly in a topic space (and therefore assigning them to a particular namespace). The ad-hoc topic space is a well-defined namespace with the following URI: `http://www.ibm.com/xmlns/stdwip/web-services/WS-Notification/adHoc`. You should use this topic space with caution because there is no way for the subscriber to know beforehand about it or about topics defined within it. It should be used only for dynamic topics where there is additional out-of-bands communication of topic meta-data between the notification producer and subscribers.

TopicPathExpressions

To this point, we've only mentioned topic expressions in passing. Topic expressions appear in subscribe requests and several other places in WS-Notification. They can contain a wide variety of expression types, from simple, QName-based topic names to path expressions (like hierarchical file paths in a computer's filesystem) to rich wildcard-enabled expression languages. The type of expression is determined by the dialect attribute of a topic expression. The `dialect` attribute contains a URI that identifies the language used by the topic expression. WS-Topics defines several dialects, and their standard URIs are specified in that document.

The simplest topic expression dialect, identified by the URI `http://www.ibm.com/xmlns/stdwip/web-services/WS-Topics/TopicExpression/simple`, can contain only QNames of root topics. This language is quite limited in that it can only identify root topics. However, in many circumstances, simple (nonhierarchical) topic spaces are sufficient. Here is an example simple topic expression that identifies the `orderPlacement` topic:

```
<wsnt:TopicExpression dialect=
"http://www.ibm.com/xmlns/stdwip/web-services/WS-Topics/TopicExpression/
➥simple">
        crm:orderPlacement
</wsnt:TopicExpression>
```

The second topic expression dialect defined by WS-Topics is a straightforward path language that's similar to file paths in hierarchical directory structures. This path-based dialect is identified by the URI http://www.ibm.com/xmlns/stdwip/web-services/WS-Topics/TopicExpression/concreteTopicPath. This is a so-called *concrete* topic expression dialect because expressions in this dialect identify exactly one topic. This is more powerful than the simple dialect, in that child topics can be identified. In this dialect, topic expressions are combinations of topic names and topic paths (topic names separated by slashes, /, to denote hierarchical parent topic/child topic structures). Note that this dialect builds on the simple dialect: The concrete topic expression dialect also allows the QName expressions found in the simple dialect.

Here's an example concrete topic expression, identifying the VIPComplaint child topic of the complaint topic.

```
<wsnt:TopicExpression dialect=
"http://www.ibm.com/xmlns/stdwip/web-services/WS-Topics/TopicExpression/
➥concreteTopicPath">
        crm: telephoneContact/complaint/VIPComplaint
</wsnt:TopicExpression>
```

A third topic expression dialect defined by WS-Topics is the full topic expression dialect. The full topic expression dialect builds on the concrete topic dialect by adding wildcard (*) characters and including a conjunction (|) to allow you to express the logical *or* of two topic expressions. With a topic expression using this full dialect, you can specify one or more topics in a single expression:

- Topic expressions containing a wildcard (*) may identify any number of topics. The wildcard can appear anywhere in the topic expression, either at the beginning of the topic expression, matching any root topic; or part way through a topic expression, matching any child topic at a particular level in the hierarchy.

- A topic expression consisting just of the * character matches any topic. If this were the parameter of a subscribe request, it would suggest that the subscriber was interested in all topics supported by that notification producer.

- A topic expression containing a wildcard after a / symbol indicates a match for all the topics at a particular level in the topic tree. For example, the topic expression crm:telephoneContact/* matches all the child topics of crm:telephoneContact. The expression crm:telephoneContact/* doesn't match the crm:telephoneContact topic itself. To match an entire subtree of topics rooted at a particular node, you use the //. construct. So the topic expression crm:telephoneContact//. matches all the topics in the entire topic tree rooted at crm:telephoneContact.

- The | character evaluates to the set union of the topics from both expressions. This allows a subscriber to use one subscription to receive notifications from a combination of different topics. For example, if the subscriber wanted to subscribe to receive notifications on the crm:telephoneContact and the crm:emailContact topics, they would use the following topic expression: crm:telephoneContact | crm:emailContact.

> `TopicExpressions` **and XPath**
>
> Although the authors of WS-Topics could have chosen XPath as the language to describe topic paths, it turned out that doing so wasn't straightforward. Early design attempts to make the topic expression language simple XPath (or a subset thereof) turned out to require that the topic space XML document look extremely awkward. So, the designers faced a choice: either specify an XPath subset as the topic expression language and have a very awkward-looking topic space document, or choose to have a straightforward-looking topic model in XML and develop a simple, path-based expression language. On balance, the designers chose the lesser of two evils.

Rounding Out the XML Model of Topics: `aliasRef`

There is one other topic component we haven't covered: `AliasRef`. WS-Notification provides a mechanism that allows one topic to *alias* or point to another topic, perhaps another topic in the same topic tree, a topic in a different topic tree, or a topic in a different topic space. The purpose of an `aliasRef` topic is to help organize topics when the domain isn't strictly hierarchical. You can see this in the CRM example. The `orderPlacement` subtopic of `telephoneContact` is an alias for another topic:

```
<wsnt:Topic name="telephoneContact">
    <wsnt:Topic name="inquiry" ...
    <wsnt:Topic name="complaint" ...
    <wstop:Topic name="orderPlacement">
      <wstop:AliasRef dialect=
"http://www.ibm.com/xmlns/stdwip/web-services/WS-Topics/TopicExpression/
➥concreteTopicPath" >
        crm:orderContact
      </wstop:AliasRef>
    </wstop:Topic>
  </wsnt:Topic>
```

The value of an `AliasRef` child element is a topic expression that can resolve to potentially multiple topics (of course, depending on the dialect). When a subscriber subscribes to a topic that is an `aliasRef`, it's the same as if the subscriber subscribed to all the topics the `aliasRef` topic expression resolves to. In this case, subscribing to the `crm:telephoneContact/orderPlacement` topic is the same as subscribing to the `crm:orderContact` topic. But why bother with the `aliasRef`? One reason comes into play when you consider wildcard topic expressions. Consider the topic expression `crm:telephone/*`: because of the `aliasRef`, this expression will pick up notification messages posted to the `crm:orderContact` topic as well, because the `orderPlacement` topic `aliasRef`'s that topic.

Resource Properties of a Notification Producer

WS-Notification requires that notification producers must include two resource properties within the XML schema definition of its resource properties document: `wsnt:Topic` and `wsnt:FixedTopicSet`.

The wsnt:Topic resource property is a sequence of topic expressions describing one or more topics supported by the notification producer. There can be many topic expressions within any individual wsnt:Topic resource properties element. If a topic is identified by a topic expression in the wsnt:Topic resource property, a subscriber has a reasonable level of assurance that a subscribe request on that given topic is likely to be successful. This isn't a guarantee that a notification consumer will receive a notification message on that topic—for example, a situation may never arise that causes a notification message to be associated with the topic.

In our example of the POPortType, the resource properties document includes the following resource property element.

```
<wsnt:Topic>poRP:status</wsnt:Topic>
...
```

This indicates that the PurchaseOrder Web service supports (among potentially many other topics) the topic corresponding to value changes in the poRP:status resource property.

The other resource property required on notification producers is wsnt:FixedTopicSet. This resource property is a Boolean and indicates whether the topic set is fixed (that is, whether it's possible that the list of topics within the wsnt:Topics resource property element can change). Certain notification producers are flexible and change the set of topics they support over time (for example, based on the changing needs of its notification consumers). In these cases, FixedTopicSet would be set to false.

Notification producers also include a resource property called TopicExpressionDialects, which contains the URIs of the topic expression dialects they can understand.

The Other Notification Producer Operation:
GetCurrentMessage

The subscribe operation is by far the most important operation provided by a notification producer. Several other operations are also specified as part of a notification producer's portType.

GetCurrentMessage allows a requestor to pull notification messages from one of the topics provided by the notification producer. The requestor specifies a topic as a parameter of the GetCurrentMessage request message and, in response, the notification producer returns the last notification message (if any) that was associated with that topic. This operation might be used in combination with a subscribe message. For example, right after subscribing for changes to the poRP:status topic, The Skateboard Warehouse can immediately issue a GetCurrentMessage on that topic, capturing the current message associated with the poRP:status topic. The Skateboard Warehouse can use a GetCurrentMessage operation on any topic supported by our PurchaseOrder WS-Resource, even topics they aren't subscribed to.

Notification of Value Changes on Resource Properties

One aspect of WS-ResourceProperties that we haven't thoroughly examined yet is subscribing for value changes on a resource property. WS-ResourceProperties defines a convention on WS-Notification topics to standardize the way subscribers can subscribe to changes in a resource property. Essentially, WS-ResourceProperties declares a convention that for each resource property, a topic is defined to correspond to the QName of that resource property. This topic is associated with notification messages that depict value changes of that resource property.

For example, for the resource property named poRP:status, there exists a corresponding root topic named status in a topic space whose target namespace is the same as the namespace identified by the poRP prefix. In this way, it's simple to describe a topic expression for the topic containing notification messages for the situation where the value of a given resource property changes. That topic expression is the QName of the resource property.

If The Skateboard Warehouse is interested in subscribing to changes in the status of its PurchaseOrder, the subscription request contains the QName of the poRP:status resource property, as in the following portion of a subscribe request:

```
<wsnt:Subscribe>
  <wsnt:ConsumerReference>
    <wsa:Address>
        http://www.skateswarehouse.com/services/inventoryManagement
    </wsa:Address>
  </wsnt:ConsumerReference>
  <wsnt:TopicExpression dialect=
"http://www.ibm.com/xmlns/stdwip/web-services/WS-Topics/TopicExpression/
⇒simple">
      poRP:status
  </wsnt:TopicPathExpression>
...
  </wsnt: Subscribe>
```

This is exactly the subscribe request we saw earlier in the chapter. For this subscribe request to work, the following things must hold:

- The Web service component of the WS-Resource must support the operations from the NotificationProducer portType. If the Web service doesn't include the operations from NotificationProducer, it's impossible to subscribe to anything associated with that Web service, including value changes on any WS-Resource it's associated with.

- The Web service component of the WS-Resource must include the poRP:status topic as a value within its Topic resource property. Recall from the section "Resource Properties of a Notification Producer" that all Web services that include the NotificationProducer operations must include this element in their resource properties document definition. If the Web service doesn't include a topic corresponding to a resource property in its `Topic` resource property, then it doesn't support value changes on that resource property. This situation may arise when the resource property changes too frequently or it's too expensive to detect the resource property change situation.

Even if the these conditions hold, and a subscriber successfully subscribes for value changes on a particular resource property, there is no guarantee that the notification consumer will receive a notification message tracking each and every value change of the resource property. This could happen because the resource property changes too frequently, or changes occur that the Web service is unable to detect.

All topics associated with a resource property value change situation contain the same pattern: the notification message must contain an element called `ResourcePropertyValueChangeNotification` defined by the WS-ResourceProperties specification. This element contains two parts: an optional `oldValue` element (the value of the resource property before the change situation occurred) and a mandatory `newValue` element (the value of the resource property after the change situation was detected).

Because the notification message of a resource property value change notification is well defined, subscribers can be sophisticated in using the selector component of the subscribe request. For example, if The Skateboard Warehouse wants to subscribe to receive notification when the status of its `PurchaseOrder` transitions from `received` to `posted`, it can issue a subscription expression targeting the `poRP:status` resource property value change notification topic with an XPath selector expression to narrow the particular notification message of interest:

```
<wsnt:Subscribe>
  <wsnt:ConsumerReference>
    <wsa:Address>
       http://www.skateswarehouse.com/services/inventoryManagement
    </wsa:Address>
  </wsnt:ConsumerReference>
  <wsnt:TopicExpression dialect=
"http://www.ibm.com/xmlns/stdwip/web-services/WS-Topics/TopicExpression/
➥simple">
      poRP:status
  </wsnt:TopicExpression>
  <wsnt:Selector
        dialect="http://www.w3.org/TR/1999/REC-xpath-19991116">
        boolean(/*/wsrp:OldValue/poRP:status/="received" and
                 /*/wsrp:NewValue/poRP:status="posted")
  </wsnt:Selector>
</wsnt: Subscribe>
```

This subscription will deliver a notification message to the notification consumer only if the notification message on the topic caused the selector expression to evaluate to true.

In this case, it would be a message that looks like

```
<wsrp:ResourcePropertyValueChangeNotification
  xmlns:wsrp=
  "http://www.ibm.com/xmlns/stdwip/web-services/WS-ResourceProperties"
  xmlns:poRP="http://www.skatestown.com/ns/poResourceProperties">
  <wsrp:OldValue>
    <poRP:status>received</poRP:status>
  </wsrp:OldValue>
  <wsrp:NewValue>
    <poRP:status>posted</poRP:status>
  </wsrp:NewValue>
</wsrp:ResourcePropertyValueChangeNotification>
```

Notification Consumers

We haven't said much about notification consumers. Essentially, a notification consumer is any Web service. WS-BaseNotification defines an optional operation called `Notify` that consumers may choose to implement. If a consumer chooses to implement a `Notify` operation, then there is a simple, clearly defined operation that notification producers can invoke in order to deliver a notification message. However, WS-Notification allows the message to be delivered directly to the notification producer, without wrapping the notification message in additional XML to make it conform to a well-known operation signature.

The format of a `Notify` message is

```
<wsnt:Notify>
   <wsnt:NotificationMessage>
      <wsnt:Topic dialect="xsd:anyURI">
         {any}
      </wsnt:Topic>
      <wsnt:ProducerReference>?
         wsa:EndpointReference
      </wsnt:ProducerReference>
      <wsnt:Message>xsd:any</wsnt:Message>
   <wsnt:NotificationMessage>+
</wsnt:Notify>
```

A `Notify` message can contain multiple individual notification message payloads. This grouping of messages allows a notification producer to deliver multiple notifications in a single Web service message exchange. Each notification message includes the topic associated with the message (the part of the subscription that causes the notification to be delivered to the notification consumer), an optional endpoint reference to the Web service that created the notification, and, of course, the message payload itself.

`Notify` is a one-way message. No response or fault message is expected back from the notification consumer.

Notification Brokers

In addition to the point-to-point model of pub/sub described by the notification producer role, the WS-BrokeredNotification specification adds an additional role called a *notification broker* 📖. The notification broker acts as an intermediary between entities that detect situations and produce notification messages (a *publisher* 📖) and the subscribers and notification consumers. These roles are depicted in Figure 8.5.

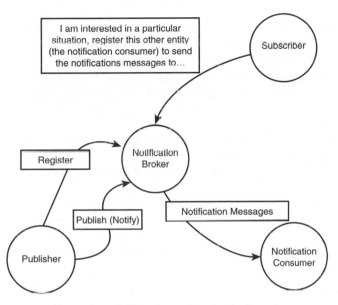

Figure 8.5 Adding the notification broker role

The notification broker relieves the publisher of the burden of creating and maintaining subscriptions, notifying notification consumers based on their subscriptions, and so on. The notification broker also provides the ability to keep publishers and consumers anonymous, in cases where it's important that the publisher isn't known to the consumer, or where the consumer doesn't care which publisher produces the notification message. The notification broker also has the potential of a value-added intermediary logging the notification messages for auditing purposes, for example, or using sophisticated message-oriented middleware to perform the pub/sub operations efficiently.

WS-BrokeredNotification defines a notification broker as an extension of a notification producer. So, a notification broker is everything a notification producer is—a Web service that accepts subscribe requests, provides a list of topics through a wsnt:Topics resource properties element, and so forth.

In addition to the base notification producer operations, the notification broker also supports a RegisterPublisher operation (to allow publishers to register prior to publishing notifications on particular topics). Not all brokers require preregistration of publishers. The publisher can tell whether it needs to preregister by examining the `RequiresRegistration` resource property of the notification broker. If this resource property is true, publishers are required to preregister before they attempt to publish. `RegisterPublisher` is similar to the subscribe request, in that it's a factory for a particular kind of WS-Resource, a `PublisherRegistration`. A `PublisherRegistration` WS-Resource maintains information about the publisher's registration, including duration (using WS-ResourceLifetime, of course) and the list of topics the publisher is permitted to publish on.

The notification broker also implements the `Notify` operation. Publishers send a notify message to the notification broker in order to publish a notification message on one or more topics. Because the publish function is implemented by sending the notify message, a notification broker looks like any other notification consumer to the publisher. This allows notification brokers to be inserted into the message flow (for auditing purposes, for example) without the publisher needing to change the way it sends its notification messages.

WS-Notification and WS-Eventing

WS-Notification isn't the only notification- or eventing-style Web service standard to be proposed. In January 2004, Microsoft, together with BEA and Tibco, proposed a specification called WS-Eventing. WS-Eventing is similar to WS-Notification in that it describes a mechanism for entities to subscribe to receive messages (events) asynchronously. However, WS-Eventing doesn't have the topic notion for categorization of situations and notification messages. WS-Eventing also doesn't have the notion of a notification broker, allowing scalability and better affinity with existing message-oriented middleware.

However, the Web services community doesn't benefit from having two notification standards. The community expects that the companies involved will work together to reconcile WS-Notification with WS-Eventing in some fashion.

Resource Lifetime

We discussed previously how resources are created: Some sort of operation (like the `doSubmission` operation) on a Web service creates a new WS-Resource and returns a WS-Resource–qualified endpoint reference to the requestor. We call this sort of operation a WS-Resource factory. However, we haven't discussed the other aspect of a resource's lifetime: its termination.

WS-ResourceLifetime is a part of the WS-Resource Framework family of specifications that standardizes how WS-Resources are terminated. There are two mechanisms for terminating a resource: immediate and scheduled termination. Designers are free to use either or both of these mechanisms to specify how their resources can be destroyed. You encode this decision into the `portType` definition of the Web service responsible for the WS-Resource in a style similar to how WS-ResourceProperties operations were mixed into the operation: by copying the WSDL operation definitions.

SkatesTown decided to allow both forms of resource termination, immediate and scheduled, to act on `PurchaseOrder` WS-Resources. In certain cases, customers want to be able to explicitly and immediately destroy a `PurchaseOrder` resource. In other cases, customers place an order and then occasionally renew interest in the `PurchaseOrder` resource; or, if business needs change, they abandon the `PurchaseOrder` and have it automatically terminate after a period of inactivity. In fact, as you'll see toward the end of this section, SkatesTown also implemented the part of WS-ResourceLifetime that allows its customers to subscribe for notification messages when their `PurchaseOrder` WS-Resources are destroyed.

Immediate Termination

Immediate termination of a WS-Resource is straightforward. If the Web service associated with the WS-Resource supports the immediate termination form of resource termination, then the requestor can terminate the resource at any time by sending a destroy request message to the Web service. Of course, the exact resource to destroy is identified using the implied resource pattern. After the destroy request is received, the Web service must destroy the WS-Resource and respond with a normal destroy response or a fault message if it can't be destroyed.

If a normal response is received, the requestor knows the WS-Resource has been destroyed; the WS-Resource can no longer be used as context for another Web service message. The implementation is free to reclaim whatever system resources were used to support the WS-Resource. This is a synchronous style of termination, and it should be used only if WS-Resource destruction can be accomplished and assured relatively quickly. If it's complicated or time-consuming to destroy a WS-Resource, you should use the scheduled termination mechanism instead (see the next section).

In order for a Web service to support immediate termination, you must copy and paste the WSDL operation definition for the destroy operation from the `portType` defined in the `WS-ResourceLifetime` specification. The `POPortType` supports immediate termination of `PurchaseOrder` resources. Here is the part of the `POPortType` WSDL that defines this operation:

```
. . .
  xmlns:wsrl=
 "http://www.ibm.com/xmlns/stdwip/web-services/WS-ResourceLifetime"
. . .
    <!-- ==== extends wsrl:ImmediateResourceTermination ========= -->
    <wsdl:operation name="Destroy">
      <wsdl:input message="wsrl:DestroyRequest" />
      <wsdl:output message="wsrl:DestroyResponse" />
      <wsdl:fault name="ResourceUnknownFault"
                  message="wsrl:ResourceUnknownFault" />
      <wsdl:fault name="ResourceNotDestroyedFault"
                  message="wsrl:ResourceNotDestroyedFault" />
    </wsdl:operation>
```

The `wsrl:` prefix is a conventional prefix to denote the WS-ResourceLifetime namespace.

That's all there is to it. Without this form of standardization, the way to terminate resources would vary between applications. Some Web services would call the operation `destroy`; others might call the operation `terminate`, `kill`, or `exit`. Providing standardization removes this impediment to interoperability.

Scheduled Termination

An alternate form of WS-Resource termination is called *scheduled termination*. This is a time-based mechanism to manage the lifetime of a WS-Resource. In a scheduled or time-based approach to resource termination, the WS-Resource is created with an initial *termination time*—a time in the future that marks when the WS-Resource will be terminated. Entities in the system, like user applications, that want to keep working with the WS-Resource will periodically attempt to reset the termination time to extend the lifetime of the WS-Resource. If the termination time elapses, because no other entity was interested in (or capable of) extending the lifetime of the WS-Resource, the WS-Resource is destroyed.

Scheduled termination is a little more complicated than immediate termination. In order for a WS-Resource's lifetime to be managed in this time-based way, its Web service must implement two resource property elements (`CurrentTime` and `TerminationTime`)and one operation (`SetTerminationTime`).

The `wsrl:CurrentTime` resource property element allows requestors to query (using WS-ResourceProperties operations like `GetResourceProperty`) the current time according to the Web service managing a particular WS-Resource. This resource property helps requestors understand how much time remains before a WS-Resource is scheduled to be terminated. Note that the `wsrl:CurrentTime` resource property is read-only; it can't be set by the WS-ResourceProperties' `SetResourceProperties` operation.

Times in WS-ResourceLifetime follow the `dateTime` type defined by XML Schema. XML Schema provides an optional component of the `dateTime` type to specify time zone. In WS-ResourceLifetime, the absence of this time zone component means that the time is to be interpreted in universal time (UTC) format.

The `wsrl:TerminationTime` resource property element allows the requestor to query when the WS-Resource is scheduled to be destroyed. This is the resource property that is updated when requestors attempt to reset the termination time of the WS-Resource. When the termination time has expired, the WS-Resource may be destroyed by its hosting environment. The timing and nature of this destruction are implementation dependent; however, the requestor shouldn't count on the WS-Resource being available after its termination time has elapsed.

Some resources have a value of `xsi:nil` for their termination time. This value indicates that the WS-Resource has indefinite lifetime; it won't be destroyed using a time-based mechanism. When a WS-Resource is set to an indefinite lifetime, it can be destroyed only using the immediate termination operation.

The `wsrl:TerminationTime` resource property element is also read-only, like `wsrl:CurrentTime`. In order to reset the termination time of a WS-Resource, a requestor needs to use the `SetTerminationTime` operation. Although the designers of WS-ResourceLifetime could have used the `SetResourceProperties` operation to change the value of the `TerminationTime` resource property, the semantics of the `SetTerminationTime` operation are slightly more sophisticated than a simple update.

Here is the section of the `PurchaseOrder` WS-Resource's resource properties document definition that contains the necessary scheduled termination resource property element definitions:

```
...
  <xsd:element name="poResourceProperties">
    <xsd:complexType>
      <xsd:sequence>
...
<!-- ==== Resource Properties for ScheduledResourceTermination ==== -->
        <xsd:element ref="wsrl:CurrentTime" minOccurs="1" maxOccurs="1"/>
        <xsd:element ref="wsrl:TerminationTime" minOccurs="1" maxOccurs="1"/>
...
```

If a requestor wishes to change the termination time of a WS-Resource, it uses the `SetTerminationTime` operation to give the WS-Resource a new termination time. If the implementation of the WS-Resource is willing to accept the new termination time, then the request causes the `wsrl:TerminationTime` resource property to have a new value.

Consider the following series of exchanges from our `PurchaseOrder` WS-Resource example. The Skateboard Warehouse created a `PurchaseOrder` WS-Resource. At any time, their applications can examine the current value of the termination time of the `PurchaseOrder` by issuing a `GetResourceProperty` operation (from WS-ResourceProperties) to get the current value of the `wsrl:TerminationTime` resource property. In fact, it's often handy to retrieve both the termination time and the current time, as shown in the following `GetMultipleResourceProperties` SOAP request:

```
<soap:Envelope
...
  <soap:Header>
...
    <!-- the reference property to id the PO -->
    <poRP:POResourceID>43871</poRP:POResourceID>
  </soap:Header>
  <soap:Body>
    <wsrp:GetMultipleResourceProperties>
      <wsrp:ResourceProperty>wsrl:TerminationTime</wsrp:ResourceProperty>w
      <wsrp:ResourceProperty>wsrl:CurrentTime</wsrp:ResourceProperty>w
    </wsrp:GetMultipleResourceProperties>
  </soap:Body>
</soap:Envelope>
```

By asking for both the termination time and the current time, the application has a better sense of how much time remains before the termination time elapses. The application can then estimate how much longer it will need the PurchaseOrder and calculate a new termination time. The application can then send a SetTerminationTime request to update the termination time of the PurchaseOrder:

```
<soap:Envelope
...
  <soap:Header>
...
    <!-- the reference property to id the PO -->
    <poRP:POResourceID>43871</poRP:POResourceID>
  </soap:Header>
  <soap:Body>
    <wsrl:SetTerminationTime>
      <wsrl:RequestedTerminationTime>
        2004-03-02T12:00:00
      </wsrl:RequestedTerminationTime>
    </wsrl:SetTerminationTime>
  </soap:Body>
</soap:Envelope>
```

This new termination time must be in the future relative to the WS-Resource's current time. If the requestor requests a termination time in the past relative to the WS-Resource's current time, then the requestor is saying that it wants the WS-Resource destroyed immediately. This is subtly different from immediate destruction; whereas immediate destruction is a synchronous operation, using the SetTerminationTime operation and passing in a termination time in the past is an asynchronous means to achieve immediate destruction of the WS-Resource. The actual process of destroying the WS-Resource and reclaiming system resources used to support the WS-Resource happens at any time, independently of when the SetTerminationTime operation responds to the requestor. The implementation could even fail to destroy the WS-Resource.

The requestor can also try to give the WS-Resource an indefinite lifetime by using xsi:nil as the parameter of the SetTerminationTime operation. For example, if The Skateboard Warehouse wishes to make its PurchaseOrder WS-Resource permanent, then it sends the following request message:

```
<soap:Envelope
...
  <soap:Header>
...
    <!-- the reference property to id the PO -->
    <poRP:POResourceID>43871</poRP:POResourceID>
  </soap:Header>
  <soap:Body>
    <wsrl:SetTerminationTime>
      <wsrl:RequestedTerminationTime xsi:nil="true"/>
    </wsrl:SetTerminationTime>
```

```
    </soap:Body>
</soap:Envelope>
```

Of course, the Web service managing the WS-Resource may not accept the new termination time suggested by the requestor in the SetTerminationTime request. For example, the implementation may be unwilling to allocate the system resources required to support the WS-Resource for as long as requested. Many implementations may be unlikely to accept the attempt to give the WS-Resource an indefinite lifetime. If an implementation rejects the termination time request, it might give information in the fault response to indicate how long it's willing to extend the termination time.

Just as with the immediate termination, you indicate that a WS-Resource can be managed using scheduled termination by inserting the definition for the SetTerminationTime operation into the WSDL definition of the Web service managing that WS-Resource. For example, the POPortType was extended to include the SetTerminationTime by copying and pasting the WSDL operation definition for SetTerminationTime:

```
...
  <wsdl:portType name="POPortType"
...
    <!-- ==== extends wsrl:ScheduledResourceTermination ========= -->
    <wsdl:operation name="SetTerminationTime">
      <wsdl:input message="wsrl:SetTerminationTimeRequest" />
      <wsdl:output message="wsrl:SetTerminationTimeResponse" />
      <wsdl:fault name="ResourceUnknownFault"
                  message="wsrl:ResourceUnknownFault" />
      <wsdl:fault name="UnableToSetTerminationTimeFault"
                  message="wsrl:UnableToSetTerminationTimeFault" />
      <wsdl:fault name="TerminationTimeChangeRejectedFault"
                  message="wsrl:TerminationTimeChangeRejectedFault" />
    </wsdl:operation>
...
```

Initializing Termination Time

For those WS-Resources that use the scheduled termination mechanism, there is no standard way for the requestor to initialize the termination time when the WS-Resource is created. There are several examples (the subscribe request in WS-Notification, for instance) where the application-specific semantic of a component of the request message is to initialize the termination time of a WS-Resource. Part of the subscribe request message is an optional InitialTerminationTime element. Here is a complete subscribe request from the partial example shown earlier (in the section "Subscribing for Notification"):

```
<soap:Envelope
    xmlns:wsnt=
        "http://www.ibm.com/xmlns/stdwip/web-services/WS-BaseNotification"
```

```
      xmlns:wsrl=
  "http://www.ibm.com/xmlns/stdwip/web-services/WS-ResourceLifetime"
...
  <soap:Header>
    <wsa:Action>
      http://www.ibm.com/xmlns/stdwip/web-services/WS-BaseNotification/Subscribe
    </wsa:Action>
...
    <poRP:POResourceID>43871</poRP:POResourceID>

  </soap:Header>
  <soap:Body>
    <wsnt:Subscribe>
      <wsnt:ConsumerReference>
        <wsa:Address>
          http://www.skateboardwarehouse.com/services/inventoryManagement
        </wsa:Address>
      </wsnt:ConsumerReference>
...
      <wsnt:InitialTerminationTime>
        2004-03-01T00:00:00.00000Z
      </wsnt:InitialTerminationTime>
    </wsnt: Subscribe>
  </soap:Body>
</soap:Envelope>
```

Notification of WS-Resource Termination

WS-ResourceLifetime also standardizes the way WS-Notification can be used to inform interested parties about the termination of a WS-Resource. There is a standardized topic (recall the topics concept we discussed in the section "Topics") in the WS-ResourceLifetime namespace ResourceTermination. Requestors can use this topic to subscribe for a notification message when a WS-Resource of interest is terminated.

In order for this facility to work, the following pieces must be in place:

- The Web service component of the WS-Resource must support the notification producer operations (for example, the subscribe operation).

- The Web service component of the WS-Resource must include the wsrl:ResourceTermination topic in its list of topics (recall the Topics resource property described in the section "Resource Properties of a Notification Producer").

SkatesTown's POPortType Web service supports generating the notification messages on the ResourceTermination topic as described earlier. The Skateboard Warehouse can issue a subscribe operation as follows to register interest in when a PurchaseOrder WS-Resource is destroyed:

```
<soap:Envelope
...
  <soap:Header>
...
    <!-- the reference property to id the PO -->
    <poRP:POResourceID>43871</poRP:POResourceID>

  </soap:Header>
  <soap:Body>
    <wsnt:Subscribe>
      <wsnt:ConsumerReference>
        <wsa:Address>
          http://www.skateboardwarehouse.com/services/inventoryManagement
        </wsa:Address>
      </wsnt:ConsumerReference>
      <wsnt:TopicExpression dialect=
"http://www.ibm.com/xmlns/stdwip/web-services/WS-Topics/TopicExpression/
simple">
        wsrl:ResourceTermination
      </wsnt:TopicPathExpression>
...
    </wsnt: Subscribe>
  </soap:Body>
</soap:Envelope>
```

When the `PurchaseOrder` WS-Resource is terminated, a notification message will be delivered to the notification consumer indicating (among other information) the time the WS-Resource was terminated and the reason for its termination. WS-ResourceLifetime specifies that the notification message must contain an element of the following form:

```
<wsrl:TerminationNotification>
  <wsrl:TerminationTime>xsd:dateTime</wsrl:TerminationTime>
  <wsrl:TerminationReason>xsd:any</wsrl:TerminationReason>?
</wsrl:TerminationNotification>
```

Other WS-Resource Framework Specifications

When the WS-Resource Framework was announced in January 2004, a total of five specifications were included in the framework. Simultaneous with the announcement, two of the specifications were published: WS-ResourceProperties and WS-ResourceLifetime, along with a whitepaper that discussed the WS-Resource concept ("Modeling Stateful Resources Using Web Services").

The remaining three specifications were discussed, but weren't published at that time. This section presents a brief sketch of the specifications that will be made public sometime in the first half of 2004.

WS-RenewableReferences

The uses of a WS-Addressing endpoint reference are many. An endpoint reference can be returned as part of a response message, as you saw in the updated doSubmission operation. An endpoint reference can be passed as part of an input message to a Web service. A requestor can receive an endpoint reference by some non–Web services means, such as in an email message. An endpoint reference can also be a resource property of a WS-Resource.

You can imagine that many copies of an endpoint reference can be made and shared with any number of other entities in a distributed computing system (more than is reasonable to keep track of). This poses an interesting challenge: What happens when an endpoint reference needs to change? Consider the scenario where SkatesTown wishes to migrate the location of its PurchaseOrder service to another IP address, perhaps as a result of a load balancing requirement, or due to a severe hardware or software problem on its server. Now the Address components of all the endpoint references to the PurchaseOrder service reflect an incorrect URL. How can all the copies of the endpoint reference to the PurchaseOrder be updated? This is solved by the concept of a renewable reference.

The WS-RenewableReference specification standardizes the *renewable reference* 📖. WS-RenewableReferences uses WS-Policy to indicate how a requestor can renew or refresh an endpoint reference when it has become stale or incoherent due to a change made by the service provider. The policy specifies the location of one or more Web services that understands how to renew the endpoint reference to its current form.

WS-ServiceGroup

WS-ServiceGroups is a standard means of declaring a by-value collection of Web services or WS-Resources (essentially, anything that can be pointed to by an endpoint reference). This collection is a WS-Resource and therefore can be manipulated, through a Web service in a fashion similar to what you've seen in this chapter: resource property queries, notifications on topics, lifetime management through WS-ResourceLifetime, and so on. A ServiceGroup can be used to collect Web services or WS-Resources for all sorts of purposes; for example, it can be used as a registry of available WS-Resources.

SkatesTown, for example, could use a WS-ServiceGroup to collect all the PurchaseOrder WS-Resources that are currently in process. By having a single WS-Resource, business intelligence monitoring tools can be built to occasionally query this WS-ServiceGroup to get status on the health of SkatesTown's order pipeline.

WS-BaseFaults

WS-BaseFaults is a simple specification, rounding out the WS-Resource Framework. It describes an XML Schema complexType for error messages associated with Web services fault messages, along with a means by which a hierarchy of application-specific extensions to this base error message complexType should be constructed. A standardized form of error messages allows tooling to be built to make the job of reporting Web services errors to applications a little easier.

> **Note**
>
> You can see the final, complete WSDL for the `POPortType`, which manages the `PurchaseOrder` WS-Resources for SkatesTown, at the Sams Publishing Web site: `www.samspublishing.com`. Remember that the bulk of this WSDL is copied from WSDL `portType` definitions defined by the various WS-Resource Framework specifications. At the Web site, you can also view the full XML Schema definition for the resource properties document of a `PurchaseOrder`.

Summary

In this chapter, we introduced the WS-Resource Framework, a collection of specifications and conventions that standardize how stateful resources are represented in the Web services world. We examined how one particular stateful resource, a `PurchaseOrder`, is modeled by SkatesTown's use of the WS-Resource Framework. We reviewed the concept of a WS-Resource and the implied resource pattern, which is a conventional use of the endpoint reference facility from WS-Addressing to point to a WS-Resource. We explored the WS-ResourceProperties specification, which describes how elements of a WS-Resource can be queried and updated by requestors.

We outlined the WS-Notification family of specifications, which standardizes the notion of publish and subscribe (asynchronous notification) in Web services. You saw how SkatesTown used WS-Notification to replace an older, SkatesTown-proprietary approach to notification. We also reviewed the WS-ResourceLifetime specification that standardizes two means by which a requestor can terminate WS-Resources: immediate and scheduled termination.

Finally, we finished our review of the WS-Resource Framework by summarizing three other specifications that will be completed and published soon.

9

Securing Web Services

IN PART I, "WEB SERVICES BASICS," you saw how SOAP enables applications to interact with each other, and how Web Services Definition Language (WSDL) and Universal Description, Discovery, and Integration (UDDI) integrate applications among businesses. With Web services technologies, applications can be coupled loosely—that is, in a decentralized manner beyond the enterprise boundary. This situation suggests a new challenge related to security: Most existing technologies are only concerned with how to protect applications within a single *security domain* 📖. Soon, however, we'll have to be concerned with how to federate security domains, because each enterprise has its own security boundary. The Web services security roadmap document (referred as *the roadmap document* in this chapter) addresses this issue; it not only provides a security model, but also shows a collection of specifications to be published.

In this chapter, we'll look at the concept of Web services security and review its pending specifications. Because the specification drafts are often abstract (especially for non–security experts), we'll provide concrete examples using SkatesTown scenarios. In particular, we'll first review existing security technologies and take a closer look at the mapping from Web services security onto those technologies. In addition, we'll review how Web services security technologies are integrated into enterprise applications using the J2EE model.

Example Scenario

In our discussion of security, we'll continue our SkatesTown example. SkatesTown's CTO, Dean Caroll, is becoming concerned with security now that the business is expanding. SkatesTown is doing business with a large number of companies, and most of them aren't Fortune 500 companies. Currently, SkatesTown's Web services are secured only with Secure Socket Layer (SSL) and HTTP Basic Authentication. The combination of the two won't be enough in the future because SkatesTown has to transact with various business partners, some of which may want to use other security technologies such as Kerberos. Specifically, when SOAP messages travel through intermediaries, end-to-end security may be required. Dean can see that the combination of SSL and HTTP Basic Authentication can support point-to-point security. However, he doesn't know what kind of security mechanisms SkatesTown should support.

To ease Dean's concern, Al Rosen of Silver Bullet Consulting has been asked to advise Dean about what kind of security features to address in the next development phase. This hasn't been an easy task for Al either, because numerous security technologies and specifications are available; it won't be possible or meaningful for him to cover all of them. Therefore, he has addressed Web services security and considered how its mechanisms would fit into SkatesTown's SOAP-based transactions, as we'll present throughout this chapter.

Security Basics

In this section, we'll introduce basic security concepts and technologies that are relevant to Web services security. We'll begin by reviewing security requirements, and then discuss a collection of security technologies. Finally, we'll describe a requirement specific to Web services: the federation of security domains.

Note that we won't discuss security risks in a generic sense; instead, we'll address network security. For example, physical site security and insider problems are outside the scope of this chapter. It's also worthwhile to clarify that we're assuming machine-to-machine interactions rather than human-to-machine interactions.

Security Requirements

E-business relies on the exchange of information between trading partners over insecure networks (often the Internet). There are always security risks, because messages could be stolen, lost, or modified.

Four security requirements must be addressed to ensure the safety of information exchanged among trading partners:

- *Confidentiality* 📖 guarantees that exchanged information is protected against eavesdroppers. For example, purchase orders and invoices shouldn't be exposed to outsiders. Your credit card information shouldn't be wiretapped by third parties.

- *Integrity* 📖 refers to the assurance that a message isn't modified accidentally or deliberately in transit. For example, an invoice or order shouldn't be modified as it moves between a buyer and a seller.

- *Authentication* 📖 guarantees that access to e-business applications and data is restricted to those who can provide appropriate proof of identity. For example, when a buyer accesses a seller's site for a purchase order, the buyer is typically required to give an ID and password as proof of their identity.

- *Nonrepudiation* 📖 guarantees that the message's sender can't deny having sent it. This requirement is important when you exchange business documents such as a purchase order or bill, because document recipients want transaction records with proof. With nonrepudiation, once a purchase order is submitted, the buyer can't repudiate it.

In addition to these requirements for message protection, you must consider how to protect resources such as data and applications such that only appropriate entities are allowed to access them. A fifth requirement is as follows:

- *Authorization* 📖 is a process that decides whether an entity with a given identity can access a particular resource. For example, authorized buyers can view a product list and submit a purchase order. The former indicates authorization on data, and the latter indicates authorization on an application—that is, an order-management system.

Message protection requires you to define how to include security information in exchanged messages. On the other hand, authorization often doesn't affect messages, but is provided as a mechanism embedded in a platform such as a Web server, an application server, or a database management system. We'll use the J2EE platform as an example to explain authorization in the "Enterprise Security" section of this chapter.

Cryptography

Cryptography technologies provide a basis for protecting messages exchanged between trading partners. Confidentiality and integrity can be ensured with *encryption* 📖 and *digital signature* 📖 technologies, respectively. These cryptography technologies can be categorized into two types in terms of an orthogonal dimension: symmetric and asymmetric keys. Table 9.1 shows four categories based on the two dimensions; the table classifies widely used algorithms. The following subsections review each category in more detail.

Table 9.1   **Classification of Cryptography Algorithms**

Technology	Symmetric Key	Asymmetric Key
Encryption	3DES, AES, RC4	RSA15
Digital signature	HMAC-SHA1, HMAC-MD5	RSA-SHA1

Symmetric Encryption

Symmetric encryption 📖 requires that you use the same key for encryption and decryption. For example, assume that Alice wants to send data to Bob. According to standard cryptography terminology, the original data is called *plaintext* 📖 and the encrypted data is called *ciphertext* 📖. As shown in Figure 9.1, Alice encrypts the plaintext with a key to send it to Bob, and Bob decrypts the ciphertext with the same key to extract the plaintext. Because the same keys are used at the both endpoints, this kind of encryptions is referred to as symmetric, and the keys used are often called *symmetric keys*.

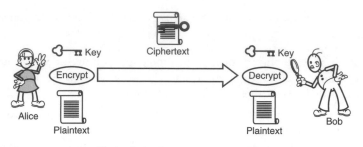

Figure 9.1   Symmetric encryption

This category of encryption includes Triple DES (3DES), which is a minor variation of the Data Encryption Standard (DES) developed by an IBM team 30 years ago; and the Advanced Encryption Standard (AES), which has been proposed as a replacement for 3DES by the National Institute of Standards and Technology (NIST). RC4, which was designed at RSA Laboratories by Ron Rivest in 1987, is also widely used with SSL.

Asymmetric Encryption

Asymmetric encryption 📖 allows you to make your encryption key public and thus simplifies key distribution. Two different keys are used: a *public key* 📖 and a *private key* 📖. Assume that Bob has a pair of private and public keys, and he only publishes the public key. Alice encrypts her plaintext with the public key to send it to Bob, and Bob decrypts the ciphertext with his private key (see Figure 9.2).

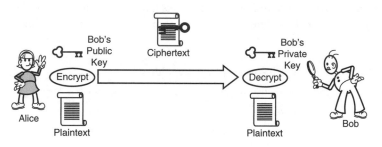

Figure 9.2   Asymmetric encryption

Unlike symmetric encryption schema, different keys are used at the endpoints. The keys are called *asymmetric keys*, reflecting their asymmetric nature. An example of an algorithm in this category is RSAES-PKCS1-v1_5 (RSA-15), which is specified in RFC 2437.

Message Authentication Code

Although the next category of security technology is symmetric digital signature, it's called *Message Authentication Code (MAC)* 📖 in cryptography terminology. It relies on mathematical algorithms known as *hashing functions* 📖 to ensure data integrity. A hashing function takes data as input and produces smaller data called a *digest* 📖 as output. If the original data changes even slightly, the digest is different. MAC is an extension of this idea: A digest is created with a key in addition to the input data. Such an extension is necessary because an attacker could otherwise capture both the data and the digest, and then tamper with the data and construct a new digest. As shown in Figure 9.3, MAC requires the same key at both ends; hence Bob can check the integrity of Alice's data with the key.

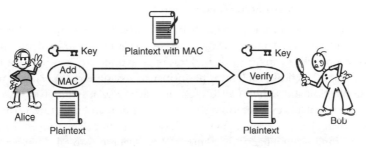

Figure 9.3 Message Authentication Code (MAC)

Keyed-Hashing for Message Authentication Code (HMAC) is an example of MAC. HMAC must be combined with hashing functions such as MD5 and SHA-1. Therefore, the algorithm names are HMAC-SHA1, HMAC-MD5, and so on, as listed in Table 9.1.

Digital Signature

The asymmetric digital signature technology is referred to as *digital signature* 📖. As shown in Figure 9.4, Alice signs the plaintext with her private key. *Signing* here means creating a signature value that's sent with the original plaintext. Bob can verify the integrity of the incoming message by generating the signature value from the plaintext with Alice's public key; he can compare this value with the signature value that accompanies the incoming plaintext.

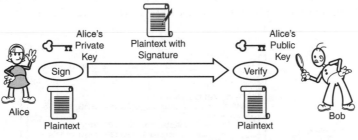

Figure 9.4 Digital signature

Like MAC algorithms, digital signature algorithms are also combined with hashing functions such as SHA-1. Table 9.1 shows an example: in RSA-SHA1, a digest is calculated with SHA-1, and a signature value on the digest is created with a private key.

You can use the digital signature technology to ensure nonrepudiation as well as integrity. In Figure 9.4, Bob can make sure that the incoming plaintext is signed by Alice, because he uses Alice's public key. However, how can he know that Alice is the holder of the public key? Public Key Infrastructure (PKI) provides a solution: An authority issues digital certificates, each of which binds a party to a public key. PKI and X.509 digital certificates are reviewed later in this chapter.

Asymmetric Versus Symmetric Technologies

Asymmetric keys may seem more useful than symmetric ones because the former can solve the issue of key distribution—symmetric keys must be transmitted and managed carefully so that attackers can't steal them. However, asymmetric keys have some limitations. One of their practical problems is performance. Asymmetric operations with private keys (decryption and signing) are a great deal slower than symmetric key operations. Even asymmetric public key operations such as encryption and signature verification are much slower than symmetric key operations. Based on such performance characteristics, it's best to combine asymmetric and symmetric key operations to take advantage of both benefits.

Authentication

Password authentication 📖 is the most commonly used authentication method on the Internet. A client shows its ID or username and password, and the server checks the ID/password pair by referring to a user registry that manages a collection of such pairs.

Password authentication to access Web servers over HTTP is called HTTP Basic Authentication (BASIC-AUTH); it's defined in RFC 2617. The specification defines an interaction protocol between Web browser and Web server in addition to how to encode the ID/password into the HTTP header (see the sidebar "HTTP Basic Authentication").

HTTP Basic Authentication

You've probably experienced being required to enter a user ID and password while visiting a Web site. This process is based on HTTP Basic Authentication (BASIC-AUTH), which is defined in RFC 2617. The typical BASIC-AUTH interaction between a Web browser and a Web server is illustrated in Figure 9.5.

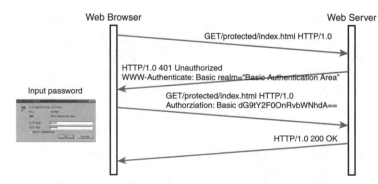

Figure 9.5 Interaction protocol for HTTP Basic Authentication

When the Web browser sends an HTTP request to access a protected Web resource, the Web server returns an HTTP response that includes the error code "401 Unauthorized" and the following HTTP header:

```
WWW-Authenticate: Basic realm="Realm Name"
```

Realm is a name given to a set of Web resources; it's a unit to be protected. *Basic* in front of *realm* indicates a type of authentication—in this case, BASIC-AUTH. Based on this information, the Web browser shows a login dialog to the user. Then, the Web browser sends an HTTP request again, including the following HTTP header:

```
Authorization: Basic credential
```

Although the credential looks like encrypted text, it's logically plaintext because its format is *UserName:Password* encoded with *Base64* —for example, dG9tY2F0OnRvbWNhdA in Figure 9.5 can be decoded to SkateboardWarehouse:wsbookexample. Because BASIC-AUTH isn't secure alone, it's combined with another security mechanism such as SSL.

The Web server authenticates the user with the user ID and password included in the credential. If the given user ID and password are wrong, "401 Unauthorized" is returned. Moreover, the Web server has an *access control list* (ACL) that specifies who can access what and checks whether the authenticated user can access the Web resource. If the check succeeds, then "200 OK" is returned; otherwise, "401 Unauthorized" is returned.

The digital signature technology can also be used for authentication. As we mentioned in the previous section, a message's signature can be bound to a digital certificate. Because the certificate is bound to a particular entity such as a user or a trading partner, you can identify a holder of the certificate.

Authentication with a digital signature is in principle more convenient than password authentication because you can assume that a certificate authority manages certificates. However, client certificates aren't widely used, because it isn't easy for Web browser users to install certificates. On the other hand, server certificates are commonly used when Web browsers authenticate servers.

Security Protocols

Symmetric and asymmetric keys each have pros and cons, so combining them is a good idea. There has been a great deal of research in the area of network security to define *security protocols*, with which symmetric keys can be shared between two parties in a secure manner. In a simple protocol, two parties only agree on a key, exchanging random numbers. However, commonly used protocols also perform authentications during the key agreement process.

The Secure Socket Layer (SSL) defined by Netscape for Web browsers is the most widely used protocol on the Internet. With SSL, two parties can share a symmetric key, and authentication is also performed. The protocol works as follows:

1. The client accesses a server.

2. The server returns its certificate.

3. The client prepares a random number that is a seed for generating a symmetric key, encrypts the seed number with a public key contained in the server certificate, and sends the encrypted data to the server.

4. The server decrypts the received data to extract the seed number.

5. Both the client and the server have the same seed number, so they can generate a symmetric key from it.

Note that authentication isn't based on digital signature technology, but on encryption. After the negotiation has been completed, the client sends its application data, encrypting it with the symmetric key. If the server's response is properly encrypted, the client can authenticate the server.

The server can authenticate the client two ways. First, when the client sends a request after the SSL negotiation, the server can return an HTTP "401 Unauthorized" message to the client (see the sidebar "HTTP Basic Authentication"). Then the client attaches the username and password to be authenticated by the server. Second, the server can use another variation of the SSL negotiation protocol, where the client is required to decrypt a random number encrypted with its public key. If the decryption is performed properly, the server can authenticate the client.

Security Infrastructures

It's difficult for developers to combine security technologies properly, so *security infrastructures* 📖 have been developed and are used today in real systems. Essentially, a security infrastructure is a basis on which applications can interact with each other securely. As illustrated in Figure 9.6, applications and the communication between them can be protected.

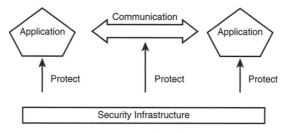

Figure 9.6 Security infrastructure

Each security infrastructure has different design requirements. Although we listed five items in the "Security Protocols" section of this chapter, not all of them have to be addressed in each infrastructure. Security infrastructures vary in terms of their design and architecture. In this section we'll review three security infrastructures that are commonly used in real-world systems: user registries, PKI, and Kerberos.

User Registries

One of the most basic security infrastructures is the *user registry* 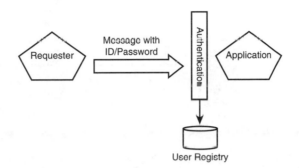. User registries ordinarily manage user IDs and their associated passwords, which are used for authentication. As shown in Figure 9.7, an authentication module sitting in front of the applications checks each ID/password pair with the user registry. Only authenticated users can access the applications.

Figure 9.7   User registry for password authentication

One of the advantages of this mechanism is its simplicity. Most commonly used systems such as operating systems, database management systems, and HTTP servers incorporate user registries. Furthermore, although only authentication is involved, this simple system can be combined with other infrastructures to meet additional security requirements, if necessary.

On the other hand, user registries may be brittle. Once a password is stolen, an attacker can easily access a system using the ID and the password. In spite of such low-security level, password authentication is often chosen because its development and management are much cheaper than for sophisticated mechanisms. This decision is reasonable when the cost of any potential damage is much lower than the cost of implementing the user registry.

Public Key Infrastructure

As we reviewed in the "Cryptography" section, asymmetric key operations offer an advantage. Because public keys can be shown to anyone, you don't have to worry about key delivery. One remaining issue is how to bind a public key to a particular party. *Public Key Infrastructure (PKI)* provides a basis to certify holders of public keys. The key constructs of PKI are the certificate and the certificate authority:

- A *certificate* is a proof of identity. With a certificate, you can relate an entity such as a trading party to its public key. Because the certificate is digitally signed, you can trust its contents as long as you can trust the certificate's issuer. Although there are alternative certificate formats such as Pretty Good Privacy (PGP) and X.509, we mainly use X.509 in our examples.

- A *certificate authority (CA)* is an entity that issues certificates. If you can trust the CA, you can trust certificates issued by the CA. PKI assumes a fairly small number of CAs (such as VeriSign) and allows a CA to issue certificates for other CAs. As a result, certificates are organized into a hierarchy, as shown in Figure 9.8. The root is called a *root CA*, intermediary nodes are called *subordinate CAs*, and terminal nodes are called *end entities*. The path for an end entity to a root CA is called a *certificate path*. If two end entities have a common CA, they can establish trust with each other.

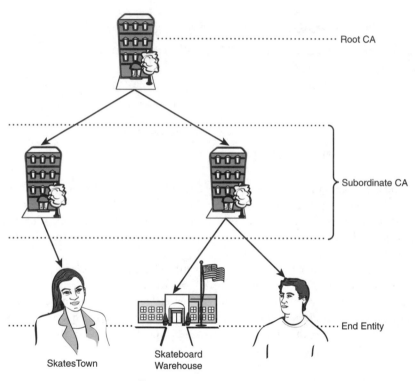

Figure 9.8 PKI trust model

Figure 9.9 illustrates how to use a certificate. First, a requestor registers its public key with the CA, and a certificate is issued. The requestor signs a message with the private key and sends the signed messages to a service provider, attaching the certificate. To verify the signature, the provider performs a cryptographic operation using a public key included in the certificate. To verify the certificate, the provider checks whether the certificate is signed by the CA, potentially traversing subordinate CAs in the process.

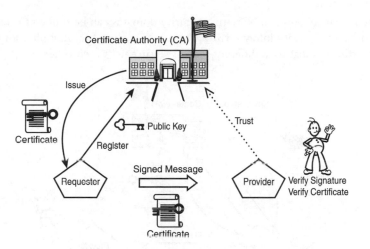

Figure 9.9 Using a certificate for a digital signature

Kerberos

Kerberos 📖 was initially developed for workstation users who wanted to access a network. One of the key requirements is *single sign-on (SSO)* 📖: A user provides an ID and a password only once to access various applications within a certain interval. Another requirement is no use of public key cryptography. With a symmetric key operation, you can achieve much higher performance.

The Kerberos architecture is illustrated in Figure 9.10. The requestor (Alice) first requests and receives a *ticket-granting ticket (TGT)* 📖 through password authentication by accessing the *Key Distribution Center (KDC)* 📖. Next, Alice requests and receives a service ticket (ST) for a provider (Bob), showing the TGT to the KDC. Alice can now access Bob by including the ST in a request message. The TGT contains Alice's ID, her session key, and TGT expiration time. Therefore, as long as the TGT is valid, Alice can get various STs without giving her ID and password. In this way, SSO is achieved.

The KDC is a core of the Kerberos system: It authenticates users to issue tickets and, more importantly, manages all participants' IDs and secret keys (called *master keys* 📖). For example, when issuing an ST for Bob, the KDC encrypts Alice's information with Bob's key. As a result, only Bob can decrypt Alice's ID in the ST, and therefore he can authenticate her. The ST contains a session key between Alice and Bob, so they can securely exchange messages with encryption and digital signatures.

Security Domains

Before moving on to Web services security, let's define the term *security domain* 📖. As you've seen, each security infrastructure has a scope of management in terms of participants and resources. A user registry or a Kerberos KDC has explicit participant databases. On the other hand, the root CA implicitly prescribes a set of participants in PKI. We call such scope a security domain. Note that security domains can be different even if they're based on the same security infrastructure. For example, there are multiple root CAs in PKI, and certificates that have different root CAs can't trust each other.

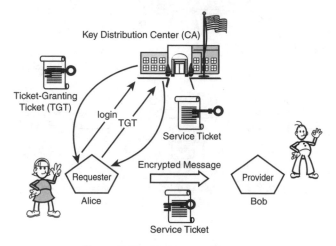

Figure 9.10   Kerberos architecture

As you can imagine, numerous security domains exist in the real world, and there is no point in considering a single security infrastructure to integrate them. Web services security—which is a main topic of this chapter—addresses how to integrate security domains that are often based on different security infrastructures.

Web Services Security

Because applications are integrated across business boundaries according to the Web services concept, Web services have specialized security requirements. As discussed in the "Security Domains" section of this chapter, numerous security domains already exist on the Internet and in intranets. Although applications and business entities belong to one or more security domains, they have to interact with one another beyond the security domain boundary. Thus, the *federation* 📖 of different security domains is extremely important, although the issue hasn't been addressed in existing security technologies. The Web services security architecture discussed in the roadmap document addresses the issue of integration of security domains.

This section examines the overall architecture of Web services security. In subsequent sections, we'll take a closer look at the security specifications.

Security Model for Web Services

Each business has its own security infrastructure and mechanism, such as PKI or Kerberos. In the context of Web services, these security systems need to interoperate over different security domains. The Web services security architecture defines an abstract model for that purpose.

As shown in Figure 9.11, three parties are identified: the requestor, the Web service, and the security token service. Each has its own claims, security token, and policy. The roadmap document defines several terms to discuss the security model, as follows:

- *Subject*—A principal (for example, a person, an application, or a business entity) about which the claims expressed in the security token apply. The subject, as the owner of the security token, possesses information necessary to prove ownership of the security token.

- *Claim*—A statement about a subject either by the subject or by a relying party that associates the subject with the claim. This specification doesn't attempt to limit the types of claims that can be made, nor does it attempt to limit how these claims may be expressed. Claims can be about keys that may be used to sign or encrypt messages. Claims can be statements the security token conveys. For example, a claim may be used to assert the sender's identity or an authorized role.

- *Security token*—A representation of security-related information (X.509 certificate, Kerberos ticket and authenticator, mobile device security token from a SIM card, username, and so on).

- *Web service endpoint policy*—Collectively, the claims and related information that Web services require in order to process messages (the Web Services have complete flexibility in specifying these claims). Endpoint policies may be expressed in XML and can be used to indicate requirements related to authentication (for example, proof of user or group identity), authorization (such as proof of execution capabilities), or other requirements.

Based on this terminology, the highly abstracted security model is designed to fit many diverse situations.

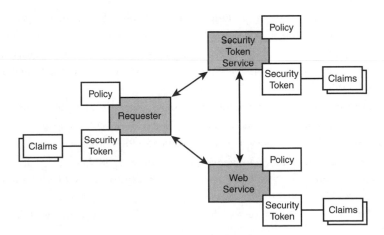

Figure 9.11   Security model for Web services

Let's examine the security model with some example scenarios. Assume that a requestor wants to invoke a Web service. The requestor has claims such as its identity and its privileges. On the other hand, the invoked Web service has a policy that requires encryption of messages and authentication of the requestor. Note that the word *policy* isn't a general term, but has a specific meaning such as "security requirements to access the Web service." Therefore, the requestor has to send messages that meet the security policy.

When you're sending security claims, you have to consider how to represent them in messages. The Web services security model suggests that all claims are included in the security token that's attached to request messages. For example, identity via a password or X.509 certificate is a security claim; therefore it's represented as a security token.

Although the requestor creates a security token, some security tokens (such as X.509 certificates) must be issued by a third party. Such a third party is called a *Security Token Service* (STS) in the security model (see Figure 9.11). The certificate authority in PKI and the Key Distribution Center in Kerberos are good examples. Because the STS is a Web service, it has security policies, claims, and security tokens. Most security systems include security servers, each of which manages its security domain. The STS is an abstraction of such security servers.

The Web services security model attempts to define an abstraction of existing security mechanisms, aiming at a generic security model. An opposite approach would be to define a generic security *mechanism*. There are security mechanisms running already, and we don't want to replace all of them. Therefore, instead of the mechanism, we use an abstract model with which we can unite different mechanisms without changing them.

Web Services Security Specifications

No Web services security specifications have been finalized yet during the writing of this book. Rather, draft specifications have been published, and some of them are being standardized in OASIS. However, a diagram of the specification release is summarized in the roadmap document, as shown in Figure 9.12:

- *WS-Security* defines how to include security tokens in SOAP messages and how to protect messages with digital signatures and encryption.

- *WS-Policy* provides a framework for describing Web services meta-information. Based on the framework, domain-specific languages can be defined, such as WS-SecurityPolicy (described later).

- *WS-Trust* prescribes an interaction protocol to access Security Token Services.

- *WS-SecureConversation* defines a security context with which parties can share a secret key to sign and encrypt parts of messages efficiently.

- *WS-Federation* provides a framework for federating multiple security domains. For example, it defines how to get a temporary identity to access a Web service in another security domain.

- *WS-Privacy* provides a framework for describing the privacy policy of Web services.

- *WS-Authorization* defines how to exchange authorization information among parties. The authorization is defined as a security token.

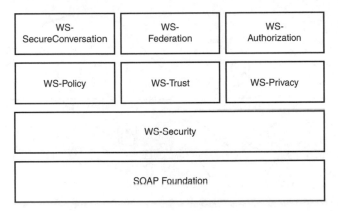

Figure 9.12   Roadmap of Web services security specifications

As of the time of this writing, draft specifications of WS-Authorization and WS-Privacy haven't been released. Other specifications are discussed in the remainder of this chapter.

Extended SkatesTown Security Scenario

Although SkatesTown's CTO, Dean Caroll, has an overview of the Web services security model, he doesn't realize how these technologies can help his business. Therefore, he asked Al Rosen of Silver Bullet Consulting to show him some scenarios that employ Web services security.

Al Rosen envisioned a buyer/seller/supplier scenario that might happen in the near future. Figure 9.13 shows the addition of a credit card company. A typical transaction is carried out as follows:

1. Buyer submits a purchase order to SkatesTown, specifying a product, a delivery date, and a credit card number.
2. SkatesTown allocates stock to Part Supplier to confirm the order.
3. If the stock is allocated, SkatesTown checks with Credit to determine whether the buyer's purchase is possible.
4. SkatesTown returns an invoice to Buyer.

Let's consider how Web services security helps protect each process in the transaction. When accepting the purchase order message, SkatesTown considers three security requirements: nonrepudiation, authentication, and confidentiality. Note that integrity is not a requirement, but nonrepudiation ensures integrity. WS-Security can be used to satisfy these requirements.

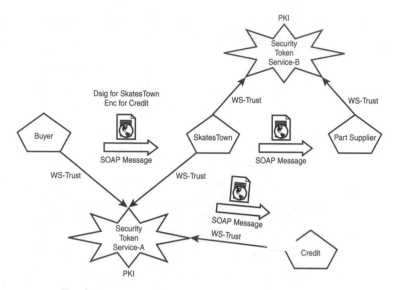

Figure 9.13   Extended SkatesTown scenario for security

A digital signature is applied to Buyer's order information as part of WS-Security. During order submission, SkatesTown wants to ensure nonrepudiation so that Buyer can't deny their request. If Buyer signs the order with its private key, SkatesTown can verify the signature with Buyer's public key.

SkatesTown also can verify Buyer's identity with Buyer's certificate. Through the signature verification, SkatesTown already has proof of possession on the certificate. Thus, authentication can be performed during the signature verification.

The card information involves a special requirement: SkatesTown can't see Buyer's number, but Credit can see it. In order to achieve this requirement, they can use the encryption feature provided in WS-Security. Specifically, the card number is encrypted with Credit's public key by Buyer and then decrypted with Credit's private key by Credit.

WS-Trust can be viewed as an API to access an STS. In this scenario, when SkatesTown receives a signed purchase order, it verifies not only the signature, but also the certificate used for the signature. In this case, SkatesTown may access an STS (STS-A in Figure 9.13) with WS-Trust in order to validate the certificate.

With WS-Policy and WS-SecurityPolicy, administrators of Web services can specify security requirements to access their services. SkatesTown requires a digital signature for purchase order submission. If such a security policy is published, buyers will be prepared to insert digital signatures into their messages.

WS-SecureConversation is used to establish a security context; it fits into the message exchange between SkatesTown and Supplier. SkatesTown interacts with many buyers but only a small number of suppliers, but the number of messages it exchanges with suppliers is much larger. Although you can apply WS-Security directly using PKI, such a solution isn't efficient because public key operations are expensive. In this case, it's a good idea to use WS-SecureConversation to establish a security context, and then communicate with partners, utilizing efficient symmetric key operations.

WS-Federation is required for authentication across security boundaries. Assume that Buyer and SkatesTown belong to security domain A, and Credit and SkatesTown belong to security domain B. In this case, Credit wants to authenticate Buyer, although Buyer can show a security token issued in domain A. WS-Federation provides a framework for resolving such federation issues as described later.

No draft specification has been published for WS-Privacy or WS-Authorization, but we'll briefly describe how they fit into this scenario. With WS-Privacy, SkatesTown could define a privacy policy dictating that purchase order information must not be used for other purposes (such as direct mail). Under such a policy, Buyer would decide whether to submit an order. WS-Privacy is provided as a specific language of WS-Policy, like WS-SecurityPolicy. This way, buyers can get the privacy policy in advance when they submit a purchase order.

WS-Authorization would define a security token for authorization. In our scenario, Supplier would have access control on its stock allocation service and would require a particular authorization token. The authorization token would prove a rank for the requestor, such as AAA or BB. Supplier would then specify the maximum amount of the transaction according to the ranking. For example, $10,000 total allocation might be allowed for an AAA requestor, but only $3,000 might be allowed for a BB requestor.

In the following sections, we'll review the specifications in more detail.

WS-Security

The WS-Security specification defines a format to include security tokens and mechanisms to protect SOAP messages. Digital signatures serve as integrity and/or nonrepudiation checks to ensure message protection, and encryption guarantees confidentiality. In addition, WS-Security provides a flexible mechanism to include various claims in SOAP messages with security tokens. With message protection and security tokens, WS-Security can provide a basis for other specifications in the roadmap.

Listing 9.1 illustrates the syntax of WS-Security. A `Security` element is defined and included in a SOAP header. Under the `Security` element can appear a `Signature` element (defined in the XML Digital Signature specification), an encryption-related element such as `EncryptedKey` (defined in the XML Encryption specification), and security tokens such as `UsernameToken` (defined in WS-Security). The following sections review digital signatures, encryption, and security tokens.

Listing 9.1   **Basic Syntax of WS-Security**

```
<S:Envelope xmlns:S="http://schemas.xmlsoap.org/soap/envelope/" >
   <S:Header>
      <wsse:Security xmlns:wsse="http://schemas.xmlsoap.org/ws/2003/06/secext" >
         <Signature xmlns="http://www.w3.org/2000/09/xmldsig#">
         </Signature>
```

Listing 9.1   **Continued**

```
        <EncryptedKey xmlns="http://www.w3.org/2001/04/enc-enc-enc#">
        </EncryptedKey>
        <wsse:UsernameToken xmlns="http://schemas.xmlsoap.org/ws/2003/06/secext">
        </wsse:UsernameToken>
      </wsse:Security>
  </S:Header>
  <S:Body>
    ...
  </S:Body>
</S:Envelope>
```

Digital Signatures

Returning to the example scenario, Dean Caroll now understands an immediate problem: Without nonrepudiation, the buyer can deny their purchase order even if the buyer
sent the order request, or the buyer can claim that the number of products ordered is
wrong. With respect to the exchange of messages between two parties, a digital signature
provides a means to prove that the sending party created the message. Al Rosen emphasized that WS-Security incorporates the *World Wide Web Consortium (W3C)* 📖/IETF
standard, the XML Digital Signature specification.

The XML Digital Signature specification defines how to sign part of an XML document in a flexible manner. Whereas in the "Cryptography" section we assumed that data
is signed, we are now concerned with how to create the signed data from an XML
document. The specification defines ways to specify parts of the document and accompa-
nying canonicalization methods, as we'll review later. The specification also permits
signature algorithms. As we discussed earlier, digital signatures and Message
Authentication Code (MAC) are similar—the difference only involves their use of asymmetric and symmetric keys. Based on this similarity, both digital signatures and MAC are
handled in an integrated manner in the specification. For example, you can specify
HMAC-SHA1 (see Table 9.1) as a signature algorithm. In that case, you can only ensure
integrity—that is, you can only ensure that the message hasn't been modified during
transmission.

In our extended example, Buyer sends a purchase order document and receives an
invoice document. In practice, these two documents should be signed; otherwise, one of
the parties can repudiate that it sent the document. Listing 9.2 shows a digitally signed
purchase order document. The Signature element includes a signature on the purchase
order and specifies a collection of parameters to create the signature.

Listing 9.2   **Digital Signature Sample**

```
<SOAP-ENV:Envelope xmlns:SOAP-ENC=http://schemas.xmlsoap.org/soap/encoding/
  xmlns:SOAP-ENV="http://schemas.xmlsoap.org/soap/envelope/"
  xmlns:xsd="http://www.w3.org/2001/XMLSchema"
  SOAP-ENV:encodingStyle="http://schemas.xmlsoap.org/soap/encoding/">
```

Listing 9.2 **Continued**

```
<SOAP-ENV:Header>
    <wsse:Security xmlns:wsse="http://schemas.xmlsoap.org/ws/2003/06/secext">
        <wsse:BinarySecurityToken xmlns:wsu=
        "http://schemas.xmlsoap.org/ws/2003/06/utility"
        EncodingType="wsse:Base64Binary" ValueType="wsse:X509v3" wsu:Id="bst_id">
        MIIDQTCCAqqgAwIBAgICAQQwDQYJKoZIhvcNAQEFBQAwTjELMAkGA1UEBhMCS1AxETAP
        BgNVBAgTCEthbmFnYXdhMQwwCgYDVQQKEwNJQk0xDDAKBgNVBAsTA1RSTDEQMA4GA1UE
        ...
        </wsse:BinarySecurityToken>
        <Signature xmlns="http://www.w3.org/2000/09/xmldsig#">
            <SignedInfo>
                <CanonicalizationMethod Algorithm=
                "http://www.w3.org/2001/10/xml-exc-c14n#">
                    </CanonicalizationMethod>
                <SignatureMethod Algorithm=
                "http://www.w3.org/2000/09/xmldsig#rsa-sha1">
                    </SignatureMethod>
                <Reference URI="#body_id">
                    <Transforms>
                        <Transform Algorithm="http://www.w3.org/2001/10/xml-exc-c14n#">
                        </Transform>
                    </Transforms>
                    <DigestMethod Algorithm="http://www.w3.org/2000/09/xmldsig#sha1">
                    </DigestMethod>
                    <DigestValue>U2BIJSk6OL0W0mGXXiGVn5XPV54=</DigestValue>
                </Reference>
            </SignedInfo>
            <SignatureValue>
            Ojjw8nkT3jJoNN/AxsdOwTqWnhfZewubBWpOSa0vJTTjQBrnKRl8brODc8byuwVf2v
            iFdvMY4mT7Iumk/ZRLRNF1tEBCFRki2++W2LIXBIXVtmwo1riS98kmFZo6dBvhFOnX
            wKE1ag6C8x/UgAMVU+YzYdllKqNXtpwvi9Ydoq4=
            </SignatureValue>
            <KeyInfo>
                <wsse:SecurityTokenReference>
                    <wsse:Reference URI="#bst_id"></wsse:Reference>
                </wsse:SecurityTokenReference>
            </KeyInfo>
        </Signature>
    </wsse:Security>
</SOAP-ENV:Header>
<SOAP-ENV:Body xmlns:wsu="http://schemas.xmlsoap.org/ws/2003/06/utility"
wsu:Id=" body_id">
    <po xmlns="http://www.skatestown.com/ns/po" id="43871" submitted=
    "2004-01-05" customerId="73852">
        <billTo>
```

Listing 9.2 **Continued**

```
            <company>The Skateboard Warehouse</company>
            <street>One Warehouse Park</street>
            <street>Building 17</street>
            <city>Boston</city>
            <state>MA</state>
            <postalCode>01775</postalCode>
        </billTo>
        <shipTo>
            <company>The Skateboard Warehouse</company>
            <street>One Warehouse Park</street>
            <street>Building 17</street>
            <city>Boston</city>
            <state>MA</state>
            <postalCode>01775</postalCode>
        </shipTo>
        <order>
            <item sku="318-BP" quantity="5">
                <description>Skateboard backpack; five pockets</description>
            </item>
            <item sku="947-TI" quantity="12">
                <description>Street-style titanium skateboard.</description>
            </item>
            <item sku="008-PR" quantity="1000">
            </item>
        </order>
    </po>
  </SOAP-ENV:Body>
</SOAP-ENV:Envelope>
```

In the XML Digital Signature specification (XML Signature), an element Signature is defined with its descendants under the namespace http://www.w3.org/2000/09/xmldsig#. The WS-Security specification defines how to embed the Signature element in SOAP messages as a header entry. You can sign all or part of the message. In our example, the body part is signed. The digest value of the body part is calculated, and the value is signed and included in the Signature element.

Let's review how to get the digest value of the target. The target is specified by Reference under the SignedInfo element. Its URI attribute indicates the target in such a way that the id attribute of the body element is referenced. The target is transformed by EXC-C14N—that is, an exclusive *canonicalization* 📖 method for XML. (Exclusive canonicalization is a W3C Recommendation to generate a canonical form for physically different but logically equivalent XML documents.) With EXC-C14N, you can check whether XML documents are semantically equivalent using a standardized code set, the order of attributes, tab processing, and so on.

Let's look at a canonicalization example. The following two documents appear quite different at a glance:

```
<?xml version="1.0" encoding="us-ascii"?>
<foo
    b="b"
    a="a"
></foo>
```

```
<?xml version="1.0" encoding="us-ascii"?>
<foo a="a" b="b"/>
```

However, with canonicalization, they're both translated into the following document:

```
<?xml version="1.0" encoding="us-ascii"?>
<foo a="a" b="b"></foo>
```

The rules applied here are as follows:

- White spaces and new line feeds in a begin tag are normalized to a single white space.
- Attributes in a begin tag are sorted in alphabetical order.
- An empty element is converted to a start-end tag pair.
- Characters are encoded with UTF-8 (although you can't see it in the printed text).

There are two specifications for XML canonicalization: XML-C14N and EXC-C14N. The key difference is how to handle namespaces. Specifically, the outer element namespace can affect the canonicalization of the inner elements with XML-C14N. However, this behavior isn't good when you want to insert a signed part into another XML document, such as a SOAP envelope. For this reason, in WS-Security, EXC-C14N is recommended rather than XML-C14N.

After translation with EXC-C14N, a digest value is calculated with an algorithm specified by the DigestMethod element. Here *SHA1* is used. The calculated value is inserted in the DigestValue element, represented in Base64 format.

The value of the target isn't signed directly. Rather, the SignedInfo element is signed. An algorithm specified by the CanonicalizationMethod element—that is, XML-C14N—canonicalizes SignedInfo. The canonicalized SignedInfo is signed with an algorithm specified by SignatureMethod: RSA-SHA1. This algorithm calculates a digest value of the SignedInfo subtree and then signs it with an RSA private key. The calculated value is inserted into the SignatureValue element, represented in Base64 format.

Optionally, the signer can include a KeyInfo element to attach key information. More specifically, the example includes a reference (via SecurityTokenReference and Reference elements) to a BinarySecurityToken element that contains an X.509 certificate. (Security tokens are discussed in more detail in the "Security Tokens" section.)

So far, we've reviewed the XML Signature syntax in the signature-processing process.
Verification is carried out in the same manner. First, you check the value of the
`DigestValue` element according to EXC-C14N and SHA1. Next, you calculate a digest
value for the `SignedInfo` subtree to compare it with the value in the `SignatureValue`
element. More precisely, the signature value is decrypted with the public key and then
compared to the calculated value.

Encryption

In our scenario, credit card information should be encrypted, because SkatesTown
doesn't have to know the card number. The XML Encryption specification defines a
means to encrypt portions of XML documents; this selective encryption feature is incorporated into WS-Security.

We can now update the purchase order document to include credit card information,
as shown in Listing 9.3. Instead of a `billTo` element, we insert `cardInfo` so that the
service requestor can pay with the card. When it receives the document from Buyer,
SkatesTown doesn't have to know the credit card information. Rather, SkatesTown wants
verify with Credit that SkatesTown can charge the purchase on the card. In order to
achieve this scenario, the credit card information must be encrypted in such a way that
only Credit can decrypt it.

Listing 9.3 **Purchase Order that Includes Card Information**

```
<po xmlns="http://www.skatestown.com/ns/po-with-card" id="43871"
submitted="2004-01-05" customerId="73852">
   <cardInfo>
      <name>The Skateboard Warehouse</name>
      <company>VISA</company>
      <expiration>02/2005</expiration>
      <number>1234123412341234</number>
   </cardInfo>
   <shipTo>
      <company>The Skateboard Warehouse</company>
      <street>One Warehouse Park</street>
      <street>Building 17</street>
      <city>Boston</city>
      <state>MA</state>
      <postalCode>01775</postalCode>
   </shipTo>
   <order>
      <item sku="318-BP" quantity="5">
         <description>Skateboard backpack; five pockets</description>
      </item>
      <item sku="947-TI" quantity="12">
         <description>Street-style titanium skateboard.</description>
      </item>
```

Listing 9.3   **Continued**

```
        <item sku="008-PR" quantity="1000">
        </item>
    </order>
</po>
```

XML Encryption Example

Let's look at a simple XML Encryption sample first. Listing 9.4 is an encrypted version of the purchase order document. In this example, we assume that two parties share a common symmetric key indicated by a key name. Note that the namespace ds is a prefix for the XML Digital Signature namespace; the XML Encryption specification reuses elements from the XML Digital Signature namespace as much as possible.

Listing 9.4   **Encrypted Purchase Order Document**

```
<po xmlns="http://www.skatestown.com/ns/po-with-card"
id-"43871" submitted="2004-01-05" customerId="73852""">
    <enc:EncryptedData
        Type="http://www.w3.org/2001/04/xmlenc#Element">
        <enc:EncryptionMethod
            Algorithm="http://www.w3.org/2001/04/xmlenc#tripledes-cbc"/>
        <ds:KeyInfo>
            <ds:KeyName>Shared key</ds:KeyName>
        </ds:KeyInfo>
        <enc:CipherData>abCdeF...</enc:CipherData>
    </enc:EncryptedData>
    <shipTo>
        <company>The Skateboard Warehouse</company>
        <street>One Warehouse Park</street>
        <street>Building 17</street>
        <city>Boston</city>
        <state>MA</state>
        <postalCode>01775</postalCode>
    </shipTo>
    <order>
        <item sku="318-BP" quantity="5">
            <description>Skateboard backpack; five pockets</description>
        </item>
        <item sku="947-TI" quantity="12">
            <description>Street-style titanium skateboard.</description>
        </item>
        <item sku="008-PR" quantity="1000">
        </item>
    </order>
</po>
```

The EncryptedData element is a root element for the encrypted part, and its Type attribute indicates that the encrypted data is an XML element. The EncryptionMethod element specifies an encryption algorithm, and KeyInfo specifies a secret key. Based on the secret key and the algorithm, the credit card information is encrypted and stored in the CipherData element. The data to be encrypted must be a portion of the XML document encoded with UTF-8.

Listing 9.5 shows encryption with a public key.

Listing 9.5   **Encryption with a Public Key**

```
<po xmlns="http://www.skatestown.com/ns/po-with-card" id="43871"
submitted="2004-01-05" customerId="73852">
   <enc:EncryptedData
      Type="http://www.w3.org/2001/04/xmlenc#Element">
      <enc:EncryptionMethod
         Algorithm="http://www.w3.org/2001/04/xmlenc#tripledes-cbc"/>
      <ds:KeyInfo>
         <enc:EncryptedKey>
            <enc:EncryptionMethod
               Algorithm="http://www.w3.org/2001/04/xmlenc#rsa-1_5"/>
            <ds:KeyInfo>
               <ds:KeyName>Receiver's key</ds:KeyName>
            </ds:KeyInfo>
            <enc:CipherData>ghIjkL...</enc:CipherData>
         </enc:EncryptedKey>
      </ds:KeyInfo>
      <enc:CipherData>abCdeF...</enc:CipherData>
   </enc:EncryptedData>
   <shipTo>
      <company>The Skateboard Warehouse</company>
      <street>One Warehouse Park</street>
      <street>Building 17</street>
      <city>Boston</city>
      <state>MA</state>
      <postalCode>01775</postalCode>
   </shipTo>
   <order>
      <item sku="318-BP" quantity="5">
         <description>Skateboard backpack; five pockets</description>
      </item>
      <item sku="947-TI" quantity="12">
         <description>Street-style titanium skateboard.</description>
      </item>
      <item sku="008-PR" quantity="1000">
      </item>
   </order>
</po>
```

The idea here is that a random symmetric key is generated to encrypt the data, and the symmetric key itself is encrypted with the receiver's public key. Let's first look at how the symmetric key is encrypted. EncryptedKey includes the encrypted symmetric key, specifying how it's encrypted. EncryptionMethod specifies the encryption algorithm, and the inner KeyInfo specifies the receiver's public key. Based on these elements, the encrypted key is stored in CipherData. The outer CipherData comes from an encryption based on the symmetric key and an encryption algorithm specified by the outer EncryptionAlgorithm.

WS-Security Example

Let's move on to encryption in WS-Security. Listing 9.6 shows a WS-Security example for encryption. In addition to the encrypted data in the body, the EncryptedKey element is located under the Security element. This indicates that the header element is used as an instruction to process the body.

EncryptedKey contains an encrypted symmetric key and a reference to the encrypted body. CipherData contains a symmetric key encrypted with the RSA-1.5 algorithm and a public key identified in the KeyIdentifier element. When you specify a reference to an X.509 certificate with KeyIdentifier, you have to use the SubjectKeyIdentifier attribute in the X.509 certificate.

The decrypted symmetric key is used to process the EncryptedData element in the body. DataReference in ReferenceList has a reference to the EncryptedData element.

Listing 9.6 **WS-Security Encryption Example**

```
<SOAP-ENV:Envelope xmlns:SOAP-ENC="http://schemas.xmlsoap.org/soap/encoding/"
xmlns:SOAP-ENV=http://schemas.xmlsoap.org/soap/envelope/
xmlns:xsd="http://www.w3.org/2001/XMLSchema"
SOAP-ENV:encodingStyle-"http://schemas.xmlsoap.org/soap/encoding/">
   <SOAP-ENV:Header>
      <wsse:Security xmlns:wsse=
      "http://schemas.xmlsoap.org/ws/2003/06/secext"
      SOAP-ENV:mustUnderstand="1">
         <EncryptedKey xmlns="http://www.w3.org/2001/04/xmlenc#">
            <EncryptionMethod Algorithm=
            "http://www.w3.org/2001/04/xmlenc#rsa-1_5"></EncryptionMethod>
            <KeyInfo xmlns="http://www.w3.org/2000/09/xmldsig#">
               <wsse:SecurityTokenReference>
                  <wsse:KeyIdentifier>u3AA1M+DMOAlbX/vWJWnFtOKBck=
                  </wsse:KeyIdentifier>
               </wsse:SecurityTokenReference>
            </KeyInfo>
            <CipherData>

<CipherValue>cdck0cWh94oF5xBoEm9x/LjjJfmfnVn3SmhryPr5Rui/Y5tJQz8hQq
➥729vPHETtKWwwRBkpkp6wqFlHztCw2h
```

Listing 9.6   **Continued**

```
KMBMubZzPTODzzgAU0ZvbHtjRKtqPnNuq3ZDYDGQ9RBIfyjPyVdwrwlPaR9eaXtmbLK/G3e3iGaxAW4jh
➥Lq+wM=</CipherValue>
        </CipherData>
        <ReferenceList>
          <DataReference URI=
          "#wssecurity_encryption_id_519136303015631520_1045115597786">
          </DataReference>
        </ReferenceList>
      </EncryptedKey>
    </wsse:Security>
  </SOAP-ENV:Header>
  <SOAP-ENV:Body>
    <po xmlns="http://www.skatestown.com/ns/po-with-card" id="43871"
    submitted="2004-01-05" customerId="73852">
        <EncryptedData xmlns="http://www.w3.org/2001/04/xmlenc#"
        Id="wssecurity_encryption_id_519136303015631520_1045115597786"
        Type="http://www.w3.org/2001/04/xmlenc#Content">
          <EncryptionMethod Algorithm=
          "http://www.w3.org/2001/04/xmlenc#tripledes-cbc">
          </EncryptionMethod>
          <CipherData>
            <CipherValue>Ew7Zggr8z3/uFGzKVNP69SPSij+Y65L/jyk5sggKcKjkBv1hip5npg
            ==</CipherValue>
          </CipherData>
        </EncryptedData>
        <shipTo>
          <company>The Skateboard Warehouse</company>
          <street>One Warehouse Park</street>
          <street>Building 17</street>
          <city>Boston</city>
          <state>MA</state>
          <postalCode>01775</postalCode>
        </shipTo>
        <order>
          <item sku="318-BP" quantity="5">
            <description>Skateboard backpack; five pockets</description>
          </item>
          <item sku="947-TI" quantity="12">
            <description>Street-style titanium skateboard.</description>
          </item>
          <item sku="008-PR" quantity="1000">
          </item>
        </order>
    </po>
  </SOAP-ENV:Body>
</SOAP-ENV:Envelope>
```

The `EncryptedKey` in the header is intended to be a directive to message recipients. The recipients can know in advance which portions are encrypted and how to decrypt them. In this scenario, the recipient isn't SkatesTown but Credit. Therefore, Buyer should use Credit's public key so that SkatesTown can't decrypt the data. Furthermore, the `Security` element that contains `EncryptedKey` should have an `actorURI` to specify a particular recipient.

Java Cryptography Extension

To implement digital signatures and encryption for WS-Security, you need to use *Java Cryptography Extension (JCE)* 📖. Let's review JCE to help you understand Java's cryptography architecture.

JCE provides a framework for accessing and developing core cryptographic functions. Implementation and algorithm independence are addressed so that applications are insulated from cryptographic details. In other words, you can change the cryptographic implementation and algorithms without modifying applications.

Implementation independence is achieved through the security provider architecture. If you look at the file `java-home>\jre\lib\security\java.security`, you'll find the following format:

```
security.provider.<n>=<Security Provider Class>
```

The number indicates a priority, and the right side specifies a security provider class. Each provider class is a subclass of `java.security.Provider` and supports some or all Java security algorithms, such as DSA, RSA, MD5, and SHA-1. For example:

```
security.provider.1=sun.security.provider.Sun
security.provider.2=com.sun.rsajca.Provider
security.provider.3=com.sun.net.ssl.internal.ssl.Provider
```

Note that this example also specifies an SSL provider with priority 3. When a security algorithm is required, providers are asked whether they support the particular algorithm according to the priority. For example, if `SHA1withRSA` is required, the second provider is chosen. Although the second and third providers both support it, the second one has higher priority. If SSL is required, the third provider is chosen because only it supports SSL.

Even if you want to use another provider, such as IBM JCE, you don't have to change your program. Rather, you only have to change the security configuration file.

Security Tokens

In addition to message protection with digital signatures and encryption, WS-Security defines security tokens, which can contain various requestors' claims (such as a username and optional password, an X.506 certificate, or a Kerberos ticket). As we reviewed earlier in this chapter, a key purpose of the Web services security model is to integrate various security infrastructures and domains. In these security infrastructures, security claims are represented in different ways; therefore, you need an abstraction to integrate these differences.

A security token is an XML representation that can contain security claims. Because the security token can contain any mechanism-specific security data, it serves as the integration of different security infrastructures. Let's take a closer look at two types of tokens: `UsernameToken` and `BinarySecurityToken`. In addition, we'll review other tokens that can be embedded in the WS-Security `Security` element.

UsernameToken

The simplest security token is `UsernameToken`, which contains a mandatory `Username` and an optional `Password`. Listing 9.7 shows an example.

Listing 9.7   `UsernameToken` **Example**

```
<wsse:UsernameToken>
    <wsse:Username>testName</wsse:Username>
    <wsse:Password>testPassword</wsse:Password>
</wsse:UsernameToken>
```

`UsernameToken` is used for password authentication, such as HTTP Basic Authentication (see the sidebar "HTTP Basic Authentication"). From a security point of view, this plaintext representation is extremely insecure. Therefore, BASIC-AUTH needs to be used with security protection methods such as WS-Security encryption and SSL/TLS (see the sidebar).

Without a password, `UsernameToken` can be viewed as ID assertion. If you have a secured intranet, ID assertion is enough. If you have a gateway server that maps external IDs to internal IDs, the downstream server only needs the internal ID represented with `UsernameToken`.

BinarySecurityToken

Unlike `UsernameToken`, some tokens such as X.509 certificates and Kerberos tickets are represented as binary data. `BinarySecurityToken` is defined to contain such binary data. Look at the format in Listing 9.8. The `Id` attribute with the `wsu` prefix is used for referencing from another place in the SOAP message. The `ValueType` attribute specifies the kind of data. In this example, `X509v3` indicates an X.509 v3 digital certificate; you can also specify `Kerberos5TGT` for a Kerberos ticket-granting ticket and `Kerberos5ST` for a Kerberos service ticket. The `EncodingType` attribute specifies the encoding format of the binary data. Because `Base64Binary` is specified, a Base64 representation of an X.509 certificate is included in the `BinarySecurityToken` element.

Listing 9.8   `BinarySecurityToken` **Example**

```
<wsse:BinarySecurityToken xmlns:wsu=
"http://schemas.xmlsoap.org/ws/2003/06//utility"
EncodingType="wsse:Base64Binary" ValueType="wsse:X509v3"
wsu:Id="wssecurity_binary_security_token_id_2343669525027134511_1045057262242">
```

Listing 9.8   **Continued**

```
MIIDQTCCAqqgAwIBAgICAQQwDQYJKoZIhvcNAQEFBQAwTjELMAkGA1UEBhMCS1AxETAP
BgNVBAgTCEthbmFnYXdhMQwwCgYDVQQKEwNJQk0xDDAKBgNVBAsTA1RSTDEQMA4GA1UE
...
</wsse:BinarySecurityToken>
```

As in Listing 9.2, X.509 certificates are often combined with digital signatures. Because any third party can take a certificate and include it in their messages, the certificate alone can't serve as *proof of possession* 📖. Therefore, the X.509 certificate in a binary security token should be used for authentication only when combined with an XML Signature.

Other Security Tokens

WS-Security only provides a framework to include security tokens, mentioning how to use them with signatures and encryption, defining concrete tokens is outside the scope of the specification. Rather, security tokens are defined as separate profiles. As of December 2003, profiles for username token and X.509 have been published by OASIS. For example, "Web Services Security: X509 Token Profile" defines the value type for the ValueType attribute of the BinarySecurityToken element. As you saw in the previous section, X509v3 is defined to indicate an X.509 v3 digital certificate.

In addition, "Web Services Security: Kerberos Binding" is also being discussed. It defines Kerberos5TGT for a Kerberos ticket-granting ticket and Kerberos5ST for a Kerberos service ticket. Like the X.509 sample, a Kerberos ticket can be contained in BinarySecurityToken as a Base64 representation, specifying either of the Kerberos value types in ValueType.

The Secure Assertion Markup Language (SAML) is another candidate that will be embedded in WS-Security as a security token. SAML lets you represent security assertions in XML format. The assertions are similar to claims in WS-Security, and they can relate to authentication, authorization, or attributes of entities (either human or computer). "Web Services Security: SAML Binding" defines how to represent such assertions as security tokens in accordance with WS-Security.

In order to understand security tokens from a broader perspective, let's consider a security context defined in WS-SecureConversation. As we'll review later, WS-SecureConversation defines SecurityContextToken and key derivation mechanisms. The security context is like that in SSL and is established through a security handshake. It's important to note that the context is considered a security token in the specification. This abstraction contributes to simplifying digital signatures and encryption with the security context, as you'll see in the section on WS-SecureConversation.

Security tokens are a key concept of abstraction in WS-Security. Like the security context, you can define various types of security tokens. If you define new tokens, you can use them in WS-Security—that is, you can use a new token for digital signatures and encryption. This way, you can extend WS-Security by defining your own tokens for future use.

WS-Trust

WS-Trust defines how to request and issue security tokens and how to establish trust relationships. At its heart, WS-Trust assumes a security token service that issues security tokens and manages a security domain. In Figure 9.14, we assume that STS-A is a certificate authority (CA) in PKI and STS-B is a Key Distribution Center (KDC) in Kerberos. In this section, we'll review PKI and Kerberos as examples, mapping them onto WS-Trust. Through these examples, you'll see how the STS concept abstracts existing security infrastructures. We'll also review the XML Key Management Specification (XKMS), relating it to WS-Trust.

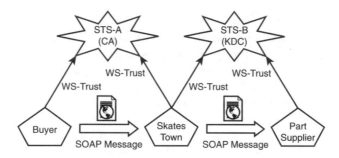

Figure 9.14   Using PKI and Kerberos with WS-Trust

Public Key Infrastructure

In terms of WS-Trust, a CA can be considered a Security Token Service (STS). Of course, in that case, the CA must implement WS-Trust. Let's review some WS-Trust examples, assuming that STS-A in Figure 9.14 is a CA. In our scenario, Buyer requires a Credit public key to encrypt credit card information. In this case, Buyer can get a Credit X.509 certificate from STS-A through WS-Trust.

As shown in Listing 9.9, the WS-Trust request is contained in the SOAP body. The `RequestSecurityToken` element is used for requesting tokens, and its child elements specify details. `wsse:X509v3` in `TokenType` indicates that an X.509 certificate is involved. `wsse:ReqIssue` in `RequestType` indicates that the required action is to issue a token. The `Base` element references a base token that is used to validate the authenticity of a request. In this example, `UsernameToken` is referred to in the header; thus the ID and password are used for authentication. Furthermore, because we need to get a Credit certificate, we want to specify it within the request. WS-Trust doesn't define how to specify a target party, so we use `AppliesTo`, which is defined in WS-Policy.

Listing 9.9   **Request to Issue an X.509 Certificate**

```
<S:Envelope xmlns:S="..." xmlns=".../secext" xmlns:wsu=".../utility>
  <S:Header wsu:Id="req">
```

Listing 9.9   **Continued**

```
    <wsse:Security>
      <wsse:UsernameToken wsu:Id='Me' >
         <wsse:Username>Buyer</wsse:Username>
         <wsse:Password>buyerPW</wsse:Password>
      </wsse:UsernameToken>
    </wsse:Security>
  </S:Header>
  <S:Body>
    <wst:RequestSecurityToken>
       <wst:TokenType>wsse:X509v3</wst:TokenType>
       <wst:RequestType>wsse:ReqIssue</wst:RequestType>
       <wst:Base>
          <wsse:Reference URI='#Me'
                 ValueType='wsse.UsernameToken' />
       </wst:Base>
       <wsp:AppliesTo
          xmlns:wsp='http://schemas.xmlsoap.org/ws/2002/12/policy' >
          <wsa:EndpointReference>
             <wsa:Address>http://credit.com/service</wsa:Address>
          </wsa:EndpointReference>
       </wsp:AppliesTo>
    </wst:RequestSecurityToken>
  </S:Body>
</S:Envelope>
```

Listing 9.10 shows a response example. `RequestedSecurityToken` in `RequestSecurityTokenResponse` contains a token. Because a Credit X.509 certificate is returned, `BinarySecurityToken` is used to contain it in a Base64 representation.

Listing 9.10   **Response for an X.509 Certificate Request**

```
<S:Envelope xmlns:S="..." xmlns="   /secext" xmlns:wsu=".../utility>
   <S:Body wsu:Id="req">
      <RequestSecurityTokenResponse>
         <RequestedSecurityToken>
           <BinarySecurityToken ValueType="wsse:X509v3"
                              EncodingType="wsse:Base64Binary">
                 MIIEZzCCA9CgAwIBAgIQEmtJZc0...
           </BinarySecurityToken>
         </RequestedSecurityToken>
      </RequestSecurityTokenResponse>
   </S:Body>
</S:Envelope>
```

Kerberos

As shown in Figure 9.14, SkatesTown and Part Supplier are managed by a Kerberos
security domain in our scenario. As we discussed earlier, users first get a ticket-granting
ticket (TGT) via password authentication, next get a Service Ticket (ST) for a particular
service, and then can access the service with the ST (see Figure 9.10). Once the user gets
a TGT, they can get other STs for other services without further authentication. In this
way, single sign-on (SSO) is achieved.

Requests from a client to KDC can be represented in a WS-Trust request. Listing
9.11 shows a request to issue a Kerberos TGT. Password authentication is required, so
UsernameToken is included and referenced from the Base element. wsse:Kerberos5TGT
is specified in TokenType.

Listing 9.11   **Request for Issuing a Kerberos TGT**

```
<S:Envelope ......>
   <S:Header>
     <Security>
         <UsernameToken wsu:Id="myToken">
            <Username>SkatesTown</Username>
             <Password>pwd</Password>
         </UsernameToken>
     </Security>
   </S:Header>
   <S:Body>
     <RequestSecurityToken>
         <TokenType>wsse:Kerberos5TGT</TokenType>
         <RequestType>wsse:ReqIssue</RequestType>
         <Base>
         <Reference URI='#myToken'
                ValueType='wsse:UsernameToken'/>
         </Base>
     </RequestSecurityToken>
   </S:Body>
</S:Envelope>
```

The client can sign and/or encrypt request messages based on the ST. Listing 9.12 shows
an example of a signature with a Kerberos ST. Notice that there isn't a significant difference between this and the X.509 signature example (Listing 9.2); the ValueType attribute in BinarySecurityToken is the only change. However, unlike PKI, a Kerberos ticket
contains a shared secret; therefore HMAC-SHA1 is used for the signature processing
instead of RSA-SHA1.

Listing 9.12   **Signature with Kerberos Service Ticket**

```
<SOAP-ENV:Envelope xmlns:SOAP-ENC="http://schemas.xmlsoap.org/soap/encoding/"
xmlns:SOAP-ENV="http://schemas.xmlsoap.org/soap/envelope/"
```

Listing 9.12 **Continued**

```
xmlns:xsd="http://www.w3.org/2001/XMLSchema"
SOAP-ENV:encodingStyle="http://schemas.xmlsoap.org/soap/encoding/">
   <SOAP-ENV:Header>
      <wsse:Security xmlns:wsse="http://schemas.xmlsoap.org/ws/2003/06/secext"
      SOAP-ENV:mustUnderstand="1">
         <wsse:BinarySecurityToken xmlns:wsu=
         "http://schemas.xmlsoap.org/ws/2003/06//utility"
         EncodingType="wsse:Base64Binary" ValueType="wsse:Kerberos5ST"
         wsu:Id-
         "wssecurity_binary_security_token_id_2343669525027134511_1045057262242">
         MIIDQTCCAqqgAwIBAgICAQQwDQYJKoZIhvcNAQEFBQAwTjELMAkGA1UEBhMCS1AxETAP
         BgNVBAgTCEthbmFnYXdhMQwwCgYDVQQKEwNJT0k0xDDAKBgNVBAsTA1RSTDEQMA4GA1UE
         AxMHSW50TENBMjAeFw0wMTEwMDEwOTU0MDZaFw0xMTEwMDEwOTU0MDZaMFQxCzAJBgNV
         BAYTAkpQMREwDwYDVQQTEwhLYW5hZ2F3YTEMMAoGA1UEChMDSUJNMQwwCgYDVQQLEwNU
         UkwxFjAUBgNVBAMTDVNPQVBSZXF1ZXN0ZXIwgZ8wDQYJKoZIhvcNAQEBBQADgY0AMIGJ
         AoGBAMy3PfZ1mPhrEsBvYiOuIlPV3Uis5Yy6hmxo2YwYC2nNDBPzKslWUi/Q+fK+DNdY
         6KEHmuDrcVcEma48J9X1a5avRlksQfKptKoVn4eBys2i/wkwyzQhDaFji79/MvnTRW8E
         Vy99FNKw4PFnhOoe1tlDcNBuIH/fIuGOz9ElTV+fAgMBAAGjggEmMIIBIjAJBgNVHRME
         AjAAMAsGA1UdDwQEAwIF4DAsBglghkgBhvhCAQ0EHxYdT3BlblNTTCBHZW5lcmF0ZWQg
         Q2VydGlmaWNhdGUwHQYDVR0OBBYEFIW3FD1cXie4j4zw1gAp4cuOAZ4lMIG6BgNVHSME
         gbIwga+AFL35INU4+WRy09vaf9zOsP7QvO9voYGSpIGPMIGMMQswCQYDVQQGEwJKUDER
         MA8GA1UECBMIS2FuYWdhd2ExDzANBgNVBAcTBllhbWF0bzEMMAoGA1UEChMDSUJNMQww
         CgYDVQQLEwNUUkwxGTAXBgNVBAMTEFNPQVAgMi4xIFRlc3QgQ0ExJjAgBgkqhkiG9w0B
         CQEWE21hcnV5YW1hQGpwLmlibS5jb22CAgEBMA0GCSqGSIb3DQEBBQUAA4GBAHkthdGD
         gCvdIL9/vXUo74xpfOQd/rr1owBmMdb1TWdOyzwbOHC7lkUlnKrkI7SofwSLSDUP571i
         iMXUx3tRdmAVCoDMMFuDXh9V7212luXccx0s1S5KN0D3xW97LLNegQC0/b+aFD8XKw2U
         5ZtwbnFTRgs097dmz09RosDKkLlM
         </wsse:BinarySecurityToken>
         <Signature xmlns="http://www.w3.org/2000/09/xmldsig#">
            <SignedInfo>
               <CanonicalizationMethod Algorithm=
               "http://www.w3.org/2001/10/xml-exc-c14n#"></CanonicalizationMethod>
               <SignatureMethod Algorithm=
               "http://www.w3.org/2000/09/xmldsig#hmac-sha1"></SignatureMethod>
               <Reference URI=
               "#wssecurity_body_id_2934309014555244973_1045057262232">
                  <Transforms>
                     <Transform Algorithm=
                     "http://www.w3.org/2001/10/xml-exc-c14n#"></Transform>
                  </Transforms>
                  <DigestMethod Algorithm=
                  "http://www.w3.org/2000/09/xmldsig#sha1"></DigestMethod>
                  <DigestValue>U2BIJSk6OL0W0mGXXiGVn5XPV54=</DigestValue>
               </Reference>
            </SignedInfo>
            <SignatureValue>
```

Listing 9.12   **Continued**

```
        Ojjw8nkT3jJoNN/AxsdOwTqWnhfZewubBWp0Sa0vJTTjQBrnKR18brODc8byuwVf2v
        iFdvMY4mT7Iumk/ZRLRNF1tEBCFRki2++W2LIXBIXVtmwo1riS98kmFZo6dBvhFOnX
        wKE1ag6C8x/UgAMVU+YzYd11KqNXtpwvi9Ydoq4=
          </SignatureValue>
          <KeyInfo>
            <wsse:SecurityTokenReference>
              <wsse:Reference URI="#wssecurity_binary_security_token_id_
➥2343669525027134511_1045057262242"></wsse:Reference>
            </wsse:SecurityTokenReference>
          </KeyInfo>
        </Signature>
      </wsse:Security>
  </SOAP-ENV:Header>
  <SOAP-ENV:Body xmlns:wsu="http://schemas.xmlsoap.org/ws/2003/06/utility"
  wsu:Id="wssecurity_body_id_2934309014555244973_1045057262232">
    <po xmlns="http://www.skatestown.com/ns/po" id="43871"
    submitted="2004-01-05" customerId="73852">
      <billTo>
        <company>The Skateboard Warehouse</company>
        <street>One Warehouse Park</street>
        <street>Building 17</street>
        <city>Boston</city>
        <state>MA</state>
        <postalCode>01775</postalCode>
      </billTo>
      <shipTo>
        <company>The Skateboard Warehouse</company>
        <street>One Warehouse Park</street>
        <street>Building 17</street>
        <city>Boston</city>
        <state>MA</state>
        <postalCode>01775</postalCode>
      </shipTo>
      <order>
        <item sku="318-BP" quantity="5">
          <description>Skateboard backpack; five pockets</description>
        </item>
        <item sku="947-TI" quantity="12">
          <description>Street-style titanium skateboard.</description>
        </item>
        <item sku="008-PR" quantity="1000">
        </item>
      </order>
    </po>
  </SOAP-ENV:Body>
</SOAP-ENV:Envelope>
```

XML Key Management Specification

Although WS-Trust provides a framework to access security token services, it doesn't encompass all aspects of key management: retrieval, registration, backup, revocation, and recovery. The XML Key Management Specification (XKMS) defines concrete operations for key managements, addressing PKI. In this section, we'll review XKMS and discuss how it relates to WS-Trust.

With XKMS, applications can interact using PKI without focusing on the myriad of fine details in PKI, such as ASN.1. There is some overlap between XKMS and WS-Trust, although they're being developed independently.

XKMS was published as a W3C Note in March 2001 by VeriSign, Microsoft, and WebMethods. XKMS has two major components: the XML Key Information Service Specification (X-KISS) and the XML Key Registration Service Specification (X-KRSS). One of the main goals of XKMS is to complement emerging W3C standards, such as XML Digital Signature and XML Encryption.

Let's go back to our example scenario, where Buyer requires a Credit X.509 certificate for encrypting credit card information. The WS-Trust request in Listing 9.9 can be represented as a XKMS request as shown in Listing 9.13. The key value of the public key can be retrieved via X-KISS, as in Listing 9.14.

Listing 9.13   **Query for Retrieving a Key Value**

```
<SOAP-ENV:Envelope xmlns:SOAP-ENV="http://schemas.xmlso ap.org/soap/envelope/">
   <SOAP-ENV:Body>
      <Locate xmlns="http://www.xkms.org/schema/xkms-2001-01-20">
         <Query>
            <KeyInfo xmlns="http://www.w3.org/2000/09/xmldsig#">
               <KeyName>
         ➥CN=Purchase Order Client, OU=Purchase Department,
         ➥O=SkateboardWarehouse, L=..., S=NY, C=US</KeyName>
            </KeyInfo>
         </Query>
         <Respond>
            <string>KeyValue</string>
         </Respond>
      </Locate>
   </SOAP-ENV:Body>
</SOAP-ENV:Envelope>
```

The Locate element includes a query on KeyInfo and a format for the response. This message requests a public key for the Distinguished Name (DN) specified by the KeyName element. Note that WS-Trust doesn't define how to specify the DN. Listing 9.14 shows its response.

Listing 9.14 **Response to the Key Value Query**

```
<SOAP-ENV:Envelope xmlns:SOAP-ENV="http://schemas.xmlsoap.org/soap/envelope/" >
  <SOAP-ENV:Body>
    <LocateResult xmlns="http://www.xkms.org/schema/xkms-2001-01-20">
      <Result>Success</Result>
      <Answer>
        <KeyInfo xmlns="http://www.w3.org/2000/09/xmldsig#" >
          <KeyValue>
            <DSAKeyValue>
              <P>
                  /X9TgR11EilS30qcLuzk5/YRt1I870QAwx4/gLZRJmlFXUAiUftZPY1
➥Y+r/F9bow9sbVWzXgTuAHTRv8mZgt2uZUKWkn5/oBHsQIsJPu6nX/rf
➥GG/g7V+fGqKYVDwT7g/bTxR7DAjVUE1oWkTL2dfOuK2HXKu/yIgMZnd
➥FIAcc=
              </P>
              <Q>l2BQjxUjC8yykrmCouuEC/BYHPU=</Q>
              <G>
                  9+GghdabPd7LvKtcNrhXuXmUr7v6OuqC+VdMCz0HgmdRWVeOutRZT+Z
➥xBxCBgLRJFn
                  Ej6EwoFhO3zwkyjMim4TwWeotUfI0o4KOuHiuzpnWRbqN/C/ohNWLx+
➥2J6ASQ7zKTx
                  vqhRkImog9/hWuWfBpKLZ16Ae1UlZAFMO/7PSSo=

              </G>
              <Y>
                  Q9N/x1cj2LSaV9ZdKPl0Sl9HhqbBdloc/AvxvY41sQREau9s/HmPwFd
➥Tgn6iRCdXrg
                  Y2HaiQYOlBdt09UW+q2XjvY1vdrWhXlxy8VdSFEdMCla926o38igZjF
➥qXF0LOlBKTK
                  LQTsCzWWxDB6sK8LkvaUikUFpudYa/rWP562GUI=
              </Y>
            </DSAKeyValue>
          </KeyValue>
        </KeyInfo>
      </Answer>
    </LocateResult>
  </SOAP-ENV:Body>
</SOAP-ENV:Envelope>
```

The value of the public key is included in the KeyValue element. With this value, you
can verify the signature of the initial SOAP message.

As shown in the example, X-KISS helps applications obtain cryptographic key information. In addition to key value retrieval, it can be used to validate a binding between a
key name and a key value. It's also useful for getting key information from an X.509 certificate. In a complementary way, X-KRSS provides key registration, revocation, and
recovery services.

As you've seen, there is overlap between WS-Trust and XKMS. Conceptually, WS-Trust is a superset of X-KISS because it can cover other security mechanisms such as Kerberos. On the other hand, XKMS defines retrieval operations more concretely than WS-Trust, addressing PKI. Furthermore, X-KRSS operations such as key registration and revocation aren't considered in WS-Trust. At this moment, we don't know whether these specifications will converge, although duplicated functions should ideally be converged.

WS-SecurityPolicy

When Buyer accesses SkatesTown services, it has to know the security requirements (the security policy) in advance. As we reviewed in Chapter 4, "Describing Web Services," WS-Policy and WS-PolicyAttachment provide a framework to describe policies and to associate them with particular services. WS-SecurityPolicy is a domain-specific language to represent policies for WS-Security. For example, you can describe your desired policy in such a way that a signature is required on a particular element and that a particular element must be encrypted.

In our scenario, SkatesTown requires a signature on Buyer's purchase order and therefore wants to represent this requirement as a policy. As in Listing 9.2, we assume that a signature is required on the SOAP `Body` element. Listing 9.15 shows a sample policy for `Signature`.

Listing 9.15   **WS-SecurityPolicy Sample for Signature**

```
<wsp:Policy xmlns:wsp="..." xmlns:wsse="...">
  <wsp:All wsp:Preference="100">
    <wsse:Integrity wsp:Usage="wsp:Required">
      <wsse:Algorithm  Type="wsse:AlgCanonicalization"
                       URI="http://www.w3.org/Signature/Drafts/xml-exc-c14n"/>
        <wsse:Algorithm Type="wsse:AlgSignature"
                       URI=" http://www.w3.org/2000/09/xmldsig#rsa-sha1"/>
        <MessageParts
               Dialect="http://schemas.xmlsoap.org/2002/12/wsse#soap">
            S:Body
        </MessageParts>
    </wsse:Integrity>
    <wsse:SecurityToken>
       <wsse:TokenType>wsse:X509v3</wsse:TokenType>
    </wsse:SecurityToken>
  </wsp:All>
</wsp:Policy>
```

Although XML Signature can be used for integrity and nonrepudiation, statements on signatures are represented with the `Integrity` element. Specifically, when you use PKI-based signatures, you can ensure the nonrepudiation of the signed message. On the other hand, if you use shared-secret-based signatures, you can't ensure nonrepudiation—only integrity.

In addition, WS-SecurityPolicy provides statements for confidentiality and security tokens. Listing 9.15 contains a `SecurityToken` statement for an X.509 certificate.

From an implementation point of view, one of the difficult aspects is verifying that necessary parts are signed or encrypted. WS-SecurityPolicy provides two mechanisms. You can use XPath to specify any parts of the message. Although this is a generic mechanism, its computational cost is often high. Therefore, if the part selection can be represented by the message part selection functions in WS-PolicyAssertion, it's recommended that you use those functions. `S:Body` in Listing 9.15 is an example of such a function.

WS-SecureConversation

SkatesTown and Part Supplier interact with each other frequently. Although you can use public-key-based signatures and encryption for such interactions, you can easily get into a performance problem. With WS-SecureConversation, the two parties can have a shared secret, making possible more effective signature and encryption algorithms.

Let's change our scenario a little, defining a security domain with PKI for SkatesTown and Part Supplier. Based on X.509 certificates, the two organizations establish a security context that contains shared secrets. With the shared secrets, they can interact with each other, ensuring integrity and confidentiality (see Figure 9.15).

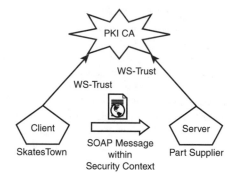

Figure 9.15 Secure conversation with PKI

The security context idea is similar to that in SSL/TLS: first establish a security context via handshake protocols, and then have a secure interaction with the security context. In this section, after we examine WS-SecureConversation, we'll review the SSL protocol in detail. Then, we'll consider a concrete authentication protocol based on WS-SecureConversation.

WS-SecureConversation Overview

WS-SecureConversation defines a format for security context mechanisms to establish a security context, and for mechanisms to derive session keys from security contexts. Let's look at an example, shown in Listing 9.16.

Listing 9.16 **Signature Based on** `SecurityContextToken`

```
<SOAP-ENV:Envelope xmlns:SOAP-ENC="http://schemas.xmlsoap.org/soap/encoding/"
xmlns:SOAP-ENV="http://schemas.xmlsoap.org/soap/envelope/" xmlns:xsd=
http://www.w3.org/2001/XMLSchema
xmlns:wsu=http://schemas.xmlsoap.org/ws/2003/06/utility
SOAP-ENV:encodingStyle="http://schemas.xmlsoap.org/soap/encoding/">
  <SOAP-ENV:Header>
    <wsse:Security xmlns:wsse="http://schemas.xmlsoap.org/ws/2003/06/secext"
    SOAP-ENV:mustUnderstand="1">
      <wsse:SecurityContextToken wsu:Id="SecContext">
        <wsu:Identifier>uuid:...</wsu:Identifier>
      </wsse:SecurityContextToken>
      <Signature xmlns="http://www.w3.org/2000/09/xmldsig#">
        <SignedInfo>
          <CanonicalizationMethod Algorithm=
          "http://www.w3.org/2001/10/xml-exc-c14n#"></CanonicalizationMethod>
          <SignatureMethod Algorithm=
          "http://www.w3.org/2000/09/xmldsig#rsa-sha1"></SignatureMethod>
          <Reference URI=
          "#wssecurity_body_id_2934309014555244973_ 1045057262232">
            <Transforms>
              <Transform Algorithm=
              "http://www.w3.org/2001/10/xml-exc-c14n#"></Transform>
            </Transforms>
            <DigestMethod Algorithm=
            "http://www.w3.org/2000/09/xmldsig#sha1"></DigestMethod>
            <DigestValue>U2BIJSkGOL0W0mGXXiGVn5XPV54=</DigestValue>
          </Reference>
        </SignedInfo>
        <SignatureValue>
Ojjw8nkT3jJoNN/AxsdOwTqWnhfZewubBWp0Sa0vJTTjQBrnKR18brODc8byuwVf2v
iFdvMY4mT7Iumk/ZRLRNF1tEBCFRki2++W2LIXBIXVtmwo1riS98kmFZo6dBvhFOnX
wKE1ag6C8x/UgAMVU+YzYd11KqNXtpwvi9Ydoq4=
        </SignatureValue>
        <KeyInfo>
          <wsse:SecurityTokenReference>
            <wsse:Reference URI="#SecContext"></wsse:Reference>
          </wsse:SecurityTokenReference>
        </KeyInfo>
      </Signature>
```

Listing 9.16   **Continued**

```
      </wsse:Security>
    </SOAP-ENV:Header>
    <SOAP-ENV:Body wsu:Id="wssecurity_body_id_2934309014555244973_1045057262232">
      <orderSupplies xmlns=
      "http://www.wheelsandboards.com/services/orderSupplies">
        <item sku="318-BP" quantity="5"/>
        <item sku="947-TI" quantity="12"/>
        <item sku="008-PR" quantity="1000"/>
      </orderSupplies>
    </SOAP-ENV:Body>
</SOAP-ENV:Envelope>
```

A security context is represented as a SecurityContextToken element. An Identifier element contains an ID for a shared secret, which is represented as a UUID or URI. Because this message is sent from a client to a server after the establishment of the security context, both parties can retrieve the secret from the ID. Note that the security context is considered a security token. As a result, the context element can be referred to from the Reference element within KeyInfo (boldface in the listing).

Although this example illustrates how to use a security context, we have to establish the context in advance. WS-SecureConversation defines three ways to do this:

- A security token service creates a SecurityContextToken.

- One of the communicating parties (particularly the initiating party) creates a SecurityContextToken.

- A SecurityContextToken is created through negotiation between the parties.

The first and second ways should be obvious. We'll discuss the third approach in more detail later in this section, using a sample negotiation protocol.

In Listing 9.16, the shared secret is used as a key for XML Signature. However, the specification recommends using keys derived from the shared secret. Listing 9.17 shows a sample for the derived key. DerivedKeyToken indicates how to derive a key from a particular shared secret. In this case, wsse:PSHA1 specified in the wsse:Algorithm attribute indicates a P_SHA-1 function defined for the TLS specification. With this function, a derived key is generated from a secret, a label, and a seed. The secret is shared already, and the label and seed are included in the Properties element. Because the P_SHA-1 function takes two parameters, the secret, label, and seed are used as follows in the function:

P_SHA1 (secret, label + seed)

Although this function generates a new secret, you can generate other secrets, applying the function to the generated secret repeatedly. You can specify how many times you need to apply the function with the Generation element, as in the example.

Listing 9.17 **Using a Derived Key from** SecurityContextToken

```
<SOAP-ENV:Envelope xmlns:SOAP-ENC="http://schemas.xmlsoap.org/soap/encoding/"
xmlns:SOAP-ENV="http://schemas.xmlsoap.org/soap/envelope/"
xmlns:xsd="http://www.w3.org/2001/XMLSchema"
SOAP-ENV:encodingStyle="http://schemas.xmlsoap.org/soap/encoding/">
  <SOAP-ENV:Header>
    <wsse:Security xmlns:wsse="http://schemas.xmlsoap.org/ws/2003/06/secext"
    SOAP-ENV:mustUnderstand="1">
      <wsse:SecurityContextToken wsu:Id="SecContext"
        <wsu:Identifier>uuid:...</wsu:Identifier>
      </wsse:SecurityContextToken>
      <Signature xmlns="http://www.w3.org/2000/09/xmldsig#">
        <SignedInfo>
          <CanonicalizationMethod Algorithm=
          "http://www.w3.org/2001/10/xml-exc-c14n#"></CanonicalizationMethod>
          <SignatureMethod Algorithm=
          "http://www.w3.org/2000/09/xmldsig#rsa-sha1"></SignatureMethod>
          <Reference URI=
          "#wssecurity_body_id_2934309014555244973_1045057262232">
            <Transforms>
              <Transform Algorithm=
              "http://www.w3.org/2001/10/xml-exc-c14n#"></Transform>
            </Transforms>
            <DigestMethod Algorithm=
            "http://www.w3.org/2000/09/xmldsig#sha1"></DigestMethod>
            <DigestValue>U2BIJSk6OL0W0mGXXiGVn5XPV54=</DigestValue>
          </Reference>
        </SignedInfo>
        <SignatureValue>
Ojjw8nkT3jJoNN/AxsdOwTqWnhfZewubBWp0Sa0vJTTjQBrnKR18brODc8byuwVf2v
iFdvMY4mT7Iumk/ZRLRNF1tEBCFRki2++W2LIXBIXVtmwo1riS98kmFZo6dBvhFOnX
wKE1ag6C8x/UgAMVU+YzYd11KqNXtpwvi9Ydoq4=
        </SignatureValue>
        <KeyInfo>
          <wsse:DerivedKeyToken wsse:Algorithm="wsse:PSHA1">
            <wsse:SecurityTokenReference>
              <wsse:Reference URI="#SecContext"></wsse:Reference>
            </wsse:SecurityTokenReference>
            <Properties>
            <Label>NewLabel</Label>
            <Nonce>FHFE...</Nonce>
            </Properties>
            <wsse:Generation>2</wsse:Generation>
          </wsse:DerivedKeyToken>
        </KeyInfo>
      </Signature>
```

Listing 9.17   **Continued**

```
      </wsse:Security>
   </SOAP-ENV:Header>
   <SOAP-ENV:Body wsu:Id="wssecurity_body_id_2934309014555244973_1045057262232">
      <orderSupplies xmlns=
      "http://www.wheelsandboards.com/services/orderSupplies">
         <item sku="318-BP" quantity="5"/>
         <item sku="947-TI" quantity="12"/>
         <item sku="008-PR" quantity="1000"/>
      </orderSupplies>
   </SOAP-ENV:Body>
</SOAP-ENV:Envelope>
```

In the WS-SecureConversation specification, the description of the establishment of the security context is a little abstract. In particular, no concrete negotiation protocol is mentioned. In the following section, we'll review the SSL protocol as an example of negotiation, and then we'll represent a protocol with WS-SecureConversation.

The SSL Protocol

SSL was proposed by Netscape Communications and has been used since the widespread adoption of the World Wide Web, because it's supported by Netscape Navigator and Microsoft Internet Explorer. The latest version of SSL, 3.0, has been presented to the *Internet Engineering Task Force* (IETF) 📖 for standardization.

> **Note**
>
> Another closely related protocol called *Transport Layer Security* (TLS) 📖 is currently on version 1.0, published as RFC 2246. There are no major differences between SSL and TLS. TLS hasn't yet become widely used, so SSL 3.0 is still dominant.

Figure 9.16 illustrates how a security *handshake* 📖 establishes a secure connection between the client and server. Once the handshake completes, the server and client have a common secret key with which data is encrypted and decrypted. In other words, SSL uses the public key(s) to encrypt exchange messages for the sole purpose of generating the shared secret key.

Despite the advantages of using public key encryption alone, SSL combines public and shared key encryption. It does so because the public key encryption system takes more time to encrypt and decrypt messages than the secret key encryption system. Thus, the combination used by SSL takes advantage of both the easy maintenance of public key encryption and the quicker operating speed of secret key encryption.

Let's take a closer look at the SSL handshake protocol, again referring to Figure 9.16. At phase I, the client starts the handshake and then sends a random number, a list of supported ciphers, and compression algorithms. At phase II, the server selects a cipher and a compression algorithm and notifies the client. Then it sends another random number and a server certificate (which includes a public key). At phase III, the client sends a premaster secret to the server, encrypting it with the server public key. Finally, the client might send a client certificate. Now the handshake is completed.

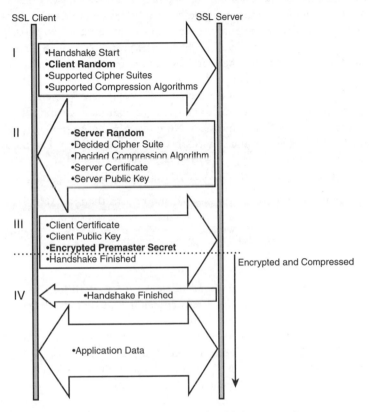

Figure 9.16 SSL security handshake protocol

The server and the client each generate a master secret by combining the random number the server sent, the random number the client sent, and the premaster secret. Several secret keys are created from the master secret. For example, one is used for encrypting transmitted data, and another is used for calculating the digest value of the date for integrity.

SSL ensures authentication (by verifying the certificates), confidentiality (by encrypting the data with a secret key), and integrity (by digesting the data). However, nonrepudiation isn't ensured with SSL because the MAC value of the transmitted data is calculated with a common secret key.

Negotiation Protocol Example

The security handshake protocol as in SSL can be represented with WS-Trust and WS-SecureConversation. WS-Trust defines a framework for challenge-response protocols, and

WS-SecureConversation defines a format for the security context token and a key derivation from a shared secret.

The idea discussed here seems similar to one in SSL. However, you don't stick to point-to-point security as in SSL. This protocol can be applied to a situation where you have a SOAP intermediary node. You can use the protocol even if two participants belong to different security domains. Thus handshake protocols in Web services security offer great advantages, especially when services and requestors are deployed on different security infrastructures and domains.

Figure 9.17 gives an overview of the protocol discussed here. The challenge-response protocol is defined with an initial `RequestSecurityToken` message and subsequent `RequestSecurityTokenResponse` messages. Note that a response message is also sent from an initial sender (Alice) to the service provider (Bob) at step 3. The protocol is performed as follows:

1. Alice sends a `RequestSecurityToken` to Bob to initiate the negotiation.

2. Bob prepares three numbers, p, g, and $r1$, and returns them to Alice. Simultaneously, he generates a secret Rb that is never exposed.

3. Alice prepares a random number $r2$ and a secret Ra, and calculates X. Then she sends X, $r1$, and $r2$ to Bob, signing them with her PKI private key. Note that $[X]_{Alice}$ indicates that X is signed with Alice's key.

4. Bob calculates Y, and sends Y, $r1$, and $r2$, signing them with his PKI private key. At the same time, a security context token containing an ID for a shared secret is sent.

The shared secrets are calculated with $K=X^Y \bmod p$ and $K=Y^X \bmod p$ respectively, and the calculated numbers are the same. Therefore, with the shared secret key K, Alice and Bob can interact with each other securely. (Note that the protocol here is prepared only for this demonstration; it isn't meant for use in a real application.)

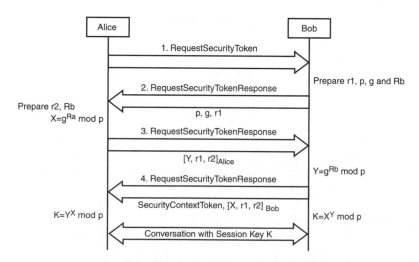

Figure 9.17 Security handshake protocol

Let's review the four messages in this scenario. Listing 9.18 shows the first message. This is a request represented in WS-Trust, and `SecurityContextToken` is specified in the `TokenType` element.

Listing 9.18   **Message 1**

```
<S:Envelope xmlns:S="http://schemas.xmlsoap.org/soap/envelope/">
   <S:Body  xmlns:wsu="http://schemas.xmlsoap.org/ws/2003/06/utility">
      <wst:RequestSecurityToken xmlns:wst=
      "http://schemas.xmlsoap.org/ws/2002/12/secext">
         <wst:TokenType>wsse:SecurityContextToken</wst:TokenType>
         <wst:RequestType>wsse:ReqIssue</wst:RequestType>
      </wst:RequestSecurityToken>
   </S:Body>
</soapenv:Envelope>
```

The second message, shown in Listing 9.19, is a first response from Bob. Because this response is considered a challenge from Bob, the `SignChallenge` element is included. We define an element `ExValue` that can contain exchanged values between Alice and Bob. In this case, p, g, and $r1$ are included in `val:P`, `val:G`, and `val:R1`, respectively.

Listing 9.19   **Message 2**

```
<S:Envelope xmlns:S="http://schemas.xmlsoap.org/soap/envelope/">
   <S:Body>
      <wst:RequestSecurityTokenResponse xmlns:wst=
      "http://schemas.xmlsoap.org/ws/2002/12/secext">
         <wst:SignChallenge>
            <wst:Challenge>
               <val:ExValue xmlns:val="http://dumml.org/exvalue">
                  <val:P>PoBmL7mRw/GI...3JSQygyzhDpRlY=</val:P>
                  <val:G>dNCglMprbcYT...GjxOCrLNczvAm=</val:G>
                  <val:R1>abcFCD...klkDDlfSGREdsfaDkF=</val:R1>
               </val:ExValue>
            </wst:Challenge>
         </wst:SignChallenge>
      </wst:RequestSecurityTokenResponse>
   </S:Body>
</S:Envelope>
```

Next, Alice returns X, $r1$, and $r2$, signing them with her PKI private key (see Listing 9.20). These values are included within the `ExValue` element. The `Signature` element is also added in the header to sign on the previous value. The signature targets the SOAP body element indicated by `Id="BODY"`.

Listing 9.20   **Message 3**

```
<S:Envelope xmlns:S=http://schemas.xmlsoap.org/soap/envelope/
xmlns:wsu="http://schemas.xmlsoap.org/ws/2003/06/utility">
   <S:Header>
      <wsse:Security xmlns:wsse="http://schemas.xmlsoap.org/ws/2003/06/secext"
      soapenv:mustUnderstand="1">
         <wsse:BinarySecurityToken
         wsu:Id=
         "wssecurity_binary_security_token_id_2148556043341261473_1054010042109">
         A1UEBxMKWWFtYXRvLXNoaTEMMAoGA1UEChMDSUJi9NI0I=.....
         </wsse:BinarySecurityToken>
         <ds:Signature xmlns:ds="http://www.w3.org/2000/09/xmldsig#">
            <Sig:SignedInfo xmlns:Sig="http://www.w3.org/2000/09/xmldsig#">
               <Sig:CanonicalizationMethod Algorithm=
               "http://www.w3.org/2001/10/xml-exc-c14n#">
               </Sig:CanonicalizationMethod>
               <Sig:SignatureMethod Algorithm=
               "http://www.w3.org/2000/09/xmldsig#rsa-sha1"></Sig:SignatureMethod>
               <Sig:Reference URI="#BODY">
                  <Sig:Transforms>
                     <Sig:Transform Algorithm=
                     "http://www.w3.org/2001/10/xml-exc-c14n#"></Sig:Transform>
                  </Sig:Transforms>
                  <Sig:DigestMethod Algorithm=
                  "http://www.w3.org/2000/09/xmldsig#sha1"></Sig:DigestMethod>
                  <Sig:DigestValue>FZEkQjaigph/bqYNlGJYpMQ6/ds=</Sig:DigestValue>
               </Sig:Reference>
            </Sig:SignedInfo>
            <ds:SignatureValue>BvwwClOX5FdF/E7tE5iSBo9htu12521ktEMkBw=.........
            </ds:SignatureValue>
            <ds:KeyInfo>
               <wsse:SecurityTokenReference>
                  <wsse:Reference URI="#wssecurity_binary_security_token_id_21485
➡56043341261473_1054010042109"></wsse:Reference>
               </wsse:SecurityTokenReference>
            </ds:KeyInfo>
         </ds:Signature>
      </wsse:Security>
   </S:Header>
   <S:Body wsu:Id="BODY">
      <wst:RequestSecurityTokenResponse xmlns:wst=
      "http://schemas.xmlsoap.org/ws/2002/12/secext">
         <wst:SignChallengeResponse>
            <val:ExValue xmlns:val="http://dumml.org/exvalue">
               <val:X>alksfdcYT...dzv112rism=</val:X>
               <val:R1>abcFCD...klkDDlfSGREdsfaDkF=</val:R1>
```

Listing 9.20   Continued

```
            <val:R2>dNCglMprbcYT...GjxOCrLNczvAm=</val:R2>
          </val:ExValue>
        </wst:SignChallengeResponse>
      </wst:RequestSecurityTokenResponse>
    </S:Body>
</soapenv:Envelope>
```

Finally, Bob sends *Y*, *r1*, and *r2* to Alice, signing them (see Listing 9.21). The message also includes `SecurityContextToken`, which contains the ID of the shared secret ($K=X^Y$ mod *p* and $K=Y^X$ mod *p*). From now on, the secret is shared and can be retrieved through the ID

Listing 9.21   Message 4

```
<soapenv:Envelope xmlns:soapenv="http://schemas.xmlsoap.org/soap/envelope/"
xmlns:wsu="http://schemas.xmlsoap.org/ws/2003/06/utility">
   <soapenv:Header>
      <wsse:Security xmlns:wsse="http://schemas.xmlsoap.org/ws/2003/06/secext"
      soapenv:mustUnderstand="1">
         <wsse:BinarySecurityToken ....>
1tYUdGOvZUtV93k9oarQ/wDy6ac0gc0z+ixDGx1VRbhN........
         </wsse:BinarySecurityToken>
         <ds:Signature xmlns:ds="http://www.w3.org/2000/09/xmldsig#">
            <Sig:SignedInfo xmlns:Sig="http://www.w3.org/2000/09/xmldsig#">
               <Sig:CanonicalizationMethod Algorithm=
               "http://www.w3.org/2001/10/xml-exc-c14n#">
               </Sig:CanonicalizationMethod>
               <Sig:SignatureMethod Algorithm=
               "http://www.w3.org/2000/09/xmldsig#rsa-sha1"></Sig:SignatureMethod>
               <Sig:Reference URI="#BODY">
                  <Sig:Transforms>
                     <Sig:Transform Algorithm=
                     "http://www.w3.org/2001/10/xml-exc-c14n#"></Sig:Transform>
                  </Sig:Transforms>
                  <Sig:DigestMethod Algorithm=
                  "http://www.w3.org/2000/09/xmldsig#sha1"></Sig:DigestMethod>
                  <Sig:DigestValue>FZEkQjaigph/bqYNlGJYpMQ6/ds=</Sig:DigestValue>
               </Sig:Reference>
            </Sig:SignedInfo>
            <ds:SignatureValue>7tE5iSBo9htu12521ktEMkBw=........
            </ds:SignatureValue>
            <ds:KeyInfo>
               <wsse:SecurityTokenReference>
                  <wsse:Reference URI="#wssecurity_binary_security_token_id_21485
➥56043341261473_1054010042109"></wsse:Reference>
```

Listing 9.21   **Continued**

```
                    </wsse:SecurityTokenReference>
                </ds:KeyInfo>
            </ds:Signature>
        </wsse:Security>
    </soapenv:Header>
    <S:Body xmlns:S="http://schemas.xmlsoap.org/soap/envelope/" wsu:Id="BODY">
        <wst:RequestSecurityTokenResponse xmlns:wst=
        "http://schemas.xmlsoap.org/ws/2002/12/secext">
            <wst:RequestedSecurityToken>
                <wsse:SecurityContextToken xmlns:wsse=
                "http://schemas.xmlsoap.org/ws/2003/06/secext">
                    <wsu:Identifier>uuid...</wsu:Identifier>
                </wsse:SecurityContextToken>
                <val:ExValue xmlns:val="http://dumml.org/exvalue">
                    <val:Y>alksfdcYT...dzvll2rism=</val:Y>
                    <val:R1>abcFCD...klkDDlfSGREdsfaDkF=</val:R1>
                    <val:R2>dNCglMprbcYT...GjxOCrLNczvAm=</val:R2>
                </val:ExValue>        </wst:RequestedSecurityToken>
            </wst:RequestedSecurityToken>
        </wst:RequestSecurityTokenResponse>
    </S:Body>
</soapenv:Envelope>
```

The protocol shown here is based on the Diffie-Hellman protocol. Although we defined a proprietary element `ExValue` for our explanation, you can use the `DHKeyValue` element defined in the XML Encryption specification in a real case.

If you look at WS-Trust and WS-SecureConversation, concrete negotiation protocols aren't included. Our example should give you a better idea of how negotiation protocols can be represented. We expect that profiles will emerge that define concrete protocols like the one we've presented here.

WS-Federation

One of the important challenges in Web services security is to federate different security domains—that is, a party in a security domain accesses another party in another domain. This process is very useful to provide users with SSO over multiple security domains. Extending the STS concept, WS-Federation defines how STS brokers security tokens such as identities, authentication, and security attributes.

Let's change our scenario a little as in Figure 9.18, where Buyer and SkatesTown belong to different security domains. In this scenario, Buyer has an ID managed by STS-A; Buyer gets a temporary ID from STS-B and accesses SkatesTown showing the temporary ID.

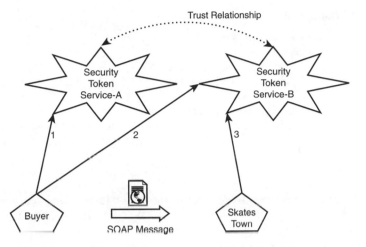

Figure 9.18   Getting a temporary ticket with federation

In message 2, a WS-Trust `RequestSecurityToken` is sent. Listing 9.22 shows a sample of the request. A Kerberos5 services ticket is required, containing an X.509 certificate issued by STS-A. The way STS-B validates the received certificate is defined by a policy or an out-of-band mechanism (Trust Relationship in the figure). After the validation, STS-B returns a temporary Kerberos ticket. Then Buyer can access SkatesTown services, including the ticket in its request messages. The request messages are no different from ones that contain Kerberos tickets issued from the same STS.

Listing 9.22   Requesting a Kerberos Ticket to Another STS

```
<S:Envelope xmlns:S="..." xmlns=".../secext" xmlns:wsu=".../utility>
    <S:Header>
        <wsse:Security xmlns:wsse="http://schemas.xmlsoap.org/ws/2003/06/secext"
        SOAP-ENV:mustUnderstand="1">
            <wsse:BinarySecurityToken xmlns:wsu=
            "http://schemas.xmlsoap.org/ws/2003/06//utility"
            EncodingType="wsse:Base64Binary" ValueType="wsse:X509v3"
            wsu:Id="myToken">
            MIIDQTCCAqqgAwIBAgICAQQwDQYJKoZIhvcNAQEFBQAwTjELMAkGA1UEBhMCS1AxETAP
            BgNVBAgTCEthbmFnYXdhMQwwCgYDVQQKEwNJQk0xDDAKBgNVBAsTA1RSTDEQMA4GA1UE
            ........
            </wsse:BinarySecurityToken>
            <Signature xmlns="http://www.w3.org/2000/09/xmldsig#">
                <SignedInfo>
                    <CanonicalizationMethod Algorithm=
                    "http://www.w3.org/2001/10/xml-exc-c14n#"></CanonicalizationMethod>
                    <SignatureMethod Algorithm=
                    "http://www.w3.org/2000/09/xmldsig#rsa-sha1"></SignatureMethod>
```

Listing 9.22   **Continued**

```
                    <Reference URI="#body_id">
                        <Transforms>
                           <Transform Algorithm=
                           "http://www.w3.org/2001/10/xml-exc-c14n#"></Transform>
                        </Transforms>
                        <DigestMethod Algorithm=
                        "http://www.w3.org/2000/09/xmldsig#sha1"></DigestMethod>
                        <DigestValue>U2BIJSk6OL0W0mGXXiGVn5XPV54=</DigestValue>
                    </Reference>
                </SignedInfo>
                <SignatureValue>
  Ojjw8nkT3jJoNN/AxsdOwTqWnhfZewubBWp0Sa0vJTTjQBrnKR18brODc8byuwVf2v
  iFdvMY4mT7Iumk/ZRLRNF1tEBCFRki2++W2LIXBIXVtmwo1riS98kmFZo6dBvhFOnX
  wKE1ag6C8x/UgAMVU+YzYd11KqNXtpwvi9Ydoq4=
                </SignatureValue>
                <KeyInfo>
                    <wsse:SecurityTokenReference>
                        <wsse:Reference URI="#myToken"></wsse:Reference>
                    </wsse:SecurityTokenReference>
                </KeyInfo>
            </Signature>
        </Security>
    </S:Header>
    <S:Body wsu:Id="req">
        <RequestSecurityToken>
            <TokenType>wsse:Kerberos5ST</TokenType>
            <RequestType>wsse:ReqIssue</RequestType>
            <Base>
                <Reference URI="#myToken"/>
            </Base>
            <wsp:AppliesTo
                xmlns:wsp='http://schemas.xmlsoap.org/ws/2002/12/policy' >
                <wsa:EndpointReference>
                    <wsa:Address>http://skatestown.com/service</wsa:Address>
                </wsa:EndpointReference>
            </wsp:AppliesTo>
        </RequestSecurityToken>
    </S:Body>
</S:Envelope>
```

In addition to the federated identity model, WS-Federation defines policy assertions, extensions of WSDL, and a UDDI profile. Let's review the policy assertions. In our example, Buyer has to know that STS-B can issue a temporary ID. Listing 9.23 shows a policy assertion for our example. RelatedServices specifies services that should be related to a policy subject. Because the policy is attached to a SkatesTown service, Buyer can send the `RequestSecurityToken` message in Listing 9.22 to an STS-B port specified in the `Address` element.

Listing 9.23   **Policy Assertion Sample for Federation**

```
<wsp:Policy>
    <wsse:RelatedService wsse:ServiceType="wsse:ServiceSTS">
        <wsa:EndpointReference>
            <wsa:Address>http://www.sts_b.com/tempIdentity</wsa:Address>
        </wsa:EndpointReference>
    </wsse:RelatedService>
</wsp:Policy>
```

Although the related service concept is generic, WS-Federation defines four service types: ServiceIP (identify provider), ServiceSTS (STS), ServiceAS (attribute service), and ServicePS (pseudonym service). In our example, Buyer requires a `BinarySecurityToken` that contains a Kerberos ticket; the ServiceSTS for it is specified in Listing 9.23.

Enterprise Security

SkatesTown's CTO, Dean Caroll, now has a good understanding of the Web services security model and has some ideas for each specification. WS-Security provides a message format to include signature, encryption and security tokens. With WS-Trust, WS-SecureConversation, and WS-Federation, you can obtain security tokens from Security Token Services (STS) in various ways.

However, it's still difficult for Dean to envision how to combine the specifications in real situations. He especially wants to see how he can extend the SkatesTown computing environment with Web services security. Addressing Dean's requirements, Al Rosen of Silver Bullet Consulting discusses the overall security architecture of SkatesTown's system.

In this section, we'll review the J2EE security model, addressing its authentication and authorization mechanisms. Then, we'll discuss how the Web services security model can be incorporated with J2EE, showing a hypothetical overall architecture.

J2EE Security

Figure 9.19 depicts the J2EE security architecture, which is based on role-based access control (RBAC). The HTTP server or Web container authenticates a requestor, referring to a user registry (an operating system [OS] user registry or a Lightweight Directory Access Protocol [LDAP] server). Within the Web container, access to Web resources is authorized based on a URL permission list. Within the EJB container, access to EJB objects is authorized based on a method permission list. Permission lists are mappings between roles and target objects: Web resources and EJB objects.

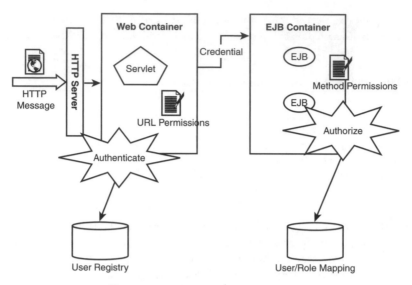

Figure 9.19 J2EE security architecture

RBAC is flexible because role assignment rules and permission lists can be independent-ly defined. There is a trick here: A credential containing a user ID travels along the method invocation path, which can span multiple containers, and roles are assigned to the requestor at each container for authorization. This concept is especially useful when the system configuration is extremely complex.

J2EE requires compliant platforms to support the following three authentication methods:

- HTTP Basic Authentication
- SSL Client Authentication
- Form-Based Authentication

In our discussion, we'll focus on HTTP Basic Authentication (BASIC-AUTH).

Authorization in J2EE

Using BASIC-AUTH, let's review how user IDs and roles are defined in J2EE. Listing 9.24 is an excerpt from `application.xml`, which is a deployment descriptor for the overall J2EE application.

Listing 9.24 **J2EE Deployment Descriptor**

```
<application>
  ...
  <security-role>
    <role-name>GoodCustomer</role-name>
```

Listing 9.24   **Continued**

```
    </security-role>
</application>
```

The `GoodCustomer` role is used in the J2EE application. J2EE doesn't prescribe any particular means for user definition and user-role mapping. Listing 9.25 is a platform-dependent format extracted from Sun's J2EE Reference Implementation.

Listing 9.25   **A Sample of User-Role Mapping**

```
<j2ee-ri-specific-information>
    <server-name></server-name>
    <rolemapping>
        <role name="GoodCustomer">
            <principals>
                <principal>
                    <name>ABCRetailer</name>
                </principal>
            </principals>
        </role>
    </rolemapping>
    ......
</j2ee-ri-specific-information>
```

With this format, you can enumerate user IDs within the `role` element. A principal indicates a user or a user group. In this example, user `ABCRetailer` can have a role `GoodCustomer`.

Let's look at a method permission definition for EJB objects. Listing 9.26 is an excerpt from `ejb.xml`, which is a deployment descriptor for EJBs.

Listing 9.26   **A Sample of Method Permission**

```
<ejb-jar>
    <display-name>OrderEjb</display-name>
    <enterprise-beans>
    </enterprise-beans>
    <assembly-descriptor>
        <security-role>
            <role-name>GoodCustomer</role-name>
        </security-role>
        <method-permission>
            <role-name>GoodCustomer</role-name>
            <method>
                <ejb-name>POProcess</ejb-name>
                <method-intf>Remote</method-intf>
                <method-name>order</method-name>
```

Listing 9.26   **Continued**

```
        <method-params>
            <method-param>java.lang.String</method-param>
            <method-param>java.lang.String</method-param>
            <method-param>java.lang.String</method-param>
            <method-param>int</method-param>
        </method-params>
      </method>
    </method-permission>
  </assembly-descriptor>
</ejb-jar>
```

The `security-role` element includes a collection of roles that are referenced some-where in this file. `method-permission` indicates who can access the target method with `role`. `role-name` specifies the role name for this method permission—in this case, `GoodCustomer`.

J2EE and Web Services Security

How can you extend J2EE servers in order to support Web services security specifica-tions? Figure 9.20 illustrates a possible extension of the J2EE architecture. Incoming SOAP messages with WS-Security are processed, potentially invoking the user registry and key/certificate registry. The registries access resources on the intranet, such as an LDAP server, and optionally invoke resources on the Internet, such as STSs and a CA. Within the extended J2EE, the security policy must be checked against incoming WS-Security messages. A security context may be established when WS-SecureConversation is used. We'll discuss in detail how each specification is processed in this architecture.

Let's look at WS-Security first. When a SOAP message uses WS-Security, you have to process digital signatures, encryption, and security tokens. When the signature is verified, a certificate (or key) should be required; therefore the key/certificate registry is invoked. In the simplest case, certificates are stored in files (such as keystore files). Certificates can also be managed by LDAP servers typically located on the intranet or external servers such STSs and CAs. For decryption, you need a private (or shared) key; therefore the key should be stored in an internal resource such as a file or an LDAP server.

The specification doesn't define a processing rule for a security token in WS-Security; only its format is defined. Security tokens are typically used for proof of identity. For example, when `UsernameToken` is used with a password, you may want to authenticate the ID/password. The authentication is equivalent to that in BASIC-AUTH. Therefore, you can reuse the module for BASIC-AUTH for this purpose. If `UsernameToken` con-tains only an identity represented in the Distinguished Name (DN), the LDAP server is accessed. Note that this solution is applicable only when you can trust the requestor node—that is, the requestor node is a gateway server of the business. An X.509 certifi-cate can also be used as a proof of identity. In that case, *proof of position* 📖 should be ensured by means of a digital signature with the certificate.

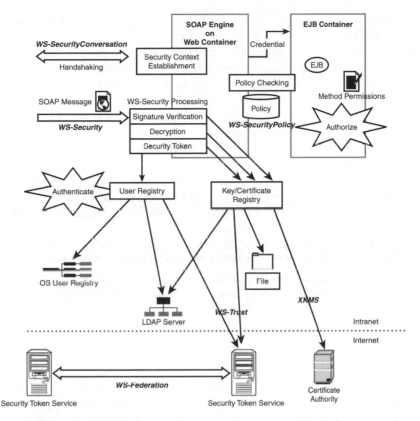

Figure 9.20   Possible integration of Web services security with J2EE

Once the requestor ID is authenticated, a credential is generated to travel along the downstream method invocation. This indicates that authorization in the downstream is exactly the same as for HTTP BASIC-AUTH. In this way, authentication with security tokens can be integrated with J2EE servers without affecting J2EE's core implementation.

The security policy described with WS-SecurityPolicy must be verified during WS-Security processing. You may have a policy that requires a signature on the message body. The signature verification only verifies whether the signature is valid; it doesn't check to see if the required part is signed. The policy-checking module in the figure needs to check such required parts, processing XPath or using the message part selection function in WS-PolicyAssertion.

In some cases, security handshaking is required to establish a security context. In that case, WS-SecureConversation performs the negotiation. Once a security context is established, a security context token is created, and its shared secret is cached for future use. When a SOAP message with the security context token is received, WS-Security processing is invoked. To process the security context token, Key/Certificate registry is invoked, and then the cached shared secret is retrieved.

There are several implementations for the key/certificate registry. When you need to retrieve an external key or certificate, you may want to use WS-Trust and XKMS. XKMS is specialized for PKI; therefore the specification is concrete. CAs such as VeriSign provide key management services with XKMS.

WS-Trust is more generic in the sense that it can be used beyond PKI. On the other hand, its specification is abstract; therefore you need further specifications (profiles). Once a collection of profiles is provided, WS-Trust becomes very useful, because you can get various security tokens with a single API.

WS-Federation defines how to integrate multiple STSs. As we reviewed in the section on WS-Federation, a temporary identity can be issued to access Web services in another security domain, for example. Thus you can achieve the ultimate goal: secure communication over multiple security domains.

Here we have envisioned how a J2EE server would be extended to support Web services security specifications. This kind of architecture discussion should help you understand Web services security more precisely, because you can imagine concrete behaviors within the J2EE architecture. Furthermore, integrating all of the specifications into a single architecture gives you an opportunity to consider the relationships among the specifications.

Security Services

XKMS suggests that key management can be outsourced to an independent third party; it could even be a Web service. In the future, a more comprehensive collection of security services may emerge. Examples include a key management service, an identity service, a signature service, an encryption service, a timer service, a rating service, and so on. Here we'll discuss a notary service as an example.

With BASIC-AUTH/SSL and/or WS-Security, you can generally fulfill the four basic security requirements: confidentiality, authentication, integrity, and nonrepudiation. However, there is a further requirement: *nonrepudiation of message receipt*. At the client side, for example, if SkatesTown receives a purchase order document from Skateboard Warehouse, it should return an invoice document. Then, it begins processing the order—that is, shipping products in the order. However, Skateboard Warehouse might not receive the invoice because of network trouble, or it might claim that the invoice wasn't delivered. Or, if the invoice delivery takes more than 10 days, Skateboard Warehouse can, by policy, consider the order unplaced or misplaced.

We want to ensure that the message has been received at the destination, and to determine when it was received. In the context of SOAP, it might be a good idea to include a notary service as a SOAP intermediary between the trading parties, as shown in Figure 9.21. The notary service provider is trusted by both SkatesTown and its customers. When there is a disagreement over message delivery between two parties, the notary service can arbitrate the problem on the basis of its log database.

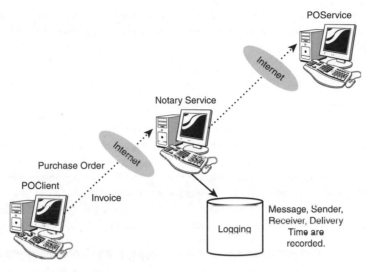

Figure 9.21 Notary service as a SOAP intermediary

From a business perspective, this structure is beneficial for all three parties. Trading parties can perform business transactions safely by contracting with the notary service. The notary service can earn money according to the transaction volume. The only problem is whether the notary service is a *real* trusted party. A number of notary services have emerged already, such as VeriSign. Most of them aim solely at trusted storage of data such as medical records. However, once they're trusted widely, they could play the role of a notary in a business structure like the one in our example.

The notary service is just one example of security services. Recently, componentization of business processes has become a trend because businesses must improve their efficiency and sharpen their competency. Considering this trend, it's possible that security services will be outsourced. After STS and XKMS become popular, we will probably see more interesting security services like our example notary service.

Three Steps to Ensure Security

You can follow a concrete process to protect your computing environment. This process consists of the following three steps:

1. *Evaluate risk*   Identify resources that you need to protect, and evaluate the value of each resource. Then, predict how much money you would lose if the resource was attacked.

2. *Decide on a policy*   Decide on an appropriate policy, referring to the risk evaluation as your context. If the amount of money that could potentially be lost is low and protection from the risk requires a huge budget, you may choose to accept the risk.

3. *Choose a protection method*   Once you decide to protect a resource, you need to specify a protection method. The protection is a process that may include system administrators, system developers, and application users. Technologies should be integrated in the process.

As you can see, technologies like Web services security are just a piece of the complete protection method. Before introducing technologies, you must consider the balance between your investment and your predicted results.

Summary

In this chapter, we've reviewed the Web services security model and looked more closely at its specifications. We've also discussed how Web services security specifications can be implemented, extending the J2EE architecture. As a future trend, we have reviewed a notary service as an example of security services.

Web services security addresses the federation of different security domains, which will be required for application integration both in intranets and on the Internet. In order to satisfy this requirement, an abstract security model is defined; as a result, we can use and integrate existing security infrastructures through the abstract model.

Let's briefly review the specifications. WS-Security is the basis in that it defines how to include security tokens, signatures, and encryption. WS-Trust defines a means to access Security Token Services (STSs), and thus defines how to obtain security tokens. WS-SecureConversation and WS-Federation define other ways to obtain security tokens. The former addresses the security context and key derivation from the security context. The latter defines federation, assuming that there are multiple STSs. In contrast to the other specifications, WS-SecurityPolicy defines security requirements that are necessary to access particular Web services.

Resources

- *AES*—NIST FIPS 197, "Advanced Encryption Standard (AES)" (NIST, November 2001), `http://csrc.nist.gov/publications/fips/fips197/fips-197.pdf`

- *ASN.1*—ITU-T Recommendation X.680, "Information Technology—Abstract Syntax Notation One (ASN.1): Specification of Basic Notation" (ITU-T, July 2002), `http://www.itu.int/rec/recommendation.asp?type=folders&lang=e&parent=T-REC-X.680`

- *Base64*—RFC 2045, "Multipurpose Internet Mail Extensions (MIME) Part One: Format of Internet Message Bodies" (IETF, November 1996), `http://www.ietf.org/rfc/rfc2045.txt`

- *BASIC-AUTH*—RFC 2617, "HTTP Authentication: Basic and Digest Access Authentication" (IETF, June 1999), `http://www.ietf.org/rfc/rfc2617.txt`

- *C14N*—"Canonical XML Version 1.0" (W3C, March 2001), `http://www.w3.org/TR/2001/REC-xml-c14n-20010315`

- *DES/3DES*—NIST FIPS 46-3, "Data Encryption Standard (DES)" (NIST, October 1999), `http://csrc.nist.gov/publications/fips/fips46-3/fips46-3.pdf`

- *Diffie-Hellman*—RFC 2631, "Diffie-Hellman Key Agreement Method" (IETF, 1999), `http://www.ietf.org/rfc/rfc2631.txt`

- *EXC-C14N*—"Exclusive XML Canonicalization, Version 1.0" (W3C, July 2002), `http://www.w3.org/TR/2002/REC-xml-exc-c14n-20020718/`

- *HMAC*—RFC 2104, "HMAC: Keyed-Hashing for Message Authentication" (IETF, Feb 1997), `http://www.ietf.org/rfc/rfc2104.txt`

- *J2EE*—"Java 2 Platform, Enterprise Edition (J2EE)" (Sun Microsystems, November 2003), `http://java.sun.com/j2ee/`

- *JAAS*—"Java Authentication and Authorization Service (JAAS)" (Sun Microsystems), `http://java.sun.com/products/jaas/`

- *JCE*—"Java Cryptography Extension (JCE)" (Sun Microsystems), `http://java.sun.com/products/jce/`

- *JSSE*—"Java Secure Socket Extension (JSSE)" (Sun Microsystems), `http://java.sun.com/products/jsse/`

- *Kerberos*—RFC 1510, "The Kerberos Network Authentication Service (V5)" (IETF, September 1993), `http://www.ietf.org/rfc/rfc1510.txt`

- *LDAP*—RFC 3377, "Lightweight Directory Access Protocol (v3): Technical Specification" (IETF, September 2002), `ftp://ftp.rfc-editor.org/in-notes/rfc3377.txt`

- *OASIS* (Organization for the Advancement of Structured Information Standards)—`http://www.oasis-open.org/`

- *PGP*—RFC 1991, "PGP Message Exchange Formats" (IETF, August 1996), `http://www.ietf.org/rfc/rfc1991.txt`

- *PKCS*—"Public-Key Cryptography Standards" (RSA Laboratories), `http://www.rsasecurity.com/rsalabs/pkcs/index.html`

- *PKI/X.509*—RFC 2510, "Internet X.509 Public Key Infrastructure Certificate Management Protocols" (IETF, March 1999), `http://www.ietf.org/rfc/rfc2510.txt`

- *RFC 2437*—"PKCS #1: RSA Cryptography Specifications Version 2.0" (IETF, October 1998), `http://www.ietf.org/rfc/rfc2437.txt`

- *Roadmap document*—"Security in a Web Services World: A Proposed Architecture and Roadmap" (IBM and Microsoft, April 2002), `http://www-106.ibm.com/developerworks/webservices/library/ws-secmap/`

- *SAML*—"Assertions and Protocol for the OASIS Security Assertion Markup Language (SAML) V1.1" (OASIS,   September 2003), `http://www.oasis-open.org/committees/download.php/3406/oasis-sstc-saml-core-1.1.pdf`

- *SHA-1*—FIPS 180-1, "Secure Hash Standard" (U.S. Dept. of Commerce/National Institute of Standards and Technology, April 1995), `http://csrc.nist.gov/publications/fips/fips180-1/fip180-1.txt`

- *SSL*—"The SSL Protocol Version 3.0" (Netscape Communications, November 1996), `http://home.netscape.com/eng/ssl3/draft302.txt`

- *TLS*—RFC 2246, "The TLS Protocol Version 1.0" (IETF, January 1999), `http://www.ietf.org/rfc/rfc2246.txt`

- *VeriSign Inc.*—`http://www.verisign.com/`

- *WS-Federation*—"Web Services Federation Language (WS-Federation)" (IBM and Microsoft, July 2003), `http://www-106.ibm.com/developerworks/library/ws-fed/`

- *WS-SecureConversation*—"Web Services Secure Conversation (WS-SecureConversation)"   (IBM and Microsoft, December 2002), `http://www-106.ibm.com/developerworks/library/ws-secon/`

- *WS-Security*—"Web Services Security: SOAP Message Security " (OASIS, August 2003), `http://www.oasis-open.org/committees/download.php/3281/WSS-SOAPMessageSecurity-17-082703-merged.pdf`

- *WS-Security Kerberos Binding*—"Web Services Security Kerberos Binding"   (IBM and Microsoft, December 2003), `http://msdn.microsoft.com/webservices/understanding/specs/default.aspx?pull=/library/en-us/dnglobspec/html/ws-security-kerberos.asp`

- *WS-Security SAML Profile*—"Web Services Security: SAML Token Profile" (OASIS, December 2003), `http://www.oasis-open.org/committees/download.php/4534/WSS-SAML-08.pdf`

- *WS-Security UsernameToken Profile*—"Web Services Security: UsernameToken Profile" (OASIS, August 2003), `http://www.oasis-open.org/committees/download.php/3154/WSS-Username-04-081103-merged.pdf`

- *WS-Security X.509 Profile*—"Web Services Security: X.509 Certificate Token Profile" (OASIS, August 2003), `http://www.oasis-open.org/committees/download.php/3214/WSS-X509%20draft%2010.pdf`

- *WS-SecurityPolicy*—"Web Services Security Policy (WS-SecurityPolicy)"   (IBM and Microsoft, December 2002), `http://www-106.ibm.com/developerworks/webservices/library/ws-secpol/`

- *WS-Trust*—"Web Services Trust Language (WS-Trust)"   (IBM and Microsoft, December 2002), `http://www-106.ibm.com/developerworks/webservices/library/ws-trust/`

- *X.500 Distinguished Name*—ITU-T Recommendation X.500, "Information Technology—Open Systems Interconnection—The Directory: Overview of Concepts, Models and Services" (ITU-T, February 2001), `http://www.itu.int/rec/recommendation.asp?type=folders&lang=e&parent=T-REC-X.500`

- *XKMS*—"XML Key Management Specification (XKMS)" (W3C, March 2001), `http://www.w3.org/TR/2001/NOTE-xkms-20010330/`

- *XKMS2*—"XML Key Management Specification (XKMS) Version 2.0" (W3C, April 2003), `http://www.w3.org/TR/2003/WD-xkms2-20030418/`

- *XML Encryption*—"XML Encryption Syntax and Processing" (W3C, December 2002), `http://www.w3.org/TR/2002/REC-xmlenc-core-20021210/`

- *XML Signature*—"XML-Signature Syntax and Processing" (W3C, February 2002), `http://www.w3.org/TR/2002/REC-xmldsig-core-20020212/`

10

Web Services Reliable Messaging

I N THE PREVIOUS CHAPTER, we started to explore how the basic SOAP protocol can be extended in order to be successful in real-world scenarios. The reality is, we don't live in a perfect world; therefore, adding features like security to messaging protocols has become a given. In the same vein, we must learn to deal with problems that may arise during message delivery. Certain situations, such as network outages or hiccups, are bound to occur. Some of these situations are already handled by the underlying transport protocol (like TCP/IP). But other failure situations can't be addressed by the transport protocol. In this chapter, we will explore a new specification that was written to try to overcome these problems by extending the SOAP protocol to add a "reliability" aspect to it.

Background of the Web Services Reliable Messaging Protocol (WS-RM)

Figure 10.1 shows the various parties involved with sending a single (one-way) message over HTTP between a client application and a Web service.

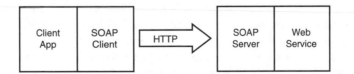

Figure 10.1   Basic message flow/components

In the simplest case, a client application issues a SOAP request by, in essence, calling the SOAP client with a message. The SOAP client then uses a network transport (such as HTTP) to send that message over to a SOAP server listening for requests. The SOAP server then locates and dispatches the message to the appropriate Web service. If this case was expanded into a two-way request/response flow, then any response message from the Web service would follow the same pattern in reverse.

The most obvious (and probably most likely) point of failure is the network itself. Although HTTP and TCP/IP are the most commonly used transports for SOAP messages, they aren't the most reliable. For human beings using a Web browser, errors such as "404 not found" are part of everyday life—we've all had to hit the Refresh button when our browser says a Web site can't be found (even though we know that isn't true). It's amazing how forgiving most of the Web community is when they encounter network glitches. Unfortunately, in the business world, we don't have that flexibility.

For some people, the most natural solution is to use a more reliable transport—perhaps message queuing, provided by products like IBM's MQSeries. These reliable transports are specifically designed to manage the instability inherent in networks. But the reality is that HTTP and TCP/IP are the de facto standard for Web services. This standard is acceptable for the Web community, which presumes that a human being is available at runtime to cope with network glitches in a graceful manner; but it isn't good enough for Web services, which are often used to do application-to-application integration and can't assume that a human being is present at runtime. Also, it isn't reasonable to complicate each application with sophisticated network error recovery capabilities. Business applications using Web services need a middleware solution to provide reliable message delivery.

Even if we ignore delivery errors due to the network itself, there are still other potential points of failure: the SOAP client and SOAP server. Once the client application gives the SOAP client the message for delivery, it's possible (in the asynchronous case) that the client application assumes its message has been delivered to the Web service and returns to its other tasks. However, what if the SOAP client crashes after receiving the message? In this case, the message will most likely be lost, and the client application will never be aware of the failure. The same type of failure can occur on the server—the SOAP server can successfully receive the message (or appear to, from the SOAP client's point of view) but then immediately crash without having a chance to deliver the message to the Web service. Again, the message is lost without the client application being aware of it.

Imagine you're trying to purchase something over the Web—you've entered your credit card information and clicked Submit. What if the Web site returns a generic "500 Internal Server Error" message? Did it accept your order? If you click Refresh, will you have placed your order twice? This uncertainty is annoying for a Web surfer and can be very costly in a business-to-business scenario. As SkatesTown interacts with its business partners, it can't afford to have such situations occur. Losing an order, or duplicating orders, could cost it money, time, and customers.

One possible solution is to add retry logic at appropriate places in the message path. This approach sounds easy enough, but it could lead to a new set of problems. What if the client thinks a message wasn't received by the SOAP server and sends the message again—but the message was received the first time? The Web service could potentially receive the same message more than once. When you're sending messages that involve money (such as purchase orders), this could lead to serious negative side effects.

Without trying to depress you too much, there's another potential message-delivery problem. Let's say the client application is trying to send a series of messages to a Web service, and it expects those messages to be delivered not just reliably but in the same order they were sent. For example, the processing of banking transactions is very order dependent—processing a deposit out of order could cause an overdraft error. It's possible that asynchronous processing or retry logic used by one of the components in the message path could cause the messages to arrive at the endpoint in a different order than they were sent. This reordering may also occur within the network. If the application and Web service need assurance of message order, then their developers must add order verification (and potentially reorder) logic to their code. However, doing so complicates application logic; application programmers should rely on middleware to take care of these sorts of situations.

Scenarios such as once-and-only-once delivery, message order, and so on are the driving force behind the need for reliable messaging. All the problems discussed in this chapter are situations that application developers would prefer to delegate to middleware. Although these issues could be solved using additional logic in the application, the Web service, or the specific SOAP implementation, it would be more desirable to handle them using a standard (and therefore interoperable) approach. Keep in mind that although one application or SOAP implementation might develop a way to solve a problem, it doesn't resolve the end-to-end problem if the receiving side doesn't solve it the same way. This is why interoperability and standards are key to successful Web services interactions. Networks and the Web will never be homogeneous.

A group of companies (IBM, Microsoft, TIBCO, and BEA) got together to develop a SOAP extension model to help solve these types of problems, and the result was *WS-ReliableMessaging* (WS-RM; this acronym may not be unique to this specification, but we will use it for convenience). Note that WS-RM is just one proposed solution—other companies have developed similar solutions, and no single, widely accepted specification has been produced by a standards body. However, we've chosen to examine WS-RM in detail in this book.

The WS-RM Specification

The WS-RM specification can be found at `http://www.ibm.com/developerworks/webservices/library/ws-rm/`. WS-RM uses the SOAP extension model to annotate SOAP messages with additional information so the sender and the receiver can cooperate to ensure proper delivery of messages. Actually, the term *ensure* isn't completely accurate; although this is the goal of WS-RM, there will always be situations where a message can't be delivered—one obvious case is when the receiver isn't there. So, WS-RM's goal isn't just reliable delivery of messages but also reliable notification to the client application regarding failures. Such notification ensures that the appropriate recovery action can be taken.

In the following sections, the XML snippets will include prefixes and namespaces that are associated as follows:

- wsa—http://schemas.xmlsoap.org/ws/2003/03/addressing
- wsrm—http://schemas.xmlsoap.org/ws/2003/03/rm
- wsp—http://schemas.xmlsoap.org/ws/2002/12/policy
- wsu—http://schemas.xmlsoap.org/ws/2002/07/utility

One of the nice things about the WS-RM specification is that it's relatively short and simple. At its most basic level, WS-RM is concerned with saving and communicating state information about the messages being sent between a sender and receiver. Each of the problems mentioned could be solved with a fairly trivial solution—and with that in mind, the authors of WS-RM kept WS-RM simple. So, as with most of the Web service specifications, the real innovation isn't contained in the details of the specification but rather in the acceptance of the specification by the various SOAP vendors—simplicity can go a long way toward increasing ubiquity.

WS-RM Processing Model

Using Figure 10.1 as a starting point, let's see how WS-RM modifies the message path to achieve reliable delivery of a single one-way message. For our purposes, we'll examine how a SkatesTown customer could use WS-RM to reliably deliver a purchase order to SkatesTown. The overall flow is as follows:

1. A client application sends a new message to the SOAP client.
2. The SOAP client, working with the WS-RM client code, associates a unique identifier for this message and saves it in a *persistent store* 📖.
3. The WS-RM client tries to send the message to the target server. If it fails, it retries until it reaches some time-out period as specified by a WS-RM configuration.
4. Upon receiving the message, the WS-RM server code acknowledges receipt of the message by sending back an *acknowledgment header* 📖. It may be sent three ways:
   - In the HTTP response flow
   - *Piggy-backed* 📖 on another message that's going to the From address
   - In a new SOAP message that's sent, including the acknowledgment header, to the From address
5. After receiving the acknowledgment, the WS-RM client removes the message and the state information from its persistent store.
6. The SOAP server locates and invokes the desired Web service.

7. Once the service is invoked, the message can be safely removed from the WS-RM server-side runtime persistent store.

8. After the Expires time has passed, the WS-RM server runtime can remove the state information about this particular message sequence.

Let's look at this process in detail.

Client-Side Processing

First, the customer's client application invokes the SOAP client APIs—basically, giving it a new message to send. The SOAP client invokes the WS-RM client-side code to send the message to the server. The WS-RM code begins by saving the message into some persistent store for safekeeping, as depicted in Figure 10.2.

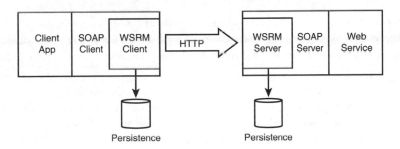

Figure 10.2   Basic WS-RM design

Now, in the asynchronous case, program control returns to the client application. In the synchronous case, the client application waits for the message to be delivered. From this point on, we can be assured that the message will be delivered even if there is some sort of failure; the WS-RM system will retain the message in its persistent store until it's delivered to the receiver. Even if the system crashes, when it's rebooted, the WS-RM component will still have a record of the message and will continue attempting to send it. It's important to note that in the asynchronous case, along with the message, the client application gives the SOAP client code a callback object that's used to notify the application when the message has been successfully delivered. In the synchronous case, the application will block until successful delivery.

Regardless of how the SOAP client was invoked, the client application should be able to query the SOAP runtime (or, more specifically, the WS-RM runtime) for the status of a message. Imagine a case where the application made a synchronous call to the SOAP client, and the system crashed after the WS-RM code received the message. In this instance, upon restarting, the application would no longer be in the wait state it was in before, so it would need to query the state of the message (or even resume its wait state—that is, wait for the message to be delivered). How the client application does this will vary between implementations, but the basic concepts should be the same.

Now that the message is safely stored in the WS-RM runtime, attempts are made to send it to the server. For the most part, there's nothing special about this action—a normal HTTP POST (if you're using HTTP) will suffice. What is different is that the SOAP envelope holds SOAP headers containing additional information about the message; this data is intended for use by the WS-RM runtime on the server. One of the key WS-RM SOAP headers is the Sequence header:

```
<wsrm:Sequence soapenv:mustUnderstand="1">
    <wsu:Identifier>urn:2ff5fdf4c0a8016413a3861</wsu:Identifier>
    <wsrm:MessageNumber>1</wsrm:MessageNumber>
    <wsrm:LastMessage/>
    <wsrm:Expires>2004-12-31T12:00:00Z</wsrm:Expires>
</wsrm:Sequence>
```

In this header, the WS-RM client tells the WS-RM server several key things:

- <wsu:Identifier>—The unique identifier for this sequence of messages. Remember, WS-RM will try to solve the problem of keeping a series of messages in order, so each series (or sequence) is uniquely identified even if it includes just one message.

- <wsrm:MessageNumber>—An element that indicates the ordinal position, in this sequence, for this message (here the ordinal position indicates that it's the first one). These message numbers must start at one and increase by one without skipping or repeating any numbers. The WS-RM runtime on the server uses these message numbers to ensure that when the Web services are called, the messages are processed in the same order in which they were sent. If the server receives two messages with the same number, then it will assume that they're duplicates. The specification doesn't say which of the duplicate messages should be kept and which should be discarded; this becomes an implementation's choice.

- <wsrm:LastMessage/>—An indication that this is the final message of the sequence. The receiver will consider any message numbers greater than the one in this Sequence header to be errors. The WS-RM runtime on the server will also use this flag to determine that it can invoke the Web services, with assurance that all the messages in the sequence have been received. In the normal case, the Web services shouldn't be called until all the messages in the sequence have been successfully delivered; but this behavior isn't mandated, so an implementation could choose to invoke each Web service as it receives each message (as long as they're done in order). We'll examine some possible exceptions later.

- <wsrm:Expires>—An element that tells the WS-RM server the time at which this sequence should be considered invalid or out of date. This will be handy later, when the WS-RM server tries to do some cleanup, if it has incomplete sequences lying around. Notice that each Sequence header (or, to put it another way, each message sent for this sequence) can optionally include this element. The last expiration time received by the server must override any previously specified time.

After sending the message to the server, the client waits for an acknowledgment from the server that it received the message; this acknowledgment comes in the form of a SOAP header (we'll look at the details in a bit). However, if the client never gets confirmation that the server received the message, then after a period of time, the client tries to send the message again—making sure to include the additional WS-RM SOAP header. This process repeats until the server successfully receives the message *and* an acknowledgment is returned, or until a timeout period has elapsed.

If the message times out, the SOAP client notifies the client application that delivery of the message isn't possible. The way in which the client application is notified varies depending on the implementation. If the message is successfully delivered, then the WS-RM client code notifies the client application of the delivery (in the asynchronous case), or the client application's call to the Web service returns (in the synchronous case). Either way, the message can now be removed from WS-RM persistence.

Client-side processing is really nothing more than a simple retry algorithm with a little persistence thrown in. For the most part, client applications using WS-RM won't need to change much; however, some WS-RM–specific tasks (such as specifying the message numbers in sequences) will probably not be hidden completely. Each implementation will handle this differently. Now, let's move on to the server side.

Server-Side Processing

On the server, a WS-RM layer between the SOAP server and the Web service manages the persistence and state information—much as you saw on the client side. In this case, when the SOAP server receives a new message, it sends the message to the WS-RM server runtime, which places it in a persistent store for safekeeping. As on the client side, this persistent store ensures that the system doesn't lose the message if something goes wrong—for example, if the system crashes.

Once all the messages for a sequence are safely in the WS-RM persistent store, the Web services are located and invoked with those messages. After that, the WS-RM runtime removes the messages from its persistent store. However, it must retain some information about the sequence (such as the sequence identifier and the message numbers) to support situations where the sequence is delivered again due to a network error. In this case, the WS-RM runtime knows that it should ignore the duplicate sequences. And, as we'll discuss later, the server must be able to tell the client which messages have been received if it's asked to do so—even after the Web service has been invoked.

This leaves open the question of when the information can be safely deleted. As of now, this is an open question—the specification authors are currently working on this issue, and a solution will probably be in the next revision of the specification. In the meantime, it's safest to assume that you can use the Expires time specified in the Sequence header as the time when you can delete any information about the sequence.

Now that the message has been successfully delivered to the server, the WS-RM server runtime must let the WS-RM client runtime know—in other words, it needs to send back the acknowledgment we discussed earlier.

> **Note**
>
> There's an important distinction to note: The WS-RM runtime is only concerned with successful delivery of the message to the WS-RM server-side runtime within the SOAP server, not to the Web service itself. If for some reason an error occurs during the invocation of the Web service, then from a WS-RM perspective, the message has still been successfully delivered. It's up to some other component (probably the SOAP server) to manage the SOAP fault that needs to be returned to the client.

Acknowledging Receipt

Let's examine the acknowledgment header that needs to be sent back to SkatesTown's customer:

```
<wsrm:SequenceAcknowledgement>
    <wsu:Identifier>urn:2ff5fdf4c0a8016413a3861</wsu:Identifier>
    <wsrm:AcknowledgementRange Lower="1" Upper="1"/>
</wsrm:SequenceAcknowledgement>
```

> **Note**
>
> The specification currently has a minor flaw, which we hope will be solved soon: its use of the words *Acknowledgement* and *Acknowledgment*. In some instances the e is included, and in others it isn't. (Our best guess about this irregularity is that both American and English authors were working on the spec and either couldn't agree or didn't notice the inconsistency.) If you work on an implementation, watch out for this issue, because such minor differences could lead to interoperability problems.

As you might expect, it contains the unique sequence identifier that was included in the `Sequence` header the client sent. It also contains an `AcknowledgementRange` element noting the range (lower and upper limits) on the message numbers (for this sequence) that were successfully received (in this case, just message 1). If this sequence included multiple messages, then we might need multiple `AcknowledgementRange` elements:

```
<wsrm:SequenceAcknowledgement>
    <wsu:Identifier>urn:2ff5fdf4c0a8016413a3861</wsu:Identifier>
    <wsrm:AcknowledgementRange Lower="1" Upper="2"/>
    <wsrm:AcknowledgementRange Lower="4" Upper="5"/>
</wsrm:SequenceAcknowledgement>
```

The header in this example indicates that message numbers 1, 2, 4, and 5 (for this particular sequence) have all been received, but message number 3 has not.

Obviously, the WS-RM client will use this acknowledgment header to determine which messages have been received, so that it can better manage its persistent store and ascertain which messages may require a resend. Remember, the WS-RM client must attempt to resend any messages until it gets confirmation of their delivery, so these `SequenceAcknowledgement` headers are crucial.

The only piece of the scenario that's missing is how, or when, this acknowledgment is sent back to the WS-RM client. In a simple HTTP transport scenario, this acknowledgment can be included in the SOAP response that's sent back to the client. However, this only works well when we're using a synchronous request/response-messaging pattern (when the client is explicitly waiting for the response from the Web service). A very slow Web service could lead the WS-RM client runtime to think that the message was never received, and it might attempt to resend the message. We can't assume the Web service invocation will be fast, so we need to examine the other possible ways in which this acknowledgment can be sent back to the WS-RM client.

First, let's examine exactly where this acknowledgment is supposed to go. In the message the client sent, it included WS-Address elements such as `To`, `From`, and `ReplyTo`. The `From` header is meant to contain the location of the client—and, more specifically, the address to which the acknowledgment should be sent. There is one exception: If the `From` URI is defined as the anonymous URI (`http://schemas.xmlsoap.org/ws/2003/03/addressing/role/anonymous`), then the server has no choice but to send the acknowledgment back to the client that initiated the HTTP connection, because it doesn't have an address for the message originator. Said another way, normally the HTTP response to the receipt of a WS-RM message is an empty HTTP message (with an HTTP return code of "202 Accepted"). This is because typically the `From` URI contains a real address; and since we can't know for sure that this address points to the same party that opened the connection, we need to create a new connection to send the acknowledgment. If the anonymous URI is used, we have no endpoint to which we can open the connection; so, we have no option but to try to send the acknowledgment back to the sender of the original message on the same connection on which we received the message (the HTTP response). This process is known as sending the acknowledgment back *synchronously*.

Typically, the `From` URI contains a reference to a real endpoint; therefore, we need to send our acknowledgment there. We have two options. First, a new connection can be made from the server back to the client. In this case, it would contain a SOAP envelope with the additional acknowledgment header. In most cases, the body of the SOAP envelope would be empty. Second, the acknowledgment header can be included (or piggy-backed) on any message that happens to be going from the server to the `From` URL. This approach is typically used as an optimization. Both options have an obvious problem, though: How can we assume that the WS-RM server can open a new connection (potentially through firewalls) back to the client? This is a potentially fatal flaw in the specification that we hope will be addressed in future revisions.

In all but the synchronous case, the server determines when to send the acknowledgment, typically using configuration settings. However, the client can explicitly ask for an acknowledgment to be sent immediately, by including an `AckRequest` header in a message to the server (we'll examine this in more detail later).

We've briefly touched on the fact that WS-RM can use WS-Addressing to determine the location of the endpoints to which messages should be sent, so let's examine this topic a bit more.

WS-Addressing

While the WS-RM specification doesn't mandate how the location of the other party involved in the Web service conversation is located, it does provide some guidance through its samples. For example, in the asynchronous message case, when the server needs to send back a message to the client, the only way the WS-RM specification suggests how to determine the client's location is through the use of WS-Addressing SOAP headers from the client's original request message.

As mentioned in Chapter 8, "Web Services and Stateful Resources," WS-Addressing provides a standard way for Web services endpoints to identify key pieces of information about themselves and the messages they send. WS-RM's primary use of WS-Addressing is to locate the client-side endpoint that will receive either the acknowledgment messages or response messages from the Web service. Three of the key WS-Addressing SOAP headers used by WS-RM are To, From, and ReplyTo:

```
<wsa:To>http://www.skatestown.com/services/PO</wsa:To>
<wsa:From>http://www.myclient.com/sender</wsa:From>
<wsa:ReplyTo>
   <wsa:Address>http://www.myclient.com/receiver</wsa:Address>
</wsa:ReplyTo>
```

The To header indicates the target for this message. In most cases this will probably be the same as the HTTP URL from the HTTP POST header. As previously discussed, the From header contains the location of the endpoint that's expecting to receive the acknowledgment messages. The ReplyTo header contains all the information the message's recipient needs to locate the endpoint that will receive any response message from the Web service. In this case, it contains the URL of the SOAP server that's waiting for a message.

Going back to our simple example, we solved the problem of locating the client's SOAP endpoint by including a couple of additional SOAP headers in the message:

```
<wsa:From>http://www.myclient.com/sender</From>
<wsa:ReplyTo soapenv:mustUnderstand="1">
   <wsa:Address>http://www.myclient.com/receiver</wsa:Address>
</wsa:ReplyTo>
```

This requires the client environment to ensure that a SOAP server is running and that it can pass on any WS-RM information it receives to the WS-RM client runtime used to send the original message. Exactly how this exchange of information takes place (especially when several WS-RM clients can be running on the client side) is an implementation choice. For our examples, we'll assume that each client has its own WS-RM receiver that's waiting to receive these messages from the server.

Typically, the WS-RM server determines when to send acknowledgments back to the WS-RM client (usually through some configuration options). There is, however, another alternative: The WS-RM client can explicitly ask the WS-RM server for any acknowledgments related to the sequence in question. In this instance, the WS-RM client could send a message to the WS-RM server containing this SOAP header:

```
<wsrm:AckRequested>
    <wsu:Identifier>urn:2ff5fdf4c0a8016413a3861</wsu:Identifier>
</wsrm:AckRequested>
```

This message asks the server-side WS-RM runtime for all the acknowledgments related to the sequence identified by urn:2ff5fdf4c0a8016413a3861. Previously, we said that even after the Web service was invoked, the WS-RM server runtime code would need to maintain information about the messages it received (but not necessarily the messages themselves). This is important because, as you may have noticed, nothing guarantees that the acknowledgments are successfully delivered back to the client. For this reason, the WS-RM server-side runtime must maintain the state information for a sequence of messages until the Expires time specified in the original Sequence header. For our example, this time is 12:00pm 12/31/2004.

Now that we've successfully delivered the acknowledgment, back to the client, we're finished. As we mentioned earlier, the WS-RM authors tried to keep this solution as simple as possible. Although it isn't perfect, the basic approach is sound.

To this point we've covered the core aspects of WS-RM. The following sections will discuss some of the specification's supplementary aspects.

Sequence Faults

So far, the error situations we've discussed have been related to network or environmental issues. However, errors could also occur in the WS-RM runtime. The specification defines a standard mechanism through which each party can communicate the details of these types of errors through the use of a SequenceFault element. For example:

```
<wsrm:SequenceFault>
    <wsu:Identifier>urn:2ff5fdf4c0a8016413a3861</wsu:Identifier>
    <wsrm:FaultCode>wsrm:LastMessageNumberExceeded</wsrm:FaultCode>
</wsrm:SequenceFault>
```

This message would be included in the detail element of a SOAP fault message sent back to the client. Notice that it includes the identifier of the sequence in question and a qualified FaultCode, or reason, for the fault (in this case, a message number was used that exceeded the message number specified in the sequence's LastMessage). Following are the possible WS-RM specific FaultCodes:

- wsrm:SequenceTerminated—This fault is generated whenever either side of the conversation has encountered an unrecoverable error and can't continue to process the specified sequence. Although in many cases the error condition is so severe that a fault message can't be delivered, the attempt to do so should still be made.

- wsrm:UnknownSequence—Whenever a sequence identifier is used that is unknown to either party in the conversation, this FaultCode must be used.

- `wsrm:InvalidAcknowledgement`—This `FaultCode` is used when a server sends back a `SequenceAcknowledgement` header to the client that seems to be in error (for example, including a range of message numbers for a sequence that was never sent). In this case, the fault should also include an additional element indicating the range of messages that was actually sent:

```
<wsrm:SequenceFault>
   <wsu:Identifier>urn:2ff5fdf4c0a8016413a3861</wsu:Identifier>
   <wsrm:FaultCode>wsrm:LastMessageNumberExceeded</wsrm:FaultCode>
   <wsrm:AcknowledgmentRange Lower="1" Upper="1"/>
</wsrm:SequenceFault>
```

Here the client is telling the server that it sent only one message.

- `wsrm:MessageNumberRollover`—This fault is sent by the client when it runs out of valid message numbers (in other words, it has sent 18,446,744,073,709,551,615 messages—the maximum value of an unsigned long).
- `wsrm:SequenceRefused`—If for some reason the server can't begin processing a new sequence, this fault must be returned. This fault is for a new sequence, whereas the `SequenceTerminated` fault is for sequences that have already begun to be processed.

The list of possible WS-RM faults is fairly small, and most of them are related to very serious (or extreme) conditions; this implies that only the most serious errors should prevent a message from being delivered reliably.

> **Note**
> When one of these errors occurs, the WS-RM runtime can start over and try to resend the entire sequence—but chances are, the same error will happen again. For this reason, the client application will probably need to change (a little) to deal with these errors being propagated back up to it.

Policy Assertions

As you've seen in the previous chapters, when a SOAP conversation deviates from the case of a simple SOAP envelope moving between two endpoints, both sides must be aware of any new requirements and agree to support them. WS-Policy is the means through which these expectations are expressed. Typically, these policy statements (or assertions) are added to the Web service's WSDL document. WS-RM defines some additional policy assertions that can be used to indicate the expectations each side of the conversation can rely on.

`SpecVersion` **Assertion**

Here an endpoint specifies which version of the WS-RM specification it supports:

```
<wsrm:SpecVersion
    wsp:URI=http://schemas.xmlsoap.org/ws/2003/03/rm"/>
```

`DeliveryAssurance` **Policy**

The `DeliveryAssurance` policy is as follows:

```
<wsrm:DeliveryAssurance Value="wsrm:ExactlyOnce"/>
```

Up to this point we've only talked about using WS-RM in the case where each side is expecting each message to be delivered exactly once and in order (in the case of multiple messages in a sequence) to the Web service. However, four different types of delivery modes are available:

- `wsrm:AtMostOnce`—Specifies that each message in the sequence must not be delivered to the Web service more than once. Notice this implies that the message might not be delivered at all.
- `wsrm:AtLeastOnce`—Specifies that each message in the sequence must be delivered to the Web service at least once. It could be delivered more than once.
- `wsrm:ExactlyOnce`—Specifies that each message in the sequence must be delivered exactly once. This is the same as the previous two modes combined.
- `wsrm:InOrder`—Specifies that in the case where a sequence includes more than one message, they will be delivered to the Web service in the same order in which they were sent.

Typically, people will want to use `ExactlyOnce` and `InOrder`, but sometimes doing so isn't practical. For example, if a server is constrained with respect to storage, then it might not be able to buffer/persist all messages waiting for the `LastMessage` indicator—making it hard to guarantee the order in which messages are passed to the Web service. In this case, it might be required to send the messages to the Web service as they're received; the Web service would have to handle duplicate messages.

`SequenceExpiration` **Policy**

The `SequenceExpiration` policy establishes a date and time at which sequences should be considered invalid or out of date:

```
<wsrm:Expires>2004-12-31T12:00:00Z </wsrm:Expires>
```

One interesting aspect of this assertion is that the date/time value isn't relative, but a fixed point in time. Thus when a client requests the WSDL for a service, the endpoint serving up the WSDL has two options: dynamically update the WSDL so that it will determine the expiration time at runtime; or, in order to have static WSDL, pick a time so far in the future that it might no longer be of value. Remember, the expiration time can be used to help systems manage their persistent store, so having a time too far in the future can mean that a large amount of storage is required to maintain state information about the sequences being sent.

InactivityTimeout **Assertion**

The InactivityTimeout assertion can be used to indicate how long an endpoint should wait before it assumes that the other side is no longer processing a sequence:

```
<wsrm:InactivityTimeout Milliseconds="3000"/>
```

Here we specify a timeout of three seconds. This means either endpoint can assume that if it doesn't get any kind of message from the other side concerning a particular sequence after three seconds, it may consider the sequence inactive. Such a timeout can help with the amount of persistent storage needed in cases when large messages are being sent.

BaseRetransmissionInterval **Assertion**

We've discussed the situation in which a client believes a message has been lost and tries to resend it. An open issue is, how long should a client wait before it assumes a message needs to be resent? The BaseRetransmissionInterval assertion gives guidance:

```
<wsrm:BaseRetransmissionInterval Milliseconds="1000"/>
```

This example specifies that unacknowledged messages should be resent after one second.

AcknowledgementInterval **Assertion**

When a return message isn't available for a server to send back an acknowledgment, then the server may choose to initiate one itself. The AcknowledgementInterval assertion specifies how long a server waits before it can try to send an acknowledgment back to the client:

```
<wsrm:AcknowledgementInterval Milliseconds="30"/>
```

This example specifies that a server can wait up to 30 milliseconds for a return message to be sent back to a client.

SequenceRef **Element**

Any of the previously mentioned policy assertions can be specified in a policy document, and by default they will apply to all sequences. However, it's possible to specify that policy assertions should apply only to certain sequences through the use of the SequenceRef element:

```
<wsrm:SequenceRef Match="wsrm:Exact">
   <wsu:Identifier>urn:2ff5fdf4c0a8016413a3861</wsu:Identifier>
</wsrm:SequenceRef>
```

Here we specify that the policy assertions apply only to sequences with a sequence identifier that exactly matches urn:2ff5fdf4c0a8016413a3861. The Match attribute could be set to wsrm:Prefix, in which case it would apply to all sequences whose sequence identifier starts with the URI specified in the SequenceRef.

Flaws and Other Thoughts on the WS-RM Spec

One of the most notable aspects of the WS-RM specification is that it's designed exclusively for one-way message delivery. Even though SOAP also claims to be a one-way messaging protocol, within the specification it talks about how to deal with two-way/request-response messaging patterns. WS-RM only does so in an indirect way. Because of the nature of the problems WS-RM tries to solve (the unreliability of message exchanges), a reliable two-way message connection couldn't be guaranteed between a client and server. As a result, the WS-RM specification was written to focus on the one-way message pattern but did leave some options available to implementers to address the response message situation. Unfortunately, the authors ignored a key problem: firewalls.

As you've begun to see, in the WS-RM specification, the client can include a SOAP header indicating where any reply message should be sent. This might sound sufficient; however, let's think about what it means. In order for a return message to be sent, a WS-RM server must also be able to act as a SOAP (and WS-RM) client. Although this isn't an issue for most implementations, the server must also be able to open a new connection back to the client. This would be nearly impossible for most (if not all) environments. Today, with security concerns at their highest levels, you aren't likely to allow an external site to open a connection back into a server sitting behind a firewall. And finally, even if a connection could be made, each client would have to have the resources available to act as a SOAP server. The equivalent would be to require every Web browser to install and configure an HTTP server and a SOAP engine. The WS-RM authors are aware of this issue, and they've indicated that this issue will probably be addressed when the specification goes to a standards body. If you're interested, a solution could be as simple as adding the ability for a client to poll a server for messages destined for it—much like a client can ask (poll) the server for the acknowledgments.

Putting WS-RM into Use

We've walked through a pretty trivial example and talked about the design; now let's see WS-RM in action. The ETTK includes an implementation of the WS-RM specification along with a couple of demos that allow you to explore various aspects of the specification. For example, you can send messages between a client and server changing various WS-RM configuration options to see how it changes the message flow and behavior.

The ETTK WS-RM demos also include sample Java code showing one possible set of implementation APIs. In this section we'll explore how the client-side application might need to change, slightly, to accommodate the inclusion of WS-RM.

> **Note**
>
> The WS-RM code used is still very much under development, so the APIs will probably change dramatically by the time this book is published. Consequently, if you're interested in playing with WS-RM, we recommend that you look for the latest version of the ETTK to have the most current WS-RM code and API documentation.

Let's look at a high level at the kinds of changes that might be necessary in order to use WS-RM. Only two things need to change in the client-side code: We need to add to the MessageContext a WS-RM Context object containing all the WS-RM–specific information, and we must define a NotificationHandler so that the client can be notified when the message has been delivered. The WS-RM Context object is set up exactly as you might expect:

```
// Define a new WS-RM Context object and add it to the Call
Context wsrContext = new Context();
wsrContext.setNumber(1);             // first in this sequence
wsrContext.setLastMessage(true);     // the one and only
call.setProperty( Context.NAME, wsrContext );  // add it
```

The NotificationHandler is created by making a new class (implementing the Notification interface) and setting a property on the call object:

```
// Define a class to receive the notification event
public class NotificationHandler implements Notification,
                                            Serializable
{
  public void notify(int code,String seqId,long msgNum,String msg)
  {
    // Notification received - do something
  }
}

...

// Define and add a notification handler
Notification notificationHandler = null ;
notificationHandler = new NotificationHandler();
call.setProperty( Notification.NAME, notificationHandler );
```

This code will tell the WS-RM code on the client to call this instance of the NotificationHandler when the message has been successfully delivered to the server. The parameters passed into the notify() method allow the code to easily determine which sequence and specific message was delivered. For the most part, that is all the modification that's needed—the remainder of the code on the client and server should remain untouched.

Summary

In this chapter, we examined one of the possible solutions being proposed to deal with network unreliability. WS-ReliableMessaging is just one of several specifications in this space, but no matter which one is eventually adopted by the industry, none of them will ever be able to completely guarantee delivery of messages. Applications will always need to be able to deal with some failures. These specifications push the recoverable errors we encounter down into the infrastructure layer of the stack, helping applications to focus on their intended jobs.

Resources

- *WS-Reliable Messaging*—"Specification: Web Services Reliable Messaging Protocol (WS-Reliable Messaging)" (IBM, March 2003), `http://www.ibm.com/developerworks/webservices/library/ws-rm/`

- EETK—Emerging Technologies Toolkit (IBM), `http://www.alphaworks.ibm.com/tech/ettk`

11

Web Services Transactions

IN CHAPTER 8, "WEB SERVICES AND STATEFUL RESOURCES," you saw how a simple Web service can be extended by adding *state*. Doing so goes a long way toward enabling your Web services environment to be more enterprise ready. However, invoking individual Web services and assuming services work in isolation isn't really realistic. It's much more likely that during the course of processing a task several Web services will need to be invoked and coordinated under the scope of a single unit of work. In this chapter, we'll examine a group of specifications that are designed to aid in the coordination of Web services.

Web Services Coordination and Transaction (WS-C/Tx)

Through SOAP's natural extensibility, you've seen how a simple one-way messaging protocol can be used and enhanced to aid in the development of enterprise-level solutions. Even with all the extensions we've explored so far, the messaging has basically dealt with a single Web service. Back in Chapter 8, we added state to Web service calls, thus allowing us to perform a series of related operations over a long period of time—but even then, we used only one particular Web service for the entire sequence of Web service calls. As our enterprise grows, it's natural to assume that in order to complete a single task, several Web service calls to multiple Web services may be required.

For example, let's assume that while processing a purchase order, our SkatesTown POService needs to perform various Web service calls. Perhaps it needs to invoke a checkInventory type of operation on its various warehouses to make sure it has all the parts necessary to fulfill the order. Sounds easy enough—just iterate over each warehouse and issue a query for the part in question. Realistically though, the processing would not stop there. More procedures would be required, depending on the outcome of the query. What would happen if the warehouse had the parts in stock? A request to carry out some action with those parts would probably also take place. The warehouse might be asked to place those items on hold while the remaining parts were located, or it could even be asked to ship the parts to the assembly plant. Either way, there's a good chance that an action associated with the original PO request would take place through some other Web service invocation.

Now, let's upset the flow of this process a little. What if a request to the Skateboard platform warehouse for 1000 boards is successful, but the following request to the Skateboard wheel warehouse for 4000 wheels fails because they don't have that many in stock? An option at this point is to stop the entire PO processing request and reject it—if so, we have to go back to the warehouse that successfully accepted our request and cancel the order for 1000 boards. If SkatesTown owned the warehouse, then there might not be a major problem; but if it's owned by a third party, that vendor not be happy with the "cancel order" request. Perhaps they would only allow SkatesTown to cancel the order within the first 24 hours; after that (because production had already begun), they might charge a 5% fee to cancel the order.

In this scenario, SkatesTown has to not only manage the information related to the original PO request, but also keep track of the various parties involved in this particular transaction so that it can tell each one to take some action based on how the entire process proceeds. If there are many different suppliers that SkatesTown could use for each request, then the situation is even more complicated—SkatesTown must keep track not only of the fact that a skate wheel supplier is involved in a transaction but of which one in particular. Granted, all of this additional information could be managed by the application (POService), and some of it probably will be; but the way in which the parties involved in the overall flow talk to one another needs to be formalized. If some suppliers expected cancel requests in different formats, this would seriously complicate design and implementation. And, of course, it would limit SkatesTown's ability to migrate to a new supplier if a new set of transactional APIs had to be supported each time.

As you might have guessed, we're really discussing the coordination of various Web services under the scope of a single action, and the standardization of the interfaces used to handle this coordination. And as you'd expect, this discussion implies yet another new specification. The folks at BEA, IBM, and Microsoft have put together a set of specifications that attempts to define these interfaces.

The first one, WS-Coordination, defines a core set of APIs that standardizes how the parties involved in a coordinated set of Web service calls exchange information related to the flow (or *transaction*). If you're familiar with transactional systems, you'll immediately realize that it would be foolish to think that all systems involved in any kind of flow/transaction could get by with only one type of transactional protocol. For example, some people may want to support atomic/two-phase commit operations, while others may require a complex, long-running, business-compensating process. (If you aren't familiar with transactional systems, don't worry; the next section gives a quick overview of the concepts.) To address this need, *WS-Coordination* defines the basic mechanism for coordinating Web services and an extensible framework that lets people define specific transactional protocols on top of it.

A second specification, *WS-Transactions* 📖, uses the extensibility defined in WS-Coordination to define some of the commonly used transactions protocols, such as those previously mentioned: atomic and business activity.

Before we dive into these new specifications, let's quickly go over some basic transaction concepts. If you're familiar with transactional systems, you can skip the next section.

Transactions: A Brief Introduction

If you aren't familiar with transactional computer systems, then the term *transaction* probably brings to mind phrases like *banking transaction*—the act of depositing or withdrawing money from your bank account. That is, in fact, a transaction. You can think of a transaction as a unit of work with a distinct start and end. Even the simple act of editing a document with a word processor can be thought of as a transaction: The "start" is opening the file, and the "end" is closing the file. While you're editing the file, the operating system will probably prevent others from also editing the file—in other words, you've locked the file. There can also be certain *semantics* (behaviors) expected by the type of transaction. In this case, the "edit file" transaction has the semantics of locking the file so no one else can edit it at the same time.

These basic concepts are similar to those in true transactional systems. Let's change the sample slightly—instead of editing a file, let's edit a field in a database, such as your bank account balance. If you want to deposit $100, you might perform a series of steps as simple as reading the current balance, adding $100 to it, and saving the new balance. But what if at the exact same moment, the bank was processing a withdrawal on the account (read current value, subtract $50, save new balance), and the two sets of steps were intertwined?

1. Read current balance (for the deposit transaction)
2. Read current balance (for the withdrawal transaction)
3. Add $100 (deposit)
4. Subtract $50 (withdrawal)
5. Save new balance (deposit)
6. Save new balance (withdrawal)

The final outcome would be that you lost the $100 deposit. Much as you wanted to lock the file when you opened it for editing so others couldn't change it, you want to lock the balance field in the database to prevent this type of overwriting of data. Transactional systems help application developers manage these types of issues.

For this very simple banking example, you can solve the problem by introducing the most basic transactional features: *start* and *end* transaction operations. Let's change the basic flow of the banking transaction as follows: start new transaction, read current balance (which implicitly locks the field), add $100, save balance, end transaction (which will implicitly unlock the balance field). Now, when the deposit and withdrawal steps are intertwined, they look like this:

1. Start deposit transaction
2. Start withdrawal transaction
3. Read current balance (deposit)—locks "balance" field
4. Read current balance (withdrawal)—but blocks
5. Add $100 (deposit)
6. Save new balance (deposit)
7. End deposit transaction
8. Complete read current balance (withdrawal)
9. Subtract $50 (withdrawal)
10. Save new balance (withdrawal)

Notice that when the withdrawal transaction tries to read the current balance, it can't do so, because the deposit transaction has locked that field. The withdrawal transaction, in this case, *blocks* or waits until the transaction that's holding the lock on that field releases it. This locking ability is critical when you're trying to manage data in an environment where many people, processes, or applications share data.

Another important aspect of transactions is the notion of *unit of work* that is introduced with the use of the *start* and *end* transaction operations. These operations allow the application to clearly tell the transactional system when all of its work is completed, so that it can save or *commit* 📖 the changes and unlock resources. Using the word-processing example, the *commit* would equate to saving the file. All changes made since the file was opened are temporary until you click Save. If you exit the word processor without saving your changes, all changes will be lost.

The same concept is true for transactional systems. While the banking example has just one operation (updating the balance), you could have several operations involved in that single transaction; more important, you might want them all viewed as a single operation. Let's change the example to better explain why this is important. Instead of the balance increasing by $100 as a result of a deposit, let's assume the increase is due to a transfer of funds from another account. Now you need to subtract $100 from one account and add $100 to another, all in the same transaction.

In this new example, if an error occurs while you're trying to deposit the $100 into the target account, you've negatively impacted the original account by decreasing its balance. When this happens, you need to *roll back* the transaction as if it never existed. It now becomes critical for the transactional system to ensure that all work within a single transaction completes successfully—or, if not, that none of it is allowed to be saved. In this case, decreasing the first balance by $100 is okay as long as you don't commit your changes until you're sure you can increase the target account by $100 as well. This notion of viewing all work between the starting and ending points of a transaction as a single unit of work is known as an *atomic transaction (AT)* 📖.

Due to the nature of some types of work, it may not always be desirable to have your data locked for the entire duration of your transactions. Looking back at the original deposit and withdrawal example, the withdrawal operation was blocked and had to wait until the deposit operation completed. Not all operations can be put on hold like that. One good example is an airline reservation. From the time you first call the airline until the time your credit card is charged, you might be on the phone quite a while. During that time, you will choose a flight and seats, and perhaps change either or both during the process. However, you can't view the entire transaction as being completed until the airline charges your credit card. If the airline had to lock certain pieces of data for the entire time you were on the phone, it would greatly impact their ability to make travel plans for other customers at the same time. Because of the variety of ways in which applications need to access and manage data, there are also many different types of transactions. An AT is just one type.

To satisfy more dynamic scenarios, like that involving the travel agent, another type of transaction was developed: *business activity (BA)* . In this type of transaction, each step is allowed to complete and save its work, thus preventing the locking of data that you experience in ATs. However, if an error occurs, the transaction has the notion of a *compensate* operation that is invoked. This *compensate* operation is responsible for fixing the state of the system as a result of the error. Unlike your editor's undo feature, the *compensate* operation won't try to undo any previously completed work; it will instead try to take some other type of corrective action. In the airline example, it would remove you from any flight on which you've reserved a seat.

We've introduced just two of the many types of transactions; and even for those two, we've just scratched the surface of the available features. However, rather than spend more time on an in-depth analysis of transactions, let's turn our attention back to Web services and examine the new specifications we mentioned and how they'll help SkatesTown. We'll elaborate on some of the features of AT and BA transactions as necessary as we progress through the chapter.

WS-Coordination

As we mentioned, WS-Coordination defines the basic building blocks for managing the coordination of various back-end systems that might be used during the execution of a single flow or transaction. In more simplistic terms, it defines a coordinator that keeps track of and manages the various resources (in other words, Web services) involved in multi-party operations.

Many technology-related terms are overloaded and represent different things to different people. For our purposes, we'll use the term *transaction* to mean the scope under which several Web service calls are made—when the collection of these calls is viewed as a single unit, it equates to one transaction.

WS-Coordination defines a *coordinator* that's responsible for keeping track of transactions and the various Web services involved in each one. So, let's go back to the example we mentioned earlier: During the processing of a purchase order, SkatesTown needs to make several Web service calls to some of its suppliers. The coordinator is responsible for keeping track of which suppliers were called and the overall status of the transaction. First, let's examine how this coordinator manages the list of players involved in the transaction. When a new transaction begins, the application initiating the transaction asks the coordinator for a new `CoordinationContext` 📖. Think of a `CoordinationContext` as a unique identifier for the transaction. This piece of information is passed around with each Web service call so the parties involved know which transaction the Web service's work relates to.

The namespaces used in the following sections' XML snippets are as follows:

- `wsa`—`http://schemas.xmlsoap.org/ws/2003/03/addressing`
- `wsat`—`http://schemas.xmlsoap.org/ws/2003/09/wsat`
- `wscoor`—`http://schemas.xmlsoap.org/ws/2002/09/wscoor`
- `wsu`—`http://schemas.xmlsoap.org/ws/2002/07/utility`

Now, let's dive into the details.

The `CoordinationContext`

The `CoordinationContext` does more than just identify the scope or transaction you're working in; it can also contain additional information that helps the application that receives it to do its job. Let's look at an example:

```
<wscoor:CoordinationContext>
  <wsu:Identifier>http://skatestown.com/trans2</wsu:Identifier>
  <wsu:Expires>2003-12-25T09:00:00Z</wsu:Expires>
</wscoor:CoordinationContext>
```

Here, a unique `Identifier` (`http://skatestown.com/trans2`) is used to indicate which transaction the Web service call is for. The `Expires` element, which is optional, defines the earliest time at which the transaction can expire due to the amount of time that has elapsed. This doesn't guarantee that it will be invalidated at this time, just that it can't happen any sooner.

The example shows the bare minimum that is defined for a `CoordinationContext`—it can also include any additional application-specific elements that might be useful to the parties receiving the message. You'll see some of these extensions in a bit, but first let's continue to explore the creation of the context.

The `CreateCoordinationContext` Operation

When an application wants to start a new transaction, it asks the coordinator to create a new context. It does so by calling the `CreateCoordinationContext` operation on the coordinator, also known as the *Activation service* 📖. The coordinator is really nothing more than a Web service that exposes some transaction-related operations. Those familiar with database APIs can equate these operations to those you might see when managing a database—for example, `startTransaction` and `endTransaction`. The operations available on a particular `coordinator` will vary depending on the types of transactions supported (we'll discuss some of them later), but coordinators typically have at least two predefined operations: `CreateCoordinationContext` and `Register`.

We've already touched on the `CreateCoordinationContext` operation, but let's see what a sample request looks like:

```
<soapenv:Envelope
    xmlns:soapenv="http://schemas.xmlsoap.org/soap/envelope/"
    xmlns:wscoor="http://schemas.xmlsoap.org/ws/2002/09/wscoor">
  <soapenv:Body>
    <wscoor:CreateCoordinationContext>
      <wscoor:CoordinationType>
        http://schemas.xmlsoap.org/ws/2002/09/wsat
      </wscoor:CoordinationType>
    </wscoor:CreateCoordinationContext>
  </soapenv:Body>
</soapenv:Envelope>
```

This operation has only one required parameter, `CoordinationType`, which defines the type of transaction in use. Notice that it's a URI that uniquely identifies the type of transaction, which means it defines the behavior expected from all parties involved in this transaction (including the coordinator). For example, in this example we've specified that we want an atomic transaction (`http://schemas.xmlsoap.org/ws/2002/09/wsat`) with very simple transactional operations, such as *commit* and *rollback* 📖. The `CoordinationType` will depend on the application being developed. Also, although they aren't shown here, you can include optional elements in the `CreateCoordinationContext` call, such as `Expires` or other parameters. They allow the coordinator the option of fine-tuning how the context object is created.

The requesting application (in our example, that would be the `POService`) has asked the coordinator to create a new `CoordinationContext`, which is then returned to the POService:

```
<soapenv:Envelope
    xmlns:soapenv="http://schemas.xmlsoap.org/soap/envelope/"
      xmlns:wscoor="http://schemas.xmlsoap.org/ws/2002/09/wscoor"
      xmlns:wsu:"http://schemas.xmlsoap.org/ws/2002/07/utility"
      xmlns:wsa:"http://schemas.xmlsoap.org/ws/2003/03/addressing">
  <soapenv:Body>
    <wscoor:CreateCoordinationContextResponse>
      <wscoor:CoordinationContext>
        <wsu:Identifier>http://skatestown.com/trans2</wsu:Identifier>
        <wsu:Expires>2003-12-25T09:00:00Z</wsu:Expires>
```

```
        <wscoor:CoordinationType>
          http://schemas.xmlsoap.org/ws/2002/09/wsat
        </wscoor:CoordinationType>
        <wscoor:RegistrationService>
          <wsa:Address>http://coordinator.com/register</wsa:Address>
        </wscoor:RegistrationService>
      </wscoor:CoordinationContext>
    </wscoor:CreateCoordinationContextResponse>
  </soapenv:Body>
</soapenv:Envelope>
```

The first three parts of the CoordinationContext should be what you'd expect: a unique identifier, an optional expires time, and the transaction type (previously passed into the create operation). The remaining element, RegistrationService, contains a reference or pointer back to the coordinator's Register service (notice this is an Endpoint Reference (EPR) as defined by the WS-Addressing specification). This service is the one that each participant in the transaction will call to notify the coordinator that it's being used in the scope of this transaction. For example, as the POService calls each of SkatesTown's suppliers, those suppliers will use this address to register with the coordinator. Doing so lets the coordinator know which suppliers to contact if they need to take some action on behalf of this transaction (such as *commit* or *rollback*).

The Register Operation

Every message sent between the various participants in the transaction, including the coordinator, has the CoordinationContext header. So, when the POService invokes an operation such as checkInventory() on one of its suppliers, the *entire* CoordinationContext is included as a SOAP header (with the mustUnderstand attribute set to true). When the supplier receives the message, it verifies that it can (and wants to) participate in this transaction by looking at the information in the CoordinationContext. For example, if the CoordinationType specifies a type of transaction that the supplier can't support, then it must return an error back to the POService. After these checks, the supplier must then register with the coordinator:

```
<soapenv:Envelope
    xmlns:soapenv="http://schemas.xmlsoap.org/soap/envelope/"
    xmlns:wscoor="http://schemas.xmlsoap.org/ws/2002/09/wscoor"
    xmlns:wsu:"http://schemas.xmlsoap.org/ws/2002/07/utility">
  <soapenv:Header>
    <wscoor:CoordinationContext mustUnderstand="true">
      <wsu:Identifier>http://skatestown.com/trans2</wsu:Identifier>
      <wsu:Expires>2003-12-25T09:00:00Z</wsu:Expires>
      <wscoor:CoordinationType>
        http://schemas.xmlsoap.org/ws/2002/09/wsat
```

```
        </wscoor:CoordinationType>
        <wscoor:RegistrationService>
          <wsa:Address>http://coordinator.com/register</wsa:Address>
        </wscoor:RegistrationService>
      </wscoor:CoordinationContext>
    </soapenv:Header>
    <soapenv:Body>
      <wscoor:Register>
        <wscoor:ProtocolIdentifier>
          http://schemas.xmlsoap.org/ws/2003/09/wsat#Durable2PC
        </wscoor:ProtocolIdentifier>
        <wscoor:ParticipantProcotolService>
          <wsa:Address>http://wheels.com/2pcservice</wsa:Address>
        </wscoor:ParticipantProcotolService>
      </wscoor:Register>
    </soapenv:Body>
</soapenv:Envelope>
```

Notice that the CoordinationContext is passed as a SOAP header so the coordinator knows which transaction we're registering for. The Register operation includes two parameters: ProtocolIdentifier and ParticipantProtocolService. The first, ProtocolIdentifier, specifies how the party that is registering wants to participant in this transaction. Based on the CoordinationType already specified (and agreed to), which in this case is Atomic, a participant is allowed to further quantify its role in the transaction. For example, if it participates in read-only activities, then perhaps it just needs to be notified when the transaction is completed so it can do some cleanup. But if its role in the transaction involves something more complex (such as accepting orders), then it needs to be notified during all stages of the transaction—when it's committed or rolled back as well as completed. The exact set of values that can be used is specified by the definition of the CoordinationType; in this example, the Atomic type has a two-phase commit protocol (http://schemas.xmlsoap.org/ws/2003/09/wsat#Durable2PC). (We haven't explained what two-phase commit is yet, so for now just understand that each participant can play different roles, and this parameter lets them tell the coordinator what that role is.)

The other parameter is ParticipantProtocolService. It specifies the address that the coordinator should use when it wants to invoke any transactional operations on this participant. In our case, this supplier is telling the coordinator that when it needs to communicate some information (such as the fact that the transaction has completed), it should use http://wheels.com/2pcservice as the endpoint. All the elements under the ParticipantProtocolService element conform to the WS-Addressing specification for an EPR and can be as simple or complex as needed to fully qualify the location of the desired service.

Finally, the coordinator responds:

```
<soapenv:Envelope
    xmlns:soapenv="http://schemas.xmlsoap.org/soap/envelope/"
    xmlns:wscoor="http://schemas.xmlsoap.org/ws/2002/09/wscoor"
    xmlns:wsu:"http://schemas.xmlsoap.org/ws/2002/07/utility">
  <soapenv:Header>
    <wscoor:CoordinationContext mustUnderstand="true">
      <wsu:Identifier>http://skatestown.com/trans2</wsu:Identifier>
      <wsu:Expires>2003-12-25T09:00:00Z</wsu:Expires>
      <wscoor:CoordinationType>
        http://schemas.xmlsoap.org/ws/2002/09/wsat
      </wscoor:CoordinationType>
      <wscoor:RegistrationService>
        <wsa:Address>http://coordinator.com/register</wsa:Address>
      </wscoor:RegistrationService>
    </wscoor:CoordinationContext>
  </soapenv:Header>
  <soapenv:Body>
    <wscoor:RegisterResponse>
      <wscoor:CoordinatorProcotolService>
        <wsa:Address>http://coordinator.com/coordinator</wsa:Address>
      </wscoor:CoordinatorProcotolService>
    </wscoor:RegisterResponse>
  </soapenv:Body>
</soapenv:Envelope>
```

Here the only information the coordinator needs to return to the registering party is the address of the `CoordinatorProtocolService` (from this point on, we'll omit the `CoordinationContext` header from the listings). Depending on how the coordinator is written, the address someone uses to register for a transaction might be different than the address it should use to relay information about the transaction. As an example, once `wheels.com` has registered with the coordinator for this transaction, if something serious happens and it needs to send an *abort* message to the coordinator, it will use this address (`http://coordinator.com/coordinator`) as the endpoint.

With the completion of this `Register` operation, we've discussed the core aspects of the WS-Coordination specification. Even though the WS-Coordination specification defines just two core operations, `CreateCoordinationContext` and `Register`, it leaves open the possibility of extending the coordinator's features with additional transactional specific operations. We'll discuss those in the section on WS-Transaction. But first, let's review the concepts we've discussed. Transactional systems can appear more complex than they really are, so a high-level review of the overall flow will help reinforce the concepts. And, of course, a picture is always helpful; see Figure 11.1.

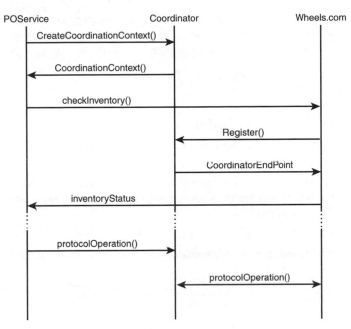

Figure 11.1   WS-Coordination flow

In the figure, you can see the overall flow we've discussed:

1. The POService, wanting to start a new transaction, creates a new CoordinationContext by invoking the CreateCoordinationContext operation on the coordinator, passing in the desired CoordinationType (transaction type) as a parameter.

2. The coordinator returns the new CoordinationContext object, containing among other values a unique identifier for this transaction and a reference to its Register service.

3. The POService invokes whatever application-specific operations it needs in order to complete its job. In this case, it calls the checkInventory() method on its supplier: wheels.com. Included in this message is the newly created CoordinationContext.

4. Each time a new participant is brought into the transaction, it uses the RegistrationService referenced in the CoordinationContext to register itself with the coordinator. In return, the coordinator tells that participant the address it should use for any further transaction-specific operations (CoordinatorEndPoint). In this example, wheels.com joins the transaction as a result of the checkInventory() call—which also returns the inventoryStatus back to the POService.

5. The protocolOperation() calls at the bottom of Figure 11.1 represent any protocol-specific operations that are invoked. For example, if the POService wants to

commit (or end) the transaction, it sends a *commit* message to the coordinator, which then takes the appropriate action for each of the participants of the transaction. In this case, the coordinator might send a *commit* message to each one.

Before we proceed with examining the transaction protocols, let's discuss a couple of additional WS-Coordination topics.

WS-Coordination Fault Codes

Errors are bound to occur, so WS-Coordination defines SOAP fault codes to be used in common WS-C error conditions:

- `wscoor:InvalidState`—This unrecoverable error indicates that one of the participants in the transaction (or the coordinator) can not recover from an error and must stop its processing.

- `wscoor:InvalidProcotol`—This unrecoverable error indicates that one of the participants in the transaction (or the coordinator) has received a message containing an invalid protocol.

- `wscoor:InvalidParameter`—This unrecoverable error indicates that one of the participants in the transaction (or the coordinator) received a message with an invalid parameter.

- `wscoor:NoActivity`—This fault indicates that there has been no activity from a participant for an extended period of time and the coordinator assumes that the participant has stopped its processing. The specification doesn't explain the reason for this assumption, nor does it say how someone might indicate an acceptable period of time. We hope this issue will be cleared up when the specification is taken to a standards body.

- `wscoor:ContextRefused`—This fault is sent by a participant to a coordinator when the context in the message it sent can't be accepted. For example, it specifies a type of transaction that can't be supported.

- `wscoor:AlreadyRegistered`—This fault is generated by the coordinator when it detects that a participant has already registered with it for a particular context, with the specified transaction protocol. Remember that when a participant registers, it includes a `ProtocolIdentifier` parameter indicating how it wishes to be included in the transaction. (A participant can register for more than one protocol in a particular transaction—this would be equivalent to combining the semantics of the specified protocols.)

When you use these SOAP fault codes, you should include any information needed to help explain the reason for the error in the detail section of the SOAP fault.

WS-Transaction: Atomic Transactions

With an understanding of WS-Coordination, we can now dive into the specific details of the transactions. As we mentioned earlier, one of the basic types of transactions is the atomic transactions (ATs). From an application's point of view, either the entire set of operations within the transaction completes successfully or the entire transaction is rolled back as if none of it ever happened. When an application creates a new `CoordinationContext` for an AT, it uses `http://schemas.xmlsoap.org/ws/2003/09/wsat` for the `CoordinationType` parameter. In order to support this type of transaction, aside from the `CreateCoordinationContext` and `Register` operations, a coordinator must also support the AT-specific operations.

WS-AT Operations

To understand what the AT-specific operations are, let's continue with the example from the previous section. We left off with the `POService` initiating a new transaction and sending a `checkInventory()` message to wheels.com, which caused wheels.com to register with the coordinator.

Now the `POService` sends a `checkInventory()` message to boards.com to ensure that it can supply the boards/platforms for the skateboards in the original order. And again, boards.com will register with the coordinator. Assuming both suppliers can fulfill the order, the `POService` then sends a *purchase* message to each one. It's important to note that on these subsequent messages to the suppliers, the suppliers don't have any interaction with the coordinator. Once they're registered, they don't need to reregister or notify the coordinator at all.

When these additional operations are completed, the `POService` is done—almost. From the `POService`'s point of view, everything is completed. However, it must still notify the coordinator that it has completed the transaction. This is important for a variety of reasons, which are best explained by examining in more detail what goes on with each of the suppliers.

When wheels.com receives the *purchase* message from the `POService`, it sets aside a portion of its inventory for this request. Likewise, boards.com does the same thing. However, participants in ATs can't assume that just because their activity completed successfully, all subsequent activities will complete as well. For example, what if boards.com decides that it can't fulfill the request (even if it said it could during the `checkInventory()` call)? In this case, boards.com would have to reject the *purchase* request, and the entire transaction would have to be undone. For this reason, even though wheels.com completed its *purchase* operation, it must wait until the coordinator tells it that all subsequent processing has completed before it can perform whatever action it needs to do to finalize its work. Remember, in ATs, either everything must succeed or the entire activity must be undone.

Commit and Rollback

Once the `POService` has received valid responses from all of its suppliers, it must send a *commit* message to the coordinator indicating that it should notify all the participants that processing has completed successfully and they can finalize their work. Here we've introduced a transaction-specific operation (*commit*) that a coordinator must support if it wants to manage ATs.

As you might imagine, we also need an operation that allows the POService to tell the coordinator that it should cancel the transaction, typically due to an error. In this case, the coordinator supports a *rollback* 📖 operation. Both operations take no parameters (because the CoordinationContext header has everything the coordinator needs to know), so the SOAP bodies looks like this:

```
<soapenv:Body>
  <wsat:Commit/>
</soapenv:Body>

<soapenv:Body>
  <wsat:Rollback/>
</soapenv:Body>
```

AT Protocols

We've examined what an AT looks like from the POService's point of view; now let's examine what happened in the coordinator and a participant.

Starting with the first Web service invocation from the POService to a supplier (the checkInventory() call), we know that wheels.com will register with the coordinator. However, with the Register operation, we need to look at another bit of information: the participant's ProtocolIdentifier. We know that wheels.com will perform its actions under an AT, but as mentioned in the WS-Coordination section, a participant can play various roles within each type of transaction. For ATs, a participant can choose to register under three different types of roles (or protocols); the first is *Completion*.

Completion Protocol

The *Completion* 📖 AT protocol means that this participant wishes to be notified at the end of the transaction. It doesn't influence the success or failure of the transaction; it will simply be told of the transaction's final result. One way to look at this protocol is as a read-only interaction. The notification at the end of the transaction allows the participant to perform some clean-up action—perhaps something as trivial as deleting any knowledge of the transaction itself. The ProtocolIdentifier used in this case would be

```
http://schemas.xmlsoap.org/ws/2003/09/wsat#Completion
```

Two-Phase Commit Protocols

The other two protocols are variants of each other; they're under the general category of *Two-Phase Commit (2PC)* 📖 protocols. At a very high level, the 2PC protocol commits (or completes) the transactions (as you might have guessed) in two phases. In the first phase, the coordinator asks each of the participants to prepare itself to commit the work it did under the scope of this transaction. By returning a "prepared" message back to the coordinator, the participant acknowledges that it can complete/commit the work and that, from its point of view, the transaction should be successfully completed. This is sometimes known as allowing each participant a *vote* on the outcome of the transaction.

If any of participants don't return *prepared* but instead return *aborted*, then that single no vote aborts the entire transaction. In that case, the coordinator sends an *abort* message to all participants, indicating that they shouldn't save any changes made under this transaction. In other words, they need to undo any work, leaving things in a state such that it would appear the transaction never happened.

A participant can return one other vote: *ReadOnly*. This means the participant is voting yes but doesn't wish to participate in the second phase of the commit. This vote is used for cases where the participant performed only read-only actions and therefore doesn't need to worry about any persistent data changes. Once the participant returns this *ReadOnly* message, it can remove any knowledge it has about this transaction.

If all participants vote yes by returning a *prepared* (or *Readonly*) message back to the coordinator, then in the second phase, the coordinator sends a *commit* message to each participant. When a participant receives this message, it should complete and save any work started under this transaction.

The 2PC protocol as just described is known as *Durable Two-Phase Commit* 📖. The `ProtocolIdentifier` used for this type of participant is `http://schemas.xmlsoap.org/ws/2003/09/wsat#Durable2PC`.

The remaining protocol (the second of the 2PCs) is called *Volatile Two-Phase Commit*. This protocol is used for resources that are transient. A good example is a resource that is a cache—one that's used because of its high performance but also has a durable resource behind the scenes acting as its true persistence.

Because volatile resources are typically associated with durable ones, the rules for processing volatile resources dictate that all volatile resources must be prepared before any durable resource is prepared. This allows the volatile resource a chance to migrate the new data back to its durable resource and be guaranteed that the durable resource hasn't yet been prepared—which would prevent this movement of data. Because the durable resource would be the true owner of the data, volatile resources aren't typically called during the second phase of the 2PC process; instead, it's assumed that the *commit* call to the durable resource suffices.

The `ProtocolIdentifier` for the volatile resource is `http://schemas.xmlsoap.org/ws/2003/09/wsat#Volatile2PC`.

Committing the Transaction

Returning to our example, `wheels.com` just received its first Web service call from the `POService`, so it must register with the coordinator. For our purposes, it registers with the Durable 2PC protocol:

```
<soapenv:Envelope
    xmlns:soapenv="http://schemas.xmlsoap.org/soap/envelope/"
    xmlns:wscoor="http://schemas.xmlsoap.org/ws/2002/09/wscoor"
```

```
     xmlns:wsu:"http://schemas.xmlsoap.org/ws/2002/07/utility">
   <soapenv:Header> …
   </soapenv:Header>
   <soapenv:Body>
     <wscoor:Register>
       <wscoor:ProtocolIdentifier>
         http://schemas.xmlsoap.org/ws/2003/09/wsat#Durable2PC
       </wscoor:ProtocolIdentifier>
       <wscoor:ParticipantProcotolService>
         <wsa:Address>http://wheels.com/2pcservice</wsa:Address>
       </wscoor:ParticipantProcotolService>
     </wscoor:Register>
   </soapenv:Body>
</soapenv:Envelope>
```

Notice the `<wsa:Address>` element contains the endpoint that the coordinator will use later when it wants to talk with `wheels.com` (for example, when it wants to prepare the transaction).

Next, the `POService` sends a *checkInventory* message to `boards.com`. It registers as well with the coordinator using the Durable 2PC protocol. Then, the `POService` sends the *purchase* message to both suppliers. Finally, when the `POService` believes that everything is done, it sends a *commit* message to the coordinator.

Upon receiving this message, the coordinator iterates over all the participants that registered for this `CoordinationContext`. For each one that registered for Volatile 2PC, it sends a *prepare* message—which in our case doesn't apply, because neither of the suppliers registered with this protocol. Then it sends a *prepare* message to all Durable 2PC participants:

```
<soapenv:Envelope
    xmlns:soapenv="http://schemas.xmlsoap.org/soap/envelope/"
    xmlns:wscoor="http://schemas.xmlsoap.org/ws/2002/09/wscoor"
    xmlns:wsu:"http://schemas.xmlsoap.org/ws/2002/07/utility">
  <soapenv:Header>
    <wscoor:CoordinationContext mustUnderstand="true">
      <wsu:Identifier>http://skatestown.com/trans2</wsu:Identifier>
      <wsu:Expires>2003-12-25T09:00:00Z</wsu:Expires>
      <wscoor:CoordinationType>
        http://schemas.xmlsoap.org/ws/2002/09/wsat
      </wscoor:CoordinationType>
      <wscoor:RegistrationService>
        <wsa:Address>http://coordinator.com/register</wsa:Address>
      </wscoor:RegistrationService>
    </wscoor:CoordinationContext>
  </soapenv:Header>
  <soapenv:Body>
    <wsat:Prepare/>
  </soapenv:Body>
</soapenv:Envelope>
```

Both `wheels.com` and `boards.com` reply with a *prepared* response:

```
<soapenv:Envelope
    xmlns:soapenv="http://schemas.xmlsoap.org/soap/envelope/"
    xmlns:wscoor="http://schemas.xmlsoap.org/ws/2002/09/wscoor"
    xmlns:wsu:"http://schemas.xmlsoap.org/ws/2002/07/utility">
  <soapenv:Header>
    <wscoor:CoordinationContext mustUnderstand="true">
      <wsu:Identifier>http://skatestown.com/trans2</wsu:Identifier>
      <wsu:Expires>2003-12-25T09:00:00Z</wsu:Expires>
      <wscoor:CoordinationType>
        http://schemas.xmlsoap.org/ws/2002/09/wsat
      </wscoor:CoordinationType>
      <wscoor:RegistrationService>
        <wsa:Address>http://coordinator.com/register</wsa:Address>
      </wscoor:RegistrationService>
    </wscoor:CoordinationContext>
  </soapenv:Header>
  <soapenv:Body>
    <wsat:Prepared/>
  </soapenv:Body>
</soapenv:Envelope>
```

After getting a yes vote from all participants, the coordinator now sends a *commit* message to each:

```
<soapenv:Envelope
    xmlns:soapenv="http://schemas.xmlsoap.org/soap/envelope/"
    xmlns:wscoor="http://schemas.xmlsoap.org/ws/2002/09/wscoor"
    xmlns:wsu:"http://schemas.xmlsoap.org/ws/2002/07/utility">
  <soapenv:Header>
    <wscoor:CoordinationContext mustUnderstand="true">
      <wsu:Identifier>http://skatestown.com/trans2</wsu:Identifier>
      <wsu:Expires>2003-12-25T09:00:00Z</wsu:Expires>
      <wscoor:CoordinationType>
        http://schemas.xmlsoap.org/ws/2002/09/wsat
      </wscoor:CoordinationType>
      <wscoor:RegistrationService>
        <wsa:Address>http://coordinator.com/register</wsa:Address>
      </wscoor:RegistrationService>
    </wscoor:CoordinationContext>
  </soapenv:Header>
  <soapenv:Body>
    <wsat:Commit/>
  </soapenv:Body>
</soapenv:Envelope>
```

And each participant responds with a *committed* response message:

```
<soapenv:Envelope
    xmlns:soapenv="http://schemas.xmlsoap.org/soap/envelope/"
    xmlns:wscoor="http://schemas.xmlsoap.org/ws/2002/09/wscoor"
    xmlns:wsu:"http://schemas.xmlsoap.org/ws/2002/07/utility">
  <soapenv:Header>
    <wscoor:CoordinationContext mustUnderstand="true">
      <wsu:Identifier>http://skatestown.com/trans2</wsu:Identifier>
      <wsu:Expires>2003-12-25T09:00:00Z</wsu:Expires>
      <wscoor:CoordinationType>
        http://schemas.xmlsoap.org/ws/2002/09/wsat
      </wscoor:CoordinationType>
      <wscoor:RegistrationService>
        <wsa:Address>http://coordinator.com/register</wsa:Address>
      </wscoor:RegistrationService>
    </wscoor:CoordinationContext>
  </soapenv:Header>
  <soapenv:Body>
    <wsat:Committed/>
  </soapenv:Body>
</soapenv:Envelope>
```

Once all the participants have successfully committed their work, the coordinator then sends a final message to any participant that registered under the Completion protocol, allowing it to be notified of the outcome of the transaction:

```
<soapenv:Envelope
    xmlns:soapenv="http://schemas.xmlsoap.org/soap/envelope/"
    xmlns:wscoor="http://schemas.xmlsoap.org/ws/2002/09/wscoor"
    xmlns:wsu:"http://schemas.xmlsoap.org/ws/2002/07/utility">
  <soapenv:Header>
    <wscoor:CoordinationContext mustUnderstand="true">
      <wsu:Identifier>http://skatestown.com/trans2</wsu:Identifier>
      <wsu:Expires>2003-12-25T09:00:00Z</wsu:Expires>
      <wscoor:CoordinationType>
        http://schemas.xmlsoap.org/ws/2002/09/wsat
      </wscoor:CoordinationType>
      <wscoor:RegistrationService>
        <wsa:Address>http://coordinator.com/register</wsa:Address>
      </wscoor:RegistrationService>
    </wscoor:CoordinationContext>
  </soapenv:Header>
  <soapenv:Body>
    <wsat:Committed/>
  </soapenv:Body>
</soapenv:Envelope>
```

Finally, the coordinator can return from the *commit* operation made by the POService, indicating that it successfully committed the work:

```
<soapenv:Envelope
    xmlns:soapenv=http://schemas.xmlsoap.org/soap/envelope/"
    xmlns:wscoor="http://schemas.xmlsoap.org/ws/2002/09/wscoor"
    xmlns:wsu:"http://schemas.xmlsoap.org/ws/2002/07/utility">
  <soapenv:Header>
    <wscoor:CoordinationContext mustUnderstand="true">
      <wsu:Identifier>http://skatestown.com/trans2</wsu:Identifier>
      <wsu:Expires>2003-12-25T09:00:00Z</wsu:Expires>
      <wscoor:CoordinationType>
        http://schemas.xmlsoap.org/ws/2002/09/wsat
      </wscoor:CoordinationType>
      <wscoor:RegistrationService>
        <wsa:Address>http://coordinator.com/register</wsa:Address>
      </wscoor:RegistrationService>
    </wscoor:CoordinationContext>
  </soapenv:Header>
  <soapenv:Body>
    <wsat:Committed/>
  </soapenv:Body>
</soapenv:Envelope>
```

Once the coordinator sends this response message, it can forget about this transaction and any data associated with it (such as the CoordinationContext). The participants can erase any knowledge of the transaction after they commit their work.

Of course, as we walked through this example, we focused just on the positive. In the real world, things do go wrong, so it's important to note that an *abort* message might be sent back to the coordinator from one of the participants. In those cases, the coordinator stops the transaction by sending an *abort* message to each participant; and instead of sending back a *committed* message to the POService, it sends an *aborted* message.

Transaction Flow Overview

We covered quite a few complicated topics in a short amount of space, especially if you aren't familiar with transactional protocols. So, as we did following our discussion of WS-Coordination, let's quickly review the example we just completed (see Figure 11.2). For the sake of brevity, the response messages have been excluded. All the steps through boards.com registering with the coordinator were covered in the WS-Coordination section. So, we'll pick up from there:

1. The POService performs additional application-specific activities. In this case, it invokes the purchase() operation.

2. The POService now wants to save any work done in this transaction by invoking the *commit* operation on the coordinator.

3. When the coordinator receives this message, it prepares each participant. Having received a *prepared* message back from each one, it then sends a *commit* message to

each participant, and finally replies back to the `POService` with a *committed* message.

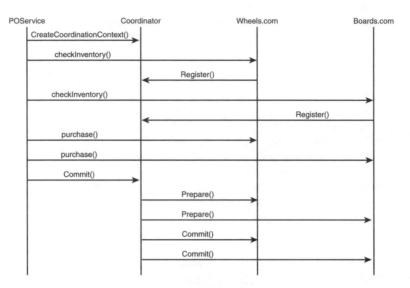

Figure 11.2   Complete AT example flow

Business Activity Protocol

ATs, as stated earlier, are one of the most basic types of transactions. However, they're not ideal for most real-world business applications. You can see one of their biggest flaws in this example. Looking at Figure 11.2, let's assume that the `checkInventory()` operation wasn't an inconsequential operation; what if instead of being a read-only type of operation, it put the items it was checking for on hold (it locked some resources)? When resources are locked, they become unavailable for other transactions to use. What if those resources were database tables? This could cause other transactions to completely block, waiting for this transaction to complete. If these transactions are short (and *short* is a very relative term), then it might not be an issue; however, if they're long-running transactions, it could dramatically reduce the response time of these automated systems. This costs money. As a result, ATs are typically not used between distributed systems such as our example; instead, other transactional protocols were developed that allowed resources to be used without being locked for extended periods of time.

The *business activity (BA)* protocol is designed for real-world scenarios—it allows long-running transactions to be used without worrying about locking resources (which would prevent other processes/transactions from completing their work).

> **Note**
>
> At the time of writing this book, the WS-Coordination and WS-Transaction specifications are in the process of being rewritten. The WS-Coordination specifications has been changed and published; however, only half of the WS-Transaction specification has been published—the AT half. The BA specification is still being modified. However, because the BA protocol is so important, there is value in discussing it here; even if the ultimate version of the specification goes through drastic changes, the key concepts should remain the same, allowing you to easily understand the new specification.

For the most part, there are only two differences between ATs and BA transactions. In ATs, either the entire transaction completes, or none of it does. In BAs, each individual Web service call is, conceptually, independent and complete. Using the SkatesTown example, each of the individual Web service calls (checkInventory() and purchase()) is committed immediately, so there is no concern about locking resources. The obvious problem is how to handle error conditions. In ATs, you can always roll back the transaction, and everything is undone. BAs have the notion of *compensation*, instead. When a transaction needs to be aborted, the coordinator sends a *compensate* message to each participant. This allows the participant to take whatever action it deems necessary to make up for previously taken (and committed) actions. Notice that unlike the AT case, where the state of the system must return to its original values (giving the appearance that nothing ever happened), in BA you accept the fact that something did happen, and you figure out how to make up for it. Using the SkatesTown example, if the *compensate* message arrives after the *checkInventory* message, perhaps the corrective action to take would be to remove the on-hold status from the inventory. However, if the *compensate* message came after the *purchase* message, then the supplier may choose to not only stop the order but also charge SkatesTown a 10% restocking fee.

Given this difference in behavior, the other difference between AT and BA should be obvious: the operations available on the coordinator and the participants. Instead of *commit* and *rollback*, the coordinator also has *complete* and *compensate*. The *complete* operation is the equivalent of *commit*—it indicates that the application successfully completed the processing of this transaction and that the coordinator should notify each participant that the transaction has completed. This allows participants to do any final processing that might be needed. The other operation, *compensate* (as discussed earlier) is called when the application wants to stop the transaction, usually due to an error. In this case, the coordinator invokes the *compensate* operator on each participant that registered for this transaction.

BA transactions are clearly better in a real-world scenario than ATs, but they're far from perfect. Although the *compensate* operation is meant to make up for any work completed, it may not be able to completely do so—some lingering side effects from operations can never be completely recovered from.

Reliable Delivery and Security

When you're working in a transactional system, if messages are lost between the parties, the result may be that more transactions are aborted than should be. For this reason, it is strongly recommended that the messages being sent use a reliable messaging scheme—for example, WS-ReliableMessaging (WS-RM). In a controlled environment, such as one that has all components in-house, this might not be an issue; however, if the systems are widely distributed or, even worse, if messages are being sent over the Internet, then adding WS-RM to the complete picture becomes even more critical.

Of course, reliable delivery is only one aspect of the Web service environment that you have to worry about. Security is probably the most important. Being able to guarantee the identity of the sender of a message, being able to be assured that no one changed a message during transit, and protecting the contents of the message from unauthorized eyes are all critical to a company's success. In the transaction space, all of these security concerns should be considered when you're building an enterprise-level solution.

> **Note**
>
> Despite our affiliation with the specification authors, in all fairness we need to issue a warning. Although the WS-Coordination/WS-Transaction specification authors are clearly very knowledgable about transactional systems, these specifications need a lot of work. The concepts presented are solid, but the presentation leaves a lot to be desired. The specifications have almost no examples, and those that are provided are incomplete at best. Even basic definitions found in other Web service–related documents, such as formal schemas for pieces of the SOAP messages, are missing, leaving the reader to guess or assume what the correct XML would be. These might be considered annoyances; however, when implementers of these specifications attempt to interoperate with each other, they will assuredly run into many more problems than they would have if a more complete specification were developed. We hope the specifications are dramatically enhanced soon.

Summary

As the evolution of Web services continues, more specifications will be written that take existing technology and give it a Web services spin. Transactional systems have been around for ages, and the WS-Coordination/WS-Transaction specifications don't try to reinvent how transactional systems should behave—they simply define a standard way to expose the technology as Web services.

In the ETTK you'll find some Web Services Coordination and Transaction demos that allow you to see, in real-time, the messages that would flow between the participants in an AT and a BA scenario.

Even if you aren't a transactions expert, this chapter has provided you with an understanding of the basic concepts and solutions proposed for the problems that transactional systems try to solve. In the next chapter, we'll continue to explore how Web services can be used to manage large enterprise-level systems by examining how to orchestrate a series of Web services.

Resources

- *WS-AT*—"Web Services Atomic Transaction (WS-AtomicTransaction)" (IBM, Microsoft, and BEA, September 2003),
  `http://www.ibm.com/developerworks/library/ws-atomtran/`

- *WS-C*—"Web Services Coordination (WS-Coordination)" (IBM, Microsoft, and BEA, September 2003),   `http://www.ibm.com/developerworks/webservices/library/ws-coor/`

12

Orchestrating Web Services

BUSINESS PROCESSES ARE INCREASINGLY IMPORTANT in both enterprise application integration and B2B scenarios. When business processes are using Web services and also exposed as Web services, they provide a powerful recursive aggregation model.

In this chapter, you'll see how existing Web services can be used to construct complex Web services. This process includes defining the business logic in terms of execution order and conditions for the invocation of orchestrated Web services.

Web services choreography languages provide the means to compose services into new complex services. We'll also introduce the *Business Process Execution Language for Web Services* 📖.

Why Are We Composing Web Services?

In the previous chapters, we looked at the concepts of Web services, examined the Web Services Description Language (WSDL), and discussed various quality of service (QoS) aspects. In most real-world scenarios, a Web service provider isn't just exposing simple and stateless services like a credit card check: Web services are reused and combined into more complex services that provide a higher value to the customer. Some services may provide multiple interactions with the customer for a single business application. In Chapter 8, "Web Services and Stateful Resources," you saw that a running instance of a service may be stateful. In many cases, business processes are stateful Web services.

Consider a business process that implements the processing of a purchase order. It's desirable to be able to not only initiate a purchase order, but also modify or cancel a running order in certain situations. Another example is a service for a loan application, where it may become necessary to ask the customer for additional information at well-defined points during the processing of the service. As you can see, you need to compose existing service into new services and also describe the order of steps and conditions for their execution.

Business processes describe service invocation and interaction patterns and are the basis for creating heterogeneous and distributed applications, also referred to as *workflow-based applications.* The aggregation of Web services to new, higher-level Web services by means of process composition allows for more flexibility. Such compositions can more quickly adapt to changing business needs, compared to hard-coded applications.

The following sections provide additional motivation for Web service composition and briefly explain the business process language evolution towards BPEL.

Two-Level Programming Model

Web services may be traditional applications, referred to as *elemental services*, or composite Web services. Composite Web services can be implemented by complex processes made up of multiple Web service invocations that are executed in a specified order.

Elemental services and composite services together constitute the paradigm of *two-level programming*: an application consists of a *process model* 📖 and service implementations. *Programming in the small* is the implementation of an elemental service with a traditional programming language. *Programming in the large* is the development of composite services in a business process language such as BPEL. On both levels, services may be reused in order to form new composite services.

Stateless and Stateful Web Services

Business processes may run for hours, days, or months, and they may invoke other long-running services. A business process can contain steps that require waiting for external events or human interaction. Thus, you need to execute the process in an interruptible fashion. We call such processes *long-running processes*.

Service requestors may either initiate the long-running process without waiting for its results or have multiple interactions with the process. In the latter case, you need to correlate the interactions with the same instance of the Web service.

We've already examined stateful Web services in Chapter 8. In this chapter, we introduce *correlation* 📖 of multiple requests with the same process instance.

Evolution of Business Process Languages

The Business Process Execution Language for Web Services (BPEL4WS, in most cases abbreviated BPEL) has been developed using combinations of concepts from the Web Service Flow Language (WSFL) and XLANG. BPEL supersedes these two language specifications.

The main objective of WSFL was to provide an XML language for the description of Web services compositions. In WSFL, you can specify a collection of Web services, the *flow model*, which is a description of a flow composition. A business process is described as a directed graph of activities (the nodes of the graph) and control connectors (the edges of the graph). Nodes and edges of the flow graph are annotated with attributes that determine the execution of the flow: for example, transition conditions for the execution of parts of the flow. In addition to flow composition, you can use WSFL to specify overall partner interactions, the *global model*. A global model is a simple recursive composition metamodel that lets you describe the interactions between existing Web services and define new Web services as compositions of existing ones.

The objective of XLANG was to provide a notation "for the specification of message exchange behavior among participating web services" in order to enable "automation of business processes based on Web services." To achieve this objective, the major constructs of XLANG include sequential and parallel control flow definition, long-running transactions with compensation, custom correlation of messages, exception handling, and dynamic service referral. An XLANG service description extends a WSDL service description with the behavioral aspects of the service. It lets you specify a set of ports in a service section of a WSDL document and extend it with a description of, for example, the sequence in which the operations provided by each port are to be used.

In July 2002, BEA, IBM, and Microsoft provided a first specification of BPEL. BPEL can be used as an implementation language for executable processes as well as for describing business protocols. It extends the Web services interaction model and enables it to support business transactions. BPEL defines an interoperable integration model that supports both the intraenterprise and the B2B spaces.

The first BPEL specification was published in May 2003 with additional contributions from SAP and Siebel, and it's the foundation for the standards work in the OASIS WS-BPEL Technical Committee.

With this introduction into the history of business process languages, let's look at SkatesTown to see how BPEL can be useful to this company.

SkatesTown Requirements

SkatesTown's business has grown over time, and the Web services it provides have become increasingly complex. The time has come to break up hard-wired service implementations into more fine-grained and manageable pieces. Processes expressed in a business process language can be changed more easily, which gives SkatesTown more flexibility and the agility to quickly react to changing business requirements.

Up to this point, SkatesTown has offered Web services that allow customers to submit purchase orders. These are now extended with a new service that lets customers cancel running purchase order requests.

Whenever SkatesTown receives purchase order requests, it initiates subsequent processing steps before a response is returned to the customer. These steps include SkatesTown-internal processing such as order request validation, stock management, delivery, and external interactions with the supplier.

During processing of a purchase order, three parties in different roles are participating in SkatesTown's overall business process:

- The customer, acting as the *buyer*. The customer may submit order requests and may now in addition cancel orders.
- SkatesTown itself, acting as the *seller*. The purchase order process that receives a customer order interacts with internal applications and optionally with services provided by a supplier.

- The *supplier.* When SkatesTown can't fulfill a purchase order because it runs out of stock, an additional interaction with the supplier is initiated in order to replenish the item(s).

Figure 12.1 provides a high-level outline of SkatesTown's overall business process. Interactions with the business partners are indicated by lanes that show, from left to right, the communication with the customer, within SkatesTown itself, and with the supplier, respectively.

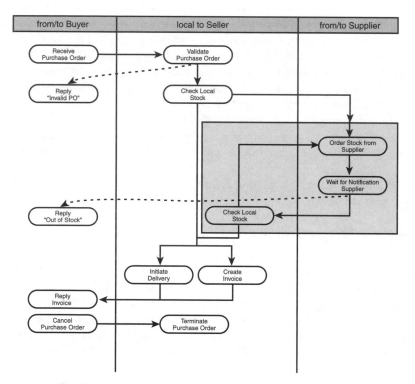

Figure 12.1   Outline of SkatesTown's purchase order process

We'll now examine more details of BPEL and give some example snippets for important elements of WSDL interfaces and BPEL processes. Finally, we'll explain how SkatesTown implements its business process with BPEL.

Business Process Execution Language for Web Services

As we mentioned earlier, BPEL is a language that allows the modeling of participant behavior in business interactions based on Web services. These include intracompany application integration scenarios as well as B2B interactions. The language is used to compose a set of Web services into new Web services. A BPEL process manifests itself as a Web service that can be consumed by other business partners and as a requestor of Web services offered by other providers.

Let's delve into the BPEL specification. We'll explain the motivation behind the key language concepts, define an external view of the business process, and then look at how you can compose services into a new business process.

Design Goals

The development of the BPEL language was guided by the following fundamental design goals:

- Business processes interact with the external world through Web services, and the interactions are described using WSDL `portType` definitions. The *process binding* (association of `portType`s to concrete service endpoints) is out of scope and addressed by the *process deployment* and/or runtime infrastructure. The operations of the `portType`s are entry points into the process.

- Business processes are described in an XML-based language. The graphical representation of business processes is outside the scope of BPEL. The language syntax is defined by a corresponding XML schema. This is a logical consequence of the fact that the business process language is built on top of Web services.

- The process language defines concepts for abstract views of business protocols and internal views of a process. Executable business processes model actual behavior of a participant in a business interaction. Business protocols, in contrast, use process descriptions that specify the mutually visible message exchange behavior of each of the parties involved in the protocol, without revealing their internal behavior.

- The language combines the benefits of both hierarchical languages (such as XLANG) and graph-oriented languages (such as WSFL).

- A limited set of constructs is provided, sufficient for simple data manipulation needed to define process-relevant data and control flow. BPEL isn't intended to be a general-purpose data-manipulation language.

- Process instances can be identified with application data defined by the business partner. No explicit factory pattern or particular instance identifier concept is required.

- Process instances are implicitly created and terminated. Additional process lifecycle operations can be addressed in the future.

- The process language defines a long-running transaction model based on scoping and compensation actions, providing backward recovery at a granularity chosen by the author of the process model.

- Web services are used as a simple recursive modularization model for process decomposition and assembly. BPEL allows you to combine structured activities to express arbitrarily complex algorithms that represent the implementation of the service.

- The language is compatible with other Web service standards, which may be developed orthogonal to the business process language itself. For example, this allows the process developer to independently address QoS attributes and process logic aspects.

The BPEL data model is built on top of WSDL 1.1 messages and XML Schema 1.0 types. All data used within a process model is defined using WSDL message definitions and XML schema types and elements. XPath 1.0 is used for data manipulation. Expressions used for the selection of data, for conditions, and for other purposes are specified as XPath expressions.

External Interface of a Process

Let's first look at business processes from an external perspective. BPEL is built on top of Web services, so WSDL plays the major role for the specification of interfaces used and exposed by a process. We'll briefly revisit standard Web services definition interfaces and then examine the external interface of a business process.

Standard WSDL: PortTypes and Messages

In Chapter 4 "Describing Web Services," we introduced the Web Service Description Language (WSDL). WSDL portTypes refer to WSDL messages with parts described by XML schema types.

The interface of a business process is specified as a collection of portTypes. Therefore, a business process is a special case of a Web service implementation. All inbound and outbound interfaces are described using WSDL. The binding of interfaces to service endpoints is outside the scope of the process language.

The following list introduces the namespaces and prefixes we use throughout this chapter:

- po—http://www.skatestown.com/ns/po

- inv—http://www.skatestown.com/ns/invoice

- pos—http://www.skatestown.com/services/interfaces/poSubmission.wsdl

- skt—http://www.skatestown.com/services/interfaces/skatestown.wsdl

- sup—http://www.wheelsandboards.com/services/interfaces/orderSupplies.wsdl

- plt—http://www.skatestown.com/processes/poSubmissionPLT

- ppa—http://www.skatestown.com/processes/poSubmissionPPA

Let's first look at the WSDL messages defined for the SkatesTown purchase order Web service. Two new messages are used for faults that may occur during purchase order processing. In addition, there's a new message for purchase order cancellations. The following WSDL snippet shows the messages used for the Web service operations exposed by the purchase order process. Note that the first two messages have already been used in the SkatesTown's purchase order Web service:

```
<message name="poSubmissionRequest">
   <part name="purchaseOrder" element="po:po"/>
</message>

<message name="poSubmissionResponse">
   <part name="invoice" element="inv:invoice"/>
</message>

<message name="poSubmissionFaultInvalidPO">
   <part name="customerID" element="xsd:ID"/>
   <part name="orderNumber" element="xsd:positiveInteger"/>
</message>

<message name="poSubmissionFaultOutOfStock">
   <part name="customerID" element="xsd:ID"/>
   <part name="orderNumber" element="xsd:positiveInteger"/>
</message>

<message name="cancelPurchaseOrderRequest">
   <part name="purchaseOrder" element="po:po"/>
</message>
```

The Web service interface provided by the WSDL portType determines the messages used as input, output, or fault messages, respectively. The next snippet shows the operations of the purchase order process. The purchase order submission request is extended with fault messages, and the purchase order cancellation operation is added to the interface:

```
<portType name="poSubmissionPortType">

   <operation name="doSubmission">
      <input message="pos:poSubmissionRequest"/>
      <output message="pos:poSubmissionResponse"/>
      <fault name="invalidPO" message="pos:poSubmissionFaultInvalidPO"/>
      <fault name="outOfStock" message="pos:poSubmissionFaultOutOfStock"/>
   </operation>

   <operation name="cancelPurchaseOrder">
      <input message="pos:cancelPurchaseOrderRequest"/>
   </operation>

</portType>
```

During the processing of a purchase order request, the process itself calls other Web services provided by SkatesTown's suppliers. These outbound invocations are defined in the same way. The following sample shows the interface of Web services that are required by the implementation of the purchase order process:

```
<portType name="orderSuppliesPortType">

    <operation name="orderSupplies">
        <input message="asp:orderSuppliesRequest"/>
    </operation>

</portType>
```

Notice that these services are one-way operations. How does information flow back into the process? The response to these one-way requests is described by a separate one-way operation called in the reverse direction. It's provided by the process and invoked by the supplier. The next WSDL snippet shows these callback interfaces. Together with the purchase order portType introduced earlier, this completes the specification of interfaces provided by the purchase order business process:

```
<portType name="orderSuppliesCallbackPortType">

    <operation name="orderSuppliesOk">
        <input message="asp:orderSuppliesResponse"/>
    </operation>

    <operation name="orderSuppliesFailed">
        <input message="asp:orderSuppliesFault"/>
    </operation>

</portType>
```

Up to this point, there was no requirement for concepts beyond the scope already covered by WSDL. Next, you'll see how multiple one-way requests can be associated with each other. PortTypes are paired in order to describe the relationship of multiple steps in an asynchronous interaction.

WSDL Extensions for Interactions with a Business Process

A business process can invoke Web services provided by other partners, provide Web services invoked by other partners, or both. The latter case can be an asynchronous response or a complex conversation that involves multiple messages flowing in both directions.

Each side of such a conversation provides Web services that are invoked by the other side. In order to describe the relationship between the two Web services, BPEL introduces a WSDL extension called *partnerLinkTypes* . PartnerLinkTypes contain one or two *roles*, which define the responsibilities of each side of the conversation. If only one partner offers a service and the other partner is only consuming this service without offering a callback operation, then the partnerLinkType only contains one role.

The role element of the partnerLinkType refers to a WSDL portType, where one partner provides one-way or request-response operations that are consumed by the other partner. *Notification* or *solicit-response* operations, described in Chapter 4, aren't supported; they're modeled by using one-way or request-response operations provided by the other side.

The following example shows the partnerLinkType for the SkatesTown portType discussed previously. This partnerLinkType has only one role: seller. The buyer role only initiates the process and doesn't offer Web service interfaces. Therefore, it isn't needed here:

```
<plnk:partnerLinkType name="purchaseOrderPartnerLinkType">

   <plnk:role name="seller">
      <plnk:portType name="pos:poSubmissionPortType"/>
   </plnk:role>

</plnk:partnerLinkType>
```

The seller role references the portType of the Web service provided to customers by SkatesTown. The implementation of this service is a BPEL process. The process refers to the portTypes that are named in the partnerLinkType roles.

In the next snippet, a partnerLinkType is shown that has two roles pointing to different portTypes. In this example, two partners are interacting with each other, and the portTypes of both partners are respectively referred to by the two roles. The portType of the seller role is another interface provided by the SkatesTown business process. It's used for asynchronous callbacks associated with an operation provided by the supplier role:

```
<plnk:partnerLinkType name="orderSuppliesPartnerLinkType">

   <plnk:role name="supplier">
      <plnk:portType name="sup:orderSuppliesPortType"/>
   </plnk:role>

   <plnk:role name="seller">
      <plnk:portType name="sup:orderSuppliesCallbackPortType"/>
   </plnk:role>

</plnk:partnerLinkType>
```

Later, we'll discuss two additional WSDL extensions: property and property alias definitions.

Overall Structure of a Process

Having specified the external interface of a BPEL process in the previous section, let's look at the internal structure of a process. The simplified example in Listing 12.1 introduces a business process to handle purchase orders: PurchaseOrderProcess. This process orchestrates the steps that are necessary to deal with the purchase order submitted by a SkatesTown customer. It fulfills the specification and requirements as outlined earlier. We'll use this process definition throughout the chapter as the means to explain the constructs provided by BPEL.

Listing 12.1   **Structure of a BPEL Process**

```
<!-- Process definition (1) -->
<process name="purchaseOrderProcess"
targetNamespace="http://www.skatestown.com/processes/purchaseOrderProcess"
xmlns:pos="http://www.skatestown.com/services/interfaces/poSubmission.wsdl"
xmlns:skt="http://www.skatestown.com/services/interfaces/skatestown.wsdl"
xmlns:sup="http://www.wheelsandboards.com/services/interfaces/orderSupplies.wsdl"
xmlns:plt="http://www.skatestown.com/processes/poSubmissionPLT"
xmlns:ppa="http://www.skatestown.com/processes/poSubmissionPPA"
xmlns:wsdl="http://schemas.xmlsoap.org/wsdl/"
xmlns="http://schemas.xmlsoap.org/ws/2003/03/business-process/">

<!-- Partner link definitions (2) -->
    <partnerLinks>
        <partnerLink name="buyer"
                    partnerLinkType="plt:purchaseOrderPartnerLinkType"
                    myRole="seller"/>

        <partnerLink name="supplier"
                    partnerLinkType="plt:allocateStockPartnerLinkType"
                    myRole="seller"
                    partnerRole="supplier"/>
        ...
    </partnerLinks>

<!-- Partner definitions (3) -->
    <partners>
        <partner name="skatestownCustomer">
            <partnerLink name="buyer"/>
        </partner>
        <partner name="skatestownSupplier">
            <partnerLink name="supplier"/>
        </partner>
        ...
    </partners>
```

Listing 12.1 **Continued**

```
<!-- Variable definitions (4) -->
    <variables>
        <variable name="poSubmissionRequest"
                  messageType="pos:poSubmissionRequest"/>
        <variable name="poSubmissionResponse"
                  messageType="pos:poSubmissionResponse"/>
        <variable name="poSubmissionFaultInvalidPO"
                  messageType="pos:poSubmissionFaultInvalidPO"/>
        ...
    </variables>

<!-- Correlation set definitions (5) -->
    <correlationSets>
        <correlationSet name="orderCorrelationSet"
                        properties="ppa:customerID ppa:orderNumber"/>
    </correlationSets>

<!-- Fault handler definitions (6) -->
    <faultHandlers>
        <catch faultName="pos:invalidPO">
            ...
        </catch>
        ...
    </faultHandlers>

<!-- Event handler definitions (7) -->
    <eventHandlers>
        <onMessage partnerLink="buyer"
                   portType="pos:poSubmisssionPortType"
                   operation="cancelPurchaseOrder" ...>
            ...
        </onMessage>
    </eventHandlers>

<!-- Body of business process (8) -->
    <sequence>
        <!-- receive purchase order from buyer (service requester) -->
        <!-- process purchase order, involves web services of supplier -->
        <!-- reply invoice to buyer (service requester) -->
        ...
    </sequence>

</process>
```

The definition of a BPEL *process* 📖 (at number 1 in the code) starts with process-specific attributes as part of its root element, such as the name of the process and its target namespace or the type of the business process. BPEL distinguishes two types of processes, and hence can be applied to two distinct usage scenarios:

- Implementing executable processes
- Describing nonexecutable *abstract processes*

Our focus is on the first scenario. We'll discuss abstract processes briefly toward the end of the chapter.

Process `PurchaseOrderProcess` involves various business partners. The customer (as the buyer) submits a purchase order. SkatesTown (as the seller) responds to the customer when the order is complete. SkatesTown also contacts the supplier when stock needs to be replenished to process the purchase order appropriately. As part of the BPEL process, interactions between partners are expressed through *partner links* 📖 (2). Often the conversation between two business partners involves multiple peer-to-peer interactions. The *partners* 📖 section (3) is a means to group multiple partner links, and as such expresses the capabilities required from a business partner.

The interaction between business partners is based on exchanging messages: The buyer sends a purchase order to the seller; the seller receives the purchase order and exchanges messages with its supplier. *Variables* 📖 (4) are the construct in BPEL to store such messages. In addition, variables can hold data that isn't exchanged with partners—data that is only needed for the internal processing of the business process.

Multiple interactions between partners might be involved in a specific business process instance that happens over a long period of time—days, months, or even years. This requires a means to identify a particular process instance that deals with, for example, a specific purchase order. BPEL introduces the notion of *correlation sets* 📖 (5) for this purpose.

The next sections of the process definition specify different kinds of handlers for the process:

- *Fault handlers* 📖 to catch process faults at the process level (6)
- *Event handlers* 📖 to deal with unsolicited events that can be received and processed in parallel with overall process execution (7)

Finally, a single activity specifies the implementation of the BPEL process: the body of the process (8). In general, this activity consists of nested activities. In our example, these are all the activities needed to handle a purchase order, and their order of execution. Since a business process is always initiated through the receipt of a message, the first step of a process needs to be an activity that can receive a message from a partner.

To summarize, the overall structure of a BPEL process consists of

- Process-specific, top-level attributes
- Partner-related specifications (partner links and partners)

- Variables
- Correlation sets
- Fault handlers and event handlers
- An activity that specifies the business logic of the overall process

Basic and Structured Activities

Activities 📖 are the composition primitives that implement the business logic of a BPEL process. BPEL distinguishes between *basic* and *structured* activities. *Structured activities* 📖 let you specify collections of nested activities and the order in which they take place. *Basic activities* 📖 represent atomic operations of a business process.

Let's first look at the basic activities BPEL provides. A basic activity can be any of the following:

- `receive` 📖—Waits to receive a request message from a partner
- `invoke` 📖—Invokes an operation on a WSDL portType provided by another partner
- `reply` 📖—Provides a response to a request message received by a `receive` activity
- `terminate` 📖—Terminates the entire process
- `throw` 📖—Indicates an exceptional situation by throwing a fault from within the process
- `assign` 📖—Allows for data manipulation of variables
- `wait` 📖—Waits either for a period of time or until a specified point in time
- `empty` 📖—Provides a no-op instruction
- `compensate` 📖—Triggers compensation for a successfully completed group of activities (a so-called *scope*)

Some activities, such as `receive` and `reply`, correspond to operations exposed by the WSDL interface of the BPEL process: operations that the process provides to its business partners and operations that the process requires from its partners.

Basic activities can be combined into more complex constructs using structured activities. BPEL provides graph-oriented constructs (such as `flow`) as well as algebraic constructs (such as `while` and `switch`). Thus, BPEL supports whichever style you prefer to express the business logic of your process.

Here are the structured activities provided by the language:

- `while` 📖—Lets you specify a loop.
- `switch` 📖—Provides a structured way of making decisions: the ability to select exactly one branch out of several choices.
- `pick` 📖—Lets you execute one out of several branches as soon as a suitable message arrives, or when a timeout occurs.

- sequence 📖—Specifies a group of activities that are executed sequentially.
- flow 📖—Specifies a collection of activities that can be executed in parallel. Links may be used to define execution order constraints including synchronization of parallel branches.
- scope 📖—Lets you define nested activities with its own set of variables, correlation sets, and handlers such as fault handlers, a compensation handler, and event handlers.

These structured activities can be combined recursively to express arbitrarily complex aggregates of activities that implement the service provided by the process.

Basic as well as structured activities can optionally have standard attributes such as the name of an activity. Later, we'll discuss additional standard attributes and elements that are applicable, for example, to activities nested in flows.

Process Lifecycle and Related Activities

The *process definition* 📖 as outlined in the section "Overall Structure of a Process" serves as a template from which specific *process instances* 📖 are created. For example, for each purchase order, a specific process instance of type PurchaseOrderProcess is responsible for the correct processing of this particular purchase order. A process instance's lifecycle begins with the creation of the instance. The lifecycle ends either upon successful completion of the business logic that implements the process or upon termination of the process instance (for example, through an unhandled fault).

The creation of a specific process instance always happens implicitly on receipt of a message. Therefore, the business logic of a process has to start with an activity that can receive such an initiating message—either a pick or receive activity. For example, the submission of a purchase order results in the creation of the process instance to handle this order.

A business process instance has completed normally if the business logic of the process could be executed successfully. However, if the process instance is terminated explicitly, or if a fault reaches the overall fault handler of the process, the completion is considered abnormal.

For explicit termination of a process instance, BPEL provides the *terminate* activity 📖. You can use this activity as part of your process logic whenever you need to terminate the entire process. The terminate activity forces the immediate termination of the process instance, including all its currently running activities.

Looking at the purchase order sample again, a customer may decide to cancel a purchase order, in which case the entire process that deals with this order is to be terminated. The terminate activity is used to implement this behavior:

```
<terminate/>
```

Partner Links

Business processes in BPEL are described as a composition of abstract services. This approach provides a higher degree of reusability for the modeled processes. Instead of referring to concrete services, only a logical name—for example, "customer" or "supplier"—and the service interface are used. The resolution to a concrete endpoint happens at a later point in time (for example, when the process is deployed).

In BPEL, this logical construct is the *partner Link* 📖 . Figure 12.2 shows the relationships between partner Links, partner Link Types, and `portTypes`. Partner Links are used for operations provided or invoked by a business process.

In the diagram, each process invokes a Web service provided by the other process. The `orderSuppliesProcess` of the supplier exists only virtually. It may be a BPEL process as well, but the BPEL partner Link Type concept doesn't require this.

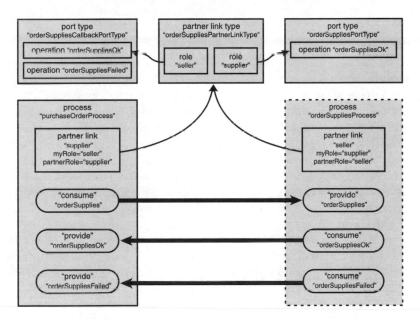

Figure 12.2   Partner Links and the associated partner Link Type

The following snippet shows an example of partner Link specifications in the purchase order process. Each partner Link declares the role of the process in the communication with the buyer, SkatesTown local services, and the supplier, respectively:

```
<process ...>

    ...

    <partnerLinks>
```

```
            <partnerLink name="buyer"
                         partnerLinkType="plt:purchaseOrderPartnerLinkType"
                         myRole="seller"/>

            <partnerLink name="local"
                         partnerLinkType="plt:localPartnerLinkType"
                         partnerRole="sellerLocal"/>

            <partnerLink name="supplier"
                         partnerLinkType="plt:orderSuppliesPartnerLinkType"
                         myRole="seller"
                         partnerRole="supplier"/>

    </partnerLinks>

    ...
</process>
```

Partner Link Binding

Partner Link Types point to WSDL portTypes with the abstract interface of a Web service. Before the Web service can be invoked, the associated partnerLink must be resolved to a concrete endpoint. The BPEL specification doesn't address the partnerLink resolution and leaves it to the infrastructure. In other words, when a BPEL process is deployed together with the WSDL portTypes that make up the Web service interfaces consumed or provided by the process, additional information is necessary to establish the relationship between the logical partner Link construct and the physical address of a Web service. In the most simple and static case, this can be a mapping of each partner Link and role to a WSDL port.

In Figure 12.3, the binding of the two roles of a partner Link to Web service endpoint is shown from SkatesTown's purchaseOrderProcess point of view. For the seller role, the WSDL port contains the address where the operations of the process itself are provided. For the supplier role, the WSDL port contains the address of the Web service provided by SkatesTown's business partner.

As an alternative to a static association of partner Link with endpoints, the process deployer can specify that the endpoint is bound to the partner Link at runtime and provide a policy that determines how this dynamic binding is performed.

For the dynamic binding of partner Link, BPEL uses the concept of *endpoint references* 📖. Endpoint references are defined by the WS-Addressing specification as a mechanism to dynamically identify and describe service endpoints and instances. They contain

- The address of a service endpoint
- Optional reference properties that are used by the service endpoint to dispatch a message to the final destination

- Optional elements that identify the WSDL portType, service, and port of the referenced endpoint
- Optional policies to describe behavior, requirements, or capabilities of a service endpoint

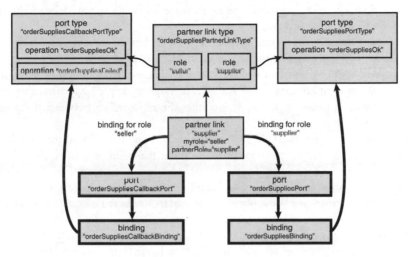

Figure 12.3   Binding a BPEL partnerLink to Web service endpoints

In BPEL, endpoint references can be dynamically assigned to or from message parts.

As an example for the use of endpoint references, consider the asynchronous interface of the supplier introduced earlier. The supplier doesn't just do business with SkatesTown; from the supplier's point of view, many business partners use its orderSupplies Web service. In order to enable the supplier to asynchronously respond to the correct partner, these partners have to identify themselves. Therefore, the request message of the orderSupplies operation contains an endpoint reference of the requester's callback service. In SkatesTown's purchase order process, this part is filled with the service end point address of the purchase order process.

You've seen how addresses of Web service endpoints can be dynamically exchanged with business partners in order to enable asynchronous conversations between them. Our example uses a callback address. In addition, we need to direct the asynchronous response back to the right purchase order. Let's look at how to correlate messages with individual stateful services.

Properties and Correlation Sets

The external interface of a BPEL process is described by portTypes; however, WSDL has no notion of a stateful Web service. Every time a new purchase order request arrives at the SkatesTown WSDL port, a new instance of the purchase order process is created.

Each process instance may perform an asynchronous interaction with the supplier Web service. Furthermore, a customer can cancel a running purchase order. We need a way to make sure all these operations take place using the same instance of a purchase order.

In order to allow the correlation of messages with process instances, each message must carry an identification of the process instance the request is targeted for. This may be a unique key associated with the process instance when it's initiated, or application data mapped to a unique instance key.

BPEL doesn't require a separate instance key. Fields within the application data are used to identify BPEL process instances. Such fields are called *properties*. A *property* 📖 is a named, typed data element that is defined as a WSDL extension element. The property value is extracted from an instance of a WSDL message by applying a message-specific XPath expression. A `propertyAlias` 📖 defines the relationship between the property and the data field in the message.

In some cases, a single data field isn't sufficient. For example, if a customer submits a new purchase order before a previous purchase order has been processed, then the customer is associated with two running purchase order instances. Therefore, just using the customer identification isn't sufficient to correlate messages to a single process instance. In addition to the customer ID, you can use an order number: The customer ID and the order number together form a unique process instance key called a *correlation set* 📖.

The diagram in Figure 12.4 shows the `poSubmissionRequest` WSDL message. It carries a part `purchaseOrder` of a complex XML schema type. The part has two key elements identified by the XPath expressions `/billTo/id` and `/id`. These elements are associated with the properties `customerId` and `orderNumber` via a property alias definition. The two properties together form the correlation set `orderCorrelationSet`, which is the unique key for one instance of the `purchaseOrderProcess`. If the customer chooses to cancel the purchase order, the cancellation request must carry the same correlation data.

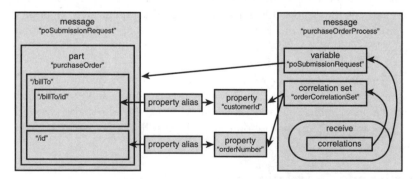

Figure 12.4   Process with correlation set

The following snippet shows a definition of the properties with their XML schema type.

```
<wsbp:property name="customerID" type="xsd:ID"/>

<wsbp:property name="orderNumber" type="xsd:positiveInteger"/>
```

For each property, a property alias definition must be provided for every WSDL message type that may contain this property. In the following property alias example, each property defined before is mapped to the WSDL message definition for the purchase order request. In addition to the message type, the property alias also names the part of the message and the XPath into the part that allows the extraction of the property value:

```
<wsbp:propertyAlias propertyName="customerID"
                    messageType="pos:poSubmissionRequest"
                    part="purchaseOrder"
                    query="/billTo/id"/>

<wsbp:propertyAlias propertyName="orderNumber"
                    messageType="pos:poSubmissionRequest"
                    part="purchaseOrder"
                    query="/id"/>
```

The two properties defined here are used together in the correlation set orderCorrelationSet. This is the key that identifies a particular instance of the purchase order process:

```
<correlationSets>
    <correlationSet name="orderCorrelationSet" properties="customerID orderNumber"/>
</correlationSets>
```

How are correlation sets associated with particular values? When a correlation set is first used within a process, the set of properties must be initialized. In a multipartner conversation, the partner starting the message exchange and creating the property values is called the *initiator*. The other partners are *followers* of the message exchange.

A correlation set can be used with all types of activities that deal with inbound (received) or outbound (sent) messages. The initialization may happen either when a message is received or when a message is sent. In the first case, the partner that sends a message to the process is setting the correlation data. In the second case, the correlation data is created by the process. The activity that refers to a correlation set explicitly states whether the correlation set is initialized. The following code snippet shows how a correlation set can be referred to from within activities; it is initiated (initialized) when it's used for the first time:

```
<!-- Receive the purchase order request message -->

    <correlations>
        <correlation set="orderCorrelationSet" initiate="yes"/>
```

```
    </correlations>

    . . .
```

After the initialization of a correlation set, it's considered immutable. All other activities referring to this correlation set must not change any of the properties.

In the following snippet, the correlation set isn't initiated. On receipt of a message, it's used to correlate the message with the correct process instance:

```
<!-- Receive the purchase order cancellation message -->

    <correlations>
        <correlation set="orderCorrelationSet" initiate="no"/>
    </correlations>


    . . .
```

If a message is sent out and the correlation set isn't initiated, then it's used to verify that the message contains the unchanged property values.

Invoking Web Services and Providing Web Services

Activities that specify interactions with partners are key to the definition of a BPEL process. Next we'll look at how to invoke operations provided by a partner, and we'll introduce activities that let you expose the entire BPEL process as a Web service.

Invoking Web Services Operations

BPEL provides a specific activity, the *invoke activity* 📖, that allows a process to call Web services provided by a business partner. As part of the specification of an `invoke` activity, you select the business partner to interact with using a partner link. You also specify the WSDL `portType` and operation to be invoked from that partner. The operation can either be a request-response operation or a one-way operation. An input variable that provides the request message for the invocation is required for both types of operations. In the case of a request-response operation, you also need to identify an output variable to store the response message of the invocation, its result.

SkatesTown employs supplier services as well as local services to process purchase orders. The following two BPEL snippets show `invoke` activities from the purchase order process. The first invokes a one-way operation of the supplier's interface to request additional supplies:

```
<invoke partnerLink="supplier"
        portType="sup:orderSuppliesPortType"
        operation="orderSupplies"
        inputVariable="orderSuppliesRequest">
    . . .
</invoke>
```

The second invokes a request-response operation of a local service to validate the purchase order request:

```
<invoke partnerLink="local"
        portType="sup:skatestownPortType"
        operation="validatePurchaseOrder"
        inputVariable="poSubmissionRequest"
        outputVariable="validatePurchaseOrderResponse">
    ...
</invoke>
```

As we explained earlier, it's sometimes necessary to correlate multiple interactions with the same process instance. For that reason, `invoke` activities support associating correlation information, correlation sets, with the outbound request message as well as the inbound response message. Correlation sets may also be initialized as a part of the invocation.

In the following example, the correlation set `orderCorrelationSet` is provided as part of the request message during the invocation of the supplier's service. It allows the supplier to interact with the same process instance again later—for example, to notify that the request for additional supplies could be fulfilled. This particular correlation set has already been initialized prior to this `invoke` activity. In addition, the sample depicts the usage of a second correlation set `anAdditionalCorrelationSet` that has not been initialized before. The attribute `initiate` specifies whether initialization should happen for a correlation set as part of the invocation, and the attribute `pattern` indicates whether the correlation set is associated with the input (pattern="in") or output (pattern="out") of a request-response operation:

```
<invoke partnerLink="supplier"
        portType="sup:orderSuppliesPortType"
        operation="orderSupplies"
        inputVariable="orderSuppliesRequest">

    <correlations>
      <correlation set="orderCorrelationSet" initiate="no" pattern="out"/>
      <correlation set="anAdditionalCorrelationSet" initiate="yes" pattern="out"/>
    </correlations>

</invoke>
```

Providing Web Services Operations

Having described what activities BPEL offers to invoke Web services operations, we'll now look at how to specify the services that a process provides to its business partners. A process can offer one-way operations as well as request-response operations. Processes implement their Web services operations using *receive activities* 📖 and *reply activities* 📖.

A `receive` activity specifies the operation of the process's WSDL interface that a partner has to invoke. The signature of the operation specifies what request message is to be passed to the process and whether the partner should expect a response message from the process. Furthermore, such invocations can result in the creation of a new process instance, or requests can be submitted to already existing process instances.

The sample process `PurchaseOrderProcess` provides the Web service operation `doSubmission`—a request-response operation. It implements this operation using a `receive` activity and a `reply` activity as shown in the following snippets. In addition, this `receive` activity needs to create a new process instance for the purchase order speci-fied by the input of operation `doSubmission`. This is achieved by setting the `createInstance` attribute of the `receive` activity to `"yes"`. Also, the correlation set `orderCorrelationSet` needs to be initialized as part of the `receive` activity for later use by the process (as shown in the supplier sample in the previous section).

```
<receive partnerLink="buyer"
        portType="pos:poSubmissionPortType"
        operation="doSubmission"
        createInstance="yes"
        variable="poSubmissionRequest">

    <correlations>
        <correlation set="orderCorrelationSet" initiate="yes"/>
    </correlations>

</receive>

...

<reply partnerLink="buyer"
       portType="pos:poSubmissionPortType"
       operation="doSubmission"
       variable="poSubmissionResponse">

</reply>
```

As mentioned in this example, the attribute `createInstance` lets you specify that a `receive` activity should create a process instance upon receipt of the corresponding mes-sage. It acts as an initiating `receive`. Otherwise, the `receive` activity happens as part of an existing process instance. If multiple initiating `receive` activities are specified for a process, only the first message targeted for one of these `receive` activities creates the instance. All the other `receive` activities wait for their corresponding messages with the same correlation set to arrive; they behave as if their `createInstance` attributes were set to `"no"`. Thus you can define processes that require multiple messages to get started, regardless of the order in which these messages arrive.

The following example shows an interaction with an existing process instance. The operation `orderSuppliesOK` represents such an interaction: It provides the supplier's response to a prior request of the process to order additional supplies. By calling this operation, the supplier indicates that the request has been completed successfully. It requires a specification to uniquely identify the existing process instance using correlation. The correlation set `orderCorrelationSet`, initialized previously, serves that purpose:

```
<receive partnerLink="supplier"
        portType="sup:orderSuppliesCallbackPortType"
        operation="orderSuppliesOK"
        createInstance="no"
        variable="orderSuppliesResponse">

    <correlations>
        <correlation set="orderCorrelationSet" initiate="no"/>
    </correlations>

</receive>
```

The *pick activity* 📖 is a variant of the `receive` activity. Whereas `receive` only allows the specification of one message to arrive, `pick` waits for the receipt of one message out of a set of specified messages or the occurrence of a timeout—whichever happens first. The timeout can be specified either by a duration (specified by a duration-valued XPath expression) or by a point in time (specified by a deadline-valued XPath expression).

Let's extend the previous example with another potential response from the supplier and a timeout specification, using a `pick` activity instead of the `receive` activity. If the supplier can't fulfill SkatesTown's request for additional supplies, the supplier comes back with a different message to indicate that the processing of the request wasn't successful. That is, the purchase order process now waits for two potential messages to arrive as the response from the supplier, only one of which might actually happen. In addition, a timeout is specified to avoid waiting forever. If the supplier doesn't respond within the given timeframe, the process continues with the activity specified as part of the `onAlarm` element:

```
<pick>
    <onMessage partnerLink="supplier"
            portType="sup:orderSuppliesCallbackPortType"
            operation="orderSuppliesOk"
            createInstance="no"
            variable="orderSuppliesResponse">
        <correlations>
            <correlation set="orderCorrelationSet" initiate="no"/>
        </correlations>
        ...
    </onMessage>
    <onMessage partnerLink="supplier"
            portType="sup:orderSuppliesCallbackPortType"
            operation="orderSuppliesFailed"
            createInstance="no"
            variable="orderSuppliesFault">
```

```
            <correlations>
                <correlation set="orderCorrelationSet" initiate="no"/>
            </correlations>
            ...
        </onMessage>
        <!-- timeout after one month -->
        <onAlarm for="P1M">
            ...
        </onAlarm>
</pick>
```

Data Handling and Related Activities

Messages initiate business processes. Processes receive messages from business partners and respond to partners via messages. Every invocation of a Web service that is orchestrated by a process is based on the exchange of messages. All these messages are specified as part of the external interface of the business process, its portTypes.

Looking at the messages from the point of view of the process definition, BPEL provides the construct for *variables* 📖 to store these messages. Variables are used for

- Messages that a process receives
- Messages that are needed as input for the invocation of Web services operations
- The result of service invocations
- Intermediate data that the internal business logic might depend on (for example, to compose messages or for conditional logic)

Variables can be typed either by WSDL message types or by XML schema types: WSDL messages types are to be specified for messages that are exchanged with partners. Variables used only for internal data handling can be typed either way.

Variables are scoped. They can be globally declared at the process level. BPEL also supports the notion of variables that are local to a BPEL scope (more details on scopes later). The scope of a variable determines its visibility and lifetime. A variable is visible within the scope it's declared in and also to all nested scopes within that scope.

The purchase order request is an example of a global variable declaration using a message type. Its declaration appears in the variables section of the process:

```
<process name="PurchaseOrderProcess"...>
    ...
    <variables>
        ...
        <variable name="poSubmissionRequest"
                  messageType="pos:poSubmissionRequest"/>
        ...
    </variables>
    ...
</process>
```

The next snippet shows an example of a local, xsd-type variable. It's declared at the scope level:

```
<scope>
    ...
    <variables>
        ...
        <variable name="itemCount"
                  type="xsd:integer"/>
        ...
    </variables>
    ...
</scope>
```

The assign Activity

Now let's look at how data can be manipulated and assigned as part of the process logic. BPEL provides a special activity type for updating variables: the *assign activity* 📖. It lets you copy type-compatible data from one variable to another; you can also construct and insert new data using general XPath expressions. Expressions also provide for simple computations—for example, to prepare data for the invocation of Web services.

The following snippets depict samples of various usages of assign activities. The first shows the copying of an entire variable:

```
<assign>
    <copy>
        <from variable="poSubmissionRequest"/>
        <to variable="trueCopyOfPoSubmissionRequest"/>
    </copy>
</assign>
```

The next sample only copies a selected part from one variable to another variable:

```
<assign>
    <copy>
        <from variable="poSubmissionRequest" part="purchaseOrder"/>
        <to variable="orderSuppliesRequest" part="orderSupplies"/>
    </copy>
</assign>
```

In the following, you see a more complex assign activity that copies two selected elements from one variable to another. This assignment is performed as an atomic operation. The selection of elements involves queries expressed in XPath as the query language:

```
<assign>
    <copy>
        <from variable="poSubmissionRequest"
```

```
                         part="purchaseOrder"
                         query="/billTo/id"/>
             <to    variable="poSubmissionFaultInvalidPO"
                         part="customerID"/>
         </copy>
         <copy>
             <from variable="poSubmissionRequest"
                         part="purchaseOrder"
                         query="/id"/>
             <to    variable="poSubmissionFaultInvalidPO"
                         part="orderNumber"/>
         </copy>
    </assign>
```

The next snippet initializes a variable using a literal value:

```
<assign>
    <copy>
        <from><xsd:integer>0</xsd:integer></from>
        <to variable="itemCount"/>
    </copy>
</assign>
```

The final `assign` sample uses an expression to perform a simple computation:

```
<assign>
    <copy>
        <from expression="bpws:getVariableData('itemCount')+1"/>
        <to variable="itemCount"/>
    </copy>
</assign>
```

The `assign` activity can also copy endpoint references to and from partner links. This aspect is useful whenever endpoint references are to be treated as data—for example, to exchange endpoint references with business partners as part of messages, or to compute endpoint references.

SkatesTown uses this feature to send its endpoint reference to the supplier. It requests additional supplies using the `orderSupplies` operation. As part of this request, SkatesTown provides its endpoint reference. This enables the supplier to asynchronously respond to the request without the need to be statically bound to one particular seller. The supplier uses this endpoint reference to submit its response—for example, to invoke the seller's `orderSuppliesOk` operation. The following BPEL snippet depicts how SkatesTown's endpoint reference is copied to the request message. The `assign` activity copies the endpoint reference from role `myRole` of partner link `supplier` to the `orderSuppliesRequest` variable. This variable then serves as input for the `orderSupplies` operation:

```
<assign>
    <copy>
```

```
            <from partnerLink="supplier" endpointReference="myRole"/>
            <to variable="orderSuppliesRequest" part="endpointReferenceOfSeller"/>
        </copy>
</assign>
```

XPath Extension Functions

Last but not least there is the need to access data from a process not only as part of assignments, but also to control the behavior of a process (for example, in conditions). In order to enable arbitrary XPath expressions to access data from the process, BPEL introduces several XPath extension functions.

The `getVariableData` function extracts arbitrary values from variables. The `partName` and `locationPath` arguments are optional:

```
getVariableData("variableName", "partName", "locationPath")
```

A variable can carry global message properties, the values of which can be extracted using the `getVariableProperty` function with the qualified name of the global property:

```
getVariableProperty("variableName", "propertyQName")
```

The `getLinkStatus` function returns a Boolean indicating the status of a link. It can only be applied in join conditions (see the section on links for details):

```
getLinkStatus("linkName")
```

The extension functions are useful for all kinds of expressions: in transition conditions, join conditions, `while` conditions, and `switch` cases, as well as for duration and deadline expressions.

More Basic Activities: `wait`, `empty`

Let's briefly discuss the remaining two basic activities: `wait` and `empty`. The `wait` activity allows the business process to wait for a specific time interval (specified by a duration-valued XPath expression) or until a certain deadline is reached (specified by a deadline-valued XPath expression). The following `wait` activity waits until New Year's Eve:

```
<wait until="2004-12-31T18:00+1:00"/>
```

This `wait` activity waits for three days and 10 hours:

```
<wait for="P3DT10H"/>
```

The `empty` activity does nothing. It may, for example, be used as implementation of a fault handler if you need to catch and suppress a fault:

```
<empty/>
```

Flows

Graph-oriented constructs are a common approach for controlling the flow of execution of several activities. The BPEL *flow activity* 📖 lets you define a collection of activities, parts of which may be performed in parallel. Activities in a flow can be wired together via *links* that specify the execution order between activities, including the synchronization of parallel execution branches within that flow. Furthermore, *transition conditions* determine the branches of a flow to be navigated, and *join conditions* specify requirements about parallel branches joining at an activity; they need to be fulfilled to execute that activity.

In SkatesTown's purchase order process, a `flow` activity controls the main processing of the purchase order, starting with its validation and finishing with the creation of the invoice and the initiation of the order's delivery:

- Some activities of this flow must be performed before others, for example, validation needs to happen first.

- Some activities can be executed in parallel, such as the creation of the invoice and the initiation of the delivery.

- The flow also uses transition conditions. For example, based on the result of the `validatePurchaseOrder` activity, processing of the order either continues normally or is discontinued by throwing the fault `invalidPO`.

Figure 12.5 outlines the graph of this flow; its activities are represented as nodes, and its links as edges.

Link Semantics

Let's look at how links and conditions are defined to support a flow's behavior:

- A link between two activities prescribes their execution order: A link's target activity can only be executed if the source activity has completed.

- A link can have an associated transition condition. The transition condition is specified as a Boolean-valued XPath expression based on the process instance's state, such as the state of its variables. It determines whether a link evaluates to true or false, and thus whether a link is followed during runtime. If a transition condition isn't specified, the link is defined to be true and therefore is always followed.

- An activity can be the source of multiple links, thus allowing for multiple branches that can be executed in parallel. Such an activity acts as a *fork activity*.

- An activity can also be the target of multiple links. Such an activity establishes a point of synchronization, because it becomes eligible for execution only when all incoming links have been evaluated. It acts as a *join activity*. In addition, this activity may have a `join` condition specified. The `join` condition is a Boolean-valued XPath expression that is based on the process instance's state, including the state of the activity's incoming links. An activity is executed only if its `join` condition evaluates to true. Omitting the specification of an activity's `join` condition means at least one incoming link has to be true.

- Activities of a flow without incoming links are started as soon as their flow is activated. They run in parallel.

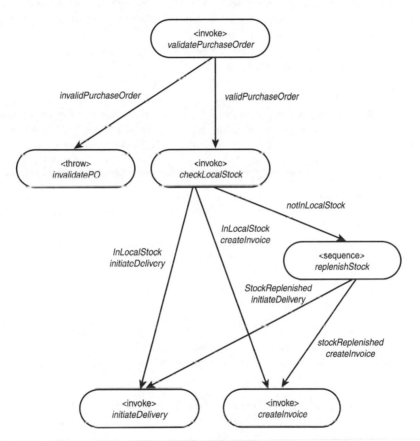

Figure 12.5 Graphical outline of sample `flow` activity with its activities and links

Join Failures and Dead Path Elimination

How does a flow continue if the `join` condition of an activity fails (evaluates to false) and the activity is not to be executed? BPEL provides two answers to this question. By specifying the attribute `suppressJoinFailure`, you can select the behavior you want to be applied to your process and its activities.

By default, a join condition failure results in throwing a BPEL standard fault called `joinFailure` followed by common BPEL fault processing.

Alternatively, the BPEL standard fault `joinFailure` can be suppressed by setting the attribute `suppressJoinFailure` to "yes," and *dead path elimination* will be performed instead. If the join condition fails, the corresponding activity is skipped, and all the activity's outgoing links are set to false (their transition conditions are ignored). From then on, navigation processing continues as usual: The target activities of the outgoing links are tested to see whether they can be executed or whether they are to be skipped as well, depending on their specifications, and so on.

The attribute `suppressJoinFailure` can be specified globally at the process level and overridden selectively at the activity level.

Putting Together the Flow Sample

Having said all that, let's get back to SkatesTown's flow as outlined in Figure 12.5. Listing 12.2 shows how this flow is expressed using the BPEL `flow` activity. The definition of a `flow` activity always starts with the specification of its links. Activities of a `flow` become the source and/or target of these links by referencing them via the standard activity elements `source` and `target`. The `transition` condition is an optional attribute of the activity's `source` element:

Listing 12.2   **Flow Activity**

```
<flow>
    <links>
        <link name="validPurchaseOrder"/>
        <link name="invalidPurchaseOrder"/>
        <link name="inLocalStock_initiateDelivery"/>
        <link name="inLocalStock_createInvoice"/>
        <link name="notInLocalStock"/>
        <link name="stockReplenished_initiateDelivery"/>
        <link name="stockReplenished_createInvoice"/>
    </links>

    <invoke partnerLink="local" portType="skt:skatestownPortType"
            operation="validatePurchaseOrder"
            inputVariable="poSubmissionRequest"
            outputVariable="validatePurchaseOrderResponse">

        <source linkName="validPurchaseOrder" transitionCondition=
          "bpws:getVariableData('validatePurchaseOrderResponse','valid')=true"/>

        <source linkName="invalidPurchaseOrder" transitionCondition=
          "bpws:getVariableData('validatePurchaseOrderResponse','valid')=false"/>
    </invoke>

    <throw faultName="pos:invalidPO">

        <target linkName="invalidPurchaseOrder"/>
```

Listing 12.2 **Continued**

```
    </throw>

    <invoke partnerLink="local" portType="skt:skatestownPortType"
            operation="checkLocalStock"
            inputVariable="poSubmissionRequest"
            outputVariable="checkLocalStockResponse">

        <target linkName="validPurchaseOrder"/>

        <source linkName="inLocalStock_createInvoice" transitionCondition=
          "bpws:getVariableData('checkLocalStockResponse','available')=true"/>
        <source linkName="inLocalStock_initiateDelivery" transitionCondition=
          "bpws:getVariableData('checkLocalStockResponse','available')=true"/>

        <source linkName="notInLocalStock" transitionCondition=
          "bpws:getVariableData('checkLocalStockResponse','available')=false"/>
    </invoke>

    <sequence name="replenishStock">

        <target linkName="notInLocalStock"/>
        <source linkName="stockReplenished_initiateDelivery"/>
        <source linkName="stockReplenished_createInvoice"/>
        ...
    </sequence>


    <invoke partnerLink="local" portType="skt:skatestownPortType"
            operation="initiateDelivery"
            inputVariable="poSubmissionRequest">

        <target linkName="inLocalStock_initiateDelivery"/>
        <target linkName="stockReplenished_initiateDelivery"/>
    </invoke>

    <invoke partnerLink="local" portType="skt:skatestownPortType"
            operation="createInvoice"
            inputVariable="poSubmissionRequest"
            outputVariable="poSubmissionResponse">

        <target linkName="inLocalStock_createInvoice"/>
        <target linkName="stockReplenished_createInvoice"/>
    </invoke>

</flow>
```

More Structured Activities: `sequence, while, switch, scope`

Besides the `pick` and `flow` activities, BPEL provides several additional types of structured activities. The *sequence activity* 📖 lets you specify that activities are to be executed in the order in which they are provided. The following snippet shows three activities from the purchase order process. They always run in the specified order; the purchase order request is received first, then processed, and finally answered:

```
<sequence>

    <receive partnerLink="buyer" portType="pos:poSubmissionPortType"
            operation="doSubmission" createInstance="yes"
            variable="poSubmissionRequest">
            ...
    </receive>

    <flow>
        ...
    </flow>

    <reply partnerLink="buyer" portType="pos:poSubmissionPortType"
          operation="doSubmission"
          variable="poSubmissionResponse">
          ...
    </reply>

</sequence>
```

The `while` activity has a nested activity that is repeatedly executed as long as a specified Boolean condition is evaluated as true. The condition is provided as an XPath expression. In our example, such an activity is used at the point where the local stock needs to be replenished. Additional goods are ordered from the supplier as long as the purchase order can't be processed from the local stock:

```
<while condition="bpws:getVariableData('checkLocalStockResponse','available')=
false">

    <!-- Replenish local stock ... -->

</while>
```

The *switch activity* 📖 can be compared to similar constructs in programming languages: for example, the `switch` statement in Java with its `case` and `default` branches. It lets you select exactly one branch out of a given set of choices. For each choice, provided as a list of `case` elements with a Boolean condition, a nested activity must be specified. The activity on the first branch (in the order of specification) whose condition evaluates to true is executed. If an otherwise element is provided, then its nested activity is executed if none of the case conditions evaluate to true:

```
<switch>

    <case condition="bpws:getVariableData(
➥'poSubmissionResponse','invoice','/totalCost')<100">
        <!-- add shipping and handling fee -->
        ...
    </case>

    <case condition="bpws:getVariableData(
➥'poSubmissionResponse','invoice','/totalCost')<800">
        <!-- do nothing -->
        <empty/>
    </case>

    <otherwise>
        <!-- subtract rebate for large orders -->
        ...
    </otherwise>

</switch>
```

The *scope activity* is used to specify visibility boundaries. Scopes have the same structure as the overall process, except for partnerLinks and partners, which can only be declared globally in the process, and a compensation handler, which can only be declared in scopes:

```
<scope ...>

    <!-- Variable definitions -->

    <!-- Correlation set definitions -->

    <!-- Fault handler definitions -->

    <!-- Compensation handler definitions -->

    <!-- Event handler definitions -->

    <!-- Body of scope: activity -->

</scope>
```

Definitions at the scope level apply to all nested activities. The only mandatory element is the nested activity, which may be a structured activity as well. Variables and correlation sets declared in a scope are only visible to activities nested within that scope.

Fault handlers, compensation handlers, and event handlers can be declared in a scope as well. Let's now examine these handlers in detail.

Fault Handling

BPEL introduces fault handlers in order to let you deal with exceptional situations, such as the following:

- A fault recognized as the result of a Web service invocation
- A fault thrown explicitly by the process logic
- A fault caused by a problem encountered by the runtime infrastructure

Let's take a closer look at these three potential sources of faults in BPEL.

Fault Situations

The outcome of a Web service invocation is either regular output or a fault, as specified by the WSDL operation. The example shows the definition of a WSDL operation with two faults. WSDL faults have a name and a reference to a message definition, as shown in the following snippet:

```
<wsdl:operation name="doSubmission">

    <wsdl:input message="pos:poSubmissionRequest"/>

    <wsdl:output message="pos:poSubmissionResponse"/>

    <wsdl:fault name="invalidPO" message="pos:poSubmissionFaultInvalidPO"/>
    <wsdl:fault name="outOfStock" message="pos:poSubmissionFaultOutOfStock"/>

</wsdl:operation>
```

BPEL also lets you raise faults explicitly by means of the `throw` activity. The `throw` activity declares a qualified name of a fault and optionally provides a variable to associate data with the fault. The following BPEL snippet shows a `throw` activity. It's used to end the execution of the normal path in the process because the validation of the received purchase order has failed:

```
<throw faultName="pos:invalidPO"/>
```

Finally, the BPEL runtime infrastructure recognizes a number of predefined exceptional situations within a running process instance. If such a situation occurs, a BPEL standard fault is raised. Examples for such standard faults are

- `mismatchedAssignmentFailure`—Incompatible types in an `assign` activity
- `forcedTermination`—Fault in an enclosing scope
- `correlationViolation`—Message contents in `receive`, `reply`, `invoke`, or `pick/onMessage` don't match correlation data

- uninitializedVariable—Attempt to access an uninitialized part of a message variable

- invalidReply—Attempt to execute a reply for which no corresponding receive activity has been processed

Fault Handlers

In BPEL, *fault handlers* 📖 are the mechanism to explicitly catch these faults and respond to them in appropriate business logic. Fault handlers are associated with a scope activity or with the overall process.

When a fault is recognized, the scope or process first stops all its nested activities. Structured activities are terminated immediately. Some types of basic activities are also interrupted, including wait, receive, reply, and invoke. Other activities are considered short-lived and aren't interrupted.

A fault handler contains an activity that runs in case the corresponding fault occurs. For example, the fault handler may contain a reply activity that notifies a partner that normal processing of the logic can't be completed.

Syntactically, a fault handler is a catch or catchAll element. The catch element lets you specify the qualified name of a fault, a fault variable, or both. The fault variable can be omitted in cases where faults don't have additional data associated with them. The catchAll element doesn't have attributes.

Following is an example of a fault handler declaration for the overall process:

```
<process ...>

    ...

    <faultHandlers>

        <catch faultName="pos:invalidPO">

            <reply partnerLink="buyer"
                   portType="pos:purchaseOrderPortType"
                   operation="submitPurchaseOrder"
                   faultName="pos:invalidPO"
                   variable="purchaseOrderFaultInvalidPO"/>

        </catch>

        <catch faultName="pos:outOfStock">

            <reply partnerLink="buyer"
                   portType="pos:poSubmissionPortType"
                   operation="poSubmission"
                   faultName="pos:outOfStock"
                   variable="poSubmissionFaultOutOfStock"/>
```

```
        </catch>

    </faultHandlers>

    ...
</process>
```

Fault handlers can be declared in the same way for scopes. They can also be declared for `invoke` activities, which is a shorthand notation for defining an enclosing scope with the fault handler.

Fault Handler Example

SkatesTown's purchase order process has multiple places that deal with faults and fault handling. As an example, the process outline in Figure 12.6 shows the invocation of the order validation step and a flow to subsequent activities. Transition conditions on the links determine whether the validation result is OK or considered failed. In the latter case, a fault is thrown explicitly. The associated fault handler sends a fault reply message back to the customer.

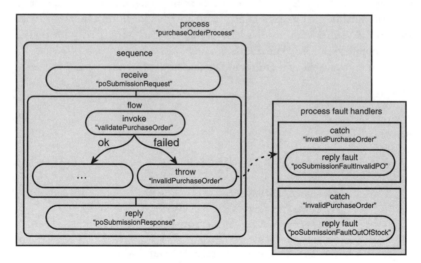

Figure 12.6 Faults and fault handlers

If a fault handler throws a fault itself, then this fault can be caught by the next higher enclosing scope. This applies to explicitly rethrown faults and to unexpected faults that occur during processing of the fault handler.

Not every scope has a fault handler specified for every possible type of fault. When a fault isn't caught by a fault handler, then a default fault handler applies. The default fault handler runs all available compensation handlers for immediately enclosed scopes in the reverse order of completion of the corresponding activities, and then rethrows the fault to the next enclosing scope.

The fault-handling concept in BPEL is similar to exception-handling in Java and other programming languages. However, business processes require additional error-handling steps. When intermediate results are made persistent, they must be reversed explicitly. Let's now take a closer look at such compensation steps.

Compensation Handling

In the previous section, we discussed fault handlers as a means to catch faults and respond to exceptional situations with appropriate business logic. As part of such logic, a common need is to undo activities that happened prior to the occurrence of the fault in order to correct the situation. For example, suppose a fault happens during the processing of a purchase order after stock has already been allocated in SkatesTown's local warehouse. When handling this fault, the allocation is to be reversed to reestablish a consistent state from which the processing of the purchase order can continue.

To do that, BPEL introduces the notion of *compensation handlers* that let you specify compensation logic to undo successfully completed activities in the case of a fault. The unit of compensation is, in its simplest form, one activity. It can also be a BPEL scope that forms a logical unit of work consisting of several activities and therefore needs to be compensated as such. A compensation handler specifically defines how to reverse the result of the particular unit it's associated with.

The following BPEL snippet specifies compensation logic for one particular activity of the PurchaseOrderProcess sample, the allocation of stock in SkatesTown's local warehouse. The checkAndAllocateLocalStock activity has an associated compensation handler that is implemented by another invoke activity. The deallocateLocalStock activity undoes what happened during the allocation of items for a purchase order:

```
<invoke name="checkAndAllocateLocalStock"
        partnerLink="local"
        portType="skt:skatestownPortType"
        operation="checkLocalStock"
        inputVariable="poSubmissionRequest"
        outputVariable="checkLocalStockResponse">

    ...

    <compensationHandler>

        <invoke name="deallocateLocalStock"
                partnerLink="local"
                portType="skt:skatestownPortType"
                operation="deallocateLocalStock"
                inputVariable="poSubmissionRequest"/>

    </compensationHandler>

</invoke>
```

Inlining the specification of a compensation handler as part of an `invoke` activity is a shorthand notation for specifying a `scope` with the `invoke` activity as its implementation.

The next example shows how you associate a compensation handler with a scope:

```
<scope name="ALogicalUnitOfWork">
    ...
    <compensationHandler>
        <!-- compensation activity -->
    </compensationHandler>
    ...
    <!-- activity implementing the scope>
    ...
</scope>
```

During runtime processing, compensation handlers become active once the corresponding `invoke` activity or `scope` has completed successfully. In addition, a snapshot of the data accessible to the `invoke` activity or `scope` at that point in time is taken. This ensures that the compensation activity will ultimately have access to the same data that was current upon invocation of the original activity, so it can reverse what the original activity did. A compensation handler never becomes active, however, for an `invoke` activity or `scope` that terminated abnormally (for example, by means of a fault). If an `invoke` activity fails, BPEL presumes that no compensation is needed for the invoked service. In the case where a scope terminated abnormally, its fault handler must have taken care of compensating its nested activities already.

Having discussed how compensation handlers are defined and when they become active, the question remains how compensation handlers are triggered. If you don't specify a fault handler or compensation handler for your activity or scope, there will be a default implementation: As part of the default implementation for fault handlers and compensation handlers, all active compensation handlers of activities enclosed by that scope are triggered. The compensation handlers are called in the reverse order of the invocation of their respective activities.

BPEL also provides a special activity, the *compensate activity* 📖, to explicitly trigger compensation handlers. This construct can only be used from within a fault handler or compensation handler. It's applicable to immediately enclosed `invoke` activities and scopes only. Using the `scope` attribute of the `compensate` activity, you select the unit to be compensated—that is, the name of the `scope` or `invoke` activity. Here's an example:

```
<compensate scope="ALogicalUnitOfWork"/>
```

The specification of the `scope` attribute is optional. If the `scope` specification is omitted, all immediately enclosed activities are compensated:

```
<compensate/>
```

In summary, through compensation handlers and compensate activities, compensation logic becomes part of the business logic of a process. Compensation is purely local to a single business process instance.

Event Handling

Event handlers [image] can be associated with a scope or a process for concurrent processing of events. BPEL defines two types of events:

- *Message event*—Implements a request-response or one-way operation invoked by a business partner
- *Alarm event*—Implements timer-driven behavior

When a scope is active, then event handlers attached to the scope are *enabled* to receive concurrent messages or alarm events. They are *disabled* when the processing of the scope ends. Events can only be processed when the corresponding event handler is enabled. When the event handlers for a scope become disabled, running event handlers are allowed to complete. The scope is terminated when all event handlers have completed processing.

During the processing of message events, the event handler remains enabled. Therefore, it can concurrently process multiple events of the same type. In addition to flow activities, this is the second place in BPEL where concurrency is possible. Note that event handlers for a process can't create new process instances.

If an alarm event handler is specified with a duration, then this duration starts when the event handler for the scope is enabled.

In the following example, an event handler is defined that allows a partner to end the lifecycle of the process instance:

```
<eventHandlers>

    <onMessage partnerLink="buyer"
               portType="purchaseOrderPortType"
               operation="cancelPurchaseOrderRequest"
               variable="purchaseOrderCancellation">
        <correlations>
            <correlation set="orderCorrelationSet" initiate="no"/>
        </correlations>

        <terminate/>

    </onMessage>

    <onAlarm>
        ...
    </onAlarm>

</eventHandlers>
```

If a buyer chooses to cancel a previously submitted purchase order, the cancellation request is processed by a concurrent event handler. The correct process instance is located using the correlation set definition introduced earlier. In this sample, the event handler is implemented by a `terminate` activity, which causes the activities on all parallel branches of the process to stop immediately.

SkatesTown: Putting It All Together

The Web services reengineering project at SkatesTown is now complete. The hard-coded Java implementation of the `submitPurchaseOrder` Web service has been replaced by a business process, and the external interface of the service has been extended accordingly.

The purchase order BPEL process is a long-running process, and, as such, it represents a stateful Web service. The Web service interface for the purchase order submission now supports fault messages. An additional operation is provided to allow the buyer to cancel a running purchase order. In addition, the process interacts with a Web service provided by SkatesTown's supplier.

Figure 12.7 gives an overview of the BPEL and WSDL artifacts of the SkatesTown business process. The interface of the SkatesTown process and its invoked services is provided by the three WSDL documents in Listings 12.3, 12.4, and 12.5. They show the Web service interfaces of the buyer, the seller, and the supplier, respectively.

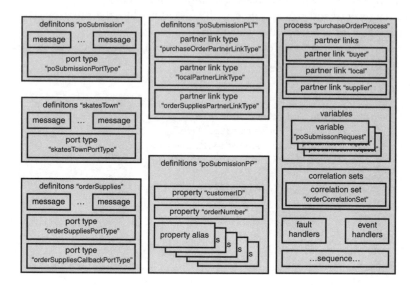

Figure 12.7   BPEL and WSDL artifacts for the SkatesTown business process

Listing 12.3   `PortType` **Offered to the Buyer**

```
<?xml version="1.0" ?>
<definitions name="poSubmission"
    targetNamespace="http://www.skatestown.com/services/interfaces/
➥poSubmission.wsdl"
```

Listing 12.3 **Continued**

```
   xmlns:pos="http://www.skatestown.com/services/interfaces/
➡poSubmission.wsdl"
   xmlns:po="http://www.skatestown.com/ns/po"
   xmlns:inv="http://www.skatestown.com/ns/invoice"
   xmlns:xsd="http://www.w3.org/2001/XMLSchema"
   xmlns:soap="http://schemas.xmlsoap.org/wsdl/soap/"
   xmlns="http://schemas.xmlsoap.org/wsdl/">

   <!-- Type definitions -->
   <types>
       <xsd:schema>
           <!-- rest of invoice schema definition from chapter 2 -->
           <xsd:import namespace="http://www.skatestown.com/ns/invoice"
                       schemaLocation="../../ns/invoice.xsd"/>
           <!-- rest of purchaseOrder schema definition from chapter 2 -->
           <xsd:import namespace="http://www.skatestown.com/ns/po"
                       schemaLocation="../../ns/po.xsd"/>
       </xsd:schema>
   </types>

   <!-- Message definitions -->
   <message name="poSubmissionRequest">
       <part name="purchaseOrder" element="po:po"/>
   </message>
   <message name="poSubmissionResponse">
       <part name="invoice" element="inv:invoice"/>
   </message>
   <message name="poSubmissionFaultInvalidPO">
       <part name="customerID" element="xsd:ID"/>
       <part name="orderNumber" element="xsd:positiveInteger"/>
   </message>
   <message name="poSubmissionFaultOutOfStock">
       <part name="customerID" element="xsd:ID"/>
       <part name="orderNumber" element="xsd:positiveInteger"/>
   </message>
   <message name="cancelPurchaseOrderRequest">
       <part name="purchaseOrder" element="po:po"/>
   </message>

   <!-- Port type definitions -->
   <portType name="poSubmissionPortType">
       <operation name="doSubmission">
           <input message="pos:poSubmissionRequest"/>
           <output message="pos:poSubmissionResponse"/>
           <fault name="invalidPO" message="pos:poSubmissionFaultInvalidPO"/>
```

Listing 12.3 **Continued**

```
            <fault name="outOfStock" message="pos:poSubmissionFaultOutOfStock"/>
        </operation>
        <operation name="cancelPurchaseOrder">
            <input message="pos:cancelPurchaseOrderRequest"/>
        </operation>
    </portType>


</definitions>
```

Listing 12.4 **PortType of SkatesTown's Local Services**

```
<?xml version="1.0" encoding="UTF-8"?>
<definitions name="skatesTown"
    targetNamespace="http://www.skatestown.com/services/interfaces/
➥skatesTown.wsdl"
    xmlns:skt="http://www.skatestown.com/services/interfaces/skatesTown.wsdl"
    xmlns:pos="http://www.skatestown.com/services/interfaces/poSubmission.wsdl"
    xmlns:po="http://www.skatestown.com/ns/po"
    xmlns:xsd="http://www.w3.org/2001/XMLSchema"
    xmlns="http://schemas.xmlsoap.org/wsdl/">

    <!-- Type definitions -->
    <types>
        <xsd:schema>
            <!-- Imports (message definitions from external interface:
                 submitPurchaseOrderRequest, submitPurchaseOrderResponse) -->
            <xsd:import namespace="http://www.skatestown.com/ns/po"
                        schemaLocation="../../ns/po.xsd"/>
        </xsd:schema>
    </types>

    <!-- Message definitions -->
    <message name="validatePurchaseOrderResponse">
        <part name="valid" element="xsd:boolean"/>
    </message>
    <message name="checkLocalStockResponse">
        <part name="available" element="xsd:boolean"/>
    </message>

    <!-- Port type definitions -->
    <portType name="skatestownPortType">
        <operation name="validatePurchaseOrder">
            <input message="submitPurchaseOrderRequest"/>
            <output message="validatePurchaseOrderResponse"/>
```

Listing 12.4 **Continued**

```
            </operation>
            <operation name="checkLocalStock">
                <input message="submitPurchaseOrderRequest"/>
                <output message="checkLocalStockResponse"/>
            </operation>
            <operation name="initiateDelivery">
                <input message="submitPurchaseOrderRequest"/>
            </operation>
            <operation name="createInvoice">
                <input message="submitPurchaseOrderRequest"/>
                <output message="submitPurchaseOrderResponse"/>
            </operation>
        </portType>


</definitions>
```

Listing 12.5 **PortTypes Offered and Used by the Supplier**

```
<?xml version="1.0" encoding="UTF-8"?>
<definitions name="orderSupplies"
    targetNamespace="http://www.wheelsandboards.com/services/interfaces/
➡orderSupplies.wsdl"
    xmlns:asp="http://www.wheelsandboards.com/services/interfaces/
➡orderSupplies.wsdl"
    xmlns:po="http://www.skatestown.com/ns/po"
    xmlns:xsd="http://www.w3.org/2001/XMLSchema"
    xmlns:wsa="http://schemas.xmlsoap.org/ws/2003/03/addressing"
    xmlns="http://schemas.xmlsoap.org/wsdl/">

    <!-- Type definitions -->
    <types>
        <xsd:schema>
            <!-- Imports (message definitions from skatestown,
                 ideally, should be shared between skatestown
                 and wheelsandboards) -->
            <xsd:import namespace="http://www.skatestown.com/ns/po"
                        schemaLocation="http://www.skatestown.com/ns/po.xsd"/>
        </xsd:schema>
    </types>

    <!-- Message definitions -->
    <message name="orderSuppliesRequest">
        <part name="orderSupplies" element="po:po"/>
        <part name="endpointReferenceOfSeller" element=
```

Listing 12.5 **Continued**

```
            "wsa:EndpointReferenceType"/>
    </message>
    <message name="orderSuppliesResponse">
        <part name="customerID" element="xsd:ID"/>
        <part name="orderNumber" element="xsd:positiveInteger"/>
    </message>
    <message name="orderSuppliesFault">
        <part name="customerID" element="xsd:ID"/>
        <part name="orderNumber" element="xsd:positiveInteger"/>
    </message>

    <!-- Port type definitions -->
    <portType name="orderSuppliesPortType">
        <operation name="orderSupplies">
            <input message="asp:orderSuppliesRequest"/>
        </operation>
    </portType>
    <portType name="orderSuppliesCallbackPortType">
        <operation name="orderSuppliesOk">
            <input message="asp:orderSuppliesResponse"/>
        </operation>
        <operation name="orderSuppliesFailed">
            <input message="asp:orderSuppliesFault"/>
        </operation>
    </portType>

</definitions>
```

The SkatesTown business process refers to three `partnerLinkTypes` for the interactions with the buyer, the supplier, and its own internal services. These `partnerLinkTypes` are defined in the WSDL shown in Listing 12.6.

Listing 12.6 **SkatesTown** `PartnerLinkType` **Definitions**

```
<?xml version="1.0" encoding="UTF-8"?>
<definitions name="poSubmissionPLT"
    targetNamespace="http://www.skatestown.com/processes/poSubmissionPLT"
    xmlns:pos="http://www.skatestown.com/services/interfaces/poSubmission.wsdl"
    xmlns:skt="http://www.skatestown.com/services/interfaces/skatesTown.wsdl"
    xmlns:sup="http://www.wheelsandboards.com/services/interfaces/
➥orderSupplies.wsdl"
    xmlns:xsd="http://www.w3.org/2001/XMLSchema"
    xmlns:plnk="http://schemas.xmlsoap.org/ws/2003/05/partner-link/"
    xmlns="http://schemas.xmlsoap.org/wsdl/">
```

Listing 12.6 **Continued**

```
    <!-- PartnerLinkType definitions -->
    <plnk:partnerLinkType name="purchaseOrderPartnerLinkType">
        <plnk:role name="seller">
            <plnk:portType name="pos:poSubmissionPortType"/>
        </plnk:role>
    </plnk:partnerLinkType>
    <plnk:partnerLinkType name="localPartnerLinkType">
        <plnk:role name="sellerLocal">
            <plnk:portType name="skt:skatesTownPortType"/>
        </plnk:role>
    </plnk:partnerLinkType>
    <plnk:partnerLinkType name="orderSuppliesPartnerLinkType">
        <plnk:role name="supplier">
            <plnk:portType name="sup:orderSuppliesPortType"/>
        </plnk:role>
        <plnk:role name="seller">
            <plnk:portType name="sup:orderSuppliesCallbackPortType"/>
        </plnk:role>
    </plnk:partnerLinkType>

    <!-- Port type definitions -->
    <import namespace="http://www.skatestown.com/services/interfaces/
➥poSubmission.wsdl"
      location="../services/interfaces/poSubmission12.wsdl"/>
    <import namespace="http://www.skatestown.com/services/interfaces/
➥skatesTown.wsdl"
      location="../services//interfaces/skatesTown.wsdl"/>
    <import
      namespace="http://www.wheelsandboards.com/services/interfaces/
➥orderSupplies.wsdl"
      location="http://www.wheelsandboards.com/services/interfaces/
➥orderSupplies.wsdl"/>

</definitions>
```

The correlation set defined as part of the SkatesTown business process names two properties. The WSDL snippet in Listing 12.7 shows the properties and their relationship to WSDL message types.

Listing 12.7 **SkatesTown Property and Property Alias Definitions**

```
<?xml version="1.0" encoding="UTF-8"?>
<definitions name="poSubmissionPPA"
    targetNamespace="http://www.skatestown.com/processes/poSubmissionPPA"
    xmlns:pos="http://www.skatestown.com/services/interfaces/poSubmission.wsdl"
```

Listing 12.7 **Continued**

```
xmlns:xsd="http://www.w3.org/2001/XMLSchema"
xmlns:wsbp="http://schemas.xmlsoap.org/ws/2003/03/business-process/"
xmlns="http://schemas.xmlsoap.org/wsdl/">

<!-- Property and property alias definitions -->
<wsbp:property name="customerID" type="xsd:ID"/>
<wsbp:property name="orderNumber" type="xsd:positiveInteger"/>

<wsbp:propertyAlias propertyName="customerID"
                    messageType="pos:poSubmissionRequest"
                    part="purchaseOrder" query="/billTo/id"/>
<wsbp:propertyAlias propertyName="orderNumber"
                    messageType="pos:poSubmissionRequest"
                    part="purchaseOrder" query="/id"/>
<wsbp:propertyAlias propertyName="customerID"
                    messageType="pos:poSubmissionResponse"
                    part="invoice" query="/billTo/id"/>
<wsbp:propertyAlias propertyName="orderNumber"
                    messageType="pos:poSubmissionResponse"
                    part="invoice" query="/id"/>
<wsbp:propertyAlias propertyName="customerID"
                    messageType="pos:poSubmissionFaultInvalidPO"
                    part="customerID"/>
<wsbp:propertyAlias propertyName="orderNumber"
                    messageType="pos:poSubmissionFaultInvalidPO"
                    part="orderNumber"/>
<wsbp:propertyAlias propertyName="customerID"
                    messageType="pos:poSubmissionFaultOutOfStock"
                    part="customerID"/>
<wsbp:propertyAlias propertyName="orderNumber"
                    messageType="pos:poSubmissionFaultOutOfStock"
                    part="orderNumber"/>
<wsbp:propertyAlias propertyName="customerID"
                    messageType="pos:cancelPurchaseOrderRequest"
                    part="purchaseOrder" query="/billTo/id"/>
<wsbp:propertyAlias propertyName="orderNumber"
                    messageType="pos:cancelPurchaseOrderRequest"
                    part="purchaseOrder" query="/id"/>

<!-- Port type definitions -->
<import namespace="http://www.skatestown.com/services/interfaces/
➥poSubmission.wsdl"
        location="../services/interfaces/poSubmission12.wsdl"/>

</definitions>
```

Finally, the complete SkatesTown business process is shown in Listing 12.8.

Listing 12.8 **The Complete SkatesTown Business Process**

```xml
<?xml version="1.0" encoding="UTF-8"?>
<process name="purchaseOrderProcess"
    targetNamespace="http://www.skatestown.com/processes/purchaseOrderProcess"
    xmlns:pos="http://www.skatestown.com/services/interfaces/poSubmission.wsdl"
    xmlns:skt="http://www.skatestown.com/services/interfaces/skatestown.wsdl"
    xmlns:sup="http://www.wheelsandboards.com/services/interfaces/
➥orderSupplies.wsdl"
    xmlns:plt="http://www.skatestown.com/processes/poSubmissionPLT"
    xmlns:ppa="http://www.skatestown.com/processes/poSubmissionPPA"
    xmlns:wsdl="http://schemas.xmlsoap.org/wsdl/"
    xmlns="http://schemas.xmlsoap.org/ws/2003/03/business-process/">

    <!-- PartnerLink definitions -->
    <partnerLinks>
        <partnerLink name="buyer"
                     partnerLinkType="plt:purchaseOrderPartnerLinkType"
                     myRole="seller"/>
        <partnerLink name="local" partnerLinkType="plt:localPartnerLinkType"
                                  partnerRole="sellerLocal"/>
        <partnerLink name="supplier"
                     partnerLinkType="plt:orderSuppliesPartnerLinkType"
                     myRole="seller" partnerRole="supplier"/>
    </partnerLinks>

    <!-- Partner definitions -->
    <partners>
        <partner name="skatestownCustomer">
            <partnerLink name="buyer"/>
        </partner>
        <partner name="skatestown">
            <partnerLink name="local"/>
        </partner>
        <partner name="skatestownSupplier">
            <partnerLink name="supplier"/>
        </partner>
    </partners>

    <!-- Variable definitions -->
    <variables>
        <variable name="poSubmissionRequest"
                  messageType="pos:poSubmissionRequest"/>
        <variable name="poSubmissionResponse"
                  messageType="pos:poSubmissionResponse"/>
```

Listing 12.8   **Continued**

```xml
            <variable name="poSubmissionFaultInvalidPO"
                     messageType="pos:poSubmissionFaultInvalidPO"/>
            <variable name="poSubmissionFaultOutOfStock"
                     messageType="pos:poSubmissionFaultOutOfStock"/>
            <variable name="cancelPurchaseOrderRequest"
                     messageType="pos:cancelPurchaseOrderRequest"/>
            <variable name="validatePurchaseOrderResponse"
                     messageType="skt:validatePurchaseOrderResponse"/>
            <variable name="checkLocalStockResponse"
                     messageType="skt:checkLocalStockResponse"/>
            <variable name="orderSuppliesRequest"
                     messageType="sup:orderSuppliesRequest"/>
            <variable name="orderSuppliesResponse"
                     messageType="sup:orderSuppliesResponse"/>
            <variable name="orderSuppliesFault"
                     messageType="sup:orderSuppliesFault"/>
        </variables>

        <!-- Correlation set definitions -->
        <correlationSets>
            <correlationSet name="orderCorrelationSet"
                           properties="ppa:customerID ppa:orderNumber"/>
        </correlationSets>

        <!-- Fault handler definitions -->
        <faultHandlers>
            <catch faultName="pos:invalidPO">
                <sequence>
                    <assign>
                        <copy>
                            <from variable="poSubmissionRequest"
                                 part="purchaseOrder" query="/billTo/id"/>
                            <to variable="poSubmissionFaultInvalidPO"
                                part="customerID"/>
                        </copy>
                        <copy>
                            <from variable="poSubmissionRequest"
                                 part="purchaseOrder" query="/id"/>
                            <to variable="poSubmissionFaultInvalidPO"
                                part="orderNumber"/>
                        </copy>
                    </assign>
                    <reply partnerLink="buyer" portType="pos:poSubmissionPortType"
                          operation="poSubmission"
                          faultName="pos:invalidPO"
```

Listing 12.8 **Continued**

```
                            variable="poSubmissionFaultInvalidPO">
                        <correlations>
                            <correlation set="orderCorrelationSet" initiate="no"/>
                        </correlations>
                    </reply>
                </sequence>
            </catch>
            <catch faultName="pos:outOfStock">
                <sequence>
                    <assign>
                        <copy>
                            <from variable="poSubmissionRequest"
                                part="purchaseOrder" query="/billTo/id"/>
                            <to variable="poSubmissionFaultInvalidPO"
                                part="customerID"/>
                        </copy>
                        <copy>
                            <from variable="poSubmissionRequest"
                                part="purchaseOrder" query="/id"/>
                            <to variable="poSubmissionFaultInvalidPO"
                                part="orderNumber"/>
                        </copy>
                    </assign>
                    <reply partnerLink="buyer" portType="pos:poSubmissionPortType"
                            operation="poSubmission"
                            faultName="pos:outOfStock"
                            variable="poSubmissionFaultOutOfStock">
                        <correlations>
                            <correlation set="orderCorrelationSet" initiate="no"/>
                        </correlations>
                    </reply>
                </sequence>
            </catch>
        </faultHandlers>

        <!-- Event handler definitions -->
        <eventHandlers>
            <onMessage partnerLink="buyer" portType="pos:poSubmissionPortType"
                    operation="cancelPurchaseOrder"
                    variable="cancelPurchaseOrderRequest">
                <correlations>
                    <correlation set="orderCorrelationSet" initiate="no"/>
                </correlations>
                <terminate/>
            </onMessage>
```

Listing 12.8 **Continued**

```
</eventHandlers>

<!-- Activity definitions -->
<sequence>

    <receive partnerLink="buyer" portType="pos:poSubmissionPortType"
            operation="poSubmission" createInstance="yes"
            variable="poSubmissionRequest">
        <correlations>
            <correlation set="orderCorrelationSet" initiate="yes"/>
        </correlations>
    </receive>

    <flow>
        <links>
            <link name="validPurchaseOrder"/>
            <link name="invalidPurchaseOrder"/>
            <link name="inLocalStock_initiateDelivery"/>
            <link name="inLocalStock_createInvoice"/>
            <link name="notInLocalStock"/>
            <link name="stockReplenished_initiateDelivery"/>
            <link name="stockReplenished_createInvoice"/>
        </links>

        <invoke partnerLink="local" portType="skt:skatestownPortType"
                operation="validatePurchaseOrder"
                inputVariable="poSubmissionRequest"
                outputVariable="validatePurchaseOrderResponse">
            <source linkName="validPurchaseOrder"
                    transitionCondition="bpws:getVariableData(
                        'validatePurchaseOrderResponse','valid')=true"/>
            <source linkName="invalidPurchaseOrder"
                    transitionCondition="bpws:getVariableData(
                        'validatePurchaseOrderResponse','valid')=false"/>
        </invoke>

        <throw faultName="pos:invalidPO">
            <target linkName="invalidPurchaseOrder"/>
        </throw>

        <invoke partnerLink="local" portType="skt:skatestownPortType"
                operation="checkLocalStock"
                inputVariable="poSubmissionRequest"
                outputVariable="checkLocalStockResponse">
            <target linkName="validPurchaseOrder"/>
```

Listing 12.8   **Continued**

```
            <source linkName="inLocalStock_initiateDelivery"
                    transitionCondition="bpws:getVariableData(
                        'checkLocalStockResponse','available')=true"/>
            <source linkName="inLocalStock_createInvoice"
                    transitionCondition="bpws:getVariableData(
                        'checkLocalStockResponse','available')=true"/>
            <source linkName="notInLocalStock"
                    transitionCondition="bpws:getVariableData(
                        'checkLocalStockResponse','available')=false"/>
    </invoke>

    <sequence name="replenishStock">

        <target linkName="notInLocalStock"/>
        <source linkName="stockReplenished_initiateDelivery"/>
        <source linkName="stockReplenished_createInvoice"/>

        <assign>
            <copy>
                <from variable="poSubmissionRequest"
                        part="purchaseOrder"/>
                <to variable="orderSuppliesRequest"
                    part="orderSupplies"/>
            </copy>
            <copy>
                <from partnerLink="supplier" endpointReference="myRole"/>
                <to variable="orderSuppliesRequest"
                    part="endpointReferenceOfSeller"/>
            </copy>
        </assign>

        <while condition="bpws:getVariableData(
                'checkLocalStockResponse','available')=false">
            <sequence>

                <invoke partnerLink="supplier"
                        portType="sup:orderSuppliesPortType"
                        operation="orderSupplies"
                        inputVariable="orderSuppliesRequest">
                    <correlations>
                        <correlation set="orderCorrelationSet"
                                    initiate="no"/>
                    </correlations>
                </invoke>
```

Listing 12.8 **Continued**

```
                            <pick>
                                <onMessage partnerLink="supplier"
                                    portType="sup:orderSuppliesCallbackPortType"
                                    operation="orderSuppliesOk" createInstance="no"
                                            variable="orderSuppliesResponse">
                                     <correlations>
                                         <correlation set="orderCorrelationSet"
                                                      initiate="no"/>
                                     </correlations>
                                     <empty/>
                                </onMessage>
                                <onMessage partnerLink="supplier"
                                    portType="sup:orderSuppliesCallbackPortType"
                                            operation="orderSuppliesFailed"
                                            createInstance="no"
                                            variable="orderSuppliesFault">
                                     <correlations>
                                         <correlation set="orderCorrelationSet"
                                                      initiate="no"/>
                                     </correlations>
                                     <throw faultName="pos:outOfStock"/>
                                </onMessage>
                                <onAlarm for="P1M">
                                     <throw faultName="pos:outOfStock"/>
                                </onAlarm>
                            </pick>

                            <invoke partnerLink="local"
                                    portType="skt:skatestownPortType"
                                    operation="checkLocalStock"
                                    inputVariable="poSubmissionRequest"
                                    outputVariable="checkLocalStockResponse"/>

                </sequence>
            </while>

        </sequence>

        <invoke partnerLink="local" portType="skt:skatestownPortType"
                operation="initiateDelivery"
                inputVariable="poSubmissionRequest">
            <target linkName="inLocalStock_initiateDelivery"/>
            <target linkName="stockReplenished_initiateDelivery"/>
        </invoke>
```

Listing 12.8 **Continued**

```
            <invoke partnerLink="local" portType="skt:skatestownPortType"
                    operation="createInvoice"
                    inputVariable="poSubmissionRequest"
                    outputVariable="poSubmissionResponse">
                <target linkName="inLocalStock_createInvoice"/>
                <target linkName="stockReplenished_createInvoice"/>
            </invoke>

        </flow>

        <reply partnerLink="buyer" portType="pos:poSubmissionPortType"
               operation="poSubmission"
               variable="poSubmissionResponse">
            <correlations>
                <correlation set="orderCorrelationSet" initiate="no"/>
            </correlations>
        </reply>

    </sequence>

</process>
```

Advanced Considerations

In addition to the concepts we've introduced, BPEL provides advanced capabilities. Let's examine abstract processes and language extensibility in more detail.

Abstract Processes

So far, we've concentrated on using BPEL to specify executable business processes. In addition, BPEL supports the definition of *business protocols* through the notion of abstract processes. A business protocol specifies the interaction of business partners via messages and their potential sequence—that is, the order in which messages between partners need to be exchanged to achieve a certain business goal. The details of what else happens internally at each partner to fulfill this goal are omitted. Typically, these messages result from internal business processes.

How are business protocols specified using abstract processes, and what distinguishes the definition of an abstract process from process definitions we have discussed so far? In general, business protocols aren't executable. An abstract process specifies the business protocol from the perspective of a partner's internal business process; however, it only provides a view of it. Business logic that describes, for example, how messages are constructed or how conditions are defined may not be part of the specification of the abstract process. An abstract process deliberately hides the details and complexity of the internal business process. It can omit variable specifications in `receive`, `reply`, `invoke`, and `pick` activities. The use of correlation sets in such cases is based on assumptions about their implicit initialization. BPEL also provides the notion of a special opaque assignment (`<from opaque="yes">`) that can only be used for abstract processes. Setting the process-level attribute `abstractProcess` to `"yes"` specifies that a BPEL process is of an abstract nature.

The constructs for specifying abstract processes are a subset of the constructs used to specify executable processes (with the one exception of the special assignment). This lets you specify an internal, executable business process and its views with the same language. It also provides for outside-in as well as inside-out approaches: You can start with the business partner's view and refine the process to become an executable process or vice versa.

SkatesTown uses an abstract process to precisely define the business protocol with its supplier. This specification is part of the contract between the two business partners. It provides the supplier with the information it needs in order to properly interact with SkatesTown. How SkatesTown actually realizes its business process isn't shared with the supplier.

Let's briefly revisit the interaction between the two partners. When SkatesTown needs to order additional supplies, it invokes the supplier's Web service operation `orderSupplies` and waits for a response from the supplier—either `orderSuppliesOK` or `orderSuppliesFailed`. If the response isn't received within a given timeframe, SkatesTown stops waiting for a response.

The example of an abstract process in Listing 12.9 expresses this interaction using a sequence that consists of an `invoke` activity (`orderSupplies`) followed by a `pick` activity (`orderSuppliesOK`, `orderSuppliesFailed`, or timeout). Details of what happened before the request was submitted to the supplier, or between the request and its response, or after the response was received, aren't of interest for the specification of this business protocol.

Listing 12.9 Abstract Process Describing Business Protocol with Supplier

```
<process name="orderSupplies"
     targetNamespace="http://www.skatestown.com/processes/purchaseOrderProcess"
     abstractProcess="yes"
     xmlns:pop="http://www.skatestown.com/services/purchaseOrder"
     xmlns:sup="http://www.wheelsandboards.com/services/orderSupplies"
     xmlns:wsdl="http://schemas.xmlsoap.org/wsdl/"
     xmlns="http://schemas.xmlsoap.org/ws/2003/03/business-process/"
     xmlns:xsi="http://www.w3.org/2001/XMLSchema-instance">

   <partnerLinks>
      <partnerLink name="supplier"
                partnerLinkType="orderSuppliesPartnerLinkType"
                myRole="seller"
```

Listing 12.9 **Continued**

```
                            partnerRole="supplier"/>
</partnerLinks>

<partners>
    <partner name="skatestownSupplier">
        <partnerLink name="supplier"/>
    </partner>
</partners>

<correlationSets>
    <correlationSet name="orderCorrelationSet"
                    properties="customerID orderNumber"/>
</correlationSets>

<sequence>

    <invoke partnerLink="supplier"
            portType="orderSuppliesPortType"
            operation="orderSupplies">
        <correlations>
            <correlation set="orderCorrelationSet"/>
        </correlations>
    </invoke>

    <pick>

        <onMessage partnerLink="supplier"
                   portType="orderSuppliesCallbackPortType"
                   operation="orderSuppliesOk">
            <correlations>
                <correlation set="orderCorrelationSet"/>
            </correlations>
            <empty/>
        </onMessage>

        <onMessage partnerLink="supplier"
                   portType="orderSuppliesCallbackPortType"
                   operation="orderSuppliesFailed">
            <correlations>
                <correlation set="orderCorrelationSet"/>
            </correlations>
            <empty/>
        </onMessage>

        <onAlarm for="P1M">
```

Listing 12.9 **Continued**

```
            <empty/>
        </onAlarm>

    </pick>

  </sequence>

</process>
```

Language Extensibility

The BPEL language may be extended by elements of other XML namespaces. You can add XML attributes and nested elements to standard BPEL elements. BPEL requires that such extensions must not change the semantics of existing BPEL elements.

We can envision a number of reasons to extend the language. However, you must be aware of the fact that every language extension may break the portability of processes or cause interoperability problems. Sample scenarios that may require BPEL extensions include

- Attributes of the BPEL process definition let you specify the query language and expression language used, for example, in assignments or conditions.

- Language elements can be added for features that have not yet been addressed by the current BPEL specification. The BPEL specification separates the notion of a core language and additional language elements for specific purposes.

- In order to accommodate new versions of other standards (for example, new versions of WSDL), elements can be added to the BPEL language.

- Elements for different types of interactions with other entities can be added. An example is the execution of inline code written in a standard programming language. Another extension would be an activity type that defines interactions with human users. Such activity types can be found in existing workflow management systems, but have not yet been provided by BPEL.

Summary

In this chapter, we've explained how you can describe executable business processes using BPEL. BPEL processes are composed with Web services and exposed as Web services. Activities in the process referring to inbound or outbound Web services specify the abstract interface.

We discussed the relationship of BPEL to other XML languages such as WSDL, XML Schema, and XPath, and you learned how BPEL is used to implement stateful Web services. We examined the following BPEL concepts in detail:

- Basic activities and structured activities are the building blocks used to aggregate Web services and add business logic to them.
- PartnerLinks and partnerLinkTypes are used to describe the relationship between the business process and the external world.
- Properties and correlation sets provide the means to associate Web service messages with instances of business processes.
- Fault handlers and compensation handlers let you deal with exceptional situations and reverse the results of business logic that successfully completed before a problem was recognized.
- Event handlers define entry points into the process with business logic executed concurrently to the main process.

BPEL has helped SkatesTown reengineer its purchase order Web service with a business process. A major objective was achieved: the implementation of a Web service that is flexible with respect to changing business needs. The recursive Web service composition model enabled SkatesTown to incorporate both internal services and business-to-business interactions within the business process. The purchase order process is a stateful service that offers the additional capability to cancel running orders.

Like SkatesTown, a growing number of companies are exploiting Web services in similar ways. In the heterogeneous environment of B2B interactions, interoperability is an absolute must. The next chapter focuses on such aspects of Web services.

Resources

- Business Process Execution Language for Web Services (BPEL4WS)

  http://dev2dev.bea.com/technologies/webservices/BPEL4WS.jsp

  http://www-106.ibm.com/developerworks/webservices/library/ws-bpel/

  http://msdn.microsoft.com/library/default.asp?url=/library/en-us/dnbiz2k2/html/bpel1-1.asp

  http://ifr.sap.com/bpel4ws/

  http://www.siebel.com/bpel

- Web Service Definition Language (WSDL)

  http://www.w3.org/TR/wsdl

  http://www.w3.org/TR/wsdl20/

- Web Services Addressing (WS-Addressing)

  http://msdn.microsoft.com/ws/2003/03/ws-addressing/

      `http://www-106.ibm.com/developerworks/webservices/library/ws-add/`

      `http://dev2dev.bea.com/technologies/webservices/ws-addressing.jsp`

- Web Services Flow Language (WSFL)

  `http://www-3.ibm.com/software/solutions/webservices/pdf/WSFL.pdf`

- XLang

  `http://www.gotdotnet.com/team/xml_wsspecs/XLANG-c/default.htm`

- XML Schema

  `http://www.w3.org/TR/xmlschema-0`

  `http://www.w3.org/TR/xmlschema-1`

  `http://www.w3.org/TR/xmlschema-2`

- XML Path Language (XPath)

  `http://www.w3.org/TR/xpath`

  `http://www.w3.org/TR/xpath20/`

III

Web Services in the Real World

13

Web Services Interoperability

ONE OF THE GREATEST PROMISES OF WEB SERVICE technology is interoperability between services that are running on different platforms and implemented using different programming languages. It's been said that the Web service standards are the *lingua franca* for the interactions between a service requestor and service provider. But the promise of interoperability between any two platforms that support Web service standards hasn't happened as quickly as most people had hoped.

The promise of Web services lies in the ability to exchange data and functionality among partners using standards-based messaging and arbitrary technological infrastructures. This not only buys you the ability to talk to many partners, it also allows you and your partners to avoid "lock in" to a particular runtime platform. If you've defined your service interfaces in terms of standards like XML, SOAP, WSDL, and UDDI, you can switch from Java to .NET and back again without disturbing your ongoing Web service–based partner relationships.

Interoperability problems occur for several reasons. Here are some examples:

- There are problems with interpreting the normative statements in a Web service specification. Most Web service–related specifications describe what should be done. In many instances, a specification implementer must interpret how to implement the functions described in the specification. Different implementations lead to products that won't interoperate with each other.

- The statements in a specification might be incorrect, incomplete, or contradictory. For example, the text within a specification may state one thing, but the schema definition may state something different.

- A specification may provide too much flexibility, in which case one platform may implement a portion of the specification and another may not contain that same level of support.

As Al Rosen developed the first set of Web services for SkatesTown, there were many instances where it was difficult to determine how to ensure the interoperability of these

Web services. Since Web service technology was fairly immature when he first started, he has continued to stay up to date on the various Web service interoperability activities.

Some of the interoperability activities that Al surveyed included the Soapbuilders Community, the various WS★ interoperability workshops, and the WS-I organization. The Soapbuilders list is a community of SOAP developers on Yahoo; it was started by Tony Hong in January 2001 and is a place where SOAP implementers discuss and resolve interoperability issues. As each of the more recent WS★ specifications (such as WS-Security and WS-ReliableMessaging) has been released, interop workshops have been held to test implementations of the specification and obtain feedback on the specification. Although both of these processes helped make Web services more interoperable, Al wasn't able to find a lot of information to help guide his development of Web services. When Al reviewed the *Web Services Interoperability (WS-I)* 📖 Organization and the profiles it's creating, the WS-I profiles seemed to provide the guidance Al was looking for, so he started to look at them in more detail.

Web Services Interoperability Organization

The WS-I Organization (`http://www.ws-i.org`) is an industry consortium whose primary goal is to promote the adoption of Web service technology. The WS-I Organization was founded by nine companies including Microsoft, IBM, BEA Systems, SAP, Oracle, and Hewlett-Packard. There are approximately 150 member companies, which include IT vendors and companies that use Web service technology, such as Diamler-Chrysler, Fidelity Investments, Kodak, and Merrill Lynch. The WS-I Organization also has associate members, including standards organizations such as OASIS (Organization for the Advancement of Structured Information Standards), RosettaNet, GGF (Global Grid Forum), OMG (Object Management Group), and OAG (Open Applications Group). By creating the associate member category, the WS-I Organization can work closely with the standards organizations that produce the standards that it profiles.

As shown in Figure 13.1, the primary deliverables from the WS-I Organization are sets of *profiles* 📖, *sample applications* 📖 based on the profiles, and *test tools* 📖 to verify conformance to the profiles. Each of these deliverables is produced by one of the working groups within the WS-I organization. For example, the Basic Profile Working Group is responsible for delivering the Basic Profile, Simple SOAP Binding Profile, and Attachments Profile, whereas the sample applications are delivered by the Sample Applications Working Group.

A profile isn't a new Web service standard. It references an existing set of Web service standards and provides guidance on how to use those standards. In some cases, the guidance limits or restricts how a standard can be used.

Most Web service standards contain normative statements with keywords such as MUST, MUST NOT, SHOULD, SHOULD NOT, or MAY. The guidance in a profile clarifies the usage of Web service standards by defining a set of requirements that turns many of the SHOULD and MAY statements into MUST statements. Doing this removes a lot of the ambiguity that may exist in the referenced Web service standards.

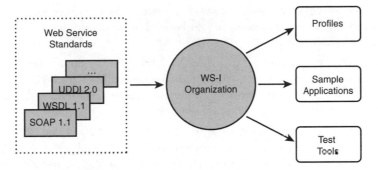

Figure 13.1   Web Services Interoperability Organization

The WS-I Basic Profile 1.0 defines a set of Web service specifications with guidelines for their usage to promote interoperability between different software platforms. After reviewing the WS-I Basic Profile 1.0, Al was convinced that he should modify the SkatesTown Web services to conform to the requirements in this profile. Doing so would provide the best opportunity to interoperate with business partners running on different platforms.

When we describe the WS-I Basic Profile in this chapter, the following namespaces are referenced using the prefixes listed here:

- `xsd`—`http://www.w3.org/2001/XMLSchema`

- `xsi`—`http://www.w3.org/2001/XMLSchema-instance`

- `soapenv`—`http://schemas.xmlsoap.org/soap/`

- `soapenc`—`http://schemas.xmlsoap.org/soap/encoding/`

- `wsdl`—`http://schemas.xmlsoap.org/wsdl/`

- `soap`—`http://schemas.xmlsoap.org/wsdl/soap/`

- `mime`—`http://schemas.xmlsoap.org/wsdl/mime/`

- `uddi`—`urn:uddi-org:api_v2`

- `wsi`—`http://ws-i.org/schemas/conformanceClaim`

- `attref`—`http://ws-i.org/ap1.0/xsd`

The specifications referenced by most of these namespaces have been described in previous chapters.

WS-I Basic Profile 1.0

A *conformance target* 📖 is an artifact that is the target of a requirement in the profile. Three types of conformance targets are defined by the WS-I Basic Profile 1.0 (`http://www.ws-i.org/Profiles/Basic/2003-08/BasicProfile-1.0a.html`):

- The first type of conformance target is for the following artifacts: SOAP messages, WSDL documents, and UDDI entries. The Basic Profile refers to these artifacts as

MESSAGE, DESCRIPTION, and REGDATA, respectively. These terms were used because they provide general names that might be used in future profiles to reference additional or different artifacts.

- The second type of conformance target is defined for the three roles defined in a service-oriented architecture: service provider (which hosts the Web service), service requestor, and service registry. In the Basic Profile, these roles are named INSTANCE, CONSUMER, and REGISTRY, respectively.

- The third type of conformance target is for a message SENDER and RECEIVER. The service provider and service requestor may receive and send messages, so both of these roles need to conform to the requirements for a SENDER and RECEIVER.

The following list summarizes the most important guidelines that appear in the Basic Profile:

- The only binding supported by the Basic Profile is the SOAP/HTTP binding. The MIME and HTTP GET/POST bindings aren't allowed, but they may appear in the same WSDL document as a conformant SOAP/HTTP binding.

- The only SOAP bindings permitted by the Basic Profile are document-literal and RPC-literal. The style attribute on the soap:binding and soap:operation elements may have a value of either document or RPC, but the use attribute on the soap:body, soap:fault, soap:header, and soap:headerfault elements may only have a value of literal. This means the RPC-encoded binding defined in the SOAP and WSDL specification isn't permitted by this profile.

- The part elements for a message that are used by an RPC-literal binding must reference a complex type definition using the type attribute. When using a document-literal binding, the part elements must use the element attribute to reference a global element definition. A global element definition may contain other element definitions, but it can't be a child of any other element definition.

- The only supported operation types are request-response and one-way. Notification and solicit-response operation types aren't allowed by the Basic Profile.

Al selected the PurchaseOrderSubmission and PriceCheck Web services to modify initially. The following sections describe the changes made to these Web services to make them more interoperable, as well as the changes that will need to be made in the future to the StockAvailableNotification Web service to make it conform to the requirements in the WS-I Basic Profile.

Each section describes the steps used to review the contents of the Basic Profile to evaluate and update the SkatesTown Web services. The steps are described based on the requirements in the Basic Profile. A *profile requirement* 📖 has an identifier with the format *Rnnnn*, where *nnnn* is a unique number. When we describe the steps in each section, references to the Basic Profile requirements will appear within brackets (for example, [R0001]).

The WSDL service description for the `PriceCheck` Web service, which was updated based on the requirements in the Basic Profile, is listed in Chapter 6, "Discovering Web Services." Listing 13.1 contains the original version of the `PriceCheck` Web service.

Listing 13.1   `PriceCheck.wsdl`

```
<?xml version="1.0"?>
<definitions name="PriceCheck"
    targetNamespace="http://www.skatestown.com/services/PriceCheck"
    xmlns:pc="http://www.skatestown.com/services/PriceCheck"
    xmlns:avail="http://www.skatestown.com/ns/availability"
    xmlns:xsd="http://www.w3.org/2001/XMLSchema"
    xmlns:soap="http://schemas.xmlsoap.org/wsdl/soap/"
    xmlns="http://schemas.xmlsoap.org/wsdl/">

    <!-- Type definitions -->
    <types>
        <xsd:schema targetNamespace="http://www.skatestown.com/ns/availability"
            xmlns:xsd="http://www.w3.org/2001/XMLSchema">
            <xsd:complexType name="availabilityType">
                <xsd:sequence>
                    <xsd:element name="sku" type="xsd:string"/>
                    <xsd:element name="price" type="xsd:double"/>
                    <xsd:element name="quantityAvailable" type="xsd:integer"/>
                </xsd:sequence>
            </xsd:complexType>
        </xsd:schema>
    </types>

    <!-- Message definitions -->
    <!-- A PriceCheckRequest is simply an item code (sku)  -->
    <message name="PriceCheckRequest">
        <part name="sku" type="xsd:string"/>
    </message>

    <!-- A PriceCheckResponse consists of an availability structure,  -->
    <!-- defined above.                                               -->
    <message name="PriceCheckResponse">
        <part name="result" type="avail:availabilityType"/>
    </message>

    <!-- Port type definitions -->
    <portType name="PriceCheckPortType">
        <operation name="checkPrice">
            <input message="pc:PriceCheckRequest"/>
            <output message="pc:PriceCheckResponse"/>
        </operation>
    </portType>
```

Listing 13.1 **Continued**

```xml
<!-- Binding definitions -->
<binding name="PriceCheckSOAPBinding" type="pc:PriceCheckPortType">
    <soap:binding style="rpc"
        transport="http://schemas.xmlsoap.org/soap/http"/>
    <operation name="checkPrice">
        <soap:operation soapAction=""/>
        <input>
            <soap:body use="encoded"
                namespace="http://www.skatestown.com/services/PriceCheck"
                encodingStyle="http://schemas.xmlsoap.org/soap/encoding/"/>
        </input>
        <output>
            <soap:body use="encoded"
                namespace="http://www.skatestown.com/services/PriceCheck"
                encodingStyle="http://schemas.xmlsoap.org/soap/encoding/"/>
        </output>
    </operation>
</binding>

<!-- Service definition -->
<service name="PriceCheckService">
    <port name="PriceCheck" binding="pc:PriceCheckSOAPBinding">
        <soap:address
            location="http://localhost:8080/axis/services/PriceCheck"/>
    </port>
</service>
</definitions>
```

Throughout this chapter, portions of the StockAvailableNotification Web service description will be used as examples that don't conform to the Basic Profile. These Web services descriptions don't conform to the profile because they were developed before the profile was published. As we identify each conformance issue, we provide a solution that will bring this Web service description into conformance with the profile. This is the same process that Al Rosen would follow to update the service description so it conformed to Basic Profile 1.0. Listing 13.2 shows the updated StockAvailableNotification Web service description, which will be referenced in subsequent sections of this chapter.

Listing 13.2 StockAvailableNotification.wsdl

```xml
<?xml version="1.0" ?>
<definitions name="StockAvailableNotification"
        targetNamespace=
            "http://www.skatestown.com/services/StockAvailableNotification"
        xmlns:tns="http://www.skatestown.com/services/StockAvailableNotification"
```

Listing 13.2   **Continued**

```
            xmlns:xsd="http://www.w3.org/2001/XMLSchema"
            xmlns:reg="http://www.skatestown.com/ns/registrationRequest"
            xmlns:soap="http://schemas.xmlsoap.org/wsdl/soap/"
            xmlns:soapenc="http://schemas.xmlsoap.org/soap/encoding/"
            xmlns:wsdl="http://schemas.xmlsoap.org/wsdl/"
            xmlns="http://schemas.xmlsoap.org/wsdl/">

<!-- Type definitions from the registration schema -->
<types>
    <xsd:schema
        targetNamespace="http://www.skatestown.com/ns/registrationRequest" >

        <xsd:import namespace="http://schemas.xmlsoap.org/soap/encoding/"
                    schemaLocation="http://schemas.xmlsoap.org/soap/encoding/"/>

        <xsd:complexType name="itemList">
          <xsd:sequence>
            <xsd:element name="item" type="xsd:string" minOccurs="1"
              maxOccurs="unbounded"/>
          </xsd:sequence>
        </xsd:complexType>

        <xsd:complexType name="registrationRequest">
          <xsd:sequence>
            <xsd:element name="items" type="reg:itemList" />
            <xsd:element name="address" type="xsd:string"/>
            <xsd:element name="transport"
                        default="smtp" minOccurs="0" >
              <xsd:simpleType>
                <xsd:restriction base="xsd:string">
                  <xsd:enumeration value="http"/>
                  <xsd:enumeration value="smtp"/>
                </xsd:restriction>
              </xsd:simpleType>
            </xsd:element>
            <xsd:element name="clientArg" type="xsd:string" minOccurs="0"/>
          </xsd:sequence>
        </xsd:complexType>

        <xsd:simpleType name="correlationID">
          <xsd:restriction base="xsd:string">
          <!-- some appropriate restriction -->
          </xsd:restriction>
        </xsd:simpleType>

        <xsd:element name="Expiration" type="xsd:dateTime" />
        <xsd:element name="ErrorString" type="xsd:string" />
```

Listing 13.2 **Continued**

```xml
        </xsd:schema>
    </types>

    <!-- Message definitions -->
    <message name="StockAvailableRegistrationRequest">
        <part name="registration" type="reg:registrationRequest"/>
        <part name="expiration" element="reg:Expiration"/>
    </message>

    <message name="StockAvailableRegistrationResponse">
        <part name="correlationID" type="reg:correlationID"/>
    </message>

    <message name="StockAvailableRegistrationError">
        <part name="errorString" element="reg:ErrorString"/>
    </message>

    <message name="StockAvailableExpirationError">
        <part name="errorString" element="reg:ErrorString"/>
    </message>

    <message name="StockAvailableCancellation">
        <part name="correlationID" type="reg:correlationID"/>
    </message>

    <message name="StockAvailableNotification">
        <part name="timeStamp" type="xsd:dateTime"/>
        <part name="correlationID" type="reg:correlationID"/>
        <part name="items" type="reg:itemList"/>
        <part name="clientArg" type="xsd:string"/>
    </message>

    <message name="StockAvailableExpirationNotification">
        <part name="timeStamp" type="xsd:dateTime"/>
        <part name="correlationID" type="reg:correlationID"/>
        <part name="items" type="reg:itemList"/>
        <part name="clientArg" type="xsd:string"/>
    </message>

    <!-- Port type definitions -->
    <portType name="StockAvailableNotificationPortType">
        <!--Registration Operation -->
        <operation name="registration">
            <input message="tns:StockAvailableRegistrationRequest"/>
            <output message="tns:StockAvailableRegistrationResponse"/>
            <fault message="tns:StockAvailableRegistrationError"
```

Listing 13.2   **Continued**

```
            name="StockAvailableNotificationErrorMessage"/>
      <fault message="tns:StockAvailableExpirationError"
         name="StockAvailableExpirationError"/>
   </operation>

   <!--Cancellation Operation -->
   <operation name="cancellation">
     <input message="tns:StockAvailableCancellation"/>
   </operation>
</portType>

<portType name="StockAvailableCallbackPortType">
   <!--Notification Operation -->
   <operation name="notification">
     <input message="tns:StockAvailableNotification"/>
   </operation>

   <!--Expiration Notification Operation -->
   <operation name="expirationNotification">
     <input message="tns:StockAvailableExpirationNotification"/>
   </operation>
</portType>

<!-- Binding definitions -->
<binding name="StockAvailableNotificationSOAPBinding"
   type="tns:StockAvailableNotificationPortType">
   <soap:binding style="rpc"
           transport="http://schemas.xmlsoap.org/soap/http"/>

   <!-- Note: the requestor must invoke the registration operation first.  >
   <operation name="registration">
     <soap:operation
       soapAction=
         "http://www.skatesTown.com/StockAvailableNotification/registration"/>
     <input>
       <soap:header message="tns:StockAvailableRegistrationRequest"
             part="expiration" use="literal" >
           <soap:headerfault message="tns:StockAvailableExpirationError"
             part="errorString" use="literal" />
       </soap:header>
       <soap:body parts="registration" use="literal"
             namespace="http://www.skatestown.com/ns/registrationRequest"/>
     </input>
     <output>
       <soap:body use="literal"
           namespace="http://www.skatestown.com/ns/registrationRequest"/>
```

Listing 13.2 **Continued**

```
            </output>
            <fault name="StockAvailableNotificationErrorMessage">
               <soap:fault name="StockAvailableNotificationErrorMessage"/>
            </fault>
         </operation>

         <operation name="cancellation">
            <soap:operation
              soapAction=
              "http://www.skatesTown.com/StockAvailableNotification/cancellation"/>
            <input>
               <soap:body use="literal"
                    namespace="http://www.skatestown.com/ns/registrationRequest"/>
            </input>
         </operation>
      </binding>

      <binding name="StockAvailableCallbackSOAPBinding"
         type="tns:StockAvailableCallbackPortType">
         <soap:binding style="rpc"
                  transport="http://schemas.xmlsoap.org/soap/http"/>

         <operation name="notification">
            <soap:operation style="rpc"/>
            <input>
               <soap:body use="literal"
                    namespace="http://www.skatestown.com/ns/registrationRequest"/>
            </input>
         </operation>

         <operation name="expirationNotification">
            <soap:operation style="rpc"/>
            <input>
               <soap:body use="literal"
                    namespace="http://www.skatestown.com/ns/registrationRequest"/>
            </input>
         </operation>
      </binding>

      <!-- Service definition -->
      <service name="StockAvailableNotification">
        <port name="StockAvailableNotification"
             binding="tns:StockAvailableNotificationSOAPBinding">
          <soap:address
           location="http://www.skatestown.com/services/StockAvailableNotification"/>
        </port>
```

Listing 13.2 **Continued**

```
  </service>

  <service name="StockAvailableCallback">
    <port name="StockAvailableCallback"
         binding="tns:StockAvailableCallbackSOAPBinding">
      <soap:address
        location="http://www.skatestown.com/services/StockAvailableCallback"/>
    </port>
  </service>
</definitions>
```

Common Requirements for SOAP Envelope, WSDL Document, and XML Schema Document

Several profile requirements are common to the SOAP envelope, WSDL document, and XML schema documents. These artifacts must be encoded using either UTF-8 or UTF-16 [R1012, R4003, R2010]. For all of these XML documents, the type of encoding is specified in the encoding attribute on the XML declaration. For the SOAP envelope, the encoding is also specified in the charset attribute on the HTTP Content-Type header field. In addition, all three types of XML documents may contain the Unicode Byte Order Mark (BOM) [R4001, R4002, R2009], which is used to indicate how the XML document was encoded.

The following example shows how to specify the encoding for a SOAP message:

```
POST /service HTTP/1.0
Content-Type: text/xml; charset=utf-8
SOAPAction: ""
Content-Length: 154

<?xml version="1.0" encoding="UTF-8"?>
<soapenv:Envelope ...>
```

In a WSDL document, the encoding is specified on the XML declaration:

```
<?xml version="1.0" encoding="UTF-8"?>
<wsdl:definitions ...>
```

In an XML schema document, the encoding is specified the same way:

```
<?xml version="1.0" encoding="UTF-8"?>
<xsd:schema ...>
```

The WSDL document and XML schema documents must be well-formed XML documents and conform to the XML 1.0 specification [R4004, R2011]. Although it isn't stated in the profile as a requirement, a SOAP envelope must also be a well-formed XML document.

All the SkatesTown Web services conformed to these profile requirements.

Understanding the WSDL Document Structure

Several requirements in the Basic Profile clarify the structure for a WSDL document. The XML schema documents for WSDL and WSDL SOAP binding elements are at the following locations:

- *WSDL namespace*—http://schemas.xmlsoap.org/wsdl/2003-02-11.xsd
- *WSDL SOAP Binding namespace*— http://schemas.xmlsoap.org/wsdl/soap/2003-02-11.xsd

These XML schema documents contain corrections to the original XML schema documents, as well as updates that are specific to the Basic Profile [R2028, R2029]. For example, the name of the `parts` attribute on the `soap:header` and `soap:headerfault` elements was corrected; it's now named the `part` attribute.

The following snippet contains the general structure for a WSDL document. For the XML elements that are children of the `wsdl:definitions` element, the `wsdl:import` and `wsdl:types` elements must precede all the other elements in the WSDL namespace except the `wsdl:documentation` element [R2022]. Also, the `wsdl:import` element must precede the `wsdl:types` element [R2023]:

```
<?xml version="1.0" encoding="UTF-8"?>
<wsdl:definitions ...>
  <wsdl:documentation .../>
  <wsdl:import .../>
  <wsdl:types .../>
  <wsdl:message .../>
  <wsdl:portType .../>
  <wsdl:binding .../>
  <wsdl:service .../>
</wsdl:definitions>
```

The Basic Profile clarifies where `wsdl:documentation` elements can be used. The `wsdl:documentation` element may appear as the first child element within any element in the WSDL namespace [R2020, R2021, R2024].

The extensibility points within a WSDL document are also clarified within the text of the profile document [Section 5.1.11]. The `wsdl:import`, `wsdl:part`, and `wsdl:portType` elements, as well as the `wsdl:input`, `wsdl:output`, and `wsdl:fault` elements within a `portType` may contain extensibility attributes. The `wsdl:definitions`, `wsdl:types`, `wsdl:message`, `wsdl:operation`, `wsdl:binding`, `wsdl:service`, and `wsdl:port` elements, as well as `wsdl:input`, `wsdl:output`, and `wsdl:fault` within a binding may contain both extensibility attributes and extensibility elements:

```
<?xml version="1.0" encoding="UTF-8"?>
<wsdl:definitions ...>
  <wsdl:documentation .../>
  <anyNS:anyElement .../>
  <wsdl:import anyNS:anyAttribute="..." .../>
  <wsdl:types anyNS:anyAttribute="...">
```

```
      <anyNS:anyElement .../>
   </wsdl:types>
   <wsdl:message  anyNS:anyAttribute="...">
      <anyNS:anyElement .../>
   </wsdl:message>
   <wsdl:portType anyNS:anyAttribute="...">
     <wsdl:operation anyNS:anyAttribute="...">
        <anyNS:anyElement .../>
        <wsdl:input anyNS:anyAttribute="..." .../>
        <wsdl:output anyNS:anyAttribute="..." .../>
        <wsdl:fault anyNS:anyAttribute="..." .../>
     </wsdl:operation>
   </wsdl:portType>
   <wsdl:binding>
      <anyNS:anyElement .../>
      <wsdl:operation anyNS:anyAttribute="...">
        <anyNS:anyElement .../>
        <wsdl:input anyNS:anyAttribute="..." ...>
          <anyNS:anyElement .../>
        </wsdl:input>
        <wsdl:output anyNS:anyAttribute="..." ...>
          <anyNS:anyElement .../>
        </wsdl:output>
        <wsdl:fault anyNS:anyAttribute="..." ...>
          <anyNS:anyElement .../>
        </wsdl:fault>
     </wsdl:operation>
   </wsdl:binding>
   <wsdl:service anyNS:anyAttribute="..." ...>>
      <anyNS:anyElement .../>
      <wsdl:port anyNS:anyAttribute="..." ...>
        <anyNS:anyElement .../>
      </wsdl:port>
   </wsdl:service>
</wsdl:definitions>
```

Two other Basic Profile requirements pertain to the content of a WSDL document. All the operations defined in a wsdl:portType must also be defined in the wsdl:binding that contains a reference to the portType [R2718]. Each wsdl:port element in a WSDL document should have a unique value for the location attribute in the soap:address element [R2711]. Although it isn't a requirement to have a unique value for the location attribute, using unique values will prevent problems when a message sent to two different locations has the same wire signature. An interoperability issue may arise in this situation, since it may not be possible to determine which wsdl:port is being invoked by the request.

After reviewing these requirements, Al determined that all the SkatesTown Web services conform to these profile requirements.

Importing XML Schema and WSDL Documents

There has been some confusion about how to import both XML schema and WSDL documents (refer to Chapter 4, "Describing Web Services," for detailed information about how to use the `wsdl:import` element). WSDL documents can be imported using only the WSDL import element [R2001]:

```
<!-- assumes interface file in same directory -->
<import
  namespace="http://www.skatestown.com/services/interfaces/poSubmission.wsdl"
  location="./poSubmission.wsdl"/>
```

When importing a WSDL document, the profile makes specific statements about the usage of the `location` and `namespace` attributes on the `wsdl:import` element. The `location` attribute must have a value [R2007], and this value should be treated as a hint [R2008] since the component processing the WSDL document may have its own method for locating the contents of the document (for example, the location information could be used to find the document in a cache or in a registry). The `namespace` attribute on the `wsdl:import` element must contain the same value as the `targetNamespace` attribute on the `wsdl:definitions` element in the imported WSDL document [R2005]. For the previous WSDL import example, the imported WSDL document contains the following `wsdl:definitions` element:

```
<definitions name="poSubmission"
      targetNamespace=
          "http://www.skatestown.com/services/interfaces/poSubmission.wsdl"
      xmlns:xsd="http://www.w3.org/2001/XMLSchema"
      xmlns:po="http://www.skatestown.com/ns/po"
      xmlns:pos="http://www.skatestown.com/services/interfaces/poSubmission.wsdl"
      xmlns:inv="http://www.skatestown.com/ns/invoice"
      xmlns:soap="http://schemas.xmlsoap.org/wsdl/soap/"
      xmlns="http://schemas.xmlsoap.org/wsdl/">
```

XML schema documents must be imported using only the XML schema `import` element [R2002], and this element must appear within an `xsd:schema` element that is a child of the `wsdl:types` element [R2003]. The `PurchaseOrderSubmission` Web service description contains an example of how to import an XML schema document:

```
<!-- Type definitions -->
<types>
  <xsd:schema>
  <!-- rest of invoice schema definition from chapter 2
       assumes XSD file is in same directory          -->
  <xsd:import namespace="http://www.skatestown.com/ns/invoice"
              schemaLocation="./invoice.xsd"/>

  <!-- rest of purchaseOrder schema definition from chapter 2
       assumes XSD file is in same directory          -->
  <xsd:import namespace="http://www.skatestown.com/ns/po"
```

```
          schemaLocation="./po.xsd"/>
    </xsd:schema>
  </types>
```

All the SkatesTown Web service descriptions conform to these requirements.

Defining the Service Interface

The service interface defines the abstract portion of the Web service description. This includes the wsdl:portType element and any elements it references (such as wsdl:import, wsdl:types, and wsdl:message)

Datatype Definitions

User-defined datatypes must be specified using XML Schema 1.0 [R2800, R2801]. The datatype definitions must be referenced in the WSDL types section. These definitions may appear within an xsd.schema element contained in the wsdl:types element, or they can be imported using the xsd:import element. The value of this targetNamespace attribute can be the same as the targetNamespace attribute on the wsdl:definitions element, but it isn't required to be the same [R2114]. The PriceCheck Web service description contains a WSDL types definition that conforms to these profile requirements:

```
<!-- Type definitions -->
<types>
   <xsd:schema
      targetNamespace="http://www.skatestown.com/ns/availability"
      xmlns:xsd="http://www.w3.org/2001/XMLSchema">

      <xsd:element name="sku" type="xsd:string" />

      <xsd:complexType name="availabilityType">
         <xsd:sequence>
            <xsd:element ref="avail:sku"/>
            <xsd:element name="price" type="xsd:double"/>
            <xsd:element name="quantityAvailable" type="xsd:integer"/>
         </xsd:sequence>
      </xsd:complexType>

      <xsd:element name="StockAvailability"
                   type="avail:availabilityType" />
   </xsd:schema>
</types>
```

When an xsd:schema element is used within the wsdl:types element, it must contain a targetNamespace attribute with a valid value unless its only child elements are xsd:import or xsd:annotation elements [R2105]. The types section from the PurchaseOrderSubmission Web service description contains an example of an xsd:schema element that adheres to this requirement:

```
<!-- Type definitions -->
<types>
   <xsd:schema>
   <!-- rest of invoice schema definition from chapter 2
        assumes XSD file is in same directory         -->
   <xsd:import namespace="http://www.skatestown.com/ns/invoice"
               schemaLocation="./invoice.xsd"/>

   <!-- rest of purchaseOrder schema definition from chapter 2
        assumes XSD file is in same directory         -->
   <xsd:import namespace="http://www.skatestown.com/ns/po"
               schemaLocation="./po.xsd"/>

   </xsd:schema>
</types>
```

Array Definitions

An array should not be defined using the soapenc:Array type [R2110] and must not reference soapenc:arrayType or use the wsdl:arrayType attribute [R2111, R2113]. Also, the array should not be declared using a name that starts with the ArrayOf prefix [R2112]. These requirements were added to the Basic Profile because the declaration of array types had been interpreted differently on different platforms, which has led to interoperability problems.

Al noted that the current StockAvailabilityNotification Web service violated all of these requirements when the ArrayOfItem datatype was defined:

```
<xsd:complexType name="ArrayOfItem"
   xmlns:soapenc="http://schemas.xmlsoap.org/soap/encoding/">
  <xsd:complexContent>
    <xsd:restriction base="soapenc:Array">
      <xsd:attribute ref="soapenc:arrayType" wsdl:arrayType="xsd:string[]"/>
    </xsd:restriction>
  </xsd:complexContent>
</xsd:complexType>
```

The correct way to define an array is to use the minOccurs and maxOccurs attributes on the element definition for the array entry; typically the array entry is contained within a wrapper element. In the next version of this Web service description, Al will use the following array definition instead of the current one:

```
<xsd:complexType name="itemList">
  <xsd:sequence>
    <xsd:element name="item" type="xsd:string" minOccurs="1"
      maxOccurs="unbounded"/>
  </xsd:sequence>
</xsd:complexType>
```

The name of this datatype definition will be changed from ArrayOfItem to itemList, and it will contain one or more item elements. This array definition will result in the following example message content:

```
<itemList>
```

```
  <item>1</item>
  <item>2</item>
  <item>...</item>
  <item>n</item>
</itemList>
```

Defining Operations

The WSDL 1.1 specification defines four operation types: request-response, one-way, solicit-response, and notification. Since the solicit-response and notification operation types aren't well defined in the WSDL specification and because there is little support for these operation types, they must not be used in a Basic Profile–compliant Web service description [R2303]. In addition, for a single portType, all of the defined operations must have a unique value for the name attribute [R2304].

When analyzing the StockAvailableNotification Web service, Al noticed that although all the operation definitions had unique names, the service contained two notification style operations:

```
    <!--Notification Operation -->
    <operation name="notification">
       <output message="tns:StockAvailableNotification"/>
    </operation>

    <!--Expiration Notification Operation -->
    <operation name="expirationNotification">
       <output message="tns:StockAvailableExpirationNotification"/>
    </operation>
```

Instead of using the notification operation style, Al decided that the next version of this Web service would use a callback design pattern similar to the one used by the WS-I Sample Applications and described in the WS-I Sample Application Supply Chain Management Architecture document (http://ws-i.org/SampleApplications/ SupplyChainManagement/2003-07/SCMArchitecture1.01-BdAD.pdf).

The purpose of the notification operation style is to define a one-way message that is pushed from the Web service to the service requestor. A callback design pattern uses two Web service interfaces: One sends requests to the service provider, and the other sends notifications to the service requestor. Since these interaction styles are asynchronous, the operations must be linked together. For this set of Web service interfaces, this is accomplished by using a correlation identifier (correlationID). This identifier is returned when the initial request is sent to the service provider, and it's included in subsequent interactions between the service provider and service requestor.

Here are the WSDL message and portType definitions for the StockAvailableCallback Web service:

```
    <!-- Message definitions -->
    <message name="StockAvailableNotification">
       <part name="timeStamp" type="xsd:dateTime"/>
       <part name="correlationID" type="cb:correlationID"/>
```

```
      <part name="items" type="cb:itemList"/>
      <part name="clientArg" type="xsd:string"/>
   </message>

   <message name="StockAvailableExpirationNotification">
      <part name="timeStamp" type="xsd:dateTime"/>
      <part name="correlationID" type="cb:correlationID"/>
      <part name="items" type="cb:itemList"/>
      <part name="clientArg" type="xsd:string"/>
   </message>

   <!-- Port type definitions -->
   <portType name="StockAvailableCallbackPortType">
      <!--Notification Operation -->
      <operation name="notification">
         <input message="tns:StockAvailableNotification"/>
      </operation>

      <!--Expiration Notification Operation -->
      <operation name="expirationNotification">
         <input message="tns:StockAvailableExpirationNotification"/>
      </operation>
   </portType>
```

The `parameterOrder` attribute on the `wsdl:operation` element is used to define the order of parts within a message, and it can indicate the return value [R2302]. When this attribute is used, at most one `wsdl:part` can be omitted from the output message [R2305]. The omitted part is the return value for the operation. If the `parameterOrder` attribute is used and no parts are omitted, then there is no return value. None of the SkatesTown Web service descriptions use the `parameterOrder` attribute.

When defining a message for an operation, the `wsdl:part` element must not contain both the `element` and `type` attributes [2306]. Only one of these attributes should be used with the `wsdl:part` element; the attribute that is used depends upon the type of SOAP binding that is being defined.

Defining a SOAP Binding

The only binding supported by the Basic Profile is the SOAP binding [R2401]. You specify a SOAP binding within a `wsdl:binding` element by using the `soap:binding` extensibility element. The `transport` attribute must be specified on the `soap:binding` element, and this attribute must have a value of `http://schemas.xmlsoap.org/soap/http` [R2701, R2702].

Here's an example from the `PurchaseOrderSubmission` Web service description:

```
<!-- Binding definitions -->
<binding name="poSubmissionSOAPBinding"
```

```
        type="pos:poSubmissionPortType">
    <soap:binding style="document"
            transport="http://schemas.xmlsoap.org/soap/http"/>
    <operation name="doSubmission">
        <soap:operation soapAction=
            "http://www.skatestown.com/services/poSubmission/submitPO"/>
        <input>
            <soap:body parts="purchaseOrder" use="literal"/>
        </input>
        <output>
            <soap:body parts="invoice" use="literal"/>
        </output>
    </operation>
</binding>
```

Although the `PriceCheckSMTP` Web service uses a SOAP binding, it doesn't use HTTP
for the transport; so, it doesn't conform to the Basic Profile and may result in interoperability problems. Here's an example of a binding that doesn't conform to the Basic
Profile but is still valid to use since some Web service consumers may need to use this
type of binding:

```
<!-- Binding definitions -->
<binding name="PriceCheckSMTPBinding" type="pc:PriceCheckPortType">
    <soap:binding style="document"
        transport="http://schemas.xmlsoap.org/soap/smtp"/>
    <operation name="checkPrice">
        <input>
            <soap:body use="literal"/>
        </input>
        <output>
            <soap:body use="literal"/>
        </output>
    </operation>
</binding>
```

Referencing PortType Operations in a SOAP Binding

All of the message parts defined for an operation in a `wsdl:portType` should be referenced by one or more of the SOAP binding extensibility elements: `soap:body`,
`soap:fault`, `soap:header`, and `soap:headerfault` [R2209]. By doing this, all the
abstract operations and messages defined by a `wsdl:portType` will be referenced by a
concrete binding. A SOAP binding may indicate that the `soapenv:Body` element in a
message will contain zero parts [R2202]. When this occurs, the `soapenv:Body` element
won't contain any content. All SkatesTown Web service descriptions conformed to these
profile requirements.

Types of SOAP Bindings Supported

The only types of SOAP bindings supported by the Basic Profile are document-literal and RPC-literal [R2705]. These are the only bindings supported because it was determined that there was no way to guarantee interoperability when using an RPC-encoded binding. In addition to the general SOAP binding requirements, there are specific requirements in the Basic Profile for both the document-literal and RPC-literal bindings.

The original `PurchaseOrderSubmission` Web service description used a document-literal binding so it didn't have to be updated to conform to the Basic Profile. Both the `PriceCheck` and `StockAvailableNotification` Web service descriptions used an RPC-encoded binding, so they had to be changed. Here's an example of the RPC-encoded binding that was originally used by the `PriceCheck` Web service:

```
<!-- Binding definitions -->
<binding name="PriceCheckSOAPBinding" type="pc:PriceCheckPortType">
   <soap:binding style="rpc"
      transport="http://schemas.xmlsoap.org/soap/http"/>
   <operation name="checkPrice">
      <soap:operation soapAction=""/>
      <input>
         <soap:body use="encoded"
             namespace="http://www.skatestown.com/services/PriceCheck"
             encodingStyle="http://schemas.xmlsoap.org/soap/encoding/"/>
      </input>
      <output>
         <soap:body use="encoded"
             namespace="http://www.skatestown.com/services/PriceCheck"
             encodingStyle="http://schemas.xmlsoap.org/soap/encoding/"/>
      </output>
   </operation>
</binding>
```

The new version of the `PriceCheck` Web service description has already been updated to use a document-literal binding. Since the current version of the `StockAvailableNotification` Web service description contains an RPC-encoded binding, it will be updated to use an RPC-literal binding.

Document-Literal Bindings

The message definition for a document-literal binding may contain any number of `wsdl:part` elements, but only one of the parts can be used to define the contents of the `soapenv:Body` element in a SOAP message [R2201]. If the `wsdl:message` element contains more than one `wsdl:part` element, then the `parts` attribute must be specified on the `soap:body` element and must contain only one part name [R2210]. If the `parts` attribute isn't specified, then the message definition may be empty (no `wsdl:part` element) or it may contain one part definition. The `wsdl:part` element that contains the definition of the `soapenv:Body` content must be defined using the `element` attribute

[R2204], and this attribute must reference a global element definition [R2206].

Both the `PriceCheck` and `PurchaseOrderSubmission` Web service descriptions have been updated from their original format to conform to these requirements. Listing 13.3 shows an example from the `PriceCheck` Web service.

Listing 13.3   **Document-Literal Binding for** `PriceCheck` **Web Service**

```
<!-- Type definitions -->
<types>
   <xsd:schema
       targetNamespace="http://www.skatestown.com/ns/availability"
       xmlns:xsd="http://www.w3.org/2001/XMLSchema"
       xmlns:avail="http://www.skatestown.com/ns/availability" >

       <xsd:element name="sku" type="xsd:string" />

       <xsd:complexType name="availabilityType">
          <xsd:sequence>
             <xsd:element ref="avail:sku"/>
             <xsd:element name="price" type="xsd:double"/>
             <xsd:element name="quantityAvailable" type="xsd:integer"/>
          </xsd:sequence>
       </xsd:complexType>

       <xsd:element name="StockAvailability"
                    type="avail:availabilityType" />
   </xsd:schema>
</types>

<!-- Message definitions -->
<!-- A PriceCheckRequest is simply an item code (sku)  -->
<message name="PriceCheckRequest">
   <part name="sku" element="avail:sku"/>
</message>

<!-- A PriceCheckResponse consists of an availability structure,   -->
<!-- defined above.                                                -->
<message name="PriceCheckResponse">
   <part name="result" element="avail:StockAvailability"/>
</message>

<!-- Port type definitions -->
<portType name="PriceCheckPortType">
   <operation name="checkPrice">
      <input message="pc:PriceCheckRequest"/>
      <output message="pc:PriceCheckResponse"/>
   </operation>
</portType>
```

Listing 13.3   **Continued**

```
<!-- Binding definitions -->
<binding name="PriceCheckSOAPBinding" type="pc:PriceCheckPortType">
  <soap:binding style="document" transport=
    "http://schemas.xmlsoap.org/soap/http" />
  <operation name="checkPrice">
    <soap:operation
      soapAction="http://www.skatestown.com/services/PriceCheck/checkPrice" />
    <input>
      <soap:body use="literal" />
    </input>
    <output>
      <soap:body use="literal" />
    </output>
  </operation>
</binding>
```

The example in Listing 13.4 shows how the PriceCheck Web service interface could be updated to define a SOAP header entry and still conform to the profile requirements defined earlier. The wsdl:message element named PriceCheckRequest contains two wsdl:part elements. The first part, which is named sku, contains the definition of the content of the soapenv:Body in a SOAP message. The second part defines the SOAP header entry.

Listing 13.4   PriceCheck **Web Service Interface with SOAP Header Definition**

```
<!-- Type definitions -->
<types>
  <xsd:schema
     targetNamespace="http://www.skatestown.com/ns/availability"
     xmlns:xsd="http://www.w3.org/2001/XMLSchema"
      xmlns:avail="http://www.skatestown.com/ns/availability">

     <xsd:element name="sku" type="xsd:string" />

     <xsd:complexType name="availabilityType">
        <xsd:sequence>
           <xsd:element ref="avail:sku"/>
           <xsd:element name="price" type="xsd:double"/>
           <xsd:element name="quantityAvailable" type="xsd:integer"/>
        </xsd:sequence>
     </xsd:complexType>

     <xsd:element name="StockAvailability"
                 type="avail:availabilityType" />
```

Listing 13.4   **Continued**

```
    <xsd:element name="Header" type="Header"/>
    <xsd:complexType name="Header">
      ...
    </xsd:complexType>
  </xsd:schema>
</types>

<!-- Message definitions -->
<!-- A PriceCheckRequest is simply an item code (sku)  -->
<message name="PriceCheckRequest">
  <part name="sku" element="avail:sku"/>
  <part name="header" element="avail:Header"/>
</message>

<!-- A PriceCheckResponse consists of an availability structure,  -->
<!-- defined above.                                               -->
<message name="PriceCheckResponse">
  <part name="result" element="avail:StockAvailability"/>
</message>

<!-- Port type definitions -->
<portType name="PriceCheckPortType">
  <operation name="checkPrice">
     <input message="pc:PriceCheckRequest"/>
     <output message="pc:PriceCheckResponse"/>
  </operation>
</portType>

<!-- Binding definitions -->
<binding name="PriceCheckSOAPBinding" type="pc:PriceCheckPortType">
 <soap:binding style="document"
    transport="http://schemas.xmlsoap.org/soap/http" />
  <operation name="checkPrice">
 <operation name="checkPrice">
  <soap:operation
    soapAction="http://www.skatestown.com/services/PriceCheck/checkPrice"/>
    <input>
      <soap:body use="literal" parts="sku"/>
      <soap:header message="tns:RequestMessage" part="header" use="literal"/>
    </input>
    <output>
      <soap:body use="literal" />
    </output>
  </operation>
```

Listing 13.4   **Continued**

```
</binding>
```

RPC-Literal Bindings

All `wsdl:part` elements that are referenced by an RPC-literal binding must use the `type` attribute instead of the `element` attribute [R2203]. The `type` attribute is used to reference a simple or complex type definition. If an RPC-literal binding contains `soap:fault`, `soap:header`, or `soap:headerfault` definitions, the corresponding part definition must use the `element` attribute to reference a global element definition [R2204, R2206]. The `namespace` attribute on the `soap:body` element must contain an absolute URI [R2717], but the `namespace` attribute on the `soap:fault`, `soap:header`, and `soap:headerfault` elements must not be specified [R2726]. For an RPC-literal binding, the child element in a `soapenv:Body` element will be a wrapper element that has a namespace whose value is the same as the value of the `namespace` attribute on the `soap:body` element. The namespace attribute on the `soap:fault`, `soap:header`, and `soap:headerfault` elements isn't needed, which is why they must not be specified.

The WSDL example in Listing 13.5 shows how the `StockAvailableNotification` Web service would be defined using an RPC-literal binding. The primary differences between this binding definition and the doc-literal binding definition are the following: The `wsdl:part` elements use the `type` attribute instead of the `element` attribute, any number of parts can be defined for a single message, and the namespace attribute must be specified on the `soap:body` element. In addition, when using the RPC-literal binding, the operation is similar to a method invocation where each typed part becomes a parameter under the wrapper element.

Listing 13.5   **RPC-Literal Binding for** `StockAvailableNotification` **Web Service**

```
<!-- Type definitions from the registration schema-->
<types>
  <xsd:schema
     targetNamespace="http://www.skatestown.com/ns/registrationRequest"
     xmlns:reg="http://www.skatestown.com/ns/registrationRequest" >

     <xsd:import namespace="http://schemas.xmlsoap.org/soap/encoding/"
                 schemaLocation="http://schemas.xmlsoap.org/soap/encoding/"/>

     <xsd:complexType name="itemList">
       <xsd:sequence>
         <xsd:element name="item" type="xsd:string" minOccurs="1"
           maxOccurs="unbounded"/>
       </xsd:sequence>
     </xsd:complexType>

     <xsd:complexType name="registrationRequest">
```

Listing 13.5   **Continued**

```xml
            <xsd:sequence>
              <xsd:element name="items" type="reg:itemList" />
               <xsd:element name="address" type="xsd:string"/>
               <xsd:element name="transport"
                            default="smtp" minOccurs="0" >
                  <xsd:simpleType>
                     <xsd:restriction base="xsd:string">
                        <xsd:enumeration value="http"/>
                        <xsd:enumeration value="smtp"/>
                     </xsd:restriction>
                  </xsd:simpleType>
               </xsd:element>
               <xsd:element name="clientArg" type="xsd:string" minOccurs="0"/>
            </xsd:sequence>
         </xsd:complexType>

         <xsd:simpleType name="correlationID">
             <xsd:restriction base="xsd:string">
             <!-- some appropriate restriction -->
             </xsd:restriction>
         </xsd:simpleType>

         <xsd:element name="Expiration" type="xsd:dateTime" />
         <xsd:element name="ErrorString" type="xsd:string" />
      </xsd:schema>
</types>

<!-- Message definitions -->
<message name="StockAvailableRegistrationRequest">
   <part name="registration" type="reg:registrationRequest"/>
   <part name="expiration" element="reg:Expiration"/>
</message>

<message name="StockAvailableRegistrationResponse">
   <part name="correlationID" type="reg:correlationID"/>
</message>

<message name="StockAvailableRegistrationError">
   <part name="errorString" element="reg:ErrorString"/>
</message>

<message name="StockAvailableExpirationError">
   <part name="errorString" element="reg:ErrorString"/>
</message>

<message name="StockAvailableCancellation">
```

Listing 13.5 **Continued**

```
        <part name="correlationID" type="reg:correlationID"/>
</message>

<!-- Port type definitions -->
<portType name="StockAvailableNotificationPortType">
    <!--Registration Operation -->
    <operation name="registration">
      <input message="tns:StockAvailableRegistrationRequest"/>
      <output message="tns:StockAvailableRegistrationResponse"/>
      <fault message="tns:StockAvailableRegistrationError"
         name="StockAvailableNotificationErrorMessage"/>
      <fault message="tns:StockAvailableExpirationError"
         name="StockAvailableExpirationError"/>
    </operation>

    <!--Cancellation Operation -->
    <operation name="cancellation">
      <input message="tns:StockAvailableCancellation"/>
    </operation>
</portType>

<!-- Binding definitions -->
<binding name="StockAvailableNotificationSOAPBinding"
    type="tns:StockAvailableNotificationPortType">
    <soap:binding style="rpc"
            transport="http://schemas.xmlsoap.org/soap/http"/>

    <!-- Note: the requestor must invoke the registration operation first. -->
    <operation name="registration">
      <soap:operation
         soapAction=
         "http://www.skatesTown.com/StockAvailableNotification/registration"/>
      <input>
        <soap:header message="tns:StockAvailableRegistrationRequest"
            part="expiration" use="literal" >
          <soap:headerfault message="tns:StockAvailableExpirationError"
            part="errorString" use="literal" />
        </soap:header>
        <soap:body parts="registration" use="literal"
            namespace="http://www.skatestown.com/ns/registrationRequest"/>
      </input>
      <output>
        <soap:body use="literal"
            namespace="http://www.skatestown.com/ns/registrationRequest"/>
      </output>
```

Listing 13.5   **Continued**

```
            <fault name="StockAvailableNotificationErrorMessage">
              <soap:fault name="StockAvailableNotificationErrorMessage"/>
            </fault>
        </operation>

        <operation name="cancellation">
          <soap:operation
            soapAction-
            "http://www.skatesTown.com/StockAvailableNotification/cancellation"/>
          <input>
            <soap:body use="literal"
                namespace="http://www.skatestown.com/ns/registrationRequest"/>
          </input>
        </operation>
    </binding>
```

Messages that are generated from an RPC-literal binding must adhere to the following
guidelines:

- The request message must have a wrapper element whose name is the operation
  (from the `name` attribute on the `wsdl:operation` element) and whose namespace
  is the value of the `namespace` attribute from the `soap:body` element in the WSDL
  binding.

- A response message must have a wrapper element whose name is the operation
  name (from the `name` attribute on the `wsdl:operation` element) with the string
  Response appended to it [R2729]. For example, if the operation name is
  `registration`, then the element name for the wrapper element would be
  `registrationResponse`.

- The `operation` wrapper element is used on both request and response messages
  and has a set of child elements called *part accessor elements*. The part accessor elements must be in no namespace [R2735].

- If the XML Schema definition for the parts of a message indicate that the parts
  should be namespace qualified (for example, the `xsd:schema` element contains
  `elementFormDefault="qualified"`), then the descendents of the part accessor
  element must be namespace qualified [R2737].

SOAP Faults, Headers, and Headerfaults

The Basic Profile contains requirements that are specific to SOAP faults, headers, and
header faults. When a `soap:fault`, `soap:header`, or `soap:headerfault` is defined in
SOAP binding, the associated `wsdl:part` definitions must use the `element` attribute
even when these elements are used with an RPC-literal binding [R2205]. When a
`soap:fault` is included in a SOAP binding, the `name` attribute must be specified

[R2721] and the value of this attribute must match the value on the parent `wsdl:fault` element.

For both faults and header faults, a `wsdl:binding` element should contain a `soap:fault` and a `soap:headerfault` for each known fault and header fault [R2740, R2741]. The detail entry in a fault for header fault is generally defined in the `wsdl:fault` and `soap:headerfault` elements, but a message may contain fault detail information that isn't described by either of these elements [R2742, R2743]. A `soap:headerfault` doesn't have to be defined if there are no known header faults [R2719].

When `soap:header` elements are included in a SOAP binding, they don't have to appear in the same order as the SOAP header blocks in a SOAP message [R2751]. In addition, the SOAP message may contain more than one instance of a SOAP header block for each `soap:header` element [R2752]. When you define a `soap:header` element, it may reference a `wsdl:part` element that is within a `wsdl:message` element that is referenced by its `soap:body` element [R2208].

The original WSDL 1.1 schema indicated that both the `soap:header` and `soap:headerfault` elements contained a `parts` element. Since the WSDL specification specified that the name of this attribute was `part` and this attribute could contain only a single part reference, the Basic Profile specified that the `part` attribute should be used instead of an attribute named `parts` [R2720, R2749].

The new `StockAvailableNotification` Web service description conforms to all of these requirements (see Listing 13.6).

Listing 13.6   StockAvailableNotification Web Service Interface with SOAP Fault, Header, and Header Fault

```
<!-- Binding definitions -->
<binding name="StockAvailableNotificationSOAPBinding"
   type="tns:StockAvailableNotificationPortType">
   <soap:binding style="rpc"
           transport="http://schemas.xmlsoap.org/soap/http"/>


   <!-- Note: the requestor must invoke the registration operation first. -->
   <operation name="registration">
     <soap:operation
       soapAction=
       "http://www.skatesTown.com/StockAvailableNotification/registration"/>
     <input>
       <soap:header message="tns:StockAvailableRegistrationRequest"
             part="expiration" use="literal" >
         <soap:headerfault message="tns:StockAvailableExpirationError"
             part="errorString" use="literal" />
       </soap:header>
       <soap:body parts="registration" use="literal"
             namespace="http://www.skatestown.com/ns/registrationRequest"/>
```

Listing 13.6 **Continued**

```
      </input>
      <output>
        <soap:body use="literal"
            namespace="http://www.skatestown.com/ns/registrationRequest"/>
      </output>
      <fault name="StockAvailableNotificationErrorMessage">
        <soap:fault name="StockAvailableNotificationErrorMessage"/>
      </fault>
    </operation>

    <operation name="cancellation">
      <soap:operation
        soapAction=
        "http://www.skatesTown.com/StockAvailableNotification/cancellation"/>
      <input>
        <soap:body use="literal"
            namespace="http://www.skatestown.com/ns/registrationRequest"/>
      </input>
    </operation>
  </binding>
```

Publishing a Service Description

The only type of service registry that is supported by the Basic Profile is UDDI. A
WSDL service description may be published by a service provider in a UDDI registry. A
uddi:bindingTemplate is used to publish a reference to the Web service endpoint.
Within the uddi:bindingTemplate element, a uddi:accessPoint element must be
used to reference the location of the Web service [R3100]:

```
<uddi:bindingTemplate bindingKey="...">
  <uddi:accessPoint>
    http://www.skatestown.com/services/PriceCheck
  </uddi:accessPoint>
  <uddi:tModelInstanceDetails>
    <uddi:tModelInstanceInfo
      tModelKey="uuid:FE462140-DD06-11D6-9D4F-000629DC0A53">
      ...
    </uddi:tModelInstanceInfo>
  </uddi:tModelInstanceDetails>
</uddi:bindingTemplate>
```

A uddi:tModel must use WSDL for a Web service description [R3002]. This means that
the uddi:tModel must be categorized using the uddi-org:types taxonomy with a categorization of wsdlSpec [R3003], and it must reference a wsdl:binding that conforms to
the Basic Profile [R3011]. The method for referencing a wsdl:binding element is

defined in the *UDDI Best Practice for Using WSDL in a UDDI Registry V1.08.* This best practice is described in Chapter 6.

In the following example, the `uddi:overviewURL` element contains a reference to a WSDL document that contains the binding definition for the Web service. The `uddi:keyedReference` element specifies the categorization for this `tModel`, which indicates that it references a WSDL-based service description:

```
<uddi:tModel tModelKey="uuid:FE462140-DD06-11D6-9D4F-000629DC0A53">
  <uddi:name>
    Service Binding
  </uddi:name>
  <uddi:overviewDoc>
    <uddi:overviewURL>
      http://www.skatestown.com/services/PriceCheck?wsdl
    </uddi:overviewURL>
  </uddi:overviewDoc>
  <uddi:categoryBag>
    <uddi:keyedReference tModelKey="uuid:C1ACF26D-9672-4404-9D70-39B756E62AB4"
        keyName="uddi-org:types"
        keyValue="wsdlSpec"/>
  </uddi:categoryBag>
</uddi:tModel>
```

HTTP and SOAP Message Content

The Basic Profile requires the use of either HTTP 1.0 or HTTP 1.1 [R1141], with a strong preference for using HTTP 1.1 since it's more clearly specified and offers performance advantages over HTTP 1.0 [R1140]. In addition, all HTTP messages sent to a Web service must use the HTTP POST method when they contain a SOAP message [R1132]. The HTTP Extension Framework can't be used to invoke a Web service [R1108]. The HTTP Extension Framework provides an extension mechanism for HTTP, but it isn't allowed by the Basic Profile because it isn't widely deployed. Here's an example of an HTTP 1.1 message with a SOAP envelope for content:

```
POST /services/PriceCheck HTTP/1.1
Content-Type: text/xml; charset=utf-8
Accept: application/soap+xml, application/dime, multipart/related, text/*
User-Agent: Axis/1.1
Host: localhost:8080
Cache-Control: no-cache
Pragma: no-cache
SOAPAction: "http://www.skatestown.com/services/PriceCheck/checkPrice"
Content-Length: 424
```

```
<?xml version="1.0" encoding="UTF-8"?>
<SOAP-ENV:Envelope
    xmlns:SOAP-ENV="http://schemas.xmlsoap.org/soap/envelope/"
    xmlns:xsd="http://www.w3.org/2001/XMLSchema"
    xmlns:xsi="http://www.w3.org/2001/XMLSchema-instance">
  <SOAP-ENV:Body>
    ...
  </SOAP-ENV:Body>
</SOAP-ENV:Envelope>
```

Specifying the SOAPAction Header

The SOAPAction HTTP header is used as a hint for SOAP processors. If the soapAction attribute is specified on the soap.operation element in the WSDL, then the value of this attribute must appear within quotes in the SOAPAction HTTP header field [R2744, R.1109] on the wire. If the soapAction attribute isn't specified, then the SOAPAction header field must have a quoted empty string as its value [R2745].

Here's the SOAP binding definition for the PriceCheck Web service, which defines a soapAction attribute value of http://www.skatestown.com/services/PriceCheck/checkPrice:

```
<!-- Binding definitions -->
<binding name="PriceCheckSOAPBinding" type="pc:PriceCheckPortType">
<soap:binding style="document"
    transport="http://schemas.xmlsoap.org/soap/http" />
  <operation name="checkPrice">
    <soap:operation
        soapAction="http://www.skatestown.com/services/PriceCheck/checkPrice" />
    <input>
      <soap:body use="literal" />
    </input>
    <output>
      <soap:body use="literal" />
    </output>
  </operation>
</binding>
```

Based on this binding definition for the PriceCheck Web service, the following SOAPAction HTTP header field must be used when sending the input message for the checkPrice operation:

```
POST /services/PriceCheck HTTP/1.1
Content-Type: text/xml; charset=utf-8
Accept: application/soap+xml, application/dime, multipart/related, text/*
User-Agent: Axis/1.1
```

```
Host: localhost:8080
Cache-Control: no-cache
Pragma: no-cache
SOAPAction: "http://www.skatestown.com/services/PriceCheck/checkPrice"
Content-Length: 424
```

SOAP Message Format

A message may not contain either a Document Type Definition (DTD) or a Processing Instruction [R1008, R1009], but it may contain an XML declaration [R1010]. The soapenv:Envelope element must not contain any child elements after the soapenv:Body element [R1011], and the children of the soapenv:Body element must be namespace qualified [R1014]. If any SOAP header in a message contains the soapenv:mustUnderstand attribute, it must have a value of 0 or 1 [R1013].

A SOAP message that contains a soapenv:Fault element must have only the following unqualified child elements: faultcode, faultstring, faultactor, and detail [R1000, R1001]. No other elements can appear within the soapenv:Fault element. The following example shows a SOAP fault message that is formatted correctly:

```
HTTP/1.1 500 Internal Server Error
Server: Apache-Coyote/1.1
Content-Type: text/xml; charset=utf-8
Content-Length: 487
Connection: close

<?xml version="1.0" encoding="UTF-8"?>
<SOAP-ENV:Envelope
    xmlns:SOAP-ENV="http://schemas.xmlsoap.org/soap/envelope/"
    xmlns:xsi="http://www.w3.org/2001/XMLSchema-instance"
    xmlns:xsd="http://www.w3.org/2001/XMLSchema">
  <SOAP-ENV:Body>
    <SOAP-ENV:Fault>
      <faultcode>SOAP-ENV:Server</faultcode>
      <faultstring>Method &amp;apos;test&amp;apos; is not supported.</faultstring>
      <faultactor>/services/PriceCheck</faultactor>
      <detail>
        <stackTrace>
          java.lang.NoSuchMethodException: StockQuoteService
          ...
      </detail>
    </SOAP-ENV:Fault>
  </SOAP-ENV:Body>
</SOAP-ENV:Envelope>
```

The soapenv:encodingStyle attribute may not be used on any element in the SOAP namespace or on any element that is a child of soapenv:Body [R1005, R1006].

Web Service Security

The profile defines some basic security requirements for a Web service. A Web service may require the use of HTTPS as a transport [R5000]. When HTTPS is used, the value of the `location` attribute on the `soap:address` element must be a URI with an `https` scheme [R5001]. Since HTTPS with mutual authentication is sometimes required, the Basic Profile allows it to be used [R5010]. When the SkatesTown Web services need transport-level security, HTTPS would be a good first step.

WS-I Conformance Claims

All the artifacts referenced by a WS-I profile may contain an indication that they conform to the requirements in the Basic Profile. A service provider can use conformance claims to indicate that their Web services adhere to specific profiles. If a service requestor has specific interoperability criteria, this information can be used when selecting the Web services they will use. For example, if a service requestor wants to use only Web services that conform to the WS-I Basic Profile, then it will look for service descriptions that contain the corresponding conformance claim.

For both a SOAP message and a WSDL document, the conformance claim has the following format:

```
<wsi:Claim conformsTo="xsd:anyURI"/>
```

The value of the `conformsTo` attribute indicates which WS-I profile an artifact conforms to. Conformance claims for Basic Profile 1.0 should use the following URI: `http://ws-i.org/profiles/basic/1.0`.

The conformance claims for a SOAP message appear in the SOAP header [R0005], and a message may contain claims for more than one profile [R0006]. Each profile claim is identified by a separate `wsi:Claims` element in the SOAP header.

The following SOAP message provides an example of a message that claims conformance to the Basic Profile 1.0:

```
<soapenv:Envelope xmlns:soapenv="http://schemas.xmlsoap.org/soap/">
  <soapenv:Header>
    <wsi:Claim xmlns:wsi="http://ws-i.org/schemas/conformanceClaim"
       conformsTo="http://wsi-org/profiles/basic/1.0"/>
  </soapenv:Header>
  <soapenv:Body>
    ...
  </soapenv:Body>
</soapenv:Envelope>
```

Within a WSDL document, a conformance claim is placed within a `wsdl:documentation` element that appears within the `wsdl:message`, `wsdl:portType`, `wsdl:operation`, `wsdl:binding`, or `wsdl:port` element [R0002, R0003].

Since the `PriceCheck` Web service description was updated to conform to the Basic Profile 1.0, it contains a conformance claim for this profile in its WSDL port definition:

```
<service name="PriceCheck">
  <port name="Pricecheck" binding="pc:PriceCheckSOAPBinding">
    <documentation>
      <wsi:Claim
        conformsTo="http://ws-i.org/profiles/basic/1.0" />
    </documentation>
    <soap:address location="http://localhost:8080/axis/services/PriceCheck"/>
  </port>
</service>
```

Conformance Claim Inheritance

Conformance claims are inherited based on the relationship of these WSDL elements: from `wsdl:port` to `wsdl:binding`, from `wsdl:binding` to `wsdl:portType`, from `wsdl:portType` to `wsdl:operation`, and from `wsdl:operation` to `wsdl:message`. Conformance claims can't be specified in a `wsdl:service` element.

Using the conformance claim from the `PriceCheck` Web service description as an example, the `wsdl:port` element contains the conformance claim. This means the `wsdl:binding` element named `pc:PriceCheckSOAPBinding`, which is referenced by the port definition, will inherit the conformance claim. The conformance claim will also be inherited by the `wsdl:portType` element referenced by the `wsdl:binding` element, the `wsdl:operation` elements within the `wsdl:portType` element, and the `wsdl:message` elements that are referenced by the `wsdl:operation` element. The conformance claim inheritance is illustrated in Figure 13.2.

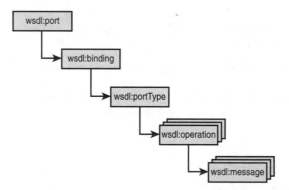

Figure 13.2   Conformance claim inheritance

Conformance Claims in UDDI Entries

A UDDI `tModel` may also contain a WS-I conformance claim [R3020, R3030, R3021]. The conformance claim for a `uddi:tModel` will appear within the `uddi:categoryBag` as a reference to the WS-I conformance categorization tModel with a key value that contains the conformance claim URI. The following listing contains the general format for a categoryBag with a conformance claim:

```
<uddi:categoryBag>
    <uddi:keyedReference tModelKey="uuid:65719168-72c6-3f29-8c20-62defb0961c0"
      keyName="{WS-I Profile Name}"
      keyValue="{WS-I Conformance Claim URI}"/>
</uddi:categoryBag>
```

A conformance claim for the WS-I Basic Profile 1.0 would have a keyName of "WS-I_conformance:BasicProfile1.0" and a keyValue of "http://ws-i.org/profiles/basic/1.0":

```
<uddi:categoryBag>
    <uddi:keyedReference tModelKey="uuid:65719168-72c6-3f29-8c20-62defb0961c0"
      keyName="WS-I_conformance:BasicProfile1.0"
      keyValue="http://ws-i.org/profiles/basic/1.0"/>
</uddi:categoryBag>
```

Any conformance claims attached to a UDDI tModel must be consistent with any conformance claims made in the wsdl:binding that the tModel references [R3004]. Only a UDDI tModel may contain a conformance claim. Other UDDI entries, such as a uddi:businessEntity, uddi:businessService, or uddi:bindingTemplate, can't contain conformance claims [R3005].

Service Provider, Requestor, and Registry Requirements

The remainder of the requirements in the Basic Profile are targeted at the service provider, service requestor, and service registry. This section describes the behavior defined in the Basic Profile for these conformance targets.

Service Provider Requirements

The most important requirement for a service provider is to make sure a Web service is described by one or both of the following: a WSDL 1.1 service description or UDDI binding template [R0001]. Also, a Web service may receive SOAP messages using a connection on port 80 [R1110], but it's acceptable to use other ports when necessary (such as port 443 for SSL support).

Several profile requirements describe the HTTP status codes that should be used by the Web service hosted by a service provider when responding to requests. When the request is processed successfully, a 2xx HTTP status code should be used for the response [R1124]. For this type of situation, it's recommended that a "200 OK" status code be used when the response contains a SOAP envelope that doesn't contain a SOAP fault [R1111]. For responses to a successful request that don't contain a SOAP envelope, either the "200 OK" or "202 Accepted" status code should be used [R1112]. When the response contains a SOAP fault, then the "500 Internal Server Error" status code must be used [R1126].

When processing a request that is defined as a one-way operation, the Web service must not return a SOAP envelope in the response [R2714]. If the service requestor receives a SOAP envelope in the response to a one-way operation, it must not be processed [R2724]. The HTTP status code in the response message for a one-way operation can't be used by the service requestor as an indicator that the message was accepted and processed [R2725].

The "307 Temporary Redirect" HTTP status code must be used by a Web service when a request is redirected to a different endpoint [R1130]. And, a service requestor may automatically redirect requests after it receives this status code [R1131].

When a Web service detects an error with the format of a request, a 4xx HTTP status code must be used for the response [R1125]. The Basic Profile recommends following 4xx status codes for the specified situations:

- *400 Bad Request*—This status code should be used when the request message contains either a malformed HTTP request or content that isn't a well-formed XML document [R1113].

- *405 Method not Allowed*—When the HTTP request message isn't sent using the POST method, then this status code should be used [R1114].

- *415 Unsupported Media Type*—This status code should be used when the Content-Type HTTP header field doesn't have a media type value of text/xml [R1115].

The method for maintaining state with HTTP is referred to as *cookies*. A Web service is allowed to use cookies [R1120], but they should conform to the RFC2965 specification [R1122]. A Web service should not require the use of cookies [R1121], and if they're used they should be used only as a hint for possible optimizations; they must not have any effect on the interaction with the Web service [R1123].

Message Receiver Requirements

A set of profile requirements is targeted at a message receiver, which can either be the service requestor or the Web service hosted by the service provider. The first set of requirements focuses on SOAP faults. To determine if a message is a SOAP fault, a message receiver must check the SOAP envelope to determine whether it contains a soapenv:Fault element [R1107]. The message receiver can't rely on the HTTP status code to determine if the message contains a SOAP fault.

A message receiver must accept SOAP fault messages under the following conditions:

- When it contains zero, one, or more elements as children of the detail element [R1002]. The child elements are allowed to support extensibility.

- When it contains a detail element with any number of attributes, as long as the namespace-qualified attributes aren't in the SOAP envelope namespace (http://schemas.xmlsoap.org/soap/envelope/) [R1003]. Similar to the previous requirement, the additional attributes are allowed to support extensibility.

- When it has an `xml:lang` attribute on the `faultstring` element [R1016]. Since a `faultstring` element contains human-readable text, this attribute is used to indicate the language used for this text.

A message receiver must generate a SOAP fault when it receives a message that doesn't contain a properly formatted SOAP envelope: `soapenv:Envelope` as the document root element [R1015]. This occurs when the SOAP message contains a well-formed XML document and a root element with a name of `Envelope` but the namespace for this element isn't `http://schemas/xmlsoap.org/soap/envelope/`. A `soapenv:mustUnderstand` fault must be returned by the message receiver when it doesn't understand a header block that contains a `soapenv:mustUnderstand` attribute with a value of 1 [R1027]. Although there is a requirement to send a `SOAPAction` HTTP header field as a quoted string, it's optional for a message receiver to return a SOAP fault if it receives an input message that contains a `SOAPAction` header field that wasn't quoted [R1119]. In general, when the message receiver generates a SOAP fault, all normal processing for a SOAP message should be stopped [R1028, R1029, R1030].

All mandatory header blocks (which will contain `soapenv:mustUnderstand` attribute with a value of 1) must be handled by a message receiver before any other processing takes place [R1027]. This requirement arises from clarifications made by the SOAP 1.2 processing model and ensures the ability of extensions to arbitrarily affect the semantics of a message. For example, if a mandatory header caused the receiver to process the remaining headers in a particular order, it would be bad if the receiver had already processed any other headers.

A message receiver can't require the sender to use the `xsi:type` attribute to indicate datatypes except when it is used to indicate a derived type [R1017]. The datatype definitions should be determined by inspecting the Web service description.

Service Registry Requirement

The only profile requirement for a service registry is the requirement to support the WS-I conformance category system [R3021]. This is done by adding the `ws-i-org:contormsTO:2002_12 LModel` to the content of the service registry.

Summary of Basic Profile 1.0 Requirements

To assist you with reviewing existing artifacts (such as SOAP messages and WSDL documents) for conformance to the Basic Profile 1.0, Table 13.1 provides a mapping of profile requirements to conformance targets. For example, if you want to understand the requirements for the `wsdl:import` element, you should read the following profile requirements: R2001, R2005, R2007, R2008, and R2022. Since some profile requirements are targeted at more than one element, a single requirement may appear more than once in this table.

Table 13.1   **Summary of Basic Profile 1.0 Requirements**

Conformance Target	Profile Requirement
WSDL document	R2025, R2026, R2028, R2029, R2101, R2102, R4002, R4003, R4004
wsdl:definitions	R2005, R2114
wsdl:documentation	R2020, R2021, R2024
wsi:Claim	R0002, R0003
wsdl:import	R2001, R2005, R2007, R2008, R2022
wsdl:types	R2023
xsd:schema	R2105, R2114, R2800, R2801
xsd:import	R2002, R2003, R2004
Imported XML schema	R2009, R2010, R2011
Array declarations	R2110, R2111, R2112
wsdl:message	R2210, R2301, R2306
wsdl:part	R2203, R2204, R2205, R2206, R2207, R2712
wsdl:portType	R2303
wsdl:operation	R2304, R2305
wsdl:binding	R2209, R2401, R2705, R2709, R2710, R2718, R2719, R2740, R2741
soap:binding	R2701, R2702
wsdl:operation	R2302
soap:operation	R2744, R2745
wsdl:input	—
wsdl:output	—
soap:body	R2201, R2202, R2204, R2207, R2210, R2706, R2707, R2716, R2717
soap:header	R2205, R2208, R2707, R2706, R2716, R2720, R2726, R2749, R2751
soap:headerfault	R2205, R2706, R2707, R2716, R2720, R2726, R2741, R2743, R2749
wsdl:fault	R2742
soap:fault	R2205, R2706, R2707, R2716, R2721, R2722, R2723, R2726, R2728, R2740, R2754
wsdl:port	R2711
wsdl:required (attribute)	R2026, R2027, R2747, R2748
SOAP envelope	R1008, R1009, R1010, R1012, R1017, R2211, R2729, R2735, R2737, R2738
soapenv:Envelope	R1011, R1015

Table 13.1   **Continued**

soapenv:Header	R2739, R2743, R2752, R2753
wsi:Claim	R0004, R0005, R0006, R0007
soapenv:Body	R1014, R2301, R2712
soapenv:Fault	R1000, R1001, R1002, R1003, R1004, R1016, R1031, R2742
soapenv:encodingStyle (attribute)	R1005, R1006, R1007
soapenv:mustUnderstand (attribute)	R1013
soapenv:arrayType (attribute)	R2113
HTTP message	R1108, R1140, R1141, R1132
Content-Type header	R1012, R1018
SOAPAction header	R1109, R1119
Cookies	R1120, R1121, R1122, R1123
HTTPS	R5000, R5001, R5010
HTTP status codes	—
HTTP 2xx status code	R1111, R1112, R1124
HTTP 3xx status code	R1130, R1131
HTTP 4xx status code	R1113, R1114, R1115, R1125
HTTP 5xx status code	R1126
UDDI entry	R3005
uddi:bindingTemplate	R3100
uddi:tModel	R3002, R3003, R3004, R3010, R3011, R3020, R3030
Roles	
Service provider	R0001, R1110, R2714, R2724, R2725
HTTP 2xx status code	R1111, R1112, R1124
HTTP 3xx status code	R1130
HTTP 4xx status code	R1113, R1114, R1115, R1125
HTTP 5xx status code	R1126
HTTP cookies	R1120, R1121, R1122, R1123
Service requestor	R2027, R2727, R2750
HTTP 3xx status code	R1131
HTTP cookies	R1123
Service registry	R3021
Message receiver	R1002, R1003, R1015, R1016, R1017, R1025, R1027, R1028, R1029, R1030, R1107, R1119, R4001

Future WS-I Profiles

After completing the Basic Profile, the WS-I organization started to work on the next version of the Basic Profile and the Basic Security Profile. The next version of the Basic Profile will add support for SOAP with attachments, and the Basic Security Profile will focus on defining the profile requirements for transport and SOAP message layer security.

As work on the next Basic Profile version progressed, it became apparent that certain profile requirements needed to be factored out into separate profiles. This resulted in three new profiles: Basic Profile 1.1, Simple SOAP Binding Profile 1.0, and Attachments Profile 1.0. By creating three profiles, the WS-I organization ensured that the requirements in these profiles can be easily composed with other profiles. The requirements in the Basic Profile 1.1 and Simple SOAP Binding Profile 1.0 should be equivalent to the requirements in the Basic Profile 1.0.

In addition to the profile requirements, these profiles also defined a set of extensibility points that have an identifier with the format E*nnnn* (where *nnnn* is a unique number). A Web service dosn't have to adhere to these extensibility points. Future versions of the WS-I Test Tools will provide an indicator that one of the extensibility points is being used by a Web service. Using an extensibility point doesn't affect conformance to a profile, but it may indicate areas where there might be interoperability problems.

At the time that this book was written, these three profiles were only available as draft documents and may change slightly before they were approved for final publication.

Basic Profile 1.1

This profile was derived from the Basic Profile 1.0. The requirements in this profile are the same as those in the Basic Profile 1.0, except for a couple of new requirements and some requirements that were factored out into the Simple SOAP Binding Profile 1.0. It also contains one additional conformance target named ENVELOPE. This conformance target corresponds to the soapenv:Envelope element and its content within a MESSAGE. This conformance target was added so that the profile requirements could distinguish between the HTTP message and SOAP message content as the target for a requirement.

Since the requirements in this profile are almost the same as those in the Basic Profile 1.0, you can refer to the Basic Profile 1.0 section for an overview of the profile requirements. This profile contains all the requirements in the Basic Profile 1.0 except the following: R1010, R1012, R1018, and R4001. All of these requirements are now in the Simple SOAP Binding Profile 1.0.

There are also some new requirements that were introduced in this profile: R1032, R2030, R2212, R2213, R2214, R2707, R2755, R2803. The soapenv:Envelope, soapenv:Header, and soapenv:Body elements in a SOAP message must not contain any attributes that are in the http://schemas.xmlsoap.org/soap/envelope/ namespace [R1032]. The wsdl:documentation element can be the first child element within the wsdl:import, wsdl:part, and wsdl:definitions elements [R2030]. A SOAP envelope must contain one part accessor element for each wsdl:part element that appears within

the body of the envelope [R2212]. When using a document-literal binding and the
`parts` attribute of a `soap:body` element is an empty string, then the `soapenv:Body` element in a message must not contain any content [R2213]. When the `parts` attribute of
a `soap:body` element is an empty string and it is defined in a RPC-literal binding, then
the `soapenv:Body` element in a message must not contain any part accessor elements
[R2214]. When a message is defined by an RPC-literal binding, the local name for the
part accessor element must be the same as the value of the `name` attribute on the corresponding `wsdl:part` element. When the `use` attribute isn't specified on the `soap:body`,
`soap:fault`, `soap:header`, or `soap:headerfault` elements, then the default value for
this attribute is `literal` [R2707]. The `namespace` attribute of a `wsdl:import` element
can't be a relative URL [R2803].

There are also some requirements that were in the Basic Profile 1.0 that aren't in the
Basic Profile 1.1: R2020, R2021, R2024, and R2728. Requirements R2020, R2021, and
R2024 were replaced by R2030, and requirement R2728 is now covered by R2707.

The conformance claim URI for this profile is `http://ws-i.org/profiles/`
`basic/1.1`.

Simple SOAP Binding Profile 1.0

The purpose of this profile is to define the requirements for the serialization of a SOAP
envelope as the only content of an HTTP message (which means the message can't contain attachments). This profile contains some new requirements, as well as some requirements derived from the Basic Profile 1.0.

New Requirements

When a SOAP envelope is sent, it must conform to the following requirements:

- The SOAP envelope must be the only payload in the body of the HTTP message
  [R9700].
- The SOAP envelope must be serialized in a format that conforms to the XML 1.0
  specification [R9701].
- The HTTP message must have a Content-Type header field [R9702].
- The Content-Type header field must have a value of `text/xml` [R9703].
- A binding within a Web service description must only use a SOAP binding
  [R9802].
- The WSDL MIME, HTTP GET/POST, and Direct Internet Message
  Encapsulation (DIME) binding extensions can't be used within a SOAP binding
  [R9801], but other binding extension elements and attributes can be used as long
  as they don't result in a message whose content doesn't conform to the profile
  [R9800].

Requirements from Basic Profile 1.0

The requirements derived from the Basic Profile 1.0 primarily describe the messaging behavior for a Web service that uses a SOAP binding. A message receiver must accept messages that contain either a SOAP envelope that includes a Byte Order Mark (BOM) [R4001] or an XML declaration [R1010]. A message must use either a UTF-8 or UTF-16 character encoding [R1012], and the character encoding must be specified using the charset attribute on the Content-Type header field [R1018]. In addition, all the message parts defined for an operation in a wsdl:portType should be referenced by one or more of the SOAP binding extensibility elements: soap:body, soap:fault, soap:header, and soap:headerfault [R2209].

Summary of Simple SOAP Binding Profile 1.0 Requirements

Table 13.2 contains a summary of the requirements for this profile mapped to the corresponding conformance targets. The profile requirements that have an identifier of R9nnn are requirements that are new and didn't exist in Basic Profile 1.0. All the other requirements originated from the Basic Profile 1.0. In addition, the conformance claim URI for this profile is http://ws-i.org/Profiles/SimpleSoapBinding/1.0.

Table 13.2 **Summary of Simple SOAP Binding Profile 1.0 Requirements**

Conformance Target	Profile Requirement
WSDL Document	—
wsdl:binding	R2209, R9800, R9801, R9802
SOAP Envelope	R1010, R1012, R9700, R9701
HTTP Message	—
Content-Type header	R1018, R9702, R9703
Roles	—
Service provider	—
Message receiver	R4001

Attachments Profile 1.0

The Attachments Profile provides support for SOAP Messages with Attachments and is intended to be used in conjunction with the Basic Profile 1.1 and Simple SOAP Binding Profile 1.0. The SOAP Messages with Attachments specification defines a method for using MIME multipart/related structure to build a message that contains a SOAP envelope with attachments. Messages with attachments are defined in a WSDL document using the WSDL MIME binding.

MIME Binding Definition

The WSDL 1.1 specification defined a MIME binding that can be used within either a wsdl:input or wsdl:output element [R2901]. When defining a MIME binding, the `mime:content` element is defined by referencing a WSDL part definition using the `part` attribute [R2946]. The part definition must be referenced by the `wsdl:operation` in the `portType` definition that corresponds to the binding [R2903]. If the `wsdl:part` is associated with the input definition, then the `mime:content` element must be defined within the binding input definition. The same condition is true for an output definition. The `mime:content` element must reference the element or type that is defined by a part definition. It can't reference a child of the element or type referenced by the `wsdl:part` element [R2904]. In addition, all of the message parts defined for a `wsdl:portType` element should be referenced by one or more of the SOAP and MIME binding extensibility elements: `soap:body`, `soap:fault`, `soap:header`, `soap:headerfault`, and `mime:content` [R2941].

The following example shows how Al Rosen could enhance the `PriceCheck` Web service description to include a MIME binding. The response message for the `checkPrice` operation has been modified to include a JPEG image of the item whose price was checked. Here are the relevant updates to the `PriceCheck` Web service description:

```
<!-- A PriceCheckResponse consists of an availability structure,   -->
<!-- defined above.                                                 -->
<message name="PriceCheckResponse">
    <part name="result" element="avail:StockAvailability"/>
    <part name="picture" type="xsd:base64Binary"/>
</message>

<!-- Port type definitions -->
<portType name="PriceCheckPortType">
    <operation name="checkPrice">
        <input message="pc:PriceCheckRequest"/>
        <output message="pc:PriceCheckResponse"/>
    </operation>
</portType>

<!-- Binding definitions -->
<binding name="PriceCheckSOAPBinding" type="pc:PriceCheckPortType">
 <soap:binding
   style="document" transport="http://schemas.xmlsoap.org/soap/http" />
 <operation name="checkPrice">
    <soap:operation
      soapAction="http://www.skatestown.com/services/PriceCheck/checkPrice" />
    <input>
      <soap:body use="literal" />
    </input>
    <output>
      <mime:multipartRelated>
        <mime:part>
          <soap:body part="result" use="literal" />
        </mime:part>
```

```
        <mime:part>
          <mime:content part="picture" type="image/jpeg" />
        </mime:part>
      </mime:multipartRelated>
    </output>
    </operation>
  </binding>
```

The `mime:content` element may reference a WSDL part definition that uses either a
`type` or `element` attribute [R2910]. When the part definition contains the `element`
attribute (which refers to a global element definition), the associated MIME part must
contain an XML serialization of this element [R2942] and the `type` attribute on the
`mime:content` element must have a value that is appropriate for this type of data
[R2944]. When the `wsdl:part` element contains a `type` attribute, its value must be
ignored and the media type value specified in the `type` attribute on the `mime:content`
element should be used instead [R2943]. In the previous example, the WSDL part
named `picture` has a `type` attribute with a value of `xsd:base64Binary`, and the corresponding MIME part has a `mime:content` element with a `type` attribute value of
`image/jpeg`. The `xsd:base64Binary` value should be ignored, since the `image/jpeg`
media type provides a better indication of the MIME part content.

The root part is identified by the `mime:part` element that contains a `soap:body` element. Since there can be only one root part, there can be only one `mime:part` element
that contains a `soap:body` element [R2911]. This `mime:part` element may appear in any
position within the list of `mime:part` elements [R2947]. The root part definition may
contain SOAP headers, but they can't be defined in a nonroot part [R2905, R2906]. The
WSDL 1.1 specification contains some inaccurate statements about the `mime:part` element: MIME parts are defined using the `mime:part` element [R2907], and this element
doesn't have a `name` attribute [R2908].

If a MIME part can contain different content types for the same data, then a
`mime:part` element may contain multiple `mime:content` definitions. Each
`mime:content` element must reference the same WSDL part definition [R2909], and the
`type` attribute must be used to indicate the different content types.

If the response to the `checkPrice` operation in the `PriceCheck` Web service description could return either a JPEG or GIF image, then the following MIME binding would
be used:

```
<!-- Binding definitions -->
<binding name="PriceCheckSOAPBinding" type="pc:PriceCheckPortType">
 <soap:binding style="document"
   transport="http://schemas.xmlsoap.org/soap/http" />
 <operation name="checkPrice">
   <soap:operation
     soapAction="http://www.skatestown.com/services/PriceCheck/checkPrice" />
   <input>
     <soap:body use="literal" />
   </input>
```

```
<output>
  <mime:multipartRelated>
    <mime:part>
      <soap:body part="result" use="literal" />
    </mime:part>
    <mime:part>
      <mime:content part="picture" type="image/jpeg" />
      <mime:content part="picture" type="image/gif" />
    </mime:part>
  </mime:multipartRelated>
</output>
</operation>
</binding>
```

A fault message can be sent either as a text/xml or multipart/related message, if the output for an operation is defined using a mime:multipartRelated element [R2913]. A fault message can be sent using attachments when the output message for an operation is defined using the MIME binding [R2920]. Faults can't be defined in a WSDL document using a MIME binding. This means that the mime:multipartRelated element can't appear as a child of the wsdl:fault element [R2930].

MIME Parts in a Message

The root part of a multipart/related message must contain the SOAP envelope [R2931], and its content must conform to the requirements for an ENVELOPE in Basic Profile 1.1 [R2927]. Since the root part contains a SOAP envelope, it must be either UTF-8 or UTF-16 encoded [R2915]. This means the charset attribute on the Content-Type header field for the root part must contain one of these two values. In addition, the type attribute on the Content-Type header field must have a value of text/xml [R2932].

All nonroot parts may have any character encoding [R2916] that is appropriate for the data contained within the part, and they may contain a SOAP envelope [R2919]. Although a nonroot part may contain a SOAP envelope, it should not be interpreted as an additional method for invoking a Web service.

The default value for the Content-Transfer-Encoding field is 7bit, but since messages may be sent or received from systems that support other types of encoding, the following values are also supported: 8bit, binary, quoted-printable, and base64 [2934]. The possible values for this field are limited to help improve interoperability between systems that support different types of transfer encoding. In addition, the content of the part must be encoded so that it conforms to the encoding value specified in the Content-Transfer-Encoding field [R2935].

The following contains an example of the Content-Type header fields for a multipart/related message:

```
MIME-Version: 1.0
Content-Type: Multipart/Related; boundary=MIME_boundary; type=text/xml;

--MIME_boundary
```

```
Content-Type: text/xml; charset=UTF-8
Content-Transfer-Encoding: 8bit
Content-ID: <rootpart@www.skatestown.com>

<?xml version='1.0' ?>
<SOAP-ENV:Envelope xmlns:SOAP-ENV="http://schemas.xmlsoap.org/soap/envelope/">
  <SOAP-ENV:Body>
    ...
  </SOAP-ENV:Body>
</SOAP-ENV:Envelope>

--MIME_boundary
Content-Type: image/jpeg
Content-Transfer-Encoding: binary
Content-ID: <picture=DE563490-EA20-5505-9DA4-45B632F52AC3@
[ic :ccc]www.skatestown.com>
>

...JPEG File...
--MIME_boundary--
```

Each part in a multipart/related message is separated by a boundary string. In the previous example, the boundary string is MIME_boundary. Each boundary string must be preceded by a carriage return (CR) and linefeed (LF), or CRLF [2936]. A CRLF is made up of two ASCII characters: CR is 13 and LF is 10.

A message must have a Content-Type field value of either text/xml or multipart/related [R2945]. When an operation is defined using the MIME binding and the definition contains only one mime:part element (for the root part), then the message that is sent based on this definition may have a Content-Type of either text/xml or multipart-related [R2917]. When the WSDL definition for an input or output message contains one or more nonroot parts, the entire message must be sent with a Content-Type HTTP header field with a value of multipart/related [R2925].

When a MIME part is defined in a Web service description by binding a part within a wsdl:message element to a mime:content element, the Content-ID for the MIME part in the message must have the following format [R2933]:

PartName=GlobalID@DomainName

The PartName, GlobalID, and DomainName variables must have the following values:

- PartName—The value of the name attribute on the wsdl:part element that is referenced by the mime:content element. Any non-ASCII characters must be represented by the escaped character %XX, where XX is the hexadecimal notation for the value of the character.
- GlobalID—A globally unique identifier, such as a UUID (Universal Unique Identifier).
- DomainName—A valid domain name that is owned by the entity that generates the message.

In the `PriceCheckSOAPBinding`, the MIME part that contains the picture references a message part with the name `picture`, as shown in the following WSDL description:

```
<!-- A PriceCheckResponse consists of an availability structure,   -->
<!-- defined above.                                                -->
<message name="PriceCheckResponse">
   <part name="result" element="avail:StockAvailability"/>
   <part name="picture" type="xsd:base64Binary"/>
</message>

...

<!-- Binding definitions -->
<binding name="PriceCheckSOAPBinding" type="pc:PriceCheckPortType">
  ...
   <output>
      <mime:multipartRelated>
         <mime:part>
           <soap:body part="result" use="literal" />
         </mime:part>
         <mime:part>
           <mime:content part="picture" type="image/jpeg" />
         </mime:part>
      </mime:multipartRelated>
   </output>
   </operation>
</binding>
```

This binding will result in a MIME part within the message that contains the following `Content-ID` value:

```
MIME-Version: 1.0
Content-Type: Multipart/Related; boundary=MIME_boundary; type=text/xml;

...

--MIME_boundary
Content-Type: image/jpeg
Content-Transfer-Encoding: binary
Content-ID: <picture=DE563490-EA20-5505-9DA4-45B632F52AC3@
➥www.skatestown.com>
>

...JPEG File...
--MIME_boundary--
```

When a message is defined using a MIME binding, the content of the message must contain all the MIME parts described by the MIME binding [R2926]. For example, if four MIME parts are defined for a message, thien all four parts must appear in the content of the message when it is sent.

MIME Part Order

The parts in a message can be in any order, but the root part must be identifiable [R2929]. The root part can be identified using the `start` attribute on the Content-Type HTTP header field. If the `start` attribute isn't specified, then the root part must be the first part in the message [R2922].

The following example shows a message where the root part isn't the first part, so the `start` attribute contains a reference to the root:

```
MIME-Version: 1.0
Content-Type: Multipart/Related; boundary=MIME_boundary; type=text/xml;
     start="<rootpart@www.skatestown.com>"

--MIME_boundary--
Content-Type: image/jpeg
Content-Transfer-Encoding: binary
Content-ID: <picture=DE563490-EA20-5505-9DA4-45B632F52AC3@
www.skatestown.com>


...JPEG File...

--MIME_boundary
Content-Type: text/xml; charset=UTF-8
Content-Transfer-Encoding: 8bit
Content-ID: <rootpart@www.skatestown.com>

<?xml version='1.0' ?>
<SOAP-ENV:Envelope xmlns:SOAP-ENV="http://schemas.xmlsoap.org/soap/envelope/">
  <SOAP-ENV:Body>
    ...
  </SOAP-ENV:Body>
</SOAP-ENV:Envelope>

--MIME_boundary
```

Attachment References from Within a SOAP Envelope

No standard method is defined for referencing attachments from within a SOAP envelope. The Attachment Profile 1.0 defines a datatype named `swaRef` that can be used for this purpose. This datatype is a URI that must resolve to an attachment in the same message as the SOAP envelope [R2928]. A WSDL message part that contains an element that references `attref:swaRef` indicates that the element must contain a URI reference to an attachment. Here's the XML schema definition for the `attref:swaRef` datatype:

```
<xsd:simpleType name="swaRef">
  <xsd:restriction base="xsd:anyURI"/>
</xsd:simpleType>
```

Using the response to the `checkPrice` operation in the `PriceCheck` Web service description as an example again, the response message could be updated so that the SOAP envelope returned the SKU for the item as well as a reference to the attachment that contains the picture of the item. This change only requires an update to the WSDL types definition:

```
<!-- Type definitions -->
<types>
   <xsd:schema
       targetNamespace="http://www.skatestown.com/ns/availability"
       xmlns:xsd=http://www.w3.org/2001/XMLSchema
       xmlns.avail="http.//www.skatestown.com/ns/availability" >

      <xsd:element name="sku" type="xsd:string" />

      <xsd:complexType name="availabilityType">
         <xsd:sequence>
            <xsd:element ref="avail:sku"/>
            <xsd:element name="price" type="xsd:double"/>
            <xsd:element name="quantityAvailable" type="xsd:integer"/>
            <xsd:element name="itemPicture" type="attref:swaRef"/>
         </xsd:sequence>
      </xsd:complexType>

      <xsd:element name="StockAvailability"
                   type="avail:availabilityType" />
   </xsd:schema>
</types>
```

When a `wsdl:part` definition contains a reference to a datatype that includes the `attref:swref` schema type definition, that part should only be referenced by a `soap:body` or `soap:header` element [R2940]. In the updated `PriceCheck` service description, the `avail:StockAvailability` element contains the attachment reference. This element is referenced by the `result` part in the `PriceCheckResponse` message. This message is output for the `checkPrice` operation, and the `result` part is referenced by the `parts` attribute on the `soap:body` element in the first MIME part definition:

```
<!-- A PriceCheckResponse consists of an availability structure, -->
<!-- defined above.                                              -->
<message name="PriceCheckResponse">
   <part name="result" element="avail:StockAvailability"/>
   <part name="picture" type="xsd:base64Binary"/>
</message>
```

...

```
   <!-- Binding definitions -->
   <binding name="PriceCheckSOAPBinding" type="pc:PriceCheckPortType">
    <soap:binding style="document"
      transport="http://schemas.xmlsoap.org/soap/http" />
    <operation name="checkPrice">
      <soap:operation
        soapAction="http://www.skatestown.com/services/PriceCheck/checkPrice" />
      <input>
        <soap:body use="literal" />
      </input>
      <output>
        <mime:multipartRelated>
          <mime:part>
            <soap:body part="result" use="literal" />
          </mime:part>
          <mime:part>
            <mime:content part="picture" type="image/jpeg" />
          </mime:part>
        </mime:multipartRelated>
      </output>
    </operation>
   </binding>
```

Based on this Web service description, the resulting response message would look like
the following:

```
MIME-Version: 1.0
Content-Type: Multipart/Related; boundary=MIME_boundary; type=text/xml;

--MIME_boundary
Content-Type: text/xml; charset=UTF-8
Content-Transfer-Encoding: 8bit
Content-ID: <rootpart@www.skatestown.com>

<?xml version='1.0' ?>
<SOAP-ENV:Envelope xmlns:SOAP-ENV="http://schemas.xmlsoap.org/soap/envelope/">
  <SOAP-ENV:Body>
    <ns1:StockAvailability xmlns:ns1="http://www.skatestown.com/ns/availability">
      <ns1:sku>...</ns1:sku>
      <ns1:price>...</ns1:price>
      <ns1:quantityAvailable>...</ns1:quantityAvailable>
      <ns1:itemPicture>
        cid:picture=DE563490-EA20-5505-9DA4-45B632F52AC3@
➥www.skatestown.com
      </ns1:itemPicture>
    </ns:StockAvailability>
  </SOAP-ENV:Body>
</SOAP-ENV:Envelope>
```

```
--MIME_boundary
Content-Type: image/jpeg
Content-Transfer-Encoding: binaryContent-ID: <picture=DE563490-EA20-5505-9DA4-
➥45B632F52AC3@www.skatestown.com>

...JPEG File...
--MIME_boundary--
```

Message Sender and Receiver Processing for Attachments

A message sender can send a message using SOAP with Attachments only when the MIME binding is specified for the associated input or output message [R2902]. Although the content of a message must contain all defined MIME parts, the message sender can include additional parts that aren't defined in the MIME binding [R2923].

When processing a message with MIME parts, the receiver of the message can't assume that the parts in the message will be in the same order as they appear in the WSDL description [R2912]. For example, the start attribute on the Content-Type HTTP header field should be used to locate the root part. In addition, the message receiver should not use the ordering of the nonroot MIME parts to infer any semantics for the message [R2921]. If an envelope contains a URI reference to an attachment within the message, the receiver is allowed to ignore this reference [R2918].

Summary of Attachments Profile 1.0 Requirements

Table 13.3 summarizes the requirements for this profile mapped to the corresponding conformance targets. Since some requirements apply to more than one target, they are listed in more than one row in this table.

For the Attachments Profile 1.0, the conformance claim URI is http://ws-i.org/profiles/attachments/1.0.

Table 13.3 **Summary of Attachments Profile 1.0 Requirements**

Conformance Target	Profile Requirement
WSDL Document	—
wsdl:message	—
wsdl:part	R2940
wsdl:binding	R2901, R2941
wsdl:operation	—
wsdl:input	—
wsdl:output	—
soap:header	R2905, R2906
mime:multipartRelated	R2911, R2917
mime:part	R2907, R2908, R2912, R2947
mime:content	R2903, R2904, R2909, R2910, R2933, R2943, R2944, R2946

Table 13.3 **Continued**

Conformance Target	Profile Requirement
wsdl:fault	R2930
SOAP envelope	R2913, R2928
HTTP message	R2915, R2916, R2919, R2925, R2926, R2927, R2929, R2931, R2934, R2935, R2936, R2942
Content-Type header	R2917, R2922, R2925, R2932, R2945
Roles	—
Service provider	R2920
Message receiver	R2912, R2918, R2921, R2922
Message sender	R2902, R2923

Basic Security Profile 1.0

At the time this book was written, the Basic Security Profile was still being developed by the WS-I Organization. This section presents an overview of the type of requirements that will appear in this profile.

The Basic Security Profile will focus on two types of conformance targets. The first type of conformance target is an *artifact*: a secure SOAP envelope that provides integrity and confidentiality protection for a SOAP envelope. The second type of conformance target is for the message sender and message receiver. The *message sender* generates and sends the message using the appropriate security protocols, and the *message receiver* receives and processes the message based on the security protocols that were used.

The Basic Security Profile will focus on the following topics. Refer to Chapter 9, "Securing Web Services," for more information on these items:

- *Transport layer security*—This portion of the profile will contain the requirements for transport protocols.
- *SOAP message security*—This level of security will be based on the Web Services Security: SOAP Message Security specification being worked on by the OASIS Web Services Security (WSS) Technical Committee (TC) (http://www.oasis-open.org/committees/tc_home.php?wg_abbrev=wss). This specification describes how to ensure the integrity and confidentiality of a SOAP message and provides single message authentication.
- *Username and X.509 certificate token profiles*—The Basis Security Profile should include requirements for how to use these token profiles, which are defined in specifications that are being worked on by the OASIS WSS TC.
- *XML Signature and XML Encryption*—The Web Service Security: SOAP Message Security specification utilizes both XML Signature and XML Encryption. This portion of the profile will define guidelines and constraints for using these two standards.

Although this profile isn't complete yet, Al Rosen has decided to review drafts as they become available. It's important for SkatesTown to have both interoperable and secure Web services.

WS-I Sample Applications

As previously noted, the WS-I Organization has three primary deliverables: profiles, sample applications, and test tools. The previous sections of this chapter described some of the profiles that are being produced by this organization. The purpose of the WS-I Sample Applications is to show how to build interoperable Web services. The sample applications are implemented based on a set of usage scenarios that conform to a WS-I profile. A complete description of the applications can be found in the WS-I Sample Application Supply Chain Management Architecture document (`http://ws-i.org/ SampleApplications/SupplyChainManagement/2003-07/SCMArchitecture1. 01-BdAD.pdf`).

The usage scenario is based on a Supply Chain Management application used by a fictional consumer electronics retailer. It consists of three systems: Retailer System, Manufacturing System, and Demo System. Figure 13.3 contains an overview of these Web services and the basic interaction patterns.

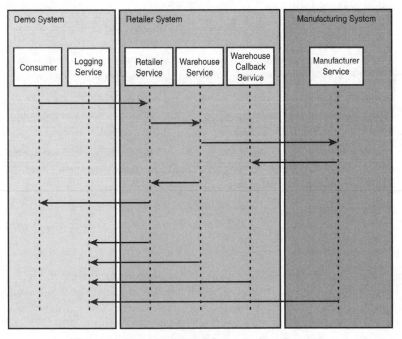

Figure 13.3   WS-I Sample Application architecture

Each system contains one or more Web service. The retailer system includes the Retailer, Warehouse, and Warehouse Callback service. The Retailer service represents the storefront for the consumer electronics retailer. This service receives orders from the consumer and then uses up to three Warehouses (each represented by a Warehouse service) to fulfill the orders. If the stock on hand drops below a preset threshold, then a warehouse will order additional inventory using one of three Manufacturer Web services in the manufacturing system. All the Web service interactions are logged using the Logging service in the demo system.

The WSDL documents for the Web services that form the WS-I Sample Application provide examples of how to build Web service descriptions that conform to the WS-I Basic Profile. For example, the Retailer and Warehouse service use an RPC-literal binding. Table 13.4 lists each Web service, the binding it supports, other primary characteristics, and the location of its Web service description.

Table 13.4 **WS-I Sample Applications**

	Service Definition	**Binding**	**Other Characteristics**
1	Retailer	RPC-literal	Message part definitions with both type and element attributes
	http://www.ws-i.org/SampleApplications/SupplyChainManagement/ 2002-08/Retailer.wsdl		
2	Warehouse	RPC-literal	Message part definitions with both type and element attributes
	http://www.ws-i.org/SampleApplications/SupplyChainManagement/ 2002-08/Warehouse.wsdl		
3	Warehouse Callback	document-literal	Callback interaction pattern
	http://www.ws-i.org/SampleApplications/SupplyChainManagement/ 2002-08/Manfacturer.wsdl		
4	Manufacturer	document-literal	SOAP faults, headers, and header faults
	http://www.ws-i.org/SampleApplications/SupplyChainManagement/ 2002-08/Manfacturer.wsdl		
5	Logging	document-literal	One-way operations
	http://www.ws-i.org/SampleApplications/SupplyChainManagement/ 2002-08/LoggingFacility.wsdl		

Ten companies implemented the WS-I Sample Applications on their Web service platforms. These implementations have been tested together through the WS-I Sample Applications Working Group to ensure that they interoperate. You can download the source code for these sample application implementations from the WS-I Web site (http://ws-i.org/implementation.aspx).

WS-I Test Tools

The third primary deliverable from the WS-I Organization is the WS-I Test Tools. These test tools provide an easy way to determine if a Web service conforms to the requirements in the WS-I Basic Profile. The latest version of the WS-I Test Tools are available on the WS-I Web site: http://www.ws-i.org/implementation.aspx. The test tools have been implemented in Java and in C#.

> **Note**
>
> Portions of this section on WS-I Test Tools are derived from an article that was published on the IBM DeveloperWorks site (http://www.ibm.com/developerworks/webservices).

The test tools consist of two tools: the monitor and analyzer. The *monitor* provides an unobtrusive way to log Web service messages using a man-in-the-middle approach, which means that the monitor sits between the service requestor and the Web service monitoring the message traffic. The WS-I monitor tool is similar in concept to the Apache Axis tcpmon application described in Chapter 5, "Implementing Web Services with Apache Axis." The purpose of the *analyzer* is to determine if a set of Web service–related artifacts conforms to the requirements in the WS-I Basic Profile. There are three basic types of artifacts:

- messages—The set of messages logged by the monitor
- description—The service description for the Web service (this includes any referenced XML schema definitions), if the location of the WSDL document is available
- discovery—The UDDI entries for a Web service, if the UDDI entries reference a WSDL-based service description

In general, the messages, description, and discovery artifacts correspond to the MESSAGE, DESCRIPTION, and REGDATA profile conformance targets, respectively. Since the test tools were designed to be noninvasive, most of the profile requirements for the INSTANCE, CONSUMER, REGISTRY, SENDER, and RECEIVER conformance targets aren't validated.

Figure 13.4 provides an overview of the WS-I Test Tools architecture.

Monitor Overview

The monitor contains two primary functions: message interceptor and message logger. The message interceptor intercepts messages that are sent from a service requestor to a Web service and from a Web service back to the service requestor. The logger formats the intercepted messages into a standard format and then writes them out to a message log. With these two functions, a single monitor can intercept and log messages from multiple Web services. The monitor functions are controlled by a configuration file that defines the association between the ports the monitor listens on for incoming messages, and the Web service location where the monitor should forward the messages.

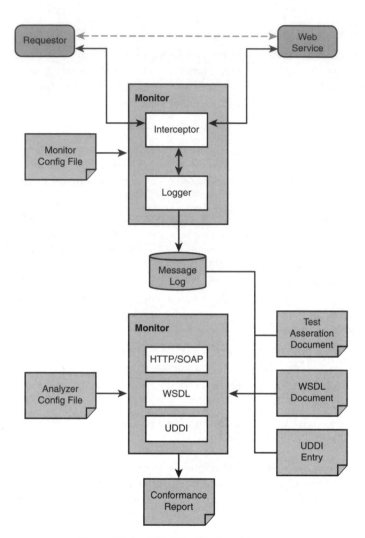

Figure 13.4   WS-I Test Tools architecture

When using the monitor, the service requestor views it as if it was the Web service. All SOAP messages are sent to the monitor instead of the Web service. Since this isn't the normal mode of operation for the requestor, there are three basic ways to do this:

- Alter the requestor to point at the monitor instead of the Web service
- Move the Web service to a new location and run the monitor in its place
- Alter the Web service endpoint information that the requestor uses (the value of the location attribute on the soap:address element in a WSDL document)

Monitor Configuration File

The monitor requires one input file: an XML document containing the configuration options that tell the monitor what it needs to monitor and where it needs to log the messages it intercepts. Listing 13.7 contains the monitor configuration file used to log messages for the `PriceCheck` Web service.

Listing 13.7   **WS–I Monitor Configuration Tile**

```
<?xml version="1.0" encoding="utf-8" ?>
<configuration xmlns="http://www.ws-i.org/testing/2003/03/monitorConfig/">
  <comment>
     This configuration file is used to log messages for
     the PriceCheck Web service.
  </comment>
  <logFile replace="true" location="log.xml">
    <addStyleSheet href="c:/wsi-test-tools/common/xsl/log.xsl" type="text/xsl"/>
  </logFile>
  <logDuration>600</logDuration>
  <cleanupTimeoutSeconds>3</cleanupTimeoutSeconds>
  <manInTheMiddle>
    <redirect>
      <comment>Redirect messages from port 4040 to localhost:8080.</comment>
      <listenPort>4040</listenPort>
      <schemeAndHostPort>http://localhost:8080</schemeAndHostPort>
      <maxConnections>1000</maxConnections>
      <readTimeoutSeconds>15</readTimeoutSeconds>
    </redirect>
  </manInTheMiddle>
</configuration>
```

A complete description of the XML elements in this file can be found in the User Guide for the WS-I Test Tools.

Message Log File

The log file created by the monitor is an XML document (see Listing 13.8). This file contains runtime information for the monitor tool, the monitor configuration information, and the messages that were intercepted while the monitor was running. The log files can be viewed as an XML document, or a stylesheet is available to view it in an HTML format.

Listing 13.8   **WS–I Message Log File**

```
<?xml version="1.0" encoding="UTF-8"?>
<?xml-stylesheet href="c:\wsi-test-tools\common\xsl\log.xsl" type="text/xsl" ?>
<log timestamp="2003-12-01T08:09:16.354"
```

Listing 13.8 **Continued**

```
    xmlns="http://www.ws-i.org/testing/2003/03/log/"
    xmlns:wsi-log="http://www.ws-i.org/testing/2003/03/log/"
    xmlns:wsi-monConfig="http://www.ws-i.org/testing/2003/03/monitorConfig/"
    xmlns:xsi="http://www.w3.org/2001/XMLSchema-instance">
  <monitor version="1.0" releaseDate="2003-10-16">
    <implementer name="Web Services Interoperability Organization"
      location="http://www.ws-i.org/implementation.aspx"/>
    <environment>
      <runtime name="Java(TM) 2 Runtime Environment, Standard Edition"
        version="1.3.1"/>
      <operatingSystem name="Windows XP" version="5.1"/>
      <xmlParser name="Apache Xerces" version="Xerces-J 2.2.1"/>
    </environment>
    <wsi-monConfig:configuration>
      <wsi-monConfig:logFile replace="true" location="traceLog.xml">
        <wsi-common:addStyleSheet href="../common/xsl/log.xsl" type="text/xsl" />
      </wsi-monConfig:logFile>
      <wsi-monConfig:logDuration>3600</wsi-monConfig:logDuration>
      <wsi-monConfig:cleanupTimeoutSeconds>3</wsi-monConfig:cleanupTimeoutSeconds>
      <wsi-monConfig:manInTheMiddle>
        <wsi-monConfig:redirect>
          <wsi-monConfig:listenPort>4040</wsi-monConfig:listenPort>
          <wsi-monConfig:schemeAndHostPort>http://localhost:8080</wsi-
➥monConfig:schemeAndHostPort>
          <wsi-monConfig:maxConnections>1000</wsi-monConfig:maxConnections>
          <wsi-monConfig:readTimeoutSeconds>15</wsi-monConfig:readTimeoutSeconds>
        </wsi-monConfig:redirect>
      </wsi-monConfig:manInTheMiddle>
    </wsi-monConfig:configuration>
  </monitor>
  <messageEntry xsi:type="wsi-log:httpMessageEntry" ID="1" conversationID="2"
    type="request" timestamp="2003-12-02T08:10:14.657">
    <messageContent>...</messageContent>
    <senderHostAndPort>127.0.0.1:1527</senderHostAndPort>
    <receiverHostAndPort>localhost:8080</receiverHostAndPort>
    <httpHeaders>...</httpHeaders>
  </messageEntry>
  <messageEntry xsi:type="wsi-log:httpMessageEntry" ID="2" conversationID="2"
    type="response" timestamp="2003-12-02T08:11:05.243">
    <messageContent>...</messageContent>
    <senderHostAndPort>localhost:8080</senderHostAndPort>
    <receiverHostAndPort>127.0.0.1:1527</receiverHostAndPort>
    <httpHeaders>...</httpHeaders>
  </messageEntry>...
</log>
```

Analyzer Overview

The analyzer tool determines whether the artifacts for a Web service conform to the Basic Profile by processing a set of test assertions. A *test assertion* is a testable expression for one or more requirements in the Basic Profile. All the test assertions are listed in a *test assertion document*, which is an XML document whose contents are segmented by artifact type (discovery, description, and messages).

The input for the analyzer includes the location of the test assertion document and references to the Web service artifacts. The output from the analyzer is a conformance report. All this information is specified in the analyzer configuration file.

Analyzer Configuration File

Just like the monitor tool, the analyzer uses an XML document to define its configuration options. Listing 13.9 contains the analyzer configuration file used to analyze the PriceCheck Web service for conformance to the WS-I Basic Profile.

Listing 13.9 **WS-I Analyzer Configuration File**

```xml
<?xml version="1.0" encoding="UTF-8"?>
<configuration name="SkatesTown StockAvailableNotification Analyzer Configuration"
    xmlns="http://www.ws-i.org/testing/2003/03/analyzerConfig/">
  <description>
    This file is used to analyze the SkatesTown PriceCheck WSDL document.
  </description>

  <verbose>false</verbose>
  <assertionResults type="all" messageEntry="true" failureMessage="true"/>
  <reportFile replace="true" location="pcReport.xml">
    <addStyleSheet href="c:/wsi-test-tools/common/xsl/report.xsl"
      type="text/xsl"/>
  </reportFile>
  <testAssertionsFile>
    c:/wsi-test-tools/common/profiles/BasicProfileTestAssertions.xml
  </testAssertionsFile>
  <wsdlReference>
    <wsdlElement type="port"
        parentElementName="PriceCheckService"
        namespace="http://www.skatestown.com/services/PriceCheck">
      PriceCheck
    </wsdlElement>
    <wsdlURI>
      pricecheck.wsdl
    </wsdlURI>
  </wsdlReference>
</configuration>
```

Test Assertion Document

Figure 13.5 contains an HTML rendering of a single test assertion. Each test assertion has a unique identifier and contains all of the information that is needed to understand how the analyzer will process the assertion. For this example, the test assertion identifier is WSI2406. The purpose of the test assertion is to analyze a WSDL binding element to verify that the value of the use attribute is "literal" when it is used on the body, fault, header, and header fault SOAP binding elements.

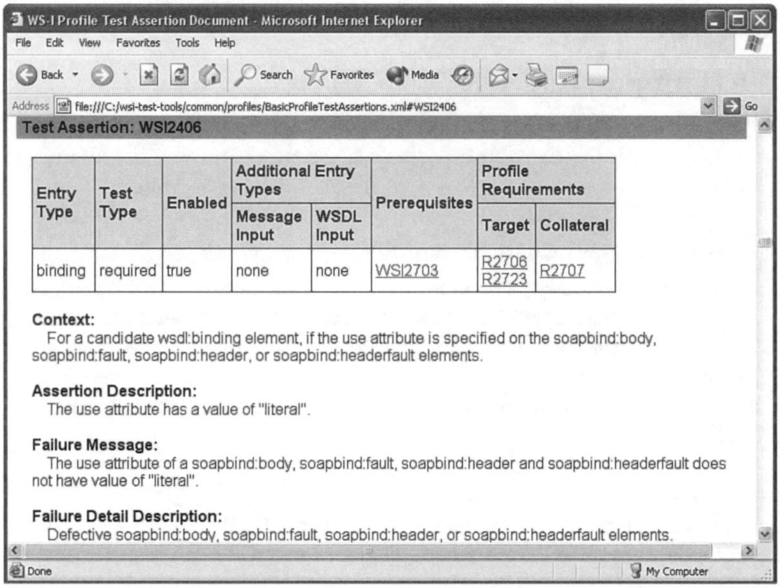

Figure 13.5   Example of a test assertion

You can find a complete description of each field in the test assertion document in the WS-I Analyzer Tool Functional Specification. When you're reviewing the results from the analyzer tool, the contents of the test assertion will help you isolate the cause of the conformance failure. For example, the `Assertion Description` field explains what was tested and the `Profile Requirements` field contains a direct reference to the requirements in the profile that are associated with the test assertion. It's important to note that a test assertion may reference one or more profile requirements, and a profile requirement may be referenced by more than one test assertion.

Profile Conformance Report

The output from the analyzer is a conformance report. The conformance report contains the results for all the test assertions that were processed. As was true with the message log file, you can view the report file as an XML document, or a stylesheet is available so that you can view it in an HTML format.

A test assertion may have one of five possible results:

- `passed`—The test assertion was processed, and it passed the stated assertion.
- `failed`—An error was detected when processing the test assertion.
- `warning`—The test assertion failed, but the test type was `recommended`.
- `notApplicable`—Either the context conditions didn't exist or a prerequisite test assertion failed.
- `missingInput`—The primary type of data wasn't specified as input to the analyzer, or it didn't exist in the specified artifact.

If any of the test assertions fails, then the Web service that was analyzed doesn't conform to the Basic Profile.

The HTML format for the report contains a couple of summaries that aren't available in the XML version of the report file. The overall summary will indicate if the specified artifacts passed or failed conformance. If the overall summary result is `failed`, then you should look through the detailed test assertion results to determine which test assertions failed. The detailed test assertion results are listed by entry (WSDL binding element, message log entry ID, and so on). Reviewing the test assertion description and the associated profile requirements will help you understand what you need to change to make your Web service conform to the Basic Profile.

Figure 13.6 shows a portion of the conformance report for the original `PriceCheck` Web service. This portion of the report shows that test assertion WSI2406 failed.

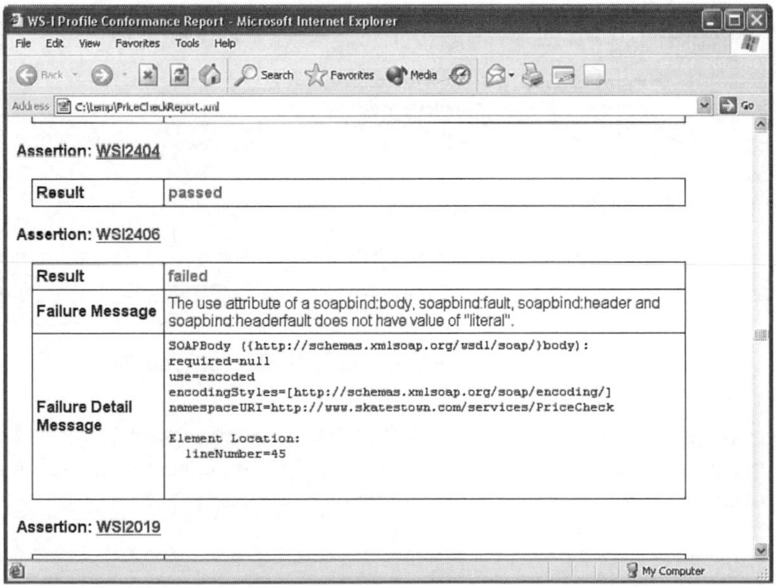

Figure 13.6   WS-I Profile conformance report for the original
`PriceCheck` Web service

This test assertion failed because the use attribute on a `soap:body`, `soap:fault`, `soap:header`, or `soap:headerfault` element didn't contain a value of `literal`. The failure detail message indicates that the use attribute for the `soap:body` element contained a value of `encoded`. By selecting the WSI2406 link, you can view the entire test assertion definition (see Figure 13.5).

The test assertion description contains a reference to the profile requirements that were used to create the test assertion. By selecting the profile requirement links, you can view the requirement description in the profile document. This test assertion contains a reference to two target profile requirements and one collateral profile requirement. The target requirements are verified by the test assertion, whereas the collateral requirements aren't. The test assertion process can use the collateral requirements when verifying the target requirements. In the example in Figure 13.7, the collateral requirement is R2707; this specifies that the default value for the use attribute on the `soap:body`, `soap:fault`, `soap:header`, and `soap:headerfault` elements is `literal`.

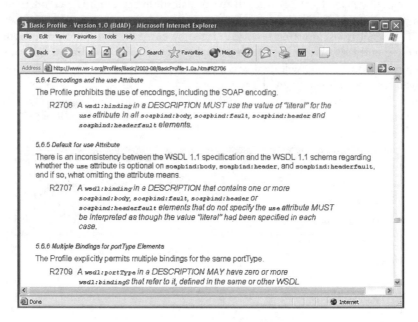

Figure 13.7 Collateral and target profile requirement

The target requirements are R2706 and R2723 (see both Figures 13.7 and 13.8), which indicate that the use attribute on the `soap:body`, `soap:fault`, `soap:header`, and `soap:headerfault` elements must have a value of `"literal"`.

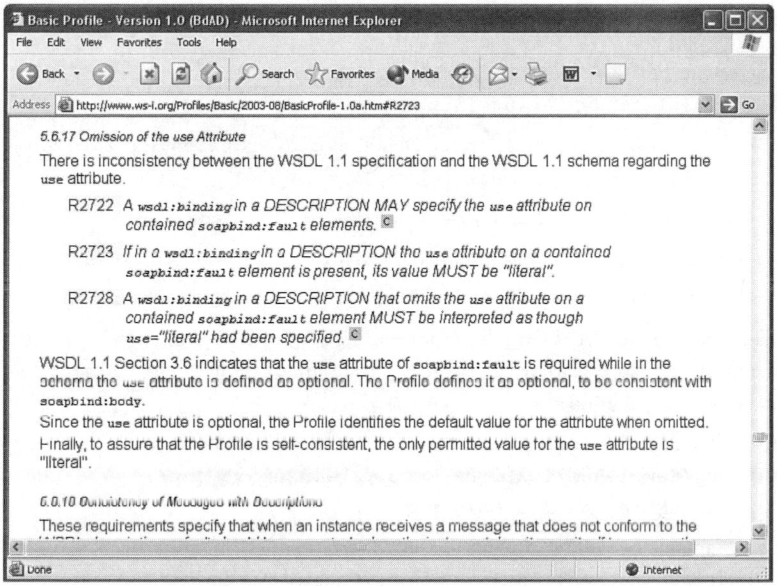

Figure 13.8   Target profile requirement

Summary

Interoperability between a Web service and the service requestor is important to the success of Web service technology. It's important to ensure that both SkatesTown's customers and business partners can use the company's Web services even when they're using different runtime platforms.

In this chapter, we've reviewed the interoperability guidelines for using Web service standards that the WS-I organization is publishing in the form of a profile. Although the Web service standards are intended to provide interoperability, in some instances ambiguities or inconsistencies make it difficult to achieve interoperability. The WS-I profiles provide clarifications and guidelines for using these standards so that you can use them to develop interoperable Web services. Conforming to these profiles will help ensure interoperability when you're using Web service technologies on different platforms.

Although the current set of profiles target the basic Web service standards, future profiles will focus on topics such as reliable messaging and business process management. Updating its Web services to conform to the current set of WS-I profiles will help SkatesTown achieve its interoperability goals for its Web services.

Resources

- *WS-I Basic Profile 1.0*—http://www.ws-i.org/Profiles/
  BasicProfile-1.0-2004-04-16.html

- *WS-I Basic Profile 1.0 Errata*—http://ws-i.org/Profiles/Basic/|2003-
  08/BasicProfile-1.0-errata-1.htm

- *WS-I Basic Profile 1.1*—http://www.ws-i.org/Documents.aspx

- *WS-I Simple SOAP Binding Profile 1.0*—http://www.ws-i.org/Documents.aspx

- *WS-I Attachment Profile 1.0*—http://www.ws-i.org/Documents.aspx

- *WS-I Basic Profile 1.0 Usage Scenarios*—http://ws-
  i.org/SampleApplications/SupplyChainManagement/
  2003-04/UsageScenarios-1.01-BdAD.pdf

- *WS-I Supply Chain Management Use Case Model*—http://
  ws-i.org/SampleApplications/SupplyChainManagement/
  2003-04/SCMUseCases1.0-BdAD.pdf

- *WS-I Sample Application Supply Chain Management Architecture*—http://
  ws-i.org/SampleApplications/SupplyChainManagement/2003-
  07/SCMArchitecture1.01-BdAD.pdf

- *WS-I Monitor Tool Functional Specification*—http://
  ws-i.org/Testing/Specs/MonitorFunctionalSpecification_BdAD_10.pdf

- *WS-I Analyzer Tool Functional Specification*—http://
  ws-i.org/Testing/Specs/AnalyzerFunctionalSpecification_BdAD_10.pdf

- *WS-I Test Assertion Document*—http://
  ws-i.org/Testing/Tools/2003/11/BasicProfileTestAssertions.xml

- *WS-I Test Tools Download Site*—http://ws-i.org/implementation.aspx

- *Eclipse Web Service Validation Tools Project*—http://eclipse.org/wsvt/

14

Web Services Pragmatics

THE AUTHORS OF THIS BOOK DEEPLY BELIEVE in the promise of Web services and are optimistic about their future. We believe that the combination of standards and technologies described so far in the book enables tremendous advances in distributed computing and systems integration. Yet we're realists, and we know that we're just at the dawn of the Web services revolution. Much work remains to be done. Some of it requires true innovation, and some of it requires time for the computing industry to rationalize and absorb the innovation that has already taken place. Remember, in early 2000 we only had SOAP. Now—well, you know how much you've had to cover to get to this point in the book.

We're conscious that we write about Web services from the bleeding edge—our companies are the thought leaders in this space. But we're also connected to the real world. We've talked to countless enterprises about their active projects and future plans in the Web services space. Technology choice is just one of the variables in a complex equation that IT organizations are trying to optimize every day. When Web services are deployed in enterprises, a plethora of issues outside the scope of core technologies emerge: organizational, budget and operations impact, vendor selection, legacy integration, and so on. These factors have a significant role to play in the ultimate decision about when and how Web services are adopted. In this chapter, we take a step back from the world of standards and technology and look more broadly at the benefits and challenges of using Web services, right now, in the enterprise.

In an ideal world, this chapter would have taught the best practices of putting Web services into production. The reality is that the Web services field is too young for proven best practices to have developed. Further, the use cases that call for Web services are too diverse and the organizations adopting them are too different for one true set of best practices to ever exist. Instead, we want to help you think about Web services in the context of your organization. After reading this chapter, you should have a framework in place that can guide you and help you ask the right questions from the broad strategy and organizational level down to the specifics of vendor selection, system architecture, and operations.

Enterprise Adoption of Web Services

Vendors of Web services technologies have a growing portfolio of standards work, infrastructure products, and tools that will greatly improve the delivery of enterprise IT services. As we mentioned in Chapter 1, "Web Services Overview and Service-Oriented Architectures," Web services significantly lower the cost of system integration. They enable business agility by making IT more responsive to business needs. They shorten the time to market for new service delivery. They facilitate tighter partnerships. In short, Web services are what IT departments have been waiting for all these years. Or are they really? The truth is more nuanced.

Clearly, Web services are a significant development. Their adoption brings multiple benefits, many of which this book has covered in depth. Eventually, Web services will change the way IT is done. However, there is much more work to do. In fact, the broad adoption of Web services has consistently failed to meet inflated industry expectations in the past several years.

Surveys like those conducted by the Software & Information Industry Association (SIIA) show that software vendors consider Web services much more important than their customers do. Enterprises have had to deal with system integration issues over decades and many platform shifts. With every shift, the IT function becomes more flexible and powerful, but the process is far from pain free. Customers have realistic expectations about what new technologies can deliver in the short run and aren't willing to rush in head-first regardless of the promises vendors make. The recent economic downturn didn't help matters. The rate of Web services deployment is therefore less related to doubts about the long-term promise of the technology and more a result of a myriad of positive and negative forces that drive or hinder the deployment of Web services. To understand the nature of these adoption drivers, it helps to look holistically at the interplay between business and technology in an enterprise's decision-making process (see Figure 14.1).

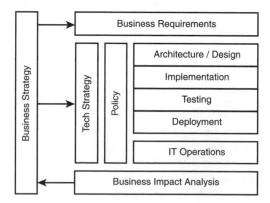

Figure 14.1   Interplay between business and technology decision
making in Web services adoption

Table 14.1 gives a flavor of some of the enabling and restraining forces companies face in rolling out SOA.

Table 14.1 **Positive and Negative Drivers for SOA Adoption**

Type of Driver	Positive Drivers	Negative Drivers
Business strategy	Agile business	Cost of implementation
	Tighter partner/supplier integration	Slower than expected adoption
Business operations	Real-time business activity monitoring (BAM)	Lack of products with mature business-level capabilities
	Access to data for business intelligence (BI)	Lagging integration into existing systems
	Consistent business exception handling	
Organizational impact	Opportunity to develop new skills and capabilities	Shortage of internal skills and understanding
	Availability of consulting services	Organizational inertia
	Headcount reduction through automation	Fear of losing jobs
Technology strategy	Mergers and acquisitions	Difficult vendor selection
	Lower cost of integration	Not a full integration solution
	Industrywide standards	Standards still in flux
	Access and exchange of data inside and outside the enterprise	
	Interoperable applications	
Architecture/design	Robust document-based interactions	Lack of consistent vocabularies and process flows
	Web services support in products	Unclear policies and best practices
	Availability of services	Lack of consistent discovery mechanisms
	Multi-layered systems	
	Composable *quality of service (QoS)* 📖	
Implementation/testing	Faster time-to-release	Tools still immature
	Availability of tools and frameworks	Some interoperability issues between platforms
	Faster/cheaper response to change	
Deployment/operations	Doesn't disturb legacy systems	Performance impact
	Adds a layer of tunable scalability/reliability	Yet another layer to include in capacity planning and root-cause analysis
	Consistent *SLA* 📖 monitoring	Immature management/monitoring tools
	Consistent exception handling	

The negative drivers fall into two main categories: those related to the state of adoption of Web services and those related to the inherent limitations of the technologies. Over the next few years, standards and technology platforms will mature, minimizing the impact of the first set of restraining forces. Minimizing the effect of the rest of the restraining forces requires significant innovations in system integration.

In a few cases, the challenges to SOA adoption have to do with limitations of companies' business models that prevent them from benefiting from the flexibility and dynamism that SOAs can enable. This is an exciting area for discussion but, unfortunately, we don't have the space to cover it here.

Time-Based Adoption Challenges

The rapid pace of evolution in the Web services space is putting strain on companies adopting the technology. On one side are the many benefits of SOAs. On the other are the costs of implementing change. Standards continue to evolve and, despite the best efforts of the industry, interoperability issues remain, especially at the higher levels of the SOA standards stacks, such as service directories and service assurances. This is to be expected, because vendors are blazing new ground in distributed computing. The good news is that if enterprises aren't broadly deploying Web services yet, they're at least seriously experimenting with them, building up the core competencies of their IT organizations.

On this stage, many small vendors focusing on Web services are vying for the attention of customers. Their value propositions cover a wide gamut:

- Being first-to-market in some area of SOA enablement, thus enabling early adopters in the enterprise and independent software vendors (ISVs) who want to deliver Web services–enabled products.

- Delivering end-to-end QoS management and monitoring capabilities independently of the implementation platform so that enterprises can deploy SOA on top of the current application server technologies while still maintaining a high level of security, reliability, and visibility.

- Developing deep expertise in Web services–based deployments in a specific vertical or a small set of verticals, including integration with industry-specific vocabularies and process flows.

- Providing consulting and best-practices expertise to push organizations that want to adopt SOA forward despite the lack of internal skills.

The economic climate following the burst of the tech bubble has not been kind to start-ups and small companies. Enterprises want guaranteed return on investment before procuring products and services from vendors that may not be around in a year or two. The *status quo* of Web services adoption is presenting them with tough vendor selection choices:

- Should enterprises delay their adoption of Web services until standards and platforms have stabilized enough to the extent that a platform vendor of choice can be selected? This wait-and-see attitude will delay the benefits of Web services.

- Should enterprises go with existing platform vendors' offerings and be prepared to fill in any gaps by leveraging existing infrastructure and custom programming? For example, should message reliability be delivered through traditional message-oriented middleware (MOM), and should the enterprise develop custom SOAP headers for facets such as logging and auditing?

- Should enterprises instead go with the basic platform vendor offering and back fill missing functionality using a startup's technology? For example, the Web services monitoring capabilities of current platforms are limited, but there are a number of small companies with platform independent offerings in this space. What process should enterprises go through to choose a reliable small vendor that is likely to survive the turbulent cycle of growth as the industry matures?

In times like these, enterprises look to best practices to help evaluate adoption options. Unfortunately, as we mentioned at the beginning of the chapter, the Web services industry is too young to have evolved solid best practices. The good news is that things should get better over time.

Inherent Limitations of SOA

At their core, Web services are about integrating software components, applications, and systems. Advances in Web services can positively impact the entire integration market. On the other hand, some of the key challenges facing the integration industry manifest themselves as roadblocks on the path to more ubiquitous Web services deployment. In Chapter 1, we claimed that application integration was a major motivator behind Web services and SOA. Completing an integration project requires a blend of product capabilities and services. Traditionally, integration projects have been service-heavy. Many services involved boilerplate work to connect systems together. SOAs promise to ease that pain.

However, it's important to understand that XML and Web services can't significantly increase the product-to-service ratio by themselves: They only offer part of the solution. Over the years, enterprises have learned that there is a lot more to integration than being able to send messages between components, applications, and systems. Two key issues that enterprises are concerned about are semantic mapping and best practices.

The Semantic Mapping Constraint

If you send a letter in English to someone who speaks only Japanese, you won't be able to communicate without the help of a translator. If you send temperature readings in Fahrenheit units to someone expecting them in Celsius units, there is potential for confusion and error unless someone makes the right conversion. This is the nature of the semantic mapping problem: How does party A know what party B is communicating about, and can party A extract the exact information that party B wants to impart? This problem is rampant in the computer industry, where applications have incompatible APIs and use proprietary data formats. Because current techniques offer no clear separation between syntax and semantics, much of the effort in integrating applications is spent negotiating between different data formats. Dozens of companies deliver data-mapping tools and technologies, but they typically solve a point integration problem between two applications and do a poor job of dealing with the next application that becomes part of the integration.

Virtual exchanges 📖 offer an architecture that scales better with the number of applications. Rather than integrate applications point-to-point, which leads to quadratic complexity (there are $N*(N-1)$ possible connections between N applications), exchanges use a hub-and-spoke model. In that architecture, all applications know how to communicate with a standard vocabulary that the exchange provides. This leads to linear complexity for the integration problem as a whole but radically increases the initial cost of integrating the first few applications. Information exchange can't begin before a standard vocabulary is agreed on. Even within narrow vertical industry segments, this type of "super-vocabulary" can take years to develop. It must cover the needs of all exchange participants. This architecture also poses significant change management challenges; it becomes difficult to evolve a vocabulary that so many applications depend on.

Web services technologies are great for discovery, description, and messaging of information, but they currently fall short of addressing the core semantic mapping problem. XML, namespaces, schema, and WSDL provide better tools than anything the industry has previously had to describe and evolve complex data formats, but they also can't deal directly with the problem. There are technical solutions to the problem, but they remain research projects. The *Semantic Web* 📖 offers one approach; it's a great vision, but it will take decades to bring to reality. More pragmatically, enterprise data dictionaries and meta-data management tools add a basic semantics layer on top of enterprise data that can facilitate faster data mapping for integration.

It doesn't help that there is some confusion in the market about the true capabilities of Web services technologies. The hype surrounding XML has made some believe that semantic mapping is no longer a big issue. They're bitterly disappointed to find that, as always, a significant portion of the integration effort is spent in this area.

Lack of Best Practices

Enterprises are process and policy driven in their adoption of technology. Best practices offer reusable templates of processes and policies that facilitate successful deployment. Encapsulating the wisdom of many successes and failures, best practices guide teams to success. They're especially useful in environments where teams implementing technologies aren't deeply experienced. Best practices are badly needed in the Web services space. Unfortunately, they're just now emerging at various levels of the technology stack, and this immaturity of best practices is a hindrance to adoption of Web services.

Enterprises are looking for three broad levels of best practices:

- *Enterprise-level policies*, dealing with how SOA should be approached from the perspective of the entire organization
- *Design-time policies*, addressing the architecture and design of Web services-based systems
- *Run-time policies*, which typically focus on the definition and enforcement of SLAs and other system behaviors important to the enterprise

Top-Down Versus Bottom-Up

SOA offers fundamental benefits that go significantly beyond the capabilities of current integration technologies. This points to a long-term trend of most applications exposing Web services interfaces. From the perspective of senior technology strategists and managers, this poses a challenge: How should enterprises go from no Web services deployments to Web services being everywhere? It may seem like a trivial question, but it has a huge impact on IT organizations and the vendors supplying them with products. The answer often determines who evaluates Web services–based projects and sets the standards for vendor selection within these projects. There are three main models for deploying Web services within an enterprise: top-down, bottom-up, and, not surprisingly, hybrid.

Top-Down Deployment

Some larger enterprises are moving toward Web services deployments as part of an overarching adoption of SOA. An indication of the presence of this approach is the existence of an enterprisewide or business–unit level standards group controlling Web services deployments. The goals of the group center on defining the mechanisms for cross-application integration, setting interoperability requirements for projects, and identifying the criteria for Web services vendor selection. Typically, these enterprises will choose one strategic vendor or integrator to help with the rollout of SOA or enable the enterprise for cross-application integration using Web services. This happens through a lengthy process: Multiple vendors are interviewed, and their products are evaluated for a pilot keystone application. The ability of a vendor or an integrator to provide design and implementation services is considered a key enabler. After the vendor selection is complete, the rollout of Web services becomes an integral part of the IT project requirements.

The main benefit of top-down SOA adoption is the consistency of project environments and integration mechanisms. The depth of knowledge within the IT organization grows significantly. IT resources can move between projects with reduced switching costs. Hardware and software are easier to procure and manage because fewer configuration types must be supported. It becomes easier to evolve the architecture across the enterprise as the industry evolves. The need for middleware negotiating the integration between applications is minimized.

At the same time, significant costs are associated with the top-down adoption process. The organizational costs of achieving agreement on a high-level SOA architecture within an enterprise or a business unit are high, similar to those of establishing technology standards. The technology requirements of various projects can be different and difficult to negotiate under a common requirements and architecture umbrella. For example, a system that uses Web services to share patient medical information between affiliated hospitals needs radically higher levels of security and compliance monitoring compared to an internal system that sends X-ray images from several radiology information systems to an image archiving application.

There is also the catch-22 of the skill and experience level of the team defining the policies for SOA adoption. How did they become experienced in Web services without going through end-to-end projects? As a rule, reading books (except this one, of course!) and going to conferences and vendor seminars are no substitutes for hands-on experience. Finally, there are the general challenges of trying to roll out anything of this scope in a large IT organization. How will compliance with the defined policies be monitored and enforced at lower levels of the organization? The bigger the scope, the more likely it is for things to go wrong and the slower the response to any change-inducing factors.

Bottom-Up Deployment

The risks associated with top-down adoption and the painful memories of failure associated with enterprisewide IT projects prompt the pendulum to swing in the opposite direction for some enterprises. They see benefits in using Web services even on a small scale: exposing the capabilities of a single service or doing point-to-point integration between two applications. They believe that only through active experimentation can their IT organization achieve a level of proficiency with Web services. Hence some organizations use a bottom-up adoption strategy. IT teams are free to use the best technologies to get the job done and encouraged to surface Web services for integration. Individual teams are in charge of vendor selection (within the context of any enterprisewide strategic vendor choices, of course). Policies and best practices emerge bottom up as teams look to one another for success and failure patterns.

You're most likely to see bottom-up adoption of Web services in enterprises with highly heterogeneous infrastructures, especially ones that have grown through mergers and acquisitions. In these environments, centralized control is limited, and it's next to impossible to drive meaningful end-to-end policies top-down.

The main benefit of a bottom-up adoption strategy is that it's well suited for an environment of rapidly evolving technologies. In effect, every IT project becomes an experiment, evaluating a particular set of Web services technologies and best practices. Since many of these experiments run in parallel, they quickly generate a lot of learning. Best practices emerge bottom-up. IT teams can maximally leverage the capabilities of Web services tools and platforms for building new applications or exposing the services of existing applications. The same applies to integrating applications—the best tools and integration platforms can be applied.

Some experienced IT professionals who have lived through point-to-point integration using old technologies (DCOM, CORBA, EAI, and so on) wince at the thought of bottom-up adoption of Web services. How can small IT teams without significant prior experience with Web services and without the benefit of consulting integration experts in the organization make optimal Web services technology choices for the long run? What are the guarantees that the products chosen for the first iteration of the project will deliver the necessary capabilities to support updates? Despite the promises of interoperability between Web services platforms, true interoperability at high levels of service assurance is a ways off. Does that mean integration between Web services exposed by different applications requires an additional layer of integration middleware that needs to be bought, configured, and managed? Further, bottom-up adoption doesn't help address the key problem of semantic mapping.

Hybrid Deployment

As with most extreme views, both top-down and bottom-up adoption pose serious limitations. Hybrid adoption strategies offer a middle ground that attempts to share some of the benefits of the other approaches while mitigating some of the risks. The basic idea is to define islands within the IT organization based on criteria that center on organizational boundaries (such as business units) or functional boundaries (such as financial systems). The IT teams within business units choose their adoption strategy for exposing services. Integration of applications between islands is based on a set of fairly broad top-down specified policies.

Here's an example of the outline of such a high-level policy from a Fortune 50 enterprise that is on the leading edge of SOA adoption:

1. All services must be registered in a corporate UDDI registry. Before a new service is introduced, the team must justify why the service is needed and why existing services can't address this need.

2. The vocabularies used by messages must be registered in a corporate schema repository. Before a new schema is introduced or a schema extended, the team needs to justify why existing schema (or schema fragments) won't satisfy requirements.

3. All services must expose a SOAP-based interface with bindings to the IBM MQSeries messaging middleware and HTTP/HTTPS. Other bindings are welcome but not required.

4. Services should expose document-oriented as opposed to RPC-oriented APIs.

5. For security, services must follow the WS-Security set of specifications unless there are serious implementation issues given the current state of tools.

6. A specified custom SOAP header must be used for auditing and logging service activity between islands. System monitoring infrastructure must be able to integrate service information across islands.

7. All exceptions must be approved by the SOA committee.

The hybrid approach allows for experimentation and the adoption of cutting-edge tools and platforms while trying to restrict the explosion of different schema, service interfaces, and products. It's a more balanced approach and thus easier to implement across an enterprise or a business unit.

Still, even the hybrid approach can't succeed without two critical factors. The first one is an organizational willingness to respect and trust the decisions of an SOA committee (typically consisting of senior enterprise architects and leaders from the emerging technologies group). The second is a set of tools that can communicate policies, monitor their use, and enforce their compliance.

Policies and Processes

In addition to the organizational-level decisions that affect Web services adoption, a number of smaller scale decisions need to be made for almost every project. The lack of SOA best practices again manifests itself through the lack of agreement around policies and processes for designing, developing, deploying, and operating systems that leverage Web services. Shared policies and processes bring consistency and predictability that reduce the risk of project failure and increase the leverage of the project. One key area of focus is reuse at all levels: vendor relations, product purchases, training and know-how, process definitions, XML vocabularies, and, of course, Web services.

There are three parts to putting useful SOA-related policies and processes in place:

- Reaching agreement and formalizing policies
- Communicating to the rest of the organization
- Monitoring and enforcing compliance

Reaching agreement is always the hardest part. The discussion of top-down versus bottom-up adoption of Web services applies here as well. It's easier to agree on best practices on a smaller scale, but the benefit is also smaller. It takes strong leadership and organizational commitment to drive best practices from the top. The fact that SOA cuts across traditional IT functions doesn't help. A Web service affects the software that exposes it, the hardware and network on which it's running, the applications that depend on it, and the security and management systems in the IT organization. As a result, there are many areas to reach agreement on in the course of adopting SOA. Common threads across all areas are vendor selection, change management as standards and vendor offerings move forward, possibility of reuse, and so on. Table 14.2 summarizes some of the key issues to focus on.

Table 14.2 **Potential Areas for SOA Policy and Process Definition**

Area	Key Issues
Service design	Vocabulary choice
	API design, including binding choices and interaction patterns
	Discovery mechanisms and additional discovery meta-data
	WS-I profile compatibility
Service implementation	SOAP version support
	Interoperability requirements
Service assurances	Levels of security, reliability, and transaction support
	Auditing, monitoring, and logging requirements for the service
System architecture	Service implementation choice
	Service assurance provision choice, such as on-host or proxy-based
	Testing, staging, and production environment specification
	Approaches to reliability, scalability, and failover
Testing	Any on-the-wire testing/debugging capabilities?
	Methods for testing interactions with partner services outside the firewall
Deployment/operations	SLA definition, monitoring, and enforcement
	Capacity planning
	Root-cause analysis
	Version management

It isn't important only to reach a level of agreement on these issues but also to formalize the agreement as a policy and communicate this policy to the organization. Doing so is easier said than done. The risk is that all the effort that goes into thinking about best practices may result in an outdated document that few people refer to. What we really need are software tools that can encapsulate key aspects of policies in machine-readable form and then integrate the communication of the policies inside the tools used for service design, implementation, testing, and deployment. The same applies on the operations side, where software can monitor and enforce SLA and policy compliance in real time. We're some time away from this world, but several software vendors are making strides in this area.

With all the challenges to SOA adoption described so far, it's no surprise that the market has been slow to develop relative to the inflated industry expectations of several years ago. Still, both established vendors and small startups are developing key capabilities to facilitate the adoption of Web services for real-world projects. The rest of the chapter covers some of the current thinking and product capabilities in this space.

Putting Web Services in Production

A few natural cases allow for initial experimentation with Web services without requiring a whole-hearted buy-in to a particular way of using Web services:

- When a new internal IT system is built, it would help to expose its services through SOAP as well as any other legacy APIs that might be required. This should be straightforward given the current level of tools. If the system's lifespan is more than a couple of years, it's likely that newer systems would want to communicate with it via Web services.

- If new systems have to gain access to a legacy system, it makes sense to encapsulate that functionality in a Web service. One exception is if the IT organization already owns an Enterprise Application Integration (EAI) platform that can cost-effectively get information in and out of the legacy system. In that case, it may be better to wait for the EAI vendor to add Web services support to the product.

- If point-to-point integration between two applications can't be done easily through the existing integration infrastructure, SOAP over HTTP/S or a message queue may be a cost-effective approach. Increasingly, the core products from major vendors offer asynchronous Web services support, which helps immensely for enterprise integration.

- Web services are an excellent mechanism for delivering information into a portal. The basic technology capabilities are part of most Web services platforms and portals. Standards are moving in that direction as well. Consider the JSR 168 *Portlet Specification* 📖 from the Java Community Process and the OASIS work on *Web Services for Interactive Applications (WSIA)* 📖, which transitioned its work to *Web Services for Remote Portlets (WSRP)* 📖. Your investment in this area would be money well spent.

- Web services are great for partner integration. Unless you and your partners are running compatible integration infrastructure, using Web services is likely to be your best bet. Doing so also insulates you to an extent from changes in your partner network, such as existing partners leaving and new partners coming on board.

In all these cases, it helps to stick to the core functionality of the current technology and rely on existing infrastructure and architectural approaches to resolve missing capabilities. For example, when possible, use enterprise message queues to get message reliability and long-running transaction support. Use HTTPS and certificates or trusted private networks to handle security. These traditional approaches to integration have worked well in some of the most demanding IT environments for years. They will do for a couple more years while Web services support is added to newer versions of current infrastructure products.

However, some desirable capabilities aren't readily available in current product offerings and don't have easy substitutes in traditional integration approaches. These include XML and Web services testing, monitoring, and analysis tools; integration, billing, and metering infrastructure; and so on. Addressing these deficiencies now requires creative leverage of existing approaches to connecting and integrating systems as well as the selective choosing of complementary products that can address gaps in functionality present in the core Web services platform offerings. Smart IT departments choose one of three adoption models:

- *Let an integrator make technology choices*—Choose an integration partner and entrust them with the task of choosing from a mix of available technologies and products. In the end, the goal is to migrate the enterprise's infrastructure to a standards-based platform provided by the products of one of the established vendors. The contract with the integrator is structured in a way that encourages parsimonious technology choices. The fewer products are bought, installed, and configured now, the less migration work in the future. Another goal is to write as little custom code as possible to ease later migration. This model is best suited for enterprises that don't have the internal IT capabilities to understand and navigate the emerging Web services market but have the money to support a long-term integration effort.

- *Rely on the internal IT team to choose technologies*—An alternative model follows the same strategy as the first but is executed by a sophisticated internal IT organization instead of an integrator. In this case, part of the reason to be on the bleeding edge of Web services deployment is motivated by the desire to develop internal know-how, skills, and capabilities in the SOA arena so that the enterprise can gradually leverage the benefits these technologies offer.

- *Adopt when the technologies improve*—The third typical strategy that enterprises follow is that of growing adoption as the core Web services platforms improve. These enterprises prefer to go around some of the limitations of current technologies either by delaying deployment or by doing internal development. For example, these enterprises invented custom security SOAP headers because their tools at the time lacked support for WS-Security. Usually, such companies have a short list of vendors of choice and don't want to complicate their infrastructure by bringing in products from other vendors.

The rest of the chapter will give you an idea of what you have to think about, the types of products that are available on the market, and some best practices for putting them to good use.

Web Services Technology Map

Putting Web services into production requires systematic thinking about a complex combination of IT and business requirements with Web services technologies and products. Making a decision requires thinking on four different levels:

- What are the technical requirements?
- How do they map to product capabilities in the Web services space?
- How are these capabilities packaged and delivered as products?
- How is a preferred vendor selected to supply the product?

The answers to the first and last questions are highly enterprise- and situation-specific and therefore difficult to go into in the context of this book. To address the third question, the next section looks at system architectures for Web services deployment; often, the boundaries of products are defined by the system architecture in which they operate. To address the section question, it helps to build a Web services technology map (see Figure 14.2).

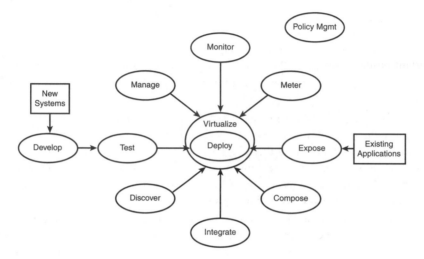

Figure 14.2   Web services technology map

The technology map isn't standard- or product-specific. Instead, it focuses on key capabilities that an enterprise Web services deployment would likely need to address. Of course, the Web services space is growing and changing rapidly, and this map is a static caricature of that market. Nevertheless, it can help us think more systematically about putting Web services into production.

Creation

The map starts with the notion that Web services are created either as part of new system development or by exposing parts of existing systems. In the former case, this requires development tools and platforms (of which there are many). The core capabilities in this category have to do with supporting the implementation of the service logic; building a service description; providing tools that link to other capabilities such as discovery, virtualization, and management/monitoring; and, if necessary, exposing the power to deal with lower-level aspects of Web services such as SOAP headers. Most developers spend their time with products in this category.

Creating Web services from existing systems requires different capabilities. Of course, if the existing systems have Web services support, all that is required is to configure them correctly. This is usually the job of a business application specialist in the IT organization. If the systems don't have Web services capabilities, the hard part of the problem is getting access to the systems through their native APIs and getting them to perform the service functionality. This is the realm of EAI and legacy extension technologies that apply a façade pattern on the existing system. For example, you can expose Web services out of a mainframe application by emulating a complex set of terminal keystrokes and screen-scraping the terminal output.

There is nothing wrong with such an approach; it extends the life and reach of an important business system at a cost that is far lower than modifying or rewriting the application. The application of a façade pattern can bring any part of IT infrastructure and applications to the Web services world. CORBA and DCOM components will be able to talk SOAP, message queues can accept messages over SOAP/HTTP, and so on. There can be some problems, however. They primarily have to do not with the core functionality of a service but with the facets surrounding it, such as security and QoS. For example, using existing tools, it's difficult to expose a secure and transactable CORBA service as an *identically* secure and transactable Web service. Even if Web services security and transaction support was broadly available, it might be tricky to map the Web services model for doing these to the legacy models. There are solutions to these problems, but they increase the overall cost and complexity of extending a legacy system to the Web services world.

In choosing a legacy extension solution that fits your needs, focus on two key areas of evaluation: the ease with which the legacy system can be controlled and the extent to which the façade logic is going to be transparent to any users of the service.

Testing

Testing Web services is another key area on the technology map. As with most new technology developments, testing capabilities have significantly lagged behind core development and platform runtime capabilities. Existing debugging and test-automation tools, including network visibility tools such as TCPMon, may not be sufficient for testing purposes. Testing applications in an SOA is more complicated than testing monolithic, client-server, or Web applications, and specialized testing capabilities can help ensure high productivity and high testing quality.

Deployment and Virtualization

At the center of the technology map is the area of deployment and virtualization. *Deployment* is broadly used in the sense of putting a service in a production environment as opposed to the narrower context of deploying on an application server, for example. *Service virtualization* refers to the task of taking a service and exposing it with the right service assurance levels: availability, scalability, reliability, security, transactability, and so on.

> **Note**
>
> *Virtualization* 📖 is an over-used term these days. We like to use the term *service virtualization* here part-ly because of the implications of upcoming utility computing where the grid can be used to automatically provision the needed level of software, hardware, and network resources as well as configure the surround-ing SOA infrastructure to support the SLA of the service. The other reason for using the term *virtualization* is to enforce the notion of separation between service implementation and the service assurances that can be wrapped around the implementation.

Discovery

When a new service has been exposed and its functionality has been tested, the service is ready to be plugged into the service fabric of the enterprise. Then comes the question of how the service should be discovered. There are two obvious approaches, neither of which is fully satisfactory. The first one follows the Web services architecture model: register the service in a UDDI repository and let service clients find it there. The second one is overly pragmatic: let clients know somehow where the service description is.

The issue is that when you look at discovery in the context of the development and deployment lifecycle, and when multiple service domains are introduced, the discovery process becomes more complicated to manage. New approaches to this task are emerging, but it will take some time for all the issues to be addressed.

Integration

With the discovery infrastructure in place, the basic SOA framework is complete. Now the benefits of using services really start to show. In the basic case, you can discover and use a service. The need for service integration quickly arises.

Suppose, for example, that an application needs a stock quote service of type X but the company that bought the application has registered for a stock quote service of type Y. The vendor building the application couldn't have designed it to use all possible stock quote services. Somehow, the mismatch between X and Y needs to be resolved. Similar to a legacy extension problem, the application of a façade on service Y will do. The difference between this scenario and legacy extension, however, is the fact that the adaptation happens in the context of SOA—from service to service. There is no need to access proprietary systems. Therefore, the same piece of infrastructure, be it a middleware component, a feature of the application server, or a network service, could do all service adaptations. That is a key benefit of adopting SOA.

Composition

With services available on the network, and with the ability to adapt their APIs, it becomes possible to combine the basic building blocks of service functionality to create high-level services that expose new capabilities. This is the nature of composable programming, another key benefit of SOA. Business Process Execution Language (BPEL), reviewed in Chapter 12, "Orchestrating Web Services," is both a specification and an execution language for composable programming. Again, a key benefit of SOA is that any piece of software enabling service composition could be used to orchestrate any set of services.

Some argue that service *orchestration* 📖 is the best way to go after *business process automation (BPA)* 📖 and *management (BPM)* 📖. Others see orchestration as potentially fragile and offer different architectures. We'll look at this important issue in depth later in the chapter.

Another angle to service composition is integrating services at the presentation tier. Most examples of Web services talk about application-to-application communication, usually in the context of a B2B exchange. However, the subject matter of many information retrieval services (such as stock quotes, weather, news, sports, and price alerts for e-commerce and auctions) is perfectly suited for human consumption.

Internet and corporate portals are all about retrieving these types of information and assembling them into dynamic pages. Traditionally, this has been done through application-specific mechanisms. If all information is exposed as Web services, if service API adaptation is possible, and if services can be composed together to create new services, then there is an opportunity to define a standards-based approach for page assembly in portals. This is what WSRP at OASIS is attempting to do. Adoption of these standards will bring another level of simplification to corporate infrastructure, this time targeting the presentation tier.

Management

In a world of lots of services integrated and composed together, IT needs a sophisticated service management platform. Too often, management is one of the last capabilities we think about when implementing and deploying new applications. The truth is, currently existing application, network, and system management tools have yet to be adapted for managing SOA. Work has just begun in the *Web Services Distributed Management (WSDM)* 📖 group in OASIS to define standards in this area. Key capabilities such as service provisioning and deprovisioning, discovery, and version management aren't part of major vendors' offerings. Yet without these capabilities, managing a network with hundreds or thousands of services exposed by different applications is difficult.

Monitoring

The monitoring and analysis of systems has traditionally been lumped under the umbrella of system management. Those products take a highly simplistic view of monitoring and analysis. A typical example is the red lights, green lights UI: Either things are OK or something is wrong; the transaction succeeded or failed. It was a big step for products to add yellow lights to the UI, meaning "things are looking like they are in between good and bad." It's easy to joke about product deficiencies, but it nevertheless helps to understand the underlying cause of the problem.

In the past, it was too difficult to extract meaningful, rich data about the behavior of systems. If all you get is a heartbeat or a few simple metrics, it's hard to go beyond the red-yellow-green metaphor. Given the heterogeneity of deployed systems and communication protocols, it was prohibitively expensive for management vendors to retrieve finer-grained system information. Web services change this situation considerably. XML messages traveling on the network can be inspected in depth (provided the inspection software has the right security permissions to see the content of the messages). With minimal customization, you can extract the stock symbol out of a stock quote request or the total payment amount from an invoice. In other words, monitoring software can finally access rich information about system behavior. This opens up significant opportunities for analyzing this information and leveraging it to improve both IT and business operations inside enterprises.

Metering

Web services are at the core of e-business; business (traditional or Internet enabled) is about money changing hands. When Web services surface existing enterprise systems such as an order-taking system on the network, billing is straightforward; it happens the way it has always happened. However, Web services allow for new kinds of e-business services that aren't based on existing enterprise systems. How should usage metering and billing happen in these cases?

One simple approach is the subscription model, which requires registration and payment up front and provides for unlimited consumption for a period of time. For example, an enterprise pays $9,995 per year for unlimited access to a real-time stock quote service. Another approach is to integrate usage metering and billing in the core fabric of SOA, which would allow for just-in-time billing, micropayments, and other more flexible arrangements between e-business partners. (The experience of *wireless service providers [WSPs]* 📖 can teach us a lot, since they've had to deal with highly dynamic pricing models for years.) That is another exciting benefit enabled by the wide adoption of Web services.

Policy Management

The final piece of the technology map in Figure 14.2 is policy management. It permeates every aspect of SOA and all parts of the technology map. From deployment guidelines to SLA definition to regulatory compliance, enterprise operations must comply with a multitude of policies at many different levels. Right now, some of these policies are formally represented by pieces of meta-data dispersed across various systems. Often, policies aren't formally represented but exist in various unstructured or unmanaged forms such as documents or email messages.

Because the complexity of a network increases with the number of its nodes and the number of connections between nodes, the complexity of networks of integrated Web services can quickly get out of hand. It's fair to say that SOA adoption will be limited until there is a way to manage policy in a coherent way across the applications and infrastructure products taking part in it.

One aspect that makes the Web services technology map complicated is that the various technology areas described don't map cleanly to products or even to product categories. The main reason is the relative immaturity of market. Product boundaries aren't clear. One way to think about this problem is to look at possible system architectures for Web services deployment and attempt to map technology capabilities to participants in the system architecture.

System Architectures for Web Services

Enterprises choosing to deploy Web services have a multitude of system architecture choices. These choices translate into a particular message path that SOAP messages must flow through between requestors and providers. Figure 14.3 shows an example of a provider-side path from the external network (on the right) to the service logic (on the left). The three components in the middle—gateway, transport, and proxy—are optional and may not be present in all situations. Any component on the message path can use an interceptor pattern to perform actions on messages (this is how handlers in Axis work). There is no limit to the type of functionality that interceptors can implement. Keep in mind that these can be both transparent interceptors and SOAP intermediaries. Let's walk through the components on the message path from the network into the service implementation and consider the type of extensibility that's available and the types of capabilities that are best exposed at that level.

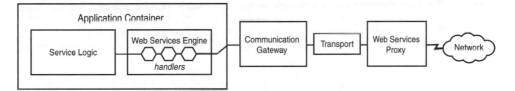

Figure 14.3   Message path for Web services

Network

The network part of the diagram refers to an area of the network that the service provider can't control directly. Therefore, any Web services–related capabilities exposed at this level must be based on standards. These will take many years to develop, but we can imagine a world, years from now, where the network provides differentiated QoS for SOAP-based messages just as it's trying to do now for streaming media traffic.

Proxies

When a SOAP message comes into the portion of the network controlled by the provider, the first opportunity to perform processing on it comes through a proxy. Proxies can operate on three levels: low-level network, high-level network, and SOA.

Low-Level Proxies

Network-level proxies are transparent from an SOA point of view. An example of a low-level network proxy is one that listens to network traffic at wire speed, figures out which traffic is Web services–related, and performs an action such as logging SOAP messages. The proxy is completely transparent; this is its main benefit and its main disadvantage. Few types of meaningful actions can be taken at this level. In particular, it can't have any side effects on the network traffic (it can only behave like a sniffer).

High-Level Proxies

This limitation doesn't exist for high-level network proxies, which typically are protocol specific. For example, an HTTP network proxy can perform smart load-balancing by looking at SOAP messages and deciding where to dispatch them. Doing that cleanly requires the typical network sophistication associated with dynamic load-balancing. It's not hard to do, but it requires careful network configuration. The benefit of network proxies is that they're completely nondisruptive to SOA. In particular, the WSDL of a service doesn't need to be modified when these proxies are introduced. This also means that it's easy to add more than one network proxy on the message path. The main disadvantage is that it's next to impossible for these proxies to perform SOA-level actions that affect the requestor. An example is interrupting processing and returning a fault.

> **Note**
>
> Products in the Web services space are changing so fast that it becomes difficult to use words such as *always*, *never*, and *impossible* and not be caught ignoring some exceptional case. Rather than qualifying every claim to protect against this possibility, we ask you to keep at the back of your head the notion that in software, everything is possible—it just isn't always well understood and easy to do.

SOA-Level Proxies

SOA-level proxies behave very differently. From a requestor's perspective, they're indistinguishable from the service endpoint. Therefore, the WSDL describing the service must change. There are no standard approaches for how this happens. In an ideal world, SOA proxies will be integrated with Web services engines and UDDI directories and will just "know" when a new service is deployed and what they should do with it. Unfortunately, this isn't the case right now. UDDI registries have a change notification mechanism, but products rarely use it because UDDI registries aren't commonly deployed. There are no standard ways to integrate with Web services engines and monitor deployments.

Finally, there are no standard ways to define the types of actions an SOA proxy must perform. Clearly, there is a need for multiple vendors to come together and resolve these issues for the benefit of their customers. Currently, most SOA proxies are manually configured post-service deployment, and then the WSDL they generate is published to potential service requestors. This process creates significant change-management problems and is one of the biggest weaknesses of SOA proxies.

Manageability issues aside, now that we're operating at the SOA level, the range of meaningful message processing that can be performed broadens. In fact, since SOA proxies have fully functioning Web services engines, you can do any of the things that can be done at the message endpoint and more. Typical capabilities include adapting transports (from HTTP to a message queue, for example), offloading processing-intensive work such as schema validation and security-related operations, transforming messages to adapt the requestor's message to a format that the provider understands, performing policy-based message dispatch, processing specific SOAP headers (for example, replacing a header containing security credentials with an SAML assertion that the requestor has been successfully authenticated), and monitoring and metering SOAP traffic.

The shear breadth of potential capabilities of an SOA proxy raises the important question of best practices. What does it make sense to do in an SOA proxy? The answer depends on the specific services and the assurances they must provide, on the system architecture, and on the capabilities of the products involved. Here are a few rules of thumb:

- If you can get away without using an SOA proxy, do so. They're yet another piece of infrastructure to buy and manage. Currently, few established vendors offer SOA proxies, and the jury is out on what functionality will end up in SOA proxies long term.

- Although proxies are built for scalability, cluster and grid architectures are inherently more scalable. Further, the deeper a proxy needs to look at a SOAP message, the more overhead it will add to message processing. Consider, for example, the task of logging the value of a SOAP header. If a handler in the Web services engine exposing the service does that, the message will be parsed only once. If a handler in an SOA proxy does that, the message will have to be parsed twice. Some proxies use hardware and software acceleration to get around this problem, but this increases their cost.

- In choosing the right combination between proxies and clusters, think about the cost implications of N backend licenses (expensive if you're using application servers, no problem if you're going open source) versus M proxy licenses to get the same work done. Proxies can be cost effective if they save you a significant number of backend licenses.

- The more functionality you have your proxy do, the higher the likelihood of change-management problems because of the lack of standards around how proxies are deployed and managed.

- Don't confuse the issues of centralized management and centralized processing. Centralized management is about making a change in one place and having all aspects of your infrastructure adapt to that change. It's easy to do centralized management by bottlenecking all traffic through a proxy, but that also centralizes processing, which isn't always good. Cluster and grid vendors are investing heavily in management, and it will soon be easy to make a centralized change to SOA policy and have that change reflected across the infrastructure.

- If all the work for a set of services is done on a single cluster, then you may not need a proxy other than for performance acceleration. On the other hand, if you've segmented your backend infrastructure, then a proxy might be helpful because there are few other good ways to do policy-based load-balancing. For example, if you process your gold-level customers on cluster A and everyone else on cluster B, a proxy can help make that switch while exposing the same WSDL to requestors.

- If you're moving toward utility computing, you should try not to adopt proxies except for low-level performance acceleration functions. The core concept of utility computing is around the notion of flexible workload distribution and ease of management. It's harder for proxies to add value in this environment.

Transport

At some point along the message path, traffic can move through transport-oriented infrastructure such as a message bus. The transport infrastructure can provide a number of services such as reliable messaging (persistence, retry logic, failure notification, and so on), prioritized routing, security, and audit logs.

Messaging systems—aka *Message-Oriented Middleware (MOM)* 📖—are the most common type of transport infrastructure deployed in enterprises. J2EE offers MOM capabilities via the *Java Messaging Service (JMS)* 📖. MOM is great for reliable asynchronous messaging and can be successfully used in the absence of broad adoption of WS-ReliableMessaging. MOMs from different vendors have poor interoperability, which is why they aren't used directly as a reliable B2B transport for SOAP messages. Fortunately, all MOM vendors are adding support for Web services and are moving to adopt WS-ReliableMessaging; this will allow reliable messaging across enterprise boundaries. Some MOM products are XML and/or SOAP aware; they offer features such as data transformation, content-based routing, and message prioritization. Beyond features covered by JMS, implementation details vary significantly between vendors and make solution portability difficult right now.

Communication Gateway

Depending on the transport, there may be one or more communications gateways on the message path right before the Web services engine. For example, for a J2EE implementation using SOAP over HTTP, there will be a Web server translating HTTP requests to application server requests and a servlet engine processing these requests. The servlet engine passes the message to the Web services engine. These communication gateways are transparent from an SOA perspective and thus typically only observe the SOAP messages passing through.

Web Services Engine

The Web services engine has a number of configurable handlers that perform operations on the SOAP message such as schema validation, header processing, data transformation, and logging. Since the Web services engine inside the application is the endpoint on the message path, it can perform any operation on the message without affecting the service description. This makes the Web services engine the best place for SOAP message processing. Change management-related headaches are also minimized, at least for homogeneous engine deployments.

Service Logic

Finally, there is the service logic. Some Web service engines can surface SOAP message context to the service implementation. Best practices suggest that service implementations should focus on the core function of the service and not perform additional processing. Dealing with data transformations, security, or other facets orthogonal to the service's purpose severely limits the reusability of the service logic.

Monitoring and Metering

Monitoring and metering of services can take place at any point in the message path as long as they're implemented purely using the observer pattern and don't affect message flow. In some cases, however, the analysis of monitoring and metering information may necessitate taking actions that affect the message flow. For example, if a monitoring system detects a message that doesn't conform to the service API, it may want to interrupt message processing. This could be one way to limit the effect of Web services–based denial of service (DoS) attacks. Another example could be usage metering logic determining that the requestor has exceeded the service invocation quota and denying the message request. It's best to put this type of processing inside an SOA-level proxy or inside the Web services engine in the application.

Processing

Processing along the SOAP message path can be significantly affected by the use of Web services security. There are three types of issues to think about:

- A *configuration management* issue arises from the difficulty associated with performing certain tasks such as logging message content or transforming messages when some of the message content is encrypted. Without access to the appropriate set of security keys, it may be impossible to see the necessary parts of the message.

- The need to distribute keys to multiple points on the message path will create a *change-management* nightmare without the help of key distribution and synchronization infrastructure.

- The need to check message signatures as well decrypt and possibly reencrypt message parts can lead to a *performance* problem since security operations are CPU intensive. To eliminate some of the performance issues related to reencryption, you may be tempted to run clear-text traffic on parts of the network. However, doing so can lead to a security problem. Consider an example where all messages go through a high-performance SOA proxy that validates schema, checks security credentials and digital signatures, authenticates and authorizes the requester, and decrypts all messages. The proxy sends SOAP messages without security precautions through the trusted internal network. From an SOA security perspective, everything looks good. However, from an overall security perspective there are two key problems: A hacker who has access to the internal network can snoop on messages; and if the backend service implementation is unprotected, the hacker is free to make calls to any services.

As you can see, the system architecture along the message path can influence where and how certain aspects of Web services processing are implemented.

> **Note**
>
> One aspect of system architecture that we don't have the space to cover is how to provide scalability, *high availability (HA)* 📖, and *disaster recovery (DR)* 📖 for SOA. Here, traditional approaches adopted to scale application server clusters and protect mission-critical systems can address most common cases. The dynamic discovery capabilities of SOA offer an extra level of flexibility.

Features, Capabilities, and Approaches

The final section of this chapter offers guidance on how to think about features that Web services products should offer and approaches for building complete Web services solutions. The section isn't meant as a definitive collection of best practices; instead, it's a collection of ideas that should aid your thinking about and analysis of Web services issues facing your organization once you've decided where to apply Web services. The ideas are presented in the context of an "ideal world"—they're things you should keep in mind or strive toward. Don't confuse this with a requirement to put these to work in all cases by acquiring products that support all mentioned features and capabilities. The mantra of this chapter is pragmatic, business-need-driven adoption of Web services. You have to contrast our ideal-world recommendations with the realization that the simpler the infrastructure on which you deploy Web services, the less you'll have to change and migrate as next-generation products come on the scene.

This section sometimes mentions vendors whose products provide significant support for Web services. The vendor list isn't meant to be complete, and the mention of vendors should not be construed as endorsement. Products change so quickly in this space that by the time the book ends up in your hands, the marketplace may have changed significantly.

Tools and Platforms

Many tools and platforms support Web services. There are four main platform categories:

- *Narrow Web services–centric platforms* that focus on core SOA functions, perhaps with the addition of basic integration and legacy extension capabilities. Examples include Systinet's offering, which is popular with *independent software vendors (ISVs)* that are looking for Web services engines to OEM into their products; and Cape Clear's offering, which started as one of the earliest Web services engines. Apache Axis also falls in this category.

- *Middleware platforms* that offer significant Web services capabilities. Examples include webMethods (with the acquisition of The Mind Electric, makers of GLUE) and Sonic Software (which extended its integration capabilities through the acquisition of Excelon). These types of platforms are best suited to integration-oriented problems.

- *Full application development and deployment platforms*: .NET from Microsoft and all the J2EE offerings from IBM, BEA, Sun, and others. These platforms are well suited for building and deploying services. All major vendors are adding integration and composition capabilities as well.

- *Business service networks (BSNs)* such as the one offered by Grand Central Communications. BSNs focus on the connection and integration of services without concern for the endpoint environments. BSNs are value-added networks (VANs) from the EDI days revved up to modern technologies such as XML and Web services; hence they're a good choice for enterprises used to that integration model.

The tools and their capabilities will depend on the choice of platform category. Regardless of your category choice, you should look for the following capabilities in the products you use:

- *Design tools that allow you to specify services at the WSDL level*—Auto-generating WSDL from a service implementation binds the service API tightly to the backend and may cause problems over time as the underlying implementation changes. It's better to have the flexibility to adapt to backend changes in the stub implementation.

- *Document-oriented as opposed to RPC APIs*—Over many years of experience with distributed systems, the use of RPCs has tended to lead to fragile APIs.

- *Auto-generated code from a schema compiler to process XML documents*—SAX, DOM, and JDOM are syntax-oriented APIs. It's easy to write fragile code that breaks even with small schema changes. Make sure the code generated by your schema compiler is robust with respect to schema changes.

- *No proprietary SOAP headers*—If you have to use them, make sure their processing is loosely tied to the infrastructure and the service implementation so you can easily migrate off them in the future.

- *Reliable, asynchronous messaging*—This is the preferred transport method for automating business processes. It offers higher workload management flexibility and scalability than synchronous messaging. Choose products that enable this and have support for long-running transactions.

- *Tool and platform integration with discovery services*—Depending on whether you're planning to use UDDI, this may become important. Walk through several change-management scenarios to be sure your platform can support your needs.

- *Design-time SOA policy management, monitoring, and enforcement capabilities*—Should be similar to the ones that companies such as WebLayers are developing.

Finally, it goes without saying that you should look for support of the WS-* set of standards, if not now, then in the near future.

SOA Testing

History tells us that concern for testing tools and methodologies for new technology platforms doesn't come until well-publicized failures. This happened with Windows GUI applications, client-server, and the Web. It's happening again with Web services. Although there are some small Web services–focused testing vendors such as MindReef, the big platform vendors and testing vendors such as Empirix and Mercury Interactive are doing little with Web services. One reason is the early stage of the market. Another reason is that few people understand what testing in an SOA world is about.

One school of thought is that Web services are just another mechanism for accessing functionality and the real problem is testing the service implementations (which can be done using standard language- and platform-specific tools). This argument makes sense in an ideal world where all Web services infrastructure works and interoperates correctly.

That world is far away. In the world we live in, Web services infrastructure is immature and significant interoperability issues remain. In addition, some aspects of SOA are unique and go beyond pure service implementation. Let's look at a couple of examples:

- How can you test your application if you don't have access to the services it will use? This isn't a silly question. Consider the cases where the client- and service-side logic are developed in parallel by two separate teams, and yours has to work on the requestors. You'll probably have to build a fake service to test against. A good testing tool can help you with that. It can also use the schema information in the WSDL to help with generating a set of valid messages. The reverse argument applies when you're the service provider and you need to create a fake client to test the service.

- Now both the service and its requestors have completed implementation, and integration testing begins. What are the chances of all calls working successfully on the first attempt? Traditionally, interoperability testing has happened at the implementation level because the wire-level protocols were impossible to work with. Web services change this situation. Visibility-oriented tools such as TCPMon can help detect interoperability issues at the protocol level. Why spend time in a debugger if you can work at a higher level?

These two simple testing scenarios cover the requester and provider implementations and the integration between the two. Now let's make things more complicated. Add WS-Security, WS-Reliability, and WS-Transactions to the picture, and simple message-level testing no longer works. Two types of messages will be on the wire this time: *logical messages* (what you see from the high-level application perspective) and *infrastructure messages* (how components of the SOA infrastructure communicate). An example infrastructure message is the registration of a transaction with a transaction coordinator. Furthermore, simple visibility tools such as TCPMon won't help much if message parts are encrypted. In that world, you need purpose-built testing tools that understand and fit in the SOA view of the world.

Now, let's start composing services together using BPEL. It's easy to see what's going on if all flows are controlled by a single BPEL engine: most process automation engines provide decent logging and monitoring capabilities. What about the cases where the process spans enterprise boundaries and no single BPEL engine is orchestrating it? A good BPEL-aware testing tool can monitor messages and note any deviations from the process specification. But how can that tool be transparently integrated to monitor all flows without affecting the application itself? (This is the Heisenberg uncertainty principle applied to SOA.) There are several choices: It can be deployed on one or more transparent proxies or communication gateways or it can be integrated with multiple Web services engines.

This last point shows the need for a link between development, testing, and deployment for Web services. TCPMon is a great tool, and you should use it; but you should also demand high-power, well-integrated Web services testing capabilities from your vendors.

Deployment and Provisioning

Let's look at a hypothetical example of deploying a mission-critical enterprise Web service that requires WS-Security and WS-Transactions on an application server cluster. First, the same version of the service needs to be deployed on all the nodes in the cluster. The locations of the WSDL and WS-Policy documents must be well defined. For the service to operate, the Web services engine exposing the service must have access to the right set of security keys (for WS-Security) and must know the location of the transaction coordinator. The service must be registered with a UDDI directory. The authorization engine used within the enterprise must receive a set of rules regarding who can access the service, who can see its WSDL and WS-Policy, and so on. The monitoring infrastructure must become aware of the new service and receive instructions about the required level of service activity logging. SLA information as well as any alerting rules must also be provided. If there are other interceptors on the message path, they also need to be notified. In some cases, the service WSDL must be adapted to take into account the behaviors of the interceptors. This affects much of the SOA infrastructure. For example, the UDDI information about the service may need to be modified. If all that doesn't sound complicated enough, imagine what happens if there is a version change in the service.

SOAs achieve high levels of flexibility to a large extent due to separation of responsibilities between description, discovery, security, reliability, transactability, and so on. This is wonderful from an architecture perspective. When you're implementing solutions, however, all that is separate must be brought together in a consistent, context-sensitive manner so that all services behave in concert, as they're supposed to. This requirement puts significant dependencies between otherwise independent parts of the SOA infrastructures and creates a huge deployment and change management problem.

This isn't an unfamiliar problem. Ask any N-tier application administrator about the hassle of managing application servers, integration servers, messaging middleware, and databases. That's before thinking about system, network, storage, and security management to keep all that software running. IT administrators are already in pain, managing complex systems; when they look at all the components of SOA, their first reaction tends to be "Oh, not more dependencies." They're right to complain, because although most vendors are busy adding support for runtime-oriented standards, few have made the deployment and provisioning of services easy.

The industry is at fault here. Consider, for example, J2EE application servers. Despite deployment descriptor specifications, deploying a nontrivial application on BEA WebLogic, IBM WebSphere, or JBoss is a different thing. Standards for managing configuration information across infrastructure layers are just starting to emerge. *Data Center Markup Language (DCML)* 📖 and *System Definition Model (SDM)* 📖—part of Microsoft's *Dynamic Systems Initiative (DSI)* 📖—are two early attempts to tackle this problem. It will take years for any standard to get significant industry traction, despite efforts of companies such as OpsWare and mValent that are delivering products capable of supporting these standards. In the meantime, lack of standards supporting deployment and provisioning can significantly slow adoption of Web services. We can only hope that OASIS or the Global Grid Forum will take on this task for SOA in the near term.

In the absence of automated approaches to deployment and provisioning, you should do the following:

- *Maximally leverage the deployment capabilities of your platform infrastructure.* Tie custom deployment scripts that propagate SOA-related configuration changes to the service deployment events of your Web service engine.

- *Document carefully what you can't automate* and define formal deployment and change management processes.

- *Ask your vendors to focus their efforts on this problem* and follow emerging standards for infrastructure management.

Business Process Automation Using Web Services

When thinking about business process automation (BPA) using Web services, most people think about BPEL and Web services orchestration. In practice, however, this is just one of at least five approaches to BPA that enterprises are taking:

- Batch integration
- Direct integration
- Integration using a Web services bus
- Rules-based message dispatch
- Orchestration

Let's look at a simple BPA example that we can use to compare and contrast these approaches. BigG Financial (BGF) is a national diversified financial services provider. A business analyst team recently completed a study of the company's data warehouse and came back with an interesting observation. The team determined that when people move from one location to another, there is a significant opportunity to sell them a variety of services: mortgages, home equity loans, insurance, college savings plans, and so on. However, there is one catch: The likelihood of people buying these additional services rapidly decreases with time. The team estimated that if a BGF representative contacted someone within 24 hours of their change of address request, the likelihood of them buying additional services was in the range of 10–15%, whereas the day after it went down to 5% and decreased from there. High-end customers bought significantly more new services. There was a significant opportunity to increase revenues, if only they could find a way to efficiently integrate the various BGF systems together to make them quickly react to address change events.

Specifically, BGF wants to do the following:

1. Generate an address change event when a person changes their address. If multiple people from the same family change their addresses, only one event should be generated. This event should result in outreach to the customer within 24 hours.

2. The address change should be propagated to all systems that maintain their own customer records, such as the mortgage mainframe system. There are more than a dozen such systems at BGF.

3. If the person is a high-end customer, a senior-level representative should contact them to go through a comprehensive analysis of their new financial situation and offer a complete set of new services for them.

4. If the person isn't a high-end customer, they should get a five-day email campaign describing new services.

This business process is simple yet realistic. It includes business event consolidation (one process instance per family), events propagation (the address update may need to be made to more than a dozen systems), exceptions (a low-end customer not having an email address on record), business rules (is this a high-end customer?), and organization-based work assignment (work goes to junior or senior representatives). Many systems are involved: the call center CRM system (because people may call with their address change requests), the client information portal (because the change address can come through the Web), the email campaign management system, the task-distribution portions of the CRM system, and various other systems that receive address changes and help evaluate dynamic business rules such as "is this a high-end customer?" Let's examine how this process automation problem maps to the various available approaches.

Batch Integration

Batch integration (Figure 14.4) provides a clean separation between data and processing. A batch process will extract all address change events for a certain period of time. Then another application, containing the core of the business process, will go over these records, process them according to the business rules, and generate change-update files for all the systems (CRM, task distribution, campaign management, mortgage, and so on) that need to receive information. When the entire processing is complete, the generated files will be imported into the systems. On the next working day, sales representatives will have work waiting for them, and email will start going to people who have moved.

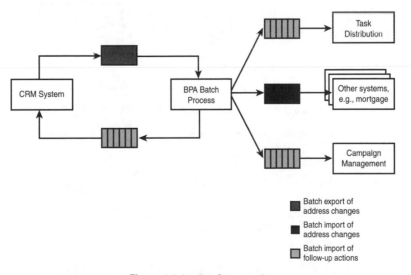

Figure 14.4 Batch processing

The main benefit of batch processing is that it doesn't require system changes: The entire processing is externalized. At the same time, batch processing has two huge disadvantages:

- *It isn't close to real-time.* In fact, this immediately disqualifies batch processing for the BPA work that BGF wants. Since batch jobs typically run outside working hours, it will be impossible to guarantee a 24-hour turnaround for the process. Many corporate systems perform batch updates once per week or once per month.

- *Batch processing requires complete centralization of the business process logic.* One piece of software has to do all the processing, decisions, and dispatch for the entire business process. This requirement severely limits flexibility and reuse.

It may seem that Web services) offer no benefits to batch processing, but this isn't the case. Traditionally, batch processing was based on custom application data import/export processes. Data was typically encoded in flat files. Web services offer the possibility for data extraction and importation to happen via open APIs and for the data to be encoded in XML for easier processing.

Direct Integration

Direct integration (Figure 14.5) is similar to batch processing in that a single piece of software is built to execute the entire business process. However, it's different from batch processing because the business process runs for every address change event and makes updates to all dependent systems as it's executing. The initial address change event can be generated directly from the CRM system, or it can be generated by a trigger that monitors changes to the CRM database. The latter approach leads to a more loosely bound system but increases the risk that a change (such as an upgrade) to the CRM system may trickle down changes to the trigger logic.

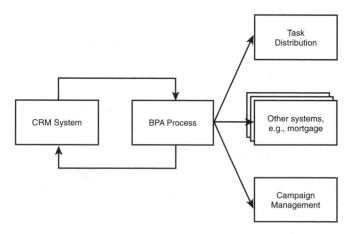

Figure 14.5 Direct integration

From the perspective of the BPA process, change events can arrive using synchronous or asynchronous operations. Clearly, the asynchronous mode has higher scalability and spreads the load on the system more evenly. Sometimes, rather than sending messages to applications, the direct integration approach changes their databases (or other information storage systems) in the same way that the batch process would have done. This helps in the case of applications that have poor integration APIs.

The main advantage of)the direct integration approach is that it can quickly propagate address changes to systems and initiate the follow-up actions. There are many disadvantages, however. This integration model is essentially a tight coupling between several point-to-point integrations. Flexibility is limited due to the monolithic implementation, and reuse is at a minimum. Further, the implementation of the BPA process in this scenario is likely to be complicated. It must know where all other systems are to direct messages to them. It has to handle all state-related processing such as event consolidation or dealing with systems that are temporarily down or undergoing scheduled maintenance. It also needs to handle all exceptions that may arise in the process.

Management and monitoring of the process are tightly bound to the implementation. Even small changes to the enterprise application environment can trigger a change to the process implementation. Any change to the implementation will require a complete test and redeployment cycle. Web services can help with connecting the systems together and passing messages between them, but they can't address the deeper problems associated with this integration approach. That is why most enterprises are moving to better solutions.

Integration Using a Web Services Bus

One way to increase the flexibility of integration and at the same time benefit from Web services is to move to an enterprise Web services bus architecture (Figure 14.6). There are two key ideas in this approach: Loosely couple the systems taking part in the integration, and break up the integration logic into pieces. The enterprise bus is a reliable asynchronous messaging system that supports both point-to-point (1-to-1) and publish/subscribe (1-to-many) messaging. In addition, the messaging system exposes services that operate on the message queues such as searching and filtering, data transformations, and so on. These operations can take advantage of the structured and introspectable nature of Web services messages.

Figure 14.6 shows one possible way to implement the address change integration scenario using a message bus:

1. The address change processing) logic is implemented as a number of event listeners, which are waiting for messages from the bus. The listeners are part of different enterprise systems (or standalone applications associated with them).

2. When an address change happens in the CRM system, a message containing the address change information is generated and put on the bus. This message targets a queue that only the event consolidator will read. (The targeting of messages is indicated by the dotted lines on the diagram.)

3. Based on a schedule (say, every hour), the event consolidator looks at the address change messages in the queue that are over an hour old and notes any that come from the same family. For every family address change, the consolidator sends one message to a queue that only the task distribution and campaign management systems listen on. It sends all address change messages to a different queue where event listeners propagating the address changes to other systems will have a chance to see the message and process it.

4. Different types of exceptions are encoded as messages and sent on the bus to a number of exception handlers whose logic decides what action should be taken.

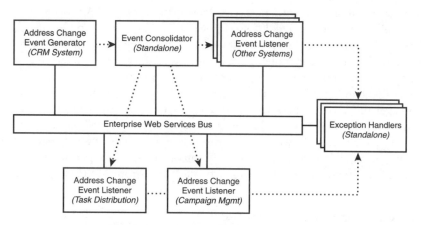

Figure 14.6   Enterprise Web services bus

The benefits of this integration approach are numerous. The complex integration process is broken into multiple smaller, manageable pieces. Changes to existing systems only affect their listeners and event generators. New applications that need address change information can be added at no extra cost. Exception handling is more robust and flexible. And, the monitoring and auditing capabilities of the message bus can be used to monitor messages and gather information for future analysis. This is a much better architecture than the previous two.

There are still a few areas)where improvements can be made. Consider, for example, the business rule that needs to determine whether someone is a high-end customer. With the architecture in Figure 14.6, this business logic will need to be replicated inside the event listeners of the campaign management and task distribution applications. We can increase reuse by encapsulating that logic in a Web service that both listeners call. This helps a little, but it doesn't remove the dependency on both applications having to make a call to that service. What if the high-level process rules change? Then we would have to change the implementation of both listeners. Perhaps a more flexible approach would be to introduce another event listener that decides whether a high-end customer changed their address and, based on the answer, dispatches a message to the campaign management or task distribution system (Figure 14.7).

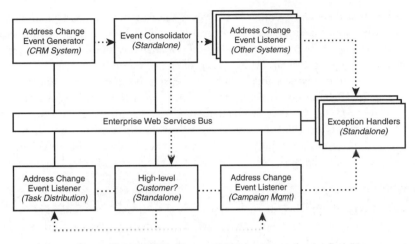

Figure 14.7 Externalizing business rules

Rules-Based Message Dispatch

Although the integration approach works in theory, in practice it creates an unmanageable number of small standalone pieces of integration logic that implement simple business rules. Each of them has to be developed, tested, deployed, and managed independently. This isn't a scalable approach that large enterprises with complex business processes can take. If, however, the message bus were smart enough to evaluate simple business rules and route messages accordingly, then we could have the best of both worlds. This is what rules-based message dispatch systems do (Figure 14.8).

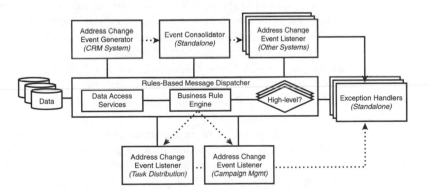

Figure 14.8 Rules-based message dispatch

A crucial feature of rules-based message dispatch systems is the quality of their data access services. Evaluating business rules often requires more information than is present in messages. For example, determining whether someone is a high-end customer may involve looking at their service order history over the past three years. This information isn't part of the address change message; it probably resides in several different systems. Data access services inside the enterprise bus offer a relatively simple, typically declarative mechanism for bringing this data within reach of the rules engine.

There are no industrywide standards for representing business rules. *Business Rules Markup Language (BRML)* 📖 is one approach. The *Object Role Modeling Markup Language (ORM-ML)* 📖 is a conceptual data querying language that can be used to bridge data access services with the rules engine. Both of these efforts are experiencing limited traction right now, but this isn't preventing vendors, such as AptSoft, from shipping good products in this space with proprietary data access and rules languages.

Orchestration

The final integration model is the orchestration-based approach we looked at in Chapter 12. The move to orchestration is driven by two main forces. First, there is the notion that business processes can be modeled formally and that the formal models can be automated through software. Second, other approaches, including rules-based message dispatch, offer limited process-level visibility. Message systems provide great reporting capabilities at the message type level, but it's difficult to get a sense of what is happening at the level of the business process. Thus, an orchestration engine provides both process automation and visibility into the state of business activities supported by business process automation.

Figure 14.9 shows how the address change integration scenario can be handled through orchestration. In this case, the process is started by an address change event. A call to a Web service determines whether this address change is a new change for a family. The diagram shows the business rule determining whether a high-end customer changes their address as an externalized Web service; the same applies for the exception handlers. External systems that need to synchronize their customer information receive Web service calls with the new customer information. These calls can be natively implemented in the systems (as a customer information update API, for example) or may be standalone services that provide façades for legacy applications.

Some orchestration engines, in addition to supporting process description and execution languages such as BPEL, offer additional capabilities such as integrated data access and transformation services, business rules engines, and so on. They can increase the power and flexibility of your integration projects at the cost of limiting portability to other orchestration platforms. The general path of replacing custom code with configuration information (meta-data) is a good one. Unfortunately, there are no standards for tying process execution to data access, transformations, and business rules; it will take several years for these to come in place. In the meantime, you have to think carefully about which orchestration products you choose.

Integrating systems using orchestration offers many advantages and has only one significant disadvantage: dealing with process complexity. There is a theory out there (it could be an urban legend, because for all we know this issue hasn't been studied in depth) that real-world business processes are really complicated. The root of the problem is that there are many more exception-oriented flows than processing-oriented flows. The basic process flow (sometimes called the *forward direction* of the process) may be simple to describe, but if all possible exception conditions are added, they will overwhelm the process description. Further, the idea goes, exception-processing rules change much more frequently than the rest of the process and rely on variable localized context, something that is difficult to formalize in a process description. Therefore, centralized approaches to integration such as orchestration can't model processes well and aren't the best way to go. Proponents of this view prefer more localized integration approaches such as enterprise message buses or rules-based message dispatch.

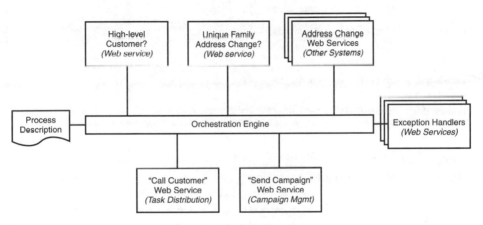

Figure 14.9   Orchestration

Experience with existing orchestration approaches suggests that there must be at least a kernel of truth in this idea. Many enterprise processes are automated only in the forward direction. In most cases, when an exception happens, a message describing the problem and the context within which it occurred is sent to a human for resolution. From supply chain automation to customer service, companies employ lots of people whose job it is to handle these exceptions. Apart from that, though, we have a hard time agreeing with the argument from a philosophical perspective. Rather than seeing this as proof positive that orchestration-based integration approaches are doomed to failure, we see it as an important set of scenarios that needs to be better understood so that we can find ways to address them appropriately through standards, technologies, and products. Formalized process modeling has too many benefits to be dismissed so easily. Unfortunately, the context of this chapter doesn't present an opportunity to discuss this interesting issue in depth. Here is just a hint of an idea of a possible solution: Make process orchestration externally reenterable so that while much of the process can be centrally managed, various pieces of it (typically associated with highly contextual and localized exception processing) can be managed locally.

Choosing an Integration Approach

You may already be wondering how to choose between all the possible approaches to integration and the multitude of products supporting them. Table 14.3 summarizes the main differences between the five approaches we've described here; this information can help you select the best possible solution for your needs.

Table 14.3 **Comparing Integration Approaches**

Integration Approach	Process Control	Exception-Handling	Real-Time Processing	Process Flexibility	Process Visibility	Product Support
Batch	Centralized	Centralized	☹	☹	☹	😐
Direct	Centralized	Centralized	😐	☹	☹	😐
Enterprise bus	Localized	Localized	☺	😐	☹	☺
Rules-based dispatch	Hybrid	Hybrid	☺	☺	😐	☹
Orchestration	Centralized	Centralized	☺	☺	☺	😐

> **Note**
>
> Having just spent many pages going over integration technologies, it helps to take a couple steps back and stress the fact that the hardest integration challenges aren't caused by technology but by business issues. It's often more difficult to scope and describe a business process than it is to automate it. A whole other set of issues that we don't have the space to discuss here concerns cross-enterprise integration. Web services do an excellent job of helping connect disparate systems. Therefore, the technical issues of integration across heterogeneous systems are reasonably well addressed by the current set of Web services standards. However, there is another set of business-related issues that we can't yet tackle easily with software: industry standard vocabularies, contract negotiation and enforcement, trust establishment, service-level agreements, activity monitoring, and so on. It's good to know we're on the right path, but we can't help wishing that we were moving faster.

Operations

Operations is the final step of the software lifecycle. It's often overlooked as something that's independent from software design and implementation. This is a short-sighted view, because the data from operations determines whether a system is behaving according to its specifications with respect to performance, reliability, business impact, and so on. That feedback cycle drives much of the change in systems over time. This is the domain of systems management tools and technologies and of the WSDM standardization effort at OASIS.

The systems management market has grown to billions of dollars across many domains: network, server, application, Web services, manufacturing and business process-es, security, and so forth. In the span of a decade, we've evolved from a world with rela-tively few, mostly disconnected devices to a complex, tightly knit fabric of integrated always-on systems. We have a host of needs—from monitoring the behavior of existing systems to lowering support costs to enforcing QoS to analyzing system behavior and performance with an eye toward improving efficiency. These are some of the technology and business forces driving the growth of systems management.

Across disparate domains, systems management plays a key role in a simple, abstract process: organizing data to produce information from which we can extract knowledge, understanding, and insight that enables us to take action. Therefore, management is often divided into three areas:

- *Visibility*—Gathering data about the behavior of systems
- *Analysis*—Processing the data to extract information
- *Control*—Taking action against the system based on that information

Some people call this the *Triple A* cycle for the combination of acquiring data, analyzing it, and acting on it. The combination of visibility and analysis is often referred to as *moni-toring*. The nature of Web services is such that it offers significant new capabilities in the system monitoring space. The key is that Web services messages are encoded in XML and can therefore be easily inspected. This allows for detailed information gathering at runtime. Further, the rich set of description information about Web services, combined with discovery services, makes it possible to significantly automate the configuration of a Web services monitoring system. For example, the system can know the API of a service as well as the service assurances that it exposes, such as security and transaction support. Finally, Web services orchestration is based on process models that can be read and ana-lyzed by Web services monitoring systems.

On the standards front, work on WSDM is steadily moving forward. The purpose of the effort is to define Web services manageability and to develop a model of Web servic-es as manageable resources. The group has defined key manageability requirements and has defined a draft architecture for Management Using Web Services (MUWS). At the time of this writing, WSDM is in draft version 0.5. Other manageability specifications, such as WS-Manageability, have been provided as input to the OASIS Technical Committee (TC). The current WSDM work will establish a solid foundation upon which vendors can provide advanced management, monitoring, and analysis capabilities. Version 1.0 of WSDM is therefore primarily concerned with the clear delineation of the roles and responsibilities of manageable resources and manager entities in an environ-ment that is SOA friendly and leverages existing investments in distributed management infrastructure. WSDM 1.0 will define key management interfaces using WSDL but won't address most of the higher-level manageability issues that we discuss in this section. All in due time...

Service Level Agreements

Service Level Agreements (SLAs) are a key notion in system operations. They define metrics for system behaviors and, in some cases, remedies for what should happen if the system behavior falls outside of the specified metrics. An example SLA would be that gold-level SkatesTown customers need to have their purchase orders processed within 30 seconds of submission with reliability equal to or exceeding 99.999% (approximately no more than 8 hours of outage per year). Another example would be that all patient records exchanged in electronic clinical trial data submissions must be encrypted with 1024-bit public key encryption.

Most SLAs are focused on technology-oriented metrics. However, there are business-oriented metrics as well. For example, you can guarantee that your preferred customers will get the best product discounts. You would break your SLA if you gave a nonpreferred customer a discount larger than the largest discount you have given a preferred customer for any product.

SLAs are a great concept, but they're often difficult to put in practice in a meaningful way because of three key problems:

- There are no accepted standards for formally specifying, discovering, and communicating SLAs. Reasons include lack of systems that could use a formal specification and high variability of SLA metrics and remedies. As a result, SLAs are typically specified in long documents, and it's up to humans to monitor whether they're being met. The SLA negotiation process, rather than being automated, happens out-of-band through phone calls and meetings.

- Most existing systems can only monitor very basic SLA metrics. Without the cooperation of system management vendors, the benefits of formally specifying and communicating SLAs won't pay for the hassle of using them. Some complex scenarios need to be handled, such as monitoring the SLA of systems outside your domain of control (as is the case with some outsourced services).

- Last but not least is the issue of enforcement. If you know an SLA isn't being met, what remedies can be made? How quickly can the situation be improved? What if it isn't improved for a prolonged period of time? Can you, for example, buy insurance to guard against failure to meet the SLAs you've promised to your partners? How about insurance in case your partners don't meet the SLAs they've promised you? Beyond automating SLA negotiation, the ultimate enforcement of SLAs boils down to the issues of trust and legal frameworks, both of which are thoroughly underdeveloped in the domain of dynamic e-business.

Here is one good reason why you should start moving toward more formal ways of specifying, communicating, monitoring, and enforcing SLAs at both the IT and business levels: without doing so, there will be no true dynamic e-business.

The most promising standards work in this space is happening as part of the WS-Agreement initiative at the *Global Grid Forum (GGF)* 📖. IBM contributed its WSLA work into this effort. The WS-Agreement work is happening as part of the *Grid Resource Allocation Agreement Protocol (GRAAP)* 📖 work at GGF. The goal is to produce a specification for the management of resources and services using negotiated SLAs that leverages SOA. This is a key emerging standard, and you would be well advised to follow its progress.

Abstraction

As with most things in information technology, the management process is about levels of abstraction. In this case, the abstractions through which we want to monitor, understand, and control a system change from physical to logical to analytic. The physical level deals with operational data about the components of a system, such as getting a heartbeat out of a network appliance or measuring response time for Web service requests. The logical level organizes component data into a coherent system-level view, typically through aggregation and dependency analysis. For example, a common logical metric in manufacturing is production line throughput. From that point on, additional processing at the analytic level can provide a deeper view into the system. A security event correlation engine might analyze hundreds of real-time security alerts coming from servers, routers, firewalls, and intrusion detection systems and reduce them to a statement that the network is under a DoS attack originating in Hong Kong. At this level, information has become knowledge, and that knowledge is actionable. In this particular scenario, a small change in a routing table could make the attack ineffective.

The boundaries between these levels of abstraction are fluid. Nevertheless, in terms of thinking about patterns in systems management, this model is helpful in outlining a roadmap for how systems management technologies evolve and how they can be applied to Web services. Table 14.4 outlines some of the facets of systems management capabilities that are common across domains, together with some examples of these capabilities. Figure 14.10 visualizes the key dependencies between the various facets as a roadmap for systems management. Darker shading indicates later stages in the roadmap. Arrows indicate ordering dependencies. There is too much detail there to discuss in the scope of this chapter, but it gives you an indication of the range of solutions available in the space. Note that Figure 14.10 paints a picture that goes far beyond the scope of WSDM; WSDM will provide the core plumbing that will enable vendors to deliver meaningful management solutions that solve real enterprise problems.

The roadmap outlined here concerns two types of operations: IT operations and business operations. IT operations are concerned with the technological footprint and behavior of a system: the hardware and software that are involved, the interconnection between servers, storage and networking, the performance and scalability of the system, its security, and any faults that occur during its operations. Business operations are concerned about the effect of systems on the business. For example, how has the deployment of supply chain automation Web services affected SkatesTown's inventory levels and out-of-stock conditions?

The end goal of both types of monitoring is action—doing something with the system or the system environment or the business to make things better. This is seen as the corrective workflow box in Figure 14.10. What information leads to the most important types of actions? From an IT perspective, there are two cases: In the case of system faults, root cause analysis enables the problem to be fixed; in the case of system changes or the system not meeting its SLAs, capacity planning leads to a new system configuration. From a business perspective, business impact analysis provides the information needed to optimize business processes.

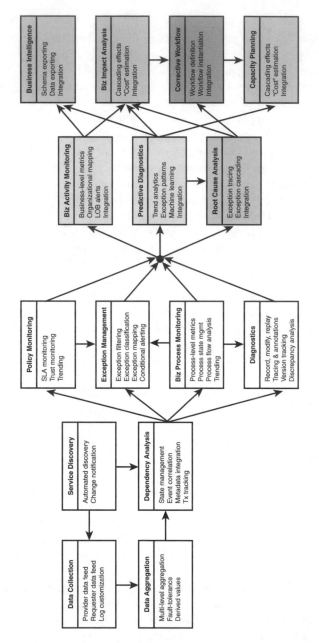

Figure 14.10   A roadmap of systems management (darker shading indicates later stages; arrows indicate ordering dependencies)

Table 14.4   **Facets of Systems Management**

Level	Capability	Description	Examples
Physical	Component discovery	Finding systems elements to monitor	Auto-discovering Web services through UDDI
	Data collection	Gathering data from all managed components	Gathering Web services response times
Physical/ logical	Data aggregation	Creating a unified data repository	Averaging response times across a cluster
Logical	Dependency analysis	Using meta-data and processing rules to establish links between system components	Auto-discovering the relations between application components and the Web services they expose
	Exception management	Applying configurable rules as to identify exception conditions and how they should be processed under different situations	Rules-based handling of SOAP faults
	Policy monitoring	Dynamic analysis of system behavior through the lens of business policy	SLA monitoring
	Diagnostics	Providing services that facilitate the isolation, analysis, and elimination of problems	Record-modify-replay of SOAP messages
Logical/ analytic	Business process monitoring (BPM)	Presenting information about the system not in terms of its components but in terms of the business processes that it supports	Exposing metrics such as start-to-finish time for entire business processes
Analytic	*Business activity monitoring (BAM)*	Analyzing real-time information about business processes	Communicating out-of-stock conditions to the right level of business user
	Business intelligence (BI)	Deep introspection as well as ad hoc analysis of system behavior	Enabling supply-chain optimization
	Business impact analysis (BIA)	Predicting the ripple effects of changes in system behavior	Determining the impact of slower-than-expected order processing
	Predictive diagnostics	Applying real-time analysis with past records to anticipate problems with the system	Predicting out-of-stock conditions based on order history
	Root cause analysis	Analyzing system information to determine the cause of specific failures	Correlating network, server, application and Web services information
	Workflow integration	Automating systems maintenance and problem resolution workflow	Trouble ticket management

If history is a lesson, *Web services management (WSM)* 📖 will follow the roadmap described here. We find proof for this when we look at other distributed management technologies such as network, system, and application management (NSAM). As Web services become more broadly deployed, customers will want all the capabilities outlined in the roadmap. However, dealing with Web services efficiently and flexibly is difficult. Processing XML tends to slow systems considerably. In addition, few products in the market can access and use all the information encapsulated in Web services messages.

This brings up the interesting question of what you should do about monitoring and managing Web services in production. The right answer depends on whether we're talking about IT or business operations. The key goals of IT operations—root cause analysis and capacity planning—can't be achieved only by looking at the Web services layer of the technology stack. Consider two simple examples. First, let's say that SkatesTown's PO submission service isn't responding. Is this happening because of a problem in the service implementation, the Web services engine exposing it, the SOA infrastructure around it, the server cluster, the network, or something else? Second, consider the example of the same service taking too long to respond. Is this due to a slow database backend, poor service implementation, overloaded servers, misconfigured network routing tables, a DoS attack in progress, or something else? In both cases, the answers can't be determined by looking at what's happening at the Web services layer alone: You need a holistic view of your system and its environment. In other words, you need the capabilities of the established management systems. This isn't to say that they will give you great Web services monitoring capabilities—right now they won't. You may need to choose a smaller, nimbler vendor, but you should make sure its monitoring capabilities integrate well with the rest of the monitoring infrastructure. Otherwise you'll never get the whole picture, and it will be difficult to take informed action.

Business operations are a different story. Information about the business sits inside the data repositories of enterprise systems and travels on the wire as Web services messages. From one perspective, this is a simpler world. All the information about a purchase order is encapsulated in a PO submission Web services message; gone is the complexity of the multiple layers of IT infrastructure. From another perspective, this is a much more complex environment because of logical dependencies between business systems. For example, a PO submission may generate a delayed shipment notification as a result of an out-of-stock condition in one of the warehouses. Understanding this level of dependencies is difficult but important for business impact analysis. It's theoretically possible for a system to take the information encapsulated in service descriptions, business process descriptions, the interaction models described in standards such as RosettaNet for the IT industry and ACORD for the global insurance industry, and all Web services messages flowing about the enterprise in order to build a model of what is going on with business processes in the enterprise and how they're related. The key advantage of such a system is that it can gather useful business information transparently. Traditional approaches to this problem, such as BAM, take an intrusive approach: They need to tie into the backend databases of enterprise systems and are therefore subject to change resulting from updates, system customizations, and so on. A system operating at the Web services message level wouldn't have these problems. In particular, change management will be easier, since much of the Web services traffic is likely to be based in industry standard vocabularies, which change more infrequently than enterprise system implementations.

You can't get a system like this from any vendor right now. Certainly, you can't get it from traditional systems management vendors, because they have been focused on solving a different problem: IT operations monitoring. Some exciting startups, such as Service Integrity, are working on this problem. The jury is out on whether they will be able to solve it; but if they do, it will be a significant achievement.

Summary

Web services are clearly the most promising technology for distributed computing and systems integration. It's easy to wonder why enterprises aren't adopting Web services faster. We hope this chapter has demonstrated that there are many reasons that go beyond technology. This chapter has also given you a framework for thinking about Web services adoption in your organization that can bring some of the benefits of the technology without exposing you to unnecessary risk and expense.

We strongly believe that the time to adopt Web services in the enterprise is now. You don't have to do an enterprisewide SOA rollout, and you don't have to reengineer systems that are working well with legacy integration solutions. However, you do need to be building the Web services skill set in your organization, because the technologies hold great promise for solving some of the tough problems facing IT organizations. The Web services tools and technologies available in the market now have achieved capability, scalability, and robustness that make them ready for prime time. Chances are that projects in your organization can benefit significantly from a pragmatic application of Web services.

As you invest more into Web services, you stand to gain more from them. The future is bright.

Resources

- *ACORD*—http://www.acord.org/
- *BRML*—Business Rules Markup Language, http://xml.coverpages.org/brml.html
- *DCML*—Data Center Markup Language, http://www.dcml.org/
- *DSI*—Dynamic Systems Initiative, http://www.microsoft.com/windowsserversystem/dsi/default.mspx
- *Gamma, et al*—*Design Patterns*, Addison-Wesley, 1995.
- *GGF*—Global Grid Forum, http://www.gridforum.org/
- *GRAAP*—Grid Resource Allocation Agreement Protocol, http://www.ggf.org/3_SRM/graap.htm
- *JSR 168*—Portlet Specification, http://jcp.org/en/jsr/detail?id=168

- *ORM-ML*—Object Role Modeling Markup Language, `http://xml.coverpages.org/orm-ml.html`

- *RosettaNet*—`http://www.rosettanet.org`

- *SDM*—System Definition Model, `http://www.microsoft.com/windowsserversystem/dsi/sdm.mspx`

- *SIIA*—Software & Information Industry Association, `http://www.siia.net`

- *WS-CAF*—Web Services Composite Applications Framework, `http://www.oasis-open.org/committees/tc_home.php?wg_abbrev=ws-caf`

- *WSIA*—Web Services Interactive Applications, `http://www.oasis-open.org/committees/tc_home.php?wg_abbrev=wsia`

- *WSLA*—Web Service Level Agreements, `http://www.research.ibm.com/wsla/`

- *WSRP*—Web Services for Remote Portlets, `http://www.oasis-open.org/committees/tc_home.php?wg_abbrev=wsrp`

15

Epilogue: Web Services Futures

NOW WE COME TO THE END OF OUR JOURNEY with this book. We've covered a lot of territory and a daunting array of technologies, all part of the Web services family of standards and technologies.

Now it's time to step back and look at the bigger picture. After summarizing the path Web services has taken since the year 2000, we conclude with a set of thoughts and predictions about where the Web services community is headed.

A Roadmap for Web Services

To help you understand the evolution of Web services technologies, let's consider three distinct but overlapping phases: invention, development, and acceptance (see Figure 15.1).

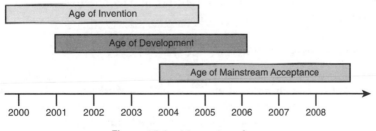

Figure 15.1   Maturation phases

All three phases overlap in time. Each phase has had a gradual introduction and will gradually reduce in importance over time.

Age of Invention (Base SOAP, WSDL, UDDI)

Web services began with a burst of innovation related to the concept of using XML as a base message exchange format to make distributed computing (particularly business application integration) easier to do. This era saw the introduction of the first versions of the core specifications: SOAP 1.1, WSDL 1.1, and UDDI 1.0.

From the initial success of the core specifications and the groundswell of industry interest and adoption, two things followed:

- There were initial preproduct releases of tools and runtimes to support early developer experience with Web services. This resulted in initial prototyping of business applications to exploit the emerging standards for Web service application integration.

- A wave of specifications was released, such as WS-Security. These specifications were prioritized by weaknesses in Web services identified by the early prototyping work.

This phase was at its peak around 2002 and 2003, with the introduction of a large number of specifications with *WS* in their names. Depending on how you count, between 40 and 50 Web services specifications are in various stages of maturation, industry acceptance, and developer adoption. What started as a simple concept—"Use XML as an interapplication messaging mechanism"—has expanded quickly. This is a sign of the importance of the technologies and, to a lesser extent, the introduction of counter productive, competitive specifications by rival factions of vendors.

This phase has also been marked by initial product-level releases of Web services technologies, usually SOAP runtime support and WSDL tools. Associated with these early product releases was the transition of many pilot applications into (often limited) production to solve real business problems. However, the lack of standards in certain areas, such as security, limited the breadth and reach of these early applications of Web services technology.

This phase is beginning to wind down. The rate at which new specifications are being introduced is slowing, product support is maturing, and more activity is dedicated to refining development practices and approaches.

Age of Development (from Hype to Delivery)

The onset of the age of development marks the end of the Wild West–style energetic land-grab for mind share and the beginning of the hard work of making these technologies useful for serious business computing. Web services are no longer at the bleeding edge; the age of innovation wanes, and the age of development pragmatics has arrived.

The age of development is marked by the second iteration of the base standards (such as SOAP 1.2, WSDL 2.0, and UDDI 3.0) and the final standardization of the second-wave specifications with narrower scope: WS-Security and, in the systems management arena, the Web Services Distributed Management (WSDM) standard. A third (and, we hope, final) wave of standards will be proposed to fill in gaps exposed by more sophisticated applications of Web services.

The maturity of the base standards is paralleled by the maturity and usefulness of second (and third) generation product support from major middleware vendors. Also associated with this phase is the emergence of an ecosystem of smaller, Web service–specific vendors that serve various niche markets with specialized Web services products and services. Overall, the focus of product and tooling development will be on the pragmatics of implementing secure, reliable, transactable, and manageable Web services.

With the maturation of Web services products comes the increasing maturity and sophistication of applications built using Web services. In this phase, companies go beyond the prototype scale; serious Web services applications are built and deployed, forming core parts of a company's application portfolio. We're beginning to see more companies put Web services applications into production.

There is also a shift in the tone of analysts' articles. In the previous phase, the bulk of such articles touted the brave new world of Web services, focusing on the promise of the brand-new technology. The beginning of the end of that phase was signaled by the appearance of skeptical articles outlining the myriad shortcomings of Web services. With the age of development, analysts' articles are dominated by those that are specific to details of a particular technology or that reflect hard lessons learned from real Web services deployments. The futurist articles now tend to focus on applying Service-Oriented Architectures (SOA) as the basis for the entire application portfolio or other broad-reaching applications of Web services and SOA.

The major theme of this era is the identification of the serious impediments to Web services exploitation and the nonglamorous tasks of addressing these issues in standards and products. Items such as enhancing the performance of SOAP messaging and managing a Web services infrastructure join security and reliability as the major focal points for innovation.

This phase will deal with the serious pragmatics of development and deployment. Chapter 14, "Web Services Pragmatics," enumerated many of these pragmatics. From the point of view of this industry-level analysis, the major pragmatic for developers will be coping with the complexity presented by Web services. The net result will be a shakeout of many superfluous standards efforts and a focusing of industry product development on the issues and standards that really matter to customers.

Age of Mainstream Acceptance (Web Services Become Boring)

As we write this text, we're one or two years away from Web services becoming truly boring. By "boring" we don't diminish the importance of the technology, but rather we describe its capacity to generate hype and industry excitement over new innovations. Java has been in this phase for some time; Java is still important, but it isn't the shiny new technology it was in the mid to late 1990s. Java is mainstream; it has been for several years, and within a couple of years, Web services will be too.

This phase will be dominated by broad adoption of Web services and SOA by almost all businesses and nonbusiness organizations. This phase will also see an increase in the use of Web services for business-to-business application integration, surpassing existing, non-Web based technologies such as Electronic Data Interchange (EDI).

In this phase, the third wave of specifications will become final standards and will be well supported within several products. During this phase, most or all of the innovation will be in industry best practices surrounding how to best exploit Web services based on real experience with Web services development projects. By this point, a dramatic shift will be observed within the industry—away from Web services standards efforts and onto more pragmatic product features and interoperability issues between vendors' products.

Since this phase has only barely begun, it's the subject of speculation on the future of Web services. We devote the rest of this chapter to discussing possible future trends with the Web services technology.

Future Trends in Web Services

We segment our predictions for the future of Web services into three parts: near term, or trends that will become visible (or be resolved) within the next year or two; medium term, or trends that will become apparent within the next 5 years; and longer term, or trends that will happen between 5 and 10 years from now. Of course, as is the case for any future trends analysis, items further out in the future are more speculative and are less certain to play out the way we predict. The near-term items reflect extrapolation of currently identified issues and are therefore more tangible in nature and more likely to happen.

Short-Term Trends and Issues

Many of the trends facing the Web services industry over the next year or two can be characterized as "gut checks." These issues are already apparent and, due to the increasing adoption of Web services for serious application development, they must be addressed short term; otherwise they risk seriously impeding the maturation of Web services standards and products.

Specification Churn

One of the things about Web services that concerns many people is the pace of change. It seems that standards bodies and groups of vendors are continually issuing new Web services specifications. Is it all worth it? A cost is associated with understanding each new specification and how it relates to the other specifications and figuring out when (or whether) to embrace it.

Some customers will adopt specifications immediately when they're released from a standards body (or even, as we saw with SOAP and WSDL, prior to release). This adoption is needs-driven: How important is functionality like reliable messaging or security for the organization's application of Web services? The greater the need, the more likely early adoption will take place. But early adoption has a price: Bleeding-edge (or pre-product level) releases of tooling and runtime offerings cost more to deploy and get working. Businesses must also consider the migration costs if a specification is adopted too early and then changes.

On the other hand, if a company waits until a specification is released and products supporting it are in the second or third release, the company will get more predictable deployment costs. However, the company may miss opportunities in the marketplace if it's slow to implement the right Web services or to be able to interact with those of its business partners.

At what point will there be "enough" Web services specifications? We claim that the rate of new specification introduction has diminished and that with the emergence of the second wave of Web services (the age of deployment), there won't be many new specifications. But have too many specifications been issued already? The answer isn't clear at this point.

It's possible (but unlikely) that the sheer rate of change of new specifications (and subsequent versions of existing specifications) can freeze adoption of Web services. The outcome of this gut check will be determined by the net cost/benefit tradeoff of adopting each new specification. This cost/benefit tradeoff is tied to the next two discussion points: complexity and composability.

Complexity

Remember when the *S* in SOAP stood for *Simple*? With the great enthusiasm for Web services in the information technology industry, the "simple" concept can no longer be applied to Web services. Have the infrastructure wizards run amok? Is the industry developing more complex infrastructure than is required by most applications?

Complexity of the Web services environment may be an impediment to adoption. The key thing to focus on is how much complexity is too much. Second-wave specifications such as WS-Security and WS-ReliableMessaging came as a result of clearly needed components in the Web services stack. But are other specifications being published that reinvent the wheel? At times, specifications are submitted by vendors as competitive alternatives to freeze the adoption of a particular Web services specification or to slow Web services adoption.

Coping with this complexity comes down to figuring out which specifications to pay attention to, learn, and adopt. But which of the many Web services specifications should a company focus on? This is a tough question, because it depends on the needs of the business application.

Clearly, the base specifications (XML, SOAP, and WSDL) are critical. Some applications will need UDDI; others won't. Some applications will need security as offered by WS-Security; others won't. You can repeat this statement for most of the technologies we've covered in this book. The material in this book should help you determine the functionality offered by these various standards and whether your business application needs that functionality.

Composability

One approach that the Web services community is taking to manage complexity is *composability* of the specifications. Web services specifications are designed to be composed with other specifications to deliver a configurable set of capabilities that suits the specific needs of an application. The idea is to define the specifications so that a designer can pick and choose which ones best suit his application and use only the concepts and specifications that are needed.

However, do all the specifications fit together? Most of the Web services specifications are designed to compose with many (but not all) of the Web services specifications that preceded them. What about the ones the specification authors missed or ignored? What about composability with specifications that aren't yet written? If the Web services stack doesn't fit together well, or if the vast majority of the specifications work in combination with only a special subset of the Web services stack, then the burden for the application designer increases along with the cost and complexity of integrating two Web services.

One way to address composability (and complexity) concerns is through tooling that integrates Web services products from a collection of emerging Web services specifications; this tooling would replace function-specific tooling that developers would otherwise integrate in an ad hoc fashion. However, tooling cannot completely mask underlying complexity.

Interoperability

To address the composability issues we just discussed, the Web services community established the WS-Interoperability Organization (WS-I; see Chapter 13, "Web Services Interoperability"). This was a good start, but just a start. If it's difficult for products built by different Web services vendors to interoperate, then the use of Web services will be limited within an organization (where it's possible to mandate the use of a single vendor's product); application integration tasks between companies will also be difficult.

Companies are also taking the initiative, outside of WS-I, to make sure interoperability becomes a reality. Since WS-I will only endorse standards that have been produced by standards bodies, its recommendations will be developed extremely late in the development cycle. To counteract this timing, specification authors have begun to host interoperability workshops to try to flesh out problem areas in their specifications that might only be visible once different implementations start to talk to one another or when their specifications are combined with other specifications. This process allows for much more complete specifications to be presented to a standards body—ideally, minimizing the changes required—and thus reduces the impact on vendors who may have chosen to take the gamble and implement the specifications early.

Performance

Many users (and all the skeptics) have voiced concerns about the performance problems associated with Web services. There have been many early attempts to speed things up, particularly at the XML level: for example, the XML–Binary work in the W3C (http://www.w3.org/TR/xop10). Not all of the proposals are standards based, and they may lead companies down a path to a proprietary lock-in of one vendor's technology. It goes without saying that proprietary solutions have a tremendous negative impact on interoperability.

Will developers have to live with the performance cost of Web services until either XML and other Web services performance improvements are developed and productized or Moore's law makes the problems less relevant? A similar situation existed with early Java. Performance concerns were addressed by a combination of improved Java Virtual Machines and garbage collection algorithms and, of course, Moore's law. Developers coped with early Java's shortcomings because of the perceived benefits. Will Web services get this same benefit of the doubt? So far it has, but performance improvements may be necessary to sustain adoption.

If performance improvements don't appear (particularly standards-based performance enhancements), then many designers will choose proprietary technologies for application integration. Such decisions will reduce the impact and evolution of Web services.

Security

Lack of a ubiquitously deployed security infrastructure based on commonly accepted open standards is often cited as an impediment to using Web services for intercompany application integration. Web services security is a useful abstraction of the currently deployed security infrastructures. Given that companies aren't likely to make significant changes in their network security infrastructures, the WS-Security approach (reviewed in Chapter 9) is an effective way to integrate various security environments.

However, we must ask a few questions. Will the current WS-Security family of specifications yield a ubiquitous security infrastructure? How long will it take for vendors to produce Web services security products based on WS-Security? How soon will companies adopt these products?

Medium-Term Trends

We expect that most of the short-term issues will be addressed (or turn out not to be real impediments to Web services adoption), and therefore we conclude that Web services will continue to be an important concept in IT for at least the next five years. Several medium-term trends are worth examining. We predict that the trends listed in this section will play out over the next five years; many of them have already started to appear and will continue to evolve, along with Web services, during the medium term.

Web Services Become Buried in the Infrastructure

Over the medium term, Web services infrastructure will no longer be a differentiator for a middleware vendor's products. Web services support will simply get buried in the application integration runtimes and tooling. This trend has already begun. BEA, IBM, Microsoft, Oracle, and others all have Web services firmly entrenched in the infrastructure.

The level of integration will be seamless and assumed in much the way that HTTP is supported in middleware products today. Over the next five years, the extent to which the entire Web services stack is supported and integrated into middleware infrastructure products will increase. The robustness of Web services support, the ease of use of the tooling and infrastructure, and other qualities of service will be key innovative differentiators for vendor middleware over this period.

In a similar light, Web services management technologies (like those being defined in the Web services distributed management technical committee in OASIS) will mature and be implemented by systems management vendors. Furthermore, the middleware and systems management products themselves will take on a service-oriented approach, blurring the distinction between traditional systems management and middleware products. By the end of the medium term, SOA-enabled systems management will be a component of an overall application integration middleware fabric.

We also expect continued evolution of the XML infrastructure, including XML-aware firewalls and other more sophisticated Web services infrastructure to protect against denial-of-service (DOS) and other security attacks.

Web Services Best Practices Emerge

Over the next five years, the focus of innovation and experimentation will shift away from the development of raw technology and standards and toward the use of Web services to solve business problems. This is not to say that developers who are exploiting Web services technologies aren't innovative; rather, in the next five years the variety of Web services technologies with which to build solutions will become greater and much more mature. This selection will allow a greater variety of solutions to be built and will therefore allow the industry to determine what combinations of Web services technologies work and what don't. Only with a rich amount of actual Web services deployment experience will we discover those Web services and SOA best practices that stand the test of time.

One example is related to the policy-based approach to building flexible information systems (we go into more detail about this in the next section). Companies everywhere will struggle with policies and processes for deploying service-oriented architectures; and from this struggle will emerge a new set of policy-oriented tools and associated best practices.

Another example of Web services best practices is associated with the widespread adoption of Business Process Execution Language (BPEL; see Chapter 12, "Orchestrating Web Services"). We predict that a two-level programming paradigm will become the preferred programming model for applications that directly reflect the business processes they support. This programming approach combines "programming in the large"—using BPEL to model the business process as an orchestration of a set of Web services—with "programming in the small"—the use of traditional programming languages for implementing Web services. This reflects an overall trend in software engineering to take a more component-oriented approach to building systems.

Two additional results are likely with the widespread adoption of BPEL. First, a market will emerge for business processes written in BPEL. This is a logical evolution of the current packaged application software market; we predict that all the current vendors (and many new vendors) will change their products over time to the BPEL-oriented two-level programming model. Second, we predict that many domain-specific standards will emerge at the business process level, and that these standards will use BPEL as the language of specification.

Policy-Based Interoperability

Once the short-term standards work is done to finalize the way policy is expressed in Web services—some combination of the WSDL 2.0 features and properties facility and WS-Policy standardization—Web services will arrive at a point of vastly improved interoperability. Policy-based interoperability exploits the composability feature of Web services, which we mentioned earlier. Systems will be built by developers who pick and choose parts of the Web services stack to exploit; no one will be forced to build and deploy the entire Web services stack for all applications.

Policy or capabilities meta-data gives designers a better idea up front of what is and isn't going to work when two parties attempt to use Web services to integrate their business processes. In other words, when you're processing the WSDL for a new Web services partner, encountering an unknown but required extension may cause a failure condition. If you have a policy description of the partner's Web service, you know exactly where to find the definition of any extension used by that Web service. This might also allow the requestor's infrastructure to acquire a plug-in component for its Web services environment, which will enable it to use the extension.

Not everyone will have (or want) every Web service extension. We'll never have a world where every machine has exactly the same stack—heterogeneity of computing infrastructure is a reality that we'll always deal with. Homogeneity isn't a desirable state, because as it tends to stifle innovation; it also increases the likelihood that more security attacks will be developed. Consider a biological analogy: Monocultures, such as we see in modern agriculture, are more susceptible to new diseases that can attack a weakness in a species, multiply rapidly, and destroy entire crops. A similar network effect for threats is less likely in ecosystems that have some diversity.

The Rise of Service-Level Agreements

During the medium term, the problem of core connectivity (getting Web services to talk to one another) will be solved for the most part. The challenge will then shift to addressing how *well* those Web services talk to one another—in other words, enhancing the quality of service (QoS) of using Web services.

This trend is related to the previous discussion of policy-based interoperability, in that it exploits additional policy meta-data describing the capabilities of the Web service (such as reliability of messaging, auditing, nonrepudiation of message sends, logging, and so on) and extends this field to include notions of monitoring and metering of use. The use of this meta-data together with third-party services that monitor and guarantee the assertions made by Web services providers enables requestors and providers to form service-level agreements that spell out the terms of use for Web services (including monetary terms and compensation terms for failure scenarios).

Standards will emerge that allow interoperability between service-level agreements authored by different parties, negotiation of terms for service-level agreements, and monitoring and enforcement of those agreements. When monetary risks and rewards are associated with providing varying QoS of Web services, businesses will have a stronger incentive to develop and deploy components to help monitor and manage the infrastructure. Technologies and standards to support mundane QoS, like failover redundancy, automated service level monitoring, usage monitoring/metering and billing, and so on, will emerge.

Watch the early work related to WS-Agreement, which is currently being standardized in the Global Grid Forum. Like many things in the Web services world, the Grid community may be early adopters and may push the envelope on Web services standards and technologies. It's hard to imagine building a Grid infrastructure without some form of service-level agreement (and commensurate charge-back structure) to go with it.

The Coming of "On Demand" Computing

Associated with the maturation of Web services standards and products and the increased uptake of Web services and service-oriented architecture concepts by vendors in their own products will be a convergence of grid, systems management, and business computing infrastructures. The distinction between these pieces will evolve from separate, standalone infrastructures, to components in a broad middleware fabric. The result of this convergence will be a more flexible Web services infrastructure that yields very flexible business solutions that are easier to manage and change. This flexibility will work in tandem with the rise of service-level agreements and the infrastructure to monitor them. The more closely integrated applications are with the infrastructure, and the more flexible the infrastructure is, the easier it is to deploy and guarantee attractive QoS at an affordable cost.

Industry Standards at the Business Level

As the core infrastructural specifications in Web services reach maturity, the standards focus will shift to standardizing Web services interfaces and policies associated with line-of-business processes. This work will be an evolution of the efforts in various industry groups to standardize on XML vocabularies associated with their business processes. This work will also be accelerated by an increased use of BPEL to model standard business processes. The net result of standardizing business processes on a Web services base will be increased interoperability between business processes.

Increasing Role of an Enterprise Service Bus

An enterprise service bus is associated with the logical evolution of current message-oriented middleware products into a service-oriented world. The concept of an enterprise service bus is analogous to a hardware bus inside a computer. Just as computers are built by attaching various components like memory, disk drives, and CPUs to a bus fabric that allows them to communicate, we envision a common approach to using a message-oriented middleware fabric to build applications by attaching software components to an enterprise service bus and using Web services messages to communicate among them.

An enterprise service bus is a combination of raw Web services support (such as SOAP) with basic message routing and delivery QoS, content and format transformation/mediation, and other value-add services such as logging, which are commonly found in message-oriented middleware products. With an enterprise service bus, new capabilities can be added to the Web services infrastructure by plugging components into the bus—for example, to provide auditing, billing, and metering. Web services messages can be explicitly (or automatically) configured to invoke these components and thereby exploit their capabilities. Enterprise service bus implementations can also be used for policy enforcement, by associating various policies (such as "log all messages from a given requestor") with an entire application domain.

Role of Portals

Within the next five years, existing portal products will evolve to exploit emerging standards such as Web Services Remote Portlets, which is being developed in OASIS. With an increasing number of Web services being deployed, businesses will be motivated to innovate on ways to present Web services results to human users by exploiting rich client interfaces. Look for spreadsheet-level ease-of-use that allows business professionals (not technical professionals) to stitch together Web services to solve simple business problems.

Rise of Business Activity Monitoring (BAM)

Businesses are looking for various ways to get better information from the raw data collected by their information systems. One approach is called business activity monitoring (BAM). With BAM, a company's messaging infrastructure is augmented with software to listen in on the message traffic coming into various business systems. The traffic is analyzed, using algorithms to detect certain patterns (like a sudden increase in sales or a sharp decrease in customer complaints). If a certain pattern is detected, alerts can be sent to decision makers, prompting further analysis and potentially corrective actions.

As Web services establish a common gateway of message flows and transactions into the organization, they provide a common focus point for companies to monitor the health of their business. Marrying Web services with BAM may yield a rich early-warning capability for businesses. Historically, BAM products focused too much on making disparate message formats into a canonical form, as a prerequisite for doing pattern analysis. This meant that most of the work went into transforming the data into a canonical form, and not enough effort was spent on efficient pattern-matching approaches and tools to help articulate which patterns were important for the business to search for. Much of the canonicalization of the data format is already being done by the XML portion of Web services; thus BAM vendors have an opportunity to focus on addressing the business value of pattern analysis.

Longer-Term Trends

Over the next 10 years, we predict that several other macro trends will emerge. Of course, when predicting this far in the future, there is an increased risk that we'll be totally off the mark.

Application Architectures Go SOA

Within the next decade, most software will be composed of services. This transformation will come in one of three forms:

- Existing software will be wrapped by a single Web service.
- Existing software will be decomposed into a collection of Web services components.
- Software will be created from inception as a collaborating network of Web service components.

A virtuous cycle, or network effect, will happen with Web services over the next 10 years. As more Web services are written, more Web services will become available for others to invoke. As more Web services can be invoked, more applications will be written to invoke them. Eventually, an ecosystem of Web services providers and requestors will be created. This process is similar to how the World Wide Web evolved into a vast, collaborative network of Web sites and client browsers.

As more companies use Web services, they will demand that their infrastructure and packaged application software vendors provide their products in a service-oriented way. In reaction to this demand, more products (particularly packaged application software) will be delivered as Web services that are easier to integrate with the work customers do to expose their existing applications as Web services. This trend may begin in the medium term, but our point is related to the firm establishment of the best practice and behavior of the majority of architects.

With the increased availability of Web services components, application designers will evolve away from thinking about application architectures as monolithic software efforts and move toward a deep exploitation of configurable, component-based, service-oriented architectures. These SOA applications will be policy based and configured to participate in standard service-level agreement management. They will be easier to configure and change: As a business process changes, components will be snapped out and replaced with newer Web services that reflect different business partners or a different orchestration of subtasks to reflect the new approach the business wants to take.

SOA-based applications will be much easier to integrate with existing business systems, a feature that will make integrating vendor-supplied software packages much easier than in the past. Furthermore, the SOA-based application software will be more easily integrated with the service-oriented infrastructure (Web service middleware and operating systems) to which it is deployed. The line between application components and infrastructure components will be blurred.

Emergence of Value Networks

The term *value networks* represents a new approach to business design that emphasizes collaboration between multiple business partners to fulfill customer needs. This work is distinguished from traditional supply-chain analysis because of its analytical focus (activities, not companies) and its emphasis on tasks that are broader than provisioning of inputs. Although the concept has been around since the mid 1990s (it was essentially derived from reorienting supply-chain management to cope with the exuberance of Web-based e-commerce), this technique hasn't gained wide acceptance.

However, the value networks concept is important in a rapidly changing business environment. A major impediment is the cost of interfacing the business processes within and among the value network. This cost is largely due to the incompatibilities between IT systems within and among member firms in the value network. This integration cost is largely due to the lack of ubiquitously deployed standards, both infrastructure-level standards and business-process-level standards.

Web services technology can unlock the value inherent in participating in a value network. This is yet another example of the convergence of business strategy, business models, and information technology.

Summary

Now we really have come to the end of the book. We have covered a lot of ground since the opening chapters, from the promise of Web services, through the detailed examinations of the various important Web services specifications and technologies, through the pragmatics of using Web services today and the outlook for the technology in the future. We hope you've learned a lot about Web services and that this book will help you successfully apply Web services concepts and technologies to your work.

Glossary

Access Control List (ACL)   The most common means by which a network security system decides to grant or deny access to network services. It is a list of the available services and the entities permitted to use each service.

acknowledgment header   A SOAP header used in the WS-RM specification that contains confirmation of a message's delivery to its intended destination.

activation service   In the transaction space, a Web service on the Coordinator that participants in a transaction will register with.

activity   A composition primitive that implements the business logic of a BPEL process. BPEL distinguishes basic and structured activities. *See also:* Business Process Execution Language for Web Services (BPEL4WS).

AdminClient   A tool used to deploy WSDD files into a running `AxisServer`.

assign activity   A BPEL construct that can be used to update the values of variables with new data.

asymmetric encryption   The process of encrypting data with a shared secret or key. *See also:* encryption.

atomic transaction (AT)   One of the various types of transactions defined in WS-Transactions. AT asserts that either all the work will be completed successfully or none of it will be done at all.

AttachmentPart   A special SAAJ message part that holds a MIME attachment (a binary object sent along with a SOAP message). *See also:* SOAP with Attachments API for Java (SAAJ).

attribute   A property of an XML element.

authentication   The process of establishing the legitimacy of a user before allowing access to requested resources. For example, the user enters a name or account number (identification) and password (authentication).

authorization   The process of determining what kinds of activities are permitted or what kind of resources are accessed.

AxisClient   The client-side `AxisEngine`, which is called via the `Call` or a stub, and ends up sending messages via a transport sender.

AxisEngine   The main message processing class in Axis, responsible for taking a `MessageContext` and invoking the appropriate handlers in order to do work.

AxisServer   The server-side `AxisEngine`, which is invoked by a transport listener, and ends up calling a service.

B2B   *See:* business-to-business (B2B).

B2C   *See:* business-to-consumer (B2C).

BAM   *See:* business activity monitoring (BAM).

basic activity   An activity that represents an atomic operation of a business process. *See also:* activity.

BI   *See:* business intelligence (BI).

BIA   *See:* business impact analysis (BIA).

bind   An operation within a service-oriented architecture. The `bind` operation describes the set of tasks associated with a service requestor preparing to invoke and invoking a Web service provided by a service provider.

binding   *See:* protocol binding.

body   The container for the essential data representing the main purpose of a given SOAP message.

BPA   *See:* Business Process Automation (BPA).

BPEL   Short for BPEL4WS. *See:* Business Process Execution Language for Web Services (BPEL4WS).

BPEL4WS   *See:* Business Process Execution Language for Web Services (BPEL4WS).

BPM   *See:* Business Process Management (BPM).

BRML   *See:* Business Rules Markup Language (BRML).

BSN   *See:* business service network (BSN).

business activity (BA)   One of the various types of transactions defined in WS-Transactions. Unlike atomic transaction (AT), BA allows each operation to complete and save its work independently of any other operation. However, a `Compensate` operation is used if an error occurs. This `Compensate` operation makes up for any previously completed work.

business activity monitoring (BAM)   Real-time access to critical business performance indicators to improve the speed and effectiveness of business operations.

business impact analysis (BIA)   Often used in the context of risk analysis and business continuity planning. BIA also stands for the ability to assess the effect of system faults on the ability of a system to support its business functions.

business intelligence (BI)   An interactive process of analyzing and exploring information to discern trends or patterns, thereby deriving insights and drawing conclusions.

Business Process Automation (BPA)   The process of transitioning interrelated manual tasks to automated task execution under process control. *See also:* Business Process Management (BPM), service orchestration.

Business Process Execution Language for Web Services (BPEL4WS)   Defines a model and a grammar for describing the behavior of a business process based on interactions between the process and its partners.

Business Process Management (BPM)   The control and execution of automated processes. *See also:* Business Process Automation (BPA), service orchestration.

Business Rules Markup Language (BRML)   An XML rule vocabulary for agent communication based on ordinary logic programs.

business service network (BSN)   *See:* virtual exchange.

business-to-business (B2B)   A characterization of interaction between businesses over the Internet. In a B2B interaction, applications between businesses communicate without human intervention being required during the interaction. Contrast with business-to-consumer (B2C).

business-to-consumer (B2C)   A characterization of interaction between a human being and a business over the Internet. In a B2C interaction, a human being, often using a Web browser, invokes applications provided by a business. Contrast with business-to-business (B2B).

Call   The central client-side class in Axis, used to directly invoke Web services.

canonicalization   A method for generating a physical representation, the *canonical form*, of an XML document that accounts for the permissible changes. For example, the order of attributes, tab processing, and a standardized code set are used to check the logical equivalence of two documents.

CDATA section   An XML construct used to escape blocks of text containing characters that would otherwise be recognized as markup. CDATA sections begin with the string `<![CDATA[` and end with the string `]]>`. They can occur in all places where character data is allowed.

certificate   A data record used for authenticating network entities such as a server or a client. A certificate contains standard information about its owner (called the *subject*) and the signing Certificate Authority (called the *issuer*), plus the owner's public key and the signature made by the CA. Network entities verify these signatures using CA certificates.

Certificate Authority (CA)   A trusted third party whose purpose is to sign certificates for network entities that it has authenticated. Other network entities can check the signature to verify that a CA has authenticated the bearer of a certificate.

chain   A collection of handlers that run sequentially and can be named and deployed as a unit.

character reference   An escape sequence for characters in XML documents. The syntax for character references is an ampersand, followed by a pound/hash sign (#), followed by either a decimal character code or lowercase *x*, followed by a hexadecimal character code, followed by a semicolon. Example: the 8-bit character code 128 will be encoded in a UTF-8 XML document as `&#x80;`.

ciphertext   Encrypted data.

cleartext   Also known as plaintext. Words and figures in unencrypted, unformatted, readable form.

client proxy   A component on the client that acts as a substitute (or proxy) for the Web service. A client proxy presents a programming language–specific interface to be used by a client application to invoke the Web service and presents the response from the Web service in a programming language–specific manner back to the client. The term *client stub* is also used as a synonym.

commit   In the transaction space, the act of ending and saving the work done under the scope of a transaction.

compensate   In the transaction space, the act of making up for any previous completed work in the event of an error.

compensate activity   A BPEL construct that lets you explicitly call a compensation handler.

compensation handler   A handler in a BPEL process that undoes the work of previous activities in the case of an error.

Completion AT protocol   A variant of the atomic transaction (AT) protocol. The participants registering under this protocol wish to be notified of the outcome (success or failure) of the transaction.

complex type   An XML element that contains subelements or carries attributes.

confidentiality   Assurance that information is shared only among authorized persons or organizations so that others can't see it.

conformance target   An entity that must conform to a profile requirement.

content   Everything between the start tag and the end tag in an XML document.

content type   An XML element's type: empty content, element-only content, or mixed content.

control characters   Also known as nonwhitespace control characters. These include the ASCII characters with codes 0 through 7, 9, 11, 12, or 14 through 31.

CoordinationContext   In the transaction space, the SOAP header that represents the transaction the current message relates to.

coordinator   In the transaction space, the administrator of the various participants in a transaction.

correlation   The relationship of message properties and BPEL process instances.

correlation ID   An identifier (usually a string) used to keep track of individual requests in a multistep series of Web services interactions.

correlation set   A set of BPEL correlation tokens defined as a set of properties shared by all messages in the correlated group. A given message can carry multiple correlation sets.

Data Center Markup Language (DCML)   A standard that provides a mechanism by which IT infrastructure assets and their relationships can be documented. *See also:* System Definition Model (SDM).

DCML   *See:* Data Center Markup Language (DCML).

declaration   A processing instruction whose target is xml. It specifies the version of XML and, optionally, the character encoding in a document. Example:
`<?xml version="1.0" encoding="UTF-8"?>`.

deserializer A Java class that parses incoming XML into Java objects.

digest A unique, mathematical summary of a document that serves to identify the document and its contents. *See also:* hashing function.

digital signature An electronic identification of a person or thing, intended to verify to a recipient the integrity of data sent to them and the identity of the sender. *See also:* certificate, Certificate Authority (CA), Public Key Infrastructure (PKI).

DIME *See:* Direct Internet Message Exchange (DIME).

Direct Internet Message Exchange (DIME) A specification from Microsoft and IBM for sending SOAP envelopes and binary attachments serialized in a binary envelope format.

disaster recovery (DR) The ability to maintain high availability across multiple locations. *See also:* high availability.

document-centric A view of processing a SOAP message that occurs when the body of the SOAP envelope is viewed as an XML document rather than as parameters forming an RPC call.

DR *See:* disaster recovery (DR).

DSI *See:* Dynamic Systems Initiative (DSI).

Durable Two-Phase Commit A variant of the Two-Phase Commit protocol in which some participants are deemed *transient*: They have no real persistent store themselves, but rather are proxies. For example, a cache might be considered transient. *See also:* Two-Phase Commit (2PC).

dynamic invocation Using the Call API instead of a stub for accessing generic Web services, with or without the use of WSDL.

Dynamic Systems Initiative (DSI) A Microsoft initiative to increase the utilization and responsiveness of IT systems while reducing operating costs. *See also:* System Definition Model (SDM).

EAR file A packaged file containing a number of other files that together make a complete J2EE application.

effective policy The policy (WS-Policy) associated with a WSDL element. This can either be a policy that is inherited or a policy that is directly attached to a WSDL element.

EJB *See:* Enterprise JavaBean (EJB).

EJB-Ref A resource reference to another EJB. *See also:* resource reference.

element A markup language term denoting the pairing of start and end tags.

element-only content An XML element that can only contain other subelements and can't contain character data.

Emerging Technologies Toolkit (ETTK) An IBM/alphaWorks product that showcases emerging technology. The toolkit provides a glimpse into what IBM is playing with at that moment with no guarantees as to any future use of the technology.

empty activity A BPEL construct identical to a no-op.

empty content An XML element that can't contain any subelements or character data.

encryption   The process by which data is temporarily rearranged into an unreadable or unintelligible form for confidentiality, transmission, or other security purposes.

endpoint reference   The component of WS-Addressing that describes a pointer or reference to a Web service at a particular deployment endpoint.

Enterprise JavaBean (EJB)   A business logic component that runs in a J2EE server.

entity   A named piece of information in an XML document. Internal entities are defined within the document. External entities have separate physical storage.

entity bean   A type of Enterprise JavaBean that is used to represent data that is long-lived. The data in an entity bean is stored persistently in a filesystem, database, or other long-term storage. *See also:* Enterprise JavaBean (EJB).

entity reference   Refers to the content of a named entity. The syntax for entity references is an ampersand (&), followed by the entity name, followed by a semicolon (;). *See also:* entity.

envelope   The main XML construct in a SOAP message. Contains a body and a header.

event handler   A handler in a BPEL process that deals with unsolicited events that can be received and processed in parallel.

fault handler   A handler in a BPEL process that deals with error situations such as faults from a Web service invocation.

feature   A unit of extensibility in SOAP. A feature specification defines a particular semantic, named with a URI, which may be implemented via SOAP modules or bindings. *See also:* module, protocol binding.

federation   Management and brokerage of the trust relationship among security domains. The concept is emphasized in Web services security in such a way that security domains are federated in a heterogeneous security environment, including support for federated identities.

`find`   An operation within a service-oriented architecture, describing a contract between a service requestor and a service registry. The `find` operation describes the steps taken by a service requestor to locate a service description of a service that meets the requirements of a component within the service requestor's application.

`flow` **activity**   A BPEL construct that allows the execution of activities in parallel in a business process.

GGF   *See:* Global Grid Forum (GGF).

global chain   A targeted chain of handlers that runs before and after the service (on the server) or the transport (on the client).

Global Grid Forum (GGF)   The leading venue for standards work focused on Grid computing.

GRAAP   *See:* Grid Resource Allocation Agreement Protocol (GRAAP).

Grid Resource Allocation Agreement Protocol (GRAAP) A standards initiative focused on resource scheduling and resource management in grid environments. *See also:* Global Grid Forum (GGF).

HA *See:* high availability (HA).

handler A message processing component in the Axis framework.

handshake An electronic exchange of signals between parties to establish that each has the necessary secret to allow secure communication.

hashing function A mathematical function used in encryption to distill the information contained in a file into a single large number, typically between 128 and 256 bits in length. Also known as a one-way hash function because it's mathematically infeasible to try to calculate the original message by computing backward from the result.

header 1: The soap:Header element. 2: (colloquial) An extensibility element inside the soap:Header.

high availability (HA) The ability to maintain continuous operations and recover from faults. *See also:* disaster recovery.

Holder A Java class that encapsulates a particular type of object so that the Holder's value can be updated in place.

hybrid parsing Parsing process that combines push, pull, and one-step parsing to best serve particular scenarios. *See also:* one-step parsing, pull parsing, push parsing.

IDL *See:* Interface Definition Language (IDL).

IETF *See:* Internet Engineering Task Force (IETF).

implied resource pattern The term in the WS-ResourceFramework for a particular pattern of Web services technology use (particularly WS-Addressing) to describe how a Web service is associated with a stateful resource.

independent software vendor (ISV) A small to medium-sized software product vendor.

inout parameter A parameter to a Web service operation that exists both in the request and in the response messages, with the understanding that the value on the client should be updated with the new value from the server.

instance Also known as an *XML instance* or *document instance*. Refers to an XML document as a specific instance from the set of possible documents allowed by a schema.

integrity Assurance that information is authentic and complete. In other words, the information hasn't been modified by an attacker during transmission between a sender and a receiver.

Interface Definition Language (IDL) A language to describe function or object interfaces in a distributed computing environment, allowing compilers to generate proxy and stub code to marshal parameters between different computers. In Web services, the IDL of choice is WSDL. *See also:* Web Services Description Language (WSDL).

interface extension   The mechanism defined in WSDL 2.0 for Web service interface composition. WSDL 2.0 defines an interface inheritance mechanism for WSDL interface elements in a fashion similar to Java interface inheritance. WSDL 2.0 defines an `extends` attribute that lets you define a WSDL interface as an extension of one or more other WSDL interfaces.

interface repository   A central store of metadata about CORBA components' interfaces. This is a CORBA-specific implementation of the Service-Oriented Architecture (SOA) services registry role.

intermediary   A SOAP node between the sender and the ultimate destination on the SOAP message path, which may do arbitrary processing of messages as they pass through.

Internet Engineering Task Force (IETF)   A large, open, international community of network designers, operators, vendors, and researchers concerned with the evolution of the Internet architecture and the smooth operation of the Internet.

invoke activity   A BPEL construct that allows the business process to invoke a one-way or request-response operation on a `portType` offered by a partner.

ISO 3166   The ISO standard for geographic location classifications.

ISV   *See:* independent software vendor (ISV).

J2EE   *See:* Java 2 Enterprise Edition (J2EE).

Java 2 Enterprise Edition (J2EE)   Defined by the Java Community Process, the overall standard that defines how to build Enterprise applications in Java. See `http://java.sun.com/j2ee/`.

Java API for XML Messaging (JAXM)   A raw API for sending/receiving SOAP messages.

Java API for XML Processing (JAXP)   A vendor-independent API for parsing and transforming XML documents.

Java API for XML-based RPC (JAX-RPC)   The JCP standard API for SOAP clients and services.

Java Architecture for XML Binding (JAXB)   A part of the J2EE specification that deals with mapping Java data structures to and from XML documents.

Java Cryptography Extension (JCE)   A Java framework and implementation of encryption, key generation, key agreement, and Message Authentication Code (MAC) algorithms. Support for encryption includes symmetric, asymmetric, block, and stream ciphers. The software also supports secure streams and sealed objects.

Java Message Service (JMS)   The standard Java interface for accessing messaging queue and publish/subscribe based messaging systems.

Java ServerPages (JSP)   HTML pages that include special directives. When deployed and run in a server, they provide dynamic web application support. The directives expand the HTML with dynamic information from the Java environment.

Java Web Service (JWS)   A method of easily deploying Java source files as Axis Web services.

JAX-RPC   *See:* Java API for XML-based RPC (JAX-RPC).

JAX-RPC handlers   Components that can access and modify a SOAP message just before it is sent and just after it is received at each end.

JAXB   *See:* Java Architecture for XML Binding (JAXB).

JAXM   *See:* Java API for XML Messaging (JAXM).

JAXP   *See:* Java API for XML Processing (JAXP).

JCE   *See:* Java Cryptography Extension (JCE).

JMS   *See:* Java Message Service (JMS).

JSP   *See:* Java ServerPages (JSP).

JSR 168   The Portlet Specification that enables interoperability between portals and portal components known as *portlets*.

JSR 109   "Implementing Enterprise Web Services." Defines how Web services are developed, deployed, consumed, and published in a J2EE application server.

JUnit   A testing framework for Java. See www.junit.org.

JWS   *See:* Java Web Service (JWS).

KDC   *See:* Key Distribution Center (KDC).

Kerberos   A trusted third-party authentication protocol developed at the Massachusetts Institute of Technology and used widely in the United States. Unlike other authentication schemes, Kerberos doesn't use public key technology. Instead, it uses symmetric ciphers and secrets shared between the Kerberos server and each individual user. Each user has a unique password, and the Kerberos server uses this password to encrypt messages sent to that user, so the message can't be read by anyone else.

Key Distribution Center (KDC)   A type of key center (used in symmetric cryptography) that implements a key distribution protocol to provide keys or tickets to two (or more) entities that wish to communicate securely. Specifically, the Kerberos server is called KDC because its main role is to issue tickets for entities. *See also:* Kerberos.

Locator   A Java class that acts as a factory for stubs.

logical structure   The organization of the concepts that define the meaning of an XML document.

MAC   *See:* Message Authentication Code (MAC).

marshalling   The process of converting application data to XML.

master keys   Keys shared by KDC and target entities. With a master key, KDC can encrypt tickets for the target entity to transmit. *See also:* Key Distribution Center (KDC).

Message   A class representing a Web service wire message, which may contain both a SOAP envelope and attachment parts.

Message Authentication Code (MAC)

A keyed-hash algorithm that is similar to secret-key digital signatures and is used to ensure data integrity. A hash value is calculated using a symmetric session key, which is included in the message itself and then recalculated at the other end by the same key to verify that the data has not been altered in transit.

message exchange pattern   A term defined by WSDL 2.0 to describe the sequence and cardinality of abstract messages listed in an operation. Message exchange patterns also define which other nodes send messages to, and receive messages from, the service implementing the operation. This term replaces the WSDL 1.1 term *transmission primitive*.

Message Exchange Pattern (MEP)

A feature defining a particular set of messages and the sequencing and rules for exchanging them. Examples include Request-Response and SOAP Response.

message path   The route a SOAP message takes from the sender to the ultimate destination, possibly through various intermediaries.

Message Transmission Optimization Mechanism (MTOM)

An abstract feature defining how to optimize the transmission of SOAP messages containing large binary content. Uses XOP for specific serialization rules.

message-driven bean (MDB)   A component that is called by the server when a message arrives, either from a JMS queue or from an inbound connector.

Message-Oriented Middleware (MOM)

Enterprise message-queuing systems that enable reliable asynchronous messaging between applications.

MessageContext   The object that is passed from Handler to Handler during Axis processing. Contains a request message, a response message, and an arbitrary number of named properties.

mixed content   An XML element that contains subelements and/or character data.

module   A SOAP extension implemented using SOAP headers. A module specification names the module with a URI and describes the rules of its operation. Modules may implement one or more features.

MOM   *See:* Message-Oriented Middleware (MOM).

MTOM   *See:* Message Transmission Optimization Mechanism (MTOM).

multireference value (multiref)   A method of encoding object graphs in XML that uses ID and href attributes to maintain referential integrity in complex graphs.

mustUnderstand   An optional flag on SOAP headers indicating that they are mandatory.

NAICS   *See:* North American Industry Classification System (NAICS).

nonrepudiation   The ability to ensure that a party to a contract or a communication can't deny the authenticity of their signature on a document or the sending of a message that they originated. On the Internet, a digital signature is used not only to ensure that a message or document has been electronically signed by the person that purported to sign the document, but also (since a digital signature can be created by only one person) to ensure that a person can't later deny that they furnished the signature.

North American Industry Classification System (NAICS)   A system for classifying businesses by industry.

notification broker   A role within WS-Notification describing an intermediary in a publish-subscribe system. A notification broker intermediates between publishers and notification consumers. Notification brokers manage the subscription creation and management capability for publishers in a WS-Notification system. The notification broker role is a specialization of the notification producer role. *See also:* notification consumer, notification producer, publisher.

notification consumer   A role within WS-Notification describing a Web service that can receive notification messages from a notification producer. *See also:* notification producer.

notification message   An XML artifact that records the information associated with a situation. In WS-Notification, notification messages are distributed to notification consumers that have subscribed to receive notification messages associated with a particular situation. *See also:* notification consumer, notification producer.

notification producer   A role within WS-Notification describing a Web service that detects the occurrence of a situation, formats a notification message artifact that records information about that situation, and can distribute copies of that notification message to notification consumers that have subscribed to receive them. Notification producers have the capability of receiving subscribe requests from subscribers creating and managing the resultant subscriptions, and matching subscriptions with notification messages. *See also:* notification consumer, notification message, publisher.

OASIS   *See:* Organization for the Advancement of Structured Information Standards (OASIS).

object graph   An abstract network of nodes and edges that represent an interconnected graph of data. Such graphs are used to model and encode programming language data structures in SOAP.

Object Role Modeling Markup Language (ORM-ML)   An XML vocabulary developed at STARLab that defines a method for designing and querying database models at a higher, conceptual level.

one-step parsing   Parsing process in which the parser generates a parse tree (typically, a DOM structure) from an XML document.

Organization for the Advancement of Structured Information Standards (OASIS)   See `http://www.oasis-open.org/`. An open standards organization responsible for many of the Web services standards including WS-Security, WS-ResourceFramework, and WS-Notification. OASIS sponsors a DTD repository at `http://www.XML.org`.

ORM-ML   *See:* Object Role Modeling Markup Language (ORM-ML).

out parameter   A parameter of a Web service operation that exists only in a response message, in order to carry additional values beyond the return type.

parse tree   A data structure generated by parsers that provides a representation of the syntax of parsed documents.

partner   A BPEL construct to group of multiple partner links, usually associated with the same business partner. *See also:* partner link.

partner link   A logical BPEL entity characterized by a partner link type and a role name that identifies the `portType` a partner must implement. *See also:* partner, partner link type.

partner link type   A BPEL construct that characterizes the relationship between two services by defining the roles played by each of the services in the relationship and specifying the `portType` provided by each role.

password authentication   An authentication method using a username and password.

PASWA   *See:* Proposed Infoset Addendum to SOAP With Attachments (PASWA).

persistent store   Storage/memory that retains its value even if the application or machine is restarted. For example, a database.

physical structure   The organization of syntax elements (elements, text, comments, and so on) in an XML document.

pick activity   A BPEL construct that lets you block and waiting for a suitable message to arrive or for a timeout alarm to go off.

piggy-back   The process of adding additional information to a message that may not be pertinent to the original purpose of the message. For example, adding an acknowledgment header to a message.

pivot   The handler at the center of a targeted chain. After the pivot processing is complete, the chain switches from request to response processing.

plaintext   *See:* cleartext.

policy   A collection of WS-Policy policy assertions. *See also:* policy assertion, policy subject.

policy assertion   The basic unit of WS-Policy. A concrete statement about the requirement, preference, capability, or other characteristic of a Web service or its operating environment.

policy subject   The component in a computing system to which a WS-Policy policy applies. A policy subject can be a Web service, a component of a Web service description, a part of the Web service's operating environment, or various other entities related to a Web service. *See also:* policy.

port   A WSDL element indicating the endpoint address of a Web service in a communications protocol–specific fashion (for example, URL for HTTP, email address for SMTP, and so on).

PortType   A WSDL element that describes a collection of message signatures (`operation` elements) that define the abstract interface of the Web service.

private key   The publicly unavailable key owned by an identity in a Public Key Cryptography system. It is used to decrypt incoming messages and sign outgoing ones.

process   The root XML element for a BPEL business process description.

process binding   The association of logical BPEL partner links with concrete Web service endpoints.

process definition   Serves as a template from which specific BPEL process instances are created.

process deployment   A step in the BPEL process development lifecycle that makes a process definition available to the runtime infrastructure.

process instance   An instance created according to a BPEL process model. Any number of instances for a given process model/definition may be executed at any time. *See also:* process definition, process model.

process model   A BPEL business process definition.

processing instruction (PI)   A special directive to the applications processing XML documents. The syntax is `<?PITarget ...?>`. The PI target is a keyword meaningful to the processing application. Everything between the PI target and the `?>` marker is considered the contents of the PI.

profile   A named group of Web service specifications that contains guidance and clarification on how to use these specifications. One of the primary deliverables from the WS-I organization.

profile requirements   The normative text in a profile. Conformance to a profile is based on adherence to each requirement in the profile. *See also:* profile.

prolog   A section of XML documents that provides metadata about the markup in the document such as information about the version of XML in use, information about the character encoding in use, information about the document's DTD, and any comments or processing instructions.

proof of possession   Information used in the process of proving ownership of a security token or set of claims. For example, proof of possession might be the private key associated with a security token that contains a public key.

property   1: A piece of abstract information or state that affects the operation of one or more SOAP features.
2: An element of a Web service request or response message; used in BPEL correlation sets.

property alias   A BPEL element that defines the relationship between a property and a WSDL message.

Proposed Infoset Addendum to SOAP With Attachments (PASWA)
A new model for considering attachments as part of the SOAP envelope infoset. Superseded by MTOM. *See also:* Message Transmission Optimization Mechanism (MTOM).

protocol binding   A specification, named with a URI, of the rules for sending and receiving SOAP messages over a particular underlying protocol such as HTTP, TCP, or email. Bindings may implement one or more features.

provider   A special kind of pivot handler inside a `SOAPService`, responsible for performing the actual Web service operation. Typically, this means calling a method on a particular Java class.

public key   The publicly available key in a Public Key Cryptography system, used to encrypt messages bound for its owner and to decrypt signatures made by its owner.

Public Key Infrastructure (PKI)
The architecture, organization, techniques, practices, and procedures that collectively support the implementation and operation of a certificate-based Public Key Cryptography system.

`publish`   An operation within a service-oriented architecture, describing a contract between a service provider and a service registry. The `publish` operation describes the steps taken by a service provider to advertise a service description in a way that one or more service requestors can find that service description and thereby be able understand what is required to invoke that service.

publisher   A role within WS-Notification describing an entity that can detect the occurrence of a situation and format a notification message artifact recording pertinent information about the situation. A notification producer is a specialization of this role. *See also:* notification producer.

pull parsing   A parsing mechanism in which the application always has to request the next piece of parsing information from the parser.

push parsing   A parsing mechanism in which the parser sends parsing events to the application processing an XML document.

QoS   *See:* Quality of Service (QoS).

Quality of Service (QoS)   A general term encompassing a set of metrics relevant to a particular distributed computing scenario. Typically these include aspects of security, transaction management, and response times.

`receive activity`   A BPEL construct that allows the business process to do a blocking wait for a matching message to arrive.

Remote Method Invocation over Internet Inter-ORB Protocol (RMI-IIOP)   A distributed computing system that allows Java components to be called over a network using the CORBA IIOP protocol. See `http://java.sun.com/products/rmi-iiop`.

Remote Procedure Call (RPC)   A design pattern using messages to serialize standard programming-language function/method calls and responses across a network.

renewable reference   In WS-ResourceFramework, an endpoint reference that has been augmented with policy information indicating how a requestor can refresh the reference in the event that some component of the reference has become invalid (or stale).

reply activity   A BPEL construct that allows the business process to send a message in reply to a message that was received earlier.

REpresentational State Transfer (REST)   An architectural pattern mirroring the design of the web. It involves a small number of common operations like GET/PUT/POST/DELETE that affect the state of resources named with URIs.

resource reference   In a J2EE system, a logical name for a resource that an application uses, such as a database, URL, or other component. This allows the application to be written independently of the actual resources it will use when it is deployed.

REST   *See:* REpresentational State Transfer (REST).

RMI-IIOP   *See:* Remote Method Invocation over Internet Inter-ORB Protocol (RMI-IIOP).

role   An optional attribute on SOAP headers that indicates the type of node that should process the header.

rollback   In the transaction space, the act of undoing work performed under the specified transaction. In an atomic transaction (AT), rolling back a transaction should have the same effect as if the transaction never happened.

root element   The first element in an XML document. The name derives from the fact that this element is the root of the element hierarchy.

root-cause analysis   The process of finding the initial factor that led to a system fault.

RPC   *See:* Remote Procedure Call (RPC).

SAAJ   *See:* SOAP with Attachments API for Java (SAAJ).

sample applications   Web service applications that are built based on usage scenarios that conform to a profile and that show how to build interoperable Web services.

scope *or* scope activity   A BPEL construct that lets you group activities with common properties.

SDM   *See:* System Definition Model (SDM).

security domain   An environment or context that is defined by a security policy, security model, or security architecture to include a set of system resources and the set of system entities that have the right to access the resources.

security infrastructures   Mechanisms or technologies used for managing participants and resources. Kerberos and Public Key Infrastructure are examples. *See also:* Kerberos, Public Key Infrastructure (PKI).

SEI   *See:* Service Endpoint Interface (SEI).

Semantic Web   An extension to the Web where information has well-defined meaning. Semantic Web work is led by W3C.

sequence activity   A BPEL construct that lets you group sequentially executed activities.

serialization   The process of emitting XML markup from a data structure.

serializer   A Java class that writes Java objects into XML.

service   A client-side object in Axis that acts as the factory for `Call` objects and the storage repository for metadata about a Web service, such as type mappings.

service description   A unit of metadata describing the capabilities of a Web service. A service description is key to a service-oriented architecture in that it describes everything a service requestor needs to know in order to invoke a Web service. The most popular form of service description is WSDL. The W3C describes a service description stack outlining all the technologies associated with describing many facets of a Web service. *See also:* Web Services Description Language (WSDL).

service discovery   The process used by the service provider to publish a Web service, and the process used by a service requestor to find the Web service.

Service Endpoint Interface (SEI)   A generated Java interface that maps to the Web service interface described in a WSDL document.

service implementation definition   A subset of WSDL elements focused on the endpoint definition of a Web service. This forms a conventional division of a WSDL document, separating the service implementation definition from service interface definition.

service interface definition   A subset of WSDL elements focused on the reusable portions of a Web service; that is, elements that are likely to be shared between many actual Web service implementations hosted by different service providers. This forms a conventional division of a WSDL document, separating the service implementation definition from service interface definition.

Service Level Agreement (SLA)   Agreements that define policies against which system behavior is measured.

service orchestration   The process of coordinating Web service invocation based on some process model such as one defined by BPEL. *See also:* Business Process Management (BPM), Business Process Automation (BPA).

service provider   A role within a Service-Oriented Architecture (SOA). Any business or entity that hosts one or more Web services for access by service requestors. Service providers publish service descriptions to one or more service registries and receive service invocations from one or more service requestors. Think of a service provider as a server in a client-server relationship with a service requestor. *See also:* service description, service requestor, Service-Oriented Architecture (SOA).

service registry   A role within a Service-Oriented Architecture (SOA). Any mechanism by which one or more service descriptions can be published by service providers and searched for or found by service requestors. *See also:* service description, service provider, service requestor, Service-Oriented Architecture (SOA).

service requestor   A role within a Service-Oriented Architecture (SOA). Any business or entity that invokes a Web service provided by a service provider. Service requestors do find operations against one or more service registries to retrieve a service description for a Web service. Based on that service description, the service requestor invokes a Web service to fulfill some task within a business process. Think of a service requestor as a client in a client-server relationship with a service provider. *See also:* service description, service provider, service registry, Service-Oriented Architecture (SOA).

service styles   Rules by which Web service invocations are mapped to Java calls. Axis supports RPC, document, wrapped, and message styles.

service virtualization   The process through which services are exposed with the right service assurance levels: availability, scalability, reliability, security, transactability, and so on.

Service-Oriented Architecture (SOA)   An abstract pattern that applies to a wide variety of Web services situations. SOA defines an architecture consisting of three roles (service provider, service registry, and service requestor) that can be fulfilled or implemented by a variety of techniques. SOA also defines the contracts between these roles in terms of three operations: publish, find, and bind. *See also:* service provider, service registry, service requestor.

service-ref   A resource reference that refers to a remote Web service. *See also:* resource reference.

session   On the server side, a data repository that enables tying particular state to individual clients. The clients require some form of session identifier in order to maintain an association with the server; this identifier is typically an HTTP cookie or a SOAP header.

session bean   A type of Enterprise JavaBean. Session beans can be stateful, which means they are instantiated on behalf of a client program; or stateless, which means they are always available. Any instance of a stateless session bean can be used by any calling component, because each instance is identical. *See also:* Enterprise JavaBean (EJB).

simple chain   A linear chain of handlers, which run one after the other when invoked.

SimpleAxisServer   A lightweight HTTP-based server that can be run standalone or embedded in your applications in order to provide Axis server functionality.

single sign-on (SSO)   A login routine in which one logon provides access to all resources on the network.

situation   In WS–Notification, a happening within a Web service's environment that is of interest to other entities. A situation may be associated with a change of state, the passage of time, or some event within the Web service's environment.

skeleton   A server-side component that intermediates between the Web services middleware (such as the Axis engine) and the target Web service implementation. A skeleton decodes information sent from the service requestor and invokes the target Web service using a programming language–specific API. The skeleton also translates the response from the target Web service back into a format expected by the Web services middleware. The term *server stub* is also used as a synonym.

SLA   *See:* Service Level Agreement (SLA).

SOAP   Originally Simple Object Access Protocol, now just SOAP. A W3C specification for a lightweight XML messaging protocol that can bind to arbitrary underlying transport protocols such as HTTP. SOAP is an XML-based protocol that consists of three parts: an envelope that defines a framework for describing what is in a message and how to process it, a set of encoding rules for expressing instances of application-defined datatypes, and a convention for representing remote procedure calls and responses. SOAP can potentially be used in combination with a variety of other protocols.

SOAP encoding   The rules by which an object graph (as specified in the SOAP data model) may be serialized into XML. *See also:* object graph.

SOAP message   The unit of communication from node to node. Contains a SOAP envelope and (potentially) other data, such as attachments.

SOAP node   A piece of software that receives and possibly sends SOAP messages. Nodes can act in particular roles. *See also:* role, SOAP message.

SOAP processing model   The rules a SOAP node must follow when receiving and acting on a message. The main point of the processing model is to ensure that mustUnderstand headers are understood prior to any meaningful work and that the correct nodes along a message path process the correct set of headers. *See also:* mustUnderstand, SOAP node.

SOAP with Attachments (SwA)   A specification defining how to package SOAP envelopes and binary attachments into MIME envelopes for transmission across the network.

SOAP with Attachments API for Java (SAAJ)   Low-level API for manipulating SOAP envelopes, messages, and attachments. Axis's message classes implement and extend the SAAJ APIs.

Soapbuilders   A grass-roots interoperability organization consisting of SOAP developers who test their implementations against each other and attempt to solve interop problems.

SOAPPart   A special part in a SAAJ message that holds the SOAP envelope. *See also:* SOAP with Attachments API for Java (SAAJ).

SOAPService   A special targeted chain that implements a Web service.

SSO   *See:* single sign-on (SSO).

structured activity   Activities that allow the specification of collections of nested activities and the order in which they take place.

stub   A Java class generated from a Web service description, which gives you an API that mirrors the Web service operations in the WSDL description and automatically handles type mappings, faults, and invoking the remote service.

subscriber   A role within WS-Notification describing an entity that can format and send subscription requests to a notification producer. Note that in many circumstances the role of subscriber and the role of notification consumer are played by the same entity. *See also:* notification consumer, notification producer.

SwA   *See:* SOAP with Attachments (SwA).

switch activity   A BPEL construct that makes decisions in a business process.

symmetric encryption   An encryption method where the same key is used both to encrypt and decrypt messages. Also called *conventional*, *secret key*, and *single key* encryption.

System Definition Model (SDM)   A Microsoft standard for modeling distributed systems. *See also:* Data Center Markup Language (DCML), Dynamic Systems Initiative (DSI).

targeted chain   A chain of handlers consisting of a request handler, a pivot handler, and a response handler. The request handler runs first, followed by the pivot, followed by the response handler, any of which may be chains.

taxonomy   The categorization scheme used to classify a business, business service, or tModel.

terminate activity   A BPEL construct that lets you immediately stop the execution of the business process.

test tools   A set of tools that can be used to determine if a Web service conforms to the requirements in a profile.

throw activity   A BPEL construct that lets you explicitly raise a fault.

ticket-granting ticket (TGT)   A ticket to access a secure server to get service tickets. In Kerberos, KDC plays the role of the secure server. The use of TGTs and tickets enable the single sign-on (SSO) feature, whereby the user need authenticate only once, after which they can access additional services without reauthenticating. *See also:* single sign-on.

topic   A unit of organization within a topic space. A topic contains the metadata description associating a situation with formats of notification messages. A topic is the unit of matching a subscription with a notification message. *See also:* topic space.

topic space   A collection of topics grouped together for some purpose. A topic space is analogous to an XML namespace. *See also:* topic.

transaction   The scope under which a unit of work is defined. The size or breadth of the amount of work will vary between applications.

transmission primitive   A characterization of the message flow associated with an operation. There are four types of transmission primitives: request-response, one-way, solicit-response, and notification. The preferred term for this concept is *message exchange pattern*.

Transport Layer Security (TSL)   A security protocol that ensures confidentiality and integrity of data exchanged over the Internet. The protocol allows client and server applications to communicate in such a way that third parties can't eavesdrop or tamper with the content of the communication. Servers are always authenticated and clients are optionally authenticated. For now, Secure Socket Layer (SSL) is widely used; TLS is its follow-on which is standardized at IETF.

transport listener   The entity responsible for accepting a transport-specific message, wrapping it in a `MessageContext`, and invoking an `AxisServer`. The default transport listener is an HTTP servlet.

transport sender   A handler responsible for sending a message and reading a response in a transport-specific fashion.

TSL   *See:* Transport Layer Security (TSL).

Two-Phase Commit (2PC)   A variant of the atomic transaction (AT) protocol where the commit process is split into two parts (or phases). In the first, each participant prepares or votes on the outcome of the transaction; in the second, each participant commits or saves its work. *See also:* atomic transaction (AT).

type-mapping registry   A framework that maps Java classes to XML type QNames and enables the location of serializers and deserializers to convert one to the other.

UDDI   *See:* Universal Description, Discovery and Integration (UDDI).

UDDI `bindingTemplate`   Contains the technical information necessary to invoke a specific Web service, and may include a reference to one or more `tModel` elements.

UDDI `businessEntity`   Provides information about the business that is a service provider, and can contain one or more `businessService` elements.

UDDI `businessService`   Contains the business description for a service and provides a way to group the different implementation details and bindings for the same logical service. A `businessService` may contain one or more `bindingTemplate` elements.

UDDI `publisherAssertion`   Provides a method to link together two or more businesses that are related to each other.

UDDI `tModel`   *There are two primary* uses for a `tModel`. First, they are used to define the technical fingerprint for a Web service. This refers to any technical specifications or prearranged agreements on how to conduct business. Second, a `tModel` can define a namespace that is used to identify business entities or classify business entities, business services, and other `tModels`.

Uniform Resource Identifier (URI)   The Web naming and addressing technology, consisting of strings that identify resources on the Web, such as documents, images, and email addresses.

Uniform Resource Locator (URL)   A subset of URIs referring to Internet addresses (for example, `http://www.example.com/doc/`). URLs consist of an access protocol specifier (`http`), a host IP specifier (`www.example.com`), and optionally the path to a file or resource residing on that host (`/doc`). *See also:* Uniform Resource Identifier (URI)

Uniform Resource Name (URN)   A URI that is globally unique and persistent. Begins with the specifier `urn:`.

Universal Description Discovery and Integration (UDDI)   A set of specifications for a service registry. UDDI is also an implementation of a services registry located at `www.uddi.org`. *See also:* service registry.

Universal Standard Products and Services Classification (UNSPSC)   A way of classifying products and services.

unmarshalling   The process of generating application data from XML.

UNSPSC   *See:* Universal Standard Products and Services Classification (UNSPSC).

URI   *See:* Uniform Resource Identifier (URI).

URL   *See:* Uniform Resource Locator (URL).

URN   *See:* Uniform Resource Name (URN).

user registry   A registry that manages users in the security domain. For example, most operating systems have such registries, so they can be used for security purposes. Lightweight Directory Access Protocol (LDAP) is another mechanism to manage user registries, providing scalability.

valid   An XML document that is well-formed and follows the constraints of some schema.

value network   A mechanism to analyze a set of activities creating value for customers, clarifying the relationships between the constituent activities in the value-creation system and the firms providing them. A value network can be thought of as a set of activities (nodes) and relationships between those activities (arcs). The value network itself is composed of organizations that create value for customers by linking business processes together and mediating exchanges between them.

variable   A BPEL entity that holds state data that is accessed by activities.

virtual exchange   A hub-and-spoke integration architecture where all data formats within a domain are mapped through a common super-vocabulary. *See also:* business service network (BSN).

virtualization   *See:* service virtualization.

vocabulary   A general term covering one or more XML Schema or DTDs used to define a set of XML structures that are used for a common purpose.

wait activity   A BPEL construct that waits for a specified period of time or point in time.

Web service   A software system designed to support interoperable machine-to-machine interaction over a network. It has an interface described in a format that the machine can process (specifically WSDL). Other systems interact with the Web service in a manner prescribed by its description using SOAP messages, typically conveyed using HTTP with an XML serialization in conjunction with other Web-related standards. See also: SOAP message, Web Services Description Language (WSDL).

Web Service Deployment Descriptor (WSDD)   An XML format used by Axis as both configuration and deployment metadata.

Web Services Description Language (WSDL)   A component of a service description that describes the interface definition of the Web service, details related to binding (network protocol and data encoding requirements), and the network location of the Web service. WSDL version 1.1 is published at http://www.w3.org/TR/wsdl. A second version, WSDL 2.0, is being standardized in the W3C and is published at http://www.w3.org/TR/wsdl20.

Web Services Distributed Management (WSDM)   An OASIS standard that defines a framework for management of distributed resources using Web services.

Web Services for Interactive Applications (WSIA)   An OASIS standard superseded by WSRP. *See also:* Web Services for Remote Portlets (WSRP).

Web Services for Remote Portlets (WSRP)   An OASIS standard that defines a framework for interoperating portals, portlets, and content aggregators using Web services.

Web Services Interoperability (WS-I)   An industry consortium formed to promote Web service interoperability by defining guidelines for using Web service specifications.

Web Services Management (WSM)   A collection of capabilities for enabling service deployment and virtualization. *See also:* service virtualization, Web Services Distributed Management (WSDM).

well-formed   A XML document that follows the rules of XML syntax.

while activity   A BPEL construct that lets you indicate that an activity should be repeated as long as a certain criteria is met.

wireless service provider (WSP)   A company that provides cell phone and other wireless services (voice, video, data, and so on).

World Wide Web Consortium (W3C)
The international body that governs
Internet standards. It was created in 1994
and is open to all interested organizations. Participation in the W3C allows
member organizations to jointly develop
protocols that promote the evolution of
the Web while ensuring its interoperability. The W3C holds the specifications for
many of the Web technologies such as
HTML, XML, and RDF, as well as many
Web services standards such as SOAP and
WSDL.

WS-Coordination   A Web services
specification that defines some basic roles
and APIs that WS-Transaction specifications build on.

WS-I   *See:* Web Services
Interoperability (WS-I).

WS-I Basic Profile   A standard that
incorporates SOAP, WSDL, and UDDI
and ensures how applications written to
use these technologies can work together. *See also:* Web Services Interoperability
(WS-I).

WS-ReliableMessaging (WS-RM)
A Web services specification that defines
a mechanism by which messages will be
reliably delivered to their destination.

WS-Resource   In the WS-
ResourceFramework, the combination of
a Web service and a stateful resource.

**WS-Resource qualified endpoint
reference**   A use of a WS-Addressing
endpoint reference to refer to a WS-
Resource.

WS-Transactions   A Web services
specification that defines a Web service
based transaction interfaces. This is akin
to a Web service version of JDBC.

WSDD   *See:* Web Service Deployment
Descriptor (WSDD).

WSDL   *See:* Web Services Description
Language (WSDL).

WSDM   *See:* Web Services Distributed
Management (WSDM).

WSIA   *See:* Web Services for Interactive
Applications (WSIA).

WSM   *See:* Web Services Management
(WSM).

WSP   *See:* wireless service provider
(WSP).

WSRP   *See:* Web Services for Remote
Portlets (WSRP).

XML Path Language (XPath)   A
W3C specification for identifying parts
of XML documents.

**XML-Binary Optimized Packaging
(XOP)**   A serialization specification for
using MIME to transmit messages optimized with MTOM.

XOP   *See:* XML-Binary Optimized
Packaging (XOP).

XPath   *See:* XML Path Language
(XPath).

Index

G

How can we make this index more useful? Email us at indexes@samspublishing.com

LF (line feed), 43
lifecycles
   activities (BPEL), 562
   Axis, 270-271
   EJBs, 349
   operations, 708-715
lifetimes
   WS-ResourceLifetime, 434-441
   XML documents, 34-35
limitations of SOA, 677-678
line feed (LF), 43
links, flow, 576-577
local attributes/elements (XML), 63
local transports, 299
logging, configuring, 302
logic, services, 694
logical structures (XML schemas), 51
long-running processes, 550
loops, object graphs, 144
low-level proxies, 691

M

MAC (Message Authentication Code), 448
mail transports, 299
mailing lists, schemas, 68
maintenance
   analyzer tool, 667-671
   Axis, 288
     AxisFault class, 288-289
     typed exceptions, 289-290
   compensation (BPEL), 585-586
   dead path elimination, 577-578
   events (BPEL), 587
   faults (BPEL), 582-585
   join failures, 577-578
   semantic mapping, 677-678
   SOAP, 113, 134-138
     encoding, 147
     headers, 138-140
   WS-Coordination fault codes, 536
   WS-I Test Tools, 663-666
   WS-RM, 517-521
   XML testing, 105-107
management, 689, 713
   interoperability, 610-611
     analyzer tool, 667-671
     Attachment Profile 1.0, 650-660

     Basic Profile 1.0 requirements, 645-647
     Basic Security Profile 1.0, 660-661
     conformance claims, 641-643
     defining service interfaces, 623-626
     future of Basic Profile 1.0, 648-650
     HTTP/SOAP messages, 638-640
     importing WSDL documents/XML schemas, 622-623
     profiles, 619
     publishing service descriptions, 637-638
     security, 641
     service providers, 643-645
     SOAP bindings, 626-633, 635-637
     WS-I Basic Profile 1.0, 611-619
     WS-I sample applications, 661-662
     WS-I Test Tools, 663-666
     WSDL documents, 620-621
   J2EE persistence, 353
   operations, 708-715
   policies, 690
   WSM, 714
Management Using Web Services (MUWS), 709
mapping
   inout/out parameters, 256-258
   invocations, 275
     document styles, 277-278
     message styles, 278-279
     RPC styles, 275
     wrapped styles, 276-277
   operation elements (Axis), 266
   properties, 357
   semantic, 677-678
   technology, 685-690
   types
     Axis, 279
     defaults, 281-284
     deserializers/serializers, 284-286
     maps, 357
     MessageElement class, 286-287
     registering, 279-281
     WSDD, 262-263
     WSDL2Java, 257-258
   user-role, 497
   WSDL, 213-214, 337
margins (XML), 42